MATHEMATICS
for Edexcel GCSE
Intermediate Tier

Tony Banks and David Alcorn

Causeway Press Limited

Published by Causeway Press Ltd
P.O. Box 13, Ormskirk, Lancashire L39 5HP

First published 2001

© Tony Banks and David Alcorn

British Library Cataloguing-in-Publication Data.
A catalogue record for this book is available from the British Library.

ISBN 1-902796-27-6

Acknowledgements
The authors and publisher wish to express their thanks and gratitude to Tony Fisher, Paul Newton, Peter Balaam and Bruce Balden for their contributions to this book.

Exam questions
Past exam questions, provided by *London Examinations, A division of Edexcel*, are marked Edexcel. The answers to all questions are entirely the responsibility of the authors/publisher and have neither been provided nor approved by Edexcel.

Every effort has been made to locate the copyright owners of material used in this book. Any omissions brought to the notice of the publisher are regretted and will be credited in subsequent printings.

Page design
Billy Johnson
Alan Fraser

Readers
Heather Doyle
David Hodgson
Gillian Rich

Artwork
David Alcorn
Alan Fraser

Cover design
Waring-Collins Partnership

Typesetting by Bibliocraft, Dundee

Printed and bound by Scotprint, Haddington, Scotland

preface

Mathematics for Edexcel GCSE - Intermediate Tier has been written to meet the requirements of the National Curriculum and provides full coverage of **Edexcel Specification A** and **Edexcel Specification B (Modular)**.

The book is suitable for students preparing for assessment at the Intermediate Tier of entry on either a 1-year or 2-year course or as a revision text.

In preparing the text, full account has been made of the requirements for students to be able to solve problems in mathematics both with and without a calculator. Whilst there has been no artificial division of subject content into calculator and non-calculator work, non-calculator questions and exercises have been incorporated throughout the book where appropriate.

The planning of topics within chapters and sections has been designed to provide efficient coverage of the specifications. Depending on how the book is to be used you can best decide on the order in which chapters are studied.

Chapters   1 - 11   Number
Chapters 12 - 19   Algebra
Chapters 20 - 33   Shape, Space and Measures
Chapters 34 - 40   Handling Data

Each chapter consists of fully worked examples with explanatory notes and commentary; carefully graded questions, a summary of key facts and skills and a review exercise.
The review exercises provide the opportunity to consolidate topics introduced within the chapter and consist of exam-style questions, which reflect how Edexcel intend to assess the work, plus lots of past examination questions (marked Edexcel).

Further opportunities to consolidate skills acquired over a number of chapters are provided with section reviews. There is a final exam questions section with a further compilation of exam and exam-style questions, organised for non-calculator and calculator practice, in preparation for the exams.

Some chapters include ideas for investigational, practical and statistical tasks and give the student the opportunity to improve and practice their skills of using and applying mathematics.

contents

CHAPTER 5 — Working with Number

CHAPTER 6 — Standard Index Form

CHAPTER 7 — Fractions

CHAPTER 29 · Volumes and Surface Areas

CHAPTER 30 · Enlargements and Similar Figures

CHAPTER 31 · Pythagoras' Theorem

CHAPTER 32 · Trigonometry

CHAPTER 1

Whole Numbers

The numbers 0, 1, 2, 3, 4, 5, . . . can be used to count objects.
Such numbers are called **whole numbers**.
There are other types of numbers, including fractions, decimals and negative numbers which you will meet in later chapters.

Place value

Our number system is made up of the digits 0, 1, 2, 3, 4, 5, 6, 7, 8 and 9.
The position a digit has in a number is called its **place value**.
In the number 5384 the digit 8 is worth 80, but in the number 4853 the digit 8 is worth 800.

Reading and writing numbers

$8543 = 8 \times 1000 + 5 \times 100 + 4 \times 10 + 3 \times 1$
The number 8543 is written or read as, "eight thousand five hundred and forty-three".
For numbers bigger than one thousand split the number into groups of three digits, starting from the units column.

EXAMPLES

1 Write the number 56843 in words.

Fifty-six *thousand* eight hundred and forty-three.

2 Write the number 4567205 in words.

Four *million* five hundred and sixty-seven *thousand* two hundred and five.

> 1. Split the numbers into groups of 3 digits.
> 2. Combine the numbers of millions and thousands with the number less than 1000.

Exercise 1.1

1 Write the following numbers in figures.
(a) three hundred and ninety-six
(b) five thousand and ten
(c) seventy thousand two hundred
(d) nine million two thousand and fifty-one
(e) seven hundred and sixty-two million five hundred and four thousand and nineteen
(f) twenty million two hundred and two thousand and twenty

2 Write the following numbers in words.
(a) 84
(b) 23590
(c) 93145670
(d) 764809
(e) 6049
(f) 9080004

3 Write answers to the following using figures.
(a) Ten less than one thousand and fourteen.
(b) One hundred more than nine hundred and thirty-five.
(c) Eight less than one thousand and ninety-four.

4 In the number 3<u>8</u>4 the value of the underlined figure is 80.
Give the value of the underlined figure in the following.
(a) 62<u>3</u>4
(b) 1<u>2</u>3 456 789
(c) 95 <u>6</u>70
(d) <u>2</u>003
(e) 9<u>4</u> 705
(f) 423<u>6</u>

5 Look at these numbers.
97, 32, 23, 28, 302, 203.
(a) Which is the largest **odd** number?
(b) Which is the smallest **even** number?

Numbers in ascending and descending order

Smallest number → ascending order → Largest number

Largest number → descending order → Smallest number

6 Write the following numbers in ascending order.
(a) 74, 168, 39, 421.
(b) 3842, 5814, 3874, 3801, 4765.

7 Write the following numbers in descending order.
(a) 399, 425, 103, 84, 429.
(b) 9434, 9646, 9951, 9653.

8 Using the digits 4, 6, 7, 1 and 5 (do not use the same digit more than once)
(a) make the biggest five-digit number,
(b) make the smallest five-digit number.
In each case explain your method.

9 By using each of the digits 5, 4, 9 and 6
(a) make the largest four-digit **even** number,
(b) make the smallest four-digit **odd** number.

10 Using the digits 8, 5, 4 and 3 make as many four-digit numbers as you can. Use each digit just once in each four-digit number, e.g. 8543.
Put your numbers in ascending order.
How many numbers begin with eight?

Non-calculator methods for addition

Writing numbers in columns

Write the numbers in tidy columns according to place value.
Add together the numbers of units, tens, hundreds, etc.
If any of these answers comes to more than 10 then something is carried to the next column.

EXAMPLE

Work out $4567 + 835$.

$$\begin{array}{r} 4567 \\ + \ 835 \\ \hline 5402 \\ \hline {\scriptstyle 1\ 1\ 1} \end{array}$$

$7 + 5 = 12$ which is 2 carry 1.
$6 + 3 + $ carried $1 = 10$, which is 0 carry 1.
$5 + 8 + $ carried $1 = 14$, which is 4 carry 1.
$4 + $ carried $1 = 5$.

Using a number line

A number line shows a different method for adding numbers.
With practice you should not need to draw a number line.

EXAMPLE

Work out $26 + 37$.

$26 + 37$ is the same as $37 + 26$.
$37 + 20 = 57$ (adding 20)
$57 + 6 = 63$ (adding 6)
So $26 + 37 = 63$.

Working in context

1. Identify the calculation required by the question.
2. Do the calculation.
3. Give the answer to the question using a short sentence.

EXAMPLE

In Year 7 the class attendances were as follows:
28 30 27 30 25
What was the total attendance?

The total attendance was 140.

$$\begin{array}{r} 28 \\ 30 \\ 27 \\ 30 \\ + \ 25 \\ \hline 140 \\ \hline {\scriptstyle 1\ 2} \end{array}$$

Do not use a calculator for this exercise.

1 Here is a number line for 18 + 15.

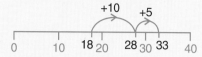

(a) What is 18 + 10?
(b) What is 18 + 15?

2 Draw a number line for each of the following sums and work out the answers.
(a) 14 + 15   (b) 13 + 18
(c) 7 + 36   (d) 18 + 25
(e) 24 + 29   (f) 19 + 27

3 What must be added to each of these numbers to make 100?
(a) 9   (b) 96   (c) 45
(d) 37   (e) 62   (f) 83

4 Work these out by writing the numbers in columns.
(a) 765 + 23   (b) 27 + 56
(c) 76 + 98   (d) 324 + 628
(e) 1273 + 729   (f) 3495 + 8708
(g) 67 + 89 + 45   (h) 431 + 865 + 245
(i) 187 + 54 + 3210
(j) 123 456 + 876 544

5 Work these out in your head.
(a) 15 + 12   (b) 24 + 32
(c) 19 + 16   (d) 37 + 17
(e) 26 + 48   (f) 29 + 41
(g) 63 + 57   (h) 13 + 99

6 This signpost is between Poole and London.

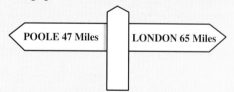

POOLE 47 Miles   LONDON 65 Miles

How far is it from Poole to London?

7

Computer Package
PC   £349
Printer   £125
Software   £65

What is the total cost of this computer package?

8

Holiday Special
CYPRUS

B & B 7 Nights   £249
Insurance   £27

What is the total cost of the holiday?

9 The class attendance in Year 7, Year 8 and Year 9 is shown.

Year 7		Year 8		Year 9	
7A	25	8A	27	9A	26
7B	29	8B	30	9B	25
7C	29	8C	25	9C	27
7D	30	8D	24	9D	29
7E	28	8E	26	9E	26

What is the total attendance
(a) in Year 7,
(b) in Year 8,
(c) in Year 9,
(d) in all fifteen classes?

10 A cinema has two screens. The table shows the number of tickets sold each day last week for Screen 1.

Mon	Tue	Wed	Thu	Fri	Sat	Sun
125	87	95	105	278	487	201

(a) How many tickets were sold for Screen 1 last week?
(b) 891 tickets were sold for Screen 2. How many tickets were sold last week by the cinema?

11 The last four attendances at a football stadium were:
21 004
19 750
18 009
22 267
What is the combined total?

Non-calculator methods for subtraction

Writing numbers in columns

Write the numbers in columns according to place value.
The order in which the numbers are written down is important.
Then, in turn, subtract the numbers of units, tens, hundreds, etc.
If the subtraction in a column cannot be done, because the number being subtracted is greater, borrow 10 from the next column.

Work out $7238 - 642$.

$$
\begin{array}{r}
\overset{6}{7}\overset{11}{2}\overset{1}{3}8 \\
-\ 642 \\
\hline
6596
\end{array}
$$

Units: $8 - 2 = 6$
Tens: $3 - 4$ cannot be done, so borrow 10 from the 2 in the next column. Now $10 + 3 - 4 = 9$.
Hundreds: $1 - 6$ cannot be done, so borrow 10 from the 7 in the next column. Now $10 + 1 - 6 = 5$.
Thousands: $6 - 0 = 6$.

You can use addition to check your subtraction.
Does $6596 + 642 = 7238$?

$$
\begin{array}{r}
6596 \\
+\ 642 \\
\hline
7238 \\
{\scriptstyle 1\ 1}
\end{array}
$$

EXAMPLES

1
$$
\begin{array}{r}
\overset{0}{1}\overset{16}{7}\overset{15}{6}\overset{1}{2} \\
-\ 873 \\
\hline
889
\end{array}
$$

2
$$
\begin{array}{r}
\overset{2}{3}\overset{9}{0}\overset{9}{0}\overset{1}{6} \\
-\ 1847 \\
\hline
1159
\end{array}
$$

3
$$
\begin{array}{r}
\overset{8}{9}\overset{9}{0}\overset{10}{1}\overset{1}{2} \\
-\ 5678 \\
\hline
3334
\end{array}
$$

Addition is the opposite (inverse) operation to subtraction.
If $\quad a - b = c$,
then $\quad c + b = a$.

Check the answers by addition.

Exercise 1.3

Do not use a calculator for this exercise.

1 Here is a number line for $43 - 16$.

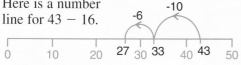

(a) What is $43 - 10$?
(b) What is $43 - 16$?

2 Draw a number line for each of the following questions and work out the answers.
(a) $56 - 28$ (b) $64 - 18$
(c) $44 - 19$ (d) $73 - 38$

3 Write down the answers to the following by working them out in your head.
(a) $100 - 95$ (b) $100 - 8$
(c) $100 - 57$ (d) $100 - 32$
(e) $100 - 24$ (f) $100 - 83$
(g) $100 - 41$ (h) $100 - 79$

4 Work these out in your head.
(a) $26 - 10$ (b) $26 - 9$
(c) $87 - 37$ (d) $87 - 38$
(e) $200 - 110$ (f) $204 - 99$
(g) $500 - 350$ (h) $500 - 199$
(i) $1000 - 425$ (j) $1003 - 999$

5 Work these out by writing the numbers in columns. Use addition to check your answers.
(a) $978 - 624$ (b) $843 - 415$
(c) $1754 - 470$ (d) $407 - 249$
(e) $5070 - 2846$ (f) $2345 - 1876$
(g) $8045 - 1777$ (h) $10\,000 - 6723$

6 A car park has spaces for 345 cars.
On Tuesday 256 spaces are used.
How many spaces are not used?

7 A school has 843 pupils.
How many are boys if there are 459 girls?

8 The table shows the milometer readings for three cars at the start and end of a year.

Which car has done the most miles in the year?

	Start	End
Car A	2501	10980
Car B	55667	67310
Car C	48050	61909

9 Here is a price list for some electrical goods.

(a) How much more does it cost to buy the TV and Video separately than to buy the Combined TV/Video?

(b) I have £500. How much more do I need to buy the Combined TV/Video, and the Music System?

TV	**£199**
Video	**£250**
Combined TV/Video	**£375**
Music System	**£185**

Multiplication of whole numbers

It is very useful to know your Multiplication Tables up to 10×10.

×	1	2	3	4	5	6	7	8	9	10
1	1	2	3	4	5	6	7	8	9	10
2	2	4	6	8	10	12	14	16	18	20
3	3	6	9	12	15	18	21	24	27	30
4	4	8	12	16	20	24	28	32	36	40
5	5	10	15	20	25	30	35	40	45	50
6	6	12	18	24	30	36	42	48	54	60
7	7	14	21	28	35	42	49	56	63	70
8	8	16	24	32	40	48	56	64	72	80
9	9	18	27	36	45	54	63	72	81	90
10	10	20	30	40	50	60	70	80	90	100

Activity

How quickly can you answer the following questions?

$$9 \times 5$$

$$6 \times 6$$

$$7 \times 4$$

$$9 \times 6$$

$$8 \times 7$$

$$9 \times 7$$

$$8 \times 8$$

Working with a partner ask each other questions from the table.

Non-calculator method for short multiplication

Short multiplication is when the multiplying number is less than 10, e.g. 165×7.
One method multiplies the units, tens, hundreds etc. in turn.

```
  1 6 5
×     7
───────
1 1 5 5
  1 4 3
```

Units: $7 \times 5 = 35$, which is 5 carry 3.

Tens: $7 \times 6 = 42$ + carried 3 = 45, which is 5 carry 4.

Hundreds: $7 \times 1 = 7$ + carried 4 = 11, which is 1 carry 1.

There are no more digits to be multiplied by 7, the carried 1 becomes 1 thousand.

EXAMPLES

1
```
  1 6 2
×     4
───────
  6 4 8
    2
```

2
```
  9 0 7 1
×       7
─────────
6 3 4 9 7
      4
```

3
```
  4 8 3 5
×       8
─────────
3 8 6 8 0
    6 2 4
```

Multiplying a whole number by 10, 100, 1000, . . .

When you multiply a whole number by:

10   The units become 10s, the 10s become 100s, the 100s become 1000s, and so on.

100   The units become 100s, the 10s become 1000s, the 100s become 10 000s, and so on.

1000   The units become 1000s, the 10s become 10 000s, the 100s become 100 000s, and so on.

EXAMPLES
$$753 \times 10 = 7530$$
$$753 \times 100 = 75\ 300$$
$$753 \times 1000 = 753\ 000$$

We can show these multiplications in a table.

100 000s	10 000s	1000s	100s	10s	Units
			7	5	3
		7	5	3	0
	7	5	3	0	0
7	5	3	0	0	0

←753 × 10
←753 × 100
←753 × 1000

$100 = 10 \times 10$
Multiplying a number by 100 is the same as multiplying the number by 10 and then by 10 again.

Explain any patterns you can see.

Multiplying a whole number by multiples of 10 (20, 30, 40, . . .)

Work out 753×20.

This can be written as:
$$753 \times 20 = 753 \times 10 \times 2$$
$$= 7530 \times 2$$
$$= 15\ 060$$

$20 = 10 \times 2$

Exercise 1.4   Do not use a calculator for this exercise.

1   I get 8 doughnuts for £1.
How many doughnuts will I get for £5?

2   When John uses a store card he gets 4 points for every pound he spends.
He spends £18.
How many points does he get?

3   A machine makes 24 jigsaws in an hour.
How many jigsaws will it make in 6 hours?

4   Linda is paid 3p for each leaflet she delivers.
She delivers 184 leaflets.
How much is she paid?

5   Work these out using a method you find easiest.
(a) 21×4
(b) 17×5
(c) 36×7
(d) 183×3
(e) 264×8
(f) 3179×5
(g) 4012×6
(h) 6012×7

6   Write down the answers to the following questions. You do not have to show any working.
(a) 132×10
(b) 123×100
(c) 47×1000
(d) 384×100

7   What number should be put in the box to make each of these statements correct?

(a) $231 \times 10 = \square$

(b) $\square \times 1000 = 514\ 000$

(c) $172 \times \square = 17\ 200$

8   A packet of 24 custard cream biscuits costs 39 pence.
I buy 10 packets.
(a)   How many biscuits do I buy?
(b)   How much will they cost altogether?

9 In each maths classroom there are 30 chairs, 20 tables, 50 pencils and 40 rulers.
There are 7 classrooms in the Maths Department.
For the whole department find the total number of
(a) chairs,   (b) tables,
(c) pencils,   (d) rulers.

10 Calculate the number of seconds in
(a) 5 minutes,   (b) 7 minutes,
(c) 20 minutes,   (d) 2 hours.

11 There are 32 classes in a school.
Each class has 30 students.
How many students are there in the school?

12 There are 400 metres in one lap of a running track.
How many metres are there in 25 laps?

13 Use a non-calculator method to calculate these products.
(a) 253×30 (b) 357×20
(c) 537×40 (d) 615×20
(e) 186×70 (f) 239×90
(g) 412×80 (h) 142×70
(i) 632×30 (j) 260×50

14 (a) Describe a method of multiplying by 200, 300, 400, and so on.
(b) Describe a method of multiplying by 2000, 3000, 4000, and so on.

Non-calculator method for short division

The process of dividing a number by a number less than 10 is called **short division**.
Short division relies on knowledge of the Multiplication Tables.
What is $32 \div 8$, $42 \div 7$, $72 \div 9$, $54 \div 6$?

Work out $882 \div 7$.

$7\overline{)8\,^18\,^42}$
  $1\,2\,6$

Starting from the left:
$8 \div 7 = 1$ remainder 1, which is 1 carry 1.
$18 \div 7 = 2$ remainder 4, which is 2 carry 4.
$42 \div 7 = 6$, with no remainder.
So $882 \div 7 = 126$.

> You may set your working out like this:
> $$\frac{1\,2\,6}{7\overline{)8\,^18\,^42}}$$

You can check your division by multiplying.
Does $126 \times 7 = 882$?

> Multiplication is the opposite (inverse) operation to division.
> If $a \div b = c$,
> then $c \times b = a$.

EXAMPLES

1 $6\overline{)1\,4\,^27\,^30}$
      $2\,4\,5$

2 $9\overline{)2\,7\,6\,^63}$
      $3\,0\,7$

Dividing a whole number by 10, 100, 1000, . . .

When you divide a whole number by:
10   The 10s become units, the 100s become 10s, the 1000s become 100s, and so on.
100   The 100s become units, the 1000s become 10s, the 10 000s become 100s, and so on.
1000   The 1000s become units, the 10 000s become 10s, the 100 000s become 100s, and so on.

Examples	10 000s	1000s	100s	10s	Units
$7530 \div 10 = 753$					
$12\,400 \div 100 = 124$		7	5	3	0
$631\,000 \div 1000 = 631$			7	5	3	←$753 \div 10$

Draw tables to show the other division sums. Explain any patterns you can see.

Dividing a whole number by multiples of 10 (20, 30, 40, . . .)

Work out $7530 \div 30$.

$7530 \div 30$
$= (7530 \div 10) \div 3$
$= 753 \div 3$ (dividing by 10)
$= 251$ (dividing by 3)

> $30 = 10 \times 3$
> Dividing by 30 is the same as dividing by 10 and then dividing by 3.

Exercise **1.5**   Do not use a calculator for this exercise.

1 Here is a price list for school equipment:

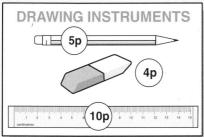

DRAWING INSTRUMENTS

5p

4p

10p

I have 80p.
(a) How many pencils can I buy?
(b) How many rubbers can I buy?
(c) How many rulers can I buy?

2 Calculate these divisions. Show your working clearly. State the remainder if there is one.
Use multiplication to check your answers.
(a) 85 ÷ 5 (b) 471 ÷ 3
(c) 816 ÷ 6 (d) 455 ÷ 6
(e) 3146 ÷ 8 (f) 824 ÷ 4
(g) 9882 ÷ 9 (h) 80 560 ÷ 4

3 Write down the answers to the following questions. You do not have to show your working.
(a) 4560 ÷ 10
(b) 465 000 ÷ 1000
(c) 64 000 ÷ 1000
(d) 65 400 ÷ 100

4 What number should be put in the box to make each of these statements correct?
(a) 56 400 ÷ ☐ = 564
(b) ☐ ÷ 1000 = 702
(c) 35 000 ÷ ☐ = 3500

5 (a) A minibus holds 20 passengers. How many minibuses are needed to carry 160 passengers?
(b) How many £50 notes are needed to pay a bill of £750?
(c) A double-decker bus holds 70 passengers. How many buses are needed to take 840 students on a trip?
(d) A class has 200 minutes of Maths each week. How many 40-minute lessons is this?
(e) How many minutes is 420 seconds?

6 Work out.
(a) 7590 ÷ 30 (b) 7110 ÷ 90
(c) 21 480 ÷ 40 (d) 7560 ÷ 60
(e) 900 ÷ 20 (f) 30 650 ÷ 50

7 (a) Describe a method to divide by multiples of 100 (200, 300, 400, ...)
(b) Work out:
(i) 13 000 ÷ 500
(ii) 263 700 ÷ 900
(iii) 329 600 ÷ 800

Long multiplication

Long multiplication is used when the multiplying number is greater than 10, e.g. 24 × 17.

Work out 24 × 17.

```
      24
    × 17
     168   ← 24 × 7 = 168
  +  240   ← 24 × 10 = 240
     408
```

A standard non-calculator method for doing long multiplication multiplies the number by:
● the units figure, then
● the tens figure, then
● the hundreds figure, and so on.

All these answers are added together.

EXAMPLES

1
```
      145
    ×  62
      290   ← 145 × 2
  +  8700   ← 145 × 60
     8990
```

2
```
      273
    × 234
     1092   ← 273 ×   4
     8190   ← 273 ×  30
  + 54600   ← 273 × 200
    63882
```

Long division

Long division is used when the dividing number is bigger than 10. It works in exactly the same way as short division, except that all the working out is written down.

Consider $952 \div 7$.

```
    1 3 6
7) 9 5 2
   7
   ---
   2 5
   2 1
   ---
     4 2
     4 2
     ---
       0
```

$9 \div 7 = 1$ and a remainder.
What is the remainder?
$1 \times 7 = 7$ (write below the 9).
$9 - 7 = 2$ (which is the remainder).
Bring down the next figure (5) to make 25.
Repeat the above process.
$25 \div 7 = 3$ and a remainder.
$3 \times 7 = 21$, $25 - 21 = 4$ (remainder).
Bring down the next figure (2) to make 42 and repeat the process.
$42 \div 7 = 6$, but there is no remainder.
$6 \times 7 = 42$, $42 - 42 = 0$ (remainder).
There are no more figures to be brought down and there is no remainder.
So $952 \div 7 = 136$.

Using short division:

$$7)9^25^42$$
$$1\ 3\ 6$$

Long division process
- $\div$ (obtain biggest answer possible)
- $\times$ } calculates
- $-$ } the remainder
- Bring down the next figure

Repeat process until there are no more figures to be brought down.

Exercise 1.6

In this exercise use non-calculator methods. Show your working clearly.

Multiplication

1 42×32

2 76×32

3 143×34

4 265×42

5 718×54

6 1038×74

7 765×451

8 9852×672

Division

9 $7871 \div 17$

10 $4582 \div 29$

11 $9471 \div 77$

12 $4864 \div 19$

13 $7560 \div 15$

14 $20\ 928 \div 32$

15 $11\ 368 \div 28$

16 $11\ 232 \div 54$

17 A coach trip costs £29 per person.
48 people go on the trip.
How much money is paid altogether?

18 Here is a price list for some office furniture:

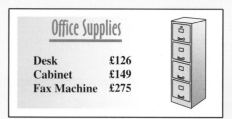

Office Supplies

Desk	£126
Cabinet	£149
Fax Machine	£275

(a) What is the cost of 14 desks?
(b) What is the cost of 23 cabinets?
(c) What is the total cost of 14 desks, 23 cabinets and 17 fax machines?

19 A train has 12 carriages.
Each carriage can seat 118 passengers.
How many passengers can be seated on this train?

20 Work these out and state the remainder each time.
(a) $410 \div 25$ (b) $607 \div 24$ (c) $800 \div 45$

21 A pint of milk costs 29 pence.
How many pints of milk can be bought for £5?
How much change will there be?

22 Tins of beans are packed in boxes of 24.
A supplier has 1000 tins of beans.
(a) How many full boxes is this?
(b) How many tins are left over?

Order of operations in a calculation

What is $4 + 3 \times 5$? It is not sensible to have two possible answers.
It has been agreed that calculations are done obeying certain rules:

First	Brackets and Division line
Second	Divide and Multiply
Third	Addition and Subtraction

EXAMPLES

1 $\quad 4 + 3 \times 5 \qquad = \quad 4 + 15 \qquad = \quad 19$

2 $\quad 10 \div 2 + 3 \qquad = \quad 5 + 3 \qquad = \quad 8$

3 $\quad 10 \div (2 + 3) \qquad = \quad 10 \div 5 \qquad = \quad 2$

4 $\quad (5 + 6) \times 3 + 4 \quad = \quad 11 \times 3 + 4 \quad = \quad 33 + 4 \quad = \quad 37$

5 $\quad \dfrac{12}{11 - 8} - 3 \qquad = \quad \dfrac{12}{3} - 3 \qquad = \quad 4 - 3 \quad = \quad 1$

This is the same as $12 \div (11 - 8) - 3$.

Exercise 1.7

Do not use a calculator for this exercise.

1 Work these out.

(a) $7 + 6 \times 5$
(b) $7 - (6 - 2)$
(c) $24 \div 6 + 5$
(d) $7 \times 6 + 8 \times 2$
(e) $10 \div 5 + 8 \div 2$
(f) $(5 - 2) \times 7 + 9$
(g) $60 \div (5 + 7)$
(h) $60 \div 5 + 7$
(i) $4 \times 3 + 2$
(j) $4 \times (3 + 2)$
(k) $12 \times (20 - 2) \div 9$
(l) $36 \div (5 + 4)$
(m) $4 \times 12 \div 8 - 6$
(n) $9 \times 9 - 5 \times 5$
(o) $(9 + 5) \times (9 - 5)$
(p) $\dfrac{22 - 4}{17 - 8} + 12 \div 3$
(q) $\dfrac{6 \times 3 - 2}{2 \times 2} + 3 \times 8$
(r) $\dfrac{(3 + 7) \times 10 - 19}{(2 + 1) \times (8 - 5)} - 3 \times 3$

2 Choose from the four signs $+$, $-$, $\times$ and $\div$ to make these sums correct.

(a) $5 \quad 6 \quad 7 = 37$
(b) $5 \quad 6 \quad 7 = 47$
(c) $15 \quad 8 \quad 9 = 87$
(d) $15 \quad 8 \quad 9 = 129$
(e) $15 \quad 8 \quad 9 = 111$
(f) $15 \quad 5 \quad 3 = 6$
(g) $5 \quad 24 \quad 6 = 1$
(h) $19 \quad 19 \quad 7 \quad 0 = 1$
(i) $4 \quad 4 \quad 7 \quad 2 = 30$

3 Using all the numbers 6, 3, 2 and 1 in this order, brackets and the signs $+$, $-$, $\times$ and $\div$ make all the numbers from 1 to 10.
$\quad 6 - 3 \times 2 + 1 = 1, \qquad 6 - 3 - 2 + 1 = 2, \qquad$ and so on.

4 The caretaker set out 17 rows of chairs. There are 15 chairs in each row. How many more chairs are needed to provide seats for 280 people?

5 Claire is 16 cm taller than Rachel. Their heights add up to 312 cm. How tall is Rachel?

6 The admission charges to a zoo are £4 for a child and £7 for an adult. Zoe is organising a trip to the zoo for a group of people and worked out that the total cost would be £336. She collected £84 from the adults in the group.
(a) How many children are in the group?
(b) What is the total number of people in the group?

What you need to know

You should be able to:
- Read and write whole numbers expressed in figures and words.
- Order whole numbers.
- Recognise the place value of each digit in a number.
- Use mental methods to carry out addition and subtraction.
- Carry out accurately non-calculator methods for addition and subtraction.
- Know the Multiplication Tables up to 10×10.
- Carry out multiplication by a number less than 10 (short multiplication).
- Multiply whole numbers by 10, 100, 1000, . . .
- Multiply whole numbers by 20, 30, 40, . . .
- Carry out division by a number less than 10 (short division).
- Divide whole numbers by 10, 100, 1000, . . .
- Divide whole numbers by 20, 30, 40, . . .
- Carry out long multiplication.
- Carry out long division.
- Know the order of operations in a calculation.

IDEAS FOR INVESTIGATION

Write down a three-digit number.
  Write in words.
    Count the letters.
    Write this number in words.
    Count the letters.
    Write this number in words
  and so on.

Example
569, five hundred and sixty-nine
23, twenty-three
11, eleven
6, six
3, three
5, five
4, four

1 Start with the number 207.
What number do you end up with?

2 Repeat the process starting with a different number.

3 Do you always end up with the same number?

Review Exercise

Do not use a calculator for this exercise.

1 (a) Write 870302 in words.
    (b) Write three million twenty-seven thousand four hundred and nine in figures.

2 By using each of the digits 4, 8, 7, 2, 9 and 5,
    (a) write the biggest six-digit number you can,
    (b) write the smallest six-digit **odd** number you can.

3 In the game of darts the scores of the three darts are added
together. These are then taken away from the current total
to calculate the new total. In each case work out the score
of the three darts and the new total.

	Current Total	1st dart	2nd dart	3rd dart	Score	New Total
(a)	501	60	18	19	[ ]	[ ]
(b)	420	19	57	38	[ ]	[ ]
(c)	301	50	25	17	[ ]	[ ]

10

4 Work out the following. Show your working.
   (a)   465 + 12 + 1582   (b)   2465 − 1878

5 Write down the answers to these questions.
   (a)   735 × 100   (b)   214 × 30   (c)   3 020 000 ÷ 1000   (d)   18 480 ÷ 40

6 The chart shows the distances in miles between some towns.

Liverpool				
35	Manchester			
109	70	Nottingham		
77	37	44	Sheffield	
102	71	87	61	York

Issac drives from Liverpool to Nottingham, from Nottingham to York and then from York back to Liverpool.
Calculate the total distance he drives.

7 Work out the following. Show your working clearly.
   (a)   718 × 9   (b)   1446 ÷ 6

8 Calculate these. Remember to do the operations in the right order.
   (a)   2 + 6 × 8   (b)   (9 − 4) × (3 + 7)   (c)   72 ÷ 8 + 1   (d) $\dfrac{(5 \times 6 - 3) - 21 \div 3}{2 \times 3 + 4}$

9 Find the cost of 15 cameras at £145 each.
Edexcel

10 Lauren does a paper round.
She delivers 47 newspapers, 6 days a week for 52 weeks a year.
How many newspapers does she deliver altogether in one year?

11 A supermarket orders 1800 kg of potatoes.
The potatoes are delivered in 15 kg bags.
How many bags are delivered?

12 One thousand chocolate biscuits are packed in boxes of 6.
   (a)   How many full boxes will there be?   (b)   How many biscuits will be left over?

13 A group of 43 people pay £379 each to go on a skiing holiday.
What is the total cost of the holiday?

14 The table shows the value of each prize and the number of winners in a lottery.
   (a)   Work out the total number of winners.
   (b)   Work out the total amount of prize money won.

Value of each prize	Number of winners
£1 000 000	1
£ 100 000	4
£ 50 000	10
£ 25 000	17
£ 10 000	44
£ 5000	87

Edexcel

15 Bob is taking 26 boys to watch a football match.
The total cost is £442.
What is the cost for each boy?

16 Sylvia has collected £1632 to provide Christmas meals for retired people.
Each meal costs £12. How many meals can she provide?

CHAPTER 2

Decimals

Numbers and quantities are not always whole numbers.

The number system you met in Chapter 1 can be extended to include **decimal numbers**, such as tenths, hundredths, thousandths, and smaller numbers.

A **decimal point** is used to separate the whole number part from the decimal part of the number.

73.26   This number is read as seventy-three point two six.

whole number   decimal part
73   2 tenths + 6 hundredths
                 (which is the same as 26 hundredths)

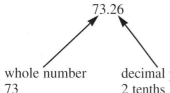

Place value

In the number 1.53 the digit 1 is worth 1 unit = 1

the digit 5 is worth 5 tenths = 0.5

the digit 3 is worth 3 hundredths = 0.03

$1.53 = 1 + 0.5 + 0.03$

1 unit = 10 tenths
1 tenth = 10 hundredths
1 hundredth = 10 thousandths
… and so on.

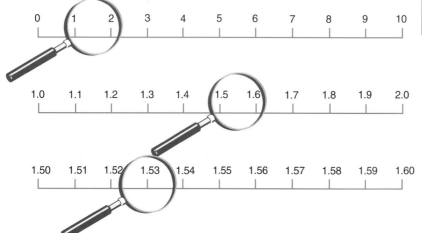

The first digit after the decimal point represents **tenths**.

The second digit after the decimal point represents **hundredths**.

The number 1.53 can be represented by a diagram.

1 unit

5 tenths

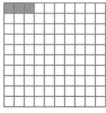

3 hundredths

Ordering decimals

Compare the numbers 52.359 and 52.36. Which number is the bigger?

You can use a grid to compare the numbers.

tens	units	.	tenths	hundredths	thousandths
5	2	.	3	5	9
5	2	.	3	6	

Start by comparing the digits with the greatest place value, the tens.
Both numbers have 5 tens, so move down to compare the units.
Both numbers have 2 units, so move down to the tenths.
Both numbers have 3 tenths, so move down to the hundredths.
52.359 has 5 hundredths but 52.36 has 6 hundredths.
So 52.36 is bigger than 52.359.

A similar method can be used to place a list of decimal numbers in order.

Exercise **2.1**

1 2.564 = 2 + 0.5 + 0.06 + 0.004
Write these numbers in the same way.
(a) 7.62   (b) 37.928
(c) 7.541   (d) 20.503

2 In the number 17.4<u>6</u>2 the value of the
underlined figure is 0.06.
Give the value of the underlined figures in
the following.
(a) 27.<u>4</u>3   (b) 36.42<u>9</u>
(c) 2<u>8</u>5.03   (d) 0.7<u>5</u>3

3 Write down the numbers shown by these
diagrams.
(a)
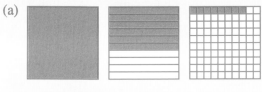

(b)
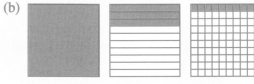

(c)

4 Look at these decimals.
      0.07, 0.6, 0.09, 0.1.
(a) Which is the smallest number?
(b) Which is the largest number?

5 On these scales what numbers are
shown by the arrows?
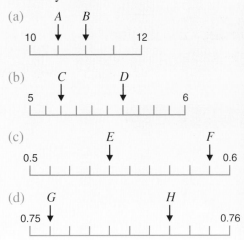

6 List the following decimals in
ascending order.
(a) 3.1, 3.01, 3.001, 3.15, 3.2.
(b) 3.567, 3.657, 3.576, 3.675.
(c) 0.1, 0.55, 0.45, 0.5, 0.15.

7 List the following decimals in
descending order.
(a) 9.87, 8.79, 9.78, 8.97.
(b) 0.00015, 0.15, 1.5, 0.015.
(c) 2.67, 2.7, 2.599, 2.701.

8 Compare the numbers 47.5074 and
47.506. Which is the bigger number?

9 Compare the numbers 93.07 and
93.072. Which is the smaller number?

Non-calculator methods for addition and subtraction of decimals

Writing numbers in columns

Write the numbers in tidy columns according to place value.
This is easily done by keeping the decimal points in a vertical column.
Start the addition or subtraction from the right, just as you did for whole numbers.
Use the same methods for carrying and borrowing as well.

EXAMPLES

1 Work out $42.6 + 0.75 + 9$

$$
\begin{array}{r}
4\,2.6 \\
0.7\,5 \\
+\;\;\;9.0 \\
\hline
5\,2.3\,5 \\
\hline
{\scriptstyle 1\;1}
\end{array}
$$

2 Work out $17.1 - 8.72$

$$
\begin{array}{r}
1\,\overset{6}{7}.\overset{10}{1}\overset{1}{0} \\
-\;\;\;8.7\,2 \\
\hline
8.3\,8 \\
\hline
\end{array}
$$

Use addition to check this answer.

You can write 9 as 9.0 or 9.00 to keep your figures tidy.
This does not change the value of the number.
42.6 can be written as 42.60
17.1 can be written as 17.10

Working mentally

Addition and subtraction of decimals can be carried out mentally, in your head.
For example, using place value, we know that $2.5 = 2 + 0.5$.
So, adding 2.5 to a number is the same as adding 2 and then adding 0.5.

EXAMPLES

1 Work out $8.31 + 3.58$.

$3.58 = 3 + 0.5 + 0.08$
$8.31 + 3.58$
$= 8.31 + 3 + 0.5 + 0.08$
$= 8.39 + 3 + 0.5$ (adding 8.31 and 0.08)
$= 8.89 + 3$ (adding 8.39 and 0.5)
$= 11.89$

$3.58 = 3 + 0.5 + 0.08$
The adding of 3, 0.5 and 0.08 can be carried out in any order.
Here, we have added the numbers in order of size, starting with the smallest.
Choose a method you find easiest.

2 Work out $25.4 - 8.7$.

$25.4 - 8.7$
$= 25.4 - 8 - 0.7$
$= 24.7 - 8$ (subtracting 0.7 from 25.4)
$= 16.7$

$8.7 = 8 + 0.7$
To subtract 8.7, first subtract 0.7 and then **subtract** 8.
Alternatively, first subtract 8 and then **subtract** 0.7.

Money

1360p can be written as £13.60

£13.60
complete number of pounds, 13   number of pence, 60

£6 can be written as £6.00
There must be exactly **two** figures after the decimal point when a decimal point is used to record amounts of money.

Other uses of decimal notation

Many measurements are recorded using decimals, including time, distance, weight, volume, etc.
The same rules for addition and subtraction can be applied if all the measurements involved are recorded using the same units.

I buy a newspaper for 45p, a set of batteries for £2.50 and a book of stamps for £2.
What is the total cost? How much change should I get from £5?

Working in pounds.

$$
\begin{array}{r}
0.4\,5 \\
2.5\,0 \\
+\ 2.0\,0 \\
\hline
4.9\,5
\end{array}
\qquad
\begin{array}{r}
5.0\,0 \\
-\ 4.9\,5 \\
\hline
0.0\,5
\end{array}
$$

The total cost is £4.95.
The change is £0.05 or 5p.

Exercise 2.2

Do this exercise without using your calculator, showing your working clearly.
Having completed the exercise you can use a calculator to check your answers.

1 (a) Work out.
   (i) 5.14 + 3.72   (ii) 7.065 + 5.384
   (iii) 11.8 + 5.69
 (b) Show how subtraction can be used to check each of the answers in part (a).

2 (a) Work out.
   (i) 9.47 − 3.24   (ii) 37.6 − 13.28
   (iii) 45.04 − 20.36
 (b) Show how addition can be used to check each of the answers in part (a).

3 Work these out in your head.
   (a) 2.5 + 8.4   (b) 0.7 + 0.95
   (c) 0.36 + 0.54   (d) 6.47 + 4.53
   (e) 2.7 − 1.5   (f) 1.3 − 0.7
   (g) 0.4 − 0.16   (h) 15.3 − 6.4

4 Work out.
   (a) 6.54 + 0.27 + 0.03
   (b) 79.1 + 7 + 0.23
   (c) 10 − 4.78
   (d) 9.57 − 4.567
   (e) 2.22 + 0.78
   (f) 9.13 − 7.89
   (g) 5.564 + 0.017 + 10.2
   (h) 17.1 − 8.82
   (i) 9.123 + 0.71 + 6.2
   (j) 9.123 − 2.85

5 Add these amounts of money. Calculate the change from the given amount.
   (a) (i) 45p, 63p, 79p, £1.43
       (ii) What is the change from £5?
   (b) (i) £2.47, £6, £1.50, £1.27
       (ii) What is the change from £15?
   (c) (i) 31p, £0.25, 27p
       (ii) What is the change from £10?
   (d) (i) £12, £3.57, 67p
       (ii) What is the change from £50?

6 I have 2.5 kg of potatoes, 0.5 kg of butter, 0.75 kg of grapes and 0.6 kg of cheese in my shopping bag.
What is the total weight of my shopping?

7 Fred cuts three pieces of wood of length 0.95 m, 1.67 m and 2.5 m from a plank 10 m long.
How much wood is left?

8 Kevin is 0.15 m shorter than Sally.
Sally is 1.7 m tall. How tall is Kevin?

9 In bobsleigh the times of four runs are added together.
Team A records: 37.03 sec   37.76 sec
                 36.89 sec   37.25 sec
Team B records: 37.27 sec   37.45 sec
                 37.64 sec   36.72 sec
Team C records: 36.87 sec   37.51 sec
                 37.03 sec   38.12 sec
   (a) Work out the total time for each team.
   (b) The team with the lowest time wins.
       Put the teams in order 1st, 2nd and 3rd.

10 Swimmer A finishes the 100 m freestyle in 51.371 seconds. Swimmer B finishes in 52.090 seconds. How long after Swimmer A does Swimmer B finish?

11 In skiing the times of two runs are added together.
   (a) Skier A has times of 47.12 seconds and 48.09 seconds. What is her total time?
   (b) Skier B completes her first run in 47.49 seconds. What time does she have to do in her second run to equal the total time of Skier A?

Multiplying and dividing decimals by powers of 10 (10, 100, 1000, . . .)

When you multiply a decimal by:

10   Each figure moves 1 place to the left.
100   Each figure moves 2 places to the left.
1000 Each figure moves 3 places to the left.
     … and so on.

When you divide a decimal by:

10   Each figure moves 1 place to the right.
100   Each figure moves 2 places to the right.
1000 Each figure moves 3 places to the right.
     … and so on.

EXAMPLES

			2 •	7	6
		2	7 •	6	
	2	7	6 •		
2	7	6	0 •		

Multiplication

←2.76 × 10 = 27.6

←2.76 × 100 = 276

←2.76 × 1000 = 2760

276 has the same value as 276.0

Noughts can be used as place fillers to locate the decimal point, as in 2.76 × 1000 = 2760. If the nought was omitted the value of all other figures would change.

3 •	4	5			
0 •	3	4	5		
0 •	0	3	4	5	
0 •	0	0	3	4	5

Division

←3.45 ÷ 10 = 0.345

←3.45 ÷ 100 = 0.0345

←3.45 ÷ 1000 = 0.00345

Exercise 2.3

Do this exercise without using a calculator.

1 Work out the following.
   (a)   25.06 × 10   (b)   25.06 × 100   (c)   25.06 × 1000
   (d)   0.93 × 10   (e)   0.93 × 100   (f)   0.93 × 1000
   (g)   0.0623 × 10   (h)   0.0623 × 100   (i)   0.0623 × 1000
   (j)   9.451 × 10   (k)   9.451 × 100   (l)   9.451 × 1000

2 Work out the following.
   (a)   37.7 ÷ 10   (b)   37.7 ÷ 100   (c)   37.7 ÷ 1000
   (d)   0.27 ÷ 10   (e)   0.27 ÷ 100   (f)   0.27 ÷ 1000
   (g)   189.02 ÷ 10   (h)   189.02 ÷ 100   (i)   189.02 ÷ 1000
   (j)   9 ÷ 10   (k)   9 ÷ 100   (l)   9 ÷ 1000

3   (a)   Multiply 0.064 by
         (i) 10   (ii) 100   (iii) 1000
    (b)   Divide 6.4 by
         (i) 10   (ii) 100   (iii) 1000

4 An ice cream costs £1.35.
   (a)   How much will 10 cost?
   (b)   How much will 100 cost?
   (c)   How much will 1000 cost?

5 A biro costs 25 pence.

(a) How much will 10 cost?   (b) How much will 100 cost?   (c) How much will 1000 cost?

6 One lap of a cycling track is 0.504 km.

(a) How far is 10 laps?   (b) How far is 100 laps?   (c) How far is 1000 laps?

7 (a) 100 calculators cost £795. How much does one cost?

(b) 1000 pencils cost £120. How much does one cost?

(c) 10 litres of petrol cost £6.69. How would the cost of 1 litre be advertised?

8 Write down pairs of calculations which give the same answer.

12.3×1000	$12.3 \div 100$	12.3×0.1	$12.3 \div 0.01$	12.3×10	$12.3 \div 0.1$
12.3×100	12.3×0.001	$12.3 \div 0.001$	$12.3 \div 10$	$12.3 \div 1000$	12.3×0.01

Multiplying decimals

The result of multiplying two numbers is called the **product**.

Activity

Use a calculator to multiply these decimals.

5.924×2.34 5.2×6.4 6×3.7 5.1×6.02 2.16×5.79

Count the total number of decimal places in the numbers to be multiplied together.
For example, 5.924 has three decimal places (there are three figures to the right of the decimal point) and 2.34 has two decimal places. The product of 5.924 and 2.34 has five decimal places. Can you find a rule?

How many decimal places does your rule predict 0.5×0.5 should have?

Non-calculator method for multiplying decimals

To multiply decimals without using a calculator:

1 Ignore the decimal points and multiply the numbers using long multiplication.

2 Count the total number of decimal places in the numbers being multiplied together.

3 Place the decimal point so that the answer has the same total number of decimal places.

EXAMPLE

1 Work out 1.752×0.23.

```
        1.7 5 2
      × 0.2 3
    ───────────
        5 2 5 6   ← 1752 × 3
      3 5 0 4 0   ← 1752 × 20
    ───────────
      0.4 0 2 9 6    The answer must have 5 decimal places because 1.752 has 3 and 0.23 has 2.
```

$1.752 \times 0.23 = 0.40296$

2 Work out 4.25×0.18.

$$
\begin{array}{r}
4.2\,5 \\
\times\,0.1\,8 \\
\hline
3\,4\,0\,0 \quad \leftarrow 425 \times 8 \\
4\,2\,5\,0 \quad \leftarrow 425 \times 10 \\
\hline
0.7\,6\,5\,0
\end{array}
$$
The answer must have 4 decimal places because 4.25 has 2 and 0.18 has 2.

$4.25 \times 0.18 = 0.7650$ This can be written as 0.765 which has the same value as 0.7650.

3 Work out 0.2×0.4.

$$
\begin{array}{r}
0.2 \\
\times\,0.4 \\
\hline
0.0\,8
\end{array}
$$
0.2 has 1 decimal place.
0.4 has 1 decimal place.
The answer has 2 decimal places.

$4 \times 2 = 8$
The answer must have 2 decimal places.
Noughts are used in the answer to locate
the decimal point and to preserve place
value.

Exercise 2.4

Do this exercise without using a calculator, showing your working clearly.
Having completed the exercise you can use a calculator to check your answers.

1 Work these out in your head.
(a) 1.7×5 (b) 1.2×0.3 (c) 2.6×0.5
(d) 0.6×0.8 (e) 0.3×0.2 (f) 1.2×1.2

2 Calculate these products.
(a) 2.5×3.5 (b) 28.7×1.9 (c) 4.12×0.25
(d) 6.9×4.32 (e) 0.01×0.07 (f) 0.1×0.1
(g) 0.01×0.01 (h) 134×0.73 (i) 10.7×5.4
(j) 0.074×0.0024

3 (a) Multiply each of these numbers by 0.6.
      (i) 5   (ii) 2.5   (iii) 0.4   (iv) 25
(b) What do you notice about the original numbers and each of your answers?

4 Work out the cost of these vegetables.
(a) 0.6 kg of carrots at 35p per kilogram.
(b) 4.6 kg of potatoes at 40p per kilogram.
(c) 1.2 kg of cabbage at 65p per kilogram.

5 What is the cost of each of these lengths of material?
(a) 7 metres of sheeting at £1.99 a metre.
(b) 4.5 metres of linen at £2.24 a metre.
(c) 7.8 metres of satin at £6.95 a metre.
(d) 3.2 metres of silk at £8.20 a metre.

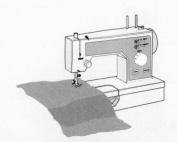

6 (a) £1 can be exchanged for 9.75 French francs. What is the value in French francs of
  (i) £3.60,   (ii) 60p,
  (iii) £54.20?

(b) £1 can be exchanged for $1.64 US dollars. What is the value in US dollars of
  (i) £7.50,   (ii) 75p,
  (iii) £36.50?

7 Work out the cost for each of these portions of cheese.
  (a) 0.7 kg of Stilton.
  (b) 1.6 kg of Cheddar.
  (c) 0.8 kg of Sage Derby.
  (d) 0.45 kg of Cotherstone.

Select
CHEESES
Price per kilogram
Cheddar   £3.20
Cotherstone £5.20
Sage Derby   £3.25
Stilton   £6.20

Dividing decimals

Non-calculator method for dividing decimals

Work out $2.4 \div 0.4$.
In other words, how many 0.4's add up to 2.4?

$0.4 + 0.4 + 0.4 + 0.4 + 0.4 + 0.4 = 2.4$
So $2.4 \div 0.4 = 6$

$2.4 \div 0.4$ can be written as $\frac{2.4}{0.4}$

$\frac{2.4}{0.4} = \frac{2.4 \times 10}{0.4 \times 10} = \frac{24}{4} = 6$

> It is easier to divide by a whole number than by a decimal.

To divide by a decimal:
1. Multiply the dividing number by a power of 10 (10, 100, 1000, …) so that it becomes a whole number.
2. Multiply the number to be divided by the same number.
3. If necessary the answer will have a decimal point in the same place.

EXAMPLES

1 Work out the following.
  (a) $4 \div 0.8$
    Multiply both numbers by 10.
    $40 \div 8 = 5$

  (b) $2 \div 0.25$
    Multiply both numbers by 100.
    $200 \div 25 = 8$

  (c) $9 \div 4$

$$4 \overline{)9.0^{1}0^{2}0}$$
$$\quad 2.2\,5$$

  (d) $16 \div 5$

$$5 \overline{)1\,6.0^{1}}$$
$$\quad 3.2$$

> Noughts are added until the division is finished.

2 8 video tapes cost £14.
How much does each tape cost?

You must work out $14 \div 8$.

$$8 \overline{)1\,4.^{6}0^{4}0}$$
$$\quad 1.7\,5$$

One video tape costs £1.75.

> Noughts can be added to the end of a decimal.
> Adding noughts does not change the value of the number. 14 has the same value as 14.00.
> Continue dividing until either there is no remainder or the required accuracy is obtained.

EXAMPLE

3 Work out 2.898 ÷ 0.23.

0.23 × **100** = 23 (whole number)
2.898 × **100** = 289.8

289.8 ÷ 23 has the same value as 2.898 ÷ 0.23 and can be worked out using long division.

2.898 ÷ 0.23 = 12.6

```
        1 2.6
2 3 ) 2 8 9.8
    − 2 3
        5 9
      − 4 6
        1 3 8
      − 1 3 8
            0
```

Exercise 2.5

Do this exercise without using a calculator, showing your working clearly. Having completed the exercise you can use a calculator to check your answers.

1 Work out.
(a) 2 ÷ 0.5   (b) 3 ÷ 0.2   (c) 6 ÷ 0.4
(d) 10 ÷ 2.5   (e) 6 ÷ 0.12

2 Work out.
(a) 7 ÷ 4   (b) 8 ÷ 5   (c) 1.2 ÷ 0.5
(d) 10.5 ÷ 6   (e) 9 ÷ 8

3 Work out.
(a) 2.46 ÷ 0.2   (b) 0.146 ÷ 0.05
(c) 2.42 ÷ 0.4   (d) 100.1 ÷ 0.07
(e) 0.0025 ÷ 0.05   (f) 0.05 ÷ 0.004
(g) 4.578 ÷ 0.7   (h) 0.3 ÷ 0.008

4 Use long division to work out the following.
(a) 81.4 ÷ 2.2   (b) 15.12 ÷ 2.7
(c) 7 ÷ 0.16   (d) 11.256 ÷ 0.24
(e) 0.1593 ÷ 0.015   (f) 16.074 ÷ 0.47

5 (a) Divide each of these numbers by 0.6.
     (i) 6   (ii) 3.6   (iii) 0.18
(b) What do you notice about the original numbers and each of your answers?

6 A steel bar is 12.73 metres long. How many pieces 0.19 metres long can be cut from it?

7 A jug holds 1.035 litres. A small glass holds 0.023 litres. How many of the small glasses would be required to fill the jug?

8 (a) A 3-litre bottle of lemonade costs £1.41. What is the cost of 1 litre of lemonade?
(b) A pack of 7 tape cassettes costs £9.45. How much does each tape cassette cost?
(c) 13 oranges cost £1.43. How much does each orange cost?
(d) 12 rolls cost £1.08. How much does each roll cost?
(e) 25 litres of petrol cost £16.70. What is the cost of 1 litre of petrol?

Changing decimals to fractions

How to change a decimal to a fraction:

Change 0.12 to a fraction.	0.12
Write the decimal without the decimal point. This will be the numerator (top number).	12
The denominator (bottom number) is a power of 10. The number of noughts is the same as the number of decimal places in the original decimal.	$\frac{12}{100}$
Divide both the numerator and denominator by the largest possible number.	Divide by 4
This gives the fraction in its simplest form.	$\frac{3}{25}$

Fractions are covered in further detail in Chapter 7.

EXAMPLE

Write the following decimals as fractions in their simplest form.

(a) $0.3 = \frac{3}{10}$ (b) $0.6 = \frac{6}{10} = \frac{3}{5}$ (c) $0.45 = \frac{45}{100} = \frac{9}{20}$

(d) $1.5 = 1 + 0.5$

$= 1 + \frac{5}{10}$

$= 1 + \frac{1}{2}$

$= 1\frac{1}{2}$

> $1\frac{1}{2}$ is called a **mixed number**.
> It is a mixture of whole numbers and fractions.

Recurring decimals

Some decimals have recurring digits.

For example, $\frac{1}{3} = 0.3333\ldots$.

The number $0.3333\ldots$ is called a **recurring decimal**.

> Recurring decimals are covered in more detail in Chapter 7.

Exercise **2.6**

1 Write the following decimals as fractions in their simplest form.
   (a) 0.25   (b) 0.5   (c) 0.75   (d) 0.1

2 Write the following decimals as fractions in their simplest form.
   (a) 0.7   (b) 0.4   (c) 0.01   (d) 0.2
   (e) 0.05   (f) 0.15   (g) 0.52   (h) 0.07
   (i) 0.125   (j) 0.65   (k) 0.6   (l) 0.95

3 Change these decimals into mixed numbers.
   (a) 1.7   (b) 2.3   (c) 1.4   (d) 3.25
   (e) 4.8   (f) 12.1   (g) 16.75   (h) 5.05

4 What fraction is equal to each of these recurring decimals?
   (a) 0.6666…   (b) 0.1111…   (c) 0.5555…

What you need to know

Without using a calculator you should be able to:

● Add and subtract decimals.

● Use decimal notation for money and other measures.

● Multiply and divide decimals by powers of 10 (10, 100, 1000, …)

● Multiply decimals by other decimals.

● Divide decimals by other decimals.

● Change decimals to fractions.

● Carry out a variety of calculations involving decimals.

● Know that:
   when a number is **multiplied** by a number between 0 and 1 the result will be **smaller** than the original number,
   when a number is **divided** by a number between 0 and 1 the result will be **larger** than the original number.

Choose any positive whole number   e.g. 20
On a calculator multiply 20 by several positive decimal numbers
e.g. 3.7, 0.24, 23.1, 0.98
$20 \times 3.7 = 74$ (bigger than 20)
$20 \times 0.24 = 4.8$ (smaller than 20)

Find a condition for a number to multiply 20 and make the answer **smaller** than 20.

Is the same condition true for any number other than 20?
*i.e. for a number to multiply 15 and make the answer **smaller** than 15.*

Now divide 20 by several positive decimal numbers e.g. 3.7, 0.24, 23.1, 0.98
$20 \div 3.7 \ = 5.405405...$ (smaller than 20)
$20 \div 0.24 = 83.33333...$ (bigger than 20)

Find a condition for a number to divide into 20 and make the answer **bigger** than 20.

Is the same condition true for any number other than 20?
*i.e. for a number to divide 15 and make the answer **bigger** than 15.*

Review Exercise

Do not use a calculator for questions 1 to 10.

1 (a) (i) $1.045 + 9.7 + 10$
        (ii) $9.89 + 0.017 + 4.5$
        (iii) $72.4 + 100.4 + 0.92 + 5.5$
    (b) (i) $9.75 - 8.88$
        (ii) $10 - 5.67$
        (iii) $4.1 - 2.57$
    (c) Check the subtractions in part (b) with an addition.

2 A 4×100 m relay team runs the four stages in 10.01 s, 9.93 s, 10.15 s and 9.91 s. What is the overall time for the team?

3 Two pieces of wood of length 97 cm and 1.78 m are sawn from a plank 5.12 m long. How much wood is left?

4 (a) Multiply 7.62 by
        (i) 10   (ii) 100   (iii) 1000
    (b) Divide 7.62 by
        (i) 10   (ii) 100   (iii) 1000

5 (a) Multiply 87.3 by
        (i) 20   (ii) 30   (iii) 40
    (b) Divide 87.3 by
        (i) 20   (ii) 30   (iii) 40

6 (a) A calculator costs £4.95. How much do 50 cost?
    (b) 20 textbooks cost £159.80. How much does one cost?

7 Calculate these products.
    (a) 7.4×6.3
    (b) 3.76×2.7
    (c) 176.5×0.6

8 Calculate these divisions.
    (a) $16.56 \div 2.3$
    (b) $98.8 \div 0.08$
    (c) $5480 \div 0.4$

9 Cakes cost 27 pence each. How many cakes can you buy with £5?

10 A tin of dog food costs 86 pence. Aimee's dog eats 1.5 tins of dog food every day. How much does she spend on tins of dog food each week?

11 Work out $\dfrac{197.6}{2.4 + 7.1}$.

12 Work out $\dfrac{4.3 \times 3.5}{4.3 - 3.5}$. Write down your full calculator display.

13 In this question you **must** use your calculator and you **may** write down any stages in your calculation.

Evaluate $\dfrac{(14.08 - 2.003) \times 1.2}{6.3 - 2.01}$.

Edexcel

CHAPTER 3

Approximation and Estimation

Approximation

In real-life it is not always necessary to use exact numbers. A number can be **rounded** to an **approximate** number. Numbers are rounded according to how accurately we wish to give details. For example, the distance to the Sun can be given as 93 million miles.

Can you think of other situations where approximations might be used?

Rounding to the nearest 10, 100, 1000

If there were 21 152 people at a football match the newspaper report could say, "21 000 at the football match".

Consider the number 7487.
The same number can be rounded to different degrees of accuracy depending on the situation.

Rounding to the nearest 10

7487 is between 7480 and 7490, but it is closer to 7490.
7487 rounded to the nearest 10 is 7490.

7480   7487   7490

Rounding to the nearest 100

7487 is between 7400 and 7500, but it is closer to 7500.
7487 rounded to the nearest 100 is 7500.

7400   7487   7500

Rounding to the nearest 1000

7487 is between 7000 and 8000, but it is closer to 7000.
7487 rounded to the nearest 1000 is 7000.

7000   7487   8000

The number 7487 can be approximated as 7490, 7500 or 7000 depending on the degree of accuracy required.

It is a convention to round a number which is in the middle to the higher number.
75 to the nearest 10 is 80.
450 to the nearest 100 is 500.
8500 to the nearest 1000 is 9000.

EXAMPLES	Rounded to the nearest 10	Rounded to the nearest 100	Rounded to the nearest 1000
7547	7550	7500	8000
973	970	1000	1000
62 783	62 780	62 800	63 000
9125	9130	9100	9000

The number of visitors to the local museum was reported as 2600, to the nearest hundred.
What is the smallest possible number of visitors?
What is the greatest possible number of visitors?

The smallest possible number of visitors is 2550.
The greatest possible number of visitors is 2649.

Exercise 3.1

1

(a) Which of these numbers:
4850, 4860, 4870, 4880, 4890
is closest to 4872?

(b) Which of these numbers:
4600, 4700, 4800, 4900, 5000
is closest to 4872?

(c) Which of these numbers:
3000, 4000, 5000, 6000
is closest to 4872?

2 Round the number 7425
(a) to the nearest 10,
(b) to the nearest 100,
(c) to the nearest 1000.

3 Copy and complete this table.

Number	Round to the nearest 10	Round to the nearest 100	Round to the nearest 1000
7613	7610	7600	8000
977			
61 115			
9714			
623			
9949			
5762			
7501			
7500			
7499			

4 Write down these figures to appropriate degrees of accuracy.
(a) There were 19 141 people at the football match.
(b) There were 259 people on the plane.
(c) Tom had 141 marbles.
(d) The class raised £49.67 for charity.
(e) There are 129 students in Year 7.
(f) The population of the town is 24 055.
(g) The land area of the country is 309 123 km^2.
(h) The distance to London is 189 km.
(i) Sarah spent £50.99 on CDs.
(j) There were 693 students in the school.

5 Write down a number each time which fits these roundings.
(a) It is 750 to the nearest 10 but 700 to the nearest 100.
(b) It is 750 to the nearest 10 but 800 to the nearest 100.
(c) It is 8500 to the nearest 100 but 8000 to the nearest 1000.
(d) It is 8500 to the nearest 100 but 9000 to the nearest 1000.

6 "43 000 spectators watch thrilling Test Match".
The number reported in the newspaper was correct to the nearest thousand.
What is the smallest possible number of spectators?

7 Carl has 140 postcards in his collection.
The number is given to the nearest ten.
What is the smallest and greatest number of postcards Carl could have in his collection?

8 "You require 2700 tiles to tile your swimming pool."
This figure is correct to the nearest 100.
What is the greatest number of tiles needed?

Rounding in real-life problems

In a real-life problem a rounding must be used which gives a common sense answer.

Penny is arranging a BBQ.
50 people have been invited.
She caters for everyone to have one burger.
Burgers are sold in packs of 12.
How many packs of burgers should she buy?

The answer is found by working out 50 ÷ 12.
In 4 packs, there are 4 × 12 = 48 burgers.
In 5 packs, there are 5 × 12 = 60 burgers.
50 ÷ 12 = 4 remainder 2.
Penny must buy 5 packs in order that everybody has one burger.
(In fact she will have 10 left over for those who might want a second burger.)

EXAMPLES

1 A Year group in a school are going to Alton Towers. There are 242 students and teachers going.
Each coach can carry 55 passengers.
How many coaches should be ordered?

242 ÷ 55 = 4.4
This should be rounded up to 5.

4 coaches can only carry 220 passengers (4 × 55 = 220).

2 Filing cabinets are to be placed along a wall.
The available space is 460 cm.
Each cabinet is 80 cm wide.
How many can be fitted in?

460 ÷ 80 = 5.75
This should be rounded down to 5.

Although the answer is nearly 6 the 6th cabinet would not fit in.

Exercise **3.2**

Do not use a calculator for this exercise.

1 49 students are waiting to go to the Sports Stadium. A minibus can take 15 passengers at a time. How many trips are required?

2 A classroom wall is 700 cm long. How many tables, each 120 cm long, could be fitted along the wall?

3 76 people are waiting to go to the top of Canary Wharf. The lift can only take 8 at a time. How many times must the lift go up?

4 A group of 175 people are going to Margate. Coaches can take 39 passengers. How many coaches should be ordered?

5 There are 210 students in a year group. They each need an exercise book. The exercise books are sold in packs of 25. How many packs should be ordered?

6 Car parking spaces should be 2.5 m wide. How many can be fitted into a car park which is 61 m wide?

7 A sweet manufacturer puts 17 sweets in a bag. How many bags can be made up if there are 500 sweets?

8 How many 26p stamps can be bought for £5?

9 How many grapefruits, each costing 29p, can be bought for £1.50?

10 Kim needs 26 candles for a cake. The candles are sold in packs of 4. How many packs must she buy?

11 Lauren needs 50 doughnuts for a party. Doughnuts are sold in packs of 12. How many packs must she buy?

Rounding using decimal places

What is the cost of 1.75 metres of material costing £1.99 a metre?

$1.75 \times 1.99 = 3.4825$

The cost of the material is £3.4825 or 348.25p.

This is a silly answer. After all you can only pay in pence.

A sensible answer is £3.48 correct to two decimal places (nearest penny).

This means that there are only two decimal places after the decimal point.

Often it is not necessary to use an exact answer.

Sometimes it is impossible, or impractical, to use the exact answer.

To round a number to a given number of decimal places

When rounding a number to one, two or more decimal places:

1. Write the number using one more decimal place than asked for.
2. Look at the last decimal place and
   - if the figure is 5 or more round up,
   - if the figure is less than 5 round down.
3. When answering a problem remember to include any units and state the degree of approximation used.

EXAMPLES

1 Write 2.76435 to 2 decimal places.
Write the number down using one more decimal place. 2.76**4**
Look at the last decimal place. **4**
This is less than 5, so round down.
Answer 2.76

2 Write 2.76285 to 3 decimal places.
Write the number using 4 decimal places.
2.762**8**
The last decimal place is 5 or more, so round up.
Answer 2.763

3 Write 7.104 to 2 decimal places.
7.104 = 7.10 to 2 d.p.
The zero is written down because it shows the accuracy used,
2 decimal places.

4 5.98 = 6.0 to 1 d.p.
Notice that the next tenth after 5.9 is 6.0.

Notation
Often decimal place is shortened to d.p.

Exercise 3.3

1 Write the number 3.9617 correct to
   (a) 3 decimal places,   (b) 2 decimal places,   (c) 1 decimal place.

2 Write the number 567.654 correct to
   (a) 2 decimal places,   (b) 1 decimal place,   (c) the nearest whole number.

3 Copy and complete this table.

Number	2.367	0.964	0.965	15.2806	0.056	4.991	4.996
d.p.	1	2	2	3	2	2	2
Answer	2.4						

26

4 The display on a calculator shows the result of 34 ÷ 7.

```
4.857142857
```

What is the result correct to two decimal places?

5 Carry out these calculations giving the answers correct to
(a) 1 d.p. (b) 2 d.p. (c) 3 d.p.
   (i) 6.12 × 7.54
   (ii) 89.1 × 0.67
   (iii) 90.53 × 6.29
   (iv) 98.6 ÷ 5.78
   (v) 67.2 ÷ 101.45

6 In each of these short problems decide upon the most suitable accuracy for the answer.
Then work out the answer.
Give a reason for your degree of accuracy.
(a) 1.74 metres of cloth at £6.99 a metre.
(b) 1.74 metres of cloth at £2.05 a metre.
(c) 0.454 kg of cheese at £5.21 a kg.
(d) 7 equal sticks measure 250 cm in total when lying end to end. How long is each stick?
(e) A packet of 6 videotapes costs £7.99. How much does one cost?
(f) Petrol costs 81.4 pence a litre. I buy 15.6 litres. How much will I have to pay?

Rounding using significant figures

Consider the calculation 600.02 × 7500.97 = 4500732.0194
To 1 d.p. it is 4500732.0, to 2 d.p. it is 4500732.02.
The answers to either 1 or 2 d.p. are very close to the actual answer and are almost as long.
There is little advantage in using either of these two roundings.
The point of a rounding is that it is a more convenient number to use.

Another kind of rounding uses **significant figures**.
The **most** significant figure in a number is the figure which has the greatest place value.

Consider the number 237.
The figure 2 has the greatest place value. It is worth 200.
So 2 is the most significant figure.

In the number 0.00328, the figure 3 has the greatest place value.
So 3 is the most significant figure.

> Noughts which are used to locate the decimal point and preserve the place value of other figures are not significant.

To round a number to a given number of significant figures

When rounding a number to one, two or more significant figures:

1. Start from the most significant figure and count the required number of figures.

2. Look at the next figure to the right of this and
   - if the figure is 5 or more round up,
   - if the figure is less than 5 round down.

3. Add noughts, as necessary, to locate the decimal point and preserve the place value.

4. When answering a problem remember to include any units and state the degree of approximation used.

EXAMPLES

1 Write 4 500 732.0194 to 2 significant figures.

The figure after the first 2 significant figures **45** is 0.
This is less than 5, so round down, leaving 45 unchanged.
Add noughts to 45 to locate the decimal point and
preserve place value.
So 4 500 732.0194 = 4 500 000 to 2 sig. fig.

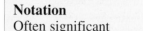

Notation
Often significant
figure is shortened to
sig. fig.

2 Write 0.000364907 to 1 significant figure.

The figure after the first significant figure 3 is 6.
This is 5 or more, so round up, 3 becomes 4.
So 0.000364907 = 0.0004 to 1 sig. fig.

Notice that the noughts before the 4 locate the decimal point and preserve place value.

Choosing a suitable degree of accuracy

In some calculations it would be wrong to use the complete answer from the calculator.
The result of a calculation involving measurement should not be given to a greater degree of accuracy
than the measurements used in the calculation.

EXAMPLE

What is the area of a rectangle measuring 4.6 cm by 7.2 cm?

$4.6 \times 7.2 = 33.12$
Since the measurements used in the calculation (4.6 cm and 7.2 cm) are given to 2 significant figures
the answer should be as well.
$33 \, cm^2$ is a more suitable answer.

Exercise **3.4**

1 Write these numbers correct to one significant figure.
    (a) 17   (b) 523   (c) 0.34   (d) 0.019   (e) 24.6

2 Copy and complete this table.

Number	sig. fig.	Answer
456 000	2	460 000
454 000	2	
7 981 234	3	
7 981 234	2	
1290	2	
19 602	1	

3 Copy and complete this table.

Number	sig. fig.	Answer
0.000567	2	
0.093748	2	
0.093748	3	
0.093748	4	
0.010245	2	
0.02994	2	

4 This display shows the result of 3400 ÷ 7.

$$485.7142857$$

What is the result correct to four significant figures?

5 Carry out these calculations giving the answers correct to
(a) 2 sig. fig.   (b) 3 sig. fig.   (c) 4 sig. fig.
   (i)   672 × 123   (ii)   6.72 × 12.3
   (iii) 78.2 × 12.8   (iv)   7.19 ÷ 987.5
   (v)   124 ÷ 65300

6 A field measures 18.6 m by 25.4 m.
Calculate the area of the field, giving your answer to a suitable degree of accuracy.

7 In each of these short problems decide upon the most suitable accuracy for the answer.
Then work out the answer, remembering to state the units.
Give a reason for your degree of accuracy.
(a) The area of a rectangle measuring 7.9 cm by 6.4 cm.
(b) The area of a rectangle measuring 13.2 cm by 11.9 cm.
(c) The area of a football pitch measuring 99 m by 62 m.
(d) The length of 13 tables was measured at 16 m.
       How long was each table?
(e) The area of a farmer's field measuring 320 m by 480 m.

Estimation

It is always a good idea to find an **estimate** for any calculation.
An estimate is used to check that the answer to the actual calculation is of the right magnitude (size).
If the answer is very different to the estimate then a mistake has possibly been made.

Estimation is done by approximating every number in the calculation to 1 significant figure.
The calculation is then done using the approximated values.

EXAMPLES

1 Estimate 421 × 48.

Round 421 to one significant figure: 400
Round 48 to one significant figure: 50
400 × 50 = 20 000

*Use long multiplication to calculate
421 × 48.
Comment on your answer.*

2 Estimate 608 ÷ 19.

Round the numbers in the calculation to one significant figure.
600 ÷ 20 = 30

*Use long division to calculate
608 ÷ 19.
Comment on your answer.*

3 Estimate $\dfrac{78.5 \times 0.51}{18.7}$

Approximating: 78.5 = 80 to 1 sig. fig.
                      0.51 = 0.5 to 1 sig. fig.
                      18.7 = 20 to 1 sig. fig.

$\dfrac{80 \times 0.5}{20} = \dfrac{40}{20} = 2$ (estimate)

Using a calculator $\dfrac{78.5 \times 0.51}{18.7} = \dfrac{40.035}{18.7} = 2.140909\ldots$

Is 2.140909 reasonably close to 2?   Yes.

Questions 1 to 7.
Do not use a calculator. Show any working clearly.

1 Make estimates to these calculations by using approximations to 1 sig. fig.
Then carry out the calculations accurately using long multiplication.
Compare your estimates with your answers.
(a) 32 × 41
(b) 12 × 66
(c) 58 × 34
(d) 72 × 45
(e) 34 × 78
(f) 17 × 219
(g) 291 × 56
(h) 312 × 23

2 Make estimates to these calculations by using approximations to 1 sig. fig.
Then carry out the calculations accurately using long division.
Compare your estimates with your answers.
(a) 594 ÷ 18
(b) 609 ÷ 21
(c) 256 ÷ 16
(d) 840 ÷ 35

3 By using approximations to 1 significant figure find estimates to these products.
Then carry out the calculations with the original figures.
Compare your estimate to the actual answer.
(a) 4.2 × 1.8
(b) 8.9 × 3.1
(c) 48.1 × 4.2
(d) 103.4 × 2.9

4 Find estimates to these divisions by using approximations to 1 significant figure.
Then carry out the calculations with the original figures.
Compare your estimate to the actual answer.
(a) 10.78 ÷ 4.9
(b) 19.68 ÷ 4.1
(c) 30.4 ÷ 3.2
(d) 203.49 ÷ 5.1.

5 (a) When estimating the answer to 29 × 48 the approximations 30 and 50 are used. Why can you tell that the estimation must be bigger than the actual answer?
(b) When estimating the answer to 182 ÷ 13 the approximations 200 and 10 are used. Will the estimate be bigger or smaller than the actual answer?

6 Bernard plans to buy a conservatory costing £5328 and furniture costing £784.
(a) By using approximations, estimate the total amount Bernard plans to spend.
(b) Find the actual cost.

7 463 people entered a store during the first hour it was open.
A further 1273 people entered the store during the second hour.
(a) Estimate how many people entered the store during the first two hours it was open.

The owners hope that 3000 people will visit their store during the first three hours.
(b) Estimate how many more people must enter the store during the third hour to meet this target.

Questions 8 and 9.
You may use a calculator to answer these questions.

8 Find estimates to these calculations by using approximations to 1 significant figure.
Then carry out the calculations with the original figures.
Compare your estimate to the actual answer.

(a) $\dfrac{7.9 \times 3.9}{4.8}$

(b) $\dfrac{400 \times 0.29}{6.2}$

(c) $\dfrac{81.7 \times 4.9}{1.9 \times 10.3}$

9 Estate Agents sometimes quote the floor area of a flat in square metres.
They quote an estimate so that buyers can easily compare one flat with another.
Write down the lengths and widths of each room to 1 significant figure.

(a) Obtain an estimate of the total floor area of the two flats.
Meadow View Flat
Reception 1   4.1 m × 6.9 m
Reception 2   3.9 m × 5 m
Bedroom 1   3.2 m × 3.7 m
Bedroom 2   2.9 m × 2.1 m
Park View Flat
Reception 1   3.9 m × 5.1 m
Reception 2   4 m × 3.8 m
Bedroom 1   4.1 m × 3.9 m
Bedroom 2   3.1 m × 2.9 m

(b) Work out the actual floor area of each flat. Compare the estimates.

- A number can be rounded to an **approximate** number.
- How to approximate using **decimal places**.
  When rounding a number to one, two or more decimal places:
  1. Write the number using one more decimal place than asked for.
  2. Look at the last decimal place and
      - if the figure is 5 or more round up,
      - if the figure is less than 5 round down.
- How to approximate using **significant figures**.
  When rounding a number to one, two or more significant figures:
  1. Start from the most significant figure and count the required number of figures.
  2. Look at the next figure to the right of this and
      - if the figure is 5 or more round up,
      - if the figure is less than 5 round down.
  3. Add noughts, as necessary, to locate the decimal point and preserve the place value.
- When answering a problem remember to include any units and state the degree of approximation used.
- Choose a suitable degree of accuracy.
- Use approximation to **estimate** that the actual answer to a calculation is of the right magnitude (size).

Review Exercise

Do not use a calculator for questions 1 to 11.

1 Round 8475
   (a) to the nearest 10
   (b) to the nearest 100
   (c) to the nearest 1000

2 Write 314.645 correct to:
   (a) the nearest whole number,
   (b) the nearest 10,
   (c) one decimal place,
   (d) one significant figure.

3 The actual number of people who watched an election broadcast was 3 967 234.
   (a) A radio report gave the number to the nearest thousand.
       What number did they use?
   (b) A newspaper headline gave the number to the nearest million.
       What number did they use?

4 Alex is asked to estimate the answer to
   $\dfrac{198.136 - 51.7}{2.973}$.
   (a) Write down approximate values for each of the numbers which Alex could use to estimate the answer.
   (b) Write down the answer she would get from using the approximations you have written down.

5 Use approximations to estimate the value of $2016 \div 49.8$.

6 (a) George uses his calculator to work out 398.9×4.05.
       The answer he gets is 16155.45.
       Use approximation to show that the answer is wrong.
   (b) Use approximation to estimate the total cost of 12 monthly mortgage payments of £497.68.

7 Kathryn marks exam papers.
   She is paid £1.86 for each paper she marks.
   In 2001 she has been asked to mark 523 papers.
   Estimate how much Kathryn will be paid altogether.
   Show all your calculations.

8 In France £1 will buy 9.64 francs.
   (a) Estimate the number of francs you could buy with £72.
   (b) Estimate the number of £'s you could buy with 5967 francs.

9 A cinema has 42 rows of seats.
   Each row has 28 seats.
   If everyone has to pay £4.75 to go to the cinema, estimate the amount of money taken when every seat is filled.

10 George needs 100 tiles to cover his kitchen floor.
The tiles are sold in boxes of 15.
How many boxes does he need to buy?

11 A school is planning a disco for 936 pupils.
Each pupil will be given 1 can of drink.
Cans of drink are sold in trays of 24.
Work out how many trays of drinks will be needed.   Edexcel

12 The display on the calculator shows the result of $179 \div 7$.

$$25.57142857$$

(a) What is the result correct to one decimal place?

(b) What is the result correct to one significant figure?

13 Calculate $72.5 \div 7.9$
(a) to 1 decimal place,
(b) to 2 decimal places.

14 Calculate $107.9 \div 72.5$
(a) to 1 significant figure,
(b) to 2 significant figures.

15 (a) Write down the numbers you could use to get an approximate answer to 593×312.
(b) Write down your approximate answer.
(c) Use a calculator to find the difference between your approximate answer and the exact answer.

16 Calculate the value of

$$\frac{21.7 \times 32.1}{16.20 - 2.19}$$

Give your answer correct to 3 significant figures.   Edexcel

17 Find estimates to these calculations by using approximations to 1 significant figure.
Then carry out these calculations with the original figures. Use a calculator.
Compare your estimate to the actual answer.

(a) $\dfrac{42.1 \times 2.97}{2.017 \times 31}$

(b) $\dfrac{38.2 + 60.17}{1.95 \times 5.12}$

(c) $\dfrac{61.4 \times 1.87}{49.2 - 28.8}$

18 Tom uses his calculator to multiply 17.8 by 0.97.
His answer is 18.236.
(a) **Without** finding the exact value of 17.8×0.97, explain why his answer must be wrong.

Sally estimates the value of $\dfrac{42.8 \times 63.8}{285}$ to be 8.
(b) Write down three numbers Sally could use to get her estimate.
                    Edexcel

19 Work out an estimate for $\dfrac{6.12 \times 193.7}{0.48}$.

20 The dimensions of a cuboid are measured.
The length is 9.8 cm, the breadth is 5.6 cm and the height is 3.7 cm.
(a) Using the formula,
Volume = length $\times$ breadth $\times$ height, calculate the volume of the cuboid.
Write down all the figures shown on your calculator.
(b) Give your answer to an appropriate degree of accuracy.
Explain why you chose this degree of accuracy.

21 Mr Mogg is going to order a new lounge carpet.
The floor of his lounge is a rectangle measuring 5.36 metres by 3.42 metres.
(a) Calculate the area of his lounge floor.
Write down all the figures shown on your calculator.
(b) What area of carpet should he order?
Give your answer to an appropriate degree of accuracy.
Explain why you chose this degree of accuracy.

CHAPTER 4

Negative Numbers

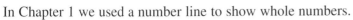

In Chapter 1 we used a number line to show whole numbers.
This number line can be extended to include **negative whole numbers**.

Negative whole numbers, zero and positive whole numbers are called **integers**.
−5 can be read as "minus five" or "negative five".
A number written without a sign before it is assumed to be positive. +5 has the same value as 5.
Real-life situations which use negative numbers include temperature, bank accounts and depths below sea-level.
Can you think of any other situations where negative numbers are used?

Ordering numbers

The thermometer

−5°C is colder than −1°C.   2°C is warmer than −3°C.
−3°C is colder than   1°C.   4°C is warmer than −5°C.
−4°C is colder than   0°C.   0°C is warmer than −3°C.
  2°C is colder than   4°C.   5°C is warmer than   2°C.

As you move up the   As you move down the
thermometer the   thermometer the
temperatures become   temperatures become
warmer.   colder.

The number line

−5 is less than −1.   2 is more than −3.
−3 is less than   1.   4 is more than −5.
−4 is less than   0.   0 is more than −3.
  2 is less than   4.   5 is more than   2.

As you move from left to   As you move from right to
right along the number line   left along the number line
the numbers become bigger.   the numbers become smaller.

EXAMPLES

1 List these temperatures from coldest to
hottest:
   3°C,   5°C,   −2°C,   0°C,   −4°C.

   −4°C,   −2°C,   0°C,   3°C,   5°C.

2 List these numbers in ascending order
(from lowest to highest):
   50,   −41,   −18,   −11,   28,   9.

   −41,   −18,   −11,   9,   28,   50.

1 Copy and complete these sentences using the words 'colder' or 'warmer' as appropriate.

(a) −2°C is ...... than −5°C.

(b) −1°C is ...... than 4°C.

(c) 2°C is ...... than −4°C.

(d) −10°C is ...... than −5°C.

2 Copy and complete these sentences using the words 'less' or 'more' as appropriate.

(a) −3 is ...... than 2.

(b) 1 is ...... than −5.

(c) −4 is ...... than −1.

(d) −4 is ...... than −10.

3 At midnight on New Year's Day the temperatures in some cities were as shown:

Edinburgh	−7°C
London	0°C
Moscow	−22°C
New York	−17°C
Rome	3°C
Colombo	21°C
Cairo	15°C

(a) Which city recorded the highest temperature?

(b) Which city recorded the lowest temperature?

(c) List the temperatures from coldest to hottest.

4 List these temperatures from coldest to hottest.

(a) 23°C, −28°C, −3°C, 19°C, −13°C.

(b) −9°C, −11°C, 12°C, 10°C, −7°C, 0°C.

(c) 27°C, 18°C, −29°C, −15°C, 2°C.

(d) 20°C, −15°C, −20°C, 0°C, −5°C, 10°C.

5 List these numbers from lowest to highest.

(a) 31, −78, 51, −39, −16, −9, 11.

(b) 5, 1, −1, −3, −5, −2, 0, 2, 4.

(c) 99, −103, 104, 5, −3, 52, −63, −19.

(d) 30, 10, −30, −50, −20, 0, 40.

(e) 27, −30, 17, 0, −15, −10, 8.

Subtracting a larger number from a smaller number

Work out 3 − 5.

To work out smaller number − larger number:

(i) Do the calculation the other way round. 3 − 5 becomes 5 − 3.

(ii) Put a minus sign in front of the answer. So 3 − 5 = −2.

This is the same as starting at 3 on a number line and going 5 places to the left, to get to −2.

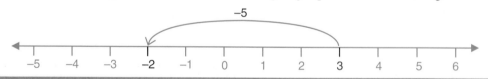

EXAMPLES

1 Work out 7 − 13.

Do 13 − 7 = 6.

Then 7 − 13 = −6.

2 Calculate 21 − 34.

Do 34 − 21 = 13.

Then 21 − 34 = −13.

3 Alec has £50 in his bank account. He writes a cheque for £80. What is his new balance?

His new balance is given by the calculation £50 − £80.

80 − 50 = 30.

So 50 − 80 = −30.

The new balance is −£30.

This means that Alec's account is overdrawn by £30.

Exercise **4.2**

Do not use a calculator for this exercise.

1 Work out the following.
(a) $4 - 7$ (b) $8 - 12$ (c) $13 - 20$ (d) $24 - 56$
(e) $20 - 20$ (f) $23 - 50$ (g) $29 - 90$ (h) $20 - 21$

2 (a) Draw a number line to show each of these statements.
(i) $7 - 10 = -3$ (ii) $3 - 6 = -3$ (iii) $-1 - 3 = -4$

(b) Explain how a number line can be used to work out the following.
(i) $5 - 6$ (ii) $4 - 8$ (iii) $-2 - 2$

3 What number should be put in the box to make each of these statements correct?

(a) $7 - \boxed{} = -2$ (b) $\boxed{} - 6 = -5$ (c) $9 - \boxed{} = -3$

(d) $-3 - 7 = \boxed{}$ (e) $\boxed{} - 50 = -20$ (f) $10 - \boxed{} = -5$

4 (a) Mr Armstrong has £25 in the bank. He writes a cheque for £100.
What is his new balance?

(b) After paying a bill of £60 by cheque, Claire's bank balance is £20 overdrawn.
What was Claire's bank balance before paying the bill?

5 Negative numbers can be used for depths below sea level.
Use negative numbers to answer the following.
(a) At what depth is the diver?
(b) At what depth is the treasure chest?

What is the difference in height between
(c) the helicopter and the parachutist,
(d) the diver and the jellyfish,
(e) the diver and the treasure chest,
(f) the bird and the jellyfish,
(g) the parachutist and the treasure chest,
(h) the kite and the jellyfish,
(i) the helicopter and the kite,
(j) the diver and the helicopter,
(k) the bird and the treasure chest?

	Helicopter	160 m above
	Parachute	100 m above
	Bird	50 m above
	Kite	30 m above
	—	Sea level
	Jellyfish	20 m below
	Diver	80 m below
	Treasure chest	200 m below

Addition and subtraction using negative numbers

Think of the number line as a series of stepping stones.

What is $-4 - 5$?
Using the number line:
Start at -4 and move 5 to the **left**.
The answer is -9.
$-4 - 5 = -9$

$-4 - 5$ can be written as:
$-4 + (-5)$ or $-4 - (+5)$.
So $-4 + (-5) = -9$,
and $-4 - (+5) = -9$.

What is $-3 - (+7)$?
$-3 - (+7)$ is the same as $-3 - 7$.
Using the number line:
Start at -3 and move 7 to the **left**.
$-3 - (+7) = -10$

$-3 - (-7)$ must start at -3 and move 7 to the **right**.
$-3 - (-7)$ is the same as $-3 + 7$.
So $-3 - (-7) = 4$,
and $-3 + 7 = 4$.

What is $-5 + (+7)$?
$+7$ can be written as 7.
$-5 + (+7)$ is the same as $-5 + 7 = 2$.

To add or subtract negative numbers:
Replace double signs with the single sign.
Start on the number line with the first number.
Then move left or right according to the single sign.

$+\ +$ can be replaced by $+$
$-\ -$ can be replaced by $+$
$+\ -$ can be replaced by $-$
$-\ +$ can be replaced by $-$

EXAMPLES

1 Work out $2+ (-6)$.

$+-$ can be replaced with $-$.
Start at 2 and move 6 to the left.
$2 + (-6) = 2 - 6 = -4$

2 Work out $-2 - (-8)$.

$--$ can be replaced with $+$.
Start at -2 and move 8 to the right.
$-2 -(-8) = -2 + 8 = 6$

3 Work out $-4 - (+6)$.

$-+$ can be replaced with $-$.
Start at -4 and move 6 to the left.
$-4 -(+6) = -4 - 6 = -10$

4 Work out $-4 + (-3) + 6 - (-5) - (+3)$.

Replace signs.
$= -4 - 3 + 6 + 5 - 3$
$= 1$

Exercise **4.3**

Do not use a calculator for this exercise.

1 Work out.
(a) $-3 + (+5)$
(b) $5 + (-4)$
(c) $-2 + (-7)$
(d) $-1 + (+9)$
(e) $7 + (-3)$
(f) $15 + (-20)$
(g) $-11 + (+4)$
(h) $11 + (-4)$
(i) $8 + (-7)$
(j) $-8 + (-7)$
(k) $3 + (+3) + (-9)$
(l) $-7 + (-5) +6$

2 Work out.
(a) $8 - (-5)$
(b) $-4 - (-10)$
(c) $10 - (+3)$
(d) $6 - (-1)$
(e) $-5 - (-10)$
(f) $-4 - (+8)$
(g) $-7 - (-6)$
(h) $7 - (-6)$
(i) $-2 - (+9)$
(j) $2 - (-9)$
(k) $5 - (+5) + 9$
(l) $-10 - (-6) + 4$

3 Work out.
(a) $-3 - (-8)$
(b) $5 + (-2)$
(c) $7 - (+4)$
(d) $-9 - (-5) + (-3)$
(e) $7 + (-8) - (+5)$
(f) $-2 - (-7) - 6$

4 Work out.
(a) $10 + 5 - 8 + 6 - 7$
(b) $12 + 8 - 15 + 7 - 20$
(c) $30 - 20 + 12 - 50$
(d) $6 + 12 - 14 - 4$
(e) $37 - 23 - 24 - 25$
(f) $12 + 13 + 14 - 20$

5 Work out.
(a) $5 + (-4) - (-3) + 2 - (-1)$
(b) $5 - 4 + (-3) - (-2) + (-1)$
(c) $10 - (-11) + (-12) + 13 - (-14)$
(d) $-7 - (-7) + 6 + (-3) + (-9)$
(e) $12 + 8 - (-8) + 9 - (-1)$
(f) $15 - (-5) + 5 - (-10) + (-20)$
(g) $-5 + (-5) + (-5) + (-5) - (-5)$
(h) $5 - (-5) - (-5) - (-5) - (-5)$
(i) $1 - (-2) - (-3) - (-4) - (-5)$
(j) $-6 + 7 - 8 + (-9) - (-10)$

6 What is the difference in temperature between
  (a) London and Rome,
  (b) Edinburgh and Rome,
  (c) Moscow and New York,
  (d) Cairo and Colombo,
  (e) Moscow and Cairo?

Edinburgh	−7°C
London	0°C
Moscow	−22°C
New York	−17°C
Rome	3°C
Colombo	21°C
Cairo	15°C

7 The temperature inside a freezer was −23°C.
After two hours the temperature had risen by 8°C.
What is the temperature in the freezer then?

Multiplying and dividing negative numbers

You will need to know these rules for multiplying and dividing negative numbers:

When multiplying:
$+ \times + = +$
$- \times - = +$
$+ \times - = -$
$- \times + = -$

When dividing:
$+ \div + = +$
$- \div - = +$
$+ \div - = -$
$- \div + = -$

The multiplication table can be extended to include negative numbers.

Describe any patterns you can see in the table.

Division is the opposite (inverse) operation to multiplication.
If $a \times b = c$,
then $c \div b = a$ and $c \div a = b$.

If $(+5) \times (-2) = -10$,
then $(-10) \div (-2) = +5$
and $(-10) \div (+5) = -2$.

Second number

F	×	−5	−4	−3	−2	−1	0	1	2	3	4	5
i	−5	25	20	15	10	5	0	−5	−10	−15	−20	−25
r	−4	20	16	12	8	4	0	−4	−8	−12	−16	−20
s	−3	15	12	9	6	3	0	−3	−6	−9	−12	−15
t	−2	10	8	6	4	2	0	−2	−4	−6	−8	−10
	−1	5	4	3	2	1	0	−1	−2	−3	−4	−5
n	0	0	0	0	0	0	0	0	0	0	0	0
u	1	−5	−4	−3	−2	−1	0	1	2	3	4	5
m	2	−10	−8	−6	−4	−2	0	2	4	6	8	10
b	3	−15	−12	−9	−6	−3	0	3	6	9	12	15
e	4	−20	−16	−12	−8	−4	0	4	8	12	16	20
r	5	−25	−20	−15	−10	−5	0	5	10	15	20	25

EXAMPLES

1 Work out $(+7) \times (-5)$.

Signs: $+ \times - = -$
Numbers: $7 \times 5 = 35$
So $(+7) \times (-5) = -35$.

2 Work out $(+8) \div (-2)$.

Signs: $+ \div - = -$
Numbers: $8 \div 2 = 4$
So $(+8) \div (-2) = -4$.

3 Work out $(-4) \times (-0.8)$.

Signs: $- \times - = +$
Numbers: $4 \times 0.8 = 3.2$
So $(-4) \times (-0.8) = 3.2$.

Work logically
Work out the sign first.
Then work out the numbers.

4 Work out $(-6) \div (-0.3)$.

Signs: $- \div - = +$
Numbers: $6 \div 0.3$ is the same as $60 \div 3 = 20$
So $(-6) \div (-0.3) = 20$.

Do not use a calculator for this exercise.

1
(a) $(+7) \times (+5)$ (b) $(-7) \times (+5)$ (c) $(-7) \times (-5)$ (d) $5 \times (+2)$
(e) $(+5) \times (-2)$ (f) $(-5) \times (-2)$ (g) $(-1) \times (-1)$ (h) $8 \times (-3)$
(i) $(-8) \times (+3)$ (j) $(-5) \times 9$ (k) $(-8) \times (-8)$ (l) $(-7) \times 6$
(m) $(-7) \times (-6)$ (n) $8 \times (-10)$ (o) $(-8) \times (+10)$ (p) $(-4) \times (-8)$

2
(a) $(+5) \times (-2) \times (+2)$ (b) $(+4) \times (-3) \times (-5)$ (c) $(-3) \times (-2) \times (-5)$
(d) $(-5) \times (+3) \times (-4)$ (e) $(-5) \times (+3) \times (+4)$ (f) $(-5) \times (-4) \times (-5)$

3
(a) $(-8) \div (+2)$ (b) $(-8) \div (-2)$ (c) $(+20) \div (+4)$ (d) $(+20) \div (-4)$
(e) $(-20) \div (+4)$ (f) $(-20) \div (-4)$ (g) $(+18) \div (+3)$ (h) $(-18) \div (+3)$
(i) $(-24) \div (-6)$ (j) $(+24) \div (-3)$ (k) $(-30) \div (-5)$ (l) $(-30) \div (+6)$

4
(a) $6 \times (-0.3)$ (b) $(-6) \times (-0.5)$ (c) $4 \times (-0.4)$ (d) $(-4) \times (-0.8)$
(e) $6 \div (-0.3)$ (f) $(-6) \div (-0.5)$ (g) $4 \div (-0.4)$ (h) $(-4) \div (-0.8)$

5
(a) $(-2.5) \div 5$ (b) $3.2 \div (-4)$ (c) $(-4.9) \div (-7)$
(d) $7.5 \div (-0.5)$ (e) $(-2.8) \div 0.7$ (f) $(-3.6) \div (-0.9)$

Using a calculator

Calculations involving negative numbers can be carried out using a calculator.
Work out $5 + (-7)$.
You should get the answer -2.

Use your calculator to check your answers to questions in Exercises 4.3 and 4.4.

What you need to know

You should be able to:
- Use **negative numbers** in context such as temperatures, bank accounts.
- Realise where negative numbers come on a **number line**.
- Put numbers in order (including negative numbers).
- Add $(+)$, subtract $(-)$, multiply $(\times)$ and divide $(\div)$ with negative numbers.

You will also meet Negative Numbers further on:
    They may be solutions to equations.
    Negative coordinates on graphs.
    They may be substituted into algebraic formulae.

Review Exercise
Do not use a calculator for questions 1 to 10.

1 Place the following numbers in order of size starting with the smallest.
    15   -5 25   0 -20

2 Calculate.
(a) $-7 - 11$
(b) $-7 + 11$
(c) $-7 - (-11)$

3 The table shows the midday temperatures in these towns one day.

Town	Selby	Poole	Woking
Temperature (°C)	-8	-2	-5

(a) Which town has the highest midday temperature?
(b) Which town has the lowest midday temperature?

4 Complete the following.

(a) $-3 + \boxed{} = -5$

(b) $3 - \boxed{} = 5$

5 The temperatures at Athens and Moscow are taken at the same time.
Athens 8°C   Moscow −5°C

(a) How many degrees colder is Moscow than Athens?

(b) At the same time, Oslo is 3°C colder than Moscow.
What is the temperature in Oslo?

6 At midnight the temperature was 2°C.
At 8 am the next day the temperature was −3°C.
By how many degrees did the temperature fall?

7 A miner is 924 metres below the ground.
A plane is 3267 metres above the ground.
How many metres is the plane above the miner?

8 One winter's day the temperatures in 3 cities were measured at the same time.
The results were:

| London . . . . −3°C |
| Paris . . . . +5°C |
| Moscow . . . . −21°C |

Work out how many degrees difference there was between the temperatures in

(a) London and Paris,

(b) Moscow and London,

(c) Moscow and Paris.   Edexcel

9 The instructions on a packet of frozen peas states:

| Store below −3°C |

The peas are kept in a freezer at −10°C.
How many degrees is this below the required storage temperature?

10 Dan has £26.40 in his bank account.
He buys a jacket for £59.95 and pays by cheque.
If the cheque is accepted by his bank how much will his account be overdrawn?

11 Carry out these multiplications.

(a) $(+6) \times (+4)$

(b) $(+6) \times (-4)$

(c) $(-6) \times (+4)$

(d) $(-6) \times (-4)$

(e) 8×5

(f) $(-8) \times 5$

(g) $8 \times (-5)$

(h) $(-8) \times (-5)$

12 Carry out these divisions.

(a) $(+50) \div (-10)$

(b) $(-12) \div (-6)$

(c) $(-18) \div 3$

(d) $24 \div 6$

13 (a) Work out.

(i) $(-3) - (-2)$

(ii) $(-2) \times (-3)$

(iii) $\dfrac{(-3) \times (-2) \times (-5)}{(-6)}$

(b) Complete the boxes.

(i) $\boxed{} \div (-2) = -3$

(ii) $(-5) + \boxed{} = -3$

14 The temperature inside a house is +17°C.
The temperature outside the house is −4°C.

(a) How much warmer is it inside the house than outside the house?

(b) Temperatures in degrees Centigrade (°C) can be changed to temperatures in degrees Fahrenheit (°F) by using this rule:

| Multiply by 9, divide by 5 and then add 32 |

Find the temperature outside the house in °F.

15 A multichoice test has 20 questions.
For each question the mark given is:

| +2 for a correct answer |
| −1 for a wrong answer |
| 0 if the question is not attempted |

(a) What is the lowest mark than could be scored on the test?

(b) Tim attempts all the questions and gets 8 correct.
Namoi attempts 13 questions and gets 8 correct.
Who scores the better mark?
Explain your answer.

CHAPTER 5

Working with Number

Multiples

A table of multiples

×	1	2	3	4	5	6	7	8	9	10	11	12	13	14	15
1	1	2	3	4	5	6	7	8	9	10	11	12	13	14	15
2	2	4	6	8	10	12	14	16	18	20	22	24	26	28	30
3	3	6	9	12	15	18	21	24	27	30	33	36	39	42	45
4	4	8	12	16	20	24	28	32	36	40	44	48	52	56	60
5	5	10	15	20	25	30	35	40	45	50	55	60	65	70	75
6	6	12	18	24	30	36	42	48	54	60	66	72	78	84	90
7	7	14	21	28	35	42	49	56	63	70	77	84	91	98	105
8	8	16	24	32	40	48	56	64	72	80	88	96	104	112	120
9	9	18	27	36	45	54	63	72	81	90	99	108	117	126	135
10	10	20	30	40	50	60	70	80	90	100	110	120	130	140	150
11	11	22	33	44	55	66	77	88	99	110	121	132	143	154	165
12	12	24	36	48	60	72	84	96	108	120	132	144	156	168	180
13	13	26	39	52	65	78	91	104	117	130	143	156	169	182	195
14	14	28	42	56	70	84	98	112	126	140	154	168	182	196	210
15	15	30	45	60	75	90	105	120	135	150	165	180	195	210	225

Numbers in the 4 times table are called **multiples** of 4.

6, 12, 18, 24, … are **multiples** of 6.

The 8th **multiple** of 7 is 8 × 7 = 56.

Multiples of 2 are called **even numbers** and end in 0, 2, 4, 6 or 8.

Odd numbers end in 1, 3, 5, 7 or 9.

What name is given to the numbers on the diagonal line, shown in blue?

Activity

The product of 1 and 12 is 1 × 12 = 12.

Write down **all** the other pairs of **whole numbers** that have a product of 12.

Write down all the pairs of whole numbers that have a product of 6.

Write down all the pairs of whole numbers that have a product of 5.

Write down all the pairs of whole numbers that have a product of 48.

When numbers are multiplied together the answer is called the **product** of the numbers.

Factors

Pairs of **whole numbers** which have a product of 6 are 1 × 6 and 2 × 3.

1, 2, 3, and 6 are called **factors** of 6.

Prime numbers

3 appears only twice in the table of multiples. It has just two factors, 1 and 3. Numbers like this are called **prime numbers**.

A prime number has exactly **two** factors, 1 and the number itself.

The first few prime numbers are: 2, 3, 5, 7, 11, 13, 17, 19, …

The number 1 is not a prime number because it has only one factor.

EXAMPLES

1 Write down the first five multiples of 5.

$1 \times 5 = 5$
$2 \times 5 = 10$
$3 \times 5 = 15$
$4 \times 5 = 20$
$5 \times 5 = 25$
The first five multiples of 5 are 5, 10, 15, 20 and 25.

2 What is the eighth multiple of 9?

The eighth multiple of 9 is $8 \times 9 = 72$.

3 The fifth multiple of a number is 30. What is the number?

$5 \times 6 = 30$.
So, the number is 6.

4 Find **all** the factors of 25.

Method 1
Find **all** the pairs of whole numbers that have a product of 25.
$25 \times 1 = 25$
$5 \times 5 = 25$

Method 2
Find **all** the whole numbers that divide exactly into 25.
$25 \div 1 = 25$ Factors 1 and 25
$25 \div 2 = 12.5$ No factors
$25 \div 3 = 8.333\ldots$ No factors
$25 \div 4 = 6.25$ No factors
$25 \div 5 = 5$ Factor 5
Why stop here?

1, 5 and 25 are all the factors of 25.

Exercise 5.1   Do not use a calculator.

1 Write down the first five multiples of:
(a) 3   (b) 7   (c) 20   (d) 12   (e) 19

2 Copy and complete the following.
(a) The fifth multiple of 4 is ….   (b) The seventh multiple of 10 is ….
(c) The …… multiple of 6 is 18.   (d) The …… multiple of 8 is 88.
(e) The twelfth multiple of … is 60.   (f) The fifteenth multiple of … is 75.

3
(a) What multiple of 6 is the third multiple of 4?
(b) What multiple of 8 is the fourth multiple of 4?
(c) What multiple of 20 is the tenth multiple of 10?
(d) What multiple of 24 is the fourth multiple of 18?

4 (a) Look at the table of multiples on Page 40.
What can you say about the following?
(i) Even multiples of an even number.
(ii) Even multiples of an odd number.
(iii) Odd multiples of an even number.
(iv) Odd multiples of an odd number.
(b) Using **O** for an odd number and **E** for an even number copy and complete these multiplication tables.

(i)
×	2	3	6	7	9
2	E				
3		O	E		
6					
7					
9					

(ii)
×	O	E
O		
E		

(c) Why are there more even numbers than odd numbers in the table of multiples?

5 (a) Find all the pairs of whole numbers that have a product of 18.

   (b) Write down all the factors of 18.

6 (a) Find all the pairs of whole numbers that have a product of 20.

   (b) Write down all the factors of 20.

7 Find all the factors of:

(a)	16	(b)	28
(c)	36	(d)	45
(e)	48	(f)	50
(g)	60	(h)	80

8 (a) Find all the factors of:

(i)	2	(ii)	3
(iii)	5	(iv)	7
(v)	11	(vi)	13

   (b) Find two more numbers with only two factors.

9 (a) Find all the factors of:

(i)	4	(ii)	9
(iii)	25	(iv)	49

   (b) Find two more numbers with only three factors.

10 (a) Find all the factors of:

(i)	6	(ii)	10
(iii)	14	(iv)	26
(v)	55	(vi)	38

   (b) Find two more numbers with only four factors.

11 (a) How many multiples of 6 are factors of 36?

   (b) How many multiples of 5 are factors of 120?

   (c) How many factors of 100 are multiples of 2?

   (d) How many factors of 96 are multiples of 4?

12 3, 4, 5, 9, 14, 20, 27, and 35. Which of the above numbers are
   (a) multiples of 7,
   (b) factors of 20,
   (c) prime numbers?

13 Draw a 100 square on squared paper.

1	2	3	4	5	6	7	8	9	10
11	12	13	14	15	16	17	18	19	20
21	22	23	24	25	26	27	28	29	30
31	32	33	34	35	36	37	38	39	40
71	72	73	74	75	76	77	78	79	80
81	82	83	84	85	86	87	88	89	90
91	92	93	94	95	96	97	98	99	100

(a) On your 100 square shade all the multiples of 2 **except** 2.

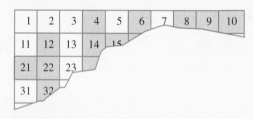

(b) Next, shade all the multiples of 3 **except** 3.

(c) All the multiples of 4 are already shaded. Explain why.

(d) Shade all the multiples of 5 **except** 5.

(e) Why have all the multiples of 6 **already** been shaded?

(f) Shade all the multiples of 7 **except** 7.

(g) Explain why 11 is the next unshaded number.
Shade all the multiples of 11 **except** 11.

(h) Continue to shade multiples of unshaded numbers (except the unshaded number).

(i) Write a list of all the unshaded numbers less than 50 (except 1). What is the special name for these numbers?

Powers

Activity

Cut a piece of paper into 2 **pieces**.

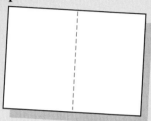

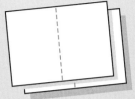

Put the pieces on top of each other.
Cut the pile in half.
How many pieces have you got?

Put **all** the pieces on top of each other.
Cut the pile in half again.
How many pieces?

Continue putting the pieces on top of each other and cutting the pile in half.

Copy and complete this table to show your results.

0 cuts gives 1 piece 1 cut gives 2 pieces 2 cuts gives 4 pieces 3 cuts gives 8 pieces 4 cuts gives . . . 5 cuts gives . . . 6 cuts gives . . .	$4 = 2 \times 2$ $8 = 2 \times 2 \times 2$	In shorthand 2×2 can be written as 2^2. In shorthand $2 \times 2 \times 2$ can be written as 2^3.

Write down the shorthand form of $2 \times 2 \times 2 \times 2 \times 2 \times 2 \times 2 \times 2 \times 2 \times 2$.
Write down the number of pieces for 20 cuts in shorthand form.
Write down the number of pieces for n cuts in shorthand form.
What are the values of 2^1 and 2^0?

Products of the same number, like $2 \times 2 \times 2 \times 2 \times 2$, can be written in a shorthand form using **powers**.
For example:

$2 \times 2 \times 2 \times 2 \times 2 = 2^5$ This is read as '2 to the power of 5'. 2^5 has the value 32.
$3 \times 3 \times 3 \times 3 = 3^4$ This is read as '3 to the power of 4'. 3^4 has the value 81.
$5 \times 5 \times 5 \times 5 \times 5 \times 5 \times 5 = 5^7$ This is read as '5 to the power of 7'. 5^7 has the value 78 125.

Use a calculator to check the values of 2^5, 3^4 and 5^7.

Index form

Numbers written in shorthand form like 2^5 are said to be in **index** form.
This is sometimes called **power** form.

An expression of the form
$a \times a \times a \times a \times a$
can be written in index form as a^5.

a^5 is read as 'a to the **power** 5'.
a is the **base** of the expression.
5 is the **index** or **power**.
(The plural of index is **indices**).

There are two special results that you might have noticed when doing the activity.

$2^0 = 1$. Also, $3^0 = 1$, $4^0 = 1$, $5^0 = 1$, ...
In general: $a^0 = 1$
Any number raised to the power zero is 1.

$2^1 = 2$. Also, $3^1 = 3$, $4^1 = 4$, $5^1 = 5$, ...
In general: $a^1 = a$
Any number raised to the power one is the number itself.

EXAMPLES

Expression	Index form	Read as	Value
$4 \times 4 \times 4 \times 4 \times 4$	4^5	'4 to the power 5'	1024
$6 \times 6 \times 6$	6^3	'6 to the power 3'	216
$2.1 \times 2.1 \times 2.1 \times 2.1$	2.1^4	'2.1 to the power 4'	19.4481

1 Write each of the following as a power.
   (a) $4 \times 4 \times 4 \times 4$
   (b) $3 \times 3 \times 3 \times 3 \times 3 \times 3 \times 3 \times 3$
   (c) $8 \times 8 \times 8 \times 8 \times 8 \times 8 \times 8$
   (d) $0.3 \times 0.3 \times 0.3$
   (e) $1.6 \times 1.6 \times 1.6 \times 1.6 \times 1.6$
   (f) $12 \times 12 \times 12 \times 12 \times 12 \times 12 \times 12$

2 (a) Copy and complete this table of the powers of 10.

Expression	Index form	Value
$10 \times 10 \times 10 \times 10 \times 10 \times 10$	10^6	1 000 000
$10 \times 10 \times 10 \times 10 \times 10$	10^5	
	10^4	
$10 \times 10 \times 10$		
		100
10		
		1

   (b) Complete a similar table for: (i) the powers of 5,   (ii) the powers of 4.
   (c) What do you notice about numbers raised to the power zero?

3 Work out the value of:
   (a) 2^3 (b) 6^2 (c) 3^4 (d) 12^2 (e) 5^4 (f) 10^7

4 Write the following as products of powers.
   For example: $2 \times 2 \times 2 \times 3 \times 3 \times 5 = 2^3 \times 3^2 \times 5$
   (a) $2 \times 2 \times 3 \times 3$
   (b) $2 \times 3 \times 3 \times 3 \times 5$ (c) $2 \times 3 \times 5 \times 5$
   (d) $2 \times 2 \times 2 \times 2 \times 3 \times 5 \times 5$
   (e) $3 \times 3 \times 3 \times 3 \times 5 \times 5 \times 7$

Prime factors

The factors of 18 are 1, 2, 3, 6, 9 and 18.
Two of these factors, 2 and 3, are prime numbers.
The **prime factors** of 18 are 2 and 3.

Those factors of a number which are prime numbers are called **prime factors**.

Products of prime factors

All numbers can be written as the product
of their prime factors.
For example:

$$6 = 2 \times 3$$
$$20 = 2 \times 2 \times 5$$
$$70 = 2 \times 5 \times 7$$
$$168 = 2 \times 2 \times 2 \times 3 \times 7$$

Powers can be used to write numbers as
the product of their prime factors in a
shorter form.
For example:

$$20 = 2^2 \times 5$$
$$168 = 2^3 \times 3 \times 7$$

A **factor tree** can be used to help write numbers as the
product of their prime factors.
For example, this factor tree shows that:

$$40 = 2 \times 20$$
$$40 = 2 \times 2 \times 10$$
$$40 = 2 \times 2 \times 2 \times 5$$
$$40 = 2^3 \times 5$$

The branches of a
factor tree stop when
a prime factor is
obtained.

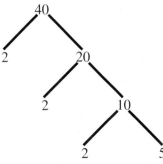

So 40 written as the product
of its prime factors is $2^3 \times 5$.

EXAMPLES

❶ Find the prime factors of 42.

First find the factors of 42.
$$42 \times 1 = 42$$
$$21 \times 2 = 42$$
$$14 \times 3 = 42$$
$$7 \times 6 = 42$$

Factors of 42 are 1, 2, 3, 6, 7, 14, 21 and 42.
2, 3 and 7 are prime numbers.
The prime factors of 42 are 2, 3 and 7.

❷ Write 50 as the product of its prime factors.

The factor tree shows that:
$$50 = 2 \times 25$$
$$50 = 2 \times 5 \times 5$$

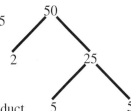

50 written as the product of its prime factors is 2×5^2.

Exercise 5.3 Do not use a calculator for questions 1 to 3.

❶ Find the prime factors of:
(a) 12   (b) 20   (c) 28   (d) 45   (e) 66

❷ Write the following numbers as products of their prime factors.
(a) 12   (b) 20   (c) 28   (d) 45   (e) 66

❸ (a) A number written as the product of its prime factors is $2^5 \times 3^3$.
Find all the factors of this number. Write them as products of their prime factors.

(b) A number written as the product of its prime factors is $5^3 \times 7^4$.
Find all the factors of this number. Write them as products of their prime factors.

❹ Each of the following numbers are written as products of their prime factors:
$2^3 \times 5^3$, $2^6 \times 5^6$, $2^2 \times 3^3 \times 5^2$, $2^4 \times 3^2 \times 5^8$, $3^2 \times 5^2 \times 11^4$, $3^3 \times 5^6 \times 13^3$.
Calculate each of the numbers.

❺ Numbers are made using the rule $a^3 \times b^2 \times c^2$ where a, b and c are different prime numbers.
The smallest number is 1800, which is given by $2^3 \times 3^2 \times 5^2$.
Find the next three numbers.

❻ Write each of the numbers 24, 40, 54 as the product of their prime factors.
What do you notice?
Find the next three numbers.

❼ Write each of the numbers 60, 84, 90 as the product of their prime factors.
What do you notice?
Find the next three numbers.

Least common multiples

The first few multiples of three are: 3, 6, 9, 12, **15**, 18, 21, 24, 27, **30**, 33, 36, 39, 42, **45**, …
The first few multiples of five are: 5, 10, **15**, 20, 25, **30**, 35, 40, **45**, 50, . . .

15, 30, 45, . . . are multiples of both 3 **and** 5.
They are called **common multiples** of 3 and 5.

The smallest number that is a multiple of both 3 and 5 is 15.
The **least common multiple** of 3 and 5 is 15.

The least common multiple (**LCM**) of two numbers is the smallest number that is a multiple of them both.

Find the least common multiple of 20 and 45.
Start with the multiples of 45: 45, 90, 135, 180, 225, 270, …
Which is the lowest multiple of 45 which is also a multiple of 20?
Multiples of 20: 20, 40, 60, 80, 100, 120, 140, 160, **180**, …

So the least common multiple of 20 and 45 is 180.

Highest common factors

The factors of 20 are: 1, 2, 4, 5, 10, 20.
The factors of 50 are: 1, 2, 5, 10, 25, 50.

1, 2, 5 and 10 are factors of both 20 **and** 50.
They are called the **common factors** of 20 and 50.

The largest number that is a factor of both 20 and 50 is 10.
The **highest common factor** of 20 and 50 is 10.

$$20 \times 1 = 20 \qquad 50 \times 1 = 50$$
$$10 \times 2 = 20 \qquad 25 \times 2 = 50$$
$$5 \times 4 = 20 \qquad 10 \times 5 = 50$$

The highest common factor (**HCF**) of two numbers is the largest number that is a factor of them both.

The factors of 18 are: 1, 2, 3, 6, 9, 18.
The factors of 45 are: 1, 3, 5, 9, 15, 45.

The common factors of 18 and 45 are: 1, 3 and 9.

The highest common factor of 18 and 45 is 9.

$$18 \times 1 = 18 \qquad 45 \times 1 = 45$$
$$9 \times 2 = 18 \qquad 15 \times 3 = 45$$
$$6 \times 3 = 18 \qquad 9 \times 5 = 45$$

Exercise 5.4   Do not use a calculator.

1 Find the least common multiple of:
   (a)   8 and 12   (b)   5 and 32   (c)   10 and 20   (d)   15 and 18
   (e)   30 and 45   (f)   4, 6 and 8   (g)   5, 8 and 10   (h)   45, 90 and 105

2 Find the highest common factor of:
   (a)   12 and 66   (b)   8 and 24   (c)   16 and 18   (d)   20 and 36
   (e)   33 and 88   (f)   16, 20 and 28   (g)   15, 39 and 45   (h)   45, 90 and 105

3 The table shows the highest common factors of pairs of numbers.

   (a)   Copy and extend the table up to at least 15 in each direction.
   (b)   Complete the table.
   (c)   Describe any patterns you see in the table.

	1	2	3	4	5	6	7
1	1						
2							
3							1
4		2					
6			3				

4 (a)   Find the value of x when $2^2 \times 3^x = 108$.
   (b)   Write 162 as a product of prime factors.
   (c)   What is the highest common factor of 108 and 162?
   (d)   What is the least common multiple of 108 and 162?

5 (a) Write 216 as a product of prime factors.
  (b) Write 288 as a product of prime factors.
  (c) What is the highest common factor of 216 and 288?
  (d) What is the least common multiple of 216 and 288?

6 The bell at St. Gabriel's church rings every 6 minutes.
  At St. Paul's, the bell rings every 9 minutes.
  Both bells ring together at 9.00 am. When is the next time both bells ring together?

Square numbers

Whole numbers raised to the power 2 are called **square numbers**.

$1^2 = 1 \times 1 = 1$ 1^2 is read as '1 squared'.   1 is a square number.
$2^2 = 2 \times 2 = 4$ 2^2 is read as '2 squared'.   4 is a square number.
$3^2 = 3 \times 3 = 9$ 3^2 is read as '3 squared'.   9 is a square number.

Square numbers can be shown
as square patterns of dots.

$1^2 = 1$ $2^2 = 4$ $3^2 = 9$

Find the next two square numbers.
Numbers that are not whole numbers can also be squared.
For example:
  $1.6^2 = 1.6 \times 1.6 = 2.56$
  2.56 is **not** a square number. *Why not?*

> To **square a number**
> multiply it by itself.

> **Squaring on a calculator**
> 1.6^2 is read as '1.6 squared'.
>
> To calculate 1.6^2 use this sequence of
> buttons: [1] [.] [6] [x^2] [=]
>
> If there is no x^2 button try this:
> [1] [.] [6] [×] [=]

Cube numbers

Whole numbers raised to the power 3 are called **cube numbers**.

$1^3 = 1 \times 1 \times 1 = 1$ 1^3 is read as '1 cubed'.   1 is a cube number.
$2^3 = 2 \times 2 \times 2 = 8$ 2^3 is read as '2 cubed'.   8 is a cube number.
$3^3 = 3 \times 3 \times 3 = 27$ 3^3 is read as '3 cubed'.   27 is a cube number.

Cube numbers can be shown using small cubes.

Draw a diagram to show 4^3.
What is the value of 4^3?

$1^3 = 1$ $2^3 = 8$ $3^3 = 27$

Numbers that are not whole numbers can also be cubed.
For example:
  $1.6^3 = 1.6 \times 1.6 \times 1.6 = 4.096$
  4.096 is **not** a cube number. *Why not?*

> 1.6^3 is read as '1.6 cubed'.

Using a scientific calculator

Powers

The **squares** of numbers and the **cubes** of numbers can also be calculated using the [x^y] button on a
scientific calculator. The [x^y] button can be used to calculate the value of a number x raised to the power y.

47

1 Calculate the value of 2.6^4.

To do the calculation enter the following sequence into your calculator.

| 2 | . | 6 | x^y | 4 | = |

This gives $2.6^4 = 45.6976$

2 Calculate the value of $5^3 \times (2^4 + 2^3)$.

To do the calculation enter the following sequence into your calculator.

| 5 | x^y | 3 | × | (| 2 | x^y | 4 | + | 2 | x^y | 3 |) | = |

This gives $5^3 \times (2^4 + 2^3) = 3\,000$

3 Find the value of x in: $\quad 2^x \times 5 = 160$

$2^x \times 5 = 160$
Dividing through by 5 gives:
$2^x = 32$
$2^5 = 32$ so $x = 5$.

Reciprocals

The **reciprocal** of a number is the value obtained when the number is divided into 1.

The reciprocal of a number x is $\frac{1}{x}$.

A number times its reciprocal equals 1.

For example, the reciprocal of 2 is $\frac{1}{2}$,

and $2 \times \frac{1}{2} = 1$.

The reciprocal of a number can be shown using an index of -1.

For example, $7^{-1} = \frac{1}{7}$.

To find the reciprocal of a number on a scientific calculator use the

| $\frac{1}{x}$ | button.

0 (zero) has no reciprocal.

Find the reciprocal of (a) 5, (b) 0.5.

(a) The reciprocal of 5 is $\frac{1}{5}$.
$1 \div 5 = 0.2$
The reciprocal of 5 is 0.2.

To find the reciprocal of 5 on your calculator use the sequence:

| 5 | $\frac{1}{x}$ |

(b) The reciprocal of 0.5 is $\frac{1}{0.5}$.
$1 \div 0.5 = 2$
The reciprocal of 0.5 is 2.

Use your calculator to check your answer.

Do not use a calculator for questions 1 and 2.

1 (a) Complete this list of square numbers from 1^2 to 20^2.
$$1^2 = 1 \times 1 = 1$$
$$2^2 = 2 \times 2 = 4$$
$$3^2 = 3 \times 3 = 9$$

(b) Explore the difference patterns in your list.

1		4		9		16		25		...
	3		5		7		9		...	
		2		2		2		...		

(c) Use the pattern to find 21^2 from 20^2.

2 (a) Complete this list of cube numbers from 1^3 to 10^3.
$$1^3 = 1 \times 1 \times 1 = 1$$
$$2^3 = 2 \times 2 \times 2 = 8$$
$$3^3 = 3 \times 3 \times 3 = 27$$

(b) Explore the difference patterns in your list.

1		8		27		64		125		...
	7		19		37		...			
		12		18		...				
			6							

3 (a) Calculate the value of:
   (i) $(-3)^2$ (ii) $(-2)^3$
   (iii) $(-4)^2$ (iv) $(-5)^3$

(b) What do you notice about the signs of your answers?

4 Consider the numbers:
8, 16, 27, 36, 64, 100.
Which of these numbers is both a square number **and** a cube number?

5 Calculate the value of:
   (a) 6.7 squared   (b) 3.4 cubed
   (c) 0.7 squared   (d) 0.04 cubed
   (e) (-0.4) squared   (f) (-0.5) cubed

6 Calculate the value of:
   (a) 0.2^0 (b) 0.3^3
   (c) 0.4^1 (d) 0.5^2

7 Calculate the value of:
   (a) 1.3^2 (b) 1.7^3
   (c) 5.4^0 (d) 4.8^1

8 Use the $\boxed{x^y}$ button on your calculator to find the value of:
   (a) (i) 13^2 (ii) 17^2 (iii) 2.5^2
       (iv) 0.8^2 (v) 9.7^2
   (b) (i) 6^3 (ii) 15^3 (iii) 2.4^3
       (iv) 0.7^3 (v) 5.6^3
   (c) (i) 3^7 (ii) 7^5 (iii) 9^6
       (iv) 0.5^4 (v) 3.8^5

9 Calculate:
   (a) 2.4^5 (b) $(-1.2)^3$
   (c) $(-0.7)^2$ (d) $3^4 + 3^2$
   (e) $2^6 - 2^2$ (f) $2^5 \times 3^3$
   (g) $3^5 \times 2^3$ (h) $4^5 \times 0.5^3$
   (i) $4^5 \div 0.5^3$ (j) $1.4^5 \div 2.5^2$

10 Calculate:
   (a) $2 + 2^2 + 2^3 + 2^4$
   (b) $3 + 3^2 - 3^3 + 3^4$
   (c) $3^3 \times (2^7 - 2^5)$
   (d) $4^2 \times (3^4 + 3^2)$
   (e) $3^3 \times 2^4 + 3^4 \times 2^3$
   (f) $(5^4 + 5^2) \div (2^7 - 2^5)$
   (g) $5^3 \times (4^5 - 4^2) + 6^3$
   (h) $3^3 \div (2^7 - 2^5)$
   (i) $(5^3 - 5^2) \times (6^3 - 2^4)$

11 (a) Find the reciprocals of these numbers without using a calculator, then use a calculator to check your answers.
   (i) 2   (ii) 5   (iii) 10
   (iv) 0.5   (v) 0.1   (vi) 0.2

(b) Use the $\boxed{\frac{1}{x}}$ button on your calculator to find the reciprocals of:
   (i) 4   (ii) 20   (iii) 25
   (iv) 0.25   (v) 0.4   (vi) 0.16

12 Show by means of an example, that a number times its reciprocal is equal to 1.

13 Calculate:
   (a) 2^{-1} (b) 4^{-1}
   (c) $(0.8)^{-1}$ (d) $\left(\frac{1}{4}\right)^{-1}$
   Give each of your answers as a decimal.

14 Find the value of x in:
   (a) $3^x \times 2 = 54$ (b) $2^x \times 7 = 7$
   (c) $3^x \times 11 = 33$ (d) $5^x \times 4 = 100$
   (e) $2^x \times 3 = 192$ (f) $5^x \times 7 = 875$
   (g) $3^x \times 5 = 405$ (h) $7^x \times 2 = 686$

Square roots

The opposite of squaring a number is called finding the **square root**.
For example:
The square root of 16 is 4 because $4^2 = 16$.

$$4 \xrightarrow{\text{square}} 16$$
$$4 \xleftarrow{\text{square root}} 16$$

The square root of 3.24 is 1.8 because $1.8^2 = 3.24$.

$$1.8 \xrightarrow{\text{square}} 3.24$$
$$1.8 \xleftarrow{\text{square root}} 3.24$$

$\sqrt{}$ This special symbol stands for the square root.

For example:

$\sqrt{9} = 3$ $\qquad$ $\sqrt{2.56} = 1.6$

The square root of a number can also be written
in index form, using an index of $\frac{1}{2}$.
For example, $9^{\frac{1}{2}} = \sqrt{9}$.

Square roots on a calculator

To calculate $\sqrt{2.56}$ use this
sequence of buttons:

$\boxed{\sqrt{}}$ $\boxed{2}$ $\boxed{\cdot}$ $\boxed{5}$ $\boxed{6}$ $\boxed{=}$

or:

$\boxed{2}$ $\boxed{\cdot}$ $\boxed{5}$ $\boxed{6}$ $\boxed{\sqrt{}}$

Cube roots

The opposite of cubing a number is called finding the **cube root**.
For example:
The cube root of 27 is 3 because $3^3 = 27$.

$$3 \xrightarrow{\text{cube}} 27$$
$$3 \xleftarrow{\text{cube root}} 27$$

The cube root of 0.125 is 0.5 because $0.5^3 = 0.125$.

$$0.5 \xrightarrow{\text{cube}} 0.125$$
$$0.5 \xleftarrow{\text{cube root}} 0.125$$

$\sqrt[3]{}$ This special symbol stands for the cube root.

The cube root of a number can also be written in index form, using an index of $\frac{1}{3}$.
For example, $27^{\frac{1}{3}} = \sqrt[3]{27}$.

Square roots and cube roots can be worked out on a calculator without using special buttons.
A method called **trial and improvement** can be used.

EXAMPLE $\quad$ You are asked to find the cube root of 18.6 but your calculator does not
have a cube root button. You know that $2^3 = 8$ and $3^3 = 27$.
Use trial and improvement, and a calculator, to find the cube root of 18.6 to an accuracy of
one decimal place. Show your method clearly.

2^3	$= 2 \times 2 \times 2$	$= 8$	so the cube root of 8 is 2	
3^3	$= 3 \times 3 \times 3$	$= 27$	so the cube root of 27 is 3	So try 2.5 *Why?*
2.5^3	$= 2.5 \times 2.5 \times 2.5$	$= 15.625$	so the cube root of 15.625 is 2.5	So try 2.6 *Why?*
2.6^3	$= 2.6 \times 2.6 \times 2.6$	$= 17.576$	so the cube root of 17.576 is 2.6	So try 2.7 *Why?*
2.7^3	$= 2.7 \times 2.7 \times 2.7$	$= 19.683$	so the cube root of 19.683 is 2.7	So try 2.65 *Why?*
2.65^3	$= 2.65 \times 2.65 \times 2.65$	$= 18.609625$	so the cube root of 18.609625 is 2.65	

This shows that the cube root of 18.6 lies between 2.6 and 2.65.
So correct to one decimal place the cube root of 18.6 is 2.6.

Remember. When using trial and improvement:
● Work methodically using trials first to the nearest whole number, then to one decimal place etc.
● Do at least one trial to one more decimal place than the required accuracy to be sure of your answer.

Exercise **5.6**

Do not use a calculator for questions 1 and 2.

1 Write down the value of:

(a) $\sqrt{25}$ (b) $100^{\frac{1}{2}}$ (c) $\sqrt{64}$ (d) $49^{\frac{1}{2}}$

2 Write down the value of:

(a) $\sqrt[3]{8}$ (b) $64^{\frac{1}{3}}$ (c) $\sqrt[3]{125}$ (d) $27^{\frac{1}{3}}$

3 Use the method of trial and improvement to find the value of:

(a) $\sqrt{20}$ (b) $\sqrt[3]{45}$ (c) $108^{\frac{1}{2}}$ (d) $200^{\frac{1}{3}}$

Give your answers to an accuracy of one decimal place.

4 Use the method of trial and improvement to find the length of the side of a square carpet of area 55 m².
Give your answer to an accuracy of two decimal places.

5 Use the method of trial and improvement to find the length of the side of an ice cube of volume 4500 mm³.
Give your answer to an accuracy of two decimal places.

Multiplying and dividing numbers with powers

EXAMPLES

This example introduces a method for multiplying powers of the same number.

1 (a) Calculate the value of $6^5 \times 6^4$ in power form.

$6^5 = 6 \times 6 \times 6 \times 6 \times 6$

$6^4 = 6 \times 6 \times 6 \times 6$

$6^5 \times 6^4 = (6 \times 6 \times 6 \times 6 \times 6) \times (6 \times 6 \times 6 \times 6)$

$= 6 \times 6 \times 6 \times 6 \times 6 \times 6 \times 6 \times 6 \times 6$

This gives: $6^5 \times 6^4 = 6^9$

(b) Calculate the value of $3^2 \times 3^6$ in power form.

$3^2 = 3 \times 3$

$3^6 = 3 \times 3 \times 3 \times 3 \times 3 \times 3$

$3^2 \times 3^6 = (3 \times 3) \times (3 \times 3 \times 3 \times 3 \times 3 \times 3)$

$= 3 \times 3 \times 3 \times 3 \times 3 \times 3 \times 3 \times 3$

This gives: $3^2 \times 3^6 = 3^8$

Check each of these results with your calculator.
Can you see a quick way of working out the power of the answer?

This example introduces a method for dividing powers of the same number.

2 (a) Calculate the value of $6^7 \div 6^4$ in power form.

$6^7 \div 6^4 = \dfrac{6 \times 6 \times 6 \times \cancel{6} \times \cancel{6} \times \cancel{6} \times \cancel{6}}{\cancel{6} \times \cancel{6} \times \cancel{6} \times \cancel{6}}$

$= 6 \times 6 \times 6$

$= 6^3$

This gives: $6^7 \div 6^4 = 6^{7-4} = 6^3$

(b) Calculate the value of $4^5 \div 4^3$ in power form.

$4^5 \div 4^3 = \dfrac{4 \times 4 \times \cancel{4} \times \cancel{4} \times \cancel{4}}{\cancel{4} \times \cancel{4} \times \cancel{4}}$

$= 4 \times 4$

$= 4^2$

This gives: $4^5 \div 4^3 = 4^{5-3} = 4^2$

Check each of these results with your calculator.

Rules for multiplying and dividing powers of the same number

Multiplying

When multiplying:
powers of the same base are **added**.

In general: $a^m \times a^n = a^{m+n}$

Dividing

When dividing:
powers of the same base are **subtracted**.

In general: $a^m \div a^n = a^{m-n}$

EXAMPLES

1 Simplify $2^6 \times 2^{-3}$.
Leave your answer in power form.

$$2^6 \times 2^{-3} = 2^{6+-3}$$
$$= 2^{6-3}$$
$$= 2^3$$

Remember
When multiplying and dividing
powers with different bases each
base must be dealt with separately.
Why?

2 Simplify $3^4 \times 2^3 \times 3^{-5} \times 2^5$.
Leave your answer in power form.

$$3^4 \times 2^3 \times 3^{-5} \times 2^5 = 3^4 \times 3^{-5} \times 2^3 \times 2^5$$
$$= 3^{4+-5} \times 2^{3+5}$$
$$= 3^{-1} \times 2^8$$

3 Simplify $10^{-4} \div 10^{-2}$.
Leave your answer in power form.

$$10^{-4} \div 10^{-2} = 10^{-4--2}$$
$$= 10^{-4+2}$$
$$= 10^{-2}$$

Exercise 5.7

Do not use a calculator in this exercise.

1 Simplify each of these expressions. Leave your answers in power form.
(a) $2^5 \times 2^2$ (b) $4^3 \times 4^6$ (c) $6^2 \times 6$
(d) $8^4 \times 8^3$ (e) $9^2 \times 9^{-2}$ (f) $2^{-3} \times 2$
(g) $5^5 \times 5^{-7}$ (h) $3^{-2} \times 3$ (i) $8^{-2} \times 8^{-3}$

2 Simplify. Leave your answers in power form.
(a) $2^5 \div 2^2$ (b) $4^7 \div 4^5$ (c) $6^2 \div 6$
(d) $8^4 \div 8^3$ (e) $3^{11} \div 3^5$ (f) $2^{-3} \div 2$
(g) $5^5 \div 5^{-7}$ (h) $11^{-2} \div 11^3$ (i) $7^{-4} \div 7^{-3}$

3 Simplify. Leave your answers in power form.
(a) $8^{-3} \times 8^5$ (b) $7^2 \div 7^7$ (c) $2.5^{-2} \div 2.5^{-1}$
(d) $4^3 \times 4^2 \times 4^{-5}$ (e) $10^{-3} \div 10^{-2}$ (f) $6^{-3} \times 6^4 \div 6^5$
(g) $0.1^{-7} \div 0.1^5$ (h) $5^{-7} \div (5^2 \times 5^6)$ (i) $4^2 \div (4^{-1} \times 4^{-2})$

4 Simplify. Leave your answers in power form.
(a) $4^{-3} \times 4^5 \times 8^5 \times 8^2$ (b) $4^{-1} \times 5^5 \times 5^{-7} \times 4^2$
(c) $2^{-5} \times 5^3 \times 2^3 \times 5^2$ (d) $3^{-1} \times 8^5 \times 3^{-2} \times 8^{-1}$

5 Simplify. Leave your answers in power form.
(a) $\dfrac{2 \times 2^5}{2^3}$ (b) $\dfrac{3^5 \times 3^{-2}}{3^2}$ (c) $\dfrac{5^{-3} \times 5^4}{5^{-2}}$

Surds

A surd is the square root of a positive integer, like $\sqrt{3}$, for which the root is not exact.

$\sqrt{4}$ is not a surd because it has an exact root.

The square root of a number can be positive or negative, for example $\sqrt{4}$ can be $+2$ or -2.

When we use surds we take the **positive square root**.

Surds are used when we want to keep an answer **exact**.

$\sqrt{3} = 1.73205\ldots$.
To keep an exact answer it is therefore necessary to keep the number in surd form and not to use a decimal approximation.

To manipulate surds we must use these rules.

1. $m\sqrt{a} + n\sqrt{a} = (m + n)\sqrt{a}$
2. $\sqrt{ab} = \sqrt{a} \times \sqrt{b}$
3. $\sqrt{\dfrac{a}{b}} = \dfrac{\sqrt{a}}{\sqrt{b}}$

To simplify surds look for factors that are square numbers.

EXAMPLES

Simplify the following leaving the answer in surd form.

(a) $\sqrt{12}$

(b) $2\sqrt{3} + 3\sqrt{3}$

(c) $\sqrt{\dfrac{15}{12}}$

(a) $\sqrt{12} = \sqrt{4} \times \sqrt{3} = 2\sqrt{3}$

(b) $2\sqrt{3} + 3\sqrt{3} = 5\sqrt{3}$

(c) $\sqrt{\dfrac{15}{12}} = \dfrac{\sqrt{3} \times \sqrt{5}}{\sqrt{4} \times \sqrt{3}} = \dfrac{\sqrt{5}}{2}$

Exercise 5.8   Do not use a calculator.

1 Which of the following are surds?

(a) $\sqrt{2}$ (b) $\sqrt{9}$ (c) $\sqrt{7}$

(d) $\sqrt{1}$ (e) $\sqrt{18}$ (f) $\sqrt{25}$

2 Write the following surds in their simplest form.

(a) $\sqrt{8}$ (b) $\sqrt{12}$ (c) $\sqrt{28}$ (d) $\sqrt{27}$

(e) $\sqrt{75}$ (f) $\sqrt{45}$ (g) $\sqrt{20}$ (h) $\sqrt{72}$

3 Simplify.

(a) $\sqrt{2} + \sqrt{2}$ (b) $2\sqrt{5} - \sqrt{5}$ (c) $5\sqrt{3} + 2\sqrt{3}$ (d) $5\sqrt{2} - 3\sqrt{2}$

4 Simplify.

(a) $\sqrt{\dfrac{9}{4}}$ (b) $\sqrt{\dfrac{25}{16}}$ (c) $\sqrt{\dfrac{6}{4}}$ (d) $\sqrt{\dfrac{18}{9}}$ (e) $\sqrt{\dfrac{12}{15}}$

5 Simplify.

(a) $\sqrt{3} \times \sqrt{3}$ (b) $\sqrt{3} \times 2\sqrt{3}$ (c) $3\sqrt{2} \times \sqrt{2}$ (d) $\sqrt{2} \times \sqrt{8}$

(e) $\sqrt{18} \times \sqrt{2}$ (f) $\sqrt{12} \times \sqrt{3}$ (g) $\sqrt{5} \times \sqrt{10}$ (h) $\sqrt{3} \times \sqrt{6}$

Working with Number

- **Multiples** of a number are found by multiplying the number by 1, 2, 3, 4, . . .
  For example: the multiples of 8 are
  $1 \times 8 = 8$, $2 \times 8 = 16$, $3 \times 8 = 24$,
  $4 \times 8 = 32$, . . .

- You can find **all** the **factors** of a number by finding all the multiplication facts that give the number.
  For example: the factors of 6 are 1, 2, 3 and 6.

- A **prime number** is a number with only two factors, 1 and the number itself.
  The first few prime numbers are:
  2, 3, 5, 7, 11, 13, 17, 19, 23, 29, 31, . . .

- The **prime factors** of a number are those factors of the number which are themselves prime numbers.

- The **Least Common Multiple** of two numbers is the smallest number that is a multiple of them both.

- The **Highest Common Factor** of two numbers is the largest number that is a factor of them both.

- An expression such as $3 \times 3 \times 3 \times 3 \times 3$ can be written in a shorthand way as 3^5.
  This is read as '3 to the power 5'.
  The number 3 is the **base** of the expression.
  5 is the **power**.

- Numbers raised to the power 2 are **squared**.
  Whole numbers squared are called **square numbers**.
  Squares can be calculated using the $\boxed{x^2}$ button on a calculator.
  The opposite of squaring a number is called finding the **square root**.
  Square roots can be calculated using the $\boxed{\sqrt{\ }}$ button on a calculator.
  The square root of a number can be written in index form.
  For example: $\sqrt{9} = 9^{\frac{1}{2}}$.

- Numbers raised to the power 3 are **cubed**.
  Whole numbers cubed are called **cube numbers**. The opposite of cubing a number is called finding the **cube root**.
  Cube roots can be calculated using the $\boxed{\sqrt[3]{\ }}$ button on a calculator.
  The cube root of a number can be written in index form.
  For example: $\sqrt[3]{27} = 27^{\frac{1}{3}}$.

- **Powers**
  The squares of numbers and the cubes of numbers can be worked out on a calculator by using the $\boxed{x^y}$ button.
  The $\boxed{x^y}$ button can be used to calculate the value of a number x raised to the power y.

- The square root of a number can be positive or negative.
  For example: $\sqrt{4}$ can be $+2$ or -2.

- **Reciprocals**
  The reciprocal of a number is the value obtained when the number is divided into 1.
  The reciprocal of a number can be found on a calculator by using the $\boxed{\frac{1}{x}}$ button.
  A number times its reciprocal equals 1.
  Zero has no reciprocal.
  The reciprocal of a number can be shown using an index of -1.
  For example: $5^{-1} = \frac{1}{5}$.

- Square roots and cube roots can be found using a method called **trial and improvement**.

- Powers of the same base are **added** when terms are **multiplied**.
  Powers of the same base are **subtracted** when terms are **divided**.
  Any number raised to the power zero equals 1.

- A surd is the square root of a positive integer, like $\sqrt{3}$, for which the root is not exact.
  $\sqrt{4}$ is not a surd because it has an exact root.

- To manipulate surds we must use these rules.

  1. $m\sqrt{a} + n\sqrt{a} = (m + n)\sqrt{a}$

  2. $\sqrt{ab} = \sqrt{a} \times \sqrt{b}$

  3. $\sqrt{\dfrac{a}{b}} = \dfrac{\sqrt{a}}{\sqrt{b}}$

1 12 written as the product of its prime factors is $2^2 \times 3$.

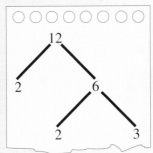

12 has 6 factors.
1, 2, 3, 4, 6 and 12

$$12 \times 1 = 12$$
$$6 \times 2 = 12$$
$$4 \times 3 = 12$$

Find the number of factors of some more numbers of the form $a^2 \times b$ where a and b are prime numbers.
What do you notice?

Investigate the number of factors of other numbers with just two prime factors.
What about numbers with any number of prime factors?

2 The squares of whole numbers can be written as the sum of consecutive odd numbers.

$$1^2 = 1 \qquad 2^2 = 1 + 3 \qquad 3^2 = 1 + 3 + 5$$

Continue this pattern. Can you find a general rule for n^2?

The cubes of whole numbers can also be written as the sum of consecutive odd numbers.

$$1^3 = 1 \qquad 2^3 = 3 + 5 \qquad 3^3 = 7 + 9 + 11$$

Continue this pattern. Can you find a general rule for n^3?

Other powers of whole numbers can also be written as the sum of consecutive odd numbers. This is how the pattern starts for the powers of 4 and 5.

$$1^4 = 1 \qquad 1^5 = 1 \qquad 2^4 = 7 + 9 \qquad 2^5 = 15 + 17$$

Investigate the connection between other powers and the sum of consecutive odd numbers.

Review Exercise

Do not use a calculator for questions 1 to 17.

1 Find all the factors of:
  (a) 12   (b) 30   (c) 96

2 Explain why 19 is a prime number.

3 The first 6 numbers in a sequence are:
    4   7   10   13   16   19
  (a) Which of these numbers is a multiple of 8?
  (b) Which of these numbers is a factor of 8?
  (c) Which of these numbers are prime numbers?

4 What is the square of 6?

5 Shirley writes down the following numbers.
    8   9   10   11   12
  Which of these numbers is:
  (a) a square number,
  (b) a cube number,
  (c) a prime number?

6 Consider the numbers:
    8, 9, 11, 17 and 121.
  (a) Write down all the factors of these numbers.
  (b) (i) Which of the numbers have only two factors?
      (ii) What special name is given to these numbers?
  (c) (i) Which of these numbers have exactly 3 factors?
      (ii) What special name is given to these numbers?

7 (a) Write down an even prime number.
  (b) Write down all the factors of 36.
  (c) Write down a multiple of 9 which is between 100 and 110.
  (d) Explain why a square number has an odd number of factors.

8 (a) Write as a product of prime factors:
    (i) 126,   (ii) 90,   (iii) 210

  (b) What is the smallest number that has 90 and 210 as factors?

  (c) What is the highest common factor of 90 and 126?

9 (a) Write 32 as a product of its prime factors.

  (b) Write 36 as a product of its prime factors.

  (c) What is the highest common factor of 32 and 36?

  (d) What is the least common multiple of 32 and 36?

10 A blue light flashes every 18 seconds and a green light flashes every 30 seconds. The two lights flash at the same time. After how many seconds will the lights next flash at the same time?

11 The number 1998 can be written as $2 \times 3^n \times p$ where n is a whole number and p is a prime number.

  (a) Work out the values of n and p.

  (b) Using your answers to part (a) or otherwise, work out the factor of 1998 which is between 100 and 200.

Edexcel

12 Write down the value of
  (a) 7^2,   (b) the square root of 81.

13 What is the value of $2^3 - \sqrt{25}$?

14 Work out the value of
  (a) 5^3,   (b) $\sqrt{36}$,   (c) $2^3 \times 3^2$

Edexcel

15 Simplify

  (a) $3\sqrt{5} - \sqrt{5}$ (b) $\sqrt{\dfrac{36}{25}}$

  (c) $\sqrt{2} \times 3\sqrt{2}$

16 Which is smaller $\sqrt{400}$ or 2^5? Show working to explain your answer.

17 (a) Work out the value of 0.2^2.

  (b) Work out the value of 0.9^3.

18 Calculate the value of:

  (a) $\sqrt{7}$ (b) $\left(\sqrt{7}\right)^2$

  (c) $\left(\sqrt{7}\right)^6$

19 What is the value of $\sqrt{50}$? Give your answer correct to one decimal place.

20 Calculate the value of $0.7^3 + \sqrt{30}$. Give your answer correct to one decimal place.

21 (a) Calculate the exact value of 8^5.

  (b) Find the reciprocal of 6. Give your answer correct to 3 decimal places.

22 Karen is using a trial and improvement method to find the cube root of 23. She calculates:

$$3 \times 3 \times 3 = 27 \qquad \text{too big}$$
$$2 \times 2 \times 2 = 8 \qquad \text{too small}$$

Continue this method to find the cube root of 23 correct to two decimal places. You **must** show all your working.

23 Write each of the following as a power of 10.
  (a) 100   (b) 1 000 000   (c) 1
  (d) 0.1   (e) 0.001

24 Write down the value of:
  (a) 1^{10} (b) 5^4 (c) $4^4 + 4^2$
  (d) $3^4 + 3^2$ (e) $5^4 - 5^3$ (f) $7^0 + 7^2$
  (g) $2^1 + 2^4 + 2^5$ (h) $3^0 + 3^1 + 3^2 + 3^3$

25 Find the value of x for each of the following equations.
  (a) $2^x = 16$ (b) $x^3 = 64$ (c) $3^x = 1$

26 Calculate the value of:
  (a) $12^5 \div 2^3$ (b) $0.3^3 + 0.3^5$
  (c) $0.3^3 \times 0.3^5$ (d) $3^4 + 2^5 \times (3^2 + 3^5)$
  (e) $2^5 \times (8^3 - 4^5)$ (f) $8^5 \times (2^3 + 4^2)$

27 Simplify fully each of these expressions. Leave your answers in power form.
  (a) $3^6 \times 3^2$ (b) $5^4 \times 5^7$ (c) $9^5 \times 9$
  (d) $4^8 \div 4^3$ (e) $7^6 \div 7$ (f) $6^7 \div 6^3$
  (g) $2^{-5} \times 2^2$ (h) $5^{-3} \times 5^{-4}$ (i) $4^{-2} \div 4$
  (j) $2^{-4} \times 7^3 \times 2^{-3} \times 7^{-1}$ (k) $3^8 \times 3^3 \div 3^2$

28 (a) Find the reciprocal of 0.27 correct to two significant figures.

  (b) Simplify, leaving your answer in power form.
$$\dfrac{5^3 \times 5^{-2}}{5^2}$$

CHAPTER 6

Standard Index Form

Standard index form is a shorthand way of writing very small and very large numbers.
Standard index form is often called **standard form** or **scientific notation**.

Very large numbers

Scientists who study the planets and the stars work with very large numbers.

Approximate distances from the Sun to some planets are:

Mercury	58 000 000 km
Venus	108 000 000 km
Earth	149 000 000 km
Mars	228 000 000 km
Pluto	5 898 000 000 km

Distances to the stars are far greater.

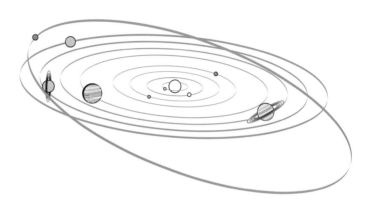

Large numbers and your calculator

A scientific calculator displays very large numbers in **standard form**.
To represent large numbers in standard form you need to use powers of 10.

Number	1 000 000	100 000	10 000	1000	100	10
Power of 10	10^6	10^5	10^4	10^3	10^2	10^1

For example: $2\,600\,000 = 2.6 \times 1\,000\,000 = 2.6 \times 10^6$
Therefore $2\,600\,000 = 2.6 \times 10^6$ in **standard form**.

Calculator displays

Work out 3 000 000 × 25 000 000 *on your calculator.*
Write down the display.

Most scientific calculators will show the answer as | 7.5   *13* |.

In **standard form** the answer should be written as 7.5×10^{13}.

A number written in standard form has **two** parts.
The first part must be a number between 1 and 10.
The second part is a power of 10.
The two parts are connected by a multiplication sign.

1 Write
  (a) 370 000 in standard form,   (b) 5.6×10^7 as an ordinary number.

  (a) $370\ 000 = 3.7 \times 100\ 000 = 3.7 \times 10^5$ (b) $5.6 \times 10^7 = 5.6 \times 10\ 000\ 000 = 56\ 000\ 000$

2 Write the calculator display | 7.3   *05* |

  (a) in standard form,   (b) as an ordinary number.

  (a) $7.3\ \ 05 = 7.3 \times 10^5$ (b) $7.3 \times 10^5 = 7.3 \times 100\ 000 = 730\ 000$

Exercise 6.1   Use a calculator for question 2 only.

1 Copy the table and fill in all the different forms of each number.

	Ordinary number	Power of 10	Standard form
	300 000	$3 \times 100\ 000$	3×10^5
(a)	75 000	$7.5 \times 10\ 000$	
(b)		$8 \times 100\ 000\ 000$	
(c)			3.5×10^{13}
(d)	62 300 000 000 000		
(e)			5.4×10^9
(f)		$6.93 \times 10\ 000\ 000$	
(g)	453 100 000 000		
(h)			6.97×10^5
(i)	453 120		
(j)		$1.097 \times 100\ 000$	

2 Use your calculator to work out each of the following. Write each of the answers:
  (i)   as on your calculator display,   (ii) in standard form,   (iii) as an ordinary number.

  (a) $300\ 000 \times 200\ 000\ 000$ (b) $120\ 000 \times 80\ 000\ 000$
  (c) $15\ 000 \times 700\ 000\ 000$ (d) $65\ 000 \times 2\ 000\ 000\ 000$
  (e) $480\ 000 \times 500\ 000\ 000$ (f) $50\ 000 \times 50\ 000\ 000$
  (g) $352\ 000\ 000 \times 40\ 000\ 000$ (h) $35\ 200 \times 6\ 500\ 000\ 000$
  (i) $3450 \times 5200 \times 45\ 000$ (j) $550\ 000 \times 8000 \times 250\ 000$

3 Write each of these numbers in standard form.
  (a) 300 000 000 000   (b) 80 000 000   (c) 700 000 000   (d) 2 000 000 000
  (e) 42 000 000   (f) 21 000 000 000   (g) 3 700 000 000   (h) 630
  (i) 3 219 000 000   (j) 654 120 000   (k) 897 213   (l) 42 670 000 000

4 Change each of these numbers to an ordinary number.
  (a) 6×10^5 (b) 2×10^3 (c) 5×10^7 (d) 9×10^8
  (e) 3.7×10^9 (f) 2.8×10^1 (g) 9.9×10^{10} (h) 7.1×10^4
  (i) 3.97×10^2 (j) 8.172×10^2 (k) 7.4312×10^6 (l) 1.234×10^9

5 Write these calculator displays   (a) in standard form,   (b) as an ordinary number.

  (i) | 4.5   *03* | (ii) | 7.8   *07* | (iii) | 5.3   *05* | (iv) | 3.25   *04* |

58

Very small numbers

Scientists who study microbiology work with numbers that are very small.
The smallest living cells are bacteria which have a diameter of
about 0.000 025 cm.
Blood cells have a diameter of about 0.000 75 cm.

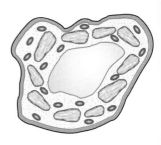

There are plenty of examples of other very small quantities.

Small numbers and your calculator

A scientific calculator displays small numbers in **standard form**.
It does this in the same sort of way that it does for large numbers.
To represent very small numbers in standard form you need to use powers of 10 for numbers less than 1.

Number	1000	100	10	1	0.1	0.01	0.001	0.000 1	0.000 01
Power of 10	10^3	10^2	10^1	10^0	10^{-1}	10^{-2}	10^{-3}	10^{-4}	10^{-5}

For example: $0.000\ 037 = 3.7 \times 0.000\ 01 = 3.7 \times 10^{-5}$
Therefore $0.000\ 037 = 3.7 \times 10^{-5}$ in **standard form**.

Calculator displays

Work out $0.000\ 007 \times 0.000\ 9$ on your calculator.
Write down the display.

Most scientific calculators will show the answer as $\boxed{\quad 6.3 \qquad -09 \quad}$.

In standard form the answer should be written as 6.3×10^{-9}.

Standard form

In **standard form** a number is written as:

a number between 1 and 10 $\times$ a power of 10

In standard form:
a **large** number has a **positive power**.
e.g. $160\ 000\ 000 = 1.6 \times 10^8$
a **small** number has a **negative power**.
e.g. $0.000\ 000\ 06 = 6 \times 10^{-8}$

EXAMPLES

1 Write
  (a) 0.000 73 in standard form,
  (b) 2.9×10^{-6} as an ordinary number.

  (a) $0.000\ 73 = 7.3 \times 0.000\ 1 = 7.3 \times 10^{-4}$
  (b) $2.9 \times 10^{-6} = 2.9 \times 0.000\ 001 = 0.000\ 002\ 9$

2 Write the calculator display $\boxed{\quad 1.5 \qquad -03 \quad}$
  (a) in standard form,
  (b) as an ordinary number.

  (a) $1.5 \quad -03 = 1.5 \times 10^{-3}$
  (b) $1.5 \times 10^{-3} = 1.5 \times 0.001 = 0.001\ 5$

Do questions 1 to 5 without using a calculator.

1 Write down the power of 10 for each of these numbers.
(a) 0.1   (b) 0.000 01   (c) 0.000 000 001
(d) 0.001   (e) 0.000 000 000 01   (f) 0.000 000 000 000 1

2 Copy and complete the following.

(a)	0.000 03	=	$3 \times 0.000\ 01$	$= 3 \times 10^{-5}$
(b)	0.007 5	=	7.5×0.001	=
(c)	0.000 008 75	=	$8.75 \times 0.000\ 001$	=
(d)	0.000 000 003 5	=		=
(e)	0.000 000 000 006 23	=		=
(f)	0.000 000 5	=		=
(g)	0.000 000 047 25	=		=
(h)	0.05	=		=
(i)	0.000 007 85	=		=

3 Change each of these numbers to an ordinary number:
(a) 3.5×10^{-1} (b) 5×10^{-4} (c) 7.2×10^{-5}
(d) 6.1×10^{-3} (e) 1.17×10^{-10} (f) 8.135×10^{-7}
(g) 6.462×10^{-2} (h) 4.001×10^{-9}

4 Write each of these numbers in standard form.
(a) 0.007   (b) 0.04   (c) 0.000 000 005
(d) 0.000 8   (e) 0.000 000 002 3   (f) 0.000 000 045
(g) 0.023 4   (h) 0.000 000 002 34   (i) 0.006 7
(j) 0.3   (k) 0.000 000 073 95   (l) 0.000 000 000 000 34

5 Change each of these numbers to an ordinary number:
(a) 5.5×10^{-6} (b) 6.5×10^{-8} (c) 3.2×10^{7}
(d) 2.9×10^{2} (e) 3.167×10^{-11} (f) 1.115×10^{4}
(g) 1.412×10^{-5} (h) 4×10^{1}

6 Use your calculator to work out each of the following. Write each of the answers:
     (i) as on the calculator display,
     (ii) in standard form,
     (iii) as an ordinary number.

(a) $0.000\ 03 \times 0.000\ 000\ 2$ (b) $0.000\ 045 \times 0.000\ 003$
(c) $0.000\ 75 \times 0.000\ 000\ 04$ (d) $0.002\ 3 \times 0.000\ 000\ 05$
(e) $0.053 \times 0.000\ 000\ 08$ (f) $0.000\ 006\ 4 \times 0.000\ 015\ 2$
(g) $0.59 \times 0.000\ 000\ 7^{2}$ (h) $0.067\ 5 \div 15\ 000^{2}$
(i) $6\ 330\ 000 \div 0.000\ 06$ (j) $7400 \div 0.002^{3}$

Using large and small numbers with a calculator

Scientific calculator

Calculations with large and small numbers can be done on a scientific calculator by:
- changing the numbers to standard form,
- entering the numbers into the calculator using the [Exp] button.

If your calculator works in a different way to the examples shown refer to the instruction booklet supplied with the calculator or ask someone for help.

EXAMPLES

1 Calculate the value of $62\,500\,000\,000 \times 0.000\,000\,003$
Give your answer both as an ordinary number and in standard form.

$62\,500\,000\,000 \times 0.000\,000\,003 = (6.25 \times 10^{10}) \times (3 \times 10^{-9})$

To do the calculation enter the following sequence into your calculator.

$\boxed{6}\ \boxed{.}\ \boxed{2}\ \boxed{5}\ \boxed{\text{Exp}}\ \boxed{1}\ \boxed{0}\ \boxed{\times}\ \boxed{3}\ \boxed{\text{Exp}}\ \boxed{9}\ \boxed{+/-}\ \boxed{=}$

Giving:
$6\,250\,000\,000 \times 0.000\,000\,03$
$= 187.5$ (ordinary number)
$= 1.875 \times 10^2$ (standard form)

Some calculators display this result as: 187.5
Other calculators give this display: 1.875 *02*

2 Calculate the value of $0.000\,000\,000\,05^4$. Give your answer in standard form.

$(0.000\,000\,000\,05)^4 = (5 \times 10^{-11})^4$

To do the calculation enter the following sequence into your calculator.

$\boxed{5}\ \boxed{\text{Exp}}\ \boxed{1}\ \boxed{1}\ \boxed{+/-}\ \boxed{x^y}\ \boxed{4}\ \boxed{=}$

This gives the calculator display:
$0.000\,000\,000\,05^4 = 6.25 \times 10^{-42}$

$\boxed{6.25 \qquad -42}$

Remember: The calculator display **must** be changed to either **standard form** or an **ordinary number**.

Solving problems involving large and small numbers

Problems can involve numbers given in standard form.

EXAMPLE

The following figures refer to the population of China and the USA in 1993.

China 1.01×10^9 USA 2.32×10^8

(a) By how much did the population of China exceed that of the USA in 1993?

(b) Calculate the total population of the two countries in 1993.

$1.01 \times 10^9 > 2.32 \times 10^8$
The greater the power . . .
. . . the bigger the number.

(a) You need to work out $1.01 \times 10^9 - 2.32 \times 10^8$
To do the calculation enter the following sequence into your calculator.

$\boxed{1}\ \boxed{.}\ \boxed{0}\ \boxed{1}\ \boxed{\text{Exp}}\ \boxed{9}\ \boxed{-}\ \boxed{2}\ \boxed{.}\ \boxed{3}\ \boxed{2}\ \boxed{\text{Exp}}\ \boxed{8}\ \boxed{=}$

Giving: $1.01 \times 10^9 - 2.32 \times 10^8 = 778\,000\,000 = 7.78 \times 10^8$

(b) You need to work out $1.01 \times 10^9 + 2.32 \times 10^8$
Enter the following sequence into your calculator.

$\boxed{1}\ \boxed{.}\ \boxed{0}\ \boxed{1}\ \boxed{\text{Exp}}\ \boxed{9}\ \boxed{+}\ \boxed{2}\ \boxed{.}\ \boxed{3}\ \boxed{2}\ \boxed{\text{Exp}}\ \boxed{8}\ \boxed{=}$

Giving: $1.01 \times 10^9 + 2.32 \times 10^8 = 1.242 \times 10^9$

*Try this example **without** a calculator.*

Use the [Exp] button on your calculator to answer these questions.

1 Give the answer to the following calculations as an ordinary number.
(a) $(5.25 \times 10^9) \times (5 \times 10^{-5})$
(b) $(5.25 \times 10^9) \div (5 \times 10^{-5})$
(c) $(8.5 \times 10^6)^2$
(d) $(5 \times 10^{-3})^3$
(e) $(7.2 \times 10^5) \div (2.4 \times 10^{-5})$
(f) $(9.5 \times 10^6) \div (1.9 \times 10^{-7})^2$

2 Give the answer to the following calculations in standard form.
(a) $33\,500\,000\,000 \times 2\,800\,000\,000$
(b) $0.000\,000\,000\,2 \times 80\,000\,000\,000$
(c) $15\,000\,000\,000\,000^2$
(d) $0.000\,000\,000\,000\,5^3$
(e) $48\,000\,000\,000 \div 0.000\,000\,000\,2$
(f) $25\,000\,000\,000 \div 500\,000\,000\,000$

3 (a) In 1992 about $1\,400\,000\,000$ steel cans and about $688\,000\,000$ aluminium cans were recycled.
What was the total number of cans that were recycled in 1992?
Give your answer in standard form.

(b) Alpha Centauri is about $40\,350\,000\,000\,000$ km from the Sun.
Alpha Cygni is about $15\,300\,000\,000\,000\,000$ km from the Sun.
How much further is it from the Sun to Alpha Cygni than from the Sun to Alpha Centauri?
Give your answer in standard form.

4 Here are the diameters of some planets.
Saturn 1.42×10^5 km   Jupiter 1.2×10^5 km   Pluto 2.3×10^3 km

(a) List the planets in order of size starting with the smallest.
(b) What is the difference between the diameters of the largest and smallest planets?
Give your answer in standard form and as an ordinary number.

5 Here are the areas of some of the world's largest deserts.
The Sahara desert in North Africa $\quad\quad\quad\quad\quad\quad$ 8.6×10^6 km²
The Gobi desert in Mongolia and North East China $\quad$ 1.166×10^6 km²
The Patagonian desert in Argentina $\quad\quad\quad\quad\quad$ 6.73×10^5 km²

(a) What is the total area of the Sahara and Patagonian deserts?
(b) What is the difference in area between the Gobi and the Patagonian deserts?
Give your answer in standard form.

6 Calculate $5.42 \times 10^6 \times 4.65 \times 10^5$ giving your answer in standard form correct to 3 significant figures.

7 Calculate $1.7 \times 10^3 \div 7.6 \times 10^7$ giving your answer in standard form correct to 2 significant figures.

8 Calculate $2.3 \times 10^{-3} \times 9.8 \times 10^{-5}$ giving your answer in standard form to an appropriate degree of accuracy.

9 Calculate $2.76 \times 10^{-5} \div 9.68 \times 10^{-3}$ giving your answer in standard form to an appropriate degree of accuracy.

10 The mass of an oxygen atom is 2.7×10^{-23} grams.
The mass of an electron at rest is approximately $30\,000$ times smaller than this.
Estimate the mass of an electron at rest.

11 The modern human appeared on the Earth about 3.5×10^4 years ago.
The Earth has been in existence for something like 1.3×10^5 times as long as this.
(a) Estimate the age of the Earth.

Reptiles appeared on the Earth about 2.3×10^8 years ago.
(b) How many times longer than the modern human have reptiles been alive?
Give your answer in standard form.

Standard form calculations without a calculator

In some standard form problems the calculations can be handled without using a calculator.

EXAMPLES

1 Calculate the value of $(3 \times 10^2) + (4 \times 10^3)$.
Give your answer in standard form.

$$3 \times 10^2 = 300 \qquad 4 \times 10^3 = 4000$$
$$(3 \times 10^2) + (4 \times 10^3) = 300 + 4000$$
$$= 4300$$
$$= 4.3 \times 10^3$$

> When adding or subtracting numbers in standard form without a calculator change to ordinary numbers first.

2 Calculate the value of ab where
$a = 8 \times 10^3$ and $b = 4 \times 10^5$.

$$ab = (8 \times 10^3) \times (4 \times 10^5)$$
$$= 8 \times 4 \times 10^3 \times 10^5$$
$$= 32 \times 10^8$$
$$= 3.2 \times 10 \times 10^8$$
$$= 3.2 \times 10^9$$

> When **multiplying** the powers are **added**.
> $10^3 \times 10^5 = 10^{3+5} = 10^8$
> $10 \times 10^8 = 10^{1+8} = 10^9$

3 Calculate the value of x^2 where $x = 7 \times 10^{-8}$.

$$x^2 = (7 \times 10^{-8})^2$$
$$= 49 \times 10^{-16}$$
$$= 4.9 \times 10 \times 10^{-16}$$
$$= 4.9 \times 10^{-15}$$

> **Remember:**
> $(7 \times 10^{-8})^2 = 7^2 \times (10^{-8})^2$
> $10 \times 10^{-16} = 10^{1-16} = 10^{-15}$

4 Calculate the value of $(1.2 \times 10^3) \div (4 \times 10^{-8})$.

$$(1.2 \times 10^3) \div (4 \times 10^{-8}) = (1.2 \div 4) \times (10^3 \div 10^{-8})$$
$$= 0.3 \times 10^{11}$$
$$= 3 \times 10^{-1} \times 10^{11}$$
$$= 3 \times 10^{10}$$

> When **dividing** the powers are **subtracted**.
> $10^3 \div 10^{-8} = 10^{3--8} = 10^{11}$

Exercise 6.4

Do not use a calculator. Give your answers in standard form.

1 For each of the following calculate the value of $p + q$.
(a) $p = 5 \times 10^3$ and $q = 2 \times 10^2$
(b) $p = 4 \times 10^5$ and $q = 8 \times 10^6$
(c) $p = 3.08 \times 10^4$ and $q = 9.2 \times 10^3$
(d) $p = 4.25 \times 10^4$ and $q = 7.5 \times 10^3$

2 For each of the following calculate the value of $p - q$.
(a) $p = 3 \times 10^3$ and $q = 2 \times 10^2$
(b) $p = 9.05 \times 10^5$ and $q = 5 \times 10^3$
(c) $p = 3.05 \times 10^7$ and $q = 5 \times 10^5$
(d) $p = 9.545 \times 10^8$ and $q = 4.5 \times 10^6$

3 For each of the following calculate the value of $p \times q$.
(a) $p = 4 \times 10^3$ and $q = 2 \times 10^4$
(b) $p = 2 \times 10^4$ and $q = 3 \times 10^3$
(c) $p = 4 \times 10^5$ and $q = 6 \times 10^2$
(d) $p = 9 \times 10^9$ and $q = 3 \times 10^5$

4 For each of the following calculate the value of $p \div q$.
(a) $p = 6 \times 10^5$ and $q = 2 \times 10^2$
(b) $p = 9 \times 10^5$ and $q = 3 \times 10^2$
(c) $p = 2.5 \times 10^5$ and $q = 5 \times 10^3$
(d) $p = 4 \times 10^8$ and $q = 2 \times 10^{-3}$
(e) $p = 1.2 \times 10^3$ and $q = 3 \times 10^{-3}$
(f) $p = 1.5 \times 10^{-5}$ and $q = 5 \times 10^{-3}$

5 $x = 3 \times 10^4$ and $y = 5 \times 10^{-5}$. Work out the value of each of these expressions.

(a) xy (b) x^3 (c) x^2y (d) y^3 (e) $\dfrac{x}{y}$

6 Find the value of each of the following.

(a) $(5 \times 10^6) \times (3 \times 10^4)$ (b) $(8 \times 10^{-5}) \times (3 \times 10^7)$

(c) $(7 \times 10^{-5}) \times (6 \times 10^{-4})$ (d) $(8 \times 10^3)^2$

(e) $(4 \times 10^5) \div (8 \times 10^3)$ (f) $(1.8 \times 10^3) \div (6 \times 10^{-7})$

(g) $(5 \times 10^{-7}) \div (8 \times 10^{-2})$ (h) $(2 \times 10^4) \div (8 \times 10^{-1})$

What you need to know

- **Standard index form**, or **standard form**, is a shorthand way of writing very large and very small numbers.

- In **standard form** a number is written as: **a number between 1 and 10 × a power of 10**.
  Large numbers (ten, or more) have a **positive** power of 10.
  Small numbers (less than one) have a **negative** power of 10.

Review Exercise

Do not use a calculator for questions 1 to 4.

1
(a) Write 7 800 000 in standard form.
(b) Write 0.000 005 in standard form.
(c) Here are some numbers written in standard form.

1.7×10^5	3.2×10^{-3}
5.675×10^4	9.75×10^{-3}

    (i) Which of these numbers is the largest?
        Write your answer as an ordinary number.
    (ii) Which of these numbers is the smallest?
        Write your answer as an ordinary number.

2 $A = 7 \times 10^5$ and $B = 5 \times 10^{-3}$.
(a) Work out $A \times B$.
    Give your answer in standard form.
(b) Work out $A \div B$.
    Give your answer in standard form.
(c) Calculate 30% of A.
(d) Calculate $\frac{3}{25}$ of B.

3
(a) Work out $\dfrac{3.6 \times 10^9}{4.5 \times 10^4}$
    Give your answer in standard form.
(b) Work out $\dfrac{4.5 \times 10^4}{3.6 \times 10^9}$
    Give your answer as an ordinary number.

4 $p = 8 \times 10^3$, $q = 2 \times 10^4$.
(a) Find the value of $p \times q$.
    Give your answer in **standard form**.
(b) Find the value of $p + q$.
    Give your answer as an **ordinary number**.

Edexcel

5 The distance from the Earth to the Moon is 250 000 miles.
(a) Express this number in standard form.

The distance from the Earth to the Sun is 9.3×10^7 miles.
(b) Calculate the value of the expression

$$\frac{\text{distance from the Earth to the Moon}}{\text{distance from the Earth to the Sun}}$$

giving your answer in standard form.

Edexcel

6

KILLICK BANK

MONTHLY REPORT - JUNE
147 million pounds was used to buy 2100 houses
AVERAGE COST OF A HOUSE IS £

(a) Write the number 147 million in standard form.
(b) Write the number 2100 in standard form.

The corner of the page showing the average cost of a house is missing.
(c) Use your answers to (a) and (b) to calculate the average cost of a house. Give your answer in standard form.

Edexcel

Fractions

Shaded fractions

What fraction of this rectangle is shaded?

The rectangle is divided into **eight** squares.
The squares are all the same size.
Three of the squares are shaded.

$\frac{3}{8}$ of the rectangle is shaded.

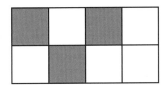

In a fraction:
The top number is
called the **numerator**.
The bottom number
is called the
denominator.

Activity

What fraction of each of these shapes is shaded?

      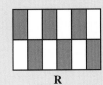

P　　　　　　Q　　　　　　R　　　　　　S

Which rectangles have the same fraction shaded?

Equivalent fractions

Fractions which are equal are called **equivalent fractions**.

Rectangle Q has $\frac{3}{12}$ shaded, $\frac{3}{12} = \frac{1}{4}$.

Rectangle S has $\frac{6}{24}$ shaded, $\frac{6}{24} = \frac{1}{4}$.

Each of the fractions $\frac{1}{4}, \frac{3}{12}, \frac{6}{24}$, is the same fraction written in different ways.

These fractions are all equivalent to $\frac{1}{4}$.

Write down two more fractions equivalent to $\frac{1}{4}$.

To write an equivalent fraction:
Multiply the numerator and
denominator by the **same** number.

For example. 　$\frac{1}{4} = \frac{1 \times 3}{4 \times 3} = \frac{3}{12}$

$\frac{1}{4} = \frac{1 \times 6}{4 \times 6} = \frac{6}{24}$

EXAMPLES

1 Write down three fractions equivalent to $\frac{5}{7}$.

The numerators are any multiples of 5.
For example: 5, 10, 15, 20, …

The denominators are the same multiples
of 7: 7, 14, 21, 28, …

This gives the fractions: $\frac{5}{7}, \frac{10}{14}, \frac{15}{21}, \frac{20}{28}, …$

2 The fraction $\frac{2}{3}$ is equivalent to the
fraction $\frac{?}{12}$.
Find the value of the unknown numerator.

3 has been multiplied by 4 to get 12.
So 2 must also be multiplied by 4 to
get the unknown numerator.
The unknown numerator is 8.

Simplifying fractions

Fractions can be simplified if the numerator and denominator have a common factor.
In its **simplest form**, the numerator and denominator of a fraction have no common factor other than 1.

To write a fraction in its simplest form divide the numerator and denominator of the fraction by their highest common factor.
This is sometimes called **cancelling** a fraction.

The numerator and denominator of $\frac{15}{25}$ have a highest common factor of 5.

$$\frac{15}{25} = \frac{15 \div 5}{25 \div 5} = \frac{3}{5}$$

3 and 5 have no common factors, other than 1.

$$\frac{15}{25} = \frac{3}{5} \text{ in its simplest form.}$$

Remember:
Multiplication and division are inverse (opposite) operations.
Equivalent fractions can also be made by dividing the numerator and denominator of a fraction by the same number.

EXAMPLES

1 Simplify $\frac{24}{30}$.

The highest common factor of 24 and 30 is 6.

$$\frac{24}{30} = \frac{24 \div 6}{30 \div 6} = \frac{4}{5}$$

2 In a class of 28 pupils there are 12 boys.
What fraction of the pupils are boys?
Write this fraction in its simplest form.

There are 12 out of 28 boys.
The fraction of boys $= \frac{12}{28}$

$$\frac{12}{28} = \frac{12 \div 4}{28 \div 4} = \frac{3}{7}$$

$$\frac{12}{28} = \frac{3}{7} \text{ in its simplest form.}$$

3 Write 42 as a fraction of 70.

42 as a fraction of 70 is $\frac{42}{70}$

2 is a common factor of 42 and 70.

$$\frac{42}{70} = \frac{42 \div 2}{70 \div 2} = \frac{21}{35}$$

7 is a common factor of 21 and 35.

$$\frac{21}{35} = \frac{21 \div 7}{35 \div 7} = \frac{3}{5}$$

$$\frac{42}{70} = \frac{3}{5} \text{ in its simplest form.}$$

We could have divided by 14.

$$\frac{42}{70} = \frac{42 \div 14}{70 \div 14} = \frac{3}{5}$$

Exercise 7.1

1 What fraction of each of these diagrams is shaded?

(a) 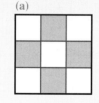 (b) 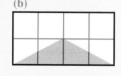 (c) 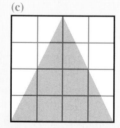 (d)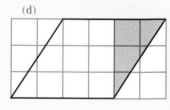

2 Write three equivalent fractions for the shaded part of this rectangle.
What is the simplest form of the shaded fraction?

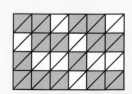

3 Look at these diagrams.

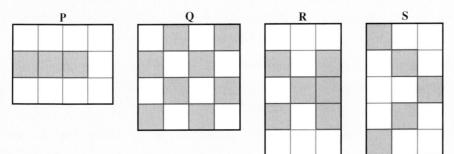

(a) Which diagram has $\frac{3}{12}$ shaded?

(b) Which diagram has $\frac{1}{4}$ shaded?

(c) Which diagram has $\frac{6}{15}$ shaded?

(d) Which diagram has $\frac{2}{5}$ shaded?

(e) Which diagram has $\frac{1}{2}$ shaded?

(f) Which diagram has $\frac{1}{3}$ shaded?

4 What fraction of each of these shapes is shaded?
Give your answers in their simplest form.

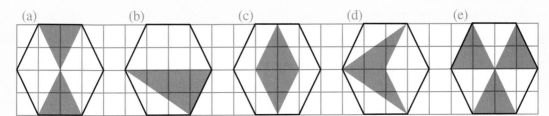

5 Write down three fractions equivalent to:

(a) $\frac{1}{3}$ (b) $\frac{2}{9}$ (c) $\frac{5}{8}$

(d) $\frac{4}{5}$ (e) $\frac{3}{10}$ (f) $\frac{7}{12}$

6 Each of these pairs of fractions are equivalent.
In each case find the value of n.

(a) $\frac{1}{3}, \frac{n}{6}$ (b) $\frac{n}{8}, \frac{6}{16}$ (c) $\frac{5}{n}, \frac{15}{18}$

(d) $\frac{n}{4}, \frac{12}{16}$ (e) $\frac{24}{64}, \frac{3}{n}$ (f) $\frac{n}{12}, \frac{56}{96}$

7 Write each of these fractions in its simplest form.

(a) $\frac{6}{8}$ (b) $\frac{12}{15}$ (c) $\frac{18}{27}$ (d) $\frac{22}{99}$

(e) $\frac{50}{75}$ (f) $\frac{16}{40}$ (g) $\frac{12}{50}$ (h) $\frac{52}{65}$

8 Write the first number as a fraction of the second.
Write the fractions in their simplest form.

(a) 4, 20   (b) 3, 12   (c) 8, 12

(d) 24, 60   (e) 60, 105

9 Mr Jones plans a car journey.

(a) The journey is 50 km long.
Mr Jones plans to stop after 35 km.
What fraction of the total distance is this?
Give your answer in its simplest form.

(b) The journey takes 60 minutes which includes a 12 minute stop.
For what fraction of the total time does Mr Jones stop on his journey?
Give your answer in its simplest form.

10 A group of students were asked some questions about how they travelled to school.
$\frac{1}{2}$ of the students said they walked.

$\frac{1}{3}$ of the students said they travelled by bus.

In the group there were more than 20 students and less than 30.

(a) How many students were in the group?

The rest of the group came by car.

(b) What fraction of the group came by car?
Give your answer in its simplest form.

Types of fractions

This diagram shows that when 5 cakes are shared equally between 2 people they get $2\frac{1}{2}$ cakes each.

This diagram shows that when 5 cakes are shared equally between 4 people they get $1\frac{1}{4}$ cakes each.

Numbers like $2\frac{1}{2}$ and $1\frac{1}{4}$ are called **mixed numbers** because they are a mixture of whole numbers and fractions.

Mixed numbers can be written as **improper** or '**top heavy**' fractions.

These are fractions where the numerator is larger than the denominator.

EXAMPLES

1 Write $3\frac{4}{7}$ as an improper fraction.

$$3\frac{4}{7} = \frac{(3 \times 7) + 4}{7} = \frac{21 + 4}{7} = \frac{25}{7}$$

2 Write $\frac{32}{5}$ as a mixed number.

$32 \div 5 = 6$ remainder 2.

$$\frac{32}{5} = 6\frac{2}{5}$$

Finding fractions of quantities

EXAMPLES

1 Find $\frac{3}{10}$ of 100.

Divide 100 into 10 equal parts.
$100 \div 10 = 10$.

10	10	10	10	10	10	10	10	10	10

Each of these parts is $\frac{1}{10}$ of 100.

Three of these parts is $\frac{3}{10}$ of 100.

10	10	10	10	10	10	10	10	10	10

So $\frac{3}{10}$ of $100 = 3 \times 10 = 30$.

2 Find $\frac{2}{5}$ of £65.

Divide £65 into 5 equal parts.
£65 $\div$ 5 = £13.

13	13	13	13	13

Each of these parts is $\frac{1}{5}$ of £65.

Two of these parts is $\frac{2}{5}$ of £65.

13	13	13	13	13

So $\frac{2}{5}$ of £65 = $2 \times$ £13 = £26.

Exercise **7.2**

Do not use a calculator in questions 1 to 3.

1 Change the following improper fractions to mixed numbers:

(a) $\frac{13}{10}$ (b) $\frac{3}{2}$ (c) $\frac{17}{8}$ (d) $\frac{15}{4}$ (e) $\frac{23}{5}$ (f) $\frac{34}{7}$

2 Change the following mixed numbers to improper fractions:

(a) $2\frac{7}{10}$ (b) $1\frac{3}{5}$ (c) $5\frac{5}{6}$ (d) $3\frac{3}{20}$ (e) $4\frac{5}{9}$ (f) $7\frac{4}{7}$

3 Calculate:

(a) $\frac{1}{4}$ of 12 (b) $\frac{1}{5}$ of 20

(c) $\frac{1}{10}$ of 30 (d) $\frac{1}{6}$ of 48

(e) $\frac{2}{5}$ of 20 (f) $\frac{3}{10}$ of 30

(g) $\frac{2}{7}$ of 42 (h) $\frac{5}{9}$ of 36

4 Calculate:

(a) $\frac{3}{10} \times 8$ (b) $\frac{3}{8} \times 20$

(c) $\frac{5}{6} \times 9$ (d) $\frac{4}{5} \times 12$

5 Tom earns £9 per hour.
Sam earns $\frac{2}{3}$ of what Tom earns.
How much does Sam earn in 10 hours?

6 Aisha has 36 balloons.
She sells $\frac{2}{9}$ of them.
How many balloons has she got left?

7 Alfie collects £120 for charity.
He gives $\frac{3}{5}$ of it to Oxfam.
How much does he give to other charities?

8 A coat costing £138 is reduced by $\frac{1}{3}$.
Find the new price of the coat.

9 In a sale of electrical goods all items are reduced by $\frac{3}{8}$.
What is the sale price of a microwave which was originally priced at £212?

10 Lauren and Amelia share a bar of chocolate.
The chocolate bar has 24 squares.
Lauren eats $\frac{3}{8}$ of the bar.
Amelia eats $\frac{5}{12}$ of the bar.

(a) How many squares has Lauren eaten?
(b) How many squares has Amelia eaten?
(c) What fraction of the bar is left?

11 Andy, Bill and Chris share a bag of sweets.
There are 60 sweets in the bag.
Andy eats $\frac{1}{6}$ of the sweets.
Bill eats $\frac{5}{12}$ of the sweets.
Chris eats $\frac{1}{5}$ of the sweets.

(a) (i) How many sweets has Andy eaten?
    (ii) How many sweets has Bill eaten?
    (iii) How many sweets has Chris eaten?
(b) What fraction of the sweets are left?

12 A publisher offers a discount of $\frac{3}{20}$ for orders of more than 100 books.
How much would a shop pay for an order of 250 books costing £3.50 each?

Adding and subtracting fractions

There are 12 sweets in a packet. Alena eats $\frac{2}{3}$ of the sweets and Sead eats $\frac{1}{4}$ of the sweets.
What fraction of the packet of sweets have they eaten altogether?

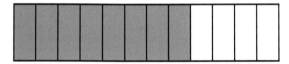

Alena eats $\frac{2}{3}$ of the sweets in the packet.
$\frac{2}{3}$ of 12 = 8 $\frac{2}{3} = \frac{8}{12}$

Sead eats $\frac{1}{4}$ of the sweets in the packet.
$\frac{1}{4}$ of 12 = 3 $\frac{1}{4} = \frac{3}{12}$

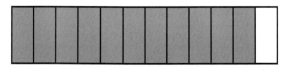

Together Alena and Sead eat $\frac{2}{3} + \frac{1}{4}$ of the packet.
$\frac{2}{3} + \frac{1}{4} = \frac{8}{12} + \frac{3}{12} = \frac{11}{12}$

Together Alena and Sead eat $\frac{11}{12}$ of the packet.

How to add and subtract fractions

Calculate $1\frac{7}{10} + \frac{5}{6}$

Change mixed numbers to improper ('top heavy') fractions.

$$1\frac{7}{10} = \frac{17}{10}$$

The calculation then becomes

$$\frac{17}{10} + \frac{5}{6}$$

Find the **lowest** common multiple of the denominators (bottom numbers).

Lowest common multiple of 10 and 6 is 30.

Change the original fractions to equivalent fractions using the lowest common multiple as the new denominator.

$$\frac{17}{10} = \frac{51}{30} \text{ and } \frac{5}{6} = \frac{25}{30}$$

Add or subtract the new numerators. Keep the new denominator the same.

$$\frac{51}{30} + \frac{25}{30} = \frac{51 + 25}{30} = \frac{76}{30}$$

Write the answer in its simplest form.

$$\frac{76}{30} = 2\frac{16}{30} = 2\frac{8}{15}$$

Fractions must have the **same denominator** before addition (or subtraction) can take place.

What happens when you use a common multiple that is not the lowest?

EXAMPLES

1 Work out $\frac{1}{2} + \frac{1}{3}$.

The lowest common multiple of 2 and 3 is 6.

$\frac{1}{2} = \frac{3}{6}$ and $\frac{1}{3} = \frac{2}{6}$

$\frac{1}{2} + \frac{1}{3} = \frac{3}{6} + \frac{2}{6}$

$\quad = \frac{5}{6}$

Remember to add the numerators only.

2 Calculate $3\frac{3}{10} - 1\frac{5}{6}$.

$3\frac{3}{10} = \frac{33}{10}$ and $1\frac{5}{6} = \frac{11}{6}$

The lowest common multiple of 10 and 6 is 30.

$\frac{33}{10} = \frac{99}{30}$ and $\frac{11}{6} = \frac{55}{30}$

$3\frac{3}{10} - 1\frac{5}{6} = \frac{99}{30} - \frac{55}{30} = \frac{44}{30}$

$\frac{44}{30} = \frac{22}{15} = 1\frac{7}{15}$

3 Work out $\frac{3}{4} + \frac{2}{3}$.

$\frac{3}{4} + \frac{2}{3} = \frac{9}{12} + \frac{8}{12}$

$\quad = \frac{17}{12} = 1\frac{5}{12}$

When the answer is an improper fraction change it into a mixed number.

Exercise **7.3** Do not use a calculator in this exercise.

1 Work out:
(a) $\frac{1}{4} + \frac{1}{8}$ (b) $\frac{1}{3} + \frac{1}{4}$ (c) $\frac{1}{2} + \frac{1}{5}$ (d) $\frac{1}{3} + \frac{1}{5}$ (e) $\frac{1}{2} + \frac{1}{7}$

2 Work out:
(a) $\frac{1}{4} - \frac{1}{8}$ (b) $\frac{1}{3} - \frac{1}{4}$ (c) $\frac{1}{2} - \frac{1}{5}$ (d) $\frac{1}{3} - \frac{1}{5}$ (e) $\frac{1}{2} - \frac{1}{7}$

3 Work out:
(a) $\frac{1}{2} + \frac{3}{4}$ (b) $\frac{2}{3} + \frac{5}{6}$ (c) $\frac{3}{4} + \frac{4}{5}$ (d) $\frac{5}{7} + \frac{2}{3}$ (e) $\frac{3}{8} + \frac{5}{6}$

4 Calculate:
(a) $\frac{5}{8} - \frac{1}{2}$ (b) $\frac{13}{15} - \frac{1}{3}$ (c) $\frac{5}{6} - \frac{5}{24}$ (d) $\frac{7}{9} - \frac{2}{5}$ (e) $\frac{7}{8} - \frac{2}{3}$ (f) $\frac{13}{16} - \frac{5}{12}$

5 Calculate:
(a) $2\frac{3}{4} + 1\frac{1}{2}$ (b) $1\frac{1}{2} + 2\frac{1}{3}$ (c) $1\frac{3}{4} + 2\frac{5}{8}$ (d) $2\frac{1}{4} + 3\frac{3}{5}$ (e) $4\frac{3}{5} + 1\frac{5}{6}$ (f) $3\frac{3}{10} + 2\frac{3}{20}$

6 Calculate:
(a) $2\frac{1}{2} - 1\frac{2}{5}$ (b) $1\frac{2}{3} - 1\frac{1}{4}$ (c) $3\frac{3}{8} - 2\frac{3}{4}$ (d) $5\frac{2}{5} - 2\frac{1}{10}$ (e) $4\frac{3}{10} - 2\frac{5}{8}$ (f) $3\frac{3}{16} - 2\frac{5}{24}$

7 Colin buys a bag of flour.

He uses $\frac{1}{3}$ to bake a cake and $\frac{2}{5}$ to make a loaf.

What fraction of the bag of flour is left?

8 Both Billy and Mary have a packet of the same sweets.

Mary eats $\frac{2}{5}$ of her packet.

Billy eats $\frac{3}{4}$ of his packet.

(a) Find the difference between the fraction Mary eats and the fraction Billy eats.

Billy gives his remaining sweets to Mary.

(b) What fraction of a packet does Mary now have?

9 A school has pupils in Years 7 to 13.

$\frac{7}{12}$ of its pupils are in Years 7 to 9.

$\frac{3}{10}$ of its pupils are in Years 10 and 11.

What fraction of the pupils in the school are in Years 12 and 13?

10 Only Andy, Billy and Cathy are candidates in a school election.

Andy got $\frac{7}{20}$ of the votes.

Billy got $\frac{5}{16}$ of the votes.

(a) What fraction of the votes did Cathy get?

(b) Which candidate won the election?

11 A bag of sweets contains chocolates, toffees and mints.

$\frac{2}{5}$ are chocolates and there are an equal number of toffees and mints.

What fraction of the sweets are toffees?

Multiplying fractions

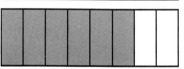

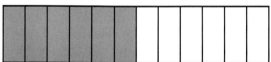
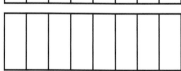

There are 12 sweets in a packet.

Alena gives $\frac{2}{3}$ of the sweets in the packet to Sead.

$\frac{2}{3}$ of 12 = 8

Sead eats $\frac{3}{4}$ of the sweets that Alena gives him.

$\frac{3}{4}$ of 8 = 6

Sead eats $\frac{6}{12}$ of the whole packet.

So ... $\frac{2}{3}$ of $\frac{3}{4}$ = $\frac{6}{12}$ = $\frac{1}{2}$

This shows that $\frac{2}{3} \times \frac{3}{4} = \frac{2 \times 3}{3 \times 4} = \frac{6}{12} = \frac{1}{2}$

How to multiply fractions

Calculate $2\frac{2}{5} \times 3\frac{1}{4}$

Change mixed numbers to improper ('top heavy') fractions. $\quad 2\frac{2}{5} = \frac{12}{5}$ and $3\frac{1}{4} = \frac{13}{4}$

The calculation then becomes $\quad \frac{12}{5} \times \frac{13}{4}$

Simplify, where possible, by cancelling. $\quad \frac{\overset{3}{\cancel{12}}}{5} \times \frac{13}{\underset{1}{\cancel{4}}}$

Multiply the numerators.
Multiply the denominators. $\quad \frac{3 \times 13}{5 \times 1} = \frac{39}{5}$

Write the answer in its simplest form. $\quad \frac{39}{5} = 7\frac{4}{5}$

To simplify:
Divide a numerator **and** a denominator by the **same number.**

In this case:
12 and 4 can be divided by 4.
$12 \div 4 = 3$ and $4 \div 4 = 1$.

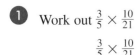

EXAMPLES

1 Work out $\frac{3}{5} \times \frac{10}{21}$

$\frac{3}{5} \times \frac{10}{21}$

Simplify by cancelling.

$= \frac{\overset{1}{\cancel{3}}}{\underset{1}{\cancel{5}}} \times \frac{\overset{2}{\cancel{10}}}{\underset{7}{\cancel{21}}}$

Multiply out.

$= \frac{1 \times 2}{1 \times 7}$

$= \frac{2}{7}$

2 Calculate $1\frac{1}{2} \times 1\frac{3}{5}$

Change mixed numbers to improper fractions.

$1\frac{1}{2} \times 1\frac{3}{5} = \frac{3}{2} \times \frac{8}{5}$

Simplify by cancelling.

$= \frac{3}{\underset{1}{\cancel{2}}} \times \frac{\overset{4}{\cancel{8}}}{5}$

Multiply out.

$= \frac{3 \times 4}{1 \times 5} = \frac{12}{5} = 2\frac{2}{5}$

Exercise 7.4

Do not use a calculator in this exercise.

1 Work out:

(a) $\frac{1}{2} \times \frac{1}{3}$ (b) $\frac{1}{4} \times \frac{1}{5}$ (c) $\frac{3}{5} \times \frac{1}{6}$ (d) $\frac{5}{7} \times \frac{1}{3}$

(e) $\frac{2}{3} \times \frac{1}{4}$ (f) $1\frac{1}{4} \times \frac{1}{5}$ (g) $2\frac{2}{5} \times \frac{1}{3}$ (h) $2\frac{5}{8} \times \frac{1}{6}$

2 Calculate:

(a) $\frac{1}{2} \times \frac{3}{4}$ (b) $\frac{3}{4} \times \frac{2}{5}$ (c) $\frac{2}{5} \times \frac{5}{6}$ (d) $\frac{2}{3} \times \frac{1}{2}$

(e) $\frac{3}{10} \times \frac{5}{8}$ (f) $\frac{2}{5} \times \frac{1}{7}$ (g) $\frac{3}{4} \times \frac{2}{3}$ (h) $\frac{3}{10} \times \frac{5}{6}$

(i) $\frac{3}{4} \times \frac{2}{9}$ (j) $\frac{5}{8} \times \frac{4}{15}$

3 Calculate:

(a) $1\frac{1}{2} \times \frac{3}{4}$ (b) $1\frac{1}{2} \times 1\frac{1}{3}$ (c) $2\frac{1}{4} \times 1\frac{2}{3}$ (d) $2\frac{3}{4} \times 1\frac{2}{5}$

(e) $1\frac{1}{2} \times 3\frac{1}{4}$ (f) $1\frac{3}{5} \times 1\frac{1}{6}$ (g) $6\frac{3}{10} \times 2\frac{2}{9}$ (h) $3\frac{3}{4} \times 3\frac{3}{5}$

(i) $1\frac{1}{4} \times 2\frac{4}{25}$ (j) $2\frac{5}{8} \times 3\frac{1}{3}$

4 Calculate:

(a) $\frac{4}{5}$ of $3\frac{1}{4}$ (b) $\frac{2}{3}$ of $5\frac{1}{4}$ (c) $\frac{3}{4}$ of $7\frac{1}{5}$ (d) $\frac{4}{5}$ of $3\frac{1}{8}$

(e) $\frac{3}{8}$ of $3\frac{5}{9}$ (f) $\frac{5}{6}$ of $4\frac{2}{7}$ (g) $\frac{5}{8}$ of $1\frac{1}{15}$ (h) $\frac{3}{10}$ of $4\frac{4}{9}$

5 Tony eats $\frac{1}{5}$ of a bag of sweets.

He shares the remaining sweets equally among Bob, Jo and David.

(a) What fraction of the bag of sweets does Bob get?

(b) What is the smallest possible number of sweets in the bag?

Dividing fractions

Activity

The diagram shows $1\frac{1}{2}$ divided into $\frac{1}{6}$'s.

Use the diagram to explain why …

(a) $1\frac{1}{2} \div \frac{1}{6} = 9$

(b) $1\frac{1}{2} \div \frac{1}{3} = 4\frac{1}{2}$

(c) $1\frac{1}{2} \div \frac{2}{3} = 2\frac{1}{4}$

Think of each of these as …

(a) How many $\frac{1}{6}$'s in $1\frac{1}{2}$?

(b) How many $\frac{1}{3}$'s in $1\frac{1}{2}$?

(c) How many $\frac{2}{3}$'s in $1\frac{1}{2}$?

How to divide fractions

The method normally used when one fraction is divided by another is to change the division to a multiplication. The fractions can then be multiplied in the usual way.

Calculate $2\frac{2}{15} \div 1\frac{3}{5}$

Change mixed numbers to improper ('top heavy') fractions. $2\frac{2}{15} = \frac{32}{15}$ and $1\frac{3}{5} = \frac{8}{5}$

Change the division to a multiplication. $\frac{32}{15} \div \frac{8}{5} = \frac{32}{15} \times \frac{5}{8}$

Simplify, where possible, by cancelling. $\frac{\overset{4}{\cancel{32}}}{\underset{3}{\cancel{15}}} \times \frac{\overset{1}{\cancel{5}}}{\underset{1}{\cancel{8}}}$

Multiply the numerators.
Multiply the denominators. $\frac{4 \times 1}{3 \times 1} = \frac{4}{3}$

Write the answer in its simplest form. $\frac{4}{3} = 1\frac{1}{3}$

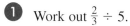 **EXAMPLES**

1 Work out $\frac{2}{3} \div 5$.

$\frac{2}{3} \div 5$

$= \frac{2}{3} \times \frac{1}{5}$

$= \frac{2}{15}$

> Divide by 5 is the same as multiply by $\frac{1}{5}$.

2 Calculate $1\frac{3}{5} \div \frac{4}{9}$.

$1\frac{3}{5} \div \frac{4}{9} = \frac{8}{5} \div \frac{4}{9}$

$= \frac{8}{5} \times \frac{9}{4}$

$= \frac{\overset{2}{\cancel{8}}}{5} \times \frac{9}{\underset{1}{\cancel{4}}}$

$= \frac{18}{5} = 3\frac{3}{5}$

> Divide by $\frac{4}{9}$ is the same as multiply by $\frac{9}{4}$.

Do not use a calculator in this exercise.

1 Work out.

(a) $\frac{1}{2} \div 5$ (b) $\frac{3}{4} \div 2$ (c) $\frac{2}{5} \div 4$

(d) $1\frac{2}{3} \div 5$ (e) $1\frac{5}{7} \div 3$ (f) $3\frac{1}{9} \div 7$

2 Calculate.

(a) $\frac{1}{2} \div \frac{1}{4}$ (b) $\frac{1}{5} \div \frac{1}{2}$ (c) $\frac{7}{8} \div \frac{1}{3}$

(d) $\frac{2}{3} \div \frac{1}{5}$ (e) $2\frac{3}{4} \div \frac{1}{8}$ (f) $1\frac{2}{9} \div \frac{1}{6}$

3 Calculate:

(a) $\frac{2}{3} \div \frac{4}{5}$ (b) $\frac{3}{8} \div \frac{2}{3}$ (c) $\frac{3}{5} \div \frac{3}{4}$

(d) $\frac{2}{5} \div \frac{3}{10}$ (e) $\frac{3}{8} \div \frac{9}{16}$ (f) $\frac{7}{12} \div \frac{7}{18}$

(g) $\frac{4}{9} \div \frac{2}{3}$ (h) $\frac{7}{10} \div \frac{3}{5}$ (i) $\frac{9}{20} \div \frac{3}{10}$

(j) $\frac{21}{25} \div \frac{7}{15}$

4 Calculate:

(a) $2\frac{3}{4} \div 4\frac{1}{8}$ (b) $1\frac{1}{2} \div 1\frac{1}{11}$ (c) $1\frac{3}{5} \div 1\frac{2}{5}$

(d) $6\frac{3}{10} \div 1\frac{7}{20}$ (e) $3\frac{3}{4} \div \frac{5}{18}$ (f) $1\frac{1}{4} \div 1\frac{9}{16}$

(g) $3\frac{1}{5} \div 2\frac{2}{15}$ (h) $2\frac{1}{4} \div 1\frac{4}{5}$ (i) $4\frac{2}{7} \div 1\frac{7}{8}$

(j) $5\frac{2}{5} \div 1\frac{2}{3}$

5 A shelf is $40\frac{3}{4}$ cm long.

(a) How many books of width $1\frac{9}{10}$ cm can be stored on the shelf?

(b) How many videos of width $1\frac{3}{4}$ cm can be stored on the shelf? In each case how much space is left on the shelf?

6 (a) $3\frac{3}{4}$ is multiplied by a number to give $2\frac{2}{3}$.
What is the number?

(b) The product of two numbers is 4. One of the numbers is $1\frac{2}{3}$.
What is the other number?

7 A jug contains $1\frac{3}{4}$ litres of milk. Mrs Jones makes a rice pudding with $1\frac{1}{3}$ litres of the milk in the jug.
What fraction of the milk in the jug does Mrs Jones use to make the rice pudding?

Problems involving fractions

1 Jenny spends $\frac{3}{5}$ of her money.
She has £1.40 left.
How much money did she start with?

Jenny has $1 - \frac{3}{5}$ of her money left.

$$1 - \frac{3}{5} = \frac{2}{5}$$

$\frac{2}{5}$ of Jenny's money is £1.40.

$\frac{1}{5}$ of Jenny's money is £1.40 ÷ 2.

Jenny started with $5 \times £0.70 = £3.50$.

2 In an experiment a weight is added to a spring. The length of the spring increases by $\frac{2}{5}$. The new length of the spring is 21 cm. What was the length of the spring before the weight was added?

$$1 + \frac{2}{5} = \frac{7}{5}$$

$\frac{7}{5}$ of the original length is 21 cm.

$\frac{1}{5}$ of the original length is $21 \div 7$.

The original length is $5 \times 3 = 15$ cm.

Do not use a calculator in this exercise.

1 Ben spends $\frac{5}{8}$ of his pocket money.
He has £1.20 left.
How much pocket money did Ben get?

2 A cyclist travels from A to B in two stages.
Stage 1 is 28 km which is $\frac{2}{7}$ of the total journey.
How long is stage 2?

3

> **Music Sale**
> $\frac{1}{4}$ off all CDs

Robert pays £9.60 for a CD in the sale.
How much did he save?

4 Sara's hourly wage is increased by $\frac{1}{10}$.
Her new hourly wage is £5.50.
What was her original hourly wage?

5 A young tree is $\frac{3}{8}$ taller in August than it was in May.
In August it is 132 centimetres tall.
How tall was it in May?

6 A factory produced 231 sofas in May, $\frac{2}{9}$ more than the number of sofas it produced in April.
How many sofas did the factory produce in April?

Fractions on a scientific calculator

Fraction calculations can be done quickly using the fraction button on a scientific calculator.
On most scientific calculators the fraction button looks like this … $\boxed{a^b/_c}$

EXAMPLES

1 Use a scientific calculator to calculate $4\frac{3}{5} \div 2\frac{1}{4}$.

This can be calculated with this calculator sequence.

$$\boxed{4}\ \boxed{a^b/_c}\ \boxed{3}\ \boxed{a^b/_c}\ \boxed{5}\ \boxed{\div}\ \boxed{2}\ \boxed{a^b/_c}\ \boxed{1}\ \boxed{a^b/_c}\ \boxed{4}\ \boxed{=}$$

This gives the answer $2\frac{2}{45}$.

2 Calculate $\frac{7}{12}$ of 32.

This can be calculated with this calculator sequence.

$$\boxed{7}\ \boxed{a^b/_c}\ \boxed{1}\ \boxed{2}\ \boxed{\times}\ \boxed{3}\ \boxed{2}\ \boxed{=}$$

This gives the answer $18\frac{2}{3}$.

Use a scientific calculator to check your answers to some of the questions in Exercises 7.3 to 7.6.

Fractions and decimals

All fractions can be written as decimals and vice versa.

Changing decimals to fractions

$0.7 = \frac{7}{10}$ $\qquad$ $0.03 = \frac{3}{100}$ $\qquad$ $0.009 = \frac{9}{1000}$

> The place value of numbers written as decimals was first covered in Chapter 2.

0.375 can be written as a fraction.
Using place value:

$0.375 = \frac{3}{10} + \frac{7}{100} + \frac{5}{1000}$

Write equivalent fractions with denominator 1000.

$\frac{3}{10} = \frac{3 \times 100}{10 \times 100} = \frac{300}{1000}$ $\qquad$ $\frac{7}{100} = \frac{7 \times 10}{100 \times 10} = \frac{70}{1000}$

$0.375 = \frac{300}{1000} + \frac{70}{1000} + \frac{5}{1000}$

$\qquad\ = \frac{375}{1000}$

>
> Adding fractions with the same denominator
> 1. Add the numerators.
> 2. Keep the denominator the same.
> *Why?*

This can be written as a fraction in its simplest form.

$\frac{375}{1000} = \frac{375 \div 125}{1000 \div 125} = \frac{3}{8}$

$0.375 = \frac{375}{1000} = \frac{3}{8}$

Fractions

Change the following decimals to fractions in their simplest form.

1 0.02 $\qquad$ 0.02 $= \dfrac{2}{100} = \dfrac{2 \div 2}{100 \div 2} = \dfrac{1}{50}$

2 0.36 $\qquad$ 0.36 $= \dfrac{36}{100} = \dfrac{36 \div 4}{100 \div 4} = \dfrac{9}{25}$

3 0.225 $\qquad$ 0.225 $= \dfrac{225}{1000} = \dfrac{225 \div 25}{1000 \div 25} = \dfrac{9}{40}$

Changing fractions to decimals

Change the following fractions to decimals.

> **Method 1**
> Write an equivalent fraction with a denominator of 10, 100, 1000, …

> **Method 2**
> $\frac{1}{5}$ means $1 \div 5$.
> $1 \div 5$ can be worked out using: short division, long division or a calculator.

1 $\dfrac{1}{5} = \dfrac{1 \times 2}{5 \times 2} = \dfrac{2}{10} = 0.2$ $\qquad$ $\dfrac{1}{5} = 1 \div 5 = 0.2$

2 $\dfrac{11}{20} = \dfrac{11 \times 5}{20 \times 5} = \dfrac{55}{100} = 0.55$ $\qquad$ $\dfrac{11}{20} = 11 \div 20 = 0.55$

3 $\dfrac{3}{8} = \dfrac{3 \times 125}{8 \times 125} = \dfrac{375}{1000} = 0.375$ $\qquad$ $\dfrac{3}{8} = 3 \div 8 = 0.375$

Remember:
$11 \div 20 = 11.00 \div 20$

$$\begin{array}{r} 0.5\,5 \\ 20\overline{)1\,1\,1.0^{11}\,0^{10}\,0} \end{array}$$

Recurring decimals

Some decimals have recurring digits. These are shown by:
$\qquad$ a single dot above a single recurring digit,
$\qquad$ a dot above the first and last digit of a set of recurring digits.

For example:

$\dfrac{1}{3} = 0.3333333\ldots = 0.\dot{3}$

$\dfrac{123}{999} = 0.123123123\ldots = 0.\dot{1}2\dot{3}$

$\dfrac{41}{70} = 0.5857142857142\ldots = 0.5\dot{8}5714\dot{2}$

$\dfrac{3}{11} = 0.27272727\ldots = 0.\dot{2}\dot{7}$

Exercise **7.7**

Do not use a calculator for questions 1 to 3.

1 Change the following decimals to fractions in their simplest form.
- (a) 0.12
- (b) 0.6
- (c) 0.32
- (d) 0.175
- (e) 0.45
- (f) 0.65
- (g) 0.22
- (h) 0.202
- (i) 0.28
- (j) 0.555
- (k) 0.625
- (l) 0.84

2 Change the following fractions to decimals.
- (a) (i) $\frac{1}{4}$ (ii) $\frac{1}{2}$ (iii) $\frac{3}{4}$
- (b) (i) $\frac{1}{10}$ (ii) $\frac{3}{10}$ (iii) $\frac{7}{10}$
- (c) (i) $\frac{2}{5}$ (ii) $\frac{3}{5}$ (iii) $\frac{4}{5}$

3 Change the following fractions to decimals.
- (a) (i) $\frac{3}{20}$ (ii) $\frac{7}{20}$ (iii) $\frac{19}{20}$
- (b) (i) $\frac{4}{25}$ (ii) $\frac{9}{25}$ (iii) $\frac{23}{25}$
- (c) (i) $\frac{7}{100}$ (ii) $\frac{23}{100}$ (iii) $\frac{106}{200}$

4 Change these fractions to decimals.
- (a) $\frac{1}{8}$
- (b) $\frac{5}{8}$
- (c) $\frac{9}{40}$
- (d) $\frac{29}{40}$

5 Write these decimals using dots to represent recurring digits.
- (a) 0.77777...
- (b) 0.11111...
- (c) 0.363636...
- (d) 0.828282...
- (e) 0.135135...
- (f) 0.216216...
- (g) 0.166666...
- (h) 0.285714285714...

6 Write each of these fractions as recurring decimals, using dots to represent recurring digits.
- (a) $\frac{8}{9}$
- (b) $\frac{4}{9}$
- (c) $\frac{17}{33}$
- (d) $\frac{8}{11}$
- (e) $\frac{1}{7}$
- (f) $\frac{6}{7}$
- (g) $\frac{1}{30}$
- (h) $\frac{7}{15}$
- (i) $\frac{5}{6}$
- (j) $\frac{17}{22}$

7 Change these fractions to decimals. Give your answers correct to two decimal places.
- (a) $\frac{1}{3}$
- (b) $\frac{2}{3}$
- (c) $\frac{3}{7}$
- (d) $\frac{5}{11}$
- (e) $\frac{7}{9}$
- (f) $\frac{5}{13}$

What you need to know

- The top number of a fraction is called the **numerator**, the bottom number is called the **denominator**.
- To write **equivalent fractions**, the numerator and denominator of a fraction are multiplied (or divided) by the **same** number.

  e.g. $\frac{3}{8} = \frac{3 \times 4}{8 \times 4} = \frac{12}{32}$

- In its **simplest form**, the numerator and denominator of a fraction have no common factor, other than 1.
- $2\frac{1}{2}$ is an example of a **mixed number**. It is a mixture of whole numbers and fractions.
- $\frac{5}{2}$ is an **improper** (or '**top heavy**') fraction.
- Fractions must have the **same denominator** before **adding** or **subtracting**.
- Mixed numbers must be changed to **improper fractions** before **multiplying** or **dividing**.
- All fractions can be written as decimals.
  Some decimals have **recurring digits**. These are shown by:

  a single dot above a single recurring digit, e.g. $\frac{2}{3} = 0.6666... = 0.\dot{6}$

  a dot above the first and last digit of a set of recurring digits, e.g. $\frac{5}{11} = 0.454545... = 0.\dot{4}\dot{5}$

Do not use a calculator for this exercise.

1 Each of these pairs of fractions are equivalent.
In each case find the value of n.
(a) $\frac{5}{8}, \frac{15}{n}$ (b) $\frac{n}{20}, \frac{5}{n}$ (c) $\frac{n}{20}, \frac{3}{15}$

2 A packet contains 24 biscuits.
Emily eats $\frac{3}{8}$ of the biscuits.
How many biscuits are left?

3 Janice is saving to buy this camera.

£77.40

She saves $\frac{2}{3}$ of the cost.
Her father gives her the rest.
How much does Janice's father give her?
Edexcel

4 Work out.
(a) $\frac{1}{4} + \frac{2}{3}$ (b) $\frac{2}{5} - \frac{1}{8}$

5 In Jimmy's class $\frac{1}{3}$ of the pupils have blue eyes and $\frac{2}{5}$ have brown eyes.
What fraction of the class do not have blue or brown eyes?

6 36 girls and 24 boys applied to go on a rock climbing course.
$\frac{2}{3}$ of the girls and $\frac{3}{4}$ of the boys went on the course.
What fraction of the 60 students who applied went on the course?
Write the fraction in its simplest form.

7 Change the following decimals to fractions in their simplest form.
(a) 0.4   (b) 0.24
(c) 0.45   (d) 0.125

8 A necklace is made from 60 beads.
$\frac{3}{10}$ of the beads are red.
$\frac{9}{20}$ of the beads are blue.
The rest of the beads are white.
What fraction of the beads are white?
Give this fraction in its simplest form.

9 Calculate:
(a) $2\frac{1}{4} + 3\frac{5}{6}$ (b) $2\frac{5}{7} + 1\frac{4}{9}$
(c) $3\frac{3}{5} - 1\frac{1}{2}$ (d) $4\frac{3}{10} - 1\frac{2}{3}$
(e) $3\frac{3}{4} \times 1\frac{1}{5}$ (f) $2\frac{2}{3} \times 3\frac{3}{4}$
(g) $3\frac{3}{5} \div 2\frac{1}{10}$ (h) $5\frac{1}{4} \div 2\frac{1}{10}$

10 The length of a rectangle is $\frac{2}{3}$ m.
The width of the rectangle is $\frac{3}{8}$ m.
(a) What is the perimeter of the rectangle?
(b) What is the area of the rectangle?

11 In a school $\frac{8}{15}$ of the pupils are girls.
$\frac{3}{16}$ of the girls are left-handed.
What fraction of the pupils in the school are left-handed girls?

12 The price of a coat is reduced by $\frac{2}{5}$ to £48.
What was the original price of the coat?

13 Change the following fractions to decimals.
(a) $\frac{4}{5}$ (b) $\frac{9}{20}$ (c) $\frac{21}{50}$ (d) $\frac{201}{500}$

14 Write down two different fractions that lie between $\frac{1}{4}$ and $\frac{1}{2}$.
Edexcel

15 An examination in French is marked out of 80.
(a) Jean scored $\frac{4}{5}$ of the marks.
How many marks did she score?
(b) Tony scored 35 marks.
What fraction of the total did he score?
Give your answer in its simplest form.

16 (a) Write $\frac{1}{6}$ as a decimal.
Give your answer correct to two decimal places.
(b) What fraction is equal to 0.375?
Give your answer in its simplest form.

17 Jim says, "I've driven 240 miles today".
Estimate the distance he has driven in kilometres if one kilometre is approximately five eighths of a mile.

18 Simon is given £9 pocket money.
He spends $\frac{1}{4}$ on a computer magazine and $\frac{4}{5}$ of the remainder on a trip to the cinema.
(a) How much did it cost to go to the cinema?
(b) What fraction of his pocket money has he got left?

CHAPTER 8

Percentages

The meaning of a percentage

'Per cent' means 'out of 100'.
The symbol for per cent is %.
A percentage can be written as a fraction with denominator 100.

> 10% means 10 out of 100.
> 10% can be written as $\frac{10}{100}$.
> 10% is read as '10 percent'.

Changing percentages to decimals and fractions

> To change a percentage to a decimal or a fraction: **divide by 100**

EXAMPLES

1 Write 38% as a fraction in its simplest form.

38% means '38 out of 100'.

This can be written as $\frac{38}{100}$.

$\frac{38}{100} = \frac{38 \div 2}{100 \div 2} = \frac{19}{50}$

$38\% = \frac{19}{50}$

> **Remember**
> To simplify a fraction divide the **numerator** (top number) and the **denominator** (bottom number) of the fraction by their highest common factor.

2 Write 72% as a fraction in its simplest form.

$72\% = \frac{72}{100} = \frac{72 \div 4}{100 \div 4} = \frac{18}{25}$

3 Write 42.5% as a decimal.

$42.5\% = \frac{42.5}{100} = 42.5 \div 100 = 0.425$

> **Remember**
> To change a fraction to a decimal divide the numerator by the denominator.

Changing decimals and fractions to percentages

> To change a decimal or a fraction to a percentage: **multiply by 100**

EXAMPLE

(a) Change these decimals to percentages.
   (i)   0.3   (ii)   0.875

(b) Change these fractions to percentages.
   (i) $\frac{7}{10}$ (ii) $\frac{11}{25}$

(a) (i) $0.3 \times 100 = 30$
        So 0.3 as a percentage is 30%.
   (ii) $0.875 \times 100 = 87.5$
        So 0.875 as a percentage is 87.5%.

(b) (i) $\frac{7}{10} \times 100 = 7 \times 100 \div 10$
        $= 700 \div 10 = 70\%$
   (ii) $\frac{11}{25} \times 100 = 11 \times 100 \div 25$
        $= 1100 \div 25 = 44\%$

Comparing fractions

Fractions can be compared by first writing them as percentages.

EXAMPLE

Ben scored 17 out of 20 in a Maths test and 21 out of 25 in a History test.
Which is Ben's better mark?

Change each mark to a percentage.

Maths: $\frac{17}{20}$ $\qquad$ $\frac{17}{20} \times 100$ $\qquad$ History: $\frac{21}{25}$ $\qquad$ $\frac{21}{25} \times 100$

$\qquad\qquad\qquad = 17 \times 100 \div 20$ $\qquad\qquad\qquad = 21 \times 100 \div 25$

$\qquad\qquad\qquad = 85\%$ $\qquad\qquad\qquad\qquad = 84\%$

So Ben's better mark was his Maths mark of 85%.

Exercise 8.1 $\qquad$ Do not use a calculator in questions 1 to 5.

1 Copy and complete this table to work out the percentage equivalents of the fractions given.

Fraction	Percentage
$\frac{1}{10}$	
$\frac{1}{5}$	
$\frac{1}{4}$	25%
$\frac{3}{10}$	
$\frac{2}{5}$	
$\frac{1}{2}$	50%
$\frac{3}{5}$	
$\frac{7}{10}$	
$\frac{3}{4}$	
$\frac{4}{5}$	
$\frac{9}{10}$	

2 Change these fractions to percentages.

(a) $\frac{17}{50}$ $\qquad$ (b) $\frac{12}{25}$

(c) $\frac{30}{200}$ $\qquad$ (d) $\frac{4}{5}$

(e) $\frac{135}{500}$ $\qquad$ (f) $\frac{13}{20}$

(g) $\frac{2}{3}$ $\qquad$ (h) $\frac{2}{9}$

3 Change these percentages to fractions in their simplest form.

(a) 10% $\qquad$ (b) 25%
(c) 18% $\qquad$ (d) 52%
(e) 23% $\qquad$ (f) 12.5%
(g) 28.5% $\qquad$ (h) 72.5%

4 Change these decimals to percentages.

(a) 0.2 $\qquad$ (b) 0.45
(c) 0.32 $\qquad$ (d) 0.125
(e) 0.07 $\qquad$ (f) 1.12
(g) 0.015 $\qquad$ (h) 0.$\dot{3}$

5 Change these percentages to decimals.

(a) 80% $\qquad$ (b) 15%
(c) 47% $\qquad$ (d) 72%
(e) 87.5% $\qquad$ (f) 150%

6 Write in order of size, lowest first:

$\frac{17}{40}$ $\qquad$ 0.42 $\qquad$ $\frac{9}{20}$ $\qquad$ 43%

7 Write in order of size, lowest first:

$\frac{23}{80}$ $\qquad$ 28% $\qquad$ $\frac{57}{200}$ $\qquad$ 0.2805

8 Peter scores 96 out of 120.
What percentage did he get?

9 Change each of these marks to a percentage.

(a) Maths: $\quad$ 27 out of 30.
(b) French: $\quad$ 34 out of 40.
(c) Science: $\quad$ 22 out of 25.
(d) Art: $\qquad$ 48 out of 60.

10 Which rectangle has the greater percentage shaded?

A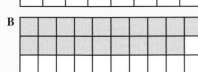

B

11 In an ice hockey competition Team A won 8 out of the 11 games they played whilst Team B won 5 of their 7 games.

Which team has the better record in the competition?

Expressing one quantity as a percentage of another

To work out one number as a percentage of another there are two steps.

Step 1	Write the numbers as a fraction.
Step 2	Change the fraction to a percentage.

EXAMPLES

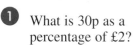
The numbers in the fraction must be in the **same** units.

1 What is 30p as a percentage of £2?

£2 = 200p

Step 1

30p as a fraction of 200p is $\frac{30}{200}$.

Step 2

$\frac{30}{200} \times 100 = 30 \times 100 \div 200 = 15\%$

So 30p as a percentage of £2 is 15%.

2 A newspaper contains 48 pages, 6 of which are Sports pages.
What percentage of the pages are Sports pages?

Step 1

6 out of 48 pages are Sports pages.

$\frac{6}{48} = 6 \div 48 = 0.125$

Step 2

$0.125 \times 100 = 12.5$

12.5% of the pages are Sports pages.

Exercise **8.2**   Do not use a calculator for questions 1 to 6.

1 What is
   (a)   30 as a percentage of 50,
   (b)   4 as a percentage of 25,
   (c)   7 as a percentage of 10,
   (d)   42 as a percentage of 200,
   (e)   63 as a percentage of 300?

2 What is
   (a)   64 pence as a percentage of £2,
   (b)   15 km as a percentage of 120 km,
   (c)   30 cm as a percentage of 600 mm,
   (d)   £3600 as a percentage of £4000,
   (e)   18 pence as a percentage of £0.60?

3 There are 8 yellow fruit drops in a packet of 25 fruit drops.
What percentage of the fruit drops are yellow?

4 A school has 800 pupils of which 160 are in Year 11.
What percentage of pupils are in Year 11?

5 James saved £30 and then spent £9.
What percentage of his savings did he spend?

6 A Youth Club has 200 members.
80 of the members are boys.
   (a) What percentage of the members are boys?
   (b) What percentage of the members are girls?

7 240 people took part in a survey.
30 of them were younger than 18.
What percentage were younger than 18?

8 A bar of chocolate has 32 squares.
Jane eats 12 of the squares.
What percentage of the bar does she eat?

9 Billy earns £4.50 per hour.
He gets a wage rise of 27 pence per hour.
What is his percentage wage rise?

10 What is
   (a) £2 as a percentage of £6,
   (b) 80 km as a percentage of 120 km,
   (c) 20 cm as a percentage of 180 cm,
   (d) £1530 as a percentage of £3600,
   (e) £105.09 as a percentage of £186?

11 A new car costs £13 500.
The dealer gives a discount of £1282.50.
What is the percentage discount?

12 There are 600 pupils in Years 9 to 13 of
a High school.
360 pupils are in Years 10 and 11.
15% of pupils are in Years 12 and 13.
What percentage of pupils are in Year 9?

Finding a percentage of a quantity

EXAMPLE

Find 20% of £56.

Step 1   Divide by 100.
£56 ÷ 100 = £0.56

Step 2   Multiply by 20.
£0.56 × 20 = £11.20
So 20% of £56 is £11.20.

Steps 1 and 2 could be done in the opposite order.
£56 × 20 = £1120
£1120 ÷ 100 = £11.20

> To find 1% of a quantity divide the quantity by 100.
>
> To find 20% of a quantity multiply 1% of the quantity by 20.
>
> This is the same as the method you would use to find $\frac{20}{100}$ of a quantity.

Percentage change

EXAMPLES

1 A shirt normally priced at £24 is
reduced by 15% in a sale.
How much does it cost in the sale?

Reduction in price = 15% of £24
15 ÷ 100 × 24 = 0.15 × 24 = 3.6
15% of £24 = £3.60
The shirt costs £24 − £3.60 = £20.40.

2 There are 440 g in a normal packet of Rice
Crunchies. A special offer packet contains
30% more than the normal packet.
How many grams of Rice Crunchies are
there in the special offer packet?

Extra contents = 30% of 440 g
                = 440 ÷ 100 × 30
                = 132 g
440 + 132 = 572
There are 572 g in a special offer packet.

Exercise 8.3 — Do not use a calculator in this exercise.

1 Find
- (a) 20% of £80
- (b) 75% of £20
- (c) 30% of £220
- (d) 15% of £350
- (e) 5% of £500
- (f) 20% of £150
- (g) 9% of £300
- (h) 20% of 20 m
- (i) 30% of 80 kg
- (j) 35% of 800
- (k) 45% of £25
- (l) 60% of 20

2 Garry has 300 marbles.
20% of the marbles are blue.
35% of the marbles are red.
The rest of the marbles are white.
- (a) How many marbles are blue?
- (b) How many marbles are red?
- (c) What percentage of the marbles are white?

3 Tim invests £400 in a building society.
He earns 5% interest per year.
How much interest does he get in one year?

4 There are 450 seats in a theatre.
60% of the seats are in the stalls.
How many seats are in the stalls?

5 A salesman earns a bonus of 3% of his weekly sales.
How much bonus does the salesman earn in a week when his sales are:
- (a) £1400,
- (b) £2350?

6 Jenny gets a 15% discount on a theatre ticket.
The normal cost is £13.
How much does she save?

7 Dipak earns £150 per week.
He gets a wage rise of 3%.
How much extra does he earn each week?

8 In a school of 1200 pupils 45% are boys.
- (a) How many are girls?

30% of the girls are under 13.
- (b) How many girls are under 13?

9 A dozen biscuits weigh 720 g.
The amount of flour in a biscuit is 40% of the weight of a biscuit.
What is the weight of flour in **each** biscuit.

10 Increase:
- (a) £400 by 20%
- (b) £300 by 40%
- (c) £2000 by 40%
- (d) £600 by 80%
- (e) £3000 by 15%
- (f) £900 by 40%
- (g) £50 by 60%
- (h) £10 by 30%
- (i) £15 by 10%
- (j) £50 by 15%

11 Decrease:
- (a) £600 by 30%
- (b) £800 by 25%
- (c) £2500 by 20%
- (d) £250 by 40%
- (e) £12 000 by 15%
- (f) £7000 by 35%
- (g) £600 by 15%
- (h) £55 by 90%
- (i) £42 by 20%
- (j) £63 by 35%

12 A mobile telephone company offers a 20% discount on calls made in March.
The normal cost of a peak time call is 30 pence per minute.
How much does a peak time call cost in March?

13 Abdul earns £200 per week.
He gets a wage rise of 7.5%.
What is his new weekly wage?

14 Prices in a sale are reduced by 18%.
The normal price of a shirt is £22.50.
Calculate its sale price.

15 A packet of breakfast cereal contains 660 g.
A special offer packet contains an extra 15%.
How many grams of breakfast cereal are in the special offer packet?

16 The price of a car is £12 500.
A dealer gives a 7% discount.
What is the price of the car after the discount?

17 35% of a magazine is pictures.
In the magazine there are 60 pages.
Each page is 25 cm long and 16 cm wide.
What is the area of pictures in the magazine?

More complicated percentage problems

Problems involving percentages can involve more complicated calculations.

1 Calculate 4×10^6 as a percentage of 2×10^8.

$$\frac{4 \times 10^6}{2 \times 10^8} = 0.02$$

$$0.02 \times 100 = 2\%$$

2 Calculate 30% of 8×10^4.

$$30 \div 100 \times 8 \times 10^4$$
$$= 24\,000$$

3 1.2×10^{10} steel cans were used in 1992. 1.4×10^9 of these were recycled. Calculate the percentage of steel cans that were **not** recycled in 1992.

$$\frac{1.4 \times 10^9}{1.2 \times 10^{10}} = 0.1166\ldots$$

$$0.1166\ldots \times 100 = 11.66\ldots$$
$$= 11.7 \text{ to 3 significant figures.}$$
Percentage recycled $= 11.7\%$
$100 - 11.7 = 88.3$
Percentage not recycled $= 88.3\%$

Exercise 8.4

Use a calculator in this exercise.
Where appropriate give your answers to
3 significant figures.

1 Prices in a sale are reduced by 24%.
The normal price of a shirt is £25.50.
Calculate its sale price.

2 (a) Jane's salary of £14 050 is increased by 3.5%. Calculate her new salary.
   (b) Petrol costs 81.9 pence a litre. What does it cost after a 2.4% increase?
   (c) Milk costs 28 pence a pint. How much does it cost after a 12.5% increase?

3 (a) The price of a gold watch is £278. What does it cost with a 12% discount?
   (b) The price of a used car is £5200. What does it cost with a 9.5% discount?
   (c) The price of a new kitchen is £3650. What does it cost with a 35% discount?

4 A 5 litre can of paint covers an area of 28 m². Harry buys 3 cans of paint to cover 70 m². What percentage of the paint does he use?

5 A car was valued at £13 500 when new. After one year it lost 22% of its value. At the end of two years it was sold for £8200.
   (a) What was the value of the car after one year?
   (b) What percentage of its original value did the car lose in its second year?

6 In 1999 house prices increased by 9.6%.
In 2000 house prices increased by 7.4%.
A house was valued at £78 000 at the beginning of 1999. What was the value of the house at the end of 2000?

7 Ben invests £650 in a building society. He earns 5.25% interest in the first year.
   (a) How much interest does he earn?

Ben leaves his original £650 plus the interest he has earned in the building society.
He earns 6.05% in the second year.
   (b) How much interest does Ben earn in the second year?

8 There are 633 pupils in a school.
  230 of the pupils walk to school, 212 travel by bus and 150 come by car.
  (a)   What percentage walk to school?
  (b)   What percentage come by car?

  18% of the pupils who normally come by car start to travel on a new bus route.
  (c)   What percentage of the pupils now travel by bus?

9 The volume of water on Earth is approximately $1.436 \times 10^9 \, \text{km}^3$. About 94% of this is contained in the Earth's oceans.
  Use these figures to estimate the volume of water in the Earth's oceans.

10 The area of the surface of the Earth is about 5.095×10^9 square miles. Approximately 29.2% of this is land. Use these figures to estimate the area of land surface on Earth.

11 James wins a lottery prize of £1.764×10^6.
  He pays £5.29×10^5 for a house.
  What percentage of his prize did he spend on the house?
  Give your answer to a suitable degree of accuracy.

12 The planet Pluto is $5.914 \times 10^9 \, \text{km}$ from the Sun.
  The Earth is $1.496 \times 10^8 \, \text{km}$ from the Sun.
  Express the distance of the Earth from the Sun as a percentage of the distance of Pluto from the Sun.

Percentage increase and decrease

Sadik and Chandni took Maths tests in October and June.

My mark went up from 54% to 72%.

My mark went up from 42% to 60%.

Who has made the most improvement?

They have both improved by a score of 18% so by one measure they have both improved equally.
Another way of comparing their improvement is to use the idea of a percentage increase.

$$\text{Percentage increase} = \frac{\text{actual increase}}{\text{initial value}} \times 100\%$$

Comparing percentage increases is the best way to decide whether Sadik or Chandni has made the most improvement.
Explain why.

Remember
To calculate
  % increase or % decrease
always use the initial value.

For Sadik
% increase $= \frac{18}{54} \times 100\% = 33.3\%$

For Chandni
% increase $= \frac{18}{42} \times 100\% = 42.9\%$

Both calculations are correct to one decimal place.

A percentage decrease can be calculated in a similar way.

$$\text{Percentage decrease} = \frac{\text{actual decrease}}{\text{initial value}} \times 100\%$$

1 A sample of soil is dried in an oven.
Its mass reduces from 65 g to 45 g.
Find the percentage decrease in the mass.

Actual decrease = 65 − 45 = 20 g

% decrease = $\frac{20}{65} \times 100$

$\qquad$ = 30.8%, correct to one decimal place.

2 A shop buys pens for 15 pence
and sells them for 21 pence.
What is their percentage profit?

Actual profit = 21 − 15

$\qquad$ = 6 pence

% profit = $\frac{6}{15} \times 100 = 40\%$

Exercise 8.5 $\qquad$ Do questions 1 to 5 without a calculator.

1 A school buys calculators for £5 and sells them for £6. Find the percentage profit.

2 Sara's wages of £7.50 per hour are increased to £9.00 per hour.
Find the percentage increase in her earnings.

3 A man buys a car for £3500 and sells it for £2625. Find his percentage loss.

4 In October, Sam scored 50% in an English test. In January he improved to 66%.
In the same tests, Becky scored 40% and 56%.
Who has made the most improvement? Explain your answer.

5 During 1998 the rent on Karen's flat increased from £80 to £90 per week.
(a) Find the percentage increase in her rent.
In the same period Karen's wages increased from £250 per week to £280 per week.
(b) Find the percentage increase in her wages.
Comment on your answers.

6 A book goes up in price from £5.99 to £6.99.
What is the percentage increase in the price?

7 John's weekly wage rises from £150 to £168.
What is John's percentage wage rise?

8 The value of car A when new was £13 000.
The value of car B when new was £16 500.
After one year the value of car A is £11 200 and the value of car B is £13 500.
Calculate the percentage loss in the values of cars A and B after one year.

9 In a school the number of pupils increased as shown in the table:

Year	1995	1996	1997	1998	1999
Number	554	605	643	679	734

In which year is the percentage increase in the number of pupils the greatest?

10 During 1995 the population of a village decreased from 323 to 260.
Find the percentage decrease in the population.

11 Between 1980 and 1990 the population of the UK increased from 5.7×10^7 to 5.9×10^7.
Find the percentage increase in the population of the UK between 1980 and 1990.

12 At the start of May a flower was 12.3 cm high.
In May it grew by 14.5%.
At the start of July it was 16.7 cm high.
What was its percentage growth during June?

13 A rectangle has length 12 cm and width 8.5 cm.
The length is increased by 8.5% and the width decreased by 13.5%.
(a) Calculate the change in the area of the rectangle.
(b) Find the change in area as a percentage of the original area of the rectangle.

14 In 1998 Miles bought £2000 worth of shares.
In 1999 the value of his shares decreased by 10%.
In 2000 the value of his shares increased by 20%.
By what percentage has the value of his shares changed from 1998 to 2000?

15 The price of a micro-scooter is reduced by 10%.
In a sale, the new price is reduced by a further 10%.
By what percentage has the original price of the micro-scooter been reduced in the sale?

16 The price of telephone calls is increased by 15%.
Companies are given a 10% discount off the new price.
What is the percentage increase in the price of calls for companies?

Reverse percentage problems

EXAMPLES

1 A shop sells videos with a 20% discount.
Petra buys a video and pays £10.
How much does the video normally cost?

Discount price is normal price less 20%.
So 80% of normal price = £10.
So 1% of normal price = £10 ÷ 80
= £0.125
So normal price = £0.125 × 100
= £12.50

2 Tara gets a 5% wage rise.
Her new wage is £126 per week.
What was Tara's wage before her wage rise?

New wage = old wage + 5%
So 105% of old wage = £126
1% of old wage is 126 ÷ 105 = £1.20
Old wage = 1.2 × 100 = £120

Exercise **8.6**   Do questions 1 to 4 without a calculator.

1 A special bottle of pop contains 10% more than a normal bottle.
The special bottle contains 660 ml.
How much does the normal bottle contain?

2 Jim saves 15% of his monthly salary.
Each month he saves £90.
What is his monthly salary?

3 May gets a 20% wage rise.
Her new wage is £264 per week.
What was May's wage before her wage rise?

4 Mary and Sam take a History and a Geography test.
(a) Sam scored 60 marks in History.
Sam's score was 20% better than his score in Geography.
What was Sam's score in Geography?
(b) Mary scored 72 marks in History.
Mary's score was 20% worse than her score in Geography.
What was Mary's score in Geography?

5 In a high jump event, Nick jumps 1.8 metres.
This is 5% lower than the best height he can jump.
What is the best height he can jump?

6 A house is valued at £350 000.
This is a 12% increase on the value of the house a year ago.
What was the value of the house a year ago?

7 30 grams of a breakfast cereal provides 16.2 mg of vitamin C.
This is 24% of the recommended daily intake.
What daily intake of vitamin C is recommended?

8 Tom gets a 3% increase in his salary.
His new salary is £1462.60 per month.
What was Tom's salary before his wage rise?

9 A one year old car is worth £1344.
This is a decrease of 16% of its value from new.
What was the price of the new car?

10 Here is some data about the changes in the number of pupils in schools A and B.
School A's numbers increased by 4% to 442.
School B's numbers decreased by 6% to 423.
How many pupils were in schools A and B before the change in numbers?

11 John sells his computer to Dan and makes a 15% profit.
Dan then sells the computer to Ron for £391.
Dan makes a 15% loss.
How much did John pay for the computer?
Explain why it is not £391.

12 Kim sells her bike to Sara.
Sara sells it to Tina for £121.50.
Both Kim and Sara make a 10% loss.
How much did Kim pay for the bike?
Explain why it is not 20% more than £121.50.

What you need to know

- 'Per cent' means 'out of 100'.
  The symbol for per cent is %.

- A percentage can be written as a fraction with denominator 100.
  For example: 10% can be written as $\frac{10}{100}$.

- To change a decimal or a fraction to a percentage - **multiply by 100**.
  For example:
  0.12 as a percentage is $0.12 \times 100 = 12\%$.
  $\frac{3}{25}$ as a percentage is $\frac{3}{25} \times 100 = 3 \times 100 \div 25 = 12\%$.

- To change a percentage to a decimal or a fraction - **divide by 100**.
  For example:
  18% as a decimal is $18 \div 100 = 0.18$.
  18% as a fraction is $\frac{18}{100}$ which in its simplest form is $\frac{9}{50}$.

IDEAS FOR INVESTIGATION

Increasing and decreasing

200 increased by 10% and then decreased by 10%	500 decreased by 10% and then increased by 30%
$200 \rightarrow +10\% \rightarrow 220 \rightarrow -10\% \rightarrow 198$	$500 \rightarrow -10\% \rightarrow 450 \rightarrow +30\% \rightarrow 585$
Actual change $= 200 - 198$ $= $ decrease of 2	Actual change $= 585 - 500$ $= $ increase of 85
$\frac{2}{200} = \frac{2}{200} \times 100 = 2 \times 100 \div 200 = 1\%$	$\frac{85}{500} = \frac{85}{500} \times 100 = 85 \times 100 \div 500 = 17\%$
2 as a percentage of 200 is 1%. The combined result of a 10% increase followed by a 10% decrease is a 1% decrease.	85 as a percentage of 500 is 17%. The combined result of a 10% decrease followed by a 30% increase is a 17% increase.

Investigate increasing and decreasing different quantities by different percentages.
You might find a spreadsheet useful.

1 A bag contains 60 beads.
(a) Emily uses 30% of the beads to make a necklace.
How many beads does she use?
(b) Laura uses 12 beads to make a bracelet.
What percentage of the beads does she use?

2 In a sale rolls of wallpaper are sold at a 30% discount.

A roll of wallpaper normally costs £12.60. How much will a roll of wallpaper cost in the sale?

3 A roll of carpet is 20 m long.
Beryl buys 18 m of carpet from the roll.
What percentage of the roll did she buy?

4 A train has 1200 seats.
85% of the seats are occupied.
How many seats are empty?

5 $\frac{5}{8}$ of the cost of building a house is labour.
What percentage of the cost of building a house is labour?

6 A pizza takeaway sells 500 pizzas a week.
87% of the pizzas have a cheese topping.
How many pizzas sold each week do not have a cheese topping?

7 The Stokoe family's electricity bill one year was £350.
They had to pay 5% VAT on this.
(a) Work out 5% of £350.

The Stokoe's electricity bill for the next year increased from £350 to £388.50.
(b) Work out the percentage increase.
Edexcel

8 A year ago Joan weighed 84 kg.
She now weighs 5% less.
Calculate her weight now.
Give your answer to a suitable degree of accuracy.

9 Sue buys a pack of 12 cans of cola for £4.80.
She sells the cans for 50p each.
She sells all of the cans.
Work out her percentage profit.
Edexcel

10 Jo got 36 out of 80 in an English test.
(a) Work out 36 out of 80 as a percentage.

Jo got 65% of the total number of marks in a French test.
Jo got 39 marks.
(b) Work out the total number of marks for the French test.
Edexcel

11 In 1988 a house was bought for £240 000.
In 2000 the house was sold for £325 000.
Calculate the percentage increase in the price of the house.
Give your answer correct to two significant figures.

12 Calculate 18% of 2.4×10^5.

13 In a sale the price of a suit is reduced by 10%.
The sale price is £72.
What was the price of the suit before the sale?

14 A shop is having a sale. Each day, prices are reduced by 20% of the price on the previous day.
Before the start of the sale, the price of a television is £450.
On the first day of the sale, the price is reduced by 20%.
(a) Work out the price of the television on
(i) the first day of the sale,
(ii) the third day of the sale.

On the first day of the sale, the price of a cooker is £300.
(b) Work out the price of the cooker before the start of the sale.
Edexcel

15 David has a 4% wage rise.
His new wage is £220.80 per week.
What was his weekly wage before his wage rise?

Time and Money

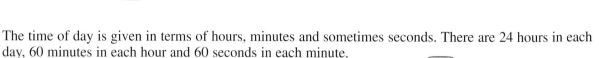

The time of day is given in terms of hours, minutes and sometimes seconds. There are 24 hours in each day, 60 minutes in each hour and 60 seconds in each minute.

24-hour clock and 12-hour clock times

The time can be given using the 12-hour clock or the 24-hour clock.

The watch and the digital clock both show the same time.
The time on the watch is 5.45 pm using 12-hour clock time.
The digital clock shows 5.45 pm as 1745 using 24-hour clock time.

> **12-hour clock times**
> Times before midday are given as am.
> Times after midday are given as pm.

> **24-hour clock times**
> The first two figures give the hours.
> The last two figures give the minutes.

EXAMPLES

1 A video recorder uses 24-hour clock times.
  (a) What time is shown by the video recorder at 6.30 pm?
  (b) The video is set to record programmes from 1120 to 1645.
      What are these times in 12-hour clock time?

(a) 6.30pm is equivalent to 1830.

(b) 1120 is equivalent to 11.20 am.
     1645 is equivalent to 4.45 pm.

> **12-hour to 24-hour clock times**
> Times before midday:
>   use the same figures.
> Times after midday:
>   add 12 to the hours.

> **24-hour to 12-hour clock times**
> Times before midday:
>   use the same figures and
>   include **am**.
> Times after midday:
>   subtract 12 from the hours and
>   include **pm**.

2 A motorist left Liverpool at 10.50 am and arrived in Birmingham at 1.20 pm.
How long did the journey take?

Method 1 (subtraction)

```
1 3.2 0
1 0.5 0
───────
```

1. Write the times as 24-hour clock times.
2. Subtract the minutes.
   20 − 50 cannot be done.
   Exchange 1 hour for 60 minutes.
   60 + 20 − 50 = 30 minutes.
3. Subtract the hours.
   12 − 10 = 2.

```
   2  6 0
1 3̷.2 0
1 0.5 0
───────
   2.3 0
```

The journey took 2 hours 30 minutes.

Method 2 (adding on)

10.50 to 11.00 =	10 minutes
11.00 to 13.00 = 2 hours	
13.00 to 13.20 =	20 minutes

Total time   = 2 hours 30 minutes

The journey took 2 hours 30 minutes.

Exercise **9.1**

1 Write these 12-hour clock times in 24-hour clock time.
(a) 10.30 am   (b) 10.30 pm   (c) 1.45 am
(d) 1.45 pm   (e) 7.50 am   (f) 11.50 pm

2 Write these 24-hour clock times in 12-hour clock time.
(a) 1415   (b) 0525   (c) 2320
(d) 1005   (e) 0940   (f) 1705

3 The times of some Sunday evening BBC 1
programmes are shown.
(a) Give the times of these programmes
using 24-hour clock time.
(b) How many minutes does
"Holiday Guide to Australia" last?
(c) How many minutes does
"Antiques Roadshow" last?

BBC 1
6 35 Antiques Roadshow
7 20 Holiday Guide to Australia
8 00 Ballykissangel
8 50 News

4 A train left Paddington at 1315 and arrived in Exeter at 1605.
(a) At what time did the train leave in 12-hour clock time?
(b) How long did the journey take?

5 A train left Manchester at 9.10 am and arrived in Reading at 1.25 pm.
(a) What was the arrival time in 24-hour clock time?
(b) How long did the journey take?

6 A coach leaves Bournemouth at 10.50 am to travel to London.
The journey takes 2 hours 40 minutes.
At what time does the coach reach London?
Give your answer in   (a) 12-hour clock time,   (b) 24-hour clock time.

7 Mrs Hill took 3 hours 56 minutes to drive from Bath to Blackpool.
She left Bath at 1045. At what time did she arrive in Blackpool?
Give your answer in   (a) the 24-hour clock,   (b) the 12-hour clock.

Timetables

Bus and rail timetables are usually given in 24-hour clock time.
Here is part of a rail timetable.

Kidderminster	1035	1115	1155	1240	1325	1410
Bewdley	1050	1130	—	1300	—	1430
Arley	1105	1148	—	1318	1403	1448
Highley	1114	1158	—	1328	—	1458
Hampton Loade	1125	1210	—	1340	1425	1510
Bridgnorth	1140	1225	1310	1355	1440	1525

Some trains do not
stop at every station.
This is shown by a
dash on the timetable.

How many minutes does the journey take on the 1035 train from Kidderminster to Arley?

Jean catches the 1155 train from Kidderminster to Bridgnorth.
What is her arrival time in 12-hour clock time?
How long does the journey take?

Alex lives in Bewdley.
What is the time of the last train he can catch to keep an appointment in Bridgnorth at 1.15 pm?

1 The times of some trains from Hastings to Charing Cross are shown.

Hastings	0702	0802	0857	0900	0957	1102	1257
Crowhurst	—	—	0908	—	1008	—	1308
Battle	0715	0815	0912	—	1012	—	1312
Tunbridge Wells	0745	0845	0943	0940	1043	1141	1342
Sevenoaks	0805	0905	1003	—	1103	1201	1403
Charing Cross	0834	0934	1032	1025	1132	1230	1432

(a) John catches the 0745 from Tunbridge Wells to Charing Cross.
How many minutes does the journey take?

(b) Aimee catches the 0857 from Hastings to Charing Cross.
How long does the journey take?

(c) Sarah catches the 1257 from Hastings to Tunbridge Wells.
What is her arrival time using the 12-hour clock?

(d) Keith wants to be in Charing Cross by 1030.
What is the latest train he can catch from Battle?

2 Some of the rail services from Manchester to Birmingham are shown.

Manchester	0925	1115	1215	1415	1555
Stockport	0933	—	1223	—	1603
Stoke	1007	1155	1255	1459	1636
Stafford	1027	—	1318	—	1656
Wolverhampton	1056	1234	1336	1535	1716
Birmingham	1121	1257	1359	1558	1742

(a) David has to be in Wolverhampton by 2 pm.
What is the time of the latest train he can catch from Manchester?

(b) Pam catches the 0933 from Stockport to Birmingham.
How long does the journey take?

(c) What time does the 1555 from Manchester arrive in Birmingham in 12-hour clock time?

3 Some of the rail services from Poole to Waterloo are shown.

Poole	0544	0602	—	0640	—	0740	0825	0846
Bournemouth	0558	0616	—	0654	0715	0754	0839	0900
Southampton	0634	0655	0714	0738	0754	0838	0908	0938
Eastleigh	0646	—	—	0750	—	0852	—	0951
Waterloo	0804	0810	0844	0901	0908	1005	1018	1112

(a) Sid arrives at Bournemouth station at 0830.
What is the time of the next train to Eastleigh?

(b) Paul catches the 0654 from Bournemouth to Southampton.
How many minutes does the journey take?

(c) Emma catches the 0544 from Poole to Waterloo.
How long does the journey take?

4 Some of the coach services from Woking to Heathrow airport are shown.

Woking	0610	0650	0720	0750	0820	Then	1830	1900	2000
Terminal 1	0650	0730	0800	0830	0900	every	1900	1930	2030
Terminal 2	0655	0735	0805	0835	0905	30	1905	1935	2035
Terminal 3	0700	0740	0810	0840	0910	mins	1910	1940	2040
Terminal 4	0710	0750	0820	0850	0920	until	1920	1950	2050

(a) Helen arrives at Woking at 3 pm. She catches the next coach to Heathrow.
　(i)　At what time does it leave Woking?
　(ii)　At what time does it arrive at Terminal 3?
(b) Leroy needs to be at Terminal 2 at 6 pm.
　What is the latest time he can catch a coach from Woking?

Wages

Hourly pay

Many people are paid by the hour for their work. In most cases they receive a **basic hourly rate** for a fixed number of hours and an **overtime rate** for any extra hours worked.

EXAMPLE

A car-park attendant is paid £4.20 per hour for a basic 40-hour week.
Overtime is paid at time and a half.
One week an attendant works 48 hours.
How much does he earn?

Basic Pay:　　　　£4.20 × 40　= £168.00
Overtime:　1.5 × £4.20 × 8　= 　£50.40

　　　　　　Total pay　= £218.40

Overtime paid at 'time and a half' means 1.5 × normal hourly rate.
In this example, the hourly overtime rate is given by:
1.5 × £4.20

Common overtime rates are 'time and a quarter', 'double time', etc.

Commission

As an incentive for their employees to work harder some companies pay a basic wage (fixed amount) plus commission. The amount of commission is usually expressed as a percentage of the value of the sales made by the employee.

EXAMPLE

An estate agent is paid a salary of £11 000 per year plus commission of 0.5% on the sales of all houses.
In 1998 the estate agent sold houses to the value of £2 040 500.
How much did the estate agent earn?

Annual salary:　　　　　　　　£11 000
Commission:　0.005 × £2 040 500 = £10 202.50

　　　　　　Total pay　= £21 202.50

Remember:
$0.5\% = \frac{0.5}{100} = 0.005$

1 A secretary earns £352.80 a week.
She is paid £9.80 per hour.
How many hours a week does she work?

2 A chef is paid £5.60 per hour for a basic 38-hour week.
Overtime is paid at time and a half.
How much does the chef earn in a week in which she works 50 hours?

3 A mechanic is paid £6.40 per hour for a basic 40-hour week.
Overtime is paid at time and a quarter.
One week the mechanic works 42 hours. How much does he earn?

4 A hairdresser is paid £4.80 per hour for a basic 35-hour week.
One week she works two hours overtime at time and a half and $3\frac{1}{2}$ hours overtime at time and a quarter.
How much is she paid that week?

5 A driver is paid £68.85 for $4\frac{1}{2}$ hours of overtime.
Overtime is paid at time and a half.
What is his basic hourly rate of pay?

6 A furniture salesperson is paid an annual salary of £9600 plus commission of 2% on sales.
In 1998 the salesperson sold £300 000 worth of furniture.
How much did the salesperson earn?

7 A car salesperson is paid an annual salary of £10 200 plus commission of 1.5% on sales.
How much does the salesperson earn in a year in which cars to the value of £868 000 are sold?

8 A double glazing salesperson is paid £480 per month plus commission of 5% on sales.
How much does he earn in a month in which he makes sales of £12 600?

9 An estate agent is paid 1.5% commission on the sales of houses.
Last month he was paid £12 000 commission.
Calculate the total value of the houses he sold.

10 A florist is paid £159.60 per week plus commission of 3% on the sales of flowers.
Last week she was paid £202.80.
Calculate the total value of the flowers she sold.

Income tax

The amount you earn for your work is called your **gross pay**.
Your employer will make deductions from your gross pay for
income tax, National Insurance, etc. Pay after all deductions
have been made is called **net pay**.

The amount of **income tax** you pay will depend on how much you earn.
Everyone is allowed to earn some money which is not taxed, this is called
a **tax allowance**. Any remaining money is your **taxable income**.

The rates of tax and
the bands (ranges of
income) to which
they apply vary.

> **EXAMPLE**
>
> George earns £5800 per year. His tax allowance is £4385 per year
> and he pays tax at 10p in the £ on his taxable income.
> How much income tax does George pay per year?
>
> Taxable income: £5800 − £4385 = £1415
> Income tax: £1415 × 0.10 = £141.50
>
> George pays income tax of £141.50 per year.

An income tax rate of 10% is often expressed as '10p in the pound (£)'.

Exercise 9.4

1 Lyn earns £5600 per year. Her tax allowance is £4385 per year and she pays tax at 10p in the £ on her taxable income.
How much income tax does she pay per year?

2 Brian earns £594 per month. His tax allowance is £5765 per year and he pays tax at 10p in the £ on his taxable income.
How much income tax does he pay per month?

3 Kay has an annual salary of £23 700. Her tax allowance is £4385 per year. She pays tax at 10p in the £ on the first £1500 of her taxable income and 22p in the £ on the remainder.
How much income tax does she pay per year?

4 Julie earns £865 per month. Her tax allowance is £4385 per year and she pays tax at 10p in the £ on the first £1500 of her taxable income and 22p in the £ on the remainder.
How much income tax does she pay per month?

5 Jim is paid £186 per week for 52 weeks a year. His tax allowance is £4385 per year.
He pays tax at 10p in the £ on the first £1500 of his taxable income and 22p in the £ on the remainder.
How much income tax does he pay per week?

6 Les has an annual salary of £18 600. His tax allowance is £4385 per year. He pays tax at 10p in the £ on the first £1500 of his taxable income and 22p in the £ on the remainder.
He is paid monthly. How much income tax does he pay per month?

7 Alf's income is £23 850 per year.
He pays 9% of his gross income into a pension scheme on which he does not pay tax.
Alf also has a tax allowance of £4385 per year.
He pays tax at 10p in the £ on the first £1500 of his taxable income and 22p in the £ on the remainder.
Calculate how much income tax he pays per year.

8 Reg has an annual salary of £46 380. His tax allowance is £4385 per year. He pays tax at 10p in the £ on the first £1500 of his taxable income, 22p in the £ on the next £26 500 and 40p in the £ on the remainder.
Calculate how much income tax he pays per year.

9 Alex has an annual salary of £35 240. Her tax allowance is £4385 per year. She pays tax at 10p in the £ on the first £1500 of her taxable income, 22p in the £ on the next £26 500 and 40p in the £ on the remainder.
She is paid monthly. How much income tax does she pay per month?

Spending

Spending money is part of daily life. Every day people have to deal with many different situations involving money. Money is needed to buy fares for journeys, for purchases at shops, for hiring cars and equipment and for buying large items such as furniture.

When a large sum of money is needed to make a purchase, **credit** may be arranged. This involves paying for the goods over a period of time by agreeing to make a number of weekly or monthly repayments. It may also involve paying a **deposit**. The cost of credit may be more than paying cash.

EXAMPLES

1 Hamish pays £2.73 for 1 kg of pears and 2 kg of apples.
Pears cost 89p per kilogram.
How much per kilogram are apples?

2 kg of apples cost $273 - 89 = 184$p
1 kg of apples costs $184 \div 2 = 92$p
Apples cost 92p per kilogram.

Use the same units:
£2.73 is 273p

2 A motor home costs £6450. It can be bought on credit by paying a deposit of £1500 and 36 monthly payments of £150.
How much more is paid for the motor home when it is bought on credit?

Deposit: £1500
Payments: £150 × 36 = £5400

Credit Price: £6900

Difference: £6900 − £6450 = £450
Credit price is £450 more.

Exercise 9.5

Do not use a calculator for this exercise.

1 Esther pays £30.47 for a wheelbarrow, a fork and a spade.
The fork costs £7.49.
The spade costs £6.99.
How much did the wheelbarrow cost?

2 Mr Grey pays £3.40 for 2 adult fares and 3 child fares on the bus.
The fare for an adult is 95p.
How much is the fare for a child?

3 Sam pays £56.40 for 200 bricks and 9 paving slabs.
The bricks cost 21p each.
How much is a paving slab?

4 Mushrooms cost £2.10 per kilogram.
Tomatoes cost 96p per kilogram.
James buys 200 g of mushrooms and 500 g of tomatoes.
How much does James have to pay?

5 Mr Jones pays £3.32 for 400 g of Brie and 250 g of Stilton.
Stilton costs £5.60 per kilogram.
How much per kilogram is Brie?

6 A building supplier hires out cement mixers.
There is a delivery charge of £15 and a hire charge of £8 per day.
(a) How much would it cost for the delivery and hire of a cement mixer for 4 days?
(b) A builder pays £95 for the delivery and hire of a cement mixer.
For how many days did he hire it?

7

£30 per day
+
20p per mile driven

VAN FOR HIRE

(a) Alex hires a van for one day and
drives 45 miles.
How much is the total hire charge?

(b) Bob hires a van for 3 days.
The total hire charge is £114.
How many miles did Bob drive?

8 The price of a pram is £299. It can be
bought on credit by paying a deposit of
£50 and 10 monthly payments of
£27.50. How much more is paid for the
pram when it is bought on credit?

9 A car costs £4950. It can be bought on
credit by paying a deposit of £2000 and
24 monthly payments of £149.50.
How much more is paid for the car
when it is bought on credit?

10 The cash price of a settee is £900. It can
be bought on credit by paying a deposit
of 10% of the cash price and 30 monthly
payments of £32.50.
How much more is paid for the settee
when it is bought on credit?

11 A washing machine costs £475. It can
be bought on credit by paying a deposit
of 10% of the cash price and 24 monthly
payments of £19.50.
How much more is paid for the washing
machine when it is bought on credit?

Best buys

When shopping we often have to make choices between products which are packed in various sizes and priced differently. If we want to buy the one which gives the better value for money we must compare prices using the same units.

EXAMPLE

Peanut butter is available in small or large jars, as shown.
Which size is the better value for money?

Compare the number of grams per penny for each size.
Small: $250 \div 58 = 4.31\ldots$ grams per penny.
Large: $454 \div 106 = 4.28\ldots$ grams per penny.

The small size gives more grams per penny and is better value.

SMALL
250 g
58p

LARGE
454 g
£1.06

Exercise 9.6

In each question you must show all your
working.

1 Milk is sold in 1 pint, 2 pint and 4 pint
containers.
The cost of a 1 pint container is 28p, the
cost of a 2 pint container is 55p and the
cost of a 4 pint container is 89p.

(a) How much per pint is saved by
buying a 2 pint container instead of
two 1 pint containers?

(b) How much per pint is saved by
buying a 4 pint container instead of
two 2 pint containers?

2 Mushroom soup is sold in two sizes.
A small tin costs 43p and weighs 224 g.
A large tin costs 89p and weighs 454 g.
Which size gives more grams per penny?

3 Strawberry jam is sold in two sizes.
A small pot costs 52p and weighs 454 g.
A large pot costs 97p and weighs 822 g.
Which size gives more grams per penny?

4 Jars of pickled onions are sold at the
following prices: 460 g at 65p or 700 g
at 98p.
Which size is better value for money?

5 Honey is sold in two sizes.
A large pot costs £1.28 and weighs 454 g.
A small pot costs 56p and weighs 185 g.
Which size is better value for money?

6 Cottage cheese costs 85p for 120 g, £1.55 for 250 g and £6 for 1 kg.
Which size is the best value for money?

7 Two bottles of sauce are shown.

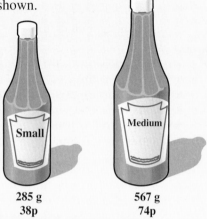

285 g   567 g
38p   74p

Which size gives better value for money?

8 Which of these two bottles of "Active" drink is better value for money?

1.5 litre   2 litre
ACTIVE   ACTIVE
90p   £1.30

9 Toothpaste is sold in small, medium and large sizes.
The small size contains 72 ml and costs 58p.
The medium size contains 125 ml and costs 98p.
The large size contains 180 ml and costs £1.44.
Which size is the best value for money?

10 Oscar wants to buy a camcorder.
He looks at two different advertisements.

(a) Find the actual selling price of each camcorder.
(b) Which camcorder has the bigger discount?

DAISY'S
OUR PRICE 30% OFF
Recommended price £640

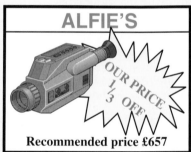

ALFIE'S
OUR PRICE 1/3 OFF
Recommended price £657

Household bills

The cost of living includes many bills for services provided to our homes. Electricity, gas and telephone charges are all examples of **quarterly bills** which are sent out four times a year. Each bill is made up of two parts:
A fixed (standing) charge, for providing the service.
A charge for the quantity of the service used (amount of gas/electricity, duration of telephone calls, etc.)

Other household bills include taxes payable to the local council, water charges and the cost of the insurance of the house (structure) and its contents.

Exercise 9.7

1 Last year the Evans family received four quarterly gas bills.

March	£134.26
June	£52.00
September	£33.49
December	£80.25

(a) What was their total bill for the year?
(b) The family can pay for their gas by 12 equal monthly instalments.
How much would each instalment be?

2 Mrs Cotton uses 1064 units of electricity during one quarter.
Find the cost of her electricity bill if each unit costs 6.16 pence and the quarterly charge is £9.30.

3 Mr Jones receives an electricity bill for £59.20.
The bill includes a quarterly charge of £9.30 and the cost per unit is 6.16 pence.
Calculate to the nearest whole number, the number of units he has used.

4 Mrs Madan receives a gas bill for £179.53.
The bill includes a standing charge and the cost of the gas used. During the quarter the gas used is equivalent to 13 377 kWh at 1.295 pence per kWh.
How much is the standing charge?
Give your answer to a suitable degree of accuracy.

5 Mr Peters has an annual council tax of £1123.05.
He pays the council tax in 10 instalments.
The first instalment is £115.05 and the remaining amount is payable in 9 instalments of equal value.
How much is the second instalment?

6 Mrs Dear checks her water bill.
She has used 46 cubic metres of water at 77.76 pence per cubic metre and there is a standing charge of £11.
How much is her bill?

7 George insures his house valued at £134 000 and its contents valued at £27 500. The annual premiums for the insurance are:
Buildings: £1.35 per £1000 of cover,
Contents: 56p per £100 of cover.
Calculate the total cost of the insurance premium.

8 The table shows the premiums charged by an insurance company to insure a house and its contents.

Buildings and Contents Insurance		
	Buildings	Contents
Annual premium for each £1000 insured.	£1.50 Minimum £20 per year	£5.00

(a) Mrs Adams has a flat valued at £38 000.
What premium would she pay to insure the flat?

(b) Jim has bought a house valued at £54 000.
How much would he pay to insure the house?

(c) The cost for Mr Brown to insure his house is £126.
What is the value of his house?

(d) Mrs Crow insures the contents of her house for £19 000.
What is the annual premium?

(e) Mr Rowe insures his house valued at £74 000 and its contents valued at £23 000.
What is the total cost of the insurance premium?

(f) Andy insures his flat valued at £42 000 and its contents valued at £9000.
Calculate the total cost of the insurance premium.

9 Naomi rents a flat and pays £69.44 to insure its contents.
Contents insurance costs 56p for each £100 insured.
For how much are the contents insured?

VAT

Some goods and services are subject to a tax called **value added tax**, or **VAT**, which is calculated as a percentage of the price or bill.

Total amount payable = cost of item or service + VAT

For most purchases the rate of VAT is 17.5%.
For gas and electricity the rate of VAT is 5%.
Some goods are exempt from VAT.

1 A bill at a restaurant is £24 + VAT at 17.5%.
What is the total bill?

Remember:
$17.5\% = \frac{17.5}{100} = 0.175$

VAT: £24 × 0.175 = £4.20

Total bill: £24 + £4.20 = £28.20

The total bill is £28.20.

2 An electricity bill of £49.14 includes VAT at 5%.
How much VAT is paid?

Cost = cost without VAT + 5% VAT.
£49.14 = 105% of cost without VAT.

1% of cost without VAT is given by
£49.14 ÷ 105 = £0.468

VAT = 5% of cost without VAT,
so VAT = £0.468 × 5 = £2.34.

Exercise 9.8   Do not use a calculator for questions 1 and 2.

1 Naomi's gas bill is £120 plus VAT at 5%.
How much VAT does she have to pay?

2 Joe receives an electricity bill for £70 plus VAT at 5%.
(a) Calculate the amount of VAT charged.
(b) What is the total bill?

3 A washing machine costs £340 plus VAT at 17.5%.
(a) Calculate the amount of VAT charged.
(b) What is the total cost of the washing machine?

4 A car service costs £90 plus VAT at 17.5%.
(a) Calculate the amount of VAT charged.
(b) What is the total cost of the service?

5 Mrs Swan receives a gas bill for £179.53.
VAT at 5% is added to the bill.
(a) How much VAT does she have to pay?
(b) What is the total bill?

6 A bike costs £248 plus VAT at 17.5%.
What is the total cost of the bike?

7 A ladder costs £145 plus VAT at 17.5%.
What is the total cost of the ladder?

8 Joyce buys a greenhouse for £184 plus VAT.
VAT is charged at 17.5%.
What is the total cost of the greenhouse?

9 James receives a telephone bill for £37.56 plus VAT at 17.5%.
How much is the total bill?

10 George buys vertical blinds for his windows.
He needs three blinds at £65 each and two blinds at £85 each.
VAT at 17.5% is added to the cost of the blinds.
How much do the blinds cost altogether?

11
> **CAR HIRE CHARGES**
> £25 per day, plus 10p for every mile driven.

A car is hired for two days and driven 90 miles.
VAT at 17.5% is added to the car charges.
How much does it cost to hire the car altogether?

12 A computer costs £1233.75 including VAT at 17.5%.
How much of the cost is VAT?

13 A gas bill of £33.60 includes VAT at 5%.
How much VAT is paid?

14 VAT at 17.5% on a washing machine is £43.75.
What is the price of the washing machine including VAT?

15 The bill for a new central heating boiler includes £436.10 VAT.
VAT is charged at 17.5%.
What is the total bill?

Savings

Money invested in a savings account or a bank or building society earns **interest**, which is usually paid once a year.

Banks and building societies advertise the **yearly rates** of interest payable.
For example, 6% per year.

Interest, usually calculated annually, can also be calculated for shorter periods of time.

Simple Interest

With **Simple Interest**, the interest is paid out each year and not added to your account.
The amount of Simple Interest an investment earns can be calculated using:

$$\text{Simple Interest} = \frac{\text{Amount invested}}{} \times \frac{\text{Time in years}}{} \times \frac{\text{Rate of interest per year}}{}$$

Compound Interest

With **Compound Interest**, the interest earned each year is added to your account and also earns interest the following year.

For example, an investment of 5% per annum means that the amount invested earns £5 for every £100 invested for one year.

So, after the first year of the investment, every £100 invested becomes £100 + 5% of £100.
£100 + 5% of £100 = £100 + £5 = £105
So, after the second year of the investment, every £100 of the original investment becomes £105 + 5% of £105.
£105 + 5% of £105 = £105 + £5.25 = £110.25

This can also be calculated as: $100 \times (1.05)^2 = £110.25$
Explain why this works.

EXAMPLES

  Find the Simple Interest paid on £600 invested for 6 months at 8% per year.

Simple Interest
$$= 600 \times \frac{6}{12} \times \frac{8}{100}$$
$$= 600 \times 0.5 \times 0.08$$
$$= £24$$

The Simple Interest paid is £24.

Note:
Interest rates are given 'per year'.
The length of time for which an investment is made is also given in years.
6 months = $\frac{6}{12}$ years.
Explain why.

2 Find the Compound Interest paid on £600 invested for 3 years at 6% per year.

1st year	Investment	= £600
	Interest: £600 × 0.06	= £ 36
	Value of investment after one year	= £636
2nd year	Investment	= £636
	Interest: £636 × 0.06	= £ 38.16
	Value of investment after two years	= £674.16
3rd year	Investment	= £674.16
	Interest: £674.16 × 0.06	= £ 40.45
	Value of investment after three years	= £714.61

Compound Interest = Final value − Original value
$$= £714.61 - £600$$
$$= £114.61$$

This could also be calculated as follows:
$$600 \times (1.06)^3 - 600 = £114.61$$

Do not use a calculator for questions 1 to 8.

1 Find the simple interest paid on £200 for 1 year at 5% per year.

2 Calculate the simple interest on £500 invested at 6% per year after
(a) 1 year, (b) 6 months.

3 A school savings account pays interest at 8% per year.
Find the simple interest paid on savings of £50 after 6 months.

4 Calculate the simple interest paid on an investment of £6000 at 7.5% per year after 6 months.

5 Find the simple interest on £800 invested for 9 months at 8% per year.

6 Calculate the simple interest on £10 000 invested for 3 months at 9% per year.

7 Jenny invests £200 at 10% per annum compound interest.
What is the value of her investment after 2 years?

8 Geof invests £300 at 5% per annum compound interest.
What is the value of his investment after 2 years?

9 Which of the following investments earn more interest?
(a) £200 for 3 years at 5% compound.
(b) £300 for 2 years at 5% compound.

10 £10 000 is to be invested for 3 years.
Calculate the final value of the investment if the interest rate per annum is:
(a) 5% (b) 6% (c) 7% (d) 8%
Give your answers to a suitable degree of accuracy.

11 Interest on a loan of £2000 is charged at the rate of 21% per annum. Interest is calculated on the outstanding loan at the **start** of each year.
(a) How much is owed immediately the loan is taken out?
Repayments are £600 per year.
(b) How much is owed at the **start** of the third year of the loan?

Foreign currency

When we go abroad we have to pay for goods and services in the currency of the country we are visiting. We therefore need to change pounds (£) into other currencies. The rate of exchange varies from day to day.
The table below shows the exchange rate in May 1998.

EXCHANGE RATE	
Each £1 will buy	
France	9.47 francs
Germany	2.84 marks
Greece	498 drachmas
Italy	2816 lira
Spain	239 pesetas
USA	1.61 dollars

EXAMPLE What is the value, in £'s and pence, of 35 200 lira?

2816 lira = £1.
35 200 lira = 35 200 ÷ 2816
= £12.50
35 200 lira = £12.50

Use the table of exchange rates above to answer these questions.

1 How much will I receive if I change £150 into
(a) French francs,
(b) German marks,
(c) Greek drachmas,
(d) Italian lira,
(e) Spanish pesetas,
(f) USA dollars?

2 How much would each item cost in £'s?
Give your answers to the nearest penny.
(a) A vase for 90 francs.
(b) A wallet for 1250 pesetas.
(c) A radio for 71 marks.
(d) A pair of jeans for 35 dollars.
(e) A pair of shoes for 112 000 lira.
(f) A meal for 9000 drachmas.

3 (a) A tourist changes £25 into German marks.
How many marks does she receive?

(b) She pays 42 marks for a gift.
What is the cost of the gift in £'s?

4 Norman travels to Italy.
He changes £120 into Italian Lira.

(a) How many lira does he receive?

(b) He pays 80 000 lira to hire a gondola.
What is the cost of hiring the gondola in £'s?

5 Dolores travels to England from Spain.
She changes 60 000 pesetas into £.

(a) How much, in £'s and pence, does she receive?

(b) She buys a theatre ticket for £30.
What is the cost of the theatre ticket in pesetas?

6 Marcel travels to England from France.
He changes 2000 francs into £.

(a) How much, in £'s, does he receive?

(b) He pays £45 for bed and breakfast.
What is the cost of bed and breakfast in francs?

7 Sue changes £500 into dollars for a trip to the USA.

(a) How many dollars does she receive?

(b) On holiday she spends 680 dollars.
She changes the remaining dollars back into £'s.
There is a £3 charge for changing the money.
How much, in £'s, will she receive?

8 Jeff has just returned from France.
He needs to change 1280 francs back into £'s.
There is a £3 charge for changing the money.
How much, in £'s, will he receive?

9 In France a car costs 53 000 francs.
In Germany the same car costs 16 500 marks.
In which country is the car cheaper?

10 In France prices are shown in francs and Euros.
£1 = 1.6185 Euros.

(a) How much is 100 francs in Euros?

(b) How much is 100 Euros in francs?

What you need to know

- Time can be given using either the **12-hour clock** or the **24-hour clock**.
  When using the 12-hour clock:
  times **before** midday are given as am,
  times **after** midday are given as pm.

- **Timetables** are usually given using the 24-hour clock.

- **Hourly pay** is paid at a **basic rate** for a fixed number of hours.
  Overtime pay is usually paid at a higher rate such as time and a half, which means each hour's work is worth 1.5 times the basic rate.

- Everyone is allowed to earn some money which is not taxed. This is called a **tax allowance**.

- Tax is only paid on income earned in excess of the tax allowance. This is called **taxable income**.

- **Value added tax**, or **VAT**, is a tax on some goods and services and is added to the bill.

- Gas, electricity and telephone bills are paid **quarterly**. The bill consists of a standing charge plus a charge for the amount used.

- When considering a **best buy**, compare quantities by using the same units. For example, find which product gives more grams per penny.

- Money invested in a savings account at a bank or building society earns **interest**, which is usually paid once a year.
  With **Simple Interest**, the interest is paid out each year and not added to your account.

  $$\text{Simple Interest} = \frac{\text{Amount}}{\text{invested}} \times \frac{\text{Time in}}{\text{years}} \times \frac{\text{Rate of interest}}{\text{per year}}$$

  With **Compound Interest**, the interest earned each year is added to your account and also earns interest the following year.

- **Exchange rates** are used to show what £1 will buy in foreign currencies.

Do not use a calculator for questions 1 to 6.

1 The table shows some rail journeys from Waterloo to Brookwood.

Waterloo	1510	1520	1523	1538	1540
Clapham Junction	1516	—	1529	—	—
Surbiton	1528	—	—	—	1558
Woking	1542	1546	1549	1603	1612
Brookwood	1547	—	—	—	1617

(a) Nick catches the 1538 from Waterloo to Woking.
   (i) What is his time of arrival in 12-hour clock time?
   (ii) How long does the journey take?
(b) Anne-Marie arrives at Waterloo station at 3.30 pm.
   What time is the next train to Surbiton?

2 Mrs Wye pays 39p for 0.5 kg of carrots and 200 g of onions.
The onions cost 55p per kilogram.
How much per kilogram are carrots?

3 A bottle of white wine costs £2.85.
Kay buys 2 dozen bottles.
How much does she have to pay?

4 Bernadette has to pay tax at the rate of 10p in the £ on the first £1500 of her taxable income and 22p in the £ on the remainder.
Her taxable income is £1967.
How much tax does she have to pay?

5 Gerald invests £9000 at 8% per year simple interest.
(a) How much interest does he get at the end of one year?

He has the option of taking his interest as monthly income.
(b) How much would he get each month?

6

CARS 4 HIRE

Hire Charges
£27 per day
plus
9 pence per mile

Brett hires a car for 3 days.
The total hire charge is £101.79.
How many miles did he drive?

7 Mr Habib receives a gas bill for £124 + VAT.
The rate of VAT is 5%.
How much VAT does he have to pay?

8 Alan receives a quarterly electricity bill. It is made up of a standing charge and the cost of the units of electricity used.

> The standing charge is £9.51 plus VAT.
>
> The cost per unit is 6.23 pence plus VAT.
>
> VAT is charged at 5%.

What is the total bill if he has used 462 units of electricity?

9

Foodstuffs Instant Coffee 400 g £7.35

Foodstuffs Instant Coffee 125 g £2.45

Foodstuff's supermarket sell their own brand of instant coffee in two sizes of jar. Which jar is the better value?

10

£499 + VAT

A lap top computer costs £499 + VAT at $17\frac{1}{2}\%$.

What is the total cost of the computer?

11 The cash price of the saxophone is £740.
Tom buys the saxophone using a Credit Plan.
He pays a deposit of 5% of the cash price and 12 monthly payments of £65.

Saxophone

£740 for cash

*Credit Plan
available*

Work out the difference between the cost when he used the Credit Plan and the cash price.

Edexcel

12 Francis is paid £4.80 per hour for a basic 35 hour week.
One week Francis also works overtime at time and a half.
His total pay that week was £196.80.
How many hours overtime did he work that week?

13 The table shows the amount of foreign currency
that a tourist can buy with £1 in December 1999.

Pepe travels from Spain to France for a holiday.
He changes 50 000 pesetas into francs.
Calculate how many francs he will get.

TOURIST RATES		
France	10.11	francs
Germany	3.01	marks
Italy	2984	lira
Spain	256	pesetas

14 In 2000 the rate of exchange was 3.07 German marks to the £.
(a) A tourist changes £25 into marks.
     How many marks does she receive?
(b) She pays 42 marks for a gift to bring home.
     What is the cost of the gift in pounds and pence?

15 Janet invests £50 in a building society for one year.
The interest rate is 6% per year.
(a) How much interest, in pounds, does Janet get?

Nisha invests £60 in a different building society.
She gets £3 interest after one year.
(b) Work out the percentage interest rate that Nisha gets.

Edexcel

16 Hannah invests £360 in a building society account at 4.8% per year.
Find the simple interest paid on her investment after 4 months.

17 Shane invests £2000 at 7% per annum compound interest.
Calculate the value of his investment after 3 years.

18 £500 is invested for 2 years at 6% per annum compound interest.
(a) Work out the total interest earned over the 2 years.

£250 is invested for 3 years at 7% per annum compound interest.
(b) By what single number must £250 be multiplied to obtain the total amount at the end of
     the 3 years?

Edexcel

Ratio

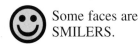 Some faces are SMILERS.

Some faces are GLUMS.

In a group of 10 faces the **ratio** of SMILERS to GLUMS is 3 : 2. This means that for every three SMILERS there are two GLUMS.

For the ratio 3 : 2 say 3 to 2.

In the group there are 6 SMILERS and 4 GLUMS.

Exercise **10.1**

1 (a) Draw 10 faces where the ratio of SMILERS to GLUMS is 4 : 1.
(b) Draw 12 faces where the ratio of SMILERS to GLUMS is:
　(i) 2 : 1
　(ii) 1 : 3
(c) Draw 20 faces where the ratio of SMILERS to GLUMS is
　(i) 4 : 1
　(ii) 2 : 3

2 The ratio of GLUMS to SMILERS is 2 : 5.

(a) How many SMILERS are there when there are …
　(i) 30 GLUMS,
　(ii) 80 GLUMS?
(b) How many GLUMS are there when there are …
　(i) 30 SMILERS,
　(ii) 80 SMILERS?
(c) How many FACES are there when there are …
　(i) 40 SMILERS,
　(ii) 40 GLUMS?

3 The ratio of SMILERS to GLUMS is 4 : 3.

(a) How many SMILERS are there when there are …
　(i) 12 GLUMS,
　(ii) 60 GLUMS?
(b) How many GLUMS are there when there are …
　(i) 12 SMILERS,
　(ii) 60 SMILERS?
(c) How many FACES are there when there are …
　(i) 48 SMILERS,
　(ii) 48 GLUMS?

4 How many SMILERS and how many GLUMS are there when …
(a) the ratio of SMILERS to GLUMS is 7 : 3 and there are:
　(i) 20 faces,
　(ii) 50 faces?
(b) the ratio of SMILERS to GLUMS is 3 : 2 and there are:
　(i) 15 faces,
　(ii) 50 faces?

Equivalent ratios

Ratios are used only to **compare** quantities.
They do not give information about actual values.

For example.
A necklace is made using red beads and white beads in the ratio **3 : 4**.
This gives no information about the actual numbers of beads in the necklace.
The ratio **3 : 4** means that for every 3 red beads in the necklace there are 4 white beads.
The **possible** numbers of beads in the necklace are shown in the table.

Red beads	White beads	Total beads
3	4	7
6	8	14
9	12	21
12	16	28
18	24	42
…	…	…

Make similar tables when the ratio of red beads to white beads in the necklace is:
(a) 4 : 5   (b) 2 : 3   (c) 3 : 1

The ratios   3 : 4,   6 : 8,   9 : 12,   … are different forms of the **same** ratio.
They are called **equivalent** ratios.
They can be found by multiplying or dividing each part of the ratio by the **same** number.

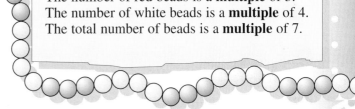

The number of red beads is a **multiple** of 3.
The number of white beads is a **multiple** of 4.
The total number of beads is a **multiple** of 7.

Simplifying ratios

A ratio in its **simplest form** has only whole numbers that have no common factor other than 1.

EXAMPLES

 1 Find 3 ratios that are equivalent to the ratio 2 : 1.

To find equivalent ratios multiply both numbers in the ratio by the same number.
$$2 \times 2 : 1 \times 2 = 4 : 2$$
$$2 \times 3 : 1 \times 3 = 6 : 3$$
$$2 \times 4 : 1 \times 4 = 8 : 4$$
3 ratios equivalent to the ratio 2 : 1 are 4 : 2, 6 : 3 and 8 : 4.

2 The ratio of boys to girls in a school is 3 : 4.
There are 72 boys.
How many girls are there?

$72 \div 3 = 24$
To find a ratio equivalent to 3 : 4 where the first number in the ratio is 72, multiply each number in the ratio by 24.
$$3 \times 24 : 4 \times 24 = 72 : 96$$
The number of girls = 96.

3 Write the ratio 15 : 9 in its simplest form.

The highest common factor of 15 and 9 is 3.
Divide both parts of the ratio by 3.
$15 \div 3 : 9 \div 3 = 5 : 3$
The ratio 15 : 9 in its simplest form is 5 : 3.

4 Write the ratio 2 cm : 50 mm in its simplest form.

This ratio compares two quantities with different units.
In its simplest form a ratio contains **only** whole numbers. There are **no units**.
In order to simplify the ratio both quantities in the ratio must be in the **same units**.

2 cm : 50 mm = 20 mm : 50 mm = 20 : 50
Divide both parts of the ratio by 10.
$20 \div 10 : 50 \div 10 = 2 : 5$
The ratio 2 cm : 50 mm in its simplest form is 2 : 5.

1 Give three ratios equivalent to the ratio:
(a) 6 : 1   (b) 7 : 2   (c) 3 : 5

2 Give the simplest form of each of these ratios.
(a) 3 : 6   (b) 9 : 27   (c) 9 : 12
(d) 10 : 25   (e) 30 : 40   (f) 22 : 55
(g) 9 : 21   (h) 18 : 8   (i) 36 : 81
(j) 35 : 15

3 Each of these pairs of ratios are equivalent.
(a) 3 : 4 and 9 : n.   (b) 2 : 7 and 8 : n.
(c) 8 : n and 2 : 25.   (d) 25 : n and 5 : 4.
In each case calculate the value of n.

4 The heights of two friends are in the ratio 7 : 9.
The shorter of the friends is 154 cm tall.
What is the height of the taller of the friends?

5 Sugar and flour are mixed in the ratio 2 : 3.
How much sugar is used with 600 g of flour?

6 The ratio of boys to girls in a school is 4 : 5.
There are 80 girls.
How many boys are there?

7

I earn £800 per month.

I earn £720 per month.

The amounts Jenny and James earn is in the ratio of their ages.
Jenny is 20 years old.
How old is James?

8 A necklace contains 30 black beads and 45 gold beads.
What is the simplest form of the ratio of black beads to gold beads on the necklace?

9 Sam spends 45p a week on comics.
Tom spends £2 a week on comics.
Write the ratio of the amounts Tom and Sam spend on comics in its simplest form.

10 Denise draws a plan of the classroom.
On her plan Denise uses 2 cm to represent 5 m.
Write the scale as a ratio in its simplest form.

11 On a map a pond is 3.5 cm long.
The pond is actually 52.5 m long.
Write the scale as a ratio in its simplest form.

12 Write each of these ratios in its simplest form.
(a) £2 : 50p   (b) 20p : £2.50
(c) £2.20 : 40p   (d) 6 m : 240 cm
(e) 2 kg : 500 g   (f) 1 kg : 425 g
(g) 90 cm : 2 m   (h) 1500 mm : 2 m
(i) 3 litres : 600 ml   (j) 3 cm² : 75 mm²
(k) 20 seconds : 5 minutes
(l) $\frac{1}{2}$ minute : 15 seconds

13 A hairdresser uses shampoo and conditioner in the ratio 5 : 2.

At the start of the day the hairdresser opens a 500 ml bottle of conditioner. During the day she uses 1 litre of shampoo.
(a) How much conditioner is left in the bottle at the end of the day?
(b) Write the ratio of the amount of conditioner **used** to the amount of conditioner **left** in the bottle in its simplest form.

14 An alloy is made of tin and zinc.
40% of the alloy is tin.
What is the ratio of tin : zinc in its simplest form?

15 A box contains blue biros and red biros.
$\frac{3}{10}$ of the biros are blue.
What is the ratio of blue biros to red biros in the box?

16 A necklace is made from 40 beads.
$\frac{2}{5}$ of the beads are white.
The rest of the beads are red.
Find the ratio of the number of red beads to the number of white beads in its simplest form.

EXAMPLES

1 Pip and Sue share £57.75 in the ratio 5 : 6.
How much do they each get?

Add the numbers in the ratio.
5 + 6 = 11.
For every £11 shared:
Pip gets £5,
Sue gets £6.
57.75 ÷ 11 = 5.25.
Pip gets £5 × 5.25 = £26.25,
Sue gets £6 × 5.25 = £31.50.

○ ○ ○ ○ ○
The number of shares is not always a whole number.

2 A box contains red, white and blue buttons in the ratio 1 : 2 : 5.
There are 104 buttons in the box.
How many of them are blue?

Add the numbers in the ratio.
1 + 2 + 5 = 8
104 ÷ 8 = 13
5 × 13 = 65
There are 65 blue counters in the box.

Exercise 10.3   Do not use a calculator for questions 1 to 10.

1
(a) Share 9 in the ratio 2 : 1.
(b) Share 20 in the ratio 3 : 1.
(c) Share 35 in the ratio 1 : 4.
(d) Share 100 in the ratio 9 : 1.
(e) Share 100 in the ratio 3 : 2.

2 A box contains gold coins and silver coins.
The ratio of gold coins to silver coins is 1 : 9.
There are 20 coins in the box.
How many silver coins are in the box?

3 Sunny and Chandni share £48 in the ratio 3 : 1.
How much do they each get?

4 A bag contains red beads and black beads in the ratio 1 : 3.
What fraction of the beads are red?

5 A box contains red biros and black biros in the ratio 1 : 4.
What percentage of the biros are black?

6 Copy and complete this table.

	Quantity	Shared in the ratio	
		4 : 1	3 : 2
(a)	40 marbles		
(b)	20 sweets		
(c)	80 kg		
(d)	200 g		
(e)	£1200		

7
(a) Share £35 in the ratio 2 : 3.
(b) Share £56 in the ratio 4 : 3.
(c) Share £5.50 in the ratio 7 : 4.

8 A necklace contains 72 beads.
The ratio of red beads to blue beads is 5 : 3.
How many red beads are on the necklace?

9 In a school the ratio of the number of boys to the number of girls is 3 : 5.
What fraction of the pupils in the school are girls?

10 The ratio of non-fiction books to fiction books in a library is 2 : 3.
Find the percentage of fiction books in the library.

11 John is 12 years old and Sara is 13 years old.
They share some money in the ratio of their ages.
What percentage of the money does John get?

12 £480 is shared in the ratio 7 : 3.
What is the difference between the larger share and the smaller share?

13 In 1901, the total population of England and Wales was 32 528 000. The ratio of the population of England to the population of Wales was 15 : 1.
What was the population of Wales in 1901?

14 In the UK there are 240 939 km² of land.
The ratio of agricultural land to non-agricultural land is approximately 7 : 3.
Estimate the area of land used for agriculture.

15 At the start of a game Jenny and Tim have 40 counters each.
At the end of the game the number of counters that Jenny and Tim each have is in the ratio 5 : 3.
(a) How many counters do Jenny and Tim have at the end of the game?
(b) How many counters did Jenny win from Tim in the game?

16 On a necklace, for every 10 black beads there are 4 red beads.
(a) What is the ratio of black beads to red beads in its simplest form?
(b) If the necklace has 15 black beads how many red beads are there?
(c) If the necklace has a total of 77 beads how many black beads are there?
(d) Why can't the necklace have a total of 32 beads?

17 The lengths of the sides of a triangle are in the ratio 4 : 6 : 9.
The total length of the sides is 38 cm.
Calculate the length of each side.

18 To make concrete a builder mixes gravel, sand and cement in the ratio 4 : 2 : 1.
The builder wants 350 kg of concrete.
How much gravel does the builder need?

19 The angles of a triangle are in the ratio 2 : 3 : 4.
Calculate each angle.

20 A bag contains some red, green and black sweets.
30% of the sweets are red.
The ratio of the numbers of green sweets to black sweets is 5 to 9.
What percentage of the total number of sweets are black?

21 Alan, Beth and Catrina share some money in the ratio 1 : 3 : 4.
(a) What percentage of the money do they each receive?
(b) What fraction of Beth's share is Alan's share?
(c) What fraction of Alan and Catrina's share is Beth's share?

Proportion

Some situations involve comparing **different** quantities.
For example, when a motorist buys fuel the more he buys the greater the cost.
In this situation the quantities can change but the ratio between the quantities stays the same.
When two different quantities are in the **same ratio** they are said to be in **direct proportion**.

EXAMPLE

4 cakes cost £1.20.
Find the cost of 7 cakes.

4 cakes cost £1.20
1 cake costs £1.20 ÷ 4 = 30p
7 cakes cost 30p × 7 = £2.10
So 7 cakes cost £2.10.

This is sometimes called the **unitary method**.
(a) **Divide** by 4 to find the cost of **1** cake.
(b) **Multiply** by 7 to find the cost of 7 cakes.

Do not use a calculator for questions 1 to 6.

1 5 candles cost 80 pence.

   (a) What is the cost of 1 candle?
   (b) What is the cost of 8 candles?

2 Georgina works for 4 hours and earns £24.
   (a) How much does she earn in 1 hour?
   (b) How much does she earn in 10 hours?

3 Alistair pays £1.90 for 2 cups of tea.
   How much would he pay for 3 cups of tea?

4 The amount a spring stretches is proportional to the weight hung on the spring.
   A weight of 5 kg stretches the spring by 60 cm.
   (a) How much does a weight of 10 kg stretch the spring?
   (b) What weight makes the spring stretch 24 cm?

5 Jean pays £168 for 10 square metres of carpet. How much would 12 square metres of carpet cost?

6 This recipe makes 20 scones.
   (a) How much dried fruit is needed to make 50 scones?
   (b) How much butter is needed to make 12 scones?

   | 500 g flour |
   | 250 g butter |
   | 100 g dried fruit |
   | water to mix |

7 Alfie is paid £28.80 for working 4 hours overtime.
   How much would he be paid for 5 hours overtime?

8 Aimee pays £1.14 for 3 kg of potatoes. How much would 7.5 kg of potatoes cost?

7.5 kg **3 kg**

9 5 litres of petrol costs £4.10.
   How much would 18 litres of petrol cost?

10 This recipe makes an apple crumble for 6 people.

   | 540 g apples |
   | 75 g butter |
   | 150 g flour |
   | 75 g sugar |

   (a) How much sugar is needed to make an apple crumble for 4 people?
   (b) How much apple is needed to make an apple crumble for 8 people?

11 9 metres of stair carpet cost £41.85. How much does 9.6 metres cost?

12 192 francs is about the same as £20. Sue spends 310 francs. How many pounds is this?

13 Mary phones her uncle in New York.
   Phone calls to New York are charged at the rate of £1.10 for a 5 minute call.

   (a) How much would a 7 minute call to New York cost?
   (b) Mary's call cost £2.64. How long was her call?

14 This recipe makes macaroni cheese for 4 people.

Macaroni	120 g
Cheese	72 g
Flour	30 g
Milk	850 ml

   (a) How much cheese is needed to make macaroni cheese for 10 people?
   (b) How much milk is needed to make macaroni cheese for 3 people?
   (c) How much macaroni is needed to make macaroni cheese for 7 people?

15 A car travels 6 miles in 9 minutes. If the car travels at the same speed:
   (a) how long will it take to travel 8 miles,
   (b) how far will it travel in 24 minutes?

16 5 litres of paint cover an area of 30 m².
   (a) What area will 2 litres of paint cover?
   (b) How much paint is needed to cover 72 m²?

17 A school is organising three trips to the zoo.

Our trip is on Monday.
There are 45 people going.
The total cost is £234.

Our trip is on Tuesday.
25 students are going.

Our trip is on Wednesday.
The total cost is £166.40.

(a) How much does Tuesday's trip cost?

(b) How many students are going to the zoo on Wednesday?

18 A 42 litre paddling pool is filled at the rate of 12 litres of water every 5 minutes. How long will it take to fill the pool?

19 50 g of flour and 90 ml of milk make 8 biscuits.
(a) How much flour is needed to make 27 biscuits?
(b) How many biscuits can be made with 225 g of flour?
Some biscuits are made with 300 g of flour.
(c) How much milk is needed?

20 A piece of beef weighs 1.5 kg and costs £5.22. How much would a piece of beef weighing 2.4 kg cost?
Give your answer to a suitable degree of accuracy.

What you need to know

- The ratio 3 : 2 is read '3 to 2'.
- A ratio is used only to **compare** quantities.
  A ratio does not give information about the exact values of quantities being compared.
- In its **simplest form**, a ratio contains whole numbers which have no common factor other than 1.
  All quantities in a ratio must have the **same units** before the ratio can be simplified.
  For example, £2.50 : 50p = 250p : 50p = 5 : 1.
- When two different quantities are always in the **same ratio** the two quantities are in **direct proportion**.
  For example, the amount and cost of fuel bought by a motorist.

IDEAS FOR INVESTIGATION

Do the squares fit?
Square P has side 3 cm and square Q has side 4 cm.
Square Q is cut into four **equal** pieces, as shown, where the ratio $a : b$ on each side is 7 : 1.

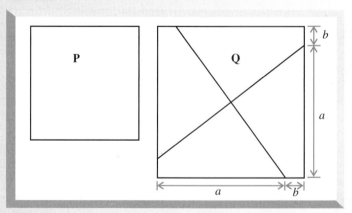

Show how square P and the four pieces of Q fit together exactly to make another square.
Repeat when square P has side 2 cm and square Q has side 6 cm.
Investigate.

Review Exercise Do not use a calculator for questions 1 to 10.

10

Ratio . . . . Ratio . . . . Ratio . . . . Ratio . . . . Ratio . . . .

1 A tin contains 21 nuts and 28 bolts. What is the ratio of nuts to bolts in its simplest form?

2 A sewing box contains pins and needles in the ratio 4 : 1. There are 36 pins in the box. How many needles are in the box?

3 In a recipe for scones, the ratio of **flour** to **fat** is 4 : 1 and the ratio of **flour** to **sugar** is 8 : 1.

RECIPE FOR SCONES
50 g fat,   … g flour,   … g sugar

Copy and complete the recipe.

Edexcel

4 In a class the ratio of students with dark hair to those with light hair is 3 : 2.
There are 18 students with dark hair. How many students have light hair?

5 This is a recipe for 8 dumplings.

100 g flour, 50 g suet, water to mix

(a) Write, in its simplest form, the ratio of flour to suet.
(b) How much flour would you need for 6 dumplings?
(c) How much suet would you need for 12 dumplings?

6 Tracey and Wayne share £7200 in the ratio 5 : 4.
Work out how much each of them receives.

Edexcel

7 (a) Peter and Jane share £36 in the ratio 5 : 7.
What is Peter's share?
(b) A bag contains 5p coins and 1p coins in the ratio 2 : 3. What percentage of the coins are 5p coins?

8 On a map the distance between two houses is 19 mm.
The actual distance between the houses is 3.8 km.
What is the scale of the map?

9 (a) A wood contains fir trees and yew trees in the ratio 3 : 4.
There are 18 fir trees in the wood.
How many yew trees are in the wood?
(b) Another wood contains 20 beech trees and 12 ash trees.
Write, in its simplest form, the ratio of beech trees to ash trees.

10 Michael wants to paint his room orange.
To make orange paint he has to mix red paint with yellow paint in the ratio 5 : 3.
He needs 2.4 litres of orange paint.
How much red paint and how much yellow paint will he need to use?

11 During a money raising appeal for charity 367 290 metal cans were collected for recycling.
The cans were either steel or aluminium.
They collected 5 times as many steel cans as aluminium cans.
How many steel cans were collected?

12 A piece of ham weighs 2.6 kg and costs £11.25.
How much would a piece of ham weighing 1.2 kg cost?
Give your answer to a suitable degree of accuracy.

13 Here are the ingredients for making 18 rock cakes.

9 ounces of flour	8 ounces of mixed
6 ounces of sugar	dried fruit
6 ounces of margarine	2 large eggs

Mark wants to make 12 rock cakes.
(a) Write down how much of each ingredient he needs for 12 rock cakes.

Mark only has 9 ounces of margarine.
He has plenty of all the other ingredients.
(b) What is the greatest number of rock cakes he can make?

Edexcel

14 Car *P* and car *Q* travel from Amfield to Barton.
Car *P* averages 10 kilometres for each litre of petrol.
It needs 45 litres of petrol for this journey.
Car *Q* averages 4 kilometres for each litre of petrol.
Work out the number of litres of petrol car *Q* needs for the same journey.

Edexcel

15 Miles, Rashid and Oliver share the cost of renting a flat in the ratio 4 : 3 : 2.
Miles plays £224 per month.
How much rent do they pay altogether each month for the flat?

Speed and Other Compound Measures

Speed

Speed is a measurement of how fast something is travelling.
It involves two other measures, **distance** and **time**.
Speed can be worked out using this formula.

$$\text{Speed} = \frac{\text{Distance}}{\text{Time}}$$

Speed can be measured in:
kilometres per hour (km/h),
metres per second (m/s),
miles per hour (mph),
and so on.

Speed can be thought of as the **distance** travelled in **one unit of time** (1 hour, 1 second, …)

Average speed

When the speed of an object is **constant** it means that the object doesn't slow down or go faster.
However, in many situations, speed is not constant.
For example:
A sprinter needs time to start from the starting blocks and is well into the race before running at top speed.
A plane changes speed as it takes off and lands.

In situations like this the idea of **average speed** can be used.
The formula for average speed is:

$$\text{Average speed} = \frac{\text{Total distance travelled}}{\text{Total time taken}}$$

The formula linking speed, distance and time can be rearranged and remembered as:

(average) **speed** = (total) **distance** ÷ (total) **time**	S = D ÷ T
(total) **distance** = (average) **speed** × (total) **time**	D = S × T
(total) **time** = (total) **distance** ÷ (average) **speed**	T = D ÷ S

EXAMPLES

 A cheetah takes 4 seconds to travel 100 m.
What is the speed of the cheetah in metres per second?

$$\text{Speed} = \frac{\text{Distance}}{\text{Time}} = \frac{100}{4} = 100 \div 4 = 25 \text{ m/s}$$

 Lisa drives at an average speed of 80 km/h on a journey that takes 3 hours.
What distance has she travelled?

Distance = Speed × Time
= 80 × 3
= 240 km

So in 3 hours she travels 240 km.

EXAMPLES

3 Lucy cycles at an average speed of 7 km/h on a journey of 21 km. How long does she take?

Time = Distance ÷ Speed
= 21 ÷ 7
= 3
So her journey takes 3 hours.

4 The Scottish Pullman travels from London to York, a distance of 302.8 km in 1 hour 45 minutes.
It then travels from York to Edinburgh, a distance of 334.7 km in 2 hours 30 minutes. Calculate the average speed of the train between London and Edinburgh.

Total distance travelled = 302.8 + 334.7
= 637.5 km
Total time taken = 1 hr 45 mins + 2 hr 30 mins
= 4 hr 15 mins = 4.25 hours

Average speed = $\frac{637.5}{4.25}$ = 150

Average speed = 150 km/h.

Exercise 11.1   Do not use a calculator for questions 1 to 11.

1 John cycles 16 miles in 2 hours. What is his average speed in miles per hour?

2 Calculate the average speed for each of the following journeys.

	Total distance travelled	Total time taken
(a)	60 km	3 hours
(b)	200 m	20 seconds
(c)	100 km	2 hours
(d)	80 cm	4 seconds
(e)	1500 m	5 minutes

3 Beverley walks for 2 hours at an average speed of 4 km/h. How many kilometres does she walk?

4 Calculate the total distance travelled on each of the following journeys.

	Total time taken	Average speed
(a)	3 hours	50 km/h
(b)	2 hours	45 km/h
(c)	50 seconds	8 m/s
(d)	10 minutes	150 m/min
(e)	½ hour	80 km/h

5 Ahmed drives 15 km at an average speed of 60 km/h. How long does the journey take?

6 Calculate the total time taken on each of the following journeys.

	Total distance travelled	Average speed
(a)	30 km	10 km/h
(b)	800 m	400 m/min
(c)	100 m	10 m/s
(d)	3000 m	30 m/min
(e)	240 km	60 km/h

7 Jackie runs 20 km in 2½ hours. What is her average speed in km/h?

8 Sam runs at 6 km/h for 30 minutes. How far does he run?

9 Lauren cycles 27 km at 12 km/h. How long does she take?

10 Joe swims 100 m in 4 minutes. What is his average speed in metres per minute?

11 Penny cycles to work at 18 km/h. She takes 20 minutes. How far does she cycle to work?

12 A train travels 36 km at an average speed of 80 km/h. How long does the journey take?

13 Bristol is 40 miles from Gloucester.

(a) How long does it take to cycle from Bristol to Gloucester at 16 miles per hour?

(b) How long does it take to drive from Bristol to Gloucester at 48 miles per hour?

14 A car travels 115 km in 2 hours.

(a) What is its average speed in kilometres per hour?

(b) How many hours would the car take to travel 115 km if it had gone twice as fast?

15 The table shows details of 5 different journeys.

Journey	(a)	(b)	(c)	(d)	(e)
Total distance	200 m			200 km	250 m
Total time	25 secs	2 hours	10 min		
Average speed		50 km/h	1.2 cm/min	200 km/h	250 m/s

Copy and complete the table.
State the units of each answer.

16 On the first part of a journey a car travels 140 km in 3 hours.
On the second part of the journey the car travels 160 km in 2 hours.

(a) What is the total distance travelled on the journey?

(b) What is the total time taken on the journey?

(c) What is the average speed of the car over the whole journey?

17 Lisa runs two laps of a 400 m running track.
The first lap takes 70 seconds.
The second lap takes 90 seconds.
What is her average speed over the two laps?

18 Jenny sets out on a journey at 10.20 am.
She completes her journey at 1.05 pm.
She travels a total distance of 27.5 km.
Calculate her average speed in kilometres per hour.

19 Here are some Olympic records for track events:

Men's 200 m	19.73 secs
Women's 200 m	21.34 secs
Men's 400 m	43.50 secs
Women's 400 m	48.64 secs
Men's 800 m	1 min 43.00 secs
Women's 800 m	1 min 53.50 secs

What was the average speed, in metres per second, of each of the record holders in these races.

20 Liam drives for 40 km at an average speed of 60 km/h.
He starts his journey at 9.50 am.
At what time does his journey end?

21 Sally cycles 38 km at an average speed of 23 km/h.
She starts her journey at 9.30 am.
At what time does she finish?
Give your answer to the nearest minute.

22 Chandni runs from Newcastle to Whitley Bay and then from Whitley Bay to Blyth.
Newcastle to Whitley Bay
    Time taken: 1 hr 20 min.
    Distance: 20 km.
Whitley Bay to Blyth
    Average speed: 0.2 km/min.
    Distance: 12 km.

(a) Calculate Chandni's average speed over the whole journey.

(b) Chandni left Newcastle at 10.50 am. At what time did she arrive in Blyth?

23 Ron runs 400 m in 1 minute 23.2 seconds.
Calculate his average speed in metres per second.

24 The distance from the Sun to the Earth is about 1.5×10^8 km.
It takes light from the Sun about 500 seconds to reach the Earth.
Calculate the speed of light in metres per second.

25 A plane travels 1.65×10^3 miles at an average speed of 7.25×10^2 miles per hour.
Calculate the time taken.
Give your answer in hours and minutes.

Distance-time graphs

Distance-time graphs are used to illustrate journeys.

Speed is given by the gradient, or slope, of the line.
The faster the speed the steeper the gradient.
Zero gradient (horizontal line) means zero speed (not moving).

EXAMPLES

1. The graph shows a bus journey.
   (a) How many times does the bus stop?
   (b) On which part of the journey does the bus travel fastest?

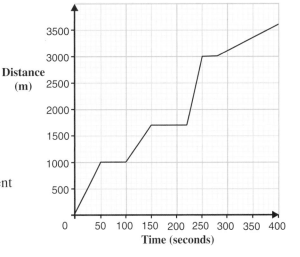

(a) At zero speed the distance-time graph is horizontal.
So the bus stops 3 times.
(b) The bus travels fastest when the gradient of the distance-time graph is steepest.
So the bus travels fastest between the second and third stops.

2. The graph represents a train journey from Woking.

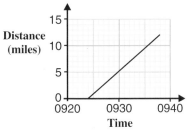

(a) At what time did the train leave Woking?
(b) How far did the train travel?

(a) 0924
(b) 12 miles

3. What speed is shown by this distance-time graph?
   Give your answer in metres per second.

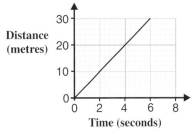

A distance of 30 metres is travelled in a time of 6 seconds.
Using Speed = Distance ÷ Time
       Speed = 30 ÷ 6
             = 5 metres per second

Exercise 11.2

1. The graph represents a bus journey from Poole.

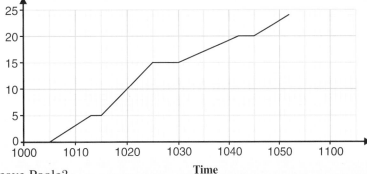

(a) At what time did the bus leave Poole?
(b) How far did the bus travel?
(c) How many times did the bus stop on the journey?

2 The graph represents the journey of a cyclist from Hambone to Boneham.
   (a) What time did the cyclist leave Hambone?
   (b) The cyclist arrived in Boneham at 1200. How far is Boneham from Hambone?
   (c) The cyclist made one stop on his journey.
      (i) At what time did the cyclist stop?
      (ii) How far was the cyclist from Boneham when he stopped?

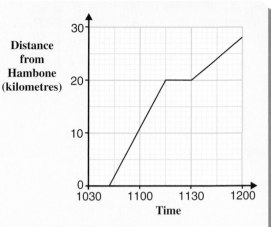

3 (a) The graph represents the journey of a car. What is the speed of the car in kilometres per hour?

(b) The graph represents the journey of a train. What is the speed of the train in metres per second?

(c) The graph represents the speed of a cyclist. What is the speed of the cyclist in miles per hour?

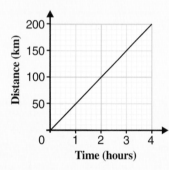
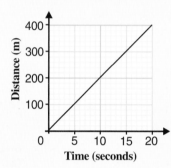
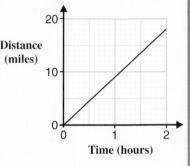

4 This graph shows the progress made by a runner during the first 20 km of a marathon race.

Find the average speed of the runner:
   (a) during the first 10 km of the race,
   (b) during the second 10 km of the race,
   (c) during the first 20 km of the race.

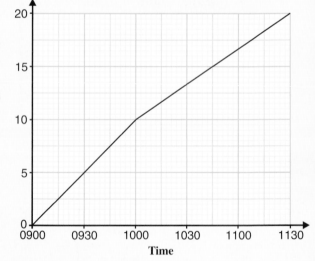

5 Selby is 20 miles from York.
   (a) Kathryn leaves Selby at 1030 and drives to York.
      She travels at an average speed of 20 miles per hour.
      Draw a distance-time graph to represent her journey.

   (b) At 1030 Matt leaves York and drives to Selby.
      He travels at an average speed of 30 miles per hour.
      (i) On the same diagram draw a distance-time graph to represent his journey.
      (ii) At what time does Matt arrive in Selby?

6 Dan walks around Bolam Lake. He starts and finishes his walk at the car park beside the lake. The distance-time graph shows his journey.

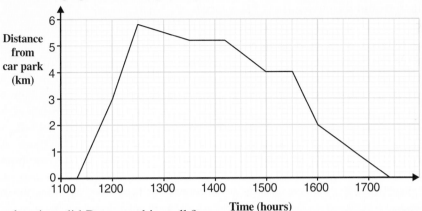

(a) At what time did Dan start his walk?
(b) At what time did Dan reach the furthest distance from the car park?
(c) How many times did Dan stop during his walk?
(d) Dan stopped for lunch at 1330.
   For how many minutes did he stop for lunch?
(e) Between what times did Dan walk the fastest?
(f) At what speed did Dan walk between 1530 and 1600?

7 The graph represents the journey of a cyclist from Bournemouth to the New Forest.

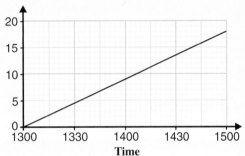

(a) What is the average speed of the cyclist in miles per hour?
(b) Another cyclist is travelling from the New Forest to Bournemouth at an average speed of 12 miles per hour. At 1300 the cyclist is 15 miles from Bournemouth.
   (i) Copy the graph and on the same diagram draw a graph to show the journey of the cyclist to Bournemouth.
   (ii) At what time does the cyclist arrive in Bournemouth?

8 Billy has a 10 km journey to school.
He leaves home at 8.05 am and takes 10 minutes to walk 1 km to Jane's house.
Billy gets a lift with Jane's mum at 8.20 am. Billy arrives at school at 8.45 am.
(a) Using 1 cm for 5 minutes on the time axis and 1 cm for 1 km on the distance axis draw a distance-time graph for Billy's journey.
(b) Find Billy's average speed for his whole journey in km/hour.

9 Emby and Ashwood are two towns 14 km apart.
Kim leaves Emby at 1000 and walks at a steady pace of 6 km/hour towards Ashwood.
Ray leaves Ashwood at 1040 and cycles towards Emby.
Ray travels at a steady speed of 21 km/hour for the first 20 minutes and then at a slower steady speed for the rest of his journey.
Ray arrives at Emby at 1130.
(a) On the same diagram and using a scale of 1 cm for 10 minutes on the time axis and 1 cm for 1 km on the distance axis, draw a distance-time graph to show both journeys.
(b) Use your diagram to find:
   (i) the time that Kim arrives at Ashwood,
   (ii) the time that Kim and Ray pass each other,
   (iii) Ray's speed for the slower part of his journey.

Other compound measures

Density

Density is a compound measure because it involves two other measures, **mass** and **volume**.
The formula for density is:

$$\text{Density} = \frac{\text{Mass}}{\text{Volume}}$$

For example, if a metal has a density of $2500\,\text{kg/m}^3$ then $1\,\text{m}^3$ of the metal weighs $2500\,\text{kg}$.

The formula linking density, mass and volume can be rearranged and remembered as:

$$\text{Volume} = \frac{\text{Mass}}{\text{Density}}$$

$$\text{Mass} = \text{Density} \times \text{Volume}$$

EXAMPLES

1 A block of metal has mass $500\,\text{g}$ and volume $400\,\text{cm}^3$.
Calculate the density of the metal.

Density $= \frac{500}{400} = 1.25\,\text{g/cm}^3$

2 The density of a certain metal is $3.5\,\text{g/cm}^3$.
A block of the metal has volume $1000\,\text{cm}^3$.
Calculate the mass of the block.

Mass $= 3.5 \times 1000 = 3500\,\text{g}$.

3 Metal A has density $3\,\text{g/cm}^3$ and metal B has density $2\,\text{g/cm}^3$.
$600\,\text{g}$ of metal A and $300\,\text{g}$ of metal B are melted down and mixed to make an alloy which is cast into a block.
(a) Calculate the volume of the block.
(b) Calculate the density of the alloy.

(a) Volume of metal A $= \frac{600}{3} = 200\,\text{cm}^3$.
Volume of metal B $= \frac{300}{2} = 150\,\text{cm}^3$.
Total volume $= 200 + 150 = 350\,\text{cm}^3$.

(b) Density $= \frac{900}{350} = 2.57\,\text{g/cm}^3$.

Population density

Population density is a measure of how populated an area is.
The formula for population density is:

$$\text{Population density} = \frac{\text{Population}}{\text{Area}}$$

EXAMPLE

The population of the county of Cumbria is 4.897×10^5.
The area of the county of Cumbria is $6824\,\text{km}^2$.
The population of the county of Surrey is 1.036×10^6.
The area of the county of Surrey is $1677\,\text{km}^2$.
Which county has the greater population density?

The population densities are:

Cumbria $\dfrac{4.897 \times 10^5}{6824} = 71.8$ people/km^2.

Surrey $\dfrac{1.036 \times 10^6}{1677} = 617.8$ people/km^2.

Surrey has the greater population density.

Exercise 11.3

You may use a calculator in this exercise.

1 A metal bar has a mass of 960 g and a volume of 120 cm³.
Find the density of the metal in the bar.

2 A block of copper has a mass of 2160 g.
The block measures 4 cm by 6 cm by 10 cm.
What is the density of copper?

3 A silver necklace has a mass of 300 g.
The density of silver is 10.5 g/cm³.
What is the volume of the silver?

4 A rectangular can measuring 30 cm by 15 cm by 20 cm is full of oil.
The density of oil is 0.8 g/cm³.
What is the mass of the oil?

5 A rectangular pane of glass measures 60 cm by 120 cm by 0.5 cm.
The density of glass is 2.6 g/cm³.
What is the mass of the glass?

6 A bag of sugar has a mass of 1 kg.
The average density of the sugar in the bag is 0.5 g/cm³.
Find the volume of sugar in the bag.

7 A block of concrete has dimensions 15 cm by 25 cm by 40 cm.
The block has a mass of 12 kg.
What is the density of the concrete?

8 A bottle holds 450 cm³ of water and has a mass of 550 g when full.
The density of water is 1 g/cm³.
What is the mass of the empty bottle?

9 The population of Northern Ireland is 1.595×10^6.
The area of Northern Ireland is 13 483 km².
Calculate the population density of Northern Ireland.

10 The table shows the total population, land area and the population densities for some countries in Europe.

	Country	Area km²	Population	Population density
(a)	Belgium	?	9.97×10^6	326.6
(b)	France	543 960	5.67×10^7	?
(c)	UK	244 090	?	235.2

Calculate the missing figures in the table.

What you need to know

- **Speed** is a compound measure because it involves **two** other measures.

- **Speed** is a measure of how fast something is travelling. It involves the measures **distance** and **time**.

    $$\text{Speed} = \frac{\text{Distance}}{\text{Time}}$$

- In situations where speed is not constant, **average speed** is used.

    $$\text{Average speed} = \frac{\text{Total distance travelled}}{\text{Total time taken}}$$

- The formula linking speed, distance and time can be rearranged and remembered as:
    (average) **speed** = (total) **distance** ÷ (total) **time**
    (total) **distance** = (average) **speed** × (total) **time**
    (total) **time** = (total) **distance** ÷ (average) **speed**

- **Distance-time graphs** are used to illustrate journeys.
    On a distance-time graph: speed can be calculated from the gradient of a line,
    the faster the speed the steeper the gradient,
    zero gradient (horizontal line) means zero speed.

- Two other commonly used compound measures are **density** and **population density**.

- **Density** is a compound measure which involves the measures **mass** and **volume**.

    $$\text{Density} = \frac{\text{Mass}}{\text{Volume}}$$

- **Population density** is a measure of how populated an area is.

    $$\text{Population density} = \frac{\text{Population}}{\text{Area}}$$

You may use a calculator in this exercise.

1 Mr Mogg took 5 hours to drive from Cardiff to Leeds.
His average speed was 48 miles per hour.
What is the distance from Cardiff to Leeds?

2 (a) Nick took 20 minutes to run 3 kilometres.
What was his average speed in kilometres per hour?
(b) Naomi cycles 12 kilometres at an average speed of 20 kilometres per hour.
For how many minutes did she cycle?

3 The chart shows the distances in kilometres between some towns.

London			
326	Manchester		
270	60	Sheffield	
129	376	334	Southampton

Mrs Hill drove from Manchester to Southampton.
She completed the journey in 4 hours.
What was her average speed for the journey in kilometres per hour?

4 (a) Ben runs 600 m at an average speed of 4.2 m/s.
How long does Ben take in seconds?
(b) Tim runs for 1 minute at an average speed of 4.2 m/s.
How far does Tim run in metres?

5 Part of a bus timetable is shown.

Bournemouth 0630 0730 0750 0810
Poole   0654 0754 0814 0834

The bus journey from Bournemouth to Poole is 8 km.
When the bus is on time what is the average speed of the bus in km/hour?

6 The distance from London to Newcastle is 285 miles.
Paul takes $4\frac{1}{2}$ hours to drive this distance.
Calculate his average speed.

7 A train travels from Bournemouth to Manchester at an average speed of 47 miles per hour. The train travels a distance of 268 miles.
How long does the journey take in hours and minutes?

8 On Monday, Gareth drove from Swindon to Newcastle.
The distance was 325 miles.
He left Swindon at 0800.
He arrived in Newcastle at 1430.
(a) Work out Gareth's average speed.

On Tuesday, Gareth left Newcastle at 1000 to drive back to Swindon.
He drove for 160 miles at an average speed of 64 miles per hour.
He stopped at a Service Station for one hour, before completing the journey.
He arrived in Swindon at 1630.
(b) Calculate Gareth's average speed from the Service Station to Swindon.
                                    Edexcel

9 Arnold runs 400 m in 1 minute.
(a) What is his average speed in metres per hour?
(b) What is his average speed in kilometres per hour?

10 The distance from Ashby to Banborough is 16 km.
The distance from Banborough to Calby is 8 km.

John leaves Ashby at noon.
He walks towards Banborough for 1 hour at an average speed of 6 km/h and then rests for 20 minutes.

John then runs the remaining distance to Banborough at an average speed of 10 km/h.

At Banborough John talks to a friend for 20 minutes and borrows his bicycle.

He then cycles to Calby at an average speed of 16 km/h.

John leaves Calby at 1600.
He cycles home over the same route arriving at 1650.

Using a scale of 1 cm for 20 minutes and 1 cm for 2 km draw a distance-time graph for John's journey.

11 Elizabeth went for a cycle ride.
The distance-time graph shows her ride.
She set off from home at 1200 and had
a flat tyre at 1400.
During her ride, she stopped for a rest.

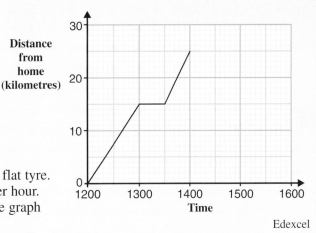

(a) (i) At what time did she stop
for a rest?
(ii) At what speed did she travel
after her rest?

It took Elizabeth 15 minutes to repair the flat tyre.
She then cycled home at 25 kilometres per hour.
(b) Copy and complete the distance-time graph
to show this information.

Edexcel

12 The distance-time graph shows the journey of a man from Durham to Leeds and back.

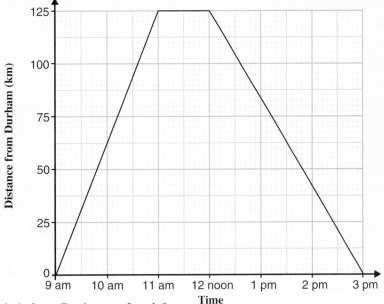

(a) How far is it from Durham to Leeds?
(b) How long did the man stop in Leeds?
(c) Did he travel at a faster speed going to Leeds or on the return journey?
Explain your answer.

13 Brass is an alloy made from zinc and copper.
The ratio of the volume of zinc to the volume of copper in the alloy is 1 : 3.
The density of zinc is 2.5 g/cm³. The density of copper is 3 g/cm³.
A block of brass in the shape of a cuboid has dimensions 10 cm by 10 cm by 40 cm.
Calculate the mass of the block.

14 The table gives some information about
various materials.
Calculate the missing figures in the table.
State the units of each answer.

Metal	Volume	Mass	Density
Steel	120 cm³	300 g	?
Concrete	?	12 kg	7.5 g/cm³
Foam	4000 cm³	?	0.05 g/cm³

15 The population density of a country is given by the formula: Population density = $\dfrac{\text{Population}}{\text{Area}}$
Find the population density of Greenland, which has an area of
840 000 square miles and a population of 56 000.

Section Review - Number

Do not use a calculator for questions 1 to 20.

1 (a) Work out
  (i) $\dfrac{7 + 2 \times 4}{5}$
  (ii) $15 \div (3 + 2) - 1$.

  (b) Write these numbers in ascending order:
  $-3 \quad 0.6 \quad 2 \quad -9 \quad 10$

  (c) Work out 0.3×0.2.

2 Tickets for a concert cost £17 each.
234 people go to the concert.
How much money is paid for tickets?

3 Work out:
  (a) $\dfrac{300 \times 200}{300 + 200}$
  (b) $\dfrac{100^2}{40}$

4 The table shows the midday temperature in two cities on one day.

London	3°C
Moscow	−8°C

  (a) How much colder is Moscow than London?
  (b) Paris is 5°C colder than London. What is the temperature in Paris?

5 (a) Lyn writes down the number 26589.
  (i) What is the value of the 6 in Lyn's number?
  (ii) Write Lyn's number to the nearest 100.

  (b) Ben writes down these five numbers:
  9, 8, 6, 5, 2.

  (i) Which number is a factor of 4?
  (ii) Which numbers are prime numbers?
  (iii) Which number is a square number?
  (iv) Which number is a cube number?
  (v) Use all five numbers to write down the smallest even number you can make.

6 John pays £2.60 for 200 g of jelly babies and 300 g of toffees.
100 g of jelly babies cost 37p.
What is the cost of 100 g of toffees?

7 To cook a leg of lamb, allow 25 minutes per 0.5 kg **plus** 25 minutes.
Dexter wants a leg of lamb, weighing 1.5 kg, to be cooked by 1 pm.
At what time should he put the lamb in the oven?

8 A crowd of 4560 watch a football match.
  (a) Two-thirds of the crowd support the home team.
  How many people support the home team?
  (b) 60% of the crowd are men.
  How many men are in the crowd?

9 (a) Write down the numbers you could use to get an approximate answer to 59×32.
  (b) Write down your approximate answer.
  (c) Find the difference between your approximate answer and the exact answer.   *Edexcel*

10

Tigers	**Cheetahs**
Admission: £2.40	Admission: £2.70
Special Offer 20% off	Special Offer $\frac{1}{3}$ off

Jugdev pays to see the Tigers.
It normally costs £2.40 but there is 20% off the price.
  (a) Work out how much he pays.

Jugdev then pays to see the Cheetahs.
It normally costs £2.70 but there is $\frac{1}{3}$ off the price.
  (b) Work out how much he pays.   *Edexcel*

11 (a) Write down a decimal that lies between $\frac{1}{4}$ and $\frac{1}{3}$.
  (b) Work out $\frac{3}{4} \times \frac{2}{3}$.

12 (a) Work out 20% of £3.60.
  (b) Work out $\frac{3}{5}$ of £130.

13　(a)　Work out $2^3 + \sqrt{25}$.

　　(b)　Given that $37 \times 249 = 9213$, find the exact value of $\frac{92.13}{3.7}$.

14　Find the values of　(a)　$\sqrt{36} + \sqrt{64}$,　　(b)　$\sqrt{36 \times 64}$.

15　Which number is smaller　3^5　or　5^3?
　　Show all your working.

16　(a)　Work out:　(i)　$\frac{1}{4} - \frac{1}{5}$　(ii)　$2\frac{1}{4} \div 1\frac{1}{5}$

　　(b)　What is the reciprocal of 4?

　　(c)　Use approximations to estimate the value of $\frac{6.135^2}{0.595}$.

17　Red tulips and yellow tulips are used for a flower display.
　　The display uses 40 tulips.
　　The ratio of red tulips to yellow tulips is 3 : 5.
　　How many tulips are red?

18　(a)　Write 36 as a product of its prime factors.

　　(b)　a and b are whole numbers.
　　　　Find the values of a and b when $2^a \times 3^b = 48$.

　　(c)　What is the highest common factor of 36 and 48?

　　(d)　What is the least common multiple of 36 and 48?

19　$A = 3 \times 10^4$　　　　$B = 5 \times 10^{-2}$

　　(a)　Calculate $A \times B$.
　　　　Give your answer in standard form.

　　(b)　Calculate $A \div B$.
　　　　Give your answer in standard form.

20　The graph represents a coach journey from Bath.

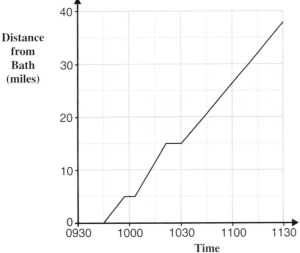

The coach completed its journey at 1130.

　　(a)　At what time did the coach leave Bath?

　　(b)　How far did the coach travel?

　　(c)　How many times did the coach stop on the journey?

　　(d)　What was the average speed of the coach between 1030 and 1130?

21 (a) Alika pays £6.46 for some cheese.
She buys 0.3 kg of brie and 0.5 kg of stilton.
The brie costs £7.20 per kilogram.
How much per kilogram is stilton?

(b) The weights and prices of two pots of natural yogurt are shown.

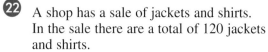

145 g
39 pence

250 g
66 pence

Which pot is better value for money?
Show **all** your working.

22 A shop has a sale of jackets and shirts.
In the sale there are a total of 120 jackets and shirts.
Shirts are to be sold at a price of
£8.00 plus VAT at $17\frac{1}{2}\%$.

(a) What is the cost of buying one shirt, including the $17\frac{1}{2}\%$ VAT?

The jackets and shirts are in the ratio 5 : 3.

(b) Work out the number of jackets.

(c) Calculate the percentage that are shirts.
                                                Edexcel

23

MOTOR BOAT

Cash price...£12 800

Credit terms...Deposit of 30% of cash price plus 36 monthly payments of £295

How much more is paid when the motorboat is bought on credit terms instead of cash?

24 Mr Mogg earns £5460 per year.
He has a tax allowance of £4385 per year and tax is paid at 10p in the £ on his taxable income. How much tax does he pay per year?

25 Calculate the value of $\dfrac{7.84 \times 2.8}{3.28 - 1.04}$
                                                Edexcel

26 Fred has a recipe for 30 biscuits.
Here is a list of ingredients for 30 biscuits.

Self-raising flour :	230 g
Butter :	150 g
Caster sugar :	100 g
Eggs :	2

Fred wants to make 45 biscuits.

(a) Write a new list of ingredients for 45 biscuits.

The recipe gives the baking temperature as 350° Fahrenheit, F.
A modern oven shows baking temperature in Celsius, C.

(b) Use the formula $C = \dfrac{5(F - 32)}{9}$
to change 350° Fahrenheit to Celsius.
Give your answer correct to the nearest degree.

Gill has only 1 kilogram of self-raising flour. She has plenty of the other ingredients.

(c) Work out the maximum number of biscuits that Gill could bake.   Edexcel

27 Calculate the simple interest on £480 invested at 7% for 6 months.

28 A mechanic is paid £7.48 per hour for a basic 35-hour week.
When he works overtime he is paid at one and a half times the basic hourly rate.

(a) One week he has to work 37 hours.
How much is he paid that week?

(b) For a different week he is paid £317.90.
How many hours overtime did he work that week?

29

EXCHANGE RATES	
£1 WILL BUY	
GERMANY	2.97 MARKS
UNITED STATES	1.40 DOLLARS

The same computer can be bought in Germany and in the United States.
In the United States it costs 950 dollars.
In Germany it costs 9% more.
How much does it cost to buy the computer in Germany?
Give your answer to a suitable degree of accuracy.

30 (a) Calculate the exact value of 5^9.

(b) Find the reciprocal of 7.
Give your answer correct to 3 decimal places.

31 Work out $2.37^2 - \sqrt{5.8}$.
Give your answer correct to two decimal places.

32 (a) $720 = 2^x \times 3^y \times 5$
Find the values of x and y.

(b) Using index notation, express 675 as a product of its prime factors.

(b) Given that $720 \times 675 = 486\,000$, express $486\,000$ as the product of its prime factors.

Edexcel

33 A farm has 427 acres of land.
135 acres are used for grazing.
What percentage of the land is used for grazing?

34 (a) Calculate $\sqrt{\dfrac{14.7}{(0.7)^3}}$

Give your answer correct to two significant figures.

(b) The distance from the Earth to the Moon is 3.81×10^5 kilometres.
Light travels at a speed of 3×10^8 metres per second.
How long does it take light to travel from the Earth to the Moon?

35 Nick invests £3000 at 7% per annum compound interest.
Calculate the value of his investment at the end of 2 years.

36 (a) A car takes 27 minutes to travel 45 km along a motorway.
What is the speed of the car in kilometres per hour?

(b) A coach overtakes a lorry on the motorway.
The speed of the coach is 60 miles per hour.
The speed of the coach is 20% more than the speed of the lorry.
What is the speed of the lorry?

37 A Building Society is going to be sold for £1 800 000 000.

(a) Write the number 1 800 000 000 in standard form.

This money is going to be shared equally between the 2.5×10^6 members of the Building Society.

(b) How much should each member get?

Later, 3×10^5 members find out that they **will not** get a share of the money.

(c) How many members **will** now receive a share of the money?
Give your answer in standard form.

Edexcel

38 The mass of one electron is   0.000 000 000 000 000 000 000 000 91 grams.

(a) Write 0.000 000 000 000 000 000 000 000 91 in standard form.

(b) Calculate the mass of five million electrons.
Give your answer, in grams, in standard form.

Edexcel

39 In Britain there are 5.8×10^7 people.
8.8% of the people in Britain live in Scotland.
How many people live in Scotland?

CHAPTER 12

Introduction to Algebra

Algebra is sometimes called the language of Mathematics.
Algebra uses letters in place of numbers.

A class of children line up.
We cannot see how many children there are altogether because of a tree.
We can say there are *n* children in the line.
The letter *n* is used in place of an unknown number.

Three more children join the line.
There are now *n* + 3 children in the line.

This picture shows two lines of *n* children.
So there are *n* + *n* or 2 × *n* children altogether.
The simplest way to write this is 2*n*.

Both *n* + 3 and 2*n* are examples of
algebraic expressions.

Exercise 12.1

Write algebraic expressions for each of the
following questions.

1 There are *n* children in a queue.
4 more children join the queue.
How many children are in the queue
now?

2 There are *n* children in a queue.
3 children leave the queue.
How many children are left in the
queue?

3 There are 3 classes with *n* children in
each class.
How many children are there altogether?

4 I have *m* marbles in a bag.
I put in another 6 marbles.
How many marbles are now in the bag?

5 I have *m* marbles. I lose 12 marbles.
How many marbles have I got left?

6 I have 8 bags of marbles.
Each bag contains *m* marbles.
How many marbles do I have
altogether?

7 There are *p* pencils in a pencil case.
I take one pencil out.
How many pencils are left in the pencil
case?

8 There are *p* pencils in a pencil case.
I put in another 5 pencils.
How many pencils are now in the pencil
case?

9 I have 25 pencil cases.
There are *p* pencils in each pencil case.
How many pencils do I have altogether?

10 I have 6 key rings.
There are *k* keys on each key ring.
How many keys do I have altogether?

11 What is the cost of b biscuits costing 5 pence each?

12 Three cakes cost a total of c pence. What is the cost of one cake?

13 Five kilograms of apples cost a pence. What is the cost of one kilogram of apples?

14 A group of 36 students are split into g groups. How many students are in each group?

15 There are t toffees in a tin. How many toffees are there in
(a)   2 tins,
(b)   10 tins?

Expressions and terms

Consider this situation:
  $2n$ students start a typing course.
  3 of the students leave the course.
  How many students remain on the course?
$2n - 3$ students remain.
$2n - 3$ is an **algebraic expression**, or simply an **expression**.
An expression is just an answer made up of letters and numbers.
$+2n$ and -3 are **terms** of the expression.

Note
A term includes the sign, $+$ or $-$.
$2n$ has the same value as $+2n$.

Simplifying expressions

Addition and subtraction

You can add and subtract terms with the same letter.
This is sometimes called **simplifying an expression**.

$a + a = 2a$ $6a - 2a = 4a$
$5k + 3k = 8k$ $2d - 3d = -d$
$3p + 5 + p - 1 = 4p + 4$ $4x - 4x = 0$

$6 + a$ cannot be simplified.
$5p - 2q$ cannot be simplified.
$x^2 + x$ cannot be simplified.
$ab + ba = 2ab$

Note that:
A simpler way to write $1d$ is just d.

$-1d$ can be written as $-d$.

$0d$ is the same as 0.

Just as with ordinary numbers you can add terms in any order.
$a - 2a + 5a = a + 5a - 2a = 4a$

EXAMPLE

Write down an expression for the perimeter of this shape.
Give your answer in its simplest form.

Perimeter is the total distance round the outside of the shape.
$y + 2x - 1 + 2y + 2x + 3$
Imagine that each term is written on a separate card.

| $+y$ | $+2x$ | -1 | $+2y$ | $+2x$ | $+3$ |

The cards can be arranged in any order.

| $+2x$ | $+2x$ | $+y$ | $+2y$ | $+3$ | -1 |

Simplify this expression to get: $4x + 3y + 2$
The perimeter of the shape is $4x + 3y + 2$.

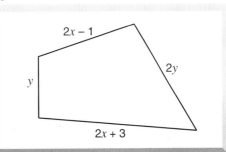

$2x - 1$
$2y$
y
$2x + 3$

1 Write simpler expressions for the following.

(a) $y + y$

(b) $c + c + c$

(c) $x + x + x + x + x$

(d) $p + p + p + p + p + p + p$

(e) $t + t + t - t$

(f) $d + d + d - d + d$

(g) $2n + n$

(h) $2y + 3y$

(i) $5g + g + 4g$

(j) $2m + 5m + m$

(k) $5z + 4z + z + 3z$

(l) $5r - 3r$

(m) $7t - 2t$

(n) $5y - y$

(o) $5j + 2j - 4j$

(p) $9c - 2c - 3c$

(q) $3x - x + 5x$

(r) $12w - 7w - 4w$

(s) $5d + 7d - 12d$

(t) $-2y - 3y$

(u) $3x - 8x$

(v) $2a - 5a - 12a + a$

(w) $3b + 5b - 4b + 2b$

(x) $m - 2m + 3m$

2 Write an expression for the perimeter of each shape.
Give each answer in its simplest form.

(a)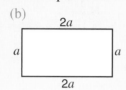

(b)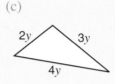

(c)

(d)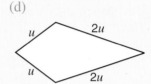

3 Which of these expressions cannot be simplified?
Give a reason for each of your answers.

(a) $v + v$

(b) $v + 4$

(c) $2v + v + 4$

(d) $v + w$

4 Simplify where possible.

(a) $5x + 3x + y$

(b) $w + 3v - v$

(c) $2a + b - 3b$

(d) $2x + 3y + 3x$

(e) $5 + 7u - 2$

(f) $p + 3q + q$

(g) $3d - 5c - 2c$

(h) $3y + 1 - y$

(i) $-a + b + 2a$

(j) $3m + n + m$

(k) $5c + 4c - d$

(l) $2x + y - x$

(m) $-p + 4p + 3p$

(n) $5 - 9k + 4k$

(o) $2a - a + 3$

5 Simplify where possible.

(a) $3a + 5a + 2b + b$

(b) $p + 2q + 2p + q$

(c) $m + 2m - n + 3n$

(d) $2x + 3y - x - 5y$

(e) $3x - x + 5y - 2y$

(f) $2d + 5 - d - 2$

(g) $3a - 5a + 2b + b$

(h) $a - 2a + 7 + a$

(i) $2a - b + 3b - a$

(j) $-f + g - f - g$

(k) $2v - w - 3w - v$

(l) $7 - 2t - 9 - 3t$

(m) $-p + 3q - 3p + q$

(n) $5 - 9k - 4 + 2k$

(o) $2c + d + 4 - c - 2d + 7$

6 Write down an expression for the perimeter of each shape. Give each answer in its simplest form.

(a)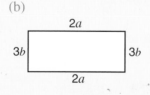

(b)

(c)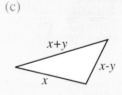

(d)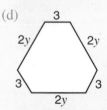

7 Simplify.

(a) $xy + yx$

(b) $3pq - qp$

(c) $5ab - 2ba$

(d) $3x^2 - x^2$

(e) $5y^2 + 4y^2$

(f) $a^2 + 5a^2 - 2a^2$

(g) $d^2 - 2g^2 - g^2 + d^2$

(h) $3t^2 + t + 2t^2 - 2t$

(i) $3m^2 - 4m^2 + 7m - m$

(j) $p^2 - 2p + p^2 + p$

Multiplying and dividing terms

$6 \times a = 6a$ $\quad 3x \times y = 3xy$

$5 \times 2a = 10a$ $\quad 5c \times 4c = 20c^2$

$a \times b = ab$ $\quad b \times b \times b = b^3$

$x \times x = x^2$

$8a \div 2 = 4a$ $\quad 9x \div x = 9$

$6y \div 2y = 3$

> **EXAMPLE**
>
> Find an expression for the area of this rectangle.
>
> Area = length × breadth
> = $3d \times d$
>
> The simplest way to write an expression for the area is $3d^2$.

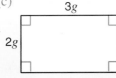

Exercise 12.3

1 Write these expressions in a simpler form.

(a) $3 \times a$ (b) $7 \times b$ (c) $2 \times 4 \times c$ (d) $3 \times 3 \times d$

(e) $e \times 4$ (f) $f \times 8$ (g) $3 \times 2p$ (h) $3q \times 5$

(i) $r \times r$ (j) $g \times g$ (k) $2g \times g$ (l) $2g \times 3g$

(m) $t \times 4t$ (n) $3t \times 4t$ (o) $5u \times 3u$ (p) $3d \times 3d$

2 Simplify.

(a) $3 \times (-y)$ (b) $y \times (-5)$

(c) $(-2) \times (-y)$ (d) $3 \times (-2y)$

(e) $t \times (-t)$ (f) $2t \times (-t)$

(g) $(-2t) \times 5t$ (h) $(-2t) \times (-5t)$

> **Remember:**
> $2 \times (-x) = -2x$
> $(-2) \times (-x) = 2x$

3 Simplify.

(a) $10a \div 2$ (b) $16b \div 4$ (c) $12x \div x$ (d) $20y \div y$

(e) $8y \div 4$ (f) $8y \div y$ (g) $8y \div 4y$ (h) $18p \div p$

(i) $18p \div 6$ (j) $18p \div 6p$ (k) $18k \div 2k$ (l) $18a \div 3a$

(m) $28g \div 7g$ (n) $10m \div 2m$ (o) $20t \div 5t$ (p) $27x \div 3x$

4 Simplify.

(a) $6y \div (-3)$ (b) $(-6y) \div 2$

(c) $(-5m) \div m$ (d) $(-5m) \div (-5)$

(e) $3a \div (-a)$ (f) $(-10d) \div 5d$

(g) $6g \div (-2g)$ (h) $(-3k) \div (-3k)$

> **Remember:**
> $2x \div (-2) = -x$
> $(-2x) \div 2 = -x$
> $(-2x) \div (-2) = x$

5 Simplify.

(a) $a \times b$ (b) $x \times y$ (c) $y \times y$ (d) $2 \times p \times q$

(e) $2 \times a \times a$ (f) $3 \times x \times y$ (g) $3 \times a \times 2 \times b$ (h) $3 \times g \times 4 \times h$

(i) $2 \times d \times 3 \times d$ (j) $3g \times g$ (k) $a \times 5b$ (l) $2g \times 3h$

(m) $a \times b \times c$ (n) $m \times m \times m$ (o) $2 \times d \times d \times d$ (p) $g \times g \times g \times 3$

(q) $2x \times 3x \times x$ (r) $5m \times m \times 2n$ (s) $3a \times b \times c$ (t) $2p \times 3q \times 3r$

6 Write an expression for the area of each shape.
Give each answer in its simplest form.

(a)   (b)   (c)   (d)

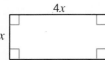

Multiplying and dividing algebraic expressions with powers

The rules for multiplying and dividing powers can be used to simplify algebraic expressions involving powers.

Remember
When multiplying or dividing expressions that include both numbers and powers:
   multiply or **divide** the **numbers**,
   add or **subtract** the **powers**.
Deal with the powers of different bases **separately**.

EXAMPLES

1 Simplify.

(a) $x^3 \times x^8 = x^{3+8} = x^{11}$

(b) $2x^2 \times 5x^7 = (2 \times 5) \times (x^2 \times x^7) = 10 \times x^{2+7} = 10x^9$

(c) $x^3y^2 \times xy^4 = (x^3 \times x) \times (y^2 \times y^4) = x^{3+1} \times y^{2+4} = x^4y^6$

(d) $(x^3y^2)^2 = (x^3y^2) \times (x^3y^2) = (x^3 \times x^3) \times (y^2 \times y^2) = x^6y^4$

(e) $(3x^4)^2 = (3x^4) \times (3x^4) = (3 \times 3) \times (x^4 \times x^4) = 9x^8$

2 Simplify.

(a) $x^8 \div x^5 = x^{8-5} = x^3$

(b) $6y^6 \div 2y^4 = (6 \div 2) \times (y^6 \div y^4) = 3 \times y^{6-4} = 3y^2$

Exercise 12.4

1 Simplify.

(a) $y^2 \times y$ (b) $t^3 \times t^2$ (c) $a^3 \times a^3$ (d) $g^7 \times g^3$

(e) $a \times a \times a^2$ (f) $m \times m^3 \times m^2$ (g) $2y \times y^2$ (h) $3d^2 \times 2d^3$

(i) $4x^2 \times 2x^3$ (j) $5y^3 \times 5y^3$ (k) $2t \times t^2 \times 3t^2$ (l) $2r \times 3r^2 \times 4r^3$

(m) $mn \times m^2n$ (n) $a^2b \times ba^2$ (o) $3rs^3 \times 2r^2s$ (p) $2x^2y \times 5x^3y^2$

2 Simplify.

(a) $(t^2)^3$ (b) $(y^3)^2$ (c) $(g^3)^3$ (d) $(x^4)^2$

(e) $(3a)^2$ (f) $(2h)^3$ (g) $2 \times (m^3)^2$ (h) $(2m^3)^2$

(i) $3 \times (d^3)^2$ (j) $(3d^3)^2$ (k) $(3a^2)^3$ (l) $(2k^3)^3$

(m) $(xy)^2$ (n) $(mn^2)^3$ (o) $(2st)^3$ (p) $(3p^2q)^2$

3 Simplify.

(a) $y^3 \div y$ (b) $a^4 \div a^3$ (c) $x^5 \div x^5$ (d) $t^7 \div t^3$

(e) $g \div g^2$ (f) $h^3 \div h^5$ (g) $6b^3 \div b$ (h) $10m^3 \div 2m^2$

(i) $8x^8 \div 2x^2$ (j) $16t^3 \div 4t^2$ (k) $15y^6 \div 3y^2$ (l) $9h^2 \div 3h^3$

(m) $xy^2 \div xy$ (n) $m^3n \div mn^2$ (o) $2p^3q \div 3pq^2$ (p) $6r^2s^3 \div 2rs$

4 Simplify.

(a) $\dfrac{t^3}{t^2}$ (b) $\dfrac{g^2}{g^3}$ (c) $\dfrac{m^2 \times m}{m}$ (d) $\dfrac{y^2 \times y^3}{y^4}$

(e) $\dfrac{y \times y^3}{y^2}$ (f) $\dfrac{m^2 \times m^3}{m^6}$ (g) $\dfrac{2t^3 \times t}{t^2}$ (h) $\dfrac{6g^2 \times g}{2g^3}$

Brackets

Some expressions contain brackets.
$2(a + b)$ means $2 \times (a + b)$.

You can multiply out brackets in an expression either by using a diagram or by expanding.

EXAMPLES

1 Multiply out the bracket $2(x + 3)$.

Diagram method
$2(x + 3)$ means $2 \times (x + 3)$.
This can be shown using a rectangle.

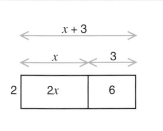

The areas of the two parts are $2x$ and 6.
The total area is $2x + 6$.
$2(x + 3) = 2x + 6$

Expanding
$2(x + 3) = 2 \times x + 2 \times 3$
$\qquad\quad = 2x + 6$

2 Multiply out the bracket $3(4a + 5)$.

Diagram method

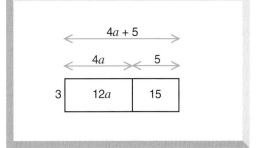

$3(4a + 5) = 12a + 15$

Expanding
$3(4a + 5) = 3 \times 4a + 3 \times 5$
$\qquad\qquad = 12a + 15$

3 Expand $x(x - 5)$.

$x \times x = x^2$ and $x \times -5 = -5x$
$x(x - 5) = x^2 - 5x$

Exercise **12.5**

1 Use the diagrams to multiply out the brackets.

(a)
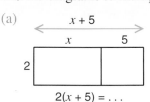

(b)
	$a + 6$	
	a	6

$3(a + 6) = \ldots$

(c)
	$2y + 3$	
	$2y$	3

$4(2y + 3) = \ldots$

2 Draw your own diagrams to multiply out these brackets.
(a) $3(x + 2)$ (b) $2(y + 5)$ (c) $2(2x + 1)$ (d) $3(p + q)$

3 Use the diagrams to multiply out the brackets.

(a)
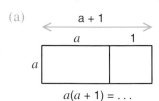

(b)
	$2 + d$	
	2	d

$d(2 + d) = \ldots$

(c)
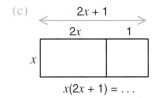

4 Multiply out the brackets by expanding.
(a) $2(x + 4)$ (b) $4(b + 1)$ (c) $4(2x + 1)$ (d) $3(t - 2)$
(e) $4(5 - a)$ (f) $3(2 - 4p)$ (g) $6(b + 2c)$ (h) $3(2m - 5n)$

5 Multiply out the brackets by expanding.
- (a) $x(x + 3)$
- (b) $y(2 + y)$
- (c) $t(t - 5)$
- (d) $g(2g + 3)$
- (e) $m(2 - 3m)$
- (f) $a(3a + 4)$
- (g) $2p(p + 3)$
- (h) $3d(2 - 3d)$
- (i) $2x(x + y)$
- (j) $5y(x - 2y)$

Remember:
Always remove brackets first, then simplify by collecting like terms together.

$$3(t + 4) + 2$$
$$= 3t + 12 + 2 \quad \text{Remove the brackets}$$
$$= 3t + 14 \quad \text{Simplify}$$

6 Multiply out the brackets and simplify.
- (a) $2(x + 1) + 3$
- (b) $3(a + 2) + 5$
- (c) $6(w - 4) + 7$
- (d) $4 + 2(p + 3)$
- (e) $3 + 3(q - 1)$
- (f) $1 + 3(2 - t)$
- (g) $4(z + 2) + z$
- (h) $5(t + 3) + 3t$
- (i) $3(c - 2) - c$
- (j) $2a + 3(a - 3)$
- (k) $y + 2(y - 5)$
- (l) $5x + 3(2 - x)$
- (m) $4(2a + 5) + 3$
- (n) $-2x + 4(3x - 3)$
- (o) $3(p - 5) - p + 4$
- (p) $3a + 2(a + b)$
- (q) $3(x + y) - 2y$
- (r) $2(p - q) - 3q$
- (s) $2x + x(3 - x)$
- (t) $a(a - 3) + a$
- (u) $y(2 - y) + y^2$

7 Remove the brackets and simplify.
- (a) $2(x + 1) + 3(x + 2)$
- (b) $3(a + 1) + 2(a + 5)$
- (c) $4(y + 2) + 5(y + 3)$
- (d) $2(3a + 1) + 3(a + 1)$
- (e) $3(2t + 5) + 5(4t + 3)$
- (f) $3(z + 5) + 2(z - 1)$
- (g) $7(q - 2) + 5(q + 6)$
- (h) $5(x + 3) + 6(x - 3)$
- (i) $8(2e - 1) + 4(e - 2)$
- (j) $2(5d + 4) + 2(d - 1)$
- (k) $m(m - 2) + m(2m - 1)$
- (l) $a(3a + 2) + 2a(a - 3)$

Remember: $\quad (-2) \times (+3) = -6$
$$(-2) \times (-3) = +6$$
so $\quad -2(x + 3) = -2x - 6$
and $\quad -2(x - 3) = -2x + 6$

8 Multiply out the brackets and simplify.
- (a) $-3(x + 2)$
- (b) $-3(x - 2)$
- (c) $-2(y - 5)$
- (d) $-2(3 - x)$
- (e) $-3(5 - y)$
- (f) $-4(1 + a)$
- (g) $5 - 2(a + 1)$
- (h) $5d - 3(d - 2)$
- (i) $4b - 2(3 + b)$
- (j) $-3(2p + 3)$
- (k) $5m - 2(3 + 2m)$
- (l) $2(3d - 1) - d + 3$
- (m) $-a(a - 2)$
- (n) $2d - d(1 + d)$
- (o) $x^2 - x(1 - x) + x$
- (p) $-3g(2g + 3)$
- (q) $t^2 - 2t(3 - 3t)$
- (r) $2m - 2m(m - 3)$

Factorising

Factorising is the opposite operation to removing brackets.
For example: to remove brackets
$$2(x + 5) = 2x + 10$$

To factorise $3x + 6$ we can see that $3x$ and 6 have a **common factor** of 3 so
$$3x + 6 = 3(x + 2)$$

Common factors
The **factors** of a number are all the numbers that will divide exactly into the number.
Factors of 6 are 1, 2, 3 and 6.

A **common factor** is a factor which will divide into two or more numbers.

EXAMPLES

❶ Factorise $4x - 6$.

Each term has a factor of 2.
So the common factor is 2.
$4x - 6 = 2(2x - 3)$

❷ Factorise $x^2 + 3x$.

Each term has a factor of x.
So the common factor is x.
$x^2 + 3x = x(x + 3)$

In some instances the terms will have both a number and a letter as common factors and **both** must be taken out.

EXAMPLE

Factorise $2x^2 - 6x$.

$$2x^2 - 6x = 2x(x - 3)$$

○○○○○○○○○○○○○○

Each term has a factor of 2.
Each term has a factor of x.
So the common factor is $2x$.

Exercise **12.6**

❶ Copy and complete.
(a) $2x + 2y = 2(\ldots + \ldots)$ (b) $3a - 6b = 3(\ldots - \ldots)$ (c) $6m + 8n = 2(\ldots + \ldots)$
(d) $x^2 - 2x = x(\quad\quad)$ (e) $ab + a = a(\quad\quad)$ (f) $2x - xy = x(\quad\quad)$
(g) $2ab - 4a = 2a(\quad\quad)$ (h) $4x^2 + 6x = 2x(\quad\quad)$ (i) $dg - dg^2 = dg(\quad\quad)$

❷ Factorise.
(a) $2a + 2b$ (b) $5x - 5y$ (c) $3d + 6e$ (d) $4m - 2n$
(e) $6a + 9b$ (f) $6a - 8b$ (g) $8t + 12$ (h) $5a - 10$
(i) $4d - 2$ (j) $3 - 9g$ (k) $5 - 20m$ (l) $4k + 4$

❸ Factorise.
(a) $xy - xz$ (b) $fg + gh$ (c) $ab - 2b$ (d) $3q + pq$
(e) $a + ab$ (f) $gh - g$ (g) $a^2 + 3a$ (h) $5t - t^2$
(i) $d - d^2$ (j) $m^2 + m$ (k) $5r^2 - 3r$ (l) $3x^2 + 2x$

❹ Factorise.
(a) $3y + 6$ (b) $t^2 - t$ (c) $2d^2 + 4d$ (d) $3m - 6mn$
(e) $2fg + 4g^2$ (f) $4pq - 8q$ (g) $6y - 15y^2$ (h) $6x^2 + 4xy$
(i) $6n^2 - 2n$ (j) $4ab + 6b$ (k) $\frac{1}{2}a - \frac{1}{2}a^2$ (l) $wx + 2x - x^2$

What you need to know

You should be able to:

- Write simple algebraic expressions.
- Simplify expressions and rules by collecting like terms together,
  e.g. $2d + 3d = 5d$ and $3x + 2 - x + 4 = 2x + 6$
- Multiply simple expressions together.
  e.g. $2a \times a = 2a^2$ and $y \times y \times y = y^3$
- Recall and use these properties of powers:
  Powers of the same base are **added** when terms are **multiplied**.
  Powers of the same base are **subtracted** when terms are **divided**.

  $$a^m \times a^n = a^{m+n}$$
  $$a^m \div a^n = a^{m-n}$$

- Multiply out brackets.
  e.g. $2(x - 5) = 2x - 10$ and $x(x - 5) = x^2 - 5x$
- Factorise expressions.
  e.g. $3x - 6 = 3(x - 2)$ and $x^2 + 5x = x(x + 5)$

1 A lollipop costs t pence.
Write an expression for the cost of 6 lollipops.

2 Tom is x years old.
Naomi is 3 years older than Tom.
How old is Naomi in terms of x?

3 Large sticks of rock cost n pence each.
(a) Write an expression for the cost of 5 large sticks of rock.
(b) A small stick of rock costs 15 pence less than a large stick.
Write an expression for the cost of a small stick of rock.
(c) Alfie buys 2 large sticks of rock and 3 small sticks of rock.
Write an expression for the total cost.
Give your answer in its simplest form.

4 In the triangle PQR, the side PQ has length x centimetres.

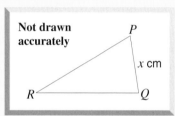

(a) PR is twice the length of PQ.
Write an expression for the length of PR.
(b) QR is 3 cm longer than PQ.
Write an expression for the length of QR.
(c) Write an expression for the perimeter of the triangle.
Give your answer in its simplest form.

5 Write down an expression, in terms of n and g, for the total cost, in pence, of n buns at 18 pence each and 5 bread rolls at g pence each. Edexcel

6 (a) Simplify (i) $n + 1 + n + 2$,
(ii) $2n \times 3n$.
(b) Multiply out and simplify $3 - 2(x - 1)$.
(c) Factorise $3x - 6$.

7 Simplify (a) $ab + 2ba$
(b) $a^2 - a + 3a$
(c) $3(x - 2) - x$

8 (a) A pint of milk costs m pence.
Write an expression for the cost of p pints of milk.
(b) Multiply out and simplify $2 - x + 3(1 - x)$.

9 (a) Simplify (i) $w + w + w$,
(ii) $2w + 5 - w - 3$,
(iii) $w \times w$.
(b) Write an expression, in terms of d, for the perimeter of this shape.

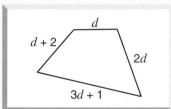

10 Factorise (a) $t^2 - 3t$ (b) $6a + 3ab$

11 Write these algebraic expressions in a simpler way.
(a) $5a + 6a - 7a$
(b) $7a + 3b - 5a - b$
(c) $5(2a + 1) - 3(a - 4)$ Edexcel

12 (a) Simplify $2n + 1 - n + 2n - 6$.
(b) Multiply out and simplify $3(a - 1) - 2(a + 2)$.
(c) Factorise $2x^2 + xy$.

13 Simplify (a) $a \times 2a \times 3a$
(b) $a \times 2b \times 3a \times 4$
(c) $(-2a) \times (+a) \times (-b)$

14 (a) Simplify $7 - 2(x - 3)$.
(b) Factorise $6xy - 2y$.
(c) Simplify $(-5m) \times (-m)$.

15 Simplify
(a) $a^6 \times a^3$ (b) $b^6 \div b^3$ (c) $\dfrac{c^3 \times c}{c^2}$

16 Simplify $\dfrac{9a^3 \times 2b}{6ab}$

17 Factorise (a) $6x - 15$, (b) $y^2 + 7y$.

18 Multiply out the brackets and simplify.
(a) $x^2 - x(1 - x)$ (b) $4 - 3(x + 1)$

19 Simplify
(a) $3y^3 \times 2y^2$ (b) $8t^6 \div 4t^3$ (c) $(2a)^3$

20 (a) Factorise
(i) $6xy - 3y^2$, (ii) $4m^2 + 6m$.
(b) Simplify
(i) $5y^3 \times 2y^2$, (ii) $6x^6 \div 2x^2$.

21 (a) Simplify $x^3 \times x^5$
(b) Simplify $y^6 \div y^2$
(c) Simplify $\dfrac{8w^7}{2w^2 \times w^3}$ Edexcel

Activity

Can you solve these puzzles?

- **Nueve** is a Spanish number.
  If you add 1 to **nueve** you get 10.
  What is **nueve**?

- What number must be put in each shape to make the statements correct?

  $\square + 3 = 8$ $\bigcirc \times 3 = 30$ $2 \times \bigcirc - 3 = 7$

These are all examples of **equations.**
Equations like these can be solved using a method known as **inspection.**
Instead of words or boxes, equations are usually written using letters for the unknown numbers.
Solving an equation means finding the numerical value of the letter which fits the equation.

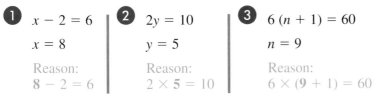

EXAMPLES Solve these equations by inspection.

1 $x - 2 = 6$
$x = 8$
Reason:
$8 - 2 = 6$

2 $2y = 10$
$y = 5$
Reason:
$2 \times 5 = 10$

3 $6(n + 1) = 60$
$n = 9$
Reason:
$6 \times (9 + 1) = 60$

Remember:
A letter or a symbol stands
for an unknown number.
$2y$ means $2 \times y$.
$6(n + 1)$ means $6 \times (n + 1)$.

Exercise **13.1**

1 What number must be put in the box to make each of these statements true?

(a) $\square + 4 = 7$ (b) $15 - \square = 11$ (c) $13 = \square + 4$ (d) $11 = \square - 5$

(e) $3 \times \square = 15$ (f) $24 = 8 \times \square$ (g) $\square \div 2 = 9$ (h) $7 = \square \div 3$

2 What number must be put in the box to make each of these statements true?

(a) $3 \times \square = 18$ (b) $24 = \square \times 4$ (c) $\square \div 2 = 7$

(d) $2 \times \square + 6 = 12$ (e) $15 - 3 \times \square = 9$ (f) $29 = 4 \times \square - 3$

(g) $\dfrac{\square}{2} + 3 = 7$ (h) $\dfrac{\square}{3} - 2 = 3$ (i) $7 - \dfrac{8}{\square} = 5$

3 Solve these equations by inspection.
(a) $a + 7 = 10$ (b) $y - 4 = 4$ (c) $4c = 20$ (d) $8 = \dfrac{d}{2}$

137

4 What is the value of x in the following?

   (a) $x - 2 = 6$ (b) $11 - x = 4$ (c) $2x = 10$

   (d) $7 = \frac{x}{4}$ (e) $3x + 1 = 10$ (f) $4x - 7 = 13$

   (g) $31 = 6x + 7$ (h) $2(x + 3) = 24$ (i) $12 = 3(5 - x)$

5 Solve the following equations.

   (a) $3y + 2 = 8$ (b) $2d - 4 = 6$ (c) $8a + 7 = 79$ (d) $6(a + 1) = 60$

Solving equations by working backwards

I think of a number, multiply it by 3 and add 4.
The answer is 19.
What is the number I thought of?

Remember

Forwards	Backwards
add	subtract
subtract	add
multiply	divide
divide	multiply

Imagine that x is the number I thought of.
The steps of the problem can be shown in a diagram.

Now work backwards, doing the opposite calculation each time.

The number I thought of is 5.

EXAMPLE

An approximate rule for changing temperatures in degrees Celsius to temperatures in degrees Fahrenheit is given by the rule: double C and add on 30

(a)   Find the value of F when C = 6.
(b)   What is the value of C when F = 58?
(c)   Write down a formula for F in terms of C.

(a)   When C = 6.
      Double C: $2 \times 6 = 12$
      Add on 30: $12 + 30 = 42$
      When C = 6, F = 42.

(b)   To find C we must use the rule in reverse.

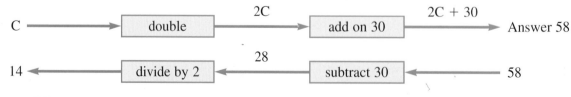

      When F = 58, C = 14.

(c) $F = 2C + 30$

1 I think of a number and then add 4.
The answer is 7.
What is my number?

2 I think of a number and then double it.
The answer is 10.
What is my number?

3 I think of a number, double it and add 4.
The answer is 16.
What is my number?

4 I think of a number, multiply it by 5 and
then add 2. The answer is 17.
What is my number?

5 I think of a number, add 4 then double
the result. The answer is 24.
What is my number?

6 I think of a number, multiply it by 3 and
then subtract 5. The answer is 7.
What is my number?

7 I think of a number, double it and add 3,
then multiply the result by 4.
The answer is 52.
What is my number?

8 Kathryn thinks of a number.
She adds 3 and then doubles the answer.
(a) What number does Kathryn start
with to get an answer of 10?
(b) Kathryn starts with x.
What is her answer?

9 Sarah thinks of a number. She subtracts
2 from it and multiplies the result by 3.
Sarah starts with x.
What is her answer?

10 Lauren uses this rule.

> Start with a number.
> Add 2.
> Multiply by 3.
> Write down the result.

(a) What is the result when Lauren
starts with 5?
(b) What is the result when Lauren
starts with -5?
(c) What is the result when Lauren
starts with x?

11 An approximate rule for changing
kilometres, K, to miles, M, is:

> multiply the number of kilometres
> by 5, then divide by 8

(a) Find the value of M when
(i) $K = 24$,
(ii) $K = 60$,
(iii) $K = 18$.
(b) What is the value of K
when $M = 10$?
(c) What is the value of K
when $M = 32$?
(d) Write down a formula for M in
terms of K.

12 A rule to find the cooking time,
C minutes, of a chicken which weighs k
kilograms, is:

> multiply the weight of the chicken
> by 40 and then add 20

(a) Find the cooking time for a chicken
which weighs 3 kg.
(b) Find the weight of a chicken which
has a cooking time of
100 minutes.
(c) Write a formula for C in terms
of k.

13 The cost of a taxi journey is:

> £3 plus
> £2 for each kilometre travelled

(a) Alex travels 5 km by taxi.
How much does it cost?
(b) A taxi journey of k kilometres costs
£C.
Write a formula for the cost, C, in
terms of k.

14 The cost of hiring a ladder is given by:

> £12 per day,
> plus a delivery charge of £8

(a) Bill hired a ladder for 3 days.
How much did he pay?
(b) Sam hired a ladder for 6 days.
How much did he pay?
(c) Fred hired a ladder for x days.
Write down a formula for the total
cost, £C, in terms of x.

The balance method

It is not always easy to solve equations by inspection.
Many equations are harder to solve than those in Exercise 13.1.
To solve harder equations a better method has to be used.
Here is a method that works a bit like a balance.

These scales are balanced.

You can add the same amount to both sides
and they still balance.

You can subtract the same amount from both sides
and they still balance.

You can double (or halve) the amount on both
sides and they still balance.

Equations work in the same way.
If you do the same to both sides of an equation, it is still true.

EXAMPLES   Use the balance method to solve these equations. Explain what you are doing.

1 Solve $d - 13 = -5$.

$d - 13 = -5$
Add 13 to both sides.
$d = 8$

2 Solve $-4a = 20$.

$-4a = 20$
Divide both sides by -4.
$a = -5$

> The aim is to find the numerical
> value of the letter, by ending up
> with **one letter** on one side of the
> equation and a **number** on the
> other side of the equation.

3 Solve $5 - 4n = -1$.

$5 - 4n = -1$
Subtract 5 from both sides.
$-4n = -6$
Divide both sides by -4.
$n = 1.5$

4 Solve $\frac{1}{2} x - 7 = -1$.

$\frac{1}{2} x - 7 = -1$
Add 7 to both sides.
$\frac{1}{2} x = 6$
Multiply both sides by 2.
$x = 12$

Look at the examples carefully.
The steps taken to solve the equations are explained.
Notice that:
Doing the same to both sides means:
    adding the **same number** to both sides,
    subtracting the **same number** from both sides,
    dividing both sides by the **same number**,
    multiplying both sides by the **same number**.

Exercise 13.3

1   Use the balance method to solve these equations.
    Write down the steps that you use to solve each equation.

(a) $x + 5 = 11$ (b) $e + 9 = 24$ (c) $d + 6 = 17$

(d) $q - 5 = 2$ (e) $n - 7 = 9$ (f) $y - 3 = 14$

(g) $5a = 20$ (h) $8p = 24$ (i) $\frac{1}{2}p = 4$

(j) $\frac{x}{3} = 5$ (k) $\frac{6}{a} = 3$ (l) $\frac{16}{y} = 2$

(m) $2p + 1 = 9$ (n) $4t - 1 = 11$ (o) $3h - 7 = 14$

(p) $3 + 4b = 11$ (q) $5d - 8 = 42$ (r) $2x + 3 = 15$

2   Solve these equations.
    There is no need to explain your working if you are confident of what you are doing.

(a) $5c + 7 = 42$ (b) $7x = 28$ (c) $8y - 5 = 27$

(d) $3x + 5 = 11$ (e) $4b + 8 = 32$ (f) $6x - 9 = 15$

(g) $6k - 7 = 5$ (h) $7b + 4 = 25$ (i) $\frac{r}{4} + 1 = 7$

(j) $\frac{1}{2}z + 2 = 7$ (k) $\frac{1}{4}t - 1 = 4$ (l) $\frac{4}{a} + 1 = 3$

3   Solve these equations.
    The solution will not always be a whole number.

(a) $5x = -10$ (b) $2y + 7 = 1$ (c) $4t + 10 = 2$

(d) $5 - a = 7$ (e) $2 - d = 5$ (f) $3 - 2g = 9$

(g) $4t = 2$ (h) $2x = 15$ (i) $5d = 7$

(j) $4a - 5 = 1$ (k) $3 + 5g = 4$ (l) $2b - 5 = 4$

4   Solve these equations.

(a) $p + 3 = -7$ (b) $6a = 15$ (c) $32 - 3t = 11$

(d) $-3 = 17 - 5n$ (e) $8c + 4 = 1.6$ (f) $2h + 1.7 = 3.1$

(g) $3 + 5x = 18$ (h) $5y + 6 = 2$ (i) $-\frac{1}{2}y + 13 = 7$

(j) $-2 = 5m + 13$ (k) $\frac{t}{3} + 21 = 15$ (l) $12 + \frac{v}{3} = 15$

(m) $\frac{1}{3}t = -0.3$ (n) $-6p - 1 = 8$ (o) $1 - \frac{x}{6} = 4$

Equations with brackets

Equations can include brackets.
Before using the balance method any brackets must be
simplified by multiplying out.
This is called **expanding**.
Once the brackets have been removed the balance method
can be used as before.

> **Remember:**
> $2(x + 3)$ means $2 \times (x + 3)$
> $2(x + 3) = 2 \times x + 2 \times 3$
> $= 2x + 6$
>
> $3(4a - 5) = 12a - 15$

Exercise 13.4

1 Solve.
(a) $2(x + 3) = 12$
(b) $4(a + 1) = 12$
(c) $5(t + 4) = 30$
(d) $2(y + 4) = 8$
(e) $3(e + 2) = 21$
(f) $6(3 + x) = 30$

2 Solve.
(a) $3(p - 2) = 9$
(b) $6(c - 2) = 24$
(c) $2(x - 1) = 4$
(d) $4(y - 3) = 24$
(e) $2(g - 3) = 16$
(f) $8(q - 3) = 40$

3 Solve.
(a) $3(a + 1) = 15$
(b) $2(b - 2) = 8$
(c) $4(c + 2) = 12$
(d) $6(d - 3) = 36$
(e) $7(2 + e) = 49$
(f) $30 = 5(f + 2)$

4 Solve.
(a) $3(2w + 1) = 15$
(b) $2(4s + 5) = 34$
(c) $4(1 + 3x) = 28$
(d) $6(3g - 7) = 12$
(e) $4(2q - 1) = 28$
(f) $8(3t - 5) = 32$
(g) $3(2w + 1) = 27$
(h) $4(7 - 2x) = 4$
(i) $25 = 5(3y - 10)$

5 Solve these equations. The solution will not always be a whole number.
(a) $3(p + 2) = 3$
(b) $2(3 - d) = 10$
(c) $2(1 - 3g) = 14$
(d) $2(x - 5) = 7$
(e) $5(y + 1) = 7$
(f) $5 = 2(1 + 3t)$
(g) $5 = 2(2t - 1)$
(h) $3(2a - 3) = 6$
(i) $5(m - 2) = 3$

Equations with letters on both sides

In some questions letters appear on both sides of the equation.

EXAMPLES

1 Solve $3x + 1 = x + 7$.

$3x + 1 = x + 7$
Subtract 1 from both sides.
$3x = x + 6$
Subtract x from both sides.
$2x = 6$
Divide both sides by 2.
$x = 3$

2 Solve $4(3 + 2x) = 5(x + 2)$.

$4(3 + 2x) = 5(x + 2)$
$12 + 8x = 5x + 10$
$8x = 5x - 2$
$3x = -2$
$x = -\frac{2}{3}$

Exercise **13.5**

1 Solve the following equations.

(a) $3x = 20 - x$ (b) $5q = 12 - q$ (c) $2t = 15 - 3t$

(d) $5e - 9 = 2e$ (e) $3g - 8 = g$ (f) $y + 3 = 5 - y$

(g) $4x + 1 = x + 7$ (h) $7k + 3 = 3k + 7$ (i) $3a - 1 = a + 7$

(j) $3p - 1 = 2p + 5$ (k) $6m - 1 = m + 9$ (l) $3d - 5 = 5 + d$

(m) $2y + 1 = y + 6$ (n) $3 + 5u = 2u + 12$ (o) $4q + 3 = q + 3$

2 Solve.

(a) $3d = 32 - d$ (b) $3q = 12 - q$ (c) $3c + 2 = 10 - c$

(d) $4t + 2 = 17 - t$ (e) $4w + 1 = 13 - 2w$ (f) $2e - 3 = 12 - 3e$

(g) $2g + 5 = 25 - 2g$ (h) $2z - 6 = 14 - 3z$ (i) $5m + 2 = 20 + 2m$

(j) $5a - 4 = 3a + 6$ (k) $3 + 4x = 15 + x$ (l) $6y - 11 = y + 4$

3 Solve these equations.
The solution will not always be a whole number.

(a) $3m + 8 = m$ (b) $2 - 4t = 12 + t$ (c) $5p - 3 = 3p - 7$

(d) $5x - 7 = 3x$ (e) $3 + 5a = a + 5$ (f) $2b + 7 = 11 - 3b$

(g) $4 - 4y = y$ (h) $7 + 3d = 10 - d$ (i) $f - 6 = 3f + 1$

4 Solve.

(a) $4t + 3 = t - 12$ (b) $3y + 1 = 9 - y$ (c) $12s = 2s + 5$

(d) $2p + 3 = 4 + 5p$ (e) $6a - 2.5 = a + 6.5$ (f) $8c + 0.7 = 1.8 - 2c$

(g) $4 - 1\frac{1}{2}p = \frac{1}{2}p - 6$ (h) $x = \frac{1}{2}x - 3$ (i) $\frac{1}{2}x - 7 = \frac{1}{4}x + 1$

5 Solve.

(a) $3(n + 5) + n = 23$ (b) $3(2z - 5) = z + 15$

(c) $4(2w + 3) + 7 = 43$ (d) $m + 2(m + 1) = 14$

(e) $2(3h - 4) = 3(h + 1) - 5$ (f) $2(3 - 2x) = 2(6 - x)$

(g) $2(3w - 1) + 4w = 28$ (h) $2(y + 4) + 3(2y - 5) = 5$

(i) $3(2v + 3) = 5 - 4(3 - v)$ (j) $5c - 2(4c - 9) = 5 + 5(2 - c)$

(k) $5(x + 2) + 2(2x - 1) = 7(x - 4)$ (l) $3(x - 4) = 5(2x - 3) - 2(3x - 5)$

Equations with fractions

You have already met some equations with fractions.
This section deals with harder equations with fractions.

For example: $\frac{3}{4}x = \frac{2}{5}$

With equations like this, it is easier to get rid of the fractions first.
To do this multiply both sides of the equation by the lowest common multiple of the denominators of the fractions.

What part of the fraction is the denominator?

The multiples of 4 are: 4, 8, 12, 16, **20**, . . .
The multiples of 5 are: 5, 10, 15, **20**, . . .
The lowest common multiple of 4 and 5 is 20.
So, the first step is to multiply both sides of the equation by 20.

$$\frac{3}{4}x \times 20 = \frac{2}{5} \times 20$$

This is the same as:

$$x \times \frac{3}{4} \times 20 = \frac{2}{5} \times 20$$

$$15x = 8$$

Divide both sides by 15.

$$x = \frac{8}{15}$$

> **Remember:**
> $\frac{3}{4} \times 20$ is the same as $\frac{3}{4}$ of 20.
> To find $\frac{3}{4}$ of 20:
> $20 \div 4 = 5$ gives $\frac{1}{4}$ of 20.
> $5 \times 3 = 15$ gives $\frac{3}{4}$ of 20.
> So, $\frac{3}{4} \times 20 = 15$.

1 Solve $\frac{2}{5}x = 6$.

$$\frac{2}{5}x = 6$$

Multiply both sides by 5.

$$5 \times \frac{2}{5}x = 5 \times 6$$
$$2x = 30$$
$$x = 15$$

2 Solve $\frac{2x}{4} = \frac{2}{5}$.

$$\frac{2x}{4} = \frac{2}{5}$$

Multiply both sides by 20.

$$20 \times \frac{2x}{4} = 20 \times \frac{2}{5}$$
$$5 \times 2x = 4 \times 2$$
$$10x = 8$$
$$x = \frac{4}{5}$$

3 Solve $\frac{x}{2} + \frac{2x}{3} = 7$.

$$\frac{x}{2} + \frac{2x}{3} = 7$$

Multiply both sides by 6.

$$6 \times \frac{x}{2} + 6 \times \frac{2x}{3} = 6 \times 7$$
$$3x + 4x = 42$$
$$7x = 42$$
$$x = 6$$

4 Solve $\frac{x-1}{3} = \frac{x+1}{4}$.

$$\frac{x-1}{3} = \frac{x+1}{4}$$

Multiply both sides by 12.

$$4(x-1) = 3(x+1)$$
$$4x - 4 = 3x + 3$$
$$4x = 3x + 7$$
$$x = 7$$

Exercise **13.6**

1 What would you multiply each of these equations by to get rid of the fractions?

(a) $\frac{2}{3}a = 5$ (b) $\frac{5}{8} = \frac{3b}{4}$ (c) $\frac{x+3}{4} = \frac{x-7}{3}$ (d) $\frac{2d}{5} + \frac{d}{3} = 3$

2 Solve these equations.

(a) $\frac{2}{3}x = 4$ (b) $\frac{3}{4}y = 6$ (c) $\frac{5a}{6} = 20$ (d) $\frac{2d}{5} = -4$

(e) $\frac{a}{8} = \frac{3}{4}$ (f) $\frac{x}{3} = \frac{3}{2}$ (g) $\frac{2m}{8} = -\frac{3}{6}$ (h) $\frac{3t}{4} = \frac{1}{3}$

3 Solve.

(a) $\frac{h+1}{4} = 3$ (b) $\frac{2x-1}{3} = 5$ (c) $\frac{3a+4}{5} = -1$

(d) $\frac{7-d}{4} = \frac{5}{2}$ (e) $\frac{2x-1}{2} = \frac{1}{4}$ (f) $\frac{2a+1}{2} = \frac{3}{5}$

(g) $\frac{4-d}{3} = \frac{1}{-2}$ (h) $\frac{2-3h}{3} = -\frac{5}{6}$ (i) $\frac{2(4x-3)}{5} = -6$

(j) $\frac{x+2}{5} = \frac{3-x}{4}$ (k) $\frac{a-1}{2} = \frac{a+1}{3}$ (l) $\frac{2x-1}{6} = \frac{2-x}{3}$

4 Solve.

(a) $\frac{x}{2} + \frac{x}{4} = 1$ (b) $\frac{x}{2} - \frac{x}{3} = 2$ (c) $\frac{x}{4} + \frac{3x}{8} = -1$

(d) $\frac{2x}{3} - \frac{x}{6} = -2$ (e) $\frac{x+1}{2} + \frac{x-1}{3} = 1$ (f) $\frac{x+2}{3} - \frac{x+1}{4} = 2$

(g) $\frac{11-x}{4} = 2 - x$ (h) $\frac{x+2}{2} + \frac{x-1}{5} = \frac{1}{10}$ (i) $\frac{2x-3}{6} + \frac{x+2}{3} = \frac{5}{2}$

Writing equations

So far, in this chapter, you have been given equations and asked to solve them.
The next step is to **write equations** (or **form equations**) using the information given in a problem.
The equations can then be solved in the usual way.
You may also be asked to use the solution to the equation to answer questions related to the initial problem.

> **Remember:** An **expression** is just an answer using letters and numbers.
> An **equation** is similar to a formula. It always has an equals sign.

EXAMPLES

1 The triangle has sides of length x cm,
$(x + 1)$ cm and $(2x - 3)$ cm.

(a) Write an expression, in terms of x,
for the perimeter of the triangle.
Give your answer in its simplest form.

(b) The triangle has a perimeter of 18 cm.
By forming an equation find the value of x.

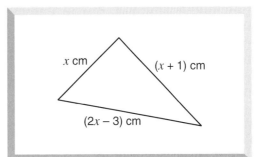

(a) The perimeter of the triangle is
$$x + (x + 1) + (2x - 3) \text{ cm}$$
$$= 4x - 2 \text{ cm}$$

(b) The perimeter of the triangle is 18 cm,
so $\quad 4x - 2 = 18$
$$4x = 20$$
$$x = 5$$

2

Birthday Party

Specials

£20, plus £5 per person

(a) Nick has a birthday party for 12 people.
How much does it cost?

(b) Tony has a birthday party for x people.
Write a formula for the cost £T, in terms of x.

(c) Jean pays £100 for her birthday party.
How many people went to the party?

(a) Nick's birthday costs: £20 + 12 × £5
$$= £80$$

(b) Cost for x people in £ $= x × 5 = 5x$
Total cost in £ $\quad = 20 + 5x$
Total cost is £T
So formula is $\quad T = 20 + 5x$

(c) Using the formula $T = 20 + 5x$.
Jean's birthday costs £100, so $T = 100$.
$$100 = 20 + 5x$$
$$5x = 80$$
$$x = 16$$
16 people went to Jean's party.

1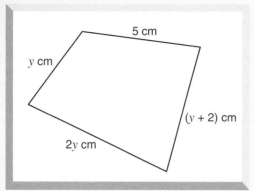

(a) Write an expression, in terms of y, for the perimeter of this shape. Give your answer in its simplest form.

(b) The shape has a perimeter of 39 cm. By forming an equation find the value of y.

2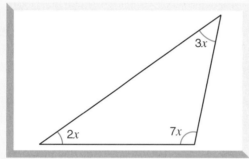

(a) Write an expression, in terms of x, for the sum of the angles of the triangle. Give your answer in its simplest form.

(b) The sum of the angles is 180°. By forming an equation find the value of x.

3 The length of a rectangle is x cm. The width of the rectangle is 4 cm less than the length.

(a) Write an expression, in terms of x, for the width of the rectangle.

(b) Write an expression for the perimeter of the rectangle in terms of x.

(c) The perimeter of the rectangle is 20 cm. By forming an equation find the value of x.

4 A teacher uses this rule to work out the number of exercise books he needs for Year 11 students.

3 books per student, plus 50 extra books

(a) This year there are 120 students in Year 11. How many books are needed?

(b) Using b for the number of books and n for the number of students, write down the teacher's rule for b in terms of n.

(c) For the next Year 11, he will need 470 books. How many students will be in Year 11 next year?

5

CARPET CLEANER HIRE

£15 PER DAY

Plus fixed delivery charge of £6

(a) How much does it cost to hire the carpet cleaner for 3 days?

(b) Using T for the total cost in £, and d for the number of days hired, write a formula for T in terms of d.

(c) Sarah paid a total of £96 to hire the carpet cleaner. For how many days did she hire the carpet cleaner?

6 Scaffolding can be hired. The hire charge is calculated using this formula:

Forty-five pounds per day plus a fixed charge of seventy pounds.

(a) How much would it cost to hire scaffolding for 5 days?

(b) Using C for the total cost in £, and n for the number of days, write a formula for C in terms of n.

(c) A builder paid £475 altogether to hire some scaffolding. For how many days did he hire the scaffolding?

7

> I think of a number.
> I multiply it by 3.
> Then I take away 7.

(a) Gail starts with the number 5.
What is her answer?

(b) What number should Gail start with to get an answer of 2?

(c) Using A for the answer, and x for the starting number, write a formula for A in terms of x.

(d) Use your formula to find the value of x when $A = 35$.

8 The cost of a pencil is x pence.
The cost of a pen is 10 pence more than a pencil.

(a) Write down, in terms of x, the cost of a pen.

(b) Write down, in terms of x, the total cost of a pencil and two pens.
Give your answer in its simplest form.

(c) The total cost of a pencil and two pens is 65 pence.
Form an equation in x and solve it to find the cost of a pencil.

9 (a) Write an expression, in terms of x, for the perimeter of this shape.

(b) The perimeter is 58 cm.
Find the value of x.

(c) What is the length of the longest side of the shape?

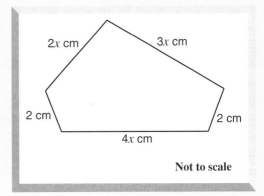

Not to scale

10 (a) Write down a simplified expression, in terms of x, for the perimeter of the triangle.

(b) The perimeter is 59 cm.
Write down an equation and solve it to find the value of x.

(c) Use your answer to find the length of each side of the triangle.

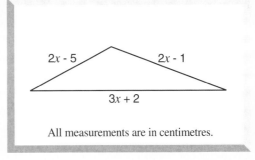

All measurements are in centimetres.

11 Geoffrey knows that the sum of the angles of this shape adds up to 540°.

(a) Write down an equation in x.

(b) Use your equation to find the size of the largest angle.

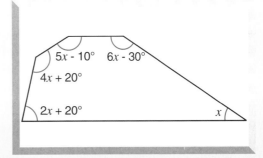

12 (a) Write an expression, in terms of x, for the area of the rectangle.

(b) The rectangle has an area of $30\,\text{cm}^2$.
By forming an equation find the value of x.

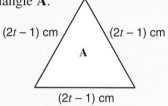

(2x + 1) cm

3 cm

13 (a) Write an expression, in terms of t, for the perimeter of triangle **A**.
Give your answer in its simplest form.

(2t – 1) cm   (2t – 1) cm

A

(2t – 1) cm

(b) Write an expression, in terms of t, for the perimeter of triangle **B**.
Give your answer in its simplest form.

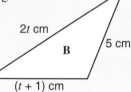

2t cm

B   5 cm

(c) The perimeters of both triangles are the same.
By forming an equation find the value of t.

(t + 1) cm

14 (a) Write down an expression, in terms of x, for the perimeter of the rectangle.

(b) The perimeter of the rectangle is equal to the perimeter of the square.
Form an equation and find the value of x.

(c) What is the perimeter of the rectangle, in centimetres?

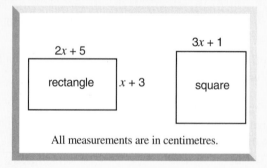

3x + 1

2x + 5

rectangle   x + 3

square

All measurements are in centimetres.

15 The areas of these rectangles are equal.

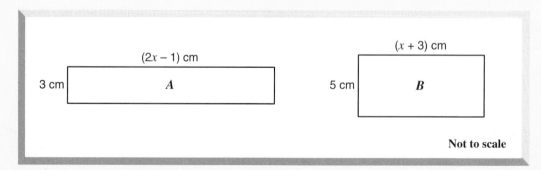

(2x – 1) cm

3 cm   **A**

(x + 3) cm

5 cm   **B**

Not to scale

By forming and solving an equation in x, find the area of A.

What you need to know

- The solution of an equation is the value of the unknown letter that fits the equation.

You should be able to:

- Solve simple equations by inspection.
  e.g. $x + 2 = 5$, $x - 3 = 7$, $2x = 10$, $\frac{x}{4} = 12$
- Solve simple equations by inspection by working backwards.
- Use the balance method to solve equations which are difficult to solve by inspection.
- Solve equations with unknowns on both sides of the equals sign.
  e.g. $3x + 1 = x + 7$
- Solve equations with brackets.
  e.g. $4(3 + 2x) = 5(x + 2)$
- Solve equations with fractions.

  e.g. $\frac{1}{4}x + 1 = 7$, $\frac{x+3}{4} = 2$, $\frac{x-1}{3} + \frac{x+1}{2} = \frac{1}{6}$

- Write, or form, equations using the information given in a problem.

Review Exercise

1 What number must be put in the box to make each of these statements correct?

(a) $\boxed{} + 5 = 9$ (b) $7 - \boxed{} = 4$

(c) $3 \times \boxed{} = 18$ (d) $\boxed{} \times 2 - 3 = 5$

2 Solve these equations.
(a) $a - 3 = 7$ (b) $6a = 30$

3 Solve these equations.
(a) $y + 3 = 5$ (b) $2t + 8 = 2$
(c) $4g = 2$ (d) $5x - 1 = 2$

4 Solve these equations.
(a) $3y + 2 = 11$ (b) $2y + 5 = 2 - y$

5 Solve.
(a) $5m - 7 = 28$,   (b) $3t + 3 = 5t - 7$.

6 Solve these equations.
(a) $2a + 3 = 7$ (b) $3(b + 1) = 15$
(c) $5c + 6 = 2c - 9$ *Edexcel*

7 Solve.
(a) $3(a - 5) = 6a$ (b) $5(x + 2) = 14$
(c) $x + 8 = 3(2 - x)$

8 Solve the equation $\frac{2x - 3}{5} = -1$.

9 Solve.
(a) $\frac{3}{4x} = \frac{1}{8}$ (b) $\frac{x-2}{2} = \frac{x+3}{3}$

10 Wilma works h hours a week.
Wilma is paid £x per hour.
Wilma is also paid a loyalty bonus of £20 a week.

(a) Write a formula for her total weekly pay, £T, in terms of h and x.
(b) Each week Wilma works 35 hours and is paid £230.
How much does Wilma get paid per hour?

11 The cost of printing business cards is:

> £5 plus 15 pence a card

(a) What is the total cost of printing 80 cards?
(b) Write a formula for the total cost, £C, of printing n cards.
(c) Fred pays £77 for some business cards to be printed.
How many cards did he have printed?

12 Bob uses this rule.

> Start with a number.
> Multiply it by 3.
> Take away 5.
> Write down the answer.

(a) What is the answer if Bob starts with x?
(b) What is the answer if Bob starts with -1?
(c) What number must Bob start with to get an answer of 16?

13 The lengths, in centemetres, of the sides of a quadrilateral are: x, $4x$, 11 and 13.

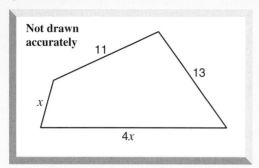

Not drawn accurately

11

13

x

$4x$

(a) Write an expression, in terms of x, for the perimeter of the quadrilateral. Give your answer in its simplest form.

The perimeter of the quadrilateral is 49 cm.
(b) By forming an equation find the value of x.

14 A bottle of drink costs x pence. A cake costs 7 pence more than a drink.
(a) Write down, in terms of x,
   (i) the cost of a cake,
   (ii) the total cost of two drinks and a cake.
(b) The total cost of two drinks and a cake is 97 pence.
Form an equation in x and solve it to find the cost of a cake.

15 A cracker costs n pence. A party hat costs 7 pence less than a cracker.

(a) Write an expression for the cost of a party hat.
(b) The cost of 10 crackers and 5 party hats is £3.40.
By forming an equation in n find the cost of a party hat.

16 The diagram shows a rectangle with length $3x + 2$ and width $2x$.

$3x + 2$

$2x$

All measurements are given in centimetres.
The perimeter of the rectangle is P centimetres.
The area of the rectangle is A square centimetres.
(a) Write down an expression in its simplest form, in terms of x, for
   (i) P, (ii) A.

$P = 44$.
(b) Work out the value of A.   Edexcel

17 This picture shows some packets of rice in the pans of a weighing machine.
Each packet of rice weighs x kg.

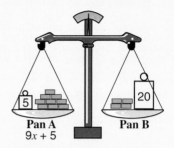

Pan A
$9x + 5$

Pan B

In pan **A** there are 9 packets of rice and a weight of 5 kg.
An expression for the total weight in kg in Pan **A** is $9x + 5$.
An expression for the total weight in kg in Pan **B** is $4x + 20$.
The total weight in each pan is the same.

(a) Write down an equation in terms of x to represent this information.
(b) Use your equation to calculate the weight, x kg, of one packet of rice.   Edexcel

18

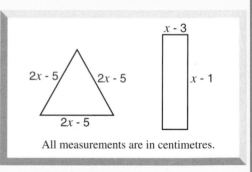

$x - 3$

$2x - 5$ $2x - 5$

$x - 1$

$2x - 5$

All measurements are in centimetres.

(a) Write down simplified expressions for the following, in terms of x.
   (i) The perimeter of the triangle.
   (ii) The perimeter of the rectangle.
(b) The perimeter of the triangle is equal to the perimeter of the rectangle.
   (i) Write down an equation in x.
   (ii) Use your equation to find the length of a side of the triangle.

CHAPTER 14

Formulae

Writing expressions and formulae

Algebra can be used in lots of situations.

The grid shows the numbers from 1 to 50.
An **L** shape has been drawn on the grid.
It is called L_{14} because the lowest number is 14.

What is the sum of the numbers in L_{14}?

The **L** shape can be moved to different parts of the grid.
We can find the sum of the numbers for each shape.

1	2	3	4	5	6	7	8	9	10
11	12	13	14	15	16	17	18	19	20
21	22	23	24	25	26	27	28	29	30
31	32	33	34	35	36	37	38	39	40
41	42	43	44	45	46	47	48	49	50

A formula for the sum of the numbers, S_n,
can be written in terms of n for shape L_n.
$S_n = n + (n + 10) + (n + 20) + (n + 21)$
$S_n = 4n + 51$

n	
$n + 10$	
$n + 20$	$n + 21$

An **expression** is just an answer using letters and numbers.

A **formula** is an algebraic rule. It always has an equals sign.

EXAMPLES

1 A fence is L metres long.
An extra 50 metres is put on one end.
Write an **expression** for the total length of the fence.

The fence is now $(L + 50)$ metres long.

2 Boxes of matches each contain 48 matches.
Write down a **formula** for the number of matches, m, in n boxes.

$m = 48 \times n$

This could be written as $m = 48n$.

Exercise 14.1

1 A pencil costs y pence.
   (a) What is the cost of 5 pencils?
   (b) A ruler costs 8 pence more than a pencil.
       What is the cost of a ruler?

2 Egg boxes hold 12 eggs each.
How many eggs are there in e boxes?

3 I am a years old.
   (a) How old will I be in 1 years time?
   (b) How old was I four years ago?
   (c) How old will I be in n years time?

4 A child is making a tower with toy bricks.
He has b bricks in his tower.
Write an expression for the number of bricks in the tower after he takes 3 bricks from the top.

5 David is h cm tall.
Sue is 12 cm taller than David.
Write down an expression for Sue's height in terms of h.

6 John has d CDs.
   (a) Carol has twice as many CDs as John.
       Write down an expression for the number of CDs that Carol has in terms of d.
   (b) Fred has 5 more CDs than Carol.
       Write down an expression for the number of CDs that Fred has in terms of d.

7 A packet of biscuits costs y pence.
Write down a formula for the cost, P pence, of another packet which costs
(a) five pence more than the first packet,
(b) two pence less than the first packet,
(c) twice the cost of the first packet.

8 David is d years old.
Copy and complete this table to show the ages, A, of these people.

Name	Clue	Age
Alec	3 years older than David.	$A = d + 3$
Ben	2 years younger than David.	
Charlotte	Twice as old as David.	
Erica	Half David's age.	

9 Write a formula for the perimeter, P, for each of these shapes in terms of the letters given.

(a)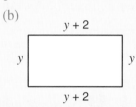

(b)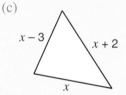

(c)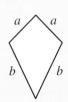

(d)

10 A caravan costs £25 per day to hire.
Write a formula for the cost, C, in £'s, to hire the caravan for d days.

11 The grid shows the numbers from 1 to 50.
An **L** shape has been drawn on the grid.
It is called $\mathbf{L_{16}}$ because the lowest number is 16.

Calculate the sum of the numbers in
(a) $\mathbf{L_1}$ (b) $\mathbf{L_{33}}$ (c) $\mathbf{L_{22}}$
(d) This diagram shows $\mathbf{L_n}$.

1	2	3	4	5	6	7	8	9	10
11	12	13	14	15	16	17	18	19	20
21	22	23	24	25	26	27	28	29	30
31	32	33	34	35	36	37	38	39	40
41	42	43	44	45	46	47	48	49	50

Copy and complete the **L** shape in terms of n.

(e) Write a formula for the sum of the numbers, $\mathbf{S_n}$, in terms of n, for shape $\mathbf{L_n}$.
Write your formula in its simplest form.

12 The grid shows the numbers from 1 to 50.
A **T** shape has been drawn on the grid.
It is called $\mathbf{T_{23}}$ because the lowest number is 23.

Calculate the sum of the numbers in
(a) $\mathbf{T_{16}}$ (b) $\mathbf{T_{28}}$ (c) $\mathbf{T_2}$

(d) The diagram on the right shows $\mathbf{T_n}$.
Copy and complete the **T** shape in terms of n.

(e) Write a formula for the sum of the numbers, $\mathbf{S_n}$,
in terms of n, for shape $\mathbf{T_n}$.
Write your answer in its simplest form.

1	2	3	4	5	6	7	8	9	10
11	12	13	14	15	16	17	18	19	20
21	22	23	24	25	26	27	28	29	30
31	32	33	34	35	36	37	38	39	40
41	42	43	44	45	46	47	48	49	50

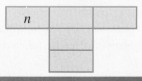

Using formulae

The formula for the perimeter of a rectangle is $P = 2L + 2W$.
By **substituting** values for the length, L, and the width, W, you can calculate the value of P.

$P = 2L + 2W$
When $L = 3$ and $W = 5$,
$P = 2 \times 3 + 2 \times 5$
$ = 6 + 10$
$ = 16$

EXAMPLES

1 A joiner earns £W for working H hours.
Her boss uses the formula
$W = 5H + 35$ to calculate her wage.
Find her wage if she works for 40 hours.

$W = 5 \times 40 + 35$
$ = 200 + 35$
$ = £235$

2 $H = 3(4x - y)$. Find the value of H
when $x = 5$ and $y = 7$.

$H = 3(4x - y)$
$ = 3(4 \times 5 - 7)$
$ = 3(20 - 7)$
$ = 3(13)$
$ = 39$

3 $A = pq - r$
What is the value of A when   (a) $p = 2$, $q = -2$ and $r = 3$,
(b) $p = 3$, $q = 2$ and $r = -2$?

(a) $A = 2 \times (-2) - 3$
$ = -4 - 3$
$ = -7$

(b) $A = 3 \times 2 - (-2)$
$ = 6 + 2$
$ = 8$

Exercise 14.2

Do not use a calculator for questions 1 to 15.

1 Find the value of $x + 3$ when
(a) $x = 2$ (b) $x = 7$ (c) $x = -2$

2 Find the value of $4a$ when
(a) $a = 5$ (b) $a = 7$ (c) $a = -3$

3 Find the value of $p - 3$ when
(a) $p = 4$ (b) $p = 5$ (c) $p = -3$

4 Find the value of $5 - d$ when
(a) $d = 3$ (b) $d = 7$ (c) $d = -3$

5 Find the value of $2x + 3$ when
(a) $x = 5$ (b) $x = -5$

6 Find the value of $4 - 2y$ when
(a) $y = 3$ (b) $y = -3$

7 Find the value of $4x$ when
(a) $x = \frac{1}{2}$ (b) $x = \frac{1}{4}$ (c) $x = \frac{1}{8}$

8 Find the value of $5y$ when
(a) $y = 0.2$ (b) $y = 0.3$ (c) $y = 0.5$

9 Find the value of $2x + 5$ when
(a) $x = \frac{1}{2}$ (b) $x = 0.4$

10 Find the value of $4y - 1$ when
(a) $y = \frac{1}{4}$ (b) $y = 0.5$

11 Find the value of $5 - 3g$ when
(a) $g = 0.5$ (b) $g = \frac{1}{3}$

12 $F = 5(v + 6)$.
What is the value of F when $v = 9$?

13 $V = 2(7 + 2x)$.
What is the value of V when $x = 3$?

14 $P = 3(5 - 2d)$.
What is the value of P when $d = 4$?

15 $C = 8(p + q)$.
What is the value of C when
(a) $p = 5$ and $q = 8$,
(b) $p = 6$ and $q = -2$?

16 $S = ax + 4$.

What is the value of S when
(a) $a = 12$ and $x = 3$,
(b) $a = 3$ and $x = -2$,
(c) $a = 5$ and $x = 0.4$?

17 $T = a(x + 4)$.

What is the value of T when
(a) $a = 5$ and $x = 3$,
(b) $a = 2$ and $x = -5$,
(c) $a = -3$ and $x = 2$,
(d) $a = -3$ and $x = -6$?

18 $K = ab + c$.

Work out the value of K when
(a) $a = 3$, $b = -2$ and $c = 5$,
(b) $a = 5$, $b = 3$ and $c = -2$.

19 $L = xy - z$.

Work out the value of L when
(a) $x = 2$, $y = 3$ and $z = -4$,
(b) $x = -4$, $y = 2$ and $z = 3$.

20 The number of matches, M, needed to make a pattern of P pentagons is given by the formula $M = 4P + 1$.
Find the number of matches needed to make 8 pentagons.

21 The distance, d metres, travelled by a lawn mower in t minutes is given by the formula: $d = 24t$.
Find the distance travelled by the lawn mower in:
(a) 4 minutes, (b) 30 minutes,
(c) 90 seconds.

22 Convert these temperatures from Fahrenheit to Centigrade using the formula:
$C = (F - 32) \div 1.8$
(a) $14°F$ (b) $-4°F$
(c) $-22°F$ (d) $-40°F$

23 Convert these temperatures from Centigrade to Fahrenheit using the formula:
$F = C \times 1.8 + 32$
(a) $10°C$ (b) $-10°C$
(c) $-30°C$ (d) $-40°C$

24 $T = 45W + 30$ is used to calculate the time in minutes needed to cook a joint of beef weighing W kilograms.
How many minutes are needed to cook a joint weighing $2.4\,kg$?

25 The voltage, V volts, in a circuit with resistance, R ohms, and current, I amps, is given by the formula $V = IR$.
Find the voltage in a circuit when $I = 12$ and $R = 20$.

26 A simple formula for the motion of a car is $F = ma + R$.
Find F when $m = 500$, $a = 0.2$ and $R = 4000$.

27 The cost, £C, of n units of gas is calculated using the formula $C = 0.08n + 3.5$.
Calculate the cost of 458 units of gas.

28 The formula $v = u + at$ gives the speed v of a particle, t seconds after it starts with speed u. Calculate v when $u = 7.8$, $a = -10$ and $t = \frac{3}{4}$.

Substitution into formulae with powers and roots

Exercise 14.3

Do not use a calculator for questions 1 to 12.

1 $S = a^2$. Find the value of S when
(a) $a = 3$ (b) $a = -3$

2 $S = 2a^2$. Find the value of S when
(a) $a = 3$ (b) $a = -3$

3 $S = (2a)^2$. Find the value of S when
(a) $a = 3$ (b) $a = -3$

4 $S = \frac{1}{2}p^2$. Find the value of S when
(a) $p = 8$ (b) $p = -8$

5 $S = \left(\frac{1}{2}p\right)^2$. Find the value of S when
(a) $p = 8$ (b) $p = -8$

6 What is the value of $3a^2 - 9$ when
(a) $a = 4$, (b) $a = 5$,
(c) $a = -4$, (d) $a = -5$?

7 What is the value of x^3 when
(a) $x = 3$, (b) $x = -3$,
(c) $x = 5$, (d) $x = -5$?

8 What is the value of $2t^3$ when
(a) $t = 4$, (b) $t = -4$?

9 What is the value of $3x - x^3$ when
  (a) $x = 2$,
  (b) $x = -2$?

10 $T = \sqrt{\dfrac{a}{b}}$

  Work out the value of T when
  (a) $a = 9$ and $b = 16$,
  (b) $a = 3$ and $b = \frac{4}{3}$.

11 $S = \sqrt[3]{pq}$

  Work out the value of S when
  (a) $p = 2$ and $q = 32$,
  (b) $p = 2\frac{1}{4}$ and $q = 1\frac{1}{2}$,
  (c) $p = 54$ and $q = -0.5$.

12 $L = \sqrt{m^2 + n^2}$

  Work out the value of L when
  (a) $m = 6$ and $n = 8$,
  (b) $m = 0.3$ and $n = 0.4$.

13 Calculate $5\sqrt{x}$ when
  (a) $x = 27$,
  (b) $x = 0.4$.
  Give your answers correct to
  one decimal place.

14 Calculate $\sqrt{5x}$ when
  (a) $x = 27$,
  (b) $x = 0.4$.
  Give your answers correct to
  two significant figures.

15 The formula $F = \dfrac{mv^2}{r}$ describes the
  motion of a cyclist rounding a corner.
  Find F when $m = 80$, $v = 6$ and $r = 20$.

16 The height, h metres, of a bullet after
  t seconds, is given by the formula
  $h = ut - \frac{1}{2}gt^2$, where $u\,\text{ms}^{-1}$ is the
  initial vertical speed and $g\,\text{ms}^{-2}$ is
  the acceleration due to gravity.
  Find h when $u = 200$ and $t = 1\frac{3}{5}$.
  Take $g = 9.8$.
  Give your answer to a suitable degree of
  accuracy.

17 The time T, for a pendulum to make a
  complete swing is given by the formula:

  $$T = 2\pi\sqrt{\dfrac{l}{g}}$$

  (a) Calculate the value of T when
       $l = 0.8$ and $g = 9.8$.
  (b) Calculate the value of T when
       $l = 1\frac{1}{2}$ and $g = 9.8$.
  Take π to be 3.14 or use the π key on
  your calculator.

18 Use the formula $v = \sqrt{u^2 + 2as}$
  to calculate the value of v when
  (a) $u = 2.4$, $a = 3.2$, $s = 5.25$,
  (b) $u = 9.1$, $a = -4.7$, $s = 3.04$.
  Give your answers correct to
  one decimal place.

Rearranging formulae

Sometimes it is easier to use a formula if you **rearrange** it first.

 EXAMPLES

1 $k = \dfrac{8m}{5}$

  Rearrange the formula to give m in terms of k.

  $k = \dfrac{8m}{5}$

  Multiply both sides by 5.
  $5k = 8m$
  Divide both sides by 8.

  $\dfrac{5k}{8} = m$

  We say we have **rearranged the formula**

  $k = \dfrac{8m}{5}$ to make m the **subject** of the formula.

2 $y = 2x + 8$

  Make x the subject of the formula.

  $y = 2x + 8$

  Subtract 8 from both sides.
  $y - 8 = 2x$
  Divide both sides by 2.
  $\frac{1}{2}y - 4 = x$

  y is the subject of $y = 2x + 8$,
  x is the subject of $x = \frac{1}{2}y - 4$.

3 $A = 3r^2$

Make r the subject of the formula.

$A = 3r^2$

Divide both sides by 3.

$\frac{A}{3} = r^2$

Take the square root of both sides.

$\pm\sqrt{\frac{A}{3}} = r$

so $r = \pm\sqrt{\frac{A}{3}}$

4 $T = a + \sqrt{b}$

Rearrange the formula to give b in terms of T and a.

$T = a + \sqrt{b}$

Take a from both sides.

$T - a = \sqrt{b}$

Square both sides.

$(T - a)^2 = b$

so $b = (T - a)^2$

Exercise 14.4

1 Make m the subject of these formulae.
   (a) $a = m + 5$ (b) $a = x + m$ (c) $a = m - 2$
   (d) $a = m - b$ (e) $a = 2 - m$ (f) $a = x - m$

2 Make x the subject of these formulae.
   (a) $y = 4x$ (b) $y = ax$ (c) $y = -ax$
   (d) $y = \frac{1}{2}x$ (e) $y = \frac{x}{a}$ (f) $y = -\frac{x}{a}$
   (g) $y = \frac{2}{x}$ (h) $y = -\frac{n}{x}$

3 Make p the subject of these formulae.
   (a) $y = 2p + 6$ (b) $t = 5p + q$ (c) $m = 3p - 2$
   (d) $r = 4p - q$ (e) $a = 3 - 2p$ (f) $d = g - 3p$
   (g) $m = \frac{p}{2} + 3$ (h) $y = \frac{p}{3} + x$ (i) $t = \frac{p}{5} - 2$
   (j) $g = h - \frac{p}{2}$ (k) $s = q + \frac{3}{p}$ (l) $y = x - \frac{a}{p}$

4 A formula for changing kilograms to pounds is $P = 0.45K$.
Rearrange the formula to give K in terms of P.

5 $F = 1.8C + 32$ changes temperatures in °C to °F.
Rearrange the formula to give C in terms of F.

6 The cost, £C, of hiring a car for n days is given by $C = 35 + 24n$.
Make n the subject of the formula.

7 The area of a trapezium is given by $A = \frac{1}{2}(a + b)h$.
Make a the subject of this formula.

8 Make c the subject of these formulae.
   (a) $y = c^2$ (b) $y = \sqrt{c}$ (c) $y = dc^2$ (d) $y = \frac{\sqrt{c}}{3}$

   (e) $y = c^2 + x$ (f) $y = x + \sqrt{c}$ (g) $y = x + \frac{c^2}{d}$ (h) $y = \frac{\sqrt{c}}{a} - x$

9 Make the bold letter the subject of these formulae.

(a) $\dfrac{V}{I} = R$ (b) $E = \boldsymbol{m}c^2$ (c) $y = a\boldsymbol{x}^2 + b$ (d) $e = \frac{1}{2}m\boldsymbol{v}^2$

10 Make a the subject of these formulae.

(a) $b = a + c^2$ (b) $a^2 = b$ (c) $4a = 8b + c$ (d) $6a = 2b$

(e) $3a = \dfrac{4b}{5}$ (f) $b = \dfrac{2a}{3}$ (g) $p = ma + d$ (h) $ma^2 = F$

11 Make x the subject of these formulae.

(a) $3(x - a) = x$ (b) $2(a + x) = 3(b - x)$ (c) $2(x + 4) = ax$

(d) $3x = a(x + b)$ (e) $ax = 3(2x - a)$ (f) $a(b + x) = b(2a - x)$

Solve problems by rearranging formulae

EXAMPLE

A cuboid has length 7.8 cm and breadth 5 cm.
The volume of the cuboid is 136.5 cm³.
Calculate the height of the cuboid.

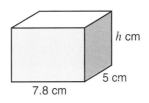
h cm
5 cm
7.8 cm

The formula for the volume of a cuboid is $V = lbh$,

     so $h = \dfrac{V}{lb}$ (by dividing both sides of $V = lbh$ by lb)

Substitute $V = 136.5$, $l = 7.8$ and $b = 5$ in $h = \dfrac{V}{lb}$.

     $h = \dfrac{136.5}{7.8 \times 5}$

     $h = 3.5$

The height of the cuboid is 3.5 cm.

The values to be substituted may include whole numbers, negative numbers, decimals or fractions.

Exercise **14.5**

Do not use a calculator for questions 1 to 5.

1 The perimeter of a square is $P = 4d$.
  (a) Change the subject to d.
  (b) Find d when $P = 2.8$ cm.

2 The area of a rectangle is $A = lb$.
  (a) Change the subject to l.
  (b) Find l when $A = 27$ cm² and $b = 4.5$ cm.

3 The speed of a car is $S = \dfrac{D}{T}$.
  (a) (i) Change the subject to D.
      (ii) Find D when $S = 48$ km/h and $T = 0.5$ hours.
  (b) (i) Change the subject to T.
      (ii) Find T when $S = 72$ km/h and $D = 90$ km.

4 The area of a wooden shape is $A = \dfrac{3}{2}pq$.
  (a) Change the subject to p.
  (b) Find p when $A = 24$ cm² and $q = 5$ cm.

5 The perimeter of a rectangle is $P = 2(l + b)$.
  (a) Change the subject to b.
  (b) Find b when $P = 18$ cm and $l = 4.8$ cm.

6 $y = mx + c$
  (a) Rearrange the formula to give x in terms of y, m and c.
  (b) Calculate x when $y = 0.6$, $m = -0.4$ and $c = 1.8$.

7 $A = \dfrac{bh}{2}$

    (a)   Rearrange the formula to give b in terms of A and h.

    (b)   Calculate b when $A = 9.8$ and $h = 0.84$.
        Give your answer correct to two significant figures.

8 $I = \dfrac{C}{d^2}$

    (a)   Rearrange the formula to give d in terms of I and C.

    (b)   Calculate d when $I = 17.4$ and $C = 23.7$.
        Give your answer correct to two decimal places.

9 $p^2 = q^2 + r^2$

    (a)   Rearrange the formula to give q in terms of p and r.

    (b)   Calculate q when $p = 7.3$ and $r = 2.7$.
        Give your answer to a suitable degree of accuracy.

10 $V = \frac{4}{3}\pi r^3$

    (a)   Rearrange the formula to give r in terms of V and π.

    (b)   Calculate r when $V = 1.6 \times 10^5$ and $\pi = 3.14$.
        Give your answer to a suitable degree of accuracy.

11 $\dfrac{x}{a} = \dfrac{b}{x}$

    (a)   Make x the subject of the formula.

    (b)   Calculate x when $a = 4.6 \times 10^3$ and $b = 3.5 \times 10^5$.
        Give your answer in standard form correct to two significant figures.

12 $m = \dfrac{1 - n}{1 + n}$

    (a)   Make n the subject of the formula.

    (b)   Calculate n when $m = 8.5 \times 10^{-2}$.
        Give your answer in standard form to a suitable degree of accuracy.

What you need to know

- A **formula** is an algebraic rule which can be rearranged to make another letter (variable) the subject.

You should be able to:

- write simple formulae,

- rearrange given formulae,

- substitute values into given formulae.

Review Exercise

1   What is the value of $2g + 3h$ when $g = 5$ and $h = -2$?

2 $V = a + bc$.
    Find the value of V when $a = -5$, $b = 3$ and $c = 4$.

3   Given that $x = 3$ and $y = -2$, find the value of
    (a) $x + y$,   (b) $x - y$,
    (c) $y - x$,   (d) xy.

4 $P = 3(m + n)$.
    Find the value of P when $m = 0.5$ and $n = 2$.

5 $S = pq + r$.
    Find the value of S when $p = -3$, $q = 4$ and $r = -2$.

6   What is the value of $3x^2$ when $x = 6$?

7   What is the value of $t^3 - t$ when
    (a) $t = 2$,   (b) $t = -2$?

8   Eve buys n pints of milk at 29 pence a pint.
    She pays for them with a £1 coin.
    She is given C pence change.
    Write down a formula for C in terms of n.

9 (a) Write down and simplify a formula for the total perimeter of this shape.

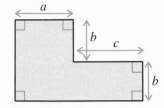

(b) Use your formula to work out the perimeter when $a = 3$, $b = 2$, $c = 4$.

Edexcel

10 Temperatures in $°F$ can be changed into $°C$ using the formula:
$$C = \tfrac{5}{9}(F - 32)$$
(a) Calculate the value of C when $F = 59$.
(b) What temperature, in $°C$, is equivalent to $5°F$?

11 The approximate area of a circle, A, is given by the formula $A = 3r^2$, where r is the radius of the circle.
Find the value of A when $r = 5$.

12 This rule is used to work out take home pay.

Take Home Pay	=	Hours Worked	×	Hourly Rate	−	Deductions

Mary's hourly rate was £5.
Her deductions were £7.
Her take home pay was £68.
Work out the number of hours she worked.

Edexcel

13 Find the exact value of $\dfrac{1}{m} - \dfrac{1}{n}$
when $m = \tfrac{2}{5}$ and $n = \tfrac{3}{4}$.

14 The cost, C pounds, of making a circular table can be worked out by using the formula
$$C = 3r + 25$$
where r is the radius of the table in centimetres.
(a) Work out the cost of making a table with a radius 48 cm.
(b) (i) Make r the subject of the formula.
(ii) A circular table cost £130 to make.
Work out the radius of the table.

15 $C = 180R + 2000$
The formula gives the capacity, C litres, of a tank needed to supply water to R hotel rooms.

$R = 5$.
(a) Work out the value of C.

$C = 3440$.
(b) Work out the value of R.

A water tank has a capacity of 3200 litres.
(c) Work out the greatest number of hotel rooms it could supply.
(d) Make R the subject of the formula $C = 180R + 2000$.

Edexcel

16 A formula is given as $s = t - uv^2$.
Calculate the value of s when $t = -6$, $u = 50$ and $v = 0.2$.

17 You are given the formula
$a = \tfrac{1}{3}(b + c)d$.
(a) Work out the value of a when $b = 5$, $c = -20$ and $d = 0.5$.
(b) Express d in terms of a, b and c.

18 $p = q - rs$
(a) Calculate the value of p when $q = 3.95$, $r = -0.65$ and $s = 5$.
(b) Express s in terms of p, q and r.

19 $p = \dfrac{2q + r}{6}$
(a) Find p when $q = 8.5$ and $r = 22$.

When $p = 12$, then $r = 42$.
(b) Form an equation and solve it to find q.

Edexcel

20 $v^2 = \dfrac{GM}{R}$
$G = 6.6 \times 10^{-11}$
$M = 6 \times 10^{24}$
$R = 6\,800\,000$
(a) Calculate the value of v.
Give your answer in standard form, correct to 2 significant figures.

(b) Rearrange the formula $v^2 = \dfrac{GM}{R}$ to make M the subject.

Edexcel

21 Rearrange the formula $s = \dfrac{t - u}{v^2}$ to give v in terms of s, t and u.

CHAPTER 15

Sequences

Continuing a sequence

A **sequence** is a list of numbers made according to some rule.
For example:

> 5,   9,   13,   17,   21,   ...

The first term is 5.
To find the next term in the sequence, add 4 to the last term.
The next term in this sequence is $21 + 4 = 25$.
What are the next three terms in the sequence?

> The numbers in a sequence are called **terms**.
> The start number is the **first term**, the next is the second term, and so on.

> **To continue a sequence:**
> 1. Work out the rule to get from one term to the next.
> 2. Apply the same rule to find further terms in the sequence.

EXAMPLES

Find the next three terms in each of these sequences.

1   5,   8,   11,   14,   17,   ...

To find the next term in the sequence, add 3 to the last term.
$17 + 3 = 20$, $20 + 3 = 23$, $23 + 3 = 26$.
The next three terms in the sequence are: 20, 23, 26.

2   2,   4,   8,   16,   ...

To find the next term in the sequence, multiply the last term by 2.
$16 \times 2 = 32$, $32 \times 2 = 64$, $64 \times 2 = 128$.
The next three terms in the sequence are: 32, 64, 128.

3   1,   1,   2,   3,   5,   8,   ...

To find the next term in the sequence, add the last two terms.
$5 + 8 = 13$, $8 + 13 = 21$, $13 + 21 = 34$.
The next three terms in the sequence are: 13, 21, 34.
This is a special sequence called the **Fibonacci sequence**.

Exercise 15.1

1   Find the next three terms in these sequences.

(a)   1, 5, 9, 13, ...   (b)   6, 8, 10, 12, ...   (c)   28, 25, 22, 19, ...

(d)   3, 8, 13, 18, 23, ...   (e)   3, 6, 12, 24, ...   (f) $\frac{1}{4}$, $\frac{1}{2}$, $\frac{3}{4}$, 1, $1\frac{1}{4}$, ...

(g)   32, 16, 8, 4, ...   (h)   0.5, 0.6, 0.7, 0.8, ...   (i)   10, 8, 6, 4, ...

(j)   80, 40, 20, 10, ...   (k)   1, 3, 6, 10, 15, ...   (l)   1, 3, 4, 7, 11, 18, ...

2 Find the missing terms from these sequences.

(a) 2, 4, 6, __, 10, 12, __, 16, …
(b) 2, 6, __, 14, 18, __, 26, …
(c) 1, 2, 4, __, 16, __, 64, …
(d) 28, 22, __, 10, 4, __, …
(e) 1, 4, 9, __, 25, __, 49, …
(f) 1, 2, 3, 5, __, 13, __, 34, …
(g) __, 8, 14, __, __, 32, 38, …
(h) __, 1.8, __, 1.4, __, 1, 0.8, …

3 Write down the rule, in words, used to get from one term to the next for each sequence.
Then use the rule to find the next two terms.

(a) 2, 9, 16, 23, 30, …   (b) 3, 5, 7, 9, 11, …
(c) 1, 5, 9, 13, 17, …   (d) 31, 26, 21, 16, …
(e) 64, 32, 16, 8, 4, …   (f) 1, 3, 9, 27, …
(g) 0.2, 0.4, 0.6, 0.8, …   (h) $\frac{3}{4}$, $1\frac{1}{2}$, $2\frac{1}{4}$, 3, …
(i) 4, 6, 10, 16, 24, …   (j) 10, 7, 4, 1, −2, …

Using rules

Sometimes you will be given a rule and asked to use it to find the terms of a sequence.
For example:
A sequence begins: 1,   4,   13,   …
The rule for the sequence is:

| multiply the last number by 3, then add 1 |

The next term in the sequence is given by:
$13 \times 3 + 1 = 39 + 1 = 40$
The following term is given by:
$40 \times 3 + 1 = 120 + 1 = 121$
So the sequence can be extended to:
1,   4,   13,   40,   121,   …
Use the rule to find the next two terms in the sequence.

The **same rule** can be used to make different sequences.
For example:
Another sequence begins:
2,   7,   22,   …
Using the same rule, the next term is given by:
$22 \times 3 + 1 = 66 + 1 = 67$
The following term is given by:
$67 \times 3 + 1 = 201 + 1 = 202$
So the sequence can be extended to:
2,   7,   22,   67,   202,   …
Use the rule to find the next two terms in the sequence.

EXAMPLE

This rule is used to find each number in a sequence from the number before it.

| Subtract 3 and then multiply by 4 |

Starting with 5 we get the following sequence:
5,   8,   20,   68,   …

(a) Write down the next number in the sequence.
(b) Using the same rule, but a different starting number, the second number is 16.
Find the starting number.

(a) $(68 − 3) \times 4 = 65 \times 4 = 260$
Notice that, following the rule, 3 is subtracted first and the result is then multiplied by 4.
The next number in the sequence is 260.

The method of working backwards was first used in Chapter 13.

(b) Imagine the first number is x.

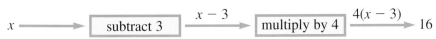

Working backwards.

The starting number is 7.

1 Write down the first five terms of these sequences.

(a) First term: 1

Rule: | add on 4 to the last term |

(b) First term: 1

Rule: | double the last term |

(c) First term: 40

Rule: | subtract 5 from the last term |

(d) First term: 4

Rule: | double the last term and then subtract 3 |

(e) First term: 47

Rule: | subtract 1 from the last term and then halve the result |

(f) First term: 2   Second term: 6

Rule: | add the last two terms and then halve the result |

2 This rule is used to get each number from the number before it:

| multiply by 2 |

Use the rule to find the next three numbers when the first number is:

(a) 1,   (b) 3,   (c) −1.

3 This rule is used to get each number from the number before it:

| add 1 and then double the result |

Use the rule to find the next three numbers when the first number is:

(a) 1,   (b) 3,   (c) −3.

4 This rule is used to find each term of a sequence from the one before:

| subtract 3 then divide by 2 |

(a) The first term is 45.
(i) What is the second term?
(ii) What is the **fourth** term?

(b) Using the same rule, but a different starting number, the second term is 17. What is the starting number for the sequence?

5 This rule is used to find each term of a sequence from the one before:

| add 5 then multiply by 3 |

(a) The first term is 7.
(i) What is the second term?
(ii) What is the **third** term?

(b) Using the same rule, but a different starting number, the second term is 45. What is the starting number for the sequence?

6 A sequence begins 1, −3, ...
The sequence is continued using the rule:

| add the previous two numbers and then multiply by 3 |

Use the rule to find the next two numbers in the sequence.

Number sequences

A number sequence which increases (or decreases) by the same amount from one term to the next is called a **linear sequence**.
For example, terms in the sequence 6, 11, 16, 21, … increase by 5 from one term to the next.
We say that the sequence has a **common difference** of 5.

By comparing a sequence with multiples of the counting numbers 1, 2, 3, 4, … we can write a rule to find the nth term of the sequence.

Sequence: 6   11   16   21   …
Multiples of 5:   5   10   15   20   …

To get the nth term add one to the multiples of 5.
So, the nth term is $5n + 1$.

> Compare the sequence with multiples of the common difference.
> In this case the common difference is 5, so compare the sequence with multiples of 5.

A table can be used to find the nth term of a sequence.
The sequence 2, 8, 14, 20, … has a common difference of 6.

Term	Term × common difference	Sequence	Difference
1	$1 \times 6 = 6$	2	$2 - 6 = -4$
2	$2 \times 6 = 12$	8	$8 - 12 = -4$
3	$3 \times 6 = 18$	14	$14 - 18 = -4$
4	$4 \times 6 = 24$	20	$20 - 24 = -4$
n	$n \times 6 = 6n$	$6n - 4$	

Term
The counting numbers. 1 represents the first term, 2 the second term, and so on. n represents the nth term.

Common difference
2nd term $-$ 1st term $= 8 - 2 = 6$.

Differences
Check that each pair of entries gives the same result.

The nth term of the sequence 2, 8, 14, 20, … is $6n - 4$.
This can be used to find the value of any term in the sequence.
To find the fifth term, substitute $n = 5$ into $6n - 4$.
$6 \times 5 - 4 = 30 - 4 = 26$. The fifth term is 26.

EXAMPLE

(a)   Find the nth term in the sequence 31, 28, 25, 22, …
(b)   Find the value of the 10th term in the sequence.

Term	Term × common difference	Sequence	Difference
1	$1 \times (-3) = -3$	31	$31 - (-3) = 34$
2	$2 \times (-3) = -6$	28	$28 - (-6) = 34$
3	$3 \times (-3) = -9$	25	$25 - (-9) = 34$
4	$4 \times (-3) = -12$	22	$22 - (-12) = 34$
n	$n \times (-3) = -3n$	$-3n + 34$	

(a)   The common difference is -3.
The nth term is $-3n + 34$.
This can also be written as $34 - 3n$.

(b)   The nth term is $34 - 3n$.
Substitute $n = 10$.
$34 - 3 \times 10 = 34 - 30 = 4$
The 10th term is 4.

1 Find the common differences of the following sequences.
- (a)   3, 6, 9, 12, …
- (b)   2, 5, 8, 11, …
- (c)   7, 13, 19, 25, …
- (d)   12, 20, 28, 36, …
- (e)   20, 18, 16, 14, …

2
- (a)   The multiples of 3 are 3, 6, 9, 12, …
  What is the nth multiple of 3?
- (b)   What is the nth multiple of 8?
- (c)   What is the nth multiple of 12?
- (d)   What is the nth even number?

3 A sequence of numbers starts: 4, 7, 10, 13, …
- (a)   What is the common difference?
- (b)   Copy and complete this table.

Term	Term × common difference	Sequence	Difference
1	$1 \times \dots =$	4	$4 - \dots =$
2	$2 \times \dots =$	7	$7 - \dots =$
3	$3 \times \dots =$	10	$10 - \dots =$
4	$4 \times \dots =$	13	$13 - \dots =$
n	$n \times \dots = \dots n$	$\dots n + \dots$	

- (c)   Write down the nth term of the sequence.
- (d)   What is the value of the 8th term of the sequence?

4 A sequence of numbers starts: 9, 11, 13, 15, …
- (a)   What is the common difference?
- (b)   Copy and complete this table.

Term	Term × common difference	Sequence	Difference
1	2	9	7
2	4	11	…
3	…	13	…
4	…	15	…
n	$\dots n$	…	

- (c)   Write down the nth term of the sequence.
- (d)   What is the value of the 20th term of the sequence?

5 A sequence of numbers starts: 20, 16, 12, 8, …
 (a) What is the common difference?
 (b) Copy and complete this table.

Term	Term × common difference	Sequence	Difference
1	…	20	…
2	…	16	…
3	…	12	…
4	…	8	…
n	…	…	

 (c) Write down the nth term of the sequence.

6 Find the nth term of the following sequences.
 (a) 1, 4, 7, 10, …   (b) 19, 16, 13, 10, …
 (c) 5, 9, 13, 17, …   (d) 4, 8, 12, 16, …
 (e) 1, 3, 5, 7, …   (f) 7, 11, 15, 19, …
 (g) 6, 4, 2, 0, …   (h) 5, 8, 11, 14, …
 (i) 3, 8, 13, 18, …   (j) 40, 35, 30, 25, …
 (k) 0, 1, 2, 3, …   (l) −1, 1, 3, 5, …

7 A sequence begins 4, 7, 13, 25, …
 The next number in the sequence can be found using the rule:

> "Multiply the last term by 2 then subtract 1."

 (a) Write down the next **two** terms in the sequence.
 (b) The 11th term in the sequence is 3073.
   Use this information to find the 10th term in the sequence.

Sequences of numbers from shape patterns

Activity

These patterns are made using squares.

Pattern 1   **Pattern 2**   **Pattern 3**
3 squares   **5 squares**   **7 squares**

How many squares are used to make Pattern 4?
How many squares are used to make Pattern 10?
How many squares are used to make Pattern 100?
Which pattern is made using 81 squares?

The number of squares used to make each pattern forms a **sequence**.

Pattern 4 is made using 9 squares.
You could have answered this: by drawing Pattern 4 or,
by continuing the sequence of numbers 3, 5, 7, …
It is possible to do the same for Pattern 10, though it would involve a lot of work, but it would be unreasonable to use either method for Pattern 100.
Instead we can investigate how each pattern is made.

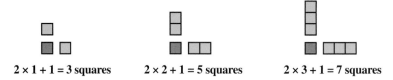

2 × 1 + 1 = 3 squares   2 × 2 + 1 = 5 squares   2 × 3 + 1 = 7 squares

Each pattern is made using a **rule**.
The rule can be **described in words**.
To find the number of squares used to make a pattern use the rule:
"Double the pattern number and add 1."
$81 = 2 \times 40 + 1$, so the 40th pattern is made using 81 squares.

Pattern number	Rule	Number of squares
4	$2 \times 4 + 1$	9
10	$2 \times 10 + 1$	21
100	$2 \times 100 + 1$	201

The same rule can be **written using symbols**.
We can then answer a very important question:
How many squares are used to make Pattern n?

Pattern n will have $2 \times n + 1$ squares.
This can be written as $2n + 1$ squares.

Special sequences of numbers

Square numbers

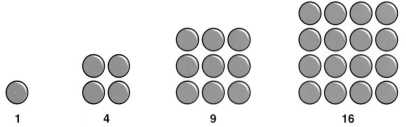

1   4   9   16

The sequence starts: 1, 4, 9, 16, …
The numbers in this sequence are called **square numbers**.

Triangular numbers

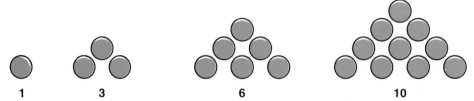

1   3   6   10

The sequence starts: 1, 3, 6, 10, …
The numbers in this sequence are called **triangular numbers**.

1 A sequence of patterns is formed using equilateral triangles.

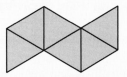
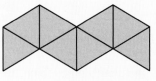

Pattern 1   Pattern 2   Pattern 3   Pattern 4

(a)   How many triangles form Pattern 5?
(b)   Explain why a pattern cannot have 27 triangles.
(c)   Write an expression, in terms of *p*, for the number of triangles in Pattern *p*.

2 A sequence of patterns is formed using sticks.

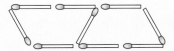
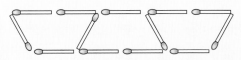

Pattern 1   Pattern 2   Pattern 3

(a)   How many sticks are used to make Pattern 4?
(b)   How many more sticks are used to make Pattern 5 from Pattern 4?
(c)   Write an expression, in terms of *n*, for the number of sticks used to make Pattern *n*.

3 Patterns are made using black and white counters.

(a)   How many white counters are
there in a pattern with
  (i)   5 black counters,
  (ii) 10 black counters,
  (iii) 100 black counters?

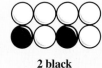

1 black   2 black   3 black
3 white   6 white   9 white

(b)   How many white counters are
there in a pattern with *n* black counters?

4 These patterns are made using matches.

(a)   How many matches are used to make
  (i)   Pattern 4,
  (ii) Pattern 20?

Pattern 1   Pattern 2   Pattern 3
6 matches   10 matches   14 matches

(b)   Which pattern uses 30 matches?

(c)   How many matches are used to make Pattern *n*?

5 Fences are made by placing fence posts 1m apart and using 2 horizontal bars between them.

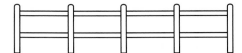

The fence above is 4m long. It has 5 posts and 8 bars.
(a)   A fence is 50 m long.
  (i)   How many posts does it have?
  (ii) How many bars does it have?

(b)   A fence is *x* metres long.
Write down expressions for
  (i)   the number of posts,
  (ii) the number of bars.

6 Linking cubes of side 1 cm are used to make rods.
This rod is made using 4 linking cubes.

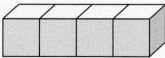

The surface area of the rod is 18 square centimetres.
(4 squares on each of the long sides plus one square at each end.)
(a) What is the surface area of a rod made using 5 linking cubes?
(b) What is the surface area of a rod made using 10 linking cubes?
(c) What is the surface area of a rod made using n linking cubes?

7 A sequence of patterns is made using sticks.

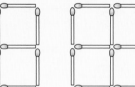 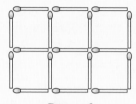 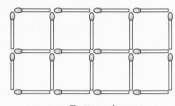

Pattern 1　　**Pattern 2**　　　　**Pattern 3**　　　　　　**Pattern 4**

(a) How many sticks are used to make Pattern 5?
(b) Pattern n uses T sticks.
Write a formula for T in terms of n.
(c) Use your formula to find the number of sticks used to make Pattern 10.
(d) One pattern uses 77 sticks. What is the pattern number?

8 These patterns are made using matches.
(a) How many matches are used to make Pattern 5?
(b) Which pattern uses 37 matches?
(c) Find a formula for the number of matches, m, in Pattern p.

Pattern 1　　**Pattern 2**　　**Pattern 3**

9 These are the first four **square numbers**.
1, 4, 9, 16, ...

(a) What is the next square number?
(b) Copy and complete this list for the first 5 square numbers.
$1^2 = 1$, $2^2 = 4$, $3^2 = 9$, $... = 16$, $5^2 = ...$

(c) Write an expression for the nth square number.
(d) Find the 15th square number.

10 (a) Find the next term in each of these sequences.
Explain how you found your answers.
(i) 2, 5, 10, 17, 26, ...
(ii) 0, 3, 8, 15, 24, ...
(iii) 4, 7, 12, 19, 28, ...
(iv) 2, 8, 18, 32, 50, ...
(v) 2, 6, 12, 20, 30, ...

(b) By comparing each of these sequences to the sequence of square numbers write an expression for the nth term of each sequence.

168

11 A sequence of shapes is made using small squares

Shape 1	Shape 2	Shape 3	Shape 4

(a) Shape n uses T small squares.
Write a formula for T in terms of n.
(b) Use your formula to find the number of small squares in shape 10.

12 These are the first four **triangular numbers**.
1, 3, 6, 10, …

(a) What is the next triangular number?
(b) Copy and complete this list for the first 5 triangular numbers.

$$\frac{1 \times 2}{2} = 1, \qquad \frac{2 \times 3}{2} = 3, \qquad \frac{3 \times 4}{2} = 6, \qquad \frac{}{2} = 10, \qquad \ldots = \ldots$$

(c) Write an expression for the nth triangular number.
(d) Find the 10th triangular number.

13 These are the first four **powers of 2**.
2, 4, 8, 16, …

(a) What is the next power of 2?
(b) Copy and complete this list for the first 5 powers of 2.
$2^1 = 2, \quad 2^2 = 4, \quad 2^3 = 8,$
$\ldots = 16, \quad \ldots = \ldots$
(c) Write an expression for the nth power of 2.
(d) Find the 10th power of 2.
(e) What power of 2 is equal to 256?

14 (a) Write down the first 5 powers of 10.
(b) Write an expression for the nth power of 10.
(c) What power of 10 is equal to one million?

15 (a) Write an expression for the nth term of this sequence:
3, 9, 27, 81, …
(b) Use your expression to find the 10th term of the sequence.

What you need to know

- A **sequence** is a list of numbers made according to some rule.
The numbers in a sequence are called **terms**.

- **To continue a sequence:**
1. Work out the rule to get from one term to the next.
2. Apply the same rule to find further terms in the sequence.

- A number sequence which increases (or decreases) by the same amount from one term to the next is called a **linear sequence**.
The sequence 2, 8, 14, 20, 26, … has a **common difference** of 6.

- Special sequences
Square numbers: 1, 4, 9, 16, 25, …
Triangular numbers: 1, 3, 6, 10, 15, …

- Patterns of shapes can be drawn to represent a number sequence.
For example, this pattern represents the sequence 3, 5, 7, …

You should be able to:
- Draw patterns of shapes which represent number sequences.

- Continue a given number sequence.

- Find the expression for the nth term of a sequence.

1 Write down the next two numbers in each of these sequences.
(a) 1, 2, 5, 10, 17, …
(b) 27, 9, 3, 1, …

2 (a) Write down the next term in this sequence.
1, 4, 7, 10, 13, …
(b) Will the number 41 be in the sequence?
Give a reason for your answer.
(c) What is the first number in the sequence which is greater than 100?

3 These sequences all begin with the numbers 3, 6.
Find the third number in each sequence.
(a) 3, 6, …, 12, …
(b) 3, 6, …, 24, …
(c) 3, 6, …, 15, …

4 A sequence begins 4, 5, …
The rule to continue this sequence is:

> Multiply the last number by 2 and then subtract 3.

(a) What is the next number in the sequence?
(b) The same rule is used for another sequence.
The sequence begins with −1.
What are the next two numbers in the sequence?

5 Here are the rules for a sequence:

If the last number is odd, add 5.
If the last number is even, halve it.

A sequence begins with the number 9.
(a) Write down the next three terms in the sequence.
(b) Explain what will happen to the sequence if you continue.

6 A sequence begins 1, 3, 6, 10, 15, …
(a) Write down the next number in the sequence.
(b) Explain how you worked out your answer.

7 A sequence begins 2, 6, 10, 14, 18, ….
One number in the sequence is x.
Write an expression, in terms of x, for the number in the sequence before x.

8 Sticks are used to make patterns of squares.

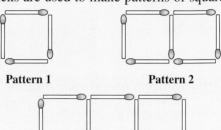

Pattern 1   **Pattern 2**

Pattern 3

(a) How many sticks are needed to make Pattern 4?
(b) How many **more** sticks are needed to make Pattern 5 from Pattern 4?
(c) Write an expression, in terms of n, for the number of sticks needed to make Pattern n.

9 A sequence begins 3, 5, 7, 9, 11, …
(a) Find, in terms of n, an expression for the nth term of the sequence.
(b) What is the 100th term of the sequence?

10 Here are the first five terms of a sequence.
17, 14, 11, 8, 5.
(a) (i) Write down the next two terms of the sequence.
(ii) Explain how your worked out your answers.
(b) Find, in terms of n, an expression for the nth term of the sequence.
(c) Find the 50th term of the sequence.
Edexcel

11 (a) Write down an expression for the nth term of the sequence
1, 4, 9, 16, 25, 36, 49, …
(b) Using your answer to (a), write down an expression for the nth term of the sequence
0, 3, 8, 15, 24, 35, 48, …   *Edexcel*

12 Crosses are arranged to form a sequence of patterns.

```
× ×      × × × ×      × × × × × ×
         × × × ×      × × × × × ×
                      × × × × × ×
```

Pattern 1   **Pattern 2**   **Pattern 3**

(a) How many crosses will be in Pattern 5?
(b) Write, in terms of n, an expression for the number of crosses in Pattern n.
(c) Which pattern number will have 128 crosses?

CHAPTER 16

Graphs

Straight line graphs

Look at these coordinates (1, 3), (2, 5), (3, 7), (4, 9).
Can you see any number patterns?

The same coordinates can be shown in a **table**.

x	1	2	3	4
y	3	5	7	9

Notice that as:
the *x* coordinate increases by 1,
the *y* coordinate increases by 2.

A **rule** connects the *x* coordinate with the *y* coordinate.
This rule can be written, in **words**, as:
"To find the *y* coordinate, multiply the
x coordinate by 2 and add 1."
The same rule can also be written, using **symbols**, as an
equation, $y = 2x + 1$.
The coordinates are used to draw the graph of
$y = 2x + 1$, as shown.

The diagram shows the coordinates plotted on a **graph**.
The points all lie on a **straight line**.
All points on the line obey the rule $y = 2x + 1$.

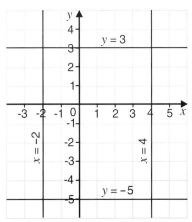

What is the value of *y* when *x* = 3.5?
Using the graph:
From 3.5 on the *x* axis, go up to meet the line
$y = 2x + 1$.
Go left to meet the *y* axis at 8.
So, when $x = 3.5$, $y = 8$.

Using the equation:
Substitute $x = 3.5$ into the equation.
$y = 2x + 1$
$y = 2 \times 3.5 + 1 = 7 + 1 = 8$
So, when $x = 3.5$, $y = 8$.

Drawing a graph from a rule

This diagram shows the graphs:

$x = 4$ $y = 3$
$x = -2$ $y = -5$

Notice that:
The graph of $x = 4$ is a **vertical** line.
All points on the line have *x* coordinate 4.

The graph of $y = 3$ is a **horizontal** line.
All points on the line have *y* coordinate 3.

$x = 0$ is the *y* axis.
$y = 0$ is the *x* axis.

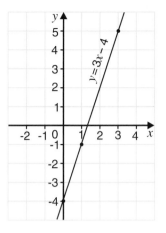

EXAMPLE

Draw the graph of the equation $y = 3x - 4$.

If values for x are not given in the question you must choose your own.

When $x = 0$, $y = 3 \times 0 - 4 = -4$.
This gives the point $(0, -4)$.

When $x = 1$, $y = 3 \times 1 - 4 = -1$.
This gives the point $(1, -1)$.

When $x = 3$, $y = 3 \times 3 - 4 = 5$.
This gives the point $(3, 5)$.

Plot the points $(0, -4)$, $(1, -1)$ and $(3, 5)$.

The straight line which passes through these points is the graph of the equation $y = 3x - 4$.

Exercise 16.1

1 Write down the equations of the lines labelled on this graph.

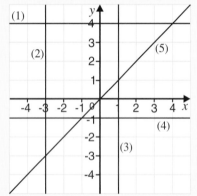

2 Copy the coordinate grid given in question 1.
Draw and label the lines:
(a) $x = 3$,   (b) $y = 2$,
(c) $x = -2$,   (d) $y = -1$.

3 (a) Copy and complete a table like the one below for each of these equations.

x	1	2	3
y			

(i) $y = x + 2$ (ii) $y = 2x$

(b) Draw graphs for each of the equations in part (a).

4 Draw tables of values and use them to draw graphs of:
(a) $y = x - 1$
Draw and label the x axis from -2 to 3 and the y axis from -4 to 3.
(b) $y = 3x + 1$
Draw and label the x axis from -1 to 3 and the y axis from -2 to 10.

5 (a) Draw these graphs **on the same diagram**:
(i) $y = x + 2$ (ii) $y = x + 1$
(iii) $y = x$ (iv) $y = x - 1$
Draw and label the x axis from 0 to 3 and the y axis from -1 to 5.
(b) What do they all have in common? What is different?

6 (a) Draw these graphs **on the same diagram**:
(i) $y = 2x + 2$ (ii) $y = 2x + 1$
(iii) $y = 2x$ (iv) $y = 2x - 1$
Draw and label the x axis from 0 to 3 and the y axis from -1 to 8.
(b) What do they all have in common? What is different?

7 (a) Draw these graphs **on the same diagram**:
(i) $y = 3x + 3$ (ii) $y = 2x + 3$
(iii) $y = x + 3$
Draw and label the x axis from -2 to 2 and the y axis from -3 to 9.
(b) What do they all have in common? What is different?

8 Draw graphs of:
    (a) $y = x - 2$ (b) $y = 3x - 1$ (c) $y = 5 - x$ (d) $y = 6 - 2x$

9 (a) Draw the graph of $y = 2x - 1$ for values of x from -2 to 3.
    (b) Use your graph to find the value of x when $y = 0$.

10 (a) Complete this table and use it to draw the straight line graph of $y = 4 - x$.
        Draw and label the x axis from -3 to 3 and the y axis from -1 to 6.

x	-2	-1	0	1	2
y		5			2

    (b) Use your graph to find the value of:
        (i) y when $x = 1.5$,   (ii) y when $x = -0.5$.

11 (a) Draw the graph of $y = 2x + 1$ for values of x from -2 to 3.
    (b) Use your graph to find the value of:
        (i) y when $x = -1.5$,   (ii) x when $y = 2$.

Gradient and intercept

Lines that are **parallel** have the same **slope** or **gradient**.

$$\text{Gradient} = \frac{\text{distance up}}{\text{distance along}}$$

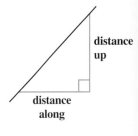

The gradient of a straight line graph is found by drawing a right-angled triangle.

The gradient of a line can be positive, zero or negative.

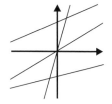 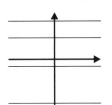 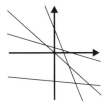

    Positive gradients   **Zero gradients**   **Negative gradients**
     go "uphill".   are "flat".   go "downhill".

The graphs of:
$y = 2x + 2$, $y = 2x + 1$, $y = 2x$, $y = 2x - 1$,
go 2 squares up for every 1 square along.
The graphs are all parallel and have a gradient of 2.

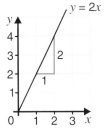

The point where a graph crosses the y axis is called the **y-intercept**.

The graphs of:
$y = 3x + 3$, $y = 2x + 3$, $y = x + 3$, $y = \frac{1}{2}x + 3$,
all cross the y axis at the point (0, 3).
The graphs each have the same y-intercept of 3.

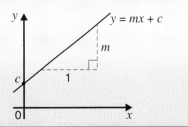

In general, the equation of any straight line can be written in the form

$$y = mx + c$$

    where m is the **gradient** of the line
      and c is the **y-intercept**.

EXAMPLES

1 Write down the gradient and y-intercept for each of the following graphs.
  (a) $y = 3x + 5$
  (b) $y = 4x - 1$
  (c) $y = 6 - x$

  (a) Gradient $= 3$, y-intercept $= 5$.
  (b) Gradient $= 4$, y-intercept $= -1$.
  (c) Gradient $= -1$, y-intercept $= 6$.

2 Write down the equation of the straight line which has gradient -7 and cuts the y axis at the point $(0, 4)$.

The general form for the equation of a straight line is $y = mx + c$.
The gradient, $m = -7$,
and the y-intercept, $c = 4$.
Substitute these values into the general equation.
The equation of the line is
  $y = -7x + 4$.
This can be written as
  $y = 4 - 7x$.

3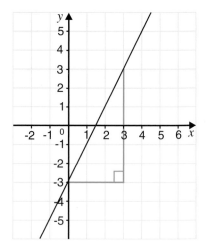

Find the equation of the line shown on this graph.

First, work out the gradient of the line. Draw a right-angled triangle.

$$\text{Gradient} = \frac{\text{distance up}}{\text{distance along}}$$

$$= \frac{6}{3}$$

$$= 2$$

The graph crosses the y axis at the point $(0, -3)$, so the y-intercept is -3.
The equation of the line is $y = 2x - 3$.

Exercise 16.2

1 (a) Write down the gradient and y-intercept of $y = 3x - 1$.
   (b) Draw the graph of $y = 3x - 1$ to check your answer.

2 Which of the following graphs are parallel?

| $y = 3x$ | | $y = x + 2$ | | $y = 2x + 3$ | | $y = 3x + 2$ |

3 Copy and complete this table.

Graph	gradient	y-intercept
$y = 4x + 3$	4	3
$y = 3x + 5$	3	
$y = 2x - 3$		
$y = 4 - 2x$		4
$y = \frac{1}{2}x + 3$		
$y = 2x$		
$y = 3$		
$y = 4 - \frac{1}{2}x$		

4 Match the following equations to their graphs.

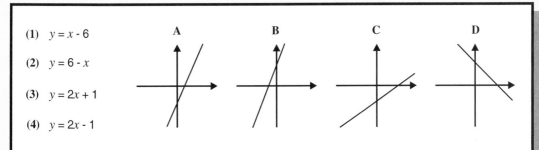

(1) $y = x - 6$

(2) $y = 6 - x$

(3) $y = 2x + 1$

(4) $y = 2x - 1$

A   B   C   D

5 (a) Write down the equation of the straight line which has gradient 5 and crosses the y axis at the point $(0, -4)$.

(b) Write down the equation of the straight line which has gradient $-\frac{1}{2}$ and cuts the y axis at the point $(0, 6)$.

6 Find the equations of the lines shown on the following graphs.

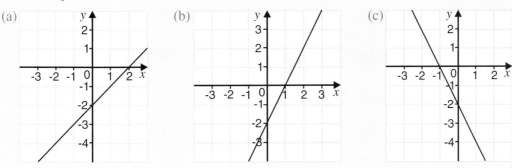

(a)   (b)   (c)

7 (a) Draw x and y axes from -8 to 8.

(b) Plot the points $A(-2, -6)$ and $B(8, 4)$.

(c) Find the gradient of the line which passes through the points A and B.

(d) Write down the coordinates of the point where the line crosses the y axis.

(e) Find the equation of the line which passes through the points A and B.

8 (a) Draw x and y axes from -8 to 8.

(b) Plot the points $P(-2, 3)$ and $Q(3, -7)$.

(c) Find the equation of the line which passes through the points P and Q.

9 What can you say about the slope of a line if the gradient is

(a) 5,   (b) -5,   (c) 0?

10 A line, with a gradient of 3, passes through the origin.
What is the equation of the line?

11 A line, with a gradient of 3, passes through the point $P(-1, 5)$.
What is the equation of the line?

12 A plumber charges a fixed call-out charge and an hourly rate.
The graph shows the charges made for jobs up to 4 hours.

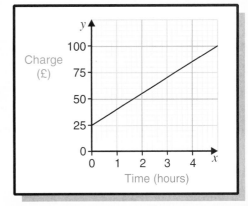

(a) What is the fixed call-out charge?

(b) What is the hourly rate?

(c) Find the equation of the line in the form $y = mx + c$.

(d) Use your equation to calculate the total charge for a job which takes 8 hours.

13 A line, with a gradient of -3, passes through the point $Q(2, 7)$.
What is the equation of the line?

14 The graph shows the taxi fare for journeys up to 3 km.

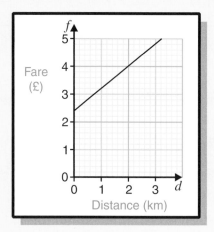

(a) Find the equation of the line, in the form $f = md + c$.
(b) Use your equation to calculate the taxi fare for a journey of 5 km.

15 In an experiment, weights are added to a spring and the length of the spring is measured.
The graph shows the results.

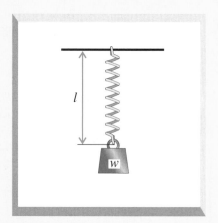 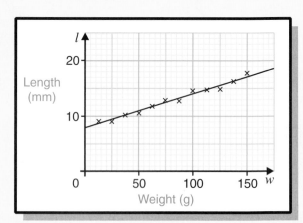

A line of best fit has been drawn.
(a) Find the equation of the line in the form $l = mw + c$.
(b) Use your equation to estimate the length of the spring for a weight of 300 g.

Rearranging equations

The general equation for a straight line graph is $y = mx + c$.
When an equation is in this form the gradient and y-intercept
are given by the values of m and c.

The equation for a straight line can also be written in the form
$px + qy = r$.
To find the gradient and y-intercept of this line we must first
rearrange the equation.

Equations of the form
$px + qy = r$ are used in
simultaneous equations.
You will meet these in
Chapter 17.

EXAMPLES

1 The graph of a straight line is given by the equation $4y - 3x = 8$.
Write this equation in the form $y = mx + c$.

$4y - 3x = 8$
Add $3x$ to both sides.
$\qquad 4y = 3x + 8$
Divide both sides by 4.
$\qquad y = \frac{3}{4}x + 2$

The line has gradient $\frac{3}{4}$ and y-intercept 2.

2 The equation of a straight line is $6x + 3y = 2$.
Write down the equation of another line which is parallel to this line.

Write the equation in the form $y = mx + c$.
$6x + 3y = 2$
Subtract $6x$ from both sides.
$\qquad 3y = -6x + 2$
Divide both sides by 3.
$\qquad y = -2x + \frac{2}{3}$

The gradient of the line is -2.
To write an equation of a parallel line keep the same gradient and change the value of the y-intercept.
For example: $y = -2x + 5$

Write the equations for two different lines which are parallel to this line.

3 Sketch the graph of the line given by the equation $4y - 3x = 12$.

Substitute $x = 0$ into the equation.
$4y = 12$
$\quad y = 3$

The line crosses the y axis at $(0, 3)$.

Substitute $y = 0$ into the equation.
$-3x = 12$
Divide both sides by -3.
$\quad x = -4$

The line crosses the x axis at $(-4, 0)$.

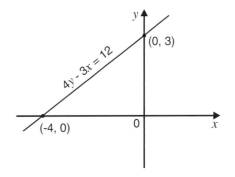

Exercise 16.3

1 The graph of a straight line is given by the equation $2y - 3x = 6$.
Write this equation in the form $y = mx + c$.

2 Write the equations of the following lines in the form $y = mx + c$.
(a) $2y + x = 4$ (b) $5y + 4x = 20$ (c) $4 - 3y = 2x$ (d) $2x - 7y = 14$

3 Find the gradients of these lines.
(a) $2y = x$ (b) $x - y = 0$ (c) $2x - y = 0$
(d) $3y + x = 0$ (e) $4y - 3x = 0$ (f) $2x + 5y = 0$

4 These lines cross the y axis at the point $(0, a)$.
Find the value of a for each line.
(a) $y = x$ (b) $2y = x + 1$ (c) $3y + 6 = x$
(d) $2y - 5 = x$ (e) $4y - 3x = 8$ (f) $x + 5y = 2$

5 Write down an equation which is parallel to each of these lines.
(a) $y = x$ (b) $y = 2x - 3$ (c) $2y = x - 4$

6 The equation of a straight line is $2y + 3x = 4$.
Write down the equation of another line which is parallel to this line.

7 The equation of a line is given by $5y - 4x = 10$.
- (a) Find the gradient of the line.
- (b) Find the y-intercept of the line.
- (c) Write down an equation of another line which has the **same** y-intercept but a **different** gradient.

8 A straight line has equation $3y + 5x = 15$.
- (a) By substituting $x = 0$ find the coordinates of the point where the line crosses the y axis.
- (b) By substituting $y = 0$ find the coordinates of the point where the line crosses the x axis.
- (c) **Sketch** the graph of the line $3y + 5x = 15$.

9 Sketch the graphs of lines with the following equations, marking clearly the coordinates of the points where the lines cross the axes.
- (a) $5y + 4x = 20$
- (b) $4x - y = 2$
- (c) $3y + 2x = 15$

10 The diagram shows a sketch of the line $2y = x + 4$.
- (a) Find the coordinates of points A and B.
- (b) What is the gradient of the line?
- (c) (i) Copy the diagram and draw the sketch of another line that has the same gradient as $2y = x + 4$.
  - (ii) What is the equation of the line you have drawn?

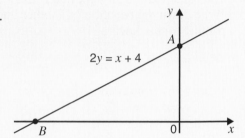

11 The diagram shows a sketch of the line $2y = 6 - x$.
- (a) Find the coordinates of points P and Q.
- (b) What is the gradient of the line?
- (c) (i) Copy the diagram and draw the sketch of another line that has the same gradient as $2y = 6 - x$.
  - (ii) What is the equation of the line you have drawn?

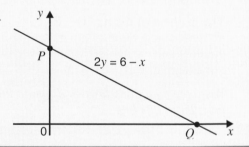

Using graphs to solve equations

The equation $2x - 3 = 2$ can be solved algebraically.

$2x - 3 = 2$
Add 3 to both sides.
$\qquad 2x = 5$
Divide both sides by 2.
$\qquad x = 2.5$

Equations can also be solved using graphs.
The diagram shows two graphs:
$y = 2x - 3$
$y = 2$

At the point where the lines cross,
both $y = 2x - 3$ and $y = 2$ are true.
The value of x at this point is the solution
to the equation $2x - 3 = 2$.
Reading from the graph, $x = 2.5$.

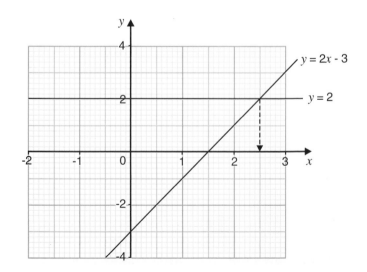

178

EXAMPLE

(a) Complete the tables for $y = x + 6$ and $y = 13 - x$.

x	1	2	3
$y = x + 6$			

x	1	2	3
$y = 13 - x$			

(b) Draw the graphs of $y = x + 6$ and $y = 13 - x$ on the same diagram.
(c) Use your graph to solve the equation $13 - x = x + 6$.

(a)

x	1	2	3
$y = x + 6$	7	8	9

x	1	2	3
$y = 13 - x$	12	11	10

(c) Reading from the graph.
$x = 3.5$

Check the graphical solution of the equation by solving $13 - x = x + 6$ algebraically.

(b)

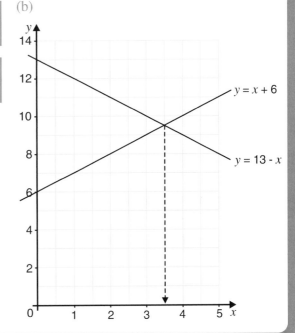

Exercise 16.4

1 (a) Copy and complete the tables for $y = x + 2$ and $y = 5 - x$.

x	1	2	3
$y = x + 2$			

x	1	2	3
$y = 5 - x$			

(b) Draw the graphs of $y = x + 2$ and $y = 5 - x$ on the same diagram.
(c) Use your graphs to solve $x + 2 = 5 - x$.

2 (a) Draw the graphs of $y = 3x + 1$ and $y = x + 6$.
(b) Use your graphs to solve the equation $3x + 1 = x + 6$.

3 (a) Draw the graphs of $y = x$ and $y = 3x - 1$.
(b) Use your graphs to solve the equation $x = 3x - 1$.

4 By drawing the graphs of $y = \frac{1}{2}x$ and $y = 3 - 2x$, solve the equation $\frac{1}{2}x = 3 - 2x$.

5 (a) Draw the graph of $y = 3 + 2x$.
(b) What graph should be drawn to solve the equation $3 + 2x = 9$?
(c) Draw the graph and use it to solve the equation $3 + 2x = 9$.

6 A delivery firm charges £25 for delivering a package.
Another firm uses the formula $y = 10 + 2x$ to calculate the charge, where y is the total cost in pounds, and x is the number of hours taken to make the delivery.
(a) Draw the graph of $y = 10 + 2x$.
(b) On the same axes draw another graph which could be used to solve the equation $10 + 2x = 25$.
(c) What does the solution to the equation in part (b) mean?

7 Two companies each use a formula to calculate the charge made for hiring out scaffolding.
Company A uses the formula $c = 20 + 5d$,
Company B uses the formula $c = 8d + 2$,
where c is the total charge, in pounds,
d is the length of the hire period, in days.
(a) Draw the horizontal axis for d from 0 to 8 and the vertical axis for c from 0 to 60.
(b) Draw the graph of $c = 20 + 5d$.
(c) Draw the graph of $c = 8d + 2$.
Use your graph to answer the following.
(d) From which company is it cheaper to hire scaffolding for 2 days?
(e) From which company is it cheaper to hire scaffolding for 8 days?
(f) For what number of days do both companies make the same charge?

Using graphs

Graphs are sometimes drawn to show real-life situations.
In most cases a quantity is measured over a period of time.

EXAMPLE

Craig drew a graph to show the amount of fuel in the family car as they travelled to their holiday destination. He also made these notes:

Part of Graph	Event
A	Leave home.
A to B	Motorway.
B to C	Car breaks down.
C to D	On our way again.
D to E	Stop for lunch.
E to F	Fill tank with fuel.
F to G	Country roads.
G	Arrive, at last!

How much fuel was in the tank at the start of the journey?

At what time did the car break down?

How long did the family stop for lunch?

How much fuel was put into the tank at the garage?

At what time did the journey end?

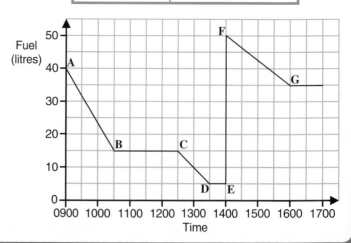

Notice that in this example and others involving graphs against time.

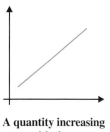

A quantity increasing with time.

A quantity decreasing with time.

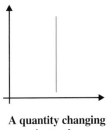

A quantity not changing, i.e. constant.

A quantity changing instantly.

Exercise 16.5

1 A climber pulls a rucksack up a vertical cliff face using a rope.
Which of the graphs below could represent the motion of the rucksack against time?

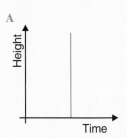

A

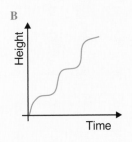

B

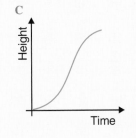

C

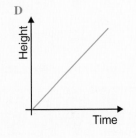

D

2 (a) Sketch a graph to show what is happening in this story:
"John leaves home at 8 am to go the shops. After 5 minutes he sees the bus coming and runs for 2 minutes. The bus has broken down so he waits for 3 minutes. He then walks slowly home, which takes 10 minutes."

(b) Write a similar story about your journey to school and draw a graph for it.

(c) Write a story for this graph.

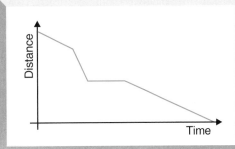

3 Match the graphs to the situations. In each graph, the horizontal axis represents time and the vertical axis represents speed.

1 A runner starts from rest and begins to pick up speed.

2 A runner keeps having to stop and start.

3 A runner gets tired and has to slow down.

4 A runner sees the finish, builds up speed and sprints to the line.

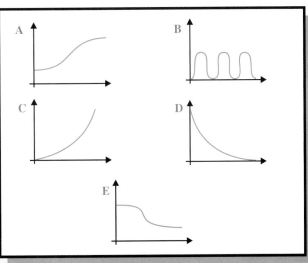

4 Cans of drink can be bought from a vending machine in the school canteen.

At 0900 one day the machine is three-quarters full.

During break, from 1045 to 1100, drinks are bought from the machine at a steady rate.

By the end of the break the machine is one-quarter full.

At 1200 the machine is filled.

The lunch break is from 1230 to 1330. Someone complains at 1315 that the machine is empty.

The machine is filled at 1400, ready for the afternoon break from 1445 to 1500.

At 1600 the machine is three-quarters full.

Sketch a graph to show the number of drinks in the machine from 0900 to 1600.

5 Water is poured into some containers at a constant rate.

Copy the axes given and sketch the graph of the depth of the water against time for each container as it is filled.

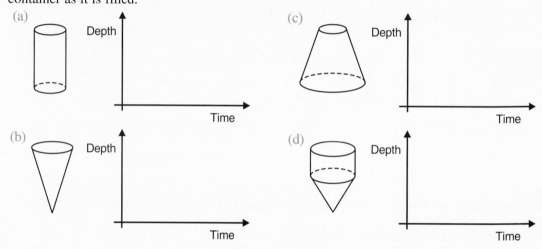

6 Water is drained from a hole in the bottom of a container.

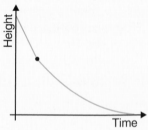

The graph shows the height of the water against time as the water is drained.

Water is drained from these containers. Each graph shows the height of the water against time.

(a) Match the containers to the graphs.

(b) Draw a container for the graph which is not matched.

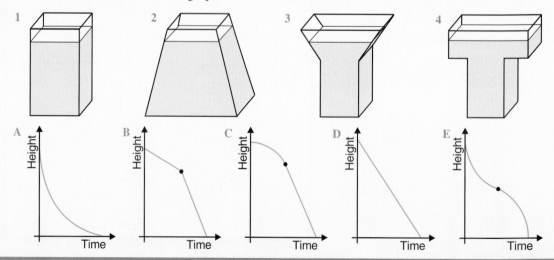

- **Coordinates** (involving positive and negative numbers) are used to describe the position of a point on a graph. For example, $A(-3, 2)$ is the point where the lines $x = -3$ and $y = 2$ cross.

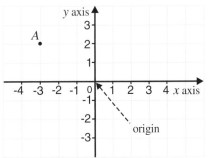

The x axis crosses the y axis at the origin.

- The **gradient** of a line can be found by drawing a right-angled triangle.

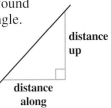

$$\text{Gradient} = \frac{\text{distance up}}{\text{distance along}}$$

Gradient can be positive, zero or negative.

In general, the equation of any straight line can be written in the form

$$y = mx + c$$

where m is the **gradient** of the line and c is the **y-intercept**.

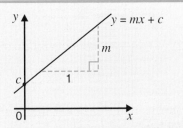

- The points where a line crosses the axes can be found:
   by reading the coordinates from a graph,
   by substituting $x = 0$ and $y = 0$ into the equation of the line.

- Equations of the form $px + qy = r$ can be **rearranged** to the form $y = mx + c$.

You should be able to:
- Plot coordinates and draw graphs.
- Find the equation for a given line.
- Solve equations and problems involving straight line graphs.
- Draw and interpret graphs which represent real-life situations.

Review Exercise

1 The graph represents $y = 3x - 2$.

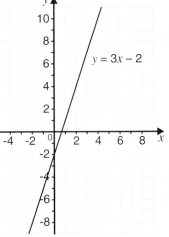

$y = 3x - 2$

(a) When $x = 2$, find the value of y.
(b) When $y = -5$, find the value of x.
(c) Explain whether or not the line $y = 3x - 2$ passes through the point $(10, 27)$. *Edexcel*

2 (a) Copy and complete the table of values for the equation $y = x + 2$.

x	-2	-1	0	1	2
y					

(b) Draw the graph of $y = x + 2$.
(c) The points $P(a, 7)$ and $Q(-5, b)$ lie on the line $y = x + 2$.
Find the values of a and b.

3 (a) On a single diagram draw and label the lines:
$y = 3x$ and $y = 4 - x$.
(b) Write down the coordinates of the point where the lines cross.

4 (a) Copy and complete the table of values for the equation $y = 2x - 1$.

x	-2	-1	0	1	2	3
y						

(b) Draw the graph of $y = 2x - 1$.

(c) Use your graph to find:
   (i)   the value of y when $x = -1.4$,
   (ii) the value of x when $y = 3.8$.

Edexcel

5 (a) On the same diagram draw and label the lines:
   $y = 3$ and $x + y = 5$.

(b) Write down the coordinates of the point where the lines cross.

6 (a) Draw and label the following lines:
   $y = 2x$ and $y = 2x + 1$.

(b) Explain why the lines are parallel.

7 The diagram shows a sketch of the graph $y = x$.

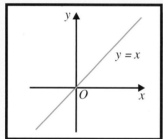

(a) Copy the diagram and, on the same axes, sketch the graph of $y = 5x - 3$. On your sketch write the coordinates of the point where your graph crosses the y axis.

(b) The line which has gradient 2 and passes through the point $(0, -1)$ has equation $y = mx + c$.
   (i)   What is the value of m?
   (ii) What is the value of c?

8 The diagram shows line L.

Write down an equation for the line.

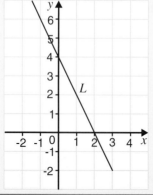

9 The table shows the cost for the delivery of different quantities of bricks.

Number of bricks	500	1200	2000
Cost (£)	140	280	440

The cost includes a fixed amount for delivery and a charge for each brick.

(a) Use this information to draw a graph.

(b) What is the fixed delivery charge?

(c) Find the equation of the line in the form $y = mx + c$.

(d) Calculate the cost for a delivery of 5000 bricks.

10

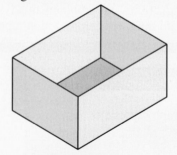

The equation of the straight line drawn on the above axes is $y = mx + c$.

(a) Find the values of c and m.

(b) Give the coordinates of the point where the line $y = 3x - 4$ crosses the y axis.

Edexcel

11 The diagram shows a water tank.

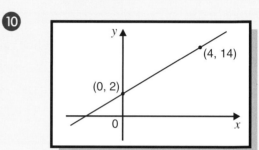

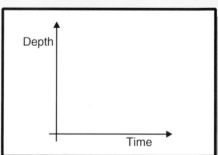

Water is poured into the tank at a constant rate until it is full.
Sketch the graph of the depth of water against time as it is being filled.

12 The graph illustrates a 10 km cycle race between Afzal and Brian.

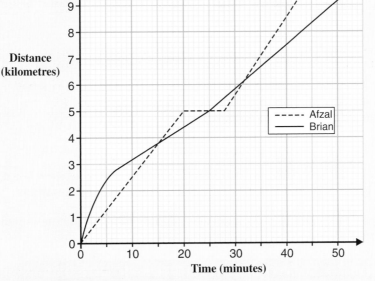

(a) Who was cycling faster at the beginning of the race?
(b) Which cyclist stopped?
(c) How far apart were the cyclists 10 minutes after the start of the race?
(d) Who won the race?

13 These two containers are full of water.
Both are emptied from taps at
the bottom of each container.
Sketch the graph of the depth
of water against time for each
container as it is being emptied.

(a)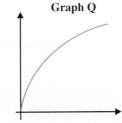

(b)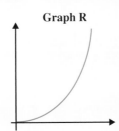

14 Which graph matches each relationship?

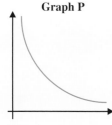   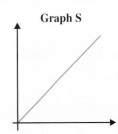

Graph P   **Graph Q**   **Graph R**   **Graph S**

A: The volume of a cube plotted against the length of its edge.
B: The cost of posting letters 1st class plotted against the number of letters posted.

15 The diagram shows a sketch of the line $y = 2x + 3$.
(a) Find the coordinates of the points marked A and B.
(b) Write down the equation of a line parallel to $y = 2x + 3$
which passes through the point $(0, -2)$.

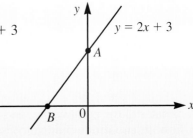

Simultaneous Equations

$x + y = 10$ is an equation with two unknown quantities x and y.
Many pairs of values of x and y fit this equation.
For example.
$x = 1$ and $y = 9$, $x = 4$ and $y = 6$, $x = 2.9$ and $y = 7.1$, $x = 1.005$ and $y = 8.995$, ...
$x - y = 2$ is another equation with the **same** two unknown quantities x and y.
Again, many pairs of values of x and y fit this equation.
For example.
$x = 4$ and $y = 2$, $x = 7$ and $y = 5$, $x = 2.9$ and $y = 0.9$, $x = -1$ and $y = -3$, ...

There is only **one** pair of values of x and y which fit **both** of these equations ($x = 6$ and $y = 4$).
Pairs of equations like $x + y = 10$ and $x - y = 2$ are called **simultaneous equations**.

To solve simultaneous equations you need to find values which fit **both** equations simultaneously.
Simultaneous equations can be solved using different methods.

Using graphs to solve simultaneous equations

Consider the simultaneous equations $x + 2y = 5$ and $x - 2y = 1$.

Draw the graphs of $x + 2y = 5$ and $x - 2y = 1$.

For $x + 2y = 5$:
When $x = 1$, $y = 2$.
This gives the point $(1, 2)$.

When $x = 5$, $y = 0$.
This gives the point $(5, 0)$.

To draw the graph of $x + 2y = 5$
draw a line through the points
$(1, 2)$ and $(5, 0)$.

For $x - 2y = 1$:
When $x = 1$, $y = 0$.
This gives the point $(1, 0)$.

When $x = 5$, $y = 2$.
This gives the point $(5, 2)$.

To draw the graph of $x - 2y = 1$
draw a line through the points
$(1, 0)$ and $(5, 2)$.

> Drawing straight line graphs was first covered in Chapter 16.

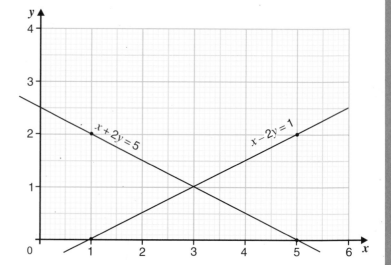

The values of x and y at the point where the lines cross give the solution to the simultaneous
equations.

The lines cross at the point $(3, 1)$.

This gives the solution $x = 3$ and $y = 1$.

To solve a pair of simultaneous equations plot the graph of each of the equations on the same diagram.
The coordinates of the point where the two lines cross:
- fit **both equations** simultaneously,
- give the **graphical solution** of the equations.

EXAMPLE

Use a graphical method to solve this pair of simultaneous equations:
$$5x + 2y = 20$$
$$y = 2x + 1$$

Find the points that fit the equations $5x + 2y = 20$ and $y = 2x + 1$.

For $5x + 2y = 20$:

When $x = 0$, $y = 10$.
This gives the point $(0, 10)$.

When $y = 0$, $x = 4$.
This gives the point $(4, 0)$.

Draw a line through the points $(0, 10)$ and $(4, 0)$.

For $y = 2x + 1$:

When $x = 0$, $y = 1$.
This gives the point $(0, 1)$.

When $x = 4$, $y = 9$.
This gives the point $(4, 9)$.

Draw a line through the points $(0, 1)$ and $(4, 9)$.

The lines cross at the point $(2, 5)$.
This gives the solution
$x = 2$ and $y = 5$.

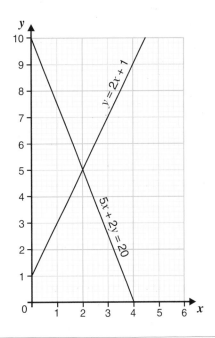

Check
You can check a graphical solution by substituting the values of x and y into the original equations.
When $x = 2$ and $y = 5$
$$5x + 2y = 5 \times 2 + 2 \times 5 = 20$$
$$y = 2x + 1 = 2 \times 2 + 1 = 5$$

Exercise 17.1

Use a graphical method to solve each of these pairs of simultaneous equations.
For each question use the sizes of axes given.
All solutions are positive whole numbers.

Drawing and labelling axes
$0 \leq x \leq 8$ means draw and label the x axis from 0 to 8 inclusive.
What does $-3 \leq y \leq 7$ mean?

1 $x + y = 6$
$y = x - 2$
Axes $0 \leq x \leq 8$, $-3 \leq y \leq 7$

2 $x + y = 8$
$y - x = 2$
Axes $0 \leq x \leq 10$, $-3 \leq y \leq 10$

3 $x + 2y = 8$
$2x + y = 7$
Axes $0 \leq x \leq 10$, $0 \leq y \leq 8$

4 $3x + 2y = 12$
$y = x + 1$
Axes $0 \leq x \leq 5$, $0 \leq y \leq 8$

5 $x + 3y = 6$
$y = 2x - 5$
Axes $0 \leq x \leq 10$, $-6 \leq y \leq 4$

6 $3x + 4y = 24$
$2y = x + 2$
Axes $-4 \leq x \leq 10$, $-2 \leq y \leq 8$

Simultaneous equations with no solution

Some pairs of simultaneous equations do not have a solution.

EXAMPLE

Show that this pair of simultaneous equations do not have a solution.

$y - 2x = 4$
$2y = 4x - 1$

Method 1
Draw the graph of each equation.

$y - 2x = 4$
When $x = 0$, $y = 4$.
When $y = 0$, $x = -2$.
Plot and draw a line through the points $(0, 4)$ and $-2, 0)$.

$2y = 4x - 1$
When $x = 0$, $y = -0.5$.
When $x = 2$, $y = 3.5$.
Plot and draw a line through the points $(0, -0.5)$ and $(2, 3.5)$.

The two lines are **parallel**.
This means they never cross and there are no values of x and y which fit both equations.
So the simultaneous equations have no solution.

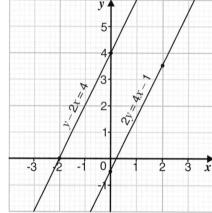

Method 2
Rearrange each equation to the form $y = mx + c$.

$y - 2x = 4$
Add $2x$ to both sides.
$y = 2x + 4$
The graph of this equation has a gradient (m) of 2 and a y-intercept (c) of 4.

$2y = 4x - 1$
Divide both sides by 2.
$y = 2x - 0.5$
The graph of this equation has a gradient (m) of 2 and a y-intercept (c) of -0.5.

Both lines have the same gradient (2) and different y-intercepts which shows that the lines are parallel.

Exercise **17.2**

1 Draw graphs to show that each of these pairs of simultaneous equations have no solution.

(a) $x + y = 6$
$y = 2 - x$

(b) $y - 4x = 8$
$y = 4x + 2$

(c) $3x + 4y = 12$
$8y = 24 - 6x$

(d) $5y - 2x = 10$
$5y = 2x + 20$

2 By rearranging each of these pairs of simultaneous equations to the form $y = mx + c$ show that they do not have a solution.

(a) $2x + y = 6$
$y = 3 - 2x$

(b) $2y - 4x = 7$
$y - 2 = 2x$

(c) $5x - 2y = 8$
$4y = 10x + 7$

(d) $4y + 12x = 5$
$1 - 2y = 6x$

3 Two of these pairs of simultaneous equations have no solution.

(a) $5x + y = 6$
$y - 5x = 2$

(b) $5x = 8 + y$
$y - 5x = 2$

(c) $2y - 10x = 5$
$4y + 20x = 5$

(d) $y + 1 = -5x$
$2y + 10x = 5$

Use an appropriate method to find which ones.
Use a graphical method to solve the other two.

188

The elimination method

The graphical method of solving simultaneous equations can be quite time consuming.
Sometimes, due to the equations involved, the coordinates of the points where the lines intersect
can be difficult to read accurately.
For these reasons, other methods of solving simultaneous equations are often used.

Consider again the simultaneous equations $x + 2y = 5$ and $x - 2y = 1$.
Both equations have the same number of x's and the same number of y's.
If the two equations are added together the y's will be **eliminated** as shown.

$$x + 2y = 5$$
$$x - 2y = 1$$

Adding gives $\quad 2x \quad\quad = 6$

So $\quad\quad x \quad\quad = 3$

Remember
$$+ 2y + -2y$$
$$= 2y - 2y = 0$$

By **substituting** the value of this letter (x) into one of the
original equations we can find the value of the other letter (y).

$$x + 2y = 5$$
$$3 + 2y = 5$$
$$2y = 2$$
$$y = 1$$

This gives the solution $x = 3$ and $y = 1$.

Remember:
If you do the same to both sides of
an equation it is still true.

EXAMPLES

1 Use the elimination method to solve this
pair of simultaneous equations:
$$2x - y = 1$$
$$3x + y = 9$$

Each equation has the **same number** of
y's but the **signs** are **different**.
To eliminate the y's the equations must
be **added**.

$$5x = 10$$
$$x = 2$$

Substitute $x = 2$ into $3x + y = 9$.
$$3 \times 2 + y = 9$$
$$6 + y = 9$$
$$y = 3$$

The solution is $x = 2$ and $y = 3$.

Check
Substitute $x = 2$ and $y = 3$ into
$$2x - y = 1$$
$$2 \times 2 - 3 = 1$$
$$4 - 3 = 1$$
$$1 = 1$$
The equation is true, so the solution
$x = 2$ and $y = 3$ is correct.

2 Use the elimination method to solve this
pair of simultaneous equations:
$$2x + 3y = 9$$
$$2x + y = 7$$

Each equation has the **same number** of
x's and the **signs** are the **same**.
To eliminate the x's one equation must
be **subtracted** from the other.

Subtract $2x + y = 7$ from $2x + 3y = 9$.
$$2y = 2$$
$$y = 1$$

Substitute $y = 1$ into $2x + y = 7$.
$$2x + 1 = 7$$
$$2x = 6$$
$$x = 3$$

The solution is $x = 3$ and $y = 1$.

Check
Substitute $x = 3$ and $y = 1$ into
$2x + 3y = 9$.
*Do this and make sure the solution is
correct.*

Simultaneous Equations

Use the elimination method to solve each of these pairs of simultaneous equations.

1 $3x - y = 1$
$x + y = 3$

2 $2x - y = 2$
$x + y = 7$

3 $4x + y = 9$
$2x - y = 3$

4 $-x + 2y = 13$
$x + y = 8$

5 $2x + y = 7$
$x + y = 4$

6 $3x + y = 9$
$2x + y = 7$

7 $2x + y = 12$
$x + y = 7$

8 $x + 5y = 14$
$x + 2y = 8$

9 $x + 2y = 13$
$x + 4y = 21$

10 $x + 4y = 11$
$x + y = 5$

11 $2x + 5y = 13$
$2x + y = 9$

12 $5x + 3y = 26$
$2x + 3y = 14$

13 $5x + 4y = 22$
$5x + y = 13$

14 $2x - y = 10$
$3x + y = 10$

15 $5x - 2y = 13$
$3x + 2y = 3$

16 $x + 5y = 14$
$-x + 2y = 7$

17 $2x + 3y = 8$
$2x + y = -4$

18 $2x + y = 4$
$4x - y = 11$

19 $3x + 4y = -8$
$x + 4y = 4$

20 $3x + 2y = 6$
$x - 2y = 6$

Further use of the elimination method

Look at this pair of simultaneous equations:
$$5x + 2y = 11$$
$$3x - 4y = 4$$

$5x + 2y = 11$ Equation A
$3x - 4y = 4$ Equation B

> A useful technique is to use capital letters to label the equations.

These equations do not have the same number of x's or the same number of y's.

To make the number of y's the same we can multiply equation A by 2.

A $\times$ 2 gives $10x + 4y = 22$ Equation C
B $\times$ 1 gives $3x - 4y = 4$ Equation D

C + D gives $13x = 26$
                 $x = 2$

> The number of y's in equations **C** and **D** is the **same** but the **signs** are **different**. To eliminate the y's the equations must be **added**.

Substitute $x = 2$ into $5x + 2y = 11$.
$$5 \times 2 + 2y = 11$$
$$10 + 2y = 11$$
$$2y = 1$$
$$y = 0.5$$

The solution is $x = 2$ and $y = 0.5$.

Check the solution by substituting $x = 2$ and $y = 0.5$ into $3x - 4y = 4$.

> In this example eliminating the y's rather than the x's is less likely to produce an error.
> *Try to solve the equations by eliminating the x's.*

EXAMPLE

Solve this pair of simultaneous equations: $3x + 7y = -2$
$4x + 9 = -3y$

Rearrange and label the equations as necessary.
$3x + 7y = -2$ A
$4x + 3y = -9$ B
These equations do not have the same number of x's or the same number of y's.
So the multiplying method can be used.

> Both equations must be in the form $px + qy = r$ before the elimination method can be used.
> You may have to **rearrange** the equations you are given.
> $4x + 9 = -3y$ can be rearranged as $4x + 3y = -9$.

Method 1
Eliminating the x's.

A × 4 gives $12x + 28y = -8$ C
B × 3 gives $12x + 9y = -27$ D

C − D gives $19y = -8 - -27$
                     $19y = -8 + 27$
                     $19y = 19$
                     $y = 1$

Substitute $y = 1$ into $3x + 7y = -2$.
    $3x + 7 \times 1 = -2$
    $3x + 7 = -2$
    $3x = -9$
    $x = -3$

The solution is $x = -3$ and $y = 1$.

Method 2
Eliminating the y's.

A × 3 gives $9x + 21y = -6$ C
B × 7 gives $28x + 21y = -63$ D

D − C gives $19x = -63 - -6$
                     $19x = -63 + 6$
                     $19x = -57$
                     $x = -3$

Substitute $x = -3$ into $3x + 7y = -2$.
    $3 \times -3 + 7y = -2$
    $-9 + 7y = -2$
    $7y = 7$
    $y = 1$

Check the solution by substituting $x = -3$ and $y = 1$ into $4x + 9 = -3y$.

Exercise 17.4

Solve each of these pairs of simultaneous equations.

1 $3x + 2y = 8$
      $2x - y = 3$

2 $x + y = 5$
      $5x - 3y = 1$

3 $2x + 3y = 9$
      $x + 4y = 7$

4 $x + 3y = 10$
      $2x + 5y = 18$

5 $5x + 2y = 8$
      $2x - y = 5$

6 $3x + y = 9$
      $x - 2y = 10$

7 $3x - 4y = 10$
      $x + 2y = 5$

8 $x + 6y = 0$
      $3x - 2y = -10$

9 $2x + 3y = 11$
      $3x + y = 13$

10 $2x + y = 10$
       $-x + 2y = 9$

11 $2x + 3y = 9$
       $4x - y = 4$

12 $2x + 3y = 8$
       $3x + 2y = 7$

13 $3x + 4y = 23$
       $2x + 5y = 20$

14 $2x - 3y = 8$
       $x - 5y = 11$

15 $3x + 4y = 5$
       $-2x + 5y = 12$

16 $3x - 2y = 4$
       $x + 4y = 6$

17 $-3x + 2y = 5$
       $4x + 3y = -1$

18 $3x + 4y = 6$
       $3y = 7 - x$

19 $5x + 3y = 16$
       $2y = 13 - x$

20 $5x - 4y = 24$
       $2x = y + 9$

21 $2x + 3y = 14$
       $8x - 5y = 5$

22 $4x - 7y = 15$
       $5x - 12 = 2y$

23 $8x + 3y = 2$
       $5x = 1 - 2y$

24 $9x = 4y - 20$
       $5x = 6y - 13$

The substitution method

For some pairs of simultaneous equations a method using **substitution** is sometimes more convenient.

EXAMPLE

Solve this pair of simultaneous equations: $5x + y = 9$

$\qquad\qquad\qquad\qquad\qquad\qquad\qquad\qquad\quad y = 4x$

$5x + y = 9 \qquad$ Equation A
$\qquad y = 4x \qquad$ Equation B
Substitute $y = 4x$ into Equation A
$\qquad 5x + 4x = 9$
$\qquad\qquad 9x = 9$
$\qquad\qquad\quad x = 1$

Substitute $x = 1$ into $y = 4x$.
$y = 4 \times 1$
$y = 4$

The solution is $x = 1$ and $y = 4$.

Check the solution by substituting
$x = 1$ and $y = 4$ into $5x + y = 9$.

Exercise 17.5   Use the substitution method to solve these pairs of simultaneous equations.

1 $\quad 2x + y = 10$
$\qquad\qquad y = 3x$

2 $\quad 3x - y = 9$
$\qquad\qquad y = 2x$

3 $\quad x + 5y = 18$
$\qquad\qquad x = 4y$

4 $\quad x + 2y = 15$
$\qquad\qquad y = 2x$

5 $\quad 2x + y = 17$
$\qquad\qquad y = 6x + 1$

6 $\quad 3x + 2y = 4$
$\qquad\qquad x = y - 2$

7 $\quad 5x + 6y = 34$
$\qquad\qquad y = x + 2$

8 $\quad 5x - 2y = 23$
$\qquad\qquad x = y + 1$

9 $\quad 5x - y = 12$
$\qquad\qquad y = 32 - 6x$

10 $\quad x + 5y = 13$
$\qquad\qquad x = 3y + 9$

11 $\quad 5x - 3y = 26$
$\qquad\qquad y = 2x + 14$

12 $\quad x + 4y = 32$
$\qquad\qquad x = 2y - 4$

Solving problems using simultaneous equations

EXAMPLE

Billy buys 5 first class stamps and 3 second class stamps at a cost of £1.93.
Jane buys 3 first class stamps and 5 second class stamps at a cost of £1.83.
Calculate the cost of a first class stamp and the cost of a second class stamp.

Let x pence be the cost of a first class stamp, and
let y pence be the cost of a second class stamp.
Billy's purchase of the stamps gives this equation.
$$5x + 3y = 193 \qquad \text{Equation A}$$
Jane's purchase of the stamps gives this equation.
$$3x + 5y = 183 \qquad \text{Equation B}$$
This gives a pair of simultaneous equations which can be solved using the elimination method.

$\qquad 5x + 3y = 193 \qquad$ A
$\qquad 3x + 5y = 183 \qquad$ B

A × 5 gives $\quad 25x + 15y = 965 \quad$ C
B × 3 gives $\quad\ \ 9x + 15y = 549 \quad$ D

C − D gives $\quad 16x = 416$
$\qquad\qquad\qquad x = 26$

Substitute $x = 26$ into $5x + 3y = 193$.
$5 \times 26 + 3y = 193$
$\qquad\qquad 3y = 63$
$\qquad\qquad\ y = 21$

So the cost of a first class stamp is 26 pence and the cost of a second class stamp is 21 pence.

Check the solution by substituting the values for x and y into the original problem.

Exercise 17.6

1 Pencils cost x pence each and pens cost y pence each.
Pam buys 6 pencils and 3 pens for 93 pence.
Ray buys 2 pencils and 5 pens for 91 pence.
(a) Write down two equations connecting x and y.
(b) By solving these simultaneous equations find the cost of a pencil and the cost of a pen.

2 Apples are x pence per kg. Oranges are y pence each.
5 kg of apples and 30 oranges cost £9.00.
10 kg of apples and 15 oranges cost £12.60.
(a) Write down two equations connecting x and y.
(b) By solving these simultaneous equations find the cost of a kilogram of apples and the cost of an orange.

3 Standard eggs cost x pence per dozen. Small eggs cost y pence per dozen.
10 dozen standard eggs and 5 dozen small eggs cost £13.60.
5 dozen standard eggs and 8 dozen small eggs cost £11.31.
By forming two simultaneous equations find the values of x and y.

4 A group of children and adults went on a coach trip to a theme park.
Ticket prices for the theme park were £10 for adults and £5 for children.
Ticket prices for the coach were £5 for adults and £2 for children.
The total cost of the tickets for the theme park was £190.
The total cost of the coach tickets was £79.
How many children and adults went on the trip?

5 Jenny types at x words per minute. Stuart types at y words per minute.
When Jenny and Stuart both type for 1 minute they type a total of 170 words.
When Jenny types for 5 minutes and Stuart types for 3 minutes they type a total of 710 words.
Calculate x and y.

6 At a café, John buys 3 coffees and 2 teas for £2.30 and Susan buys 2 coffees and 3 teas for £2.20.
Calculate the price of a coffee and the price of a tea.

7 Standard coaches hold x passengers and first class coaches hold y passengers.
A train with 5 standard coaches and 2 first class coaches carries a total of 1040 passengers.
A train with 7 standard coaches and 3 first class coaches carries a total of 1480 passengers.
By forming two simultaneous equations find the values of x and y.

What you need to know

- A pair of **simultaneous equations** are linked equations with the same unknown letters in each equation.

- To solve a pair of simultaneous equations find values for the unknown letters that fit **both** equations.

- Simultaneous equations can be solved either **graphically** or **algebraically**.

- Solving simultaneous equations **graphically** involves:
     drawing the graph of both equations,
     finding the point where the graphs cross.
  When the graphs of both equations are parallel, the equations have no solution.

- Solving simultaneous equations **algebraically** involves using either:
     the **elimination** method, or
     the **substitution** method (if it is more convenient).

1 The diagram shows the graph of the line $3y = 6 - 2x$.

(a) Copy the diagram and on the same axes draw the graph of $y = x - 1$.

(b) Use the graphs to solve the simultaneous equations: $3y = 6 - 2x$
$y = x - 1$

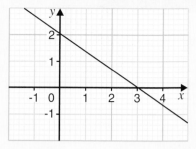

2 Use a graphical method to solve each of these simultaneous equations. For each question use the size of axes given.

(a) $x + y = 10$
$y = 2x + 1$
Axes $0 \leqslant x \leqslant 11, 0 \leqslant y \leqslant 11$

(b) $5x + 6y = 30$
$2y = x - 2$
Axes $0 \leqslant x \leqslant 8, -3 \leqslant y \leqslant 8$

3 Use a graphical method to solve the simultaneous equations: $2y = 3x + 2$
$x + y = 6$

4 Use an algebraic method to solve each of these simultaneous equations. You must show all your working.

(a) $2x + y = 8$
$x + y = 5$

(b) $3x + y = 10$
$x - 2y = 8$

(c) $3y - 5x = 1$
$5y - 3x = 7$

(d) $x + 5y = 3$
$y = 3x + 7$

5 Solve the simultaneous equations: $2x + 3y = 23$
$x - y = 4$

Edexcel

6 Solve the simultaneous equations: $2x + 6y = 17$
$3x - 2y = 20$

Edexcel

7 Solve the simultaneous equations: $2x - 3y = 12$
$x - y = 5$

8 (a) Show that the simultaneous equations $y = 2x - 2$ and $2y - 4x = 3$ have no solution.

(b) Show that the simultaneous equations $4y = x + 1$ and $8y - 2x = 3$ have no solution.

(c) The simultaneous equations $y = 3x + 2$ and $y = ax + b$ have no solution. What can you say about the values of a and b?

(d) The simultaneous equations $y = 3x + 2$ and $py + qx = r$ have no solution. Find some possible values for p, q and r.

9 Mrs Rogers bought 3 blouses and 2 scarves. She paid £26. Miss Summers bought 4 blouses and 1 scarf. She paid £28.

The cost of a blouse was x pounds. The cost of a scarf was y pounds.

(a) Use the information to write down two equations in x and y.

(b) Solve these equations to find the cost of one blouse.

Edexcel

10 Peaches cost x pence each and oranges cost y pence each. 4 peaches and one orange cost 58p. 6 peaches and 2 oranges cost 92p.

(a) Write down two equations connecting x and y.

(b) Solve these simultaneous equations to find the values of x and y.

More or Less

Activity

For all children who enter the competition we can say that
Age < 16 years

For anyone riding the Big Dipper we can say that
Height ≥ 1.2 m

For all items sold in the store we can say that
Cost ≤ £1

These are examples of inequalities.
Can you think of other situations where inequalities are used?

Inequalities

An **inequality** is a mathematical statement, such as $x > 1$ or $a \leq 2$.

In the following, x is an integer.

Sign	Meaning	Example	Possible values of x
<	is less than	$x < 4$	3, 2, 1, 0, −1, −2, −3, …
≤	is less than or equal to	$x \leq 4$	4, 3, 2, 1, 0, −1, −2, −3, …
>	is greater than	$x > 6$	7, 8, 9, 10, …
≥	is greater than or equal to	$x \geq 2$	2, 3, 4, 5, …

> Inequalities are similar to equations.

> An **integer** is a positive or negative whole number or zero.

Explain the difference between the meanings of the signs < and ≤.
Explain the difference between the meanings of the signs > and ≥.

Number lines

Inequalities can be shown on a **number line**.

-6   -5   -4   -3   -2   -1   0   1   2   3   4   5   6

As you move to the right, numbers get bigger.
As you move to the left, numbers get smaller.

Draw number lines to show the following inequalities.

1 $x < 1.5$

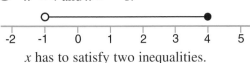

The circle is **not filled** because 1.5 is **not included**.

2 $x \geqslant -2$

The circle is **filled** because -2 is **included**.

3 $x \leqslant 4$ and $x > -1$.

x has to satisfy two inequalities.

4 $3 \leqslant x < 8$

Exercise 18.1

1 Write down the following mathematical statements and say whether each is true or false.
(a) $4 < 7$ (b) $3 > -3$ (c) $4 \geqslant 4$ (d) $-2 > -1$
(e) $-8 \leqslant -8$ (f) $1.5 \geqslant 2.1$ (g) $3 \times 5 \leqslant 7 \times 2$ (h) $-4 \times (-2) > -4 - 4$

2 Write down an integer which could replace the letter.
(a) $x < 6$ (b) $a \geqslant -2$ (c) $c + 2 < 8$ (d) $2d \leqslant 14$
(e) $f - 3 > 7$ (f) $-2 < h < 0$ (g) $t \leqslant 5$ **and** $t > 4$ (h) $r \geqslant -6$ **and** $r < -1$

3 In this question x is an integer. Write down all the values of x which satisfy these inequalities.
(a) $1 < x < 5$ (b) $-2 < x \leqslant 3$ (c) $-4 \leqslant x \leqslant -1$ (d) $-1 \leqslant x < 3$

4 Write down a mathematical statement, using inequalities, for each of these diagrams.

(a)

(b)

(c)

(d)

5 Draw number lines to show the following inequalities. For each part, draw and label a number line from -5 to 5.
(a) $-2 \leqslant x < 3$ (b) $x > -4$ (c) $x < -3$ and $x \geqslant 1$

Solving inequalities

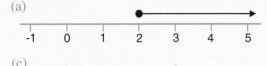

Solve means to find the values of x which make the inequality true.
The aim is to end up with **one letter** on one side of the inequality and a **number** on the other side of the inequality.

EXAMPLES

1 Solve the inequality $5x - 3 < 27$ and show the solution on a number line.

$5x - 3 < 27$
Add 3 to both sides.
$\quad 5x < 30$
Divide both sides by 5.
$\quad\quad x < 6$

The solution is shown on a number line as:

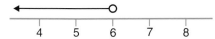

This means that the inequality is **true** for all values of x which are less than 6.

2 Solve the inequality $7a \geqslant a + 9$.

$7a \geqslant a + 9$
Subtract a from both sides.
$6a \geqslant 9$
Divide both sides by 6.
$\quad a \geqslant 1.5$

This means that the inequality is true for all values of a which are equal to 1.5, or greater.
Substitute $a = 1.5$, $a = 2$ and $a = 1$ into the original inequality.
What do you notice?

Exercise **18.2**

1 Solve each of the following inequalities and show the solution on a number line.

(a) $3n > 6$
(b) $a + 1 < 5$
(c) $2d - 5 \leqslant 1$
(d) $t + 2 < -1$
(e) $5 + 2g > 1$
(f) $4 + 3y \geqslant 4$

2 Solve the following inequalities. Show your working clearly.

(a) $a + 3 < 7$
(b) $b - 3 \geqslant -2$
(c) $-2 + b \leqslant -1$
(d) $3c > 15$
(e) $2d < -6$
(f) $\frac{1}{2}a \geqslant 3$
(g) $\frac{1}{3}b < 5$
(h) $2c + 5 \leqslant 11$
(i) $3d - 4 > 8$
(j) $4 + 3f < -2$
(k) $8g - 1 \leqslant 3$
(l) $5h < h + 8$
(m) $6j \geqslant 2j + 10$
(n) $7k > 3k - 16$
(o) $4m + 2 > 2m - 11$
(p) $7n - 3 \leqslant 13 - n$
(q) $3p - 2 > 6 + 2p$
(r) $4q + 5 > 12 - 3q$
(s) $6r + 1 \geqslant 4r - 2$
(t) $2t - 10 > t + 3$
(u) $2(u - 5) \leqslant 8$
(v) $3(4v + 1) < -15$
(w) $\frac{1}{2}w + 3 > 7$
(x) $\frac{1}{2}(5x - 1) < 3$

Multiplying (or dividing) an inequality by a negative number

Activity

$-2 < 3$

Multiply both sides by -1.
$-2 \times (-1) = 2$ and $3 \times (-1) = -3$

$2 > -3$

To keep the statement true we have to reverse the inequality sign.

Multiply both sides of these inequalities by -1.

1 $3 > 2$

2 $3 > -2$

3 $-3 < -1$

4 $5 \geqslant 4$

5 $-4 \leqslant 5$

6 $-4 \geqslant -5$

The same rules for equations can be applied to inequalities, with one exception:

When you **multiply** (or **divide**) both sides of an inequality by a negative number the inequality is reversed.

Remember:
Division is the inverse (opposite) operation to multiplication.

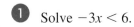

EXAMPLES

1 Solve $-3x < 6$.

Divide both sides by -3.
Because we are dividing by a negative number the inequality is reversed.
$x > -2$

2 Solve $3a - 2 \geqslant 5a - 9$.

Subtract $5a$ from both sides.
$-2a - 2 \geqslant -9$
Add 2 to both sides.
$-2a \geqslant -7$
Divide both sides by -2.
$a \leqslant 3.5$

Exercise 18.3

Solve the following inequalities. Show your working clearly.

1 $-4a > 8$

2 $-5b \leqslant -15$

3 $-3c \geqslant 12$

4 $3 - 2d < 5$

5 $14 - 3e \leqslant 4e$

6 $-5f > 4f - 9$

7 $4g < 7g + 12$

8 $5 - 3h \leqslant h - 3$

9 $-5 - j \geqslant 12j - 18$

10 $3 - 5k < 2(3 + 2k)$

11 $3(m - 2) > 5m$

12 $3(2n - 1) < 8n + 5$

13 $3p \geqslant 5 - 6p$

14 $2(q - 3) < 5 + 7q$

15 $n - 5 > 2(n - 7)$

Double inequalities

EXAMPLE

Find the values of x such that $-8 < 4x - 2 \leqslant 10$.

$-8 < 4x - 2 \leqslant 10$
Add 2 to each part of the inequality.
$-6 < 4x \leqslant 12$
Divide each part of the inequality by 4.
$-1.5 < x \leqslant 3$

Alternative method
Write the **double inequality** as two separate inequalities.
$-8 < 4x - 2$ and $4x - 2 \leqslant 10$
Solve each inequality.

$-8 < 4x - 2$
Add 2 to both sides.
$-6 < 4x$
Divide both sides by 4.
$-1.5 < x$

$4x - 2 \leqslant 10$
Add 2 to both sides.
$4x \leqslant 12$
Divide both sides by 4.
$x \leqslant 3$

So $-1.5 < x \leqslant 3$

The double inequality $-1.5 < x \leqslant 3$ gives **all** the possible values of x.
This means that the inequality $-8 < 4x - 2 \leqslant 10$ is true for all the values of x from -1.5 (not included) up to 3 (included).

Inequalities involving integers

EXAMPLE

Find the integer values of n for which $-1 \leqslant 2n + 3 < 7$.

$-1 \leqslant 2n + 3 < 7$
Subtract 3 from each part.
$-4 \leqslant 2n < 4$
Divide each part by 2.
$-2 \leqslant n < 2$

Integer values which satisfy the inequality $-1 \leqslant 2n + 3 < 7$ are: $-2, -1, 0, 1$.

Exercise 18.4

1 Solve each of the following inequalities and show the solution on a number line.
   (a) $5 < x + 4 \leqslant 9$
   (b) $-3 \leqslant x - 2 < 7$
   (c) $2 < 9 + x \leqslant 13$

2 Find the values of x such that:
   (a) $2 < 2x \leqslant 6$
   (b) $-6 \leqslant 3x < 12$
   (c) $5 < 2x - 1 < 8$
   (d) $-2 \leqslant 3x - 1 \leqslant 11$
   (e) $12 < 5x + 2 \leqslant 27$
   (f) $-9 \leqslant 4x + 3 < 27$
   (g) $-16 < 7x - 2 < 12$
   (h) $-1 \leqslant 3x - 10 < 8$
   (i) $-4 \leqslant 5 + 2x \leqslant 3$

3 Find the integer values of n for which:
   (a) $3 < n - 2 < 7$
   (b) $-2 < n + 1 \leqslant 5$
   (c) $-2 < 2n \leqslant 4$
   (d) $5 \leqslant 2n - 3 < 13$
   (e) $0 < 2n - 8 < 3$
   (f) $5 < 4n + 1 \leqslant 13$
   (g) $-4 \leqslant 5n + 6 < 11$
   (h) $-4 < 3n + 2 \leqslant 11$
   (i) $-5 \leqslant \frac{1}{2}n - 3 \leqslant 0$
   (j) $-12 < 5 - n \leqslant -3$
   (k) $-3 \leqslant 4 - 2n \leqslant 12$
   (l) $-5 < 3(n + 5) < 0$

Graphs of inequalities

Activity

Line A has equation $y = 2$.

Describe the y coordinates of points **on** line A.
Describe the y coordinates of points **below** line A.
Describe the y coordinates of points **above** line A.

Above the line is the region $y > 2$.
Below the line is the region $y < 2$.

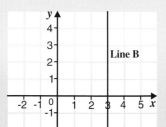

Use an inequality to describe the region to the right of line B.
Use an inequality to describe the region to the left of line B.

A line divides the graph into two **regions**.
The region $x \leqslant 2$ is to the **left** of the line $x = 2$, including the line itself.
The region $x \geqslant 2$ is to the **right** of the line $x = 2$, including the line itself.

The region $y < -3$ is **below** the line $y = -3$.
The region $y > -3$ is **above** the line $y = -3$.

A **solid line** is used when the points on the line are included.
A **broken line** is used when the points on the line are not included.

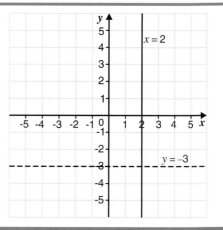

EXAMPLE

On a sketch, show the region where the inequalities $x > -2$ and $y \leqslant 1$ are both true.
Label the region R.

To do this:
1 Draw the x and y axes.
2 Draw and label the line $x = -2$, using a broken line.
3 Show the region $x > -2$ by shading out the **unwanted** region.

4 Draw and label the line $y = 1$ using a solid line.
5 Show the region $y \leqslant 1$ by shading out the **unwanted** region.

6 Label the region, R, where $x > -2$ **and** $y \leqslant 1$.
Note that the region R extends for ever to the right and downwards.

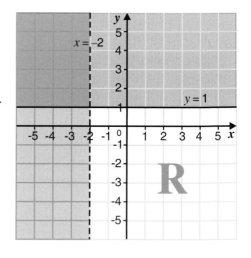

Shading regions on a graph
Unless you are told to do otherwise, always shade out the **unwanted** region.

Exercise 18.5

For each question, draw and label axes for x and y from -5 to 5. Shade the unwanted regions.
Leave the given region unshaded and label it R.

1 $x > 2$ and $y \geqslant 1$

2 $x \geqslant -3$ and $y < 4$

3 $x \geqslant -2$, $x < 1$ and $y > 2$

4 $x < 5$, $x \geqslant -1$ and $y \leqslant 3$

5 $x \leqslant 2$, $x > -2$, $y < 3$ and $y \geqslant 1$

6 $x \geqslant -2$, $x \leqslant 0$, $y \geqslant 1$ and $y \leqslant 4$

7 $x \leqslant 1.5$, $y > -1$ and $y \leqslant 2.5$

8 $x > -2.5$, $x \leqslant 1.5$ and $y \leqslant 2.5$

EXAMPLES

1 Show the region defined by the inequality $y \geq 2x - 3$.

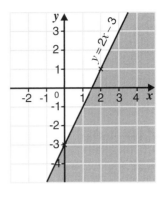

First draw the line with equation $y = 2x - 3$.
When $x = 0$, $y = -3$. Plot the point $(0, -3)$.
When $x = 2$, $y = 1$. Plot the point $(2, 1)$.

Next, draw the line through the two points.
Use a solid line because the inequality sign is $\geq$.

Now test a point above the line and a point below the line.

Point	Coordinates	Value of y	Value of $2x - 3$	Is $y \geq 2x - 3$?
Above	$(1, 3)$	3	-1	Yes
Below	$(4, -2)$	-2	5	No

The inequality $y \geq 2x - 3$ is true **above** the line, so we shade the unwanted region, below the line.

2 Show the region where the inequality $2x + 3y < 12$ is true.

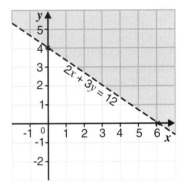

First draw the line with equation $2x + 3y = 12$.
When $x = 0$, $y = 4$. Plot the point $(0, 4)$.
When $y = 0$, $x = 6$. Plot the point $(6, 0)$.

Next, draw the line through the two points.
Use a broken line because the inequality sign is $<$.

Point	Coordinates	Is $2x + 3y < 12$?
Above	$(3, 4)$	No
Below	$(2, 1)$	Yes

The inequality $2x + 3y < 12$ is true **below** the line, so we shade the unwanted region, above the line.

Exercise 18.6

1 Draw graphs to show the following.
Leave unshaded the regions where the inequalities are true.
(a) $y \geq x$
(b) $y < 2x$
(c) $y > x + 1$
(d) $y \leq 2x - 1$
(e) $y < 3x + 1$ and $x < 2$
(f) $y \geq \frac{1}{2}x + 2$, $x > -1$ and $y \leq 5$
(g) $y > -2x + 4$, $y < 5$ and $y \geq -1$
(h) $y \leq 5 - x$, $x \geq -1$ and $y < 3$
(i) $y < x + 5$, $y < 5 - 2x$ and $y > 1$
(j) $y > -3x - 4$, $y < \frac{1}{2}x + 1$ and $y > -1$

2 Draw graphs to show the following.
Label with the letter R the region defined by the inequalities.
(a) $2x + 5y \leq 10$
(b) $3x + 4y > 12$
(c) $4x + 3y \geq 6$ and $y > 2$
(d) $x + 3y < 6$, $x > -1$ and $y > 1$
(e) $2x + 3y > 9$, $x \geq 1$ and $x \leq 6$
(f) $4x + 5y < 10$, $x \geq -1$ and $y > 0$
(g) $3x + y < 9$, $y < 6x + 9$ and $y > -1$
(h) $2x + 5y > 12$, $x + y < 6$ and $x > 0$
(i) $3x + 2y \leq 8$, $2x + 3y > 6$ and $x > -1$

3 Match each of these inequalities to its **unshaded** region.

A $2y < x + 2$ **B** $y > x$ **C** $2y < 4 - x$ **D** $y < 4 - x$

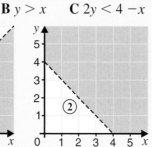

4 Copy the diagram and shade the region which satisfies all of these inequalities:
$y \geqslant 2$, $y \leqslant 2x$, $x > 0$, $x + y \leqslant 4$.

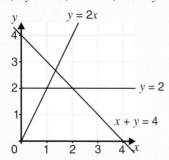

5 The shaded area can be described by three inequalities, one for each side of the shape.
One of the inequalities is $x < 3$.
Write down the other two inequalities.

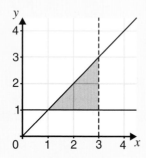

6 Use inequalities to describe the shaded region in this diagram.

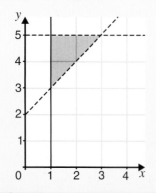

7 Use inequalities to describe the shaded region in this diagram.

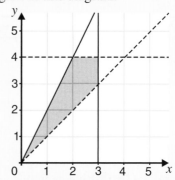

8 Use inequalities to describe the shaded region in this diagram.

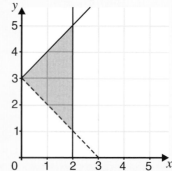

9 A point P has whole number coordinates and lies in the region
$$y < 3, 1 < x < 4 \text{ and } 2y > x.$$

(a) Copy the diagram and show the region which satisfies these inequalities.

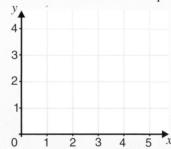

(b) Write down the coordinates of all the possible positions of P.

202

- Inequalities can be described using words or numbers and symbols.

Sign	Meaning
$<$	is less than
$\leqslant$	is less than or equal to
$>$	is greater than
$\geqslant$	is greater than or equal to

- Inequalities can be shown on a **number line**.

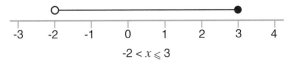

$-2 < x \leqslant 3$

The circle is:
    filled if the inequality is **included** (i.e. $\leqslant$ or $\geqslant$),
    not filled if the inequality is **not included** (i.e. $<$ or $>$).

- Solving inequalities.
  Solve means find the values of x which make the inequality true.
  The same rules for equations can be applied to inequalities, with one exception:
      When you **multiply** (or **divide**) both sides of an inequality by a negative number the inequality is reversed. For example, if $-3x < 6$ then $x > -2$.

- Inequalities can be shown on a graph. Replace the inequality sign by '=' and draw the line.
  For $>$ and $<$ the line is **broken**. For $\geqslant$ and $\leqslant$ the line is **solid**.
  Test a point on each side of the line to see whether its coordinates satisfy the inequality.
  Shade the **unwanted** region.

Review Exercise

You should be able to do all these questions without a calculator.

1 Solve these inequalities.
(a) $3x \geqslant -15$
(b) $3x < x + 6$
(c) $5x - 4 \leqslant 2x + 14$
(d) $5 - 3x < 11$

2 Draw number lines to show each of these inequalities.
(a) $x \leqslant -1$
(b) $4 < x \leqslant 9$
(c) $x < -2$ **and** $x > 5$

3 w is a whole number such that $5 < 2w < 12$.
List all the possible values of w.

4 n is an integer such that $1 < n + 3 \leqslant 5$.
List all the possible values of n.

5 Solve these inequalities and show the solution on a number line.
(a) $x - 3 < 1$
(b) $-2 < 2x \leqslant 4$
(c) $-1 \leqslant 3x + 2 < 5$
(d) $-1 < 2x + 5 < 3$

6 Solve the inequalities.
(a) $5x < -10$
(b) $3x - 7 \geqslant 8$
(c) $2x - 4 \leqslant 5 - x$

7 Find the integer values of n such that:
(a) $-4 < 2n \leqslant 8$
(b) $-3 \leqslant 3n + 6 < 12$
(c) $-4 \leqslant 5n + 6 \leqslant 1$

8 (a) y is an integer and $-2 < y < 2$.
Write down all the possible values of y.
(b) (i) Solve the inequality $3n > -8$.
(ii) Write down the smallest integer which satisfies the inequality $3n > -8$.
Edexcel

9 List all the possible values of x, where x is an integer, such that $-3 \leqslant x - 1 < 1$.

10 Solve $5a + 1 < 4$.

11 Solve the inequalities.
(a) $x - 5 > 3x + 7$
(b) $3(x - 3) < x$

12 (a) Solve the inequality $5n + 2 \leq n + 22$.

(b) Write down the maximum value of n that satisfies the inequality $5n + 2 \leq n + 22$.

Edexcel

13 (a) Solve $2(x - 3) < 5(3 - x)$.

(b) n is an integer, such that $-2 < 2(x - 3) \leq 4$.
List all the possible values of n.

Edexcel

14 Copy the grids and shade the regions where:

(a) $x < 3$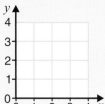

(b) $y > 2$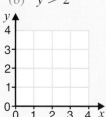

(c) $y > x$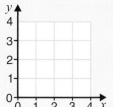

15 The diagram shows part of the graph of
$x + 2y = 8$.

Copy the diagram.
Shade in the region which satisfies all the
following three inequalities: $x + 2y \leq 8$
$x \geq 0$
$y \geq 0$

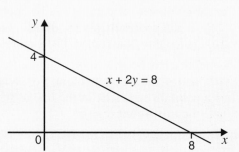

Edexcel

16 (a) Use inequalities to describe
the shaded region in this
diagram.

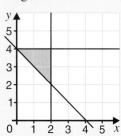

(b) Copy this grid.

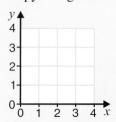

Shade the region which
satisfies **all** of these
inequalities:
$2 < x < 3$, $x + y > 3$ and $y < 3$.

17 Draw and label axes for x from -3 to 8 and for y from 0 to 7.

(a) On your diagram draw and label the lines
$y = 3$ and $x + y = 5$.

(b) Show clearly on your diagram the single region that is satisfied by all of these inequalities.
$x \geq 0$, $y \geq 3$ and $x + y \leq 5$.
Label this region R.

18 Show, on a graph, the region where the following inequalities are true.

(a) $x \leq 2$, $y > -3$ and $y < 1$.

(b) $2x + 3y < 6$, $x > -1$ and $y \geq 0$.

(c) $3x + 4y \leq 12$, $3x + y > 3$ and $y > -1$.

CHAPTER 19

Quadratic and Other Equations

Brackets

You can multiply out brackets, either by using a diagram or by expanding.

Removing brackets was first covered in Chapter 12.

EXAMPLES

1 Multiply out $2(x + 3)$.
Diagram method

$$\xleftarrow{\hspace{1.5cm}} x + 3 \xrightarrow{\hspace{1.5cm}}$$

	x	3
2	2x	6

The areas of the two parts are $2x$ and 6.
The total area is $2x + 6$.
$2(x + 3) = 2x + 6$

Expanding
$2(x + 3) = 2 \times x + 2 \times 3$
$\qquad\qquad = 2x + 6$

2 Multiply out $x(x + 3)$.

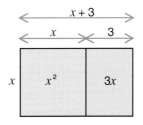

The areas of the two parts are x^2 and $3x$.
$x(x + 3) = x^2 + 3x$

More brackets

This method can be extended to multiply out $(x + 2)(x + 3)$.

The areas of the four parts are:
x^2, $3x$, $2x$ and 6.

$(x + 2)(x + 3) = x^2 + 3x + 2x + 6$
Collect like terms and simplify (i.e. $3x + 2x = 5x$)
$\qquad\qquad = x^2 + 5x + 6$

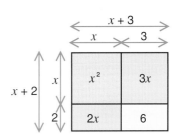

EXAMPLES

1 Expand $(2x + 3)(x + 4)$.

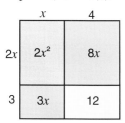

$(2x + 3)(x + 4) = 2x^2 + 8x + 3x + 12$
$\qquad\qquad\qquad = 2x^2 + 11x + 12$

2 Expand $(x + 3)(x - 5)$.

	x	-5
x	x^2	$-5x$
3	$3x$	-15

The diagram method works with negative numbers.
$(x + 3)(x - 5) = x^2 - 5x + 3x - 15$
$\qquad\qquad\qquad = x^2 - 2x - 15$

EXAMPLES

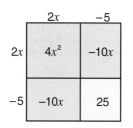

3 Expand $(2x - 5)^2$.

	$2x$	-5
$2x$	$4x^2$	$-10x$
-5	$-10x$	25

$(2x - 5)^2 = (2x - 5)(2x - 5)$
$= 4x^2 - 10x - 10x + 25$
$= 4x^2 - 20x + 25$

4 Expand $(x - 1)(2x + 3)$.
As you become more confident you may not need a diagram to expand the brackets.

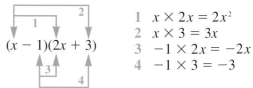

1   $x \times 2x = 2x^2$
2   $x \times 3 = 3x$
3   $-1 \times 2x = -2x$
4   $-1 \times 3 = -3$

$(x - 1)(2x + 3) = 2x^2 + 3x - 2x - 3$
$= 2x^2 + x - 3$

Exercise 19.1

Questions 1 to 6.
Use diagrams to multiply out the brackets.

1 $(x + 3)(x + 4)$

2 $(x + 1)(x + 5)$

3 $(x - 5)(x + 2)$

4 $(2x + 1)(x - 2)$

5 $(3x - 2)(x - 6)$

6 $(2x + 1)(3x + 2)$

Questions 7 to 24.
Expand the following brackets. Only draw a diagram if necessary.

7 $(x + 8)(x - 2)$

8 $(x + 5)(x - 2)$

9 $(x - 1)(x + 3)$

10 $(x - 3)(x - 2)$

11 $(x - 4)(x - 1)$

12 $(x - 7)(x + 2)$

13 $(2x + 3)(x - 1)$

14 $(3x - 1)(x + 5)$

15 $(4x - 2)(3x + 5)$

16 $(x + 3)(x - 3)$

17 $(x + 5)(x - 5)$

18 $(x + 7)(x - 7)$

19 $(x - 10)(x + 10)$

20 $(x + 3)^2$

21 $(x + 5)^2$

22 $(x - 3)^2$

23 $(x - 7)^2$

24 $(2x - 3)^2$

Factorising

Factorising is the opposite operation to removing brackets.
For example, $x^2 + 4x = x(x + 4)$
     and $3x^2 + 6 = 3(x^2 + 2)$.
You can check that you have factorised an expression correctly by multiplying out the brackets.

> Factorising was first covered in Chapter 12.

Factorising quadratic expressions

$x^2 + 8x + 15$, $x^2 - 4$ and $x^2 + 7x$ are examples of **quadratic expressions**.
You will need to be able to factorise such expressions in order to solve quadratic equations in the next section of this chapter.

> The general form of a quadratic expression is $ax^2 + bx + c$, where a cannot be equal to 0.

Common factors

A **common factor** is a factor which will divide into each term of an expression.
For example, $x^2 + 7x$ has a common factor of x.
     $x^2 + 7x = x(x + 7)$

Difference of two squares

In the expression $x^2 - 4$,
$x^2 = x \times x$ and $4 = 2^2 = 2 \times 2$.

$x^2 - 4 = (x + 2)(x - 2)$
This result is called the **difference of two squares**.
In general: $a^2 - b^2 = (a + b)(a - b)$

EXAMPLES Factorise the following.

1
$x^2 - 100$
$= x^2 - 10^2$
$= (x + 10)(x - 10)$

2
$25 - x^2$
$= 5^2 - x^2$
$= (5 + x)(5 - x)$

3
$s^2 - t^2$
$= (s + t)(s - t)$

Quadratics of the form $x^2 + bx + c$

The expression $x^2 + 8x + 15$ can be factorised.

From experience, we know that the answer is likely to be of the form:
$\quad x^2 + 8x + 15 = (x + ?)(x + ?)$,
where the question marks represent numbers.
Replacing the question marks with letters, p and q, we get:
$\quad x^2 + 8x + 15 = (x + p)(x + q)$

Multiply the brackets out, using either the diagram method or by expanding, and compare the results with
the original expression.

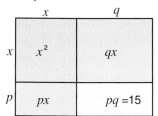

$$px + qx = x(p + q) = 8x$$
and $p \times q = 15$

$(x + p)(x + q)$

1 $x \times x = x^2$
2 $x \times q = qx$
3 $p \times x = px$
4 $p \times q = pq$

$(x + p)(x + q) = x^2 + qx + px + pq$
$\qquad\qquad\qquad = x^2 + (q + p)x + pq$
$\qquad\qquad\qquad = x^2 + 8x + 15$

Two numbers are required which: when multiplied give $+15$, **and** when added give $+8$.
$\quad +5$ and $+3$ satisfy **both** conditions.
$\quad x^2 + 8x + 15 = (x + 5)(x + 3)$

EXAMPLES

1 Factorise $x^2 + 6x + 9$.

$x^2 + 6x + 9 = (x + 3)(x + 3)$
$\qquad\qquad\quad = (x + 3)^2$
Because $3 \times 3 = 9$
and $3 + 3 = 6$.

2 Factorise $x^2 - 8x + 12$.

$x^2 - 8x + 12 = (x - 6)(x - 2)$

Because $-6 \times -2 = 12$
and $-6 + -2 = -8$.

3 Factorise $x^2 + 2x - 15$.

$x^2 + 2x - 15 = (x + 5)(x - 3)$

Because $+5 \times -3 = -15$
and $+5 + -3 = +2$.

4 Factorise $x^2 - 2x - 8$.

$x^2 - 2x - 8 = (x + 2)(x - 4)$

Because $+2 \times -4 = -8$
and $+2 + -4 = -2$.

1 Factorise these expressions.

(a) $x^2 + 5x$ (b) $x^2 - 7x$ (c) $y^2 - 6y$ (d) $2y^2 - 12y$

(e) $5t - t^2$ (f) $8y + y^2$ (g) $x^2 - 20x$ (h) $3x^2 - 60x$

2 Factorise.

(a) $x^2 - 9$ (b) $x^2 - 81$ (c) $y^2 - 25$ (d) $y^2 - 1$

(e) $x^2 - 64$ (f) $100 - x^2$ (g) $36 - x^2$ (h) $x^2 - a^2$

3 Copy and complete the following.

(a) $x^2 + 6x + 5 = (x + 5)(x + \dots)$ (b) $x^2 + 9x + 14 = (x + 7)(x + \dots)$

(c) $x^2 + 6x + 8 = (x + \dots)(x + 4)$ (d) $x^2 + 9x + 18 = (x + \dots)(x + 6)$

(e) $x^2 - 6x + 5 = (x - 5)(x - \dots)$ (f) $x^2 - 7x + 10 = (x - 5)(x - \dots)$

(g) $x^2 - 7x + 12 = (x - \dots)(x - 3)$ (h) $x^2 + 3x - 4 = (x + 4)(x - \dots)$

(i) $x^2 + 5x - 14 = (x + 7)(x - \dots)$ (j) $x^2 - 4x - 5 = (x - 5)(x + \dots)$

4 Factorise.

(a) $x^2 + 3x + 2$ (b) $x^2 + 8x + 7$ (c) $x^2 + 8x + 15$ (d) $x^2 + 8x + 12$

(e) $x^2 + 12x + 11$ (f) $x^2 + 9x + 20$ (g) $x^2 + 10x + 24$ (h) $x^2 + 13x + 36$

5 Factorise.

(a) $x^2 - 6x + 9$ (b) $x^2 - 6x + 8$ (c) $x^2 - 11x + 10$ (d) $x^2 - 16x + 15$

(e) $x^2 - 8x + 15$ (f) $x^2 - 10x + 16$ (g) $x^2 - 12x + 20$ (h) $x^2 - 11x + 24$

6 Factorise.

(a) $x^2 - x - 6$ (b) $x^2 - 5x - 6$ (c) $x^2 + 2x - 24$ (d) $x^2 + 5x - 24$

(e) $x^2 - 2x - 15$ (f) $x^2 + 3x - 18$ (g) $x^2 - 3x - 40$ (h) $x^2 - 4x - 12$

7 Factorise.

(a) $x^2 - 4x + 4$ (b) $x^2 + 11x + 30$ (c) $x^2 + 2x - 8$ (d) $x^2 - 4x - 21$

(e) $x^2 + x - 20$ (f) $x^2 + 7x + 12$ (g) $x^2 + 8x + 16$ (h) $x^2 - 2x + 1$

(i) $x^2 - 49$ (j) $t^2 + 12t$ (k) $x^2 - 9x + 14$ (l) $x^2 - 7x + 6$

(m) $x^2 + 11x + 18$ (n) $x^2 + 11x + 24$ (o) $x^2 + 19x + 18$ (p) $x^2 - y^2$

(q) $x^2 + x - 6$ (r) $y^2 + 4y$ (s) $y^2 - 10y + 25$ (t) $x^2 - 12x + 36$

Further factorising

When factorising, work logically.

     Does the expression have a common factor?

     Is the expression a difference of two squares?

     Will the expression factorise into two brackets?

EXAMPLES

1 Factorise $2x^2 - 14x$.

Common factor $2x$.
$2x^2 - 14x = 2x(x - 7)$

2 Factorise $25 - 4y^2$.

Difference of two squares.
$25 - 4y^2 = 5^2 - (2y)^2$
$\qquad\qquad = (5 + 2y)(5 - 2y)$

EXAMPLES

3 Factorise $2x^2 - 18$.

Common factor 2.
$2x^2 - 18 = 2(x^2 - 9)$
Difference of two squares.
$\qquad = 2(x + 3)(x - 3)$

4 Factorise $x^2 - 6x + 8$.

$x^2 - 6x + 8 = (x - 2)(x - 4)$

Because $-2 \times -4 = 8$
and $-2 + -4 = -6$.

Exercise **19.3**

Factorise.

1 $3x + 12y$

2 $t^2 - 16$

3 $x^2 + 4x + 3$

4 $y^2 - y$

5 $2d^2 - 6$

6 $p^2 - q^2$

7 $a^2 - 2a$

8 $x^2 - 2x + 1$

9 $2y^2 - 8y$

10 $a^2 - 6a + 9$

11 $3m^2 - 12$

12 $v^2 - v - 6$

13 $ax^2 - ay^2$

14 $-8 - 2x$

15 $4 - 4k + k^2$

16 $18 - 2x^2$

17 $50 - 2x^2$

18 $12x^2 - 27y^2$

19 $6a^2 - 3a$

20 $x^2 - 15x + 56$

Algebraic fractions

Algebraic fractions have a numerator and a denominator (just as an ordinary fraction) but at least one of them is an expression involving an unknown.

e.g $\quad \dfrac{1}{x} \qquad \dfrac{x}{2} \qquad \dfrac{2}{x - 5} \qquad \dfrac{x + 1}{x - 6} \qquad \dfrac{3}{x + 7} \qquad \dfrac{x^2 + 2x + 1}{x^2 - 1}$

Algebraic fractions can be simplified, added, subtracted, multiplied, divided and used in equations in the same way as numerical fractions.

Simplifying algebraic fractions

Fractions can be simplified if the numerator and the denominator have a common factor.
In its **simplest form**, the numerator and denominator of an algebraic fraction have no common factor other than 1.

The numerator and denominator of $\dfrac{15}{25}$ have a highest common factor of 5.

$$\dfrac{15}{25} = \dfrac{15 \div 5}{25 \div 5} = \dfrac{3}{5}$$

3 and 5 have no common factors, other than 1.

$$\dfrac{15}{25} = \dfrac{3}{5} \text{ in its simplest form.}$$

Algebraic fractions work in a similar way.

To write an algebraic fraction in its simplest form:
- factorise the numerator and denominator of the fraction,
- divide the numerator and denominator by their highest common factor.

This is sometimes called **cancelling** a fraction.

Write the following in their simplest form.

① $\dfrac{3x - 6}{3}$

$= \dfrac{3(x - 2)}{3}$

$= x - 2$

② $\dfrac{3x + 9}{4x + 12}$

$= \dfrac{3(x + 3)}{4(x + 3)}$

$= \dfrac{3}{4}$

③ $\dfrac{9 - 3y}{y - 3}$

$= \dfrac{3(3 - y)}{y - 3}$

$= \dfrac{-3(y - 3)}{(y - 3)} = -3$

Exercise 19.4

① Simplify these algebraic fractions.

(a) $\dfrac{4d + 6}{2}$

(b) $\dfrac{9x + 6}{3}$

(c) $\dfrac{8a + 10b}{2}$

(d) $\dfrac{15m - 10n}{5}$

(e) $\dfrac{8x - 4y}{2}$

(f) $\dfrac{ax + bx}{x}$

(g) $\dfrac{x^2 - x}{x}$

(h) $\dfrac{2x^2 - 4}{2}$

(i) $\dfrac{2x}{6x - 4}$

(j) $\dfrac{3x}{6x^2 - 3}$

(k) $\dfrac{3x}{6x^2 - 3x}$

(l) $\dfrac{2x - 1}{6x^2 - 3x}$

(m) $\dfrac{3m - 6}{2m - 4}$

(n) $\dfrac{m^2 + 3m}{3m + 9}$

(o) $\dfrac{x^2 - 3x}{x^2 + 2x}$

(p) $\dfrac{5x - 10}{6 - 3x}$

② Match the algebraic fractions with the values **A** to **E**.

(a) $\dfrac{3x + 6}{4x + 8}$

(b) $\dfrac{5x - 15}{2x - 6}$

(c) $\dfrac{8 - 4y}{6 - 3y}$

(d) $\dfrac{8x + 10}{4x + 5}$

(e) $\dfrac{-2x - 4}{-4x - 8}$

A 2 **B** $\dfrac{4}{3}$ **C** $2\frac{1}{2}$ **D** $\dfrac{1}{2}$ **E** $\dfrac{3}{4}$

③ Simplify these algebraic fractions.

(a) $\dfrac{x^2 + 3x}{x^2 + 4x + 3}$

(b) $\dfrac{x^2 + 3x + 2}{x^2 + 4x + 3}$

(c) $\dfrac{x^2 - 2x}{x^2 + x - 6}$

(d) $\dfrac{x^2 - x - 20}{x^2 + 7x + 12}$

(e) $\dfrac{x^2 - 4x + 4}{x^2 - 5x + 6}$

(f) $\dfrac{x^2 - 5x}{x^2 + 4x}$

(g) $\dfrac{x^2 - 1}{x + 1}$

(h) $\dfrac{x - 2}{x^2 - 4}$

(i) $\dfrac{x^2 - 2x - 3}{2x - 6}$

Solving quadratic equations

Activity

I am thinking of two numbers.
I multiply them together.
The answer is zero.

Write down 2 numbers which could be Jim's numbers.
Now write down **four** more pairs.
What can you say about Jim's numbers?

You should have discovered that at least one of Jim's
numbers must be **zero**.
We can use this fact to solve **quadratic equations**.

EXAMPLES

1 Find x if

(a) $x(x - 2) = 0$
Either $x = 0$ or $x - 2 = 0$
Because one of them must be zero.
$x = 0$ or $x = 2$

(b) $(x - 3)(x + 2) = 0$
$x - 3 = 0$ or $x + 2 = 0$
Because one of them must be zero.
$x = 3$ or $x = -2$

2 Factorise the quadratic expression and so solve the equation.

(a) $x^2 - 5x + 6 = 0$
$(x - 2)(x - 3) = 0$
$x = 2$ or $x = 3$

Check: Does $(2)^2 - 5 \times (2) + 6 = 0$
and $(3)^2 - 5 \times (3) + 6 = 0$?

(b) $x^2 - 9 = 0$
$(x - 3)(x + 3) = 0$
$x = 3$ or $x = -3$

(c) $y^2 + 7y = 0$
$y(y + 7) = 0$
$y = 0$ or $y + 7 = 0$
$y = 0$ or $y = -7$

(d) $a^2 + 4a - 5 = 0$
$(a - 1)(a + 5) = 0$
$a = 1$ or $a = -5$

Exercise **19.5**

1 Solve these equations.

(a) $(x - 2)(x - 3) = 0$
(b) $(x + 4)(x + 6) = 0$
(c) $(x - 3)(x + 1) = 0$
(d) $(x - 5)(x + 2) = 0$
(e) $x(x - 4) = 0$
(f) $3x(x + 2) = 0$

2 Solve.

(a) $x^2 - 3x + 2 = 0$
(b) $y^2 + 7y + 12 = 0$
(c) $m^2 - 2m - 8 = 0$
(d) $a^2 + a - 12 = 0$
(e) $n^2 - 5n - 36 = 0$
(f) $z^2 - 9z + 18 = 0$
(g) $k^2 + 8k + 15 = 0$
(h) $c^2 + 15c + 56 = 0$
(i) $b^2 + b - 20 = 0$
(j) $v^2 - 7v - 60 = 0$
(k) $w^2 + 8w - 48 = 0$
(l) $p^2 - p - 72 = 0$

3 Solve.

(a) $x^2 - 5x = 0$
(b) $y^2 + y = 0$
(c) $p^2 + 3p = 0$
(d) $4a - a^2 = 0$
(e) $t^2 - 6t = 0$
(f) $g^2 - 4g = 0$

4 Solve.

(a) $x^2 - 4 = 0$
(b) $y^2 - 144 = 0$
(c) $9 - a^2 = 0$
(d) $d^2 - 16 = 0$
(e) $x^2 - 100 = 0$
(f) $36 - x^2 = 0$
(g) $x^2 - 49 = 0$
(h) $2.25 - x^2 = 0$

5 Rearrange these equations and then solve them.

(a) $y^2 = 4y + 5$
(b) $x^2 = x$
(c) $x^2 = 8x - 16$
(d) $x^2 = 2x + 15$
(e) $n^2 - 10n = 24$
(f) $7 = 8m - m^2$
(g) $a(a - 5) = 24$
(h) $x^2 - 5x + 6 = 3 - x$

6 This rectangle has an area of 21 cm².

(a) Form an equation in x.
(b) By solving your equation, find the value of x.

x cm

$(x - 4)$ cm

7 The product of x and $(x - 2)$ is 63.
By forming an equation, find the value of x.

8 The sum of two numbers is 15.
Their product is 56.
By forming an equation, find the two numbers.

Solving quadratic equations graphically

The graph of a **quadratic function** is always a smooth curve and is called a **parabola**. The general equation of a quadratic function is $y = ax^2 + bx + c$, where a cannot be equal to zero.

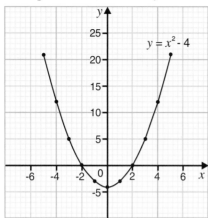

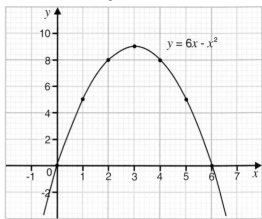

The graph of $y = x^2 - 4$ has a **minimum value** at the point $(0, -4)$.

The graph of $y = 6x - x^2$ has a **maximum value** at the point $(3, 9)$.

The values of x where the graphs of quadratic functions cross (or touch) the x axis give the **solutions to quadratic equations**.

At the point where the graph $y = x^2 - 4$ crosses the x axis the value of $y = 0$.
$x^2 - 4 = 0$
The solutions of this quadratic equation can be read from the graph. $x = -2$ and $x = 2$.

Remember:
- Your graphs should never be flat or pointed.
- Quadratic graphs are always symmetrical.
- Join plotted points using smooth curves and not a series of straight lines.

Find the solutions of the equation $6x - x^2 = 0$ from the graph of $y = 6x - x^2$.
Check the graphical solutions using the factorising method.

EXAMPLE

Draw the graph of
$y = x^2 + 3x - 2$ for values of x from -5 to 2.
Use the graph to find the solutions of the equation
$x^2 + 3x - 2 = 0$.

First make a table of values for $y = x^2 + 3x - 2$.

x	-5	-4	-3	-2	-1	0	1	2
y	8	2	-2	-4	-4	-2	2	8

The graph has a **minimum value** between $x = -2$ and $x = -1$.
To find this value substitute $x = -1.5$ into the equation.
$y = (-1.5 \times -1.5) + (3 \times -1.5) - 2$
$\quad = 2.25 - 4.5 - 2 = -4.25$
Plot the point $(-1.5, -4.25)$.

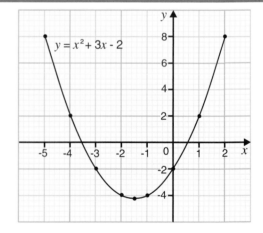

$x^2 + 3x - 2 = 0$
To solve this equation, read the values of x where the graph of $y = x^2 + 3x - 2$ crosses the x axis.
$x = -3.6$ and $x = 0.6$, correct to 1 d.p.

Cubic graphs

The general form of a **cubic function** is $y = ax^3 + bx^2 + cx + d$, where a cannot be equal to zero. As for quadratic graphs, the solutions of cubic equations can be found in a similar way.

1 (a) Copy and complete this table of values for $y = x^2$.

x	-3	-2	-1	0	1	2	3
y	9		1			4	

(b) Draw the graph of $y = x^2$.
Label the x axis from -3 to 3 and the y axis from 0 to 10.

(c) Use your graph to find the value of y when $x = 1.5$.

2 (a) Copy and complete this table of values for $y = x^2 - 2$.

x	-3	-2	-1	0	1	2	3
y		2			-1		7

(b) Draw the graph of $y = x^2 - 2$.
Label the x axis from -3 to 3 and the y axis from -3 to 8.

(c) Use your graph to find the value of y when $x = -1.5$.

(d) Write down the coordinates of the points where the graph of $y = x^2 - 2$ crosses the x axis.

3 (a) Copy and complete this table of values for $y = x^2 - 4$.

x	-3	-2	-1	0	1	2	3
y			-3				5

(b) Draw the graph of $y = x^2 - 4$.
Label the x axis from -3 to 3 and the y axis from -5 to 5.

(c) Use your graph to find the value of y when $x = -1.5$.

(d) Use your graph to find the values of x when $y = 0$.

4 Draw the graphs of $y = x^2 + 2$ and $y = x^2 - 2$ on the same diagram.
Draw the x axis from -2 to 2 and the y axis from -2 to 6.
What do you notice about the two graphs?

5 (a) Draw the graph of $y = x^2 + 1$ for values of x from -2 to 4.

(b) Use your graph to find the value of y when $x = 2.5$.

(c) Use your graph to find the values of x when $y = 4$.

6 (a) Copy and complete this table of values for $y = 2x^2$.

x	-2	-1	0	1	2
y					

(b) Draw axes marked from -2 to 2 for x and from -2 to 8 for y.
Draw the graph of $y = 2x^2$ on your axes.

(c) Use your graph to solve the equation $2x^2 = 5$.

7 (a) Copy and complete this table of values for $y = x^2 + x$.

x	-3	-2	-1	0	1	2
y						

(b) Draw axes marked from -3 to 2 for x and from -2 to 6 for y.
Draw the graph of $y = x^2 + x$ on your axes.

(c) Use your graph to solve the equation $x^2 + x = 0$.

(d) Find the coordinates of the point at which the graph has a minimum value.

8 (a) Copy and complete this table of values for $y = x^2 - x - 1$.

x	-2	-1	0	1	2	3
y						

(b) Draw axes marked from -2 to 3 for x and from -2 to 6 for y.
Draw the graph of $y = x^2 - x - 1$ on your axes.

(c) Use your graph to solve the equation $x^2 - x - 1 = 0$.

9 (a) Copy and complete this table of values for $y = 15 - 2x^2$.

x	-3	-2	-1	0	1	2	3
y							

(b) Draw axes marked from -3 to 3 for x and from -4 to 16 for y.
Draw the graph of $y = 15 - 2x^2$ on your axes.

(c) Use your graph to solve the equation $15 - 2x^2 = 0$.

10 (a) Draw the graph of $y = x^2 + 2x - 3$ for values of x from -5 to 3.

(b) Use your graph to solve the equation $x^2 + 2x - 3 = 0$.

11 (a) Copy and complete this table of values for $y = 10 - x^2$.

x	-4	-3	-2	-1	0	1	2	3	4
y									

(b) Draw axes marked from -4 to 4 for x and from -6 to 10 for y.
Draw the graph of $y = 10 - x^2$ on your axes.

(c) Use your graph to solve the equation $10 - x^2 = 0$.

(d) Find the coordinates of the point at which the graph has a maximum value.

12 Draw suitable graphs to solve the following equations.

(a) $x^2 - 8 = 0$ (b) $5 - x^2 = 0$ (c) $3x^2 = 0$ (d) $12 - 2x^2 = 0$

13 (a) Draw the graph of $y = x^3 - 3$ for values of x from -3 to 3.

(b) Draw the graph of $y = x^3 + x$ for values of x from -3 to 3.

(c) Draw the graph of $y = \frac{1}{x}$ for values of x from -4 to 4.

14 (a) Copy and complete this table of values for $y = x^3 + x^2 - 6x$.

x	-4	-3	-2	-1	0	1	2	3
y								

(b) Draw axes marked from -4 to 3 for x and from -25 to 20 for y.
Draw the graph of $y = x^3 + x^2 - 6x$ on your axes.

(c) Use your graph to solve the equation $x^3 + x^2 - 6x = 0$.

15 (a) Copy and complete this table of values for $y = x^3 - 5x + 6$.

x	-3	-2	-1	0	1	2	3
y							

(b) Draw axes marked from -3 to 3 for x and from -10 to 20 for y.
Draw the graph of $y = x^3 - 5x + 6$ on your axes.

(c) Use your graph to solve the equation $x^3 - 5x + 6 = 0$.

Trial and improvement

Some equations cannot be solved directly (as quadratics can be).
Numerical solutions can be found by making a guess and improving
the accuracy of the guess by **trial and improvement**.
This can be a time consuming method of solving equations and is
often used only as a last resort for solving equations which cannot be
easily solved by algebraic or graphical methods.

A solution to the equation $x^3 - 4x = 7$ lies between 2 and 3.
Find this solution to 1 decimal place.

First guess: $x = 2.5$ $2.5^3 - 4(2.5) = 5.625$ Too small
Second guess: $x = 2.6$ $2.6^3 - 4(2.6) = 7.176$ Too big

The solution lies between 2.5 and 2.6, but 2.6 gives an answer closer to 7.
The answer is probably 2.6, correct to 1 d.p.
To be certain, try $x = 2.55$. $2.55^3 - 4(2.55) = 6.381375$ Too small

The solution lies between 2.55 and 2.6.
2.6 is the solution, correct to 1 d.p.

Because the solution lies
between 2 and 3, notice that:
when $x = 2$
$2^3 - 4(2) = 0$
    Less than 7

when $x = 3$
$3^3 - 4(3) = 15$
    Greater than 7

We are trying to find a value
for x which produces the
answer 7.

Exercise 19.7   You will need a calculator for this exercise.

1 Use trial and improvement to solve $x^3 = 54$, correct to one decimal place.
The working can be shown in a table.

x	x^3	
3	27	Too small
4	64	Too big
3.5		

2 Use trial and improvement to solve these equations.
(a) $w^3 = 72$ (b) $4x^3 = 51$

3 A solution to the equation
$x^3 + 2x = 40$ lies between 3 and 4.
Find this solution to 1 decimal place.

x	$x^3 + 2x$	
3	33	Too small
3.5	49.875	Too big

4 A solution to the equation $x^3 + 5x = 880$
lies between 9 and 10.
Use trial and improvement to find this
solution to 1 decimal place.
Show your trials.

5 Show that a solution to $x^3 - 5x^2 = 47$
lies between 6 and 7.
Use trial and improvement to find this
solution, showing your trials,
(a) to 1 decimal place,
(b) to 2 decimal places.

6 This cuboid has dimensions:
x, $x + 2$ and $2x$.

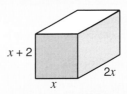

(a) Write down an expression, in
terms of x, for the volume of the
cuboid.
(b) The volume of the cuboid is
$400 \, cm^3$.
Form an equation and use trial
and improvement to find x,
correct to 1 d.p.

7 A solution to $x^4 + 5x - 20 = 0$
lies between 1 and 2.
Use trial and improvement to find this
solution correct to 2 decimal places.
Show your trials.

What you need to know

- Brackets, such as $(x + 2)(x + 5)$ can be multiplied out using:
  the **diagram method**, or by **expanding**.

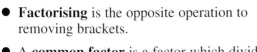

- **Factorising** is the opposite operation to
  removing brackets.

- A **common factor** is a factor which divides
  into two, or more, numbers (or terms).
  For example: $8ab + 12bc = 4b(2a + 3c)$
  where $4b$ is a common factor of $8ab$ and $12bc$.

$$(x + 2)(x + 5) = x^2 + 5x + 2x + 10$$
$$= x^2 + 7x + 10$$

- **Difference of two squares** $a^2 - b^2 = (a - b)(a + b)$

- **Algebraic fractions** have a numerator and a denominator (just as an ordinary fraction) but at
  least one of them is an expression involving an unknown.

- To write an algebraic fraction in its **simplest form**:
  factorise the numerator and denominator of the fraction,
  divide the numerator and denominator by their highest common factor.
  This is sometimes called **cancelling** a fraction.

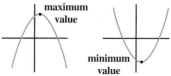
Review Exercise

1 Expand and simplify $(x - 5)(x + 2)$.

2 (a) (i) Factorise $t^2 - 4t$.
    (ii) Hence, solve $t^2 - 4t = 0$.
(b) (i) Factorise $y^2 + 3y + 2$.
    (ii) Hence, solve $y^2 + 3y + 2 = 0$.

3 (a) Expand $(2x + 1)(x + 4)$.
(b) Factorise completely $4x^2 - 6x$.
             Edexcel

4 Solve the equation $(x - 2)(x + 1) = 0$.

5 Solve $x^2 + 2x - 8 = 0$.

6 Solve the equations
(b) $x^2 - 9 = 0$,   (b) $x^2 - 8x - 9 = 0$.

7
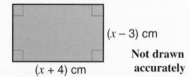

$(x - 3)$ cm

Not drawn accurately

$(x + 4)$ cm

The length of a rectangle is $(x + 4)$ cm.
The width is $(x - 3)$ cm.
The area of the rectangle is 78 cm^2.

(a) Use this information to write down an equation in terms of x.
(b) (i) Show that your equation in part (a) can be written as $x^2 + x - 90 = 0$.
    (ii) Find the values of x which are the solutions of the equation $x^2 + x - 90 = 0$.
    (iii) Write down the length and the width of the rectangle.   Edexcel

8 (a) Draw the graph of $y = 5 - x^2$ for values of x from -3 to 3.
(b) Use your graph to find
    (i) the maximum value of y,
    (ii) the solutions to the equation $5 - x^2 = 0$.

9
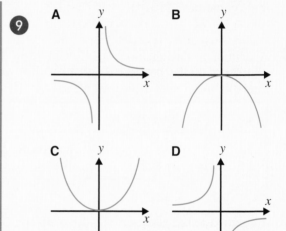

Which of the graphs could be the graph of
(a) $y = -x^2$,   (b) $xy = 12$?   Edexcel

10 A tank for holding oil is 2 m high, and has a square base of side x m.
The formula for the volume, V, of the tank is $V = 2x^2$.

(a) Copy and complete the table to show the values of V for the given values of x.

x	0.5	1	1.5	2	2.5	3
V	0.5		4.5		12.5	

(b) Use these values to draw the graph of $V = 2x^2$.
Use a scale of 4 cm to 1 unit on the x axis, and 1 cm for 2 units on the V axis.
(c) From your graph, find what value of x will give a volume of 10 m^3.
Give your answer to one decimal place.
           Edexcel

11 The equation $x^3 + x = 20$ has a solution between 2 and 3.
Use a trial and improvement method to find the solution correct to two decimal places.
Show all your working.

Section Review - Algebra

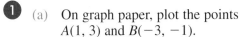

1 (a) On graph paper, plot the points
A(1, 3) and B(−3, −1).

(b) M is the midpoint of AB.
What are the coordinates of M?

2 Simplify (a) 3a − 2 − a + 3
(b) $y^2 − 2y + y^2 + y$

3 (a) Pens cost x pence each.
Write an expression for the cost of
3 pens.

(b) A ruler costs 7 pence more than a
pen.
Write an expression for the cost of
a ruler.

4 Solve (a) 8x + 4 = 20
(b) 3x − 2 = 10
(c) $\frac{1}{2} x + 2 = 8$

5 Alex uses this rule:

> Begin with a number.
> Take away 3.
> Multiply by 2.
> Write down the result.

(a) What is the result when Alex
begins with 2?

(b) What is the result when Alex
begins with x?

(c) The result is 0. What number did
Alex begin with?

6 Kim thinks of a number.
She doubles it and adds 3.
The answer is 16.
What is her number?

7 (a) What is the value of 3p − q when
p = −1 and q = 2?

(b) What is the value of $x^2 − 2x$ when
x is −3?

8 (a) What is the next number in this
sequence?
1, 5, 9, 13, …

(b) One number in the sequence is x.
Write an expression for the number
in the sequence before x.

9 (a) Simplify 3a − b + 2ab − a + ba.
(b) Expand and simplify 3(x + 1) − x.

10 Work out the value of m^3 when
(a) m = −2, (b) $m = \frac{1}{2}$.

11 Solve the equations
(a) 3(x − 1) = 6
(b) 30 + 12(n − 1) = 102

12 (a) Write down the next term in the
sequence 2, 5, 8, 11, ….

(b) Write an expression, in terms of n,
for the nth term of the sequence.

13 (a) Solve the equations
(i) 5x − 7 = 9
(ii) 3t + 1 = 7 − t

(b) Factorise 6 + 4a.

14 (a) Buns cost x pence each.
How much will 2 buns cost?

(b) A doughnut costs 5 pence less than
a bun.
How much will 3 doughnuts cost?

(c) The cost of buying 2 buns and
3 doughnuts is 95 pence.
By forming an equation find the
cost of a bun.

15 The perimeters of these two shapes are
the same.

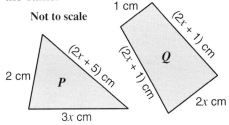

Not to scale

(a) By forming an equation calculate
the value of x.

(b) What is the perimeter of shape Q?

16 A sequence begins 7, 5, 3, 1, −1, ….
(a) What is the next term in the
sequence?

(b) What is the nth term of the
sequence?

17 (a) On the same diagram, draw and label the lines
$$y = x \quad \text{and} \quad y = 3 - x \quad \text{for values of } x \text{ from 0 to 3.}$$
(b) Explain how you can use your graph to solve the equation
$$x = 3 - x.$$
(c) Shade the region that is satisfied by all of the inequalities
$$y \geqslant x, \quad y \leqslant 3 - x \quad \text{and} \quad x \geqslant 0.$$

18 (a) Solve the equation $5x - 7 = 3(x + 1)$
(b) Solve the simultaneous equations $x - y = 3$ and $3x + y = -1$

19 (a) Solve the equations:
(i) $2x = 10$
(ii) $6y + 1 = 25$
(iii) $8p - 3 = 3p + 13$
(iv) $4x + 3 = 2(x - 3)$
(b) Solve the inequality $2x + 3 \leqslant 8$.

Edexcel

20 Factorise (a) $6p - 3$ (b) $p^2 + 2p$

21 (a) Here are the first five numbers of a sequence:
$$1, \quad 7, \quad 13, \quad 19, \quad 25.$$
Write, in terms of n, an expression for the nth term of the sequence.
(b) The nth term of the sequence $1, \quad 4, \quad 9, \quad 16, \quad 25, \quad \ldots$ is n^2.
What is the nth term of the sequence $3, \quad 6, \quad 11, \quad 18, \quad 27, \quad \ldots$?

22 (a) Draw the graph of $y = x^2$ for values of x from -3 to 3.
(b) Use your graph to find
(i) the value of y when $x = -2.4$,
(ii) the values of x when $y = 3.6$.

23 (a) Solve the inequality $3x - 5 > 4$.
(b) List the values of x, where x is an integer, such that
$$-1 \leqslant x + 2 < 1.$$

24 The air temperature, $T°C$, outside an aircraft flying at a
height of h feet is given by the formula
$$T = 26 - \frac{h}{500}$$

An aircraft is flying at a height of 27 000 feet.
(a) Use the formula to calculate the air temperature
outside the aircraft.

The air temperature outside an aircraft is $-52°C$.
(b) Calculate the height of the aircraft.

Edexcel

25 You are given the formula $V = \sqrt{\dfrac{P}{R}}$.

(a) Work out the value of V when $P = 0.35$ and $R = \frac{5}{7}$.
(b) Rearrange the formula to give P in terms of V and R.

26 (a) Solve the inequality $x + 3 < 2 - x$.
    (b) Multiply out and simplify $(x - 5)^2$.
    (c) Factorise
        (i) $3m^2 - 6m$,
        (ii) $t^2 - t - 12$.

27 (a) Draw the graph of $y = x^2 - x - 4$ for values of x between -2 and $+3$.
    (b) Use your graph to write down an estimate for
        (i) the minimum value of y,
        (ii) the solutions of the equation $x^2 - x - 4 = 0$.   Edexcel

28 The graph shows the cost of hiring a hall.

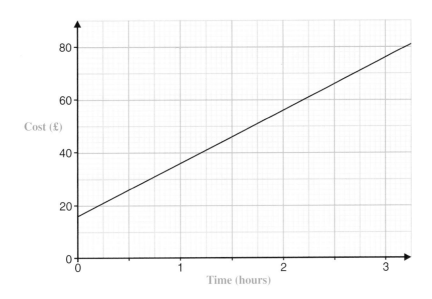

    (a) Find the equation of the line in the form $y = mx + c$.
    (b) What is the cost of hiring the hall for 5 hours?

29 Draw and label axes for x from 0 to 20 and for y from 0 to 30.
On your diagram draw the appropriate boundary lines and carefully shade the area that contains all the points satisfying the inequalities:
    $x > 5$, $y > 8$ and $y < 30 - 2x$.

30 Simplify
    (a) $8x^2 \div 4x$ (b) $3a^2 \times 5a^3$ (c) $(5t^3)^2$

31 (a) Solve $5 - \frac{2x}{3} = x$.

    (b) Solve the simultaneous equations $3x - y = 11$,
                                   $x + 2y = -1$.

    (c) List the values of n, where n is an integer, such that $-2 \leqslant 3n + 4 < 4$.

32 $V = \frac{4}{3} \pi r^3$.
    (a) Rearrange the formula to give r in terms of V.
    (b) Calculate the value of r when $V = 905$.

33 Use a trial and improvement method to solve the equation
$$x^3 - x = 15.$$
Copy and complete the working shown below to find a solution correct to one decimal place.

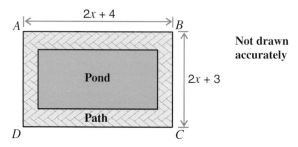

x	$x^3 - x =$	
2	6	Too small
3	24	Too big

Edexcel

34 (a) Multiply out and simplify $(x - 3)(x - 2)$.
(b) Solve the equation $x^2 + 7x - 8 = 0$.

35 The diagram shows a rectangular pond and a path.
The outside edges of the path form the rectangle $ABCD$.

2x + 4

A — B

Not drawn
accurately

Pond

2x + 3

Path

D — C

The length, in metres, of AB is $2x + 4$.
The length, in metres, of BC is $2x + 3$.
(a) Write down, in terms of x, an expression for the perimeter of the rectangle $ABCD$.
Write your expression in its simplest form.

The area of the pond is $12\,\text{m}^2$.
(b) Show that the area, in m^2, of the path is $4x^2 + 14x$.

$x = 1.2$
(c) Use the expression $4x^2 + 14x$ to find the area of the path when $x = 1.2$.

Edexcel

36 Solve the equations
(a) $y^2 + 5y = 0$
(b) $m^2 - 7m + 12 = 0$

37 The sum of two numbers is 15.
The product of the numbers is 54.
If one of the numbers is x, show that $x^2 - 15x + 54 = 0$.

38 (a) Simplify $\dfrac{a^2 + 2a}{5a + 10}$
(b) Factorise $2x^2 - 18$

39 A rectangle has length $(x + 2)\,\text{cm}$ and width $(x + 1)\,\text{cm}$.
The rectangle has an area of $6\,\text{cm}^2$.
Form an equation and show that it can be simplified
to $x^2 + 3x - 4 = 0$.

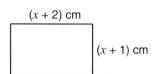

(x + 2) cm

(x + 1) cm

CHAPTER 20

Angles ●●●●●●●●●●●●●●●●●●●●●●●

The diagram shows a stopwatch with a second hand.
Every minute the second hand will make one complete turn.
An **angle** is a measure of turn.
Angles are measured in **degrees**.
In one minute the second hand will turn through an angle of 360°.

Types and names of angles

Each of these diagrams shows a quarter-turn.

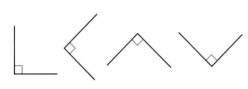

A quarter-turn is called a **right angle**.
A right angle is 90°.

An angle less than 90° is called an **acute** angle.
An angle between 90° and 180° is called an **obtuse** angle.
An angle greater than 180° is called a **reflex** angle.

Exercise **20.1**

1 Through what angle will a second hand turn in:

(a) half a minute,
(b) quarter of a minute,
(c) three-quarters of a minute,
(d) 15 seconds,
(e) 20 seconds,
(f) 1 second,
(g) 7 seconds,
(h) 2 minutes,
(i) $1\frac{1}{2}$ minutes,
(j) 135 seconds?

2 This clock shows 4.30.

(a) What size is the acute angle between the hands of the clock?

(b) What is the size of the reflex angle between the hands?

3 Through what angle will the hour hand of the clock turn between:
(a) 10.00 am and 11.30 am,
(b) 10.00 am and 10.00 pm?

4 Say whether each of the marked angles is acute, obtuse, reflex or a right angle.

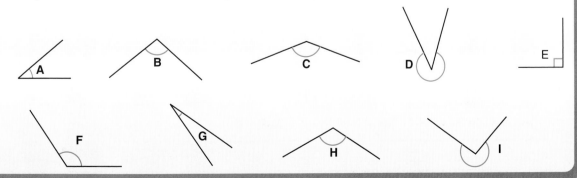

Measuring angles

To measure an angle accurately we need to use a **protractor**.

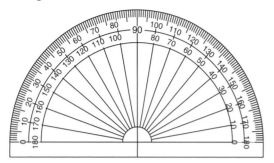

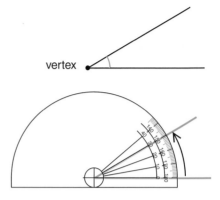

To measure an angle, the protractor is placed so that its centre point is on the corner (vertex) of the angle, with the base along one of the arms of the angle as shown.

vertex

This angle measures 30°.

How can you measure the size of a reflex angle?

Some protractors have two scales. Look at the type of angle (acute/obtuse) you are measuring and use the correct scale.

Drawing angles

Draw an angle of 74°.

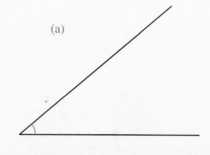

Draw a line.
Mark the vertex of the angle.

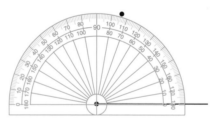

Position the protractor as if you were measuring an angle.
Mark a dot at 74°.

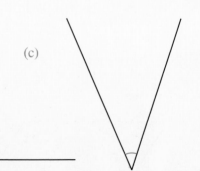

Draw a line from the vertex through the dot.

Exercise 20.2

1 Use a protractor to measure these angles.

(a)   (b)   (c)

2 Use a protractor to measure these angles.

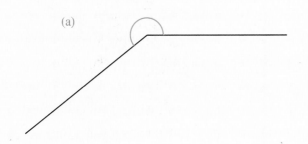

(a)

(b)

3 Draw these angles accurately.

   (a) 20°   (b) 85°   (c) 128°   (d) 205°   (e) 324°

Angles at a point

When angles meet at a point, the sum of all the angles is 360°.

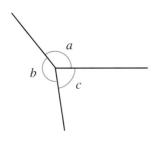

$$a + b + c = 360°$$

Supplementary angles

Angles which can be placed together on a straight line add up to 180°.
When two angles add up to 180°, the angles are called **supplementary**.

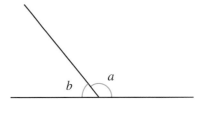

$$a + b = 180°$$

a and b are supplementary angles.

Complementary angles

When two angles add up to 90°, the angles are called **complementary**.

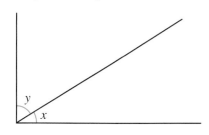

$$x + y = 90°$$

x and y are complementary angles.

Vertically opposite angles

When two lines cross each other the angles between the lines make two pairs of equal angles.

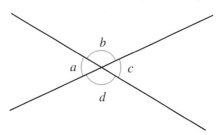

$$a = c \text{ and } b = d$$

a and c are vertically opposite angles.
b and d are vertically opposite angles.

223

EXAMPLES

1 Without measuring, work out the size of the angle marked *a*.

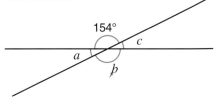

Angles at a point add up to 360°.
a + 95 + 120 = 360
a = 360 − 95 − 120
a = 145°

2 Calculate the size of the angles marked with letters.

b = 154° (vertically opposite angles)

a + 154 = 180 (supplementary angles)
a = 180 − 154
a = 26°

c = 26°

a = 26°, b = 154°, c = 26°

Exercise **20.3**

1 Without measuring, work out the size of the angles marked with letters.

(a)

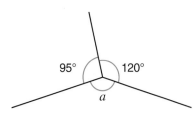

(b)

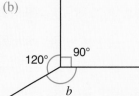

(c)

(d)

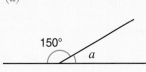

(e)

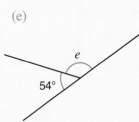

(f)

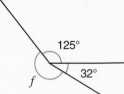

(g)

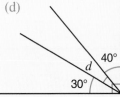

(h)

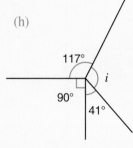

(i)

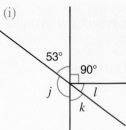

(j)

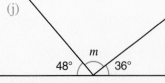

(k)

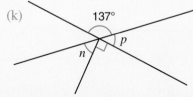

2 These diagrams are not drawn accurately. Without measuring, work out the value of x in each diagram.

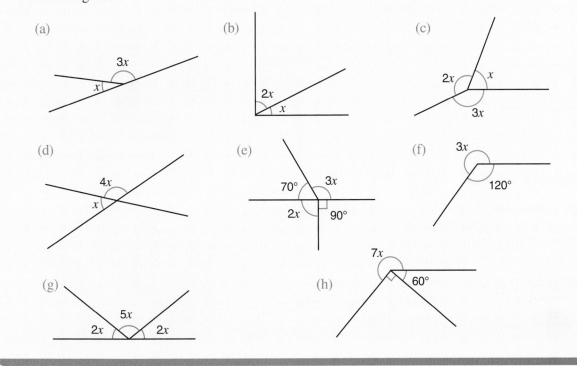

(a)

$3x$

x

(b)

$2x$

x

(c)

$2x$ x

$3x$

(d)

$4x$

x

(e)

$70°$ $3x$

$2x$ $90°$

(f)

$3x$

$120°$

(g)

$5x$

$2x$ $2x$

(h)

$7x$

$60°$

Parallel lines

Which of the following pairs of lines are parallel?

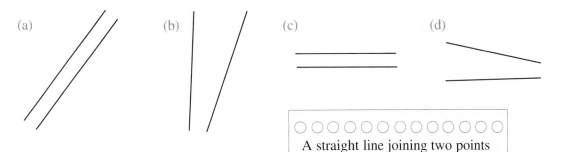

(a)

(b)

(c)

(d)

Parallel lines are lines which never meet.
The pairs of lines in (a) and (c) are parallel.

A straight line joining two points is called a **line segment**.

The diagram, in the activity below, shows two parallel lines crossed by another straight line called a **transversal**.

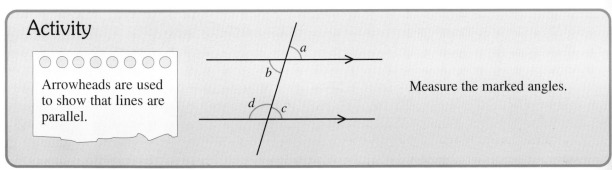

Activity

Arrowheads are used to show that lines are parallel.

a

b

d c

Measure the marked angles.

Corresponding angles

Angles *a* and *c* are equal. They are called **corresponding** angles.
Corresponding angles are always equal.
Here are some examples of corresponding angles.

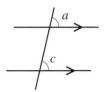 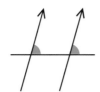

Corresponding angles are always on the same side of the transversal.

Alternate angles

Angles *b* and *c* are equal. They are called **alternate** angles.
Alternate angles are always equal.
Here are some examples of alternate angles.

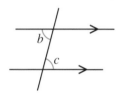 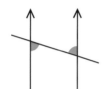

Alternate angles are always on opposite sides of the transversal.

Allied angles

Angles *b* and *d* add up to 180°. They are called **allied** angles.
Allied angles are supplementary, they always add up to 180°.
Here are some examples of allied angles.

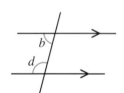

Allied angles are always between parallels on the same side of the transversal.

$b + d = 180°$

EXAMPLE

Without measuring, work out the size of the angles
marked with letters.

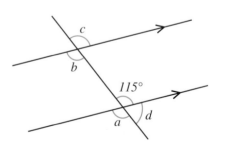

$a = 115°$ (vertically opposite angles)

$b = 115°$ (alternate angles)

$c = 115°$ (corresponding angles)

$d + 115 = 180$ (supplementary angles)
$\quad\quad d = 180 - 115$
$\quad\quad d = 65°$

Exercise 20.4

Do not use a calculator for this exercise.
The diagrams in this exercise are not drawn accurately.

1 Without measuring, work out the size of the angles marked with letters.
Give a reason for each answer.

(a)

(b)

(c)

(d)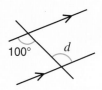

2 Without measuring, work out the size of the angles marked with letters.

(a)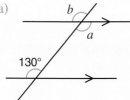

(b)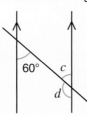

(c)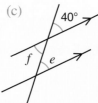

(d)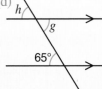

3 Calculate the size of the angles marked with letters.

(a)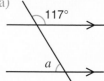

(b)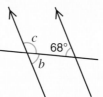

(c)

(d)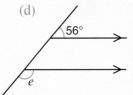

(e)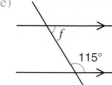

(f)

(g)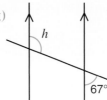

(h)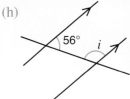

4 Calculate the size of the angles marked with letters.

(a)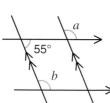

(b)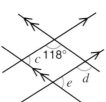

(c)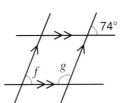

(d)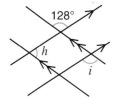

5 Calculate the size of the angles marked with letters.

(a)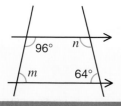

(b)

(c)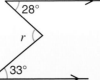

(d)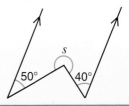

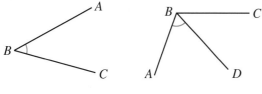

Up to now we have used small letters to name angles. This is not always convenient.
Another method is to use three capital letters.

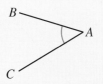

angle *ABC*
∠*ABC*

angle *ABD*
∠*ABD*

○○○○○○○○○○○○○○○○○○○○○○○
∠ means 'angle'.

∠*CBA* is the same as ∠*ABC*.
We usually write the letters either side of the
vertex (shown by the middle letter) in
alphabetical order.

Notice that the middle letter is where the angle is made.

Exercise 20.5

1 Use three letters to name the marked angles in each of these diagrams.

(a)
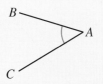

(b)
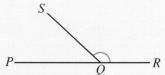

(c)
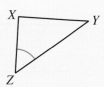

2 Use three letters to name the angles marked with small letters in this diagram.

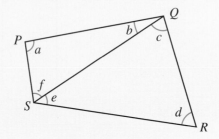

3 Use your protractor to measure accurately the size of these angles.

(a) ∠*ABH*
(b) ∠*HGF*
(c) ∠*BCD*
(d) ∠*AJE*
(e) ∠*GFJ*
(f) reflex ∠*GFJ*
(g) reflex ∠*BHG*
(h) reflex ∠*DEJ*

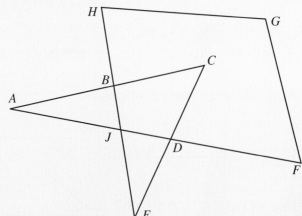

4 These diagrams have not been drawn accurately.
    (i)   Work out the size of the required angles.
    (ii) Give a reason for each of your answers.

(a) *PQ* is a straight line.
     Find ∠*QOR*.

(b) *AB* and *CD* are straight lines.
     Find ∠*AOD*.

(c) *PQ* and *RT* are parallel.
     Find ∠*XOQ*.

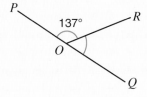
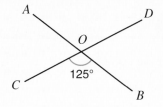
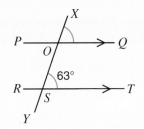

5 These diagrams are not drawn accurately. Work out the size of the required angles.

(a)
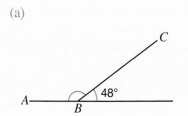
Find ∠*ABC*.

(b)
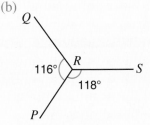
Find ∠*QRS*.

(c)
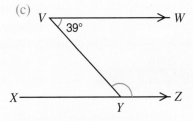
Find ∠*ZYV*.

(d)
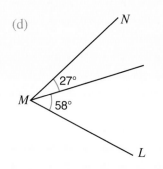
Find ∠*LMN*.

(e)
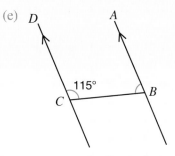
Find ∠*ABC*.

(f)
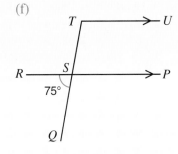
Find ∠*QSP* and ∠*STU*.

6 These diagrams are not drawn accurately. Work out the size of the required angles.

(a)
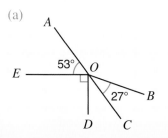
Find ∠*AOB* and ∠*COD*.

(b)
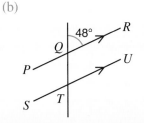
Find ∠*QTU* and ∠*QTS*.

(c)
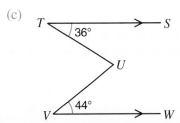
Find reflex angle *TUV*.

Direction and distance

Journeys are often described in terms of **direction** and **distance**.
When planning journeys we often use **maps**.
To interpret maps we need to understand:

      angles in order to describe **direction**,

      scales in order to find **distances**.

Compass points and **three-figure bearings** are used to describe direction.

Compass points

The diagram shows the points of the compass.

The angle between North and East is 90°.

The angle between North and North-East is 45°.

Do you know the names of any other compass points?

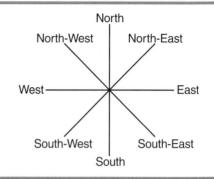

Exercise 20.6

1   (a) What is the angle between North and North-West?
     (b) What is the angle between South and North-West?
     (c) What is the angle between South-West and South-East?
     (d) What is the angle between North-West and South-West?
     (e) What is the angle between South-East and North-West?

2   (a) Lyn is facing North.
        She turns through an angle of 180°.
        In which direction is she now facing?
     (b) Tony is facing West.
        He turns through an angle of 90° clockwise.
        In which direction is he now facing?

3   (a) Claire is facing South. In which direction will she face after turning clockwise through
        an angle of 135°?
     (b) Kevin turned anticlockwise through an angle of 270°. He is now facing South-East.
        In which direction was he facing?

4   Copy and complete this table.
The first line has been
done for you.

Start facing	Amount of turn	Finish facing
South	135° clockwise	North-West
North-East	90° clockwise	
West	135° anticlockwise	
	270° clockwise	East
	45° anticlockwise	West

Three-figure bearings

Bearings are used to describe the direction in which you must travel to get from one place to another.

A bearing is an angle measured from the North line in a clockwise direction.

The angle, which can be from $0°$ to $360°$, is written as a three-figure number.

Bearings which are less than $100°$ include noughts to make up the three figures, e.g. $005°$, $087°$.

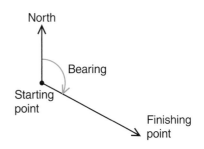

To show the direction given by a bearing

Example
The bearing of C from D is $153°$. Draw a diagram to show this information.

The bearing of C **from** D tells you that D is the starting point.
● Draw a North line. Mark and label point D on the North line.
● Using your protractor, centred on point D, mark an angle of $153°$ measured in a clockwise direction from the North line.
● Draw a line from D through the marked point.
  An arrow is drawn on the line to show the direction in which you must travel to get to C.

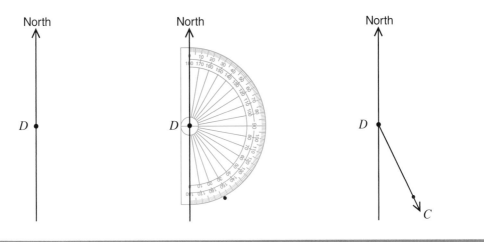

This diagram shows the positions of Bath and Poole.

The bearing of Poole from Bath is $162°$.

If you are at Bath, facing North, and turn through $162°$ in a clockwise direction you will be facing in the direction of Poole.

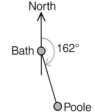

Back bearings

The return bearing of Bath from Poole is called a **back bearing**.
Back bearings can be found by using parallel lines and alternate angles.

The bearing of Poole from Bath is $162°$.

$a = 162°$ (alternate angles)

Required angle $= 180° + 162° = 342°$.
The bearing of Bath from Poole (the back bearing) is $342°$.

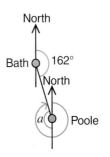

1 Use your protractor to find the three-figure bearings of A from B in each of the following.

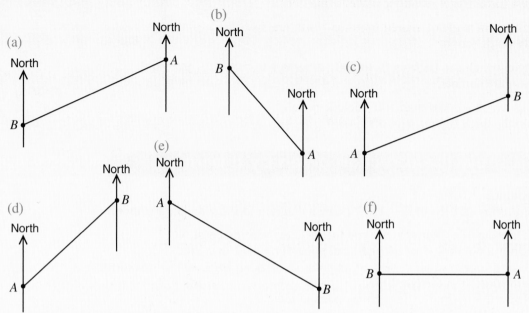

2 (a) Draw sketches to show the following information.
  (i) The bearing of F from E is 050°.   (iv) The bearing of L from B is 260°.
  (ii) The bearing of C from H is 125°.   (v) The bearing of A from J is 305°.
  (iii) The bearing of K from Q is 195°.   (vi) The bearing of X from T is 175°.
(b) Use your sketches to give the back bearings for each of the directions in part (a).

3 Copy the diagram.

North

P ●

R is on a bearing of 100° from P.
R is on a bearing of 060° from Q.
Mark the position of R on your diagram.   Q ●

4 The diagram shows the positions of
three oil rigs at A, B and C.

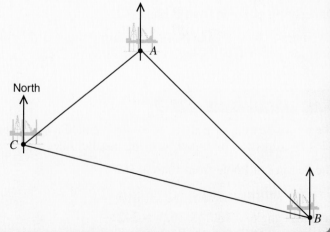

(a) What is the bearing of A from B?
(b) What is the bearing of B from A?
(c) What is the bearing of C from B?
(d) What is the bearing of B from C?
(e) What is the bearing of C from A?
(f) What is the bearing of A from C?

Scale drawing

Maps and plans are scaled down representations of real-life situations.
The **scale** used in drawing a map or plan determines the amount of detail that can be shown.

The distances between different points on a map are all drawn to the same scale.
There are two ways to describe a scale.

1 A scale of 1 cm to 10 km means that a distance of 1 cm on the map represents an actual distance of 10 km.

2 A scale of 1 : 10 000 means that all distances measured on the map have to be multiplied by 10 000 to find the real distance.

EXAMPLES

1 A road is 3.7 cm long on a map.
The scale given on the map is
'1 cm represents 10 km'.
What is the actual length of the road?

1 cm represents 10 km.
Scale up, so multiply.
3.7 cm represents 3.7 × 10 km
　　　= 37 km
The road is 37 km long.

2 A plan of a field is to be drawn using a scale of 1 : 500.
Two trees in the field are 350 metres apart.
How far apart will they be on the plan?

Scale down, so divide.
Distance on plan = 350 m ÷ 500
Change 350 m to centimetres.
　　　= 35 000 cm ÷ 500
　　　= 70 cm
The trees will be 70 cm apart on the plan.

Exercise 20.8

1 A forest walk measures 8.4 cm on a map.
The scale given on the map is
"1 cm represents 2 km".
What is the actual length of the walk in kilometres?

2 A motor-racing circuit is 9.6 km in length.
A plan of the circuit has been drawn to a scale of 1 cm to 3 km.
What is the length of the circuit on the plan?

3 The scale of a map is 1 : 200.
(a) On the map a house is 3.5 cm long.
How long is the actual house?
(b) A field is 60 m wide.
How wide is the field on the map?

4 Roy draws a plan of a boat using a scale of 2 : 125.
On Roy's plan the width of the boat is 20 cm.
What is the actual width of the boat?

5 Claire draws a diagram for a printed circuit board in the ratio 20 : 1.
On Claire's diagram the distance between two components is 35 mm.
What is the actual distance between the components?

6 Helen drew a plan of her classroom using a scale of 5 cm to represent 1 m.
(a) Write the scale Helen used in the form 1 : n.
(b) On the plan, the length of the classroom is 29 cm.
What is the actual length of the classroom?
(c) The actual width of the classroom is 4.5 m.
What is the width of the classroom on the plan?

7 Here is a map of an island.

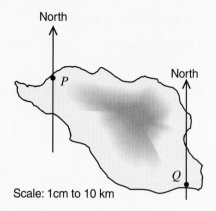

North

P

North

Q

Scale: 1cm to 10 km

(a) Use your protractor to find:
  (i) the bearing of *Q* from *P*,
  (ii) the bearing of *P* from *Q*.

(b) (i) Measure the distance between *P* and *Q* on the map.
  (ii) What is the actual distance between *P* and *Q*?

8

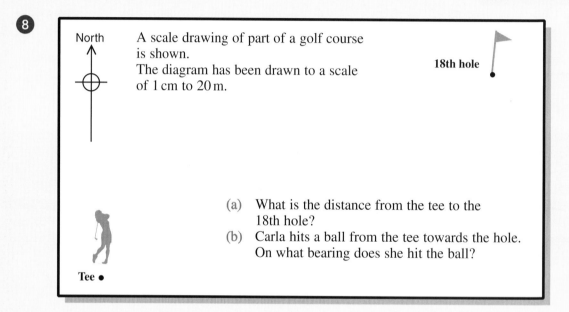

North

A scale drawing of part of a golf course is shown.
The diagram has been drawn to a scale of 1 cm to 20 m.

18th hole

(a) What is the distance from the tee to the 18th hole?
(b) Carla hits a ball from the tee towards the hole. On what bearing does she hit the ball?

Tee ●

9 The sketch shows the positions of Ayton, Boulder, Carey and Dole.

Carey is 12 km due West of Dole.
Carey is 8 km due North of Boulder.
Ayton is on a bearing 100° from Boulder and 160° from Dole.
By using a scale of 1 cm to 2 km, find by scale drawing the distance of Ayton from Carey.

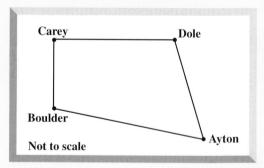

Carey

Dole

Boulder

Ayton

Not to scale

10 A boat leaves port and sails on a bearing of 144° for 4 km.
It then changes course and sails due East for 5 km to reach an island.
Find by scale drawing:
(a) the distance of the island from the port,
(b) the bearing of the island from the port,
(c) the bearing on which the boat must sail to return directly to the port.

11 A yacht sails on a bearing of 040° for 5000 m and then a further 3000 m on a bearing of 120°.
Find by scale drawing:
(a) the distance of the yacht from its starting position,
(b) the bearing on which it must sail to return directly to its starting position.

12 An aircraft leaves an airport, at *A*, and flies on a bearing of 035° for 50 km and then on a bearing of 280° for a further 40 km before landing at an airport, at *B*.
Find by scale drawing:
(a) the distance between the airports,
(b) the bearing of *B* from *A*,
(c) the bearing of *A* from *B*.

What you need to know

- An angle of 90° is called a **right angle**.
  An angle less than 90° is called an **acute angle**.
  An angle between 90° and 180° is called an **obtuse angle**.
  An angle greater than 180° is called a **reflex angle**.

- The sum of the angles at a point is 360°.

- Angles on a straight line add up to 180°.
  Angles which add up to 180° are called **supplementary angles**.
  Angles which add up to 90° are called **complementary angles**.

- When two lines cross, the opposite angles formed are equal and called **vertically opposite angles**.

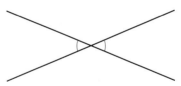

- Lines which meet at right angles are **perpendicular** to each other.

- A straight line joining two points is called a **line segment**.

- Lines which never meet and are always the same distance apart are **parallel**.

- When two parallel lines are crossed by a transversal the following pairs of angles are formed.

Corresponding angles	Alternate angles	Allied angles

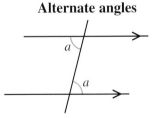 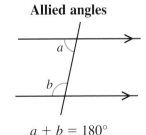

$$a + b = 180°$$

- **Scales**
  The distances between points on a map are all drawn to the same scale.
  There are two ways to describe a scale.
  1. A scale of 1 cm to 10 km means that a distance of 1 cm on the map represents an actual distance of 10 km.
  2. A scale of 1 : 10 000 means that all distances measured on the map have to be multiplied by 10 000 to find the real distance.

1 (a) What is the size of angle a?
Give a reason for your answer.

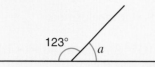

123° a

(b) What is the size of angle x?

x $5x$

2 Calculate the value of y.

210° $y°$ $y°$ $y°$

3 The diagram has two pairs of parallel lines.

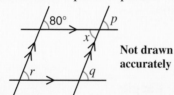

80° p x r q

Not drawn accurately

(a) Angles marked p and q are equal.
What geometrical name is given to this type of equal angles?
(b) Write down the size of angle r.
(c) (i) Write down the size of angle x.
     (ii) What geometrical name is given to the pair of angles x and q?

Edexcel

4 In the diagram, the lines AB and CD are parallel.
CRQ is a straight line.

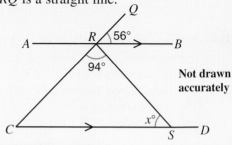

Q

A —— R 56° —— B

94°

Not drawn accurately

C $x°$ S —— D

Angle $CRS = 94°$.
Angle $QRB = 56°$.
Angle $RSC = x°$.

Find the value of x.   *Edexcel*

5 In the diagram AOB and POQ are straight lines.
Angle $ROB = 90°$.
Angle $AOP = 27°$.

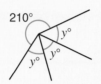

Q

A —— O —— B

27°

P R

(a) (i) Work out the size of angle AOQ.
     (ii) Work out the size of angle POR.
(b) What angle is the same size as angle AOP?

6 The diagram shows the plan of a sailboard race.
The sailboards have to go round buoys at A, B and C.
Buoy B is on a bearing of 050° from buoy A.
Angle ABC is 90°.

(a) What is the bearing of A from B?
(b) What is the bearing of C from B?

The plan has been drawn to a scale of 1 : 20 000.
(c) (i) Measure AB.
     (ii) What is the distance from A to B in metres?

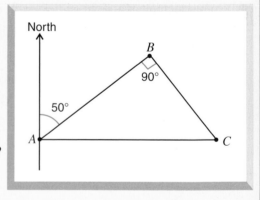

North

B

90°

50°

A C

7 Axford is 70 km from Moxley on a bearing of 065°.
Parley is 55 km from Moxley on a bearing of 125°.
(a) By using a scale of 1 cm to 10 km, draw an accurate diagram to show the positions of Axford, Parley and Moxley.
(b) What is the bearing of Moxley from Axford?
(c) By taking measurements from your diagram work out
     (i) the distance of Parley from Axford,
     (ii) the bearing of Parley from Axford.

A **triangle** is a shape made by three straight lines.

The smallest number of straight lines needed to make a shape is 3. Can you explain why?

Types of triangle

Measure the angles in each of these triangles.

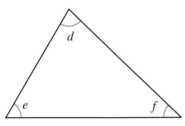 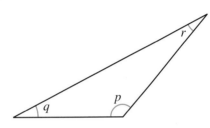 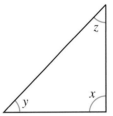

Angles *d*, *e* and *f* are all acute angles.
Triangles with three acute angles are called **acute-angled** triangles.

Angle *p* is an obtuse angle.
Triangles with an obtuse angle are called **obtuse-angled** triangles.

Angle *x* is a right angle.
Triangles with a right angle are called **right-angled** triangles.

The sum of the angles in a triangle

The sum of the three angles in a triangle is 180°.

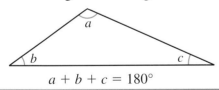

$$a + b + c = 180°$$

*Add up the three angles d, e
and f in the triangle.
Do the same for the other
two triangles.
You may not always get 180°.
Can you explain why?*

EXAMPLE

Without measuring, work out the size of the angle marked *a*.

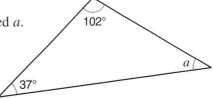

The sum of the angles in a triangle is 180°.
$$a + 102° + 37° = 180°$$
$$a + 139° = 180°$$
$$a = 180° - 139°$$
$$a = 41°$$

1 Is it possible to draw triangles with the following types of angles?
Give a reason for each of your answers.

(a) three acute angles,
(b) one obtuse angle and two acute angles,
(c) two obtuse angles and one acute angle,
(d) three obtuse angles,
(e) one right angle and two acute angles,
(f) two right angles and one acute angle.

2 Is it possible to draw a triangle with these angles.
If a triangle can be drawn, what type of triangle is it?
Give a reason for each of your answers.

(a) 95°, 78°, 7°
(b) 48°, 62°, 90°
(c) 48°, 62°, 70°
(d) 90°, 38°, 52°
(e) 130°, 35°, 15°
(f) 27°, 100°, 63°

3 Without measuring, work out the size of the third angle in each of these triangles.

(a)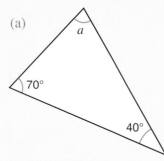

(b)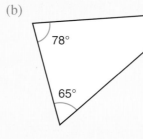

(c)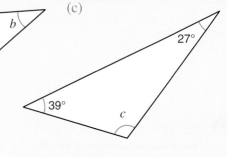

(d)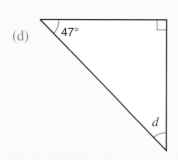

(e)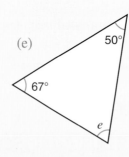

(f)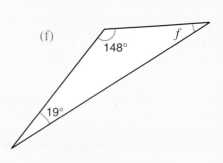

Exterior angle of a triangle

When one side of a triangle is extended, as shown, the angle formed is called an **exterior angle**.

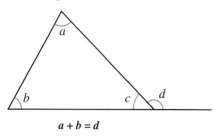

$a + b = d$

In any triangle the exterior angle is always equal to the sum of the two opposite interior angles.
Check this by measuring the angles a, b and d in the diagram.

This result can be easily proved.
$a + b + c = 180°$
(sum of angles in a triangle)
$c + d = 180°$
(supplementary angles)
$a + b + c = c + d$
$a + b = d$

EXAMPLE

Find the size of the angles marked a and b.

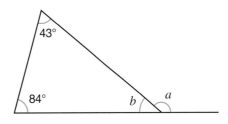

○○○○○○○○○○○○○○○○○○○○○

Short but fully accurate
In geometry we often abbreviate words and use symbols to provide the reader with full details using the minimum amount of writing.

Δ is short for triangle.
ext. $\angle$ of a Δ means exterior angle of a triangle.
supp. $\angle$'s means supplementary angles.

$a = 84° + 43°$ (ext. $\angle$ of a Δ)
$a = 127°$

$b + 127° = 180°$ (supp. $\angle$'s)
$\qquad b = 180° - 127°$
$\qquad b = 53°$

Exercise **21.2**

You should be able to do this exercise without a calculator. Having completed the exercise you can use your calculator to check your working.

1   The following diagrams have not been drawn accurately.
Work out the size of the marked angles.

(a)
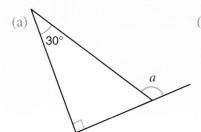

(b)
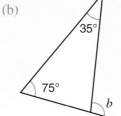

(c)
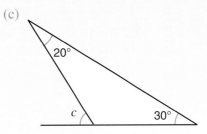

(d)
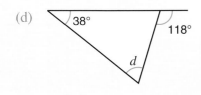

(e)
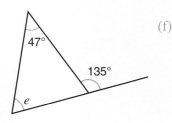

(f)
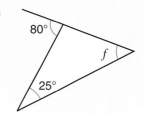

2   Work out the size of the marked angles.

(a)
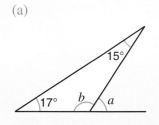

(b)
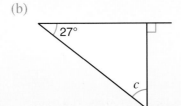

(c)
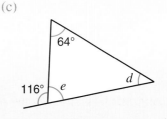

Naming parts of a triangle

Triangles are named by labelling each vertex with a capital letter.
Triangle ABC can be written as $\triangle ABC$.

Triangle ABC is formed by the sides AB, BC and AC.
Triangles and lines are often named in alphabetical order.
$\triangle ABC$ is the same as $\triangle BCA$.

The angles of a triangle are also described in terms of the vertices.
For example, the angle marked on the diagram is angle ACB or $\angle ACB$.
The middle letter is the vertex where the angle is made.

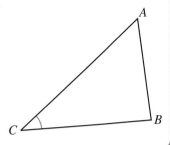

Special triangles

Scalene triangle	Isosceles triangle	Equilateral triangle	Notation used on sketch diagrams
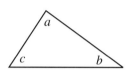		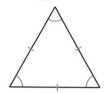	A sketch is used when an accurate drawing is not required.
The angles are all different. $a + b + c = 180°$.	Two equal sides. Two angles equal.	Three equal sides. All angles are 60°.	Dashes across lines show sides that are equal in length. Equal angles are marked using arcs.

Exercise 21.3

1 (a) What special name is given to $\triangle ABE$?
(b) What special name is given to $\triangle BDE$?
(c) Triangle BDC is scalene.
Give the three-letter name of another scalene triangle in the diagram.

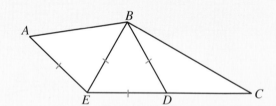

2 (a) On squared paper, draw triangles with the following coordinates:
(i) $(1, 1)$, $(6, 1)$, $(3, 5)$,
(ii) $(1, 1)$, $(5, 1)$, $(1, 4)$,
(iii) $(1, 1)$, $(5, 1)$, $(3, 4)$,
(iv) $(1, 1)$, $(6, 1)$, $(9, 5)$.

(b) Which of the following words could be used to describe each of the triangles you have drawn?
Acute-angled, Obtuse-angled or Right-angled.
Scalene, Equilateral or Isosceles.

3 On squared paper, draw an isosceles triangle with coordinates:
$A (3, 3)$, $B (9, 3)$ and $C (6, 10)$.
Which two sides are equal?
Which two angles are equal?

4 Triangle PQR is isosceles with angle $RPQ =$ angle QRP.
P is the point $(3, 5)$ and R is the point $(9, 5)$.
Give the coordinates of the two possible positions of Q so that angle PQR is a right angle.

5 These triangles have not been drawn accurately.
Work out the size of angle *a* in each triangle.

(a)
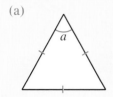

(b)
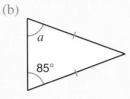

(c)
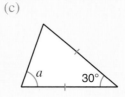

(d)
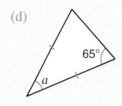

6 The following diagrams have not been drawn accurately.
Work out the size of the angles marked with letters.

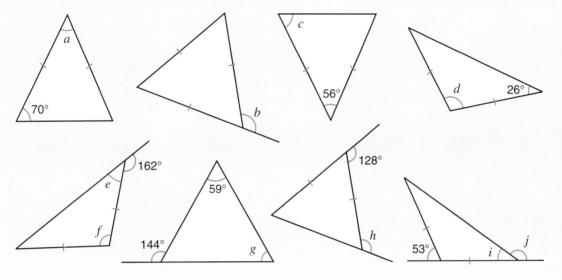

7 In the diagram $AB = BD = DA$ and $BC = CD$.
(a) What type of triangle is *BCD*?
(b) What is the size of angle *BDC*?
(c) Work out the size of angle *ADE*.

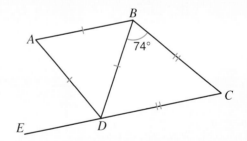

8 These diagrams have not been drawn accurately.
Work out the size of the required angles.

(a)
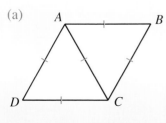

Find ∠*BCD*.

(b)
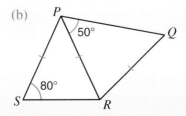

Find ∠*PRQ* and ∠*QRS*.

(c)
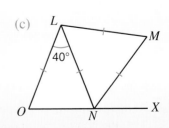

Find ∠*MNX*.

Drawing triangles

Your ruler, compasses and protractor can be used to draw triangles accurately.
Drawings can be made from written information or sketch diagrams.
Follow the instructions below to accurately draw two triangles.

Sketch diagram

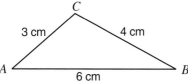

Information given:
Lengths of three sides of the triangle.

Step 1
Start by drawing the longest side, *AB*.
Draw a line 6 cm long.

A ———————————— B

Step 2
Set your compasses to a radius of 4 cm.
Draw an arc from *B*.

Step 3
Set your compasses to a radius of 3 cm.
Draw an arc from *A* to intersect (cross) the
arc drawn in step 2. Label the point *C*.

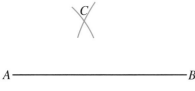

Step 4
Draw the sides *AC* and *BC*.
Add labels.

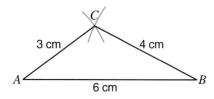

Sketch diagram

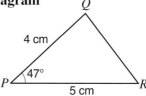

Information given:
Lengths of two sides of the triangle and the
size of the angle between the two sides.

Step 1
Start by drawing the longest side, *PR*.
Draw a line 5 cm long.

P ———————————— R

Step 2
∠*QPR* = 47° (acute angle)
Use your protractor to measure 47°.

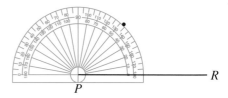

Step 3
Using the dot as a guide, draw a line,
4 cm long, from *P*. Label point *Q*.

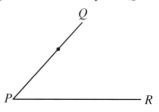

Step 4
Draw the line *QR* to complete the triangle.
Add labels.

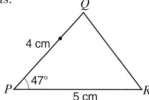

If you are given written information draw a sketch diagram first.

For example, information for triangle *ABC* could be given as:

Draw accurately triangle *ABC* with sides *AB* = 6 cm, *BC* = 4 cm and *AC* = 3 cm.

Activity

Write instructions which someone could follow to draw the following triangles accurately.

(a)

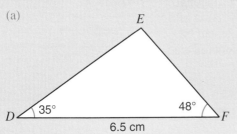

(b)

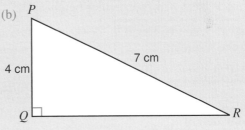

Exercise 21.4

1 Use a ruler and compasses to draw accurately triangles with the following sides.
(a) 4 cm, 5 cm, 6 cm.
(b) 3.5 cm, 4.5 cm, 5 cm.
(c) $AB = 4.8$ cm, $BC = 3.6$ cm, $AC = 6.2$ cm.
(d) $PQ = 6$ cm, $QR = 6.5$ cm, $PR = 2.5$ cm.

2 Use a ruler and compasses to construct an equilateral triangle of side 5 cm.

3 Accurately draw the triangles using the information shown in the sketch diagrams below.

(a)

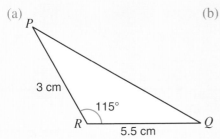

(b)

(c)

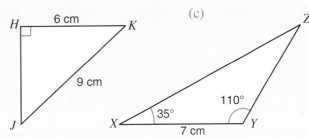

4 Use a ruler and protractor to draw the following triangles.
(a) $AB = 4$ cm, $BC = 4$ cm, $\angle ABC = 40°$.
(b) $PQ = 3.5$ cm, $PR = 5$ cm, $\angle QPR = 100°$.
(c) $XY = YZ = ZX = 4$ cm.
(d) $FG = 5$ cm, $FH = 5$ cm, $\angle FGH = 40°$.

5 A sketch of triangle PQR is shown.
(a) Make an accurate drawing of triangle PQR.
(b) Measure and write down the length of PR.
(c) Measure and write down the size of angle QPR.

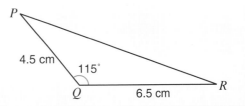

Perimeter of a triangle

The **perimeter** is the distance round the outside of a shape. The perimeter of a triangle is the sum of the lengths of its three sides.

Measure the sides of this triangle.
What is the perimeter?

You should find:
$AB = 4$ cm, $BC = 5$ cm and $AC = 6$ cm.
Perimeter $= 4 + 5 + 6 = 15$ cm.

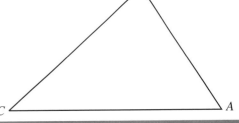

Area of a triangle

The area of a triangle is given by:

Area $= \frac{1}{2} \times$ base $\times$ perpendicular height.

> The area, A, can be found using the formula:
> $$A = \frac{1}{2} \times b \times h$$

In these triangles b is the base and h is the **perpendicular height**.

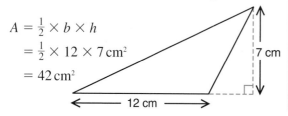

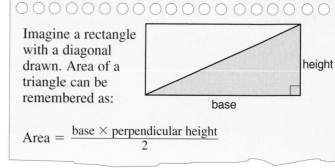

Imagine a rectangle with a diagonal drawn. Area of a triangle can be remembered as:

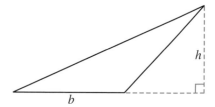

Area $= \dfrac{\text{base} \times \text{perpendicular height}}{2}$

EXAMPLES

1 Calculate the area of this triangle.

$A = \frac{1}{2} \times b \times h$

$\quad = \frac{1}{2} \times 12 \times 7\,\text{cm}^2$

$\quad = 42\,\text{cm}^2$

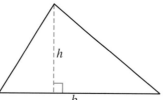

7 cm

12 cm

2 This triangle has area $36\,\text{cm}^2$. Find the height of the triangle.

$A = \frac{1}{2} \times b \times h$

$36 = \frac{1}{2} \times 16 \times h$

$36 = 8h$

$h = \frac{36}{8}$

$h = 4.5\,\text{cm}$

16 cm

Exercise 21.5

Do not use a calculator for questions 1 to 5.

1 Work out the lengths of the perimeters of these triangles.

(a)

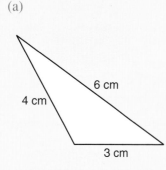

6 cm
4 cm
3 cm

(b)

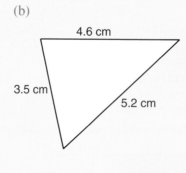

4.6 cm
3.5 cm
5.2 cm

(c)

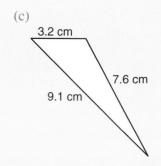

3.2 cm
7.6 cm
9.1 cm

2 Which of the triangles *PQR*, *QRS* or *RST* has the largest perimeter?

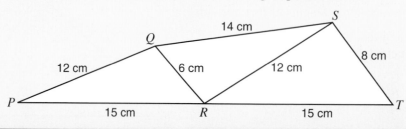

14 cm
Q
12 cm
6 cm
12 cm
S
8 cm
P
15 cm
R
15 cm
T

3 These triangles each have a perimeter of length 20 cm.
Work out the lengths of the marked sides.

(a)
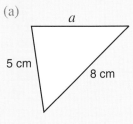
a
5 cm
8 cm

(b)
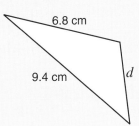
6.8 cm
9.4 cm
d

(c)
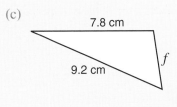
7.8 cm
9.2 cm
f

4 Calculate the areas of these triangles.

(a)
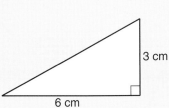
3 cm
6 cm

(b)
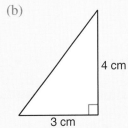
4 cm
3 cm

(c)
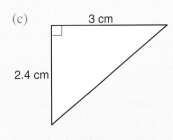
3 cm
2.4 cm

(d)
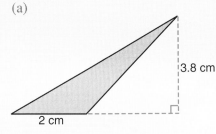
2.4 cm
6 cm

(e)
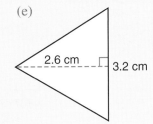
2.6 cm 3.2 cm

(f)
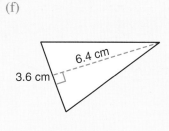
6.4 cm
3.6 cm

5 Find the areas of the shaded triangles.

(a)
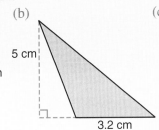
3.8 cm
2 cm

(b)
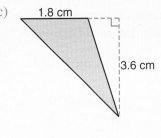
5 cm
3.2 cm

(c)
1.8 cm
3.6 cm

6 These triangles each have an area of 32 cm².
Calculate the lengths of the marked sides.

(a)
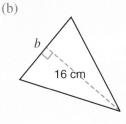
8 cm
a

(b)
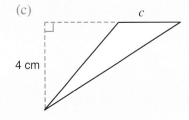
b
16 cm

(c)
c
4 cm

7 This triangle has a perimeter of 45 cm.
Calculate the area of the triangle.
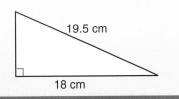
19.5 cm
18 cm

8 This triangle has an area of 37.5 cm².
Calculate the perimeter of the triangle.

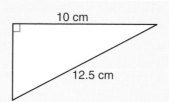
10 cm
12.5 cm

9 The shape *ABCDE* is made of two right-angled triangles.
ABCDE has an area of 28.5 cm².
Calculate the length of *ED*.

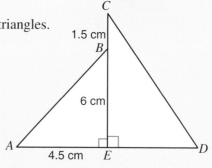

C
1.5 cm
B
6 cm
A   4.5 cm   E   D

What you need to know

- Triangles can be:

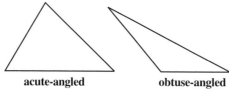

acute-angled   **obtuse-angled**   **right-angled**

- The sum of the angles in a triangle is 180°.
  $a + b + c = 180°$

- The exterior angle is equal to the sum of the two opposite interior angles.
  $a + b = d$

a
b   *c*   *d*

- Types of triangle:

Scalene triangle	Isosceles triangle	Equilateral triangle

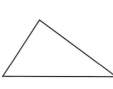

All sides have different lengths.   Two equal sides. Two equal angles.   Three equal sides. Three equal angles, 60°.

- Perimeter of a triangle is the sum of its three sides.

- Area of a triangle = $\dfrac{\text{base} \times \text{perpendicular height}}{2}$

  $A = \frac{1}{2} \times b \times h$

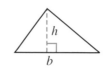

h
b
h
b

You should be able to:
- Draw triangles accurately using ruler, compasses, protractor.

1 (a) Plot the points $P(2, 1)$, $Q(4, 5)$, $R(6, 1)$.
   Join the points to form triangle PQR.
   (b) (i) What special name is given to triangle PQR?
       (ii) What is the area of the triangle?
   (c) On the same diagram draw another triangle PRS, which has the same area as triangle PQR.

2 $AB = AC$.
Work out the size of the angles marked
   (a) x,
   (b) y.

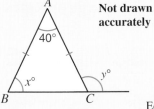

Not drawn accurately

Edexcel

3 In the diagram, triangle ABC is isosceles with $BA = AC$, and triangle ACD is right-angled with angle $CAD = 90°$.

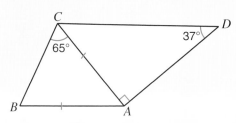

The diagram has not been drawn accurately.
   (a) Angle $ADC = 37°$.
       Work out the size of angle DCA.
   (b) Angle $ACB = 65°$.
       Work out the size of angle BAC.

4 In the triangle ABC,
$BC = 8$ cm,
angle $CBA = 24°$,
$AB = 10$ cm.

   (a) Use the information to draw triangle ABC.
   (b) (i) Measure the size of angle BAC.
       (ii) What mathematical name is given to angle BAC? Edexcel

5

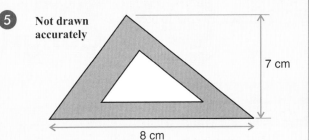

Not drawn accurately

7 cm

8 cm

In the diagram, the outer triangle has base 8 cm and height 7 cm.
   (a) Calculate the area of the outer triangle.

The base and height of the inner triangle are each half those of the outer triangle.
   (b) Calculate the area of the inner triangle.
   (c) Hence, calculate the area of the shaded part.

Edexcel

6 Calculate the area of triangle ABC.

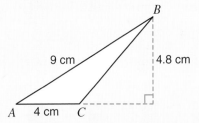

7 The diagram shows a sketch of triangle PQR.

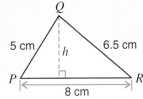

   (a) Make an accurate drawing of the triangle.
   (b) By measuring the height of your triangle calculate the area of triangle PQR.

8 The diagram shows three triangles, BAE, BED and BDC.

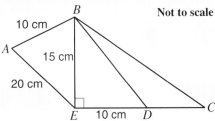

Not to scale

   (a) Calculate the perimeter of triangle BAE.
   (b) Calculate the area of triangle BED.
   (c) The areas of triangles BED and BDC are equal.
       Calculate the length of DC.

CHAPTER 22

Symmetry and Congruence

Lines of symmetry

These shapes are **symmetrical**.

When each shape is folded along the dashed line one side will fit exactly over the other side. The dashed line is called a **line of symmetry**.

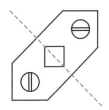

Some shapes have more than one line of symmetry.

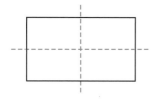
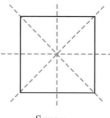

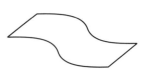

Rectangle
2 lines of symmetry.

Square
4 lines of symmetry.

Circle
Infinite number of lines of symmetry. Each diameter is a line of symmetry.

Shape with no lines of symmetry.

Rotational symmetry

Is this shape symmetrical?

The shape does not have line symmetry.

Try placing a copy of the shape over the original and rotating it about the centre of the circle.

After 180° (a half-turn) the shape fits into its own outline.
The shape has **rotational symmetry**.
The point about which the shape is rotated is called the **centre of rotation**.
The **order of rotational symmetry** is 2. When rotating the shape through 360° it fits into its own outline twice (once after a half-turn and again after a full-turn).
A shape is only described as having rotational symmetry if the order of rotational symmetry is 2 or more.

A shape can have both line symmetry and rotational symmetry.

EXAMPLES

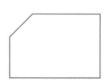

Order of rotational symmetry 5.

Order of rotational symmetry 4.
4 lines of symmetry.

Order of rotational symmetry 1.
The shape is **not** described as having rotational symmetry.

1 These shapes have **line symmetry**. Copy each shape and draw the line of symmetry.

(a)

(b)

(c)

(d)

2 The following diagrams show half a shape.
The dashed line is the line of symmetry for the complete shape.
Copy the diagrams and complete each shape.

(a)

(b)

(c)

(d)

3 These shapes have been drawn accurately.
How many lines of symmetry has each shape?

(a)

(b)

(c)

4 How many lines of symmetry has each of these letters?

A C E H K

5 What is the order of rotational symmetry for each of these shapes?

(a)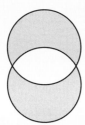

(b)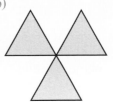

(c)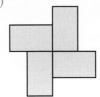

(d)

(e)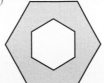

(f)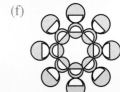

6 Look at these letters of the alphabet.

J M N O P X Y Z

   (a)   Which two letters have only line symmetry?
   (b)   Which two letters have only rotational symmetry?
   (c)   Which letters have rotational symmetry of order 2?
   (d)   Which letters have neither rotational nor line symmetry?

7 Make a copy of this shape.

   (a)   How many lines of symmetry does the
          shape have?
   (b)   (i)   Colour one square so that your shape
               has rotational symmetry of order 2.
          (ii) Mark the centre of rotational symmetry
               on your shape.

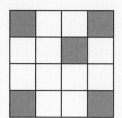

8 Make a copy of this shape.

   (a)   How many lines of symmetry does the
          shape have?
   (b)   (i)   Colour one triangle so that your shape
               has rotational symmetry of order 3.
          (ii) How many lines of symmetry does
               your shape have?

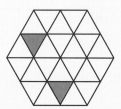

9 For each shape state   (i)   the number of lines of symmetry,
                          (ii) the order of rotational symmetry.

  (a)   (b)   (c)   (d)   (e)

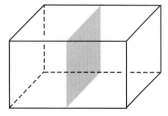 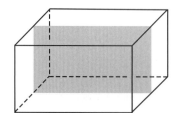 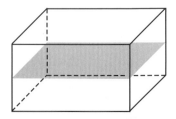

Symmetry in three-dimensions

Planes of symmetry

So far we have looked at two-dimensional (flat) shapes.
Two-dimensional shapes can have line symmetry.
Three-dimensional objects can have **plane symmetry**.
A **plane of symmetry** slices through an object so that one half is the mirror image of the other half.

A cuboid has three planes of symmetry as shown.

Axes of symmetry

A wall is built using cuboids.

In how many different ways can the next cuboid be placed in position?

If the cuboid can be placed in more than one way, it must have rotational symmetry about one or more **axes**.

A cuboid has three axes of symmetry. The diagram shows one **axis of symmetry**. The order of rotational symmetry about this axis is two.

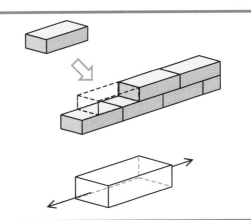

Exercise 22.2

1 How many planes of symmetry has a cube?

2 State the order of rotational symmetry about the axis shown in each of the following.

(a) Cube   (b) Square-based pyramid   (c) Cylinder   (d) Cone

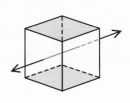

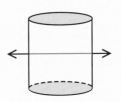

3 Each end of this cuboid is a square.
The axes of symmetry are labelled *a*, *b* and *c*.
What is the order of rotational symmetry about
(a) axis *a*,
(b) axis *b*,
(c) axis *c*?

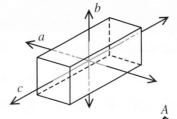

4 The diagram shows a cuboid, with a square base. On top of the cuboid is a square-based pyramid with vertex *A* above the centre of the top of the cuboid.

(a) How many planes of symmetry has the figure?
(b) How many axes of symmetry has the figure?
Give the order of rotational symmetry about each axis.

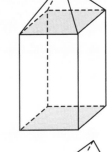

5 The diagram shows a triangular prism.
The ends of the prism are equilateral triangles.

(a) How many axes of symmetry has the prism?
(b) How many planes of symmetry has the prism?

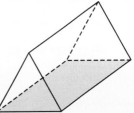

Congruent shapes

When two shapes are the same shape and size they are said to be **congruent**.
A copy of one shape would fit exactly over the second shape. Sometimes it is necessary to turn the copy over to get an exact fit.
These shapes are all congruent.

Exercise 22.3

1 Look at the shapes below. List five **pairs** of congruent shapes.

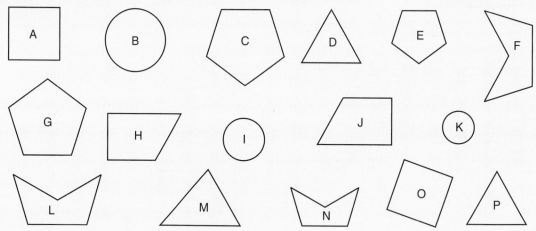

2 Which of these shapes are congruent to each other?

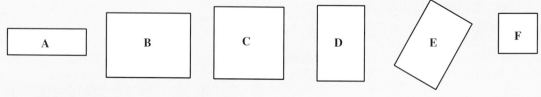

3 The diagram shows a rectangle that has been divided into five triangles.
(a) Which triangle is congruent to triangle *AFG*?
(b) Which quadrilateral is congruent to quadrilateral *ABEF*?

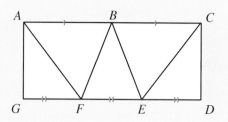

4 Triangle *ABC* has been divided into four smaller triangles as shown.

Name two pairs of congruent triangles.

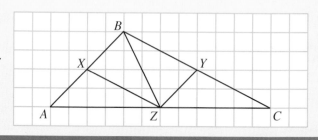

252

Congruent triangles

There are four ways to show that a pair of triangles are congruent.

1 Three sides.   SSS

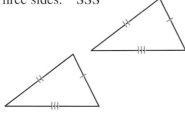

2 Two sides and the included angle.   SAS

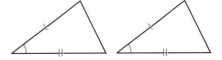

The included angle is the angle between the two sides.

3 Two angles and a corresponding side. ASA

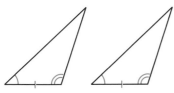

This can be written as AAS if the corresponding side is not between the angles.

4 Right angle, hypotenuse and one side. RHS

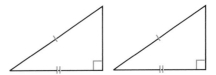

The hypotenuse is the side opposite the right angle and is the longest side in a right-angled triangle.

EXAMPLE

Show that triangles *ABC* and *PQR* are congruent.

AB = *PQ* (equal lengths, given)
AC = *PR* (equal lengths, given)
∠*BAC* = ∠*QPR* (equal angles, given)

So triangles *ABC* and *PQR* are congruent.
Reason: SAS (Two sides and the included angle.)

Since the triangles are congruent we also know that *BC* = *QR*, ∠*ABC* = ∠*PQR* and ∠*ACB* = ∠*PRQ*.

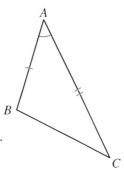
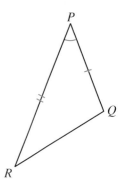

Exercise **22.4**

1 The following triangles have not been drawn accurately.
Which two of these triangles are congruent to each other?
Give a reason for your answer.

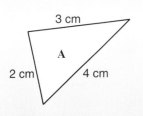
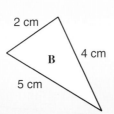
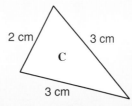
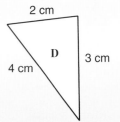

2 The following triangles have not been drawn accurately.
Which two of these triangles are congruent to each other?
Give a reason for your answer.

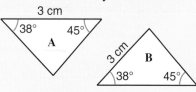
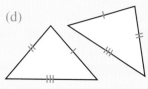
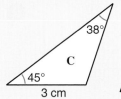
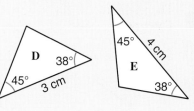

3 The following triangles have not been drawn accurately. State whether each pair of triangles is congruent or not. Where triangles are congruent give the reason.

(a)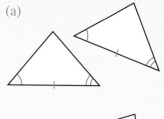

(b)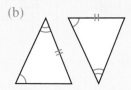

(c)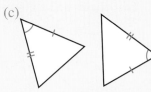

(d)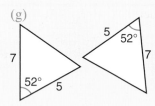

(e)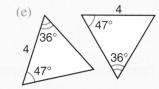

(f)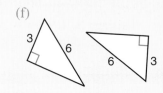

(g)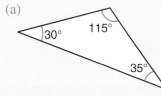

(h)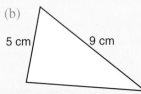

(i)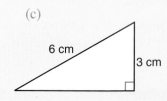

4 For each of the following, is it possible to draw a congruent triangle without taking any other measurements from the original triangle? If a triangle can be drawn give the reason for congruence which applies.

(a)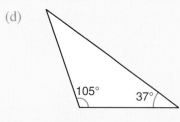

(b)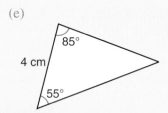

(c)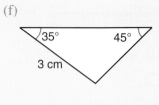

(d)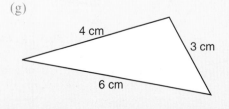

(e)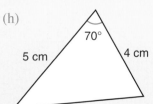

(f)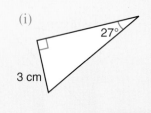

(g)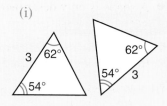

(h)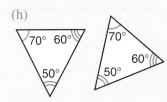

(i)

⑤ Triangle *ABC* has angles 90°, 50° and 40°.
Triangle *XYZ* also has angles 90°, 50° and 40°.
The triangles are not congruent.
Can you explain why?

⑥ Show that triangles *DEF* and *PQR* are
congruent.

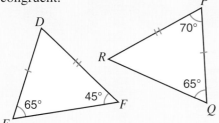

⑦ In the diagram *AB* is parallel to *CD*.
AB = *CD* = 7 cm and ∠*ABD* = 25°.

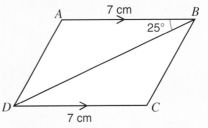

(a) What is the size of ∠*BDC*?
(b) Show that triangles *ABD* and
BCD are congruent.
(c) Name an angle which is the
same size as ∠*CBD*.

What you need to know

- A two-dimensional shape has **line symmetry** if the line divides the
shape so that one side fits exactly over the other.

- A two-dimensional shape has **rotational symmetry** if it fits into a
copy of its outline as it is rotated through 360°.

- A shape is only described as having rotational symmetry if the order
of rotational symmetry is 2 or more.

- The number of times a shape fits into its outline in a single turn is
the **order of rotational symmetry**.

- A **plane of symmetry** slices through a three-dimensional object so
that one half is the mirror image of the other half.

- Three-dimensional objects can have **axes of symmetry**.

- When two shapes are the same shape and size they are said to be
congruent.

- There are four ways to show that a pair of triangles are congruent:
  - SSS   Three equal sides.
  - SAS   Two sides and the included angle.
  - ASA   Two angles and a corresponding side.
  - RHS   Right angle, hypotenuse and one other side.

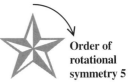

Order of
rotational
symmetry 5

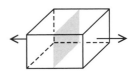

Review Exercise

❶ Half of a shape is drawn on squared paper.
AB is a line of
symmetry for the
complete shape.
Copy the diagram
and complete the
shape.

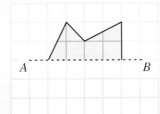

❷ Consider the letters

X   Y   Z

(a) Which of these letters has line
symmetry only?
(b) Which of these letters has
rotational symmetry but not
line symmetry?

3 Look at these diagrams.

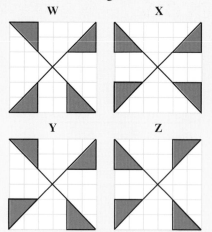

(a) Which diagram has rotational symmetry only?
(b) Which diagram has line symmetry only?
(c) Which diagram has line symmetry **and** rotational symmetry?

4 The diagram consists of three equilateral triangles.

Copy the diagram, and add another triangle so that the final diagram
(a) has rotational symmetry **and** line symmetry,
(b) has rotational symmetry **only**.

5 These shapes have both line symmetry and rotational symmetry.

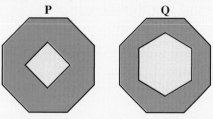

(a) How many lines of symmetry has shape **P**?
(b) What is the order of rotational symmetry of shape **Q**?

6 Copy these shapes and draw in one plane of symmetry for each.

(a)   (b)

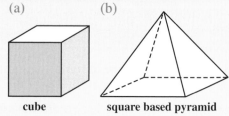

cube   square based pyramid

Edexcel

7 This diagram has been drawn accurately.
(a) Which triangle is congruent to triangle *ABC*?
(b) Which triangle is congruent to triangle *ACF*?
(c) Which quadrilateral is congruent to quadrilateral *ABCF*?

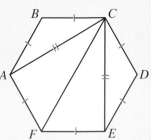

8 These triangles have not been drawn accurately.
Which two triangles are congruent to each other? Give a reason for your answer.

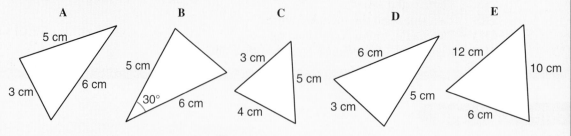

9 These triangles have not been drawn accurately.

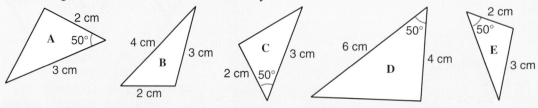

Which two of these triangles are congruent? Give a reason for your answer.

CHAPTER 23

Quarilaterals

A **quadrilateral** is a shape made by four straight lines.

Special quadrilaterals

Parallelogram

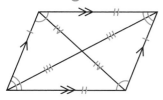

Opposite sides equal and parallel.
Opposite angles equal.
Diagonals bisect each other.

Rectangle

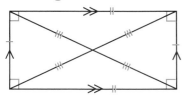

Opposite sides equal and parallel.
Angles of 90°.
Diagonals bisect each other.

Square

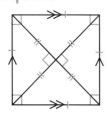

Four equal sides.
Opposite sides parallel.
Angles of 90°.
Diagonals bisect each other at 90°.

Rhombus

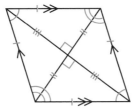

Four equal sides.
Opposite sides parallel.
Opposite angles equal.
Diagonals bisect each other at 90°.

Kite

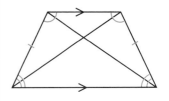

Two pairs of adjacent sides equal.
One pair of opposite angles equal.
One diagonal bisects the other at 90°.

Trapezium

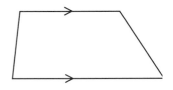

One pair of parallel sides.

Isosceles trapezium

One pair of parallel sides.
Non-parallel sides equal.
Two pairs of equal angles.
Diagonals equal.

Remember:
Sides of equal length are marked with
the same number of **dashes**.
Lines which are parallel are marked
with the same number of **arrowheads**.
Angles of equal size are marked with
the same number of **arcs**.

Sum of the angles of a quadrilateral

The sum of the four angles of a quadrilateral is 360°.

Measure the angles of this quadrilateral.
Do the angles add up to 360°?

You may not always get 360°.
Can you explain why?

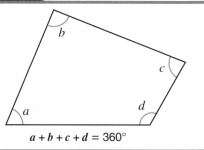

$$a + b + c + d = 360°$$

EXAMPLE

Without measuring, work out the size of the angle marked x.

PQ is parallel to RS and PS is parallel to QR.
$PQRS$ could be either a parallelogram or a rhombus.
In both types of quadrilateral the opposite angles are equal.

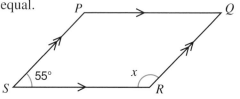

$$55° + 55° + x + x = 360°$$
$$110° + 2x = 360°$$
$$2x = 360° - 110°$$
$$2x = 250°$$
$$x = 125°$$

Symmetry of quadrilaterals

Remember:
A two-dimensional shape has line symmetry if the line divides the shape so that one side fits exactly over the other.
A two-dimensional shape has rotational symmetry if it fits into a copy of its own outline as it is rotated through 360°.

Parallelogram

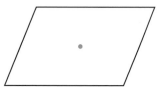

0 lines of symmetry.
Order of rotational symmetry 2.

Isosceles trapezium

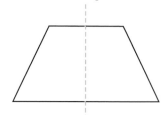

1 line of symmetry.

Rectangle

2 lines of symmetry.
Order of rotational symmetry 2.

Square

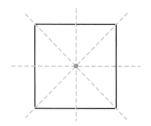

Rhombus

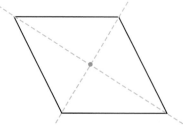

Kite

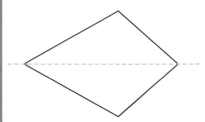

4 lines of symmetry.
Order of rotational symmetry 4.

2 lines of symmetry.
Order of rotational symmetry 2.

1 line of symmetry.

Use squared paper to answer questions 1 to 8.
You should be able to do this exercise without using your calculator.
Having completed the exercise you can use a
calculator to check your working.

1 (a) Draw quadrilaterals with the following
coordinates.
(i) $A(3, 1)$, $B(1, 3)$, $C(2, 6)$, $D(6, 2)$
(ii) $E(1, 0)$, $F(6, 2)$, $G(8, 9)$, $H(3, 7)$
(iii) $J(3, 0)$, $K(0, 4)$, $L(3, 8)$, $M(6, 4)$
(iv) $P(1, 1)$, $Q(2, 4)$, $R(4, 4)$, $S(4, 2)$
(v) $W(3, 1)$, $X(1, 3)$, $Y(3, 5)$, $Z(5, 3)$
(b) What special name is given to each of
these quadrilaterals?

2 *JKLM* is a square.
J is the point $(1, 1)$, $K(4, 1)$, $L(4, 4)$.
Find the coordinates of *M*.

3 *PQRS* is a rectangle.
P is the point $(1, 3)$, $Q(4, 6)$, $R(6, 4)$.
Find the coordinates of *S*.

4 *ABCD* is a rhombus.
A is the point $(3, 0)$, $B(0, 4)$ and $D(8, 0)$.
Find the coordinates of *C*.

5 *WXYZ* is a parallelogram.
W is the point $(1, 0)$, $X(4, 1)$, $Z(3, 3)$.
Find the coordinates of *Y*.

6 *OABC* is a kite.
O is the point $(0, 0)$, $B(5, 5)$, $C(3, 1)$.
Find the coordinates of *A*.

7 *KLMN* is an isosceles trapezium.
K is the point $(1, 1)$, $M(4, 3)$, $N(5, 1)$.
Find the coordinates of *L*.

8 *STUV* is a square with
S at $(1, 3)$ and *U* at $(5, 3)$.
Find the coordinates of *T* and *V*.

9 The following diagrams have not been drawn accurately.
Work out the size of the angles marked with letters.

(a)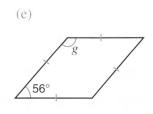

(b)

(c)

(d)

(e)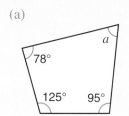

(f)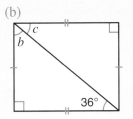

(g)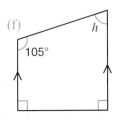

(h)

10 *PQRS* is a rhombus.

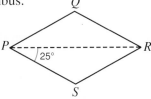

Work out the size of (a) angle *QPR*,
(b) angle *QRS*,
(c) angle *PQR*.

11 *WXYZ* is an isosceles trapezium.
Work out the size of angle *WXY* and
angle *XYZ*.

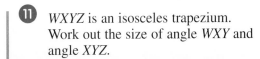
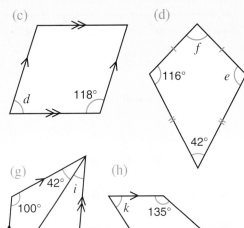

12 These quadrilaterals have been drawn on squared paper.

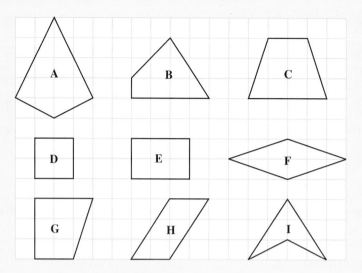

Copy and complete the table for each shape.

Shape	A	B	C	D	E	F	G	H	I
Number of lines of symmetry									
Order of rotational symmetry									

13 How many lines of symmetry has each of these quadrilaterals?

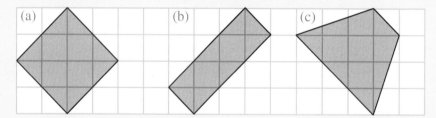

(a)   (b)   (c)

14 What is the order of rotational symmetry for each of these quadrilaterals?

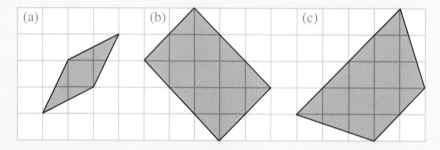

(a)   (b)   (c)

15 (a) Draw a rhombus of side 4 cm, with angles of 80° and 100°.
(b) Mark on your diagram any lines of symmetry.
(c) What order of rotational symmetry has the rhombus?

Perimeters of rectangles and squares

The **perimeter** is the distance round the outside of a shape.
The perimeter of a rectangle (or square) is the sum of the lengths of its four sides.

Measure the sides of this rectangle.
What is the perimeter of the rectangle?

You should find:
$AB = 3$ cm, $BC = 4$ cm,
$CD = 3$ cm, $DA = 4$ cm.
Perimeter $= 3 + 4 + 3 + 4$
$= 14$ cm

Area

Area is the amount of surface covered by a shape.
The standard unit for measuring area is the square centimetre, cm².
Small areas are measured using square millimetres, mm².
Large areas are measured using square metres, m², or square kilometres, km².

Area formulae

Rectangle

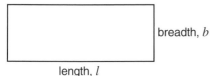
length, *l*

Area = length × breadth
$A = lb$

Square

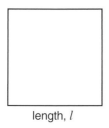
length, *l*

Area = length × breadth
In a square, length = breadth
Area = (length)²
$A = l^2$

Trapezium

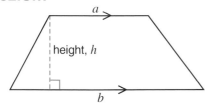

Area = half the sum of the parallel sides ×
perpendicular height

$A = \frac{1}{2}(a + b)h$

Parallelogram

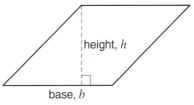
base, *b*

Area = base × height
$A = bh$

Rhombus

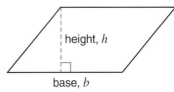
base, *b*

Area = base × height
$A = bh$

Base and perpendicular height
The **base** is the side of the shape from
which the height is measured.
The base does not have to be at the
bottom of the shape.
The height of a shape, measured at right
angles to the base, is called the
perpendicular height.

Quadrilaterals . . . Quadrilaterals . . . Quadrilaterals . . .

1 Find the area of this trapezium.

$A = \frac{1}{2}(a + b)h$
$= \frac{1}{2}(5 + 9)6$
$= \frac{1}{2} \times 14 \times 6$
$= 42\,cm^2$

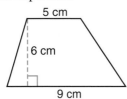

5 cm
6 cm
9 cm

2 The area of a rectangular room is $17.5\,m^2$.
The room is 5 m long.
Find the width of the room.

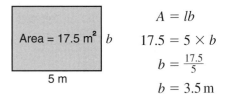

Area = 17.5 m² | b
5 m

$A = lb$
$17.5 = 5 \times b$
$b = \frac{17.5}{5}$
$b = 3.5\,m$

Exercise **23.2**

You should be able to do questions 1 and 2 without using a calculator.

1 Four rectangles are shown.

(a) Which of these rectangles have the same perimeter?

(b) Which of these rectangles have the same area?

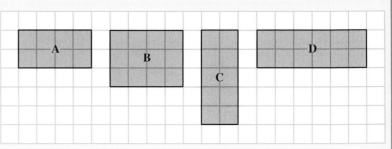

2 These shapes have been drawn on 1 cm squared paper. Find the area of each shape.

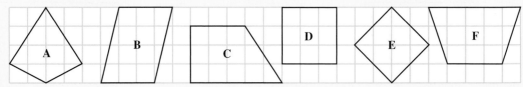

3 Calculate the perimeters and areas of these rectangles and squares.

(a)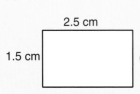
2.5 cm
1.5 cm

(b)
3.1 cm
0.9 cm

(c)
2.8 cm
2.8 cm

(d)
1.4 cm
1.4 cm

4 Calculate the areas of these shapes.

(a)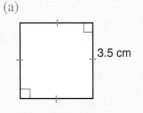
3.5 cm

(b)
2.8 cm
1.4 cm

(c)
1.8 cm
2.6 cm

(d)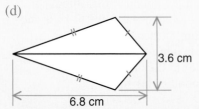
3.6 cm
6.8 cm

(e)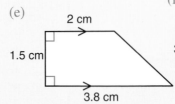
2 cm
1.5 cm
3.8 cm

(f)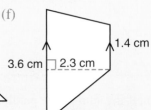
1.4 cm
3.6 cm | 2.3 cm

5 A carpet measuring 4 m by 4 m is placed on a rectangular floor measuring 5 m by 6 m. What area of floor is not carpeted?

6 The diagram shows a picture in a frame. The outer dimensions of the frame are 18 cm by 10 cm. The frame is 2 cm wide. What is the area of the picture?

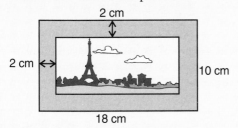

2 cm

2 cm

10 cm

18 cm

7 A rectangle has an area of 36 cm². The length of the rectangle is 9 cm. What is the breadth?

8 The diagram shows a square drawn inside a rectangle.

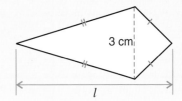

7.5 cm

5 cm

6 cm

Calculate the shaded area.

9 A rhombus of side 6 cm has an area of 48 cm². What is the perpendicular height of the rhombus?

10 A trapezium has an area of 30 cm². The two parallel sides are 7 cm and 8 cm. What is the perpendicular distance between the sides?

11 These shapes all have the same area. Calculate the values of h and l.

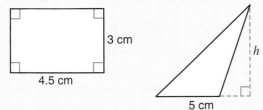

3 cm

4.5 cm

h

5 cm

3 cm

l

12 Each of these shapes has an area of 24 cm². Calculate the lengths marked with letters.

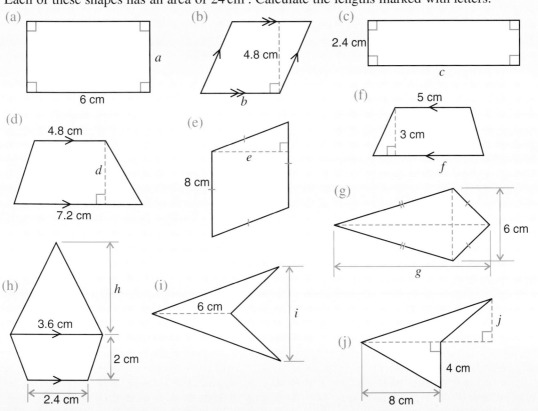

(a)

6 cm

a

(b)

4.8 cm

b

(c)

2.4 cm

c

(d)

4.8 cm

d

7.2 cm

(e)

8 cm

e

(f)

5 cm

3 cm

f

(g)

6 cm

g

(h)

3.6 cm

2.4 cm

h

2 cm

(i)

6 cm

i

(j)

4 cm

8 cm

j

- A **quadrilateral** is a shape made by four straight lines.

- The sum of the angles in a quadrilateral is 360°.

- The **perimeter** of a quadrilateral is the sum of the lengths of its four sides.

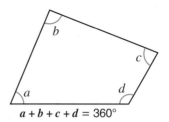

$a + b + c + d = 360°$

- Facts about these special quadrilaterals:

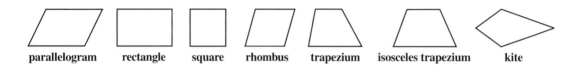

parallelogram   rectangle   square   rhombus   trapezium   isosceles trapezium   kite

Quadrilateral	Sides	Angles	Diagonals	Line symmetry	Order of rotational symmetry	Area formula
Parallelogram	Opposite sides equal and parallel	Opposite angles equal	Bisect each other	0	2	$A = bh$
Rectangle	Opposite sides equal and parallel	All 90°	Bisect each other	2	2	$A = bh$
Rhombus	4 equal sides, opposite sides parallel	Opposite angles equal	Bisect each other at 90°	2	2	$A = bh$
Square	4 equal sides, opposite sides parallel	All 90°	Bisect each other at 90°	4	4	$A = l^2$
Trapezium	1 pair of parallel sides					$A = \frac{1}{2}(a + b)h$
Isosceles trapezium	1 pair of parallel sides, non-parallel sides equal	2 pairs of equal angles	Equal in length	1	1	$A = \frac{1}{2}(a + b)h$
Kite	2 pairs of adjacent sides equal	1 pair of opposite angles equal	One bisects the other at 90°	1	1	

IDEAS FOR INVESTIGATION

The area of a quadrilateral in which the diagonals intersect at 90° can be worked out using, area = $\frac{1}{2}$ product of the diagonals.

Investigate.

1

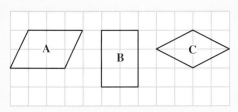

(a) How many lines of symmetry has shape **B**?
(b) Which shape has no lines of symmetry?
(c) What is the order of rotational symmetry of shape **C**?

2 *PQ* is a side of the square *PQRS*.
R is at $(1, -3)$.
What are the coordinates of *S*?

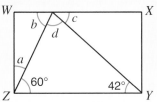

3 *WXYZ* is a rectangle.

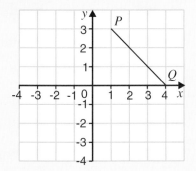

Calculate angles a, b, c and d.

4 Work out the size of angle a.
Give a reason for
your answer.

5 (a) How many lines of symmetry has a kite?
(b) Find the size of the angles marked with letters in each of these kites.

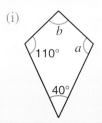

6 The diagram shows a trapezium.
Find the size of angle a and angle b.

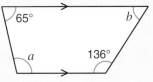

7 Three rectangles each have an area of
28 cm².
The lengths of all the sides are whole numbers of centimetres.
For each rectangle work out the lengths of the two sides.   Edexcel

8 The diagram shows the dimensions of a kite.

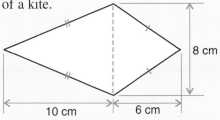

What is the area of the kite?

9 A square has a perimeter of 20 cm.
Calculate the area of the square.

10 The rectangle has an area of 54 cm².
The length of
the rectangle is
7.5 cm.
Calculate the
perimeter of the
rectangle.

7.5 cm

11 The diagram shows a square drawn
inside a rectangle.
The shaded area
is 47 cm².
What is the
perimeter of
the square?

9 cm

8 cm

12 *ABCD* is a trapezium.
The trapezium has
an area of 42 cm².

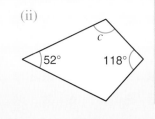

Calculate the length of *BC*.

CHAPTER 24

Polygons

A **polygon** is a shape made by straight lines.
A three-sided polygon is a **triangle**.

A four-sided polygon is called a **quadrilateral**.

A polygon is a many-sided shape.
Look at these polygons.

Pentagon
5 sides

Hexagon
6 sides

Heptagon
7 sides

Octagon
8 sides

Interior and exterior angles of a polygon

Angles formed by sides inside a polygon are called **interior angles**.

When a side of a polygon is extended, as shown, the angle formed is called an **exterior angle**.

At each vertex of the polygon:
    interior angle + exterior angle = 180°

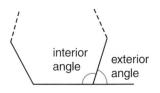

interior angle / exterior angle

Sum of the interior angles of a polygon

The diagram shows polygons with the diagonals from one vertex drawn.

P    Q 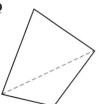   R 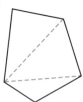   S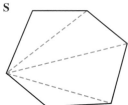

The diagonals divide the polygons into triangles.

Shape	Number of sides	Number of triangles	Sum of interior angles
P	3	1	$1 \times 180° = 180°$
Q	4	2	$2 \times 180° = 360°$
R	5	3	$3 \times 180° = 540°$
S	6	4	$4 \times 180° = 720°$

In general, for any n-sided polygon, the sum of the interior angles is $(n - 2) \times 180°$.

Sum of the exterior angles of a polygon

The sum of the
exterior angles
of **any** polygon
is 360°.

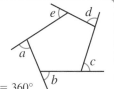

$a + b + c + d + e = 360°$

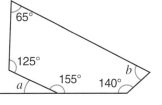

EXAMPLE

Find the size
of the angles
marked a and b.

$155° + a = 180°$ (int. angle + ext. angle = 180°)
$a = 180° - 155°$
$a = 25°$
The sum of the interior angles of a pentagon is 540°.
$b + 140° + 155° + 125° + 65° = 540°$
$b + 485° = 540°$
$b = 540° - 485°$
$b = 55°$

To find the sum of the interior
angles of a pentagon substitute
$n = 5$ into $(n - 2) \times 180°$.
  $(5 - 2) \times 180°$
  $= 3 \times 180°$
  $= 540°$

Exercise 24.1

The diagrams in this exercise have not been drawn accurately.
You should be able to do this exercise without using a calculator.
Having completed the exercise you may use a calculator to check your working.

1 Work out the size of the angles marked with letters.

(a)

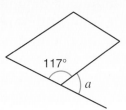

(b)

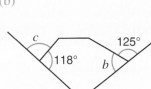

(c)

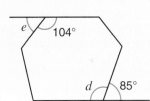

2 Work out the size of the angles marked with letters.

(a)

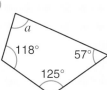

(b)

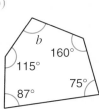

(c)

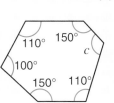

(d)

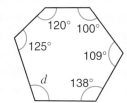

3 Work out the size of the angles marked with letters.

(a)

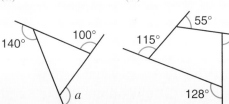

(b)

(c)

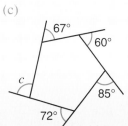

(d)

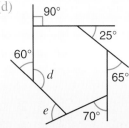

4 Work out the sum of the interior angles of these polygons.

(a) 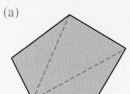   (b) 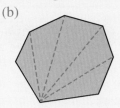   (c) 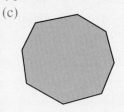   (d)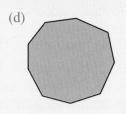

5 Work out the size of the angles marked with letters.

(a)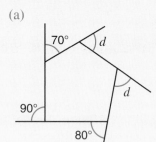

70° d
90°
80° d

(b)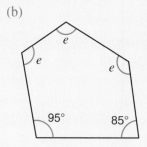

e
e e
95°   85°

(c)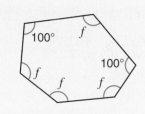

100° f
f 100°
f f

Regular polygons

A polygon with all sides equal and all angles equal is called a **regular polygon**.

A regular triangle is usually called an **equilateral triangle**.
A regular quadrilateral is usually called a **square**.

Regular hexagon   Regular octagon

Exterior angles of regular polygons

Measure the exterior angles of these regular polygons.
What do you find?

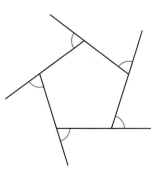

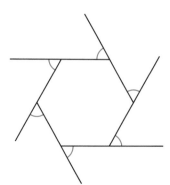

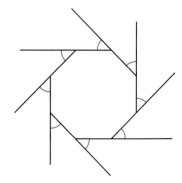

Regular pentagon   Regular hexagon   Regular octagon

You should find the exterior angles of a regular polygon are equal.

In general, for any regular n-sided polygon: exterior angle $= \frac{360°}{n}$

By rearranging the formula we can find the number of sides, n, of a regular polygon when we know the exterior angle.

$$n = \frac{360°}{\text{exterior angle}}$$

EXAMPLE

A regular polygon has an exterior angle of 30°.
(a) How many sides has the polygon?
(b) What is the size of an interior angle of
     the polygon?

Remember:
It is a good idea to write down the
formula you are using.

(a) $n = \dfrac{360°}{\text{exterior angle}}$

$n = \frac{360°}{30°}$

$n = 12$

(b) interior angle + exterior angle = 180°
   int. ∠ + 30° = 180°
   int. ∠ = 180° − 30°
   interior angle = 150°

Exercise 24.2

1 Calculate (a) the exterior angle and (b) the interior angle of these regular polygons.

(i)   (ii)   (iii)   (iv)

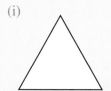  

2 A regular polygon has an exterior angle of 18°.
   How many sides has the polygon?

3 Calculate the number of sides of regular polygons with an exterior angle of:
   (a) 9°   (b) 24°   (c) 40°   (d) 60°

4 A regular polygon has an interior angle of 135°.
   How many sides has the polygon?

5 Calculate the number of sides of regular polygons with an interior angle of:
   (a) 108°   (b) 162°   (c) 171°   (d) 90°

6 (a) Calculate the size of an exterior angle of a regular pentagon.
   (b) What is the size of an interior angle of a regular pentagon?
   (c) What is the sum of the interior angles of a pentagon?

7 The following diagrams are drawn using regular polygons.
   Work out the values of the marked angles.

(a)   (b)   (c)   (d)

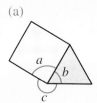 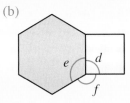 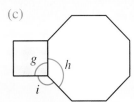 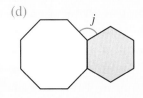

(e)   (f)   (g)   (h)

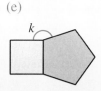 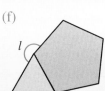 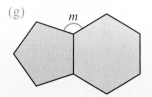 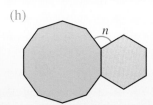

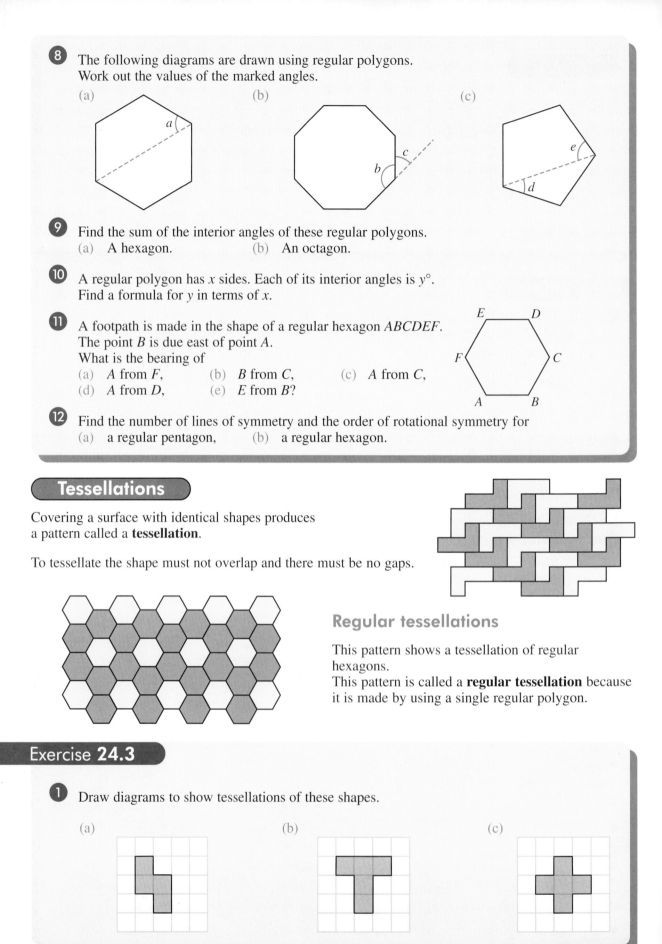

8 The following diagrams are drawn using regular polygons.
Work out the values of the marked angles.

(a)   (b)   (c)

9 Find the sum of the interior angles of these regular polygons.
(a) A hexagon.   (b) An octagon.

10 A regular polygon has x sides. Each of its interior angles is $y°$.
Find a formula for y in terms of x.

11 A footpath is made in the shape of a regular hexagon $ABCDEF$.
The point B is due east of point A.
What is the bearing of
(a) A from F,   (b) B from C,   (c) A from C,
(d) A from D,   (e) E from B?

12 Find the number of lines of symmetry and the order of rotational symmetry for
(a) a regular pentagon,   (b) a regular hexagon.

Tessellations

Covering a surface with identical shapes produces
a pattern called a **tessellation**.

To tessellate the shape must not overlap and there must be no gaps.

Regular tessellations

This pattern shows a tessellation of regular
hexagons.
This pattern is called a **regular tessellation** because
it is made by using a single regular polygon.

Exercise 24.3

1 Draw diagrams to show tessellations of these shapes.

(a)   (b)   (c)

2 Copy these regular tessellations.
Continue the tessellation by drawing four more shapes.

(a)

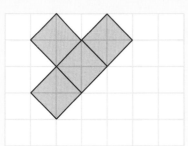

(b)

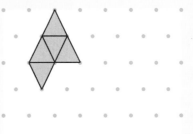

3

(a) The diagram shows part of a tessellation.
Copy the diagram.
Continue the tessellation by drawing
four more quadrilaterals.

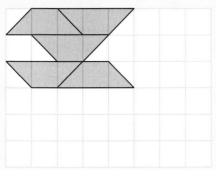

(b) Copy this quadrilateral onto card.
Use the quadrilateral to make a
tessellation.

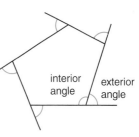

(c) All quadrilaterals tessellate.
Draw a quadrilateral of your own,
make copies, and show that it will
tessellate.

4 Explain why regular pentagons will not tessellate.

What you need to know

- A **polygon** is a many-sided shape made by straight lines.

- A polygon with all sides equal and all angles equal is called a **regular polygon**.

- Shapes you need to know: A 5-sided polygon is called a **pentagon**.
  A 6-sided polygon is called a **hexagon**.
  An 8-sided polygon is called an **octagon**.

- The sum of the exterior angles of any polygon is 360°.

- At each vertex of a polygon: interior angle + exterior angle = 180°

- The sum of the interior angles of an n-sided polygon is given by:
  $(n - 2) \times 180°$

- For a regular n-sided polygon: exterior angle $= \dfrac{360°}{n}$

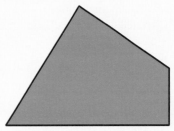

interior angle

exterior angle

- A shape will **tessellate** if it covers a surface without overlapping and leaves no gaps.

- All triangles tessellate.

- All quadrilaterals tessellate.

- Equilateral triangles, squares and hexagons can be used to make **regular tessellations**.

- A regular pentagon cannot be used to make a regular tessellation.

Inscribed regular polygons

Inscribed regular polygons can be constructed by equal divisions of a circle.
To draw an inscribed regular polygon follow these steps.

Step 1   Find the exterior angle of the polygon.

$$\text{Exterior angle} = \frac{360°}{\text{number of sides}}$$

Step 2   Draw a circle.
Divide the circle into equal sectors, where the sector angles
are equal to the exterior angle of the polygon.

Step 3   Join the divisions on the circumference of the circle to form
the polygon.

Example   Draw an inscribed regular hexagon.

| **Step 1** | **Step 2** | **Step 3** |

A hexagon has 6 sides.

$$\text{Exterior angle} = \frac{360°}{6}$$

$$= 60°$$

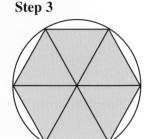

(a)   Draw an inscribed
equilateral triangle.

(b)   Draw an inscribed square.

(c)   Draw other inscribed regular polygons.

Which regular polygons are difficult to draw accurately? Explain why.

Review Exercise

1   The diagram shows a regular hexagon.
O is the point at the centre of the hexagon.
A and B are two vertices.

(a)   Write down the order of
rotational symmetry of
the regular hexagon.

(b)   Copy the diagram and draw
the lines from O to A and from O to B.
  (i)   Write down the size of angle AOB.
  (ii)   Write down the mathematical name
for triangle AOB.   *Edexcel*

2 $ABCDE$ is a regular pentagon.
O is the centre of the pentagon.

(a)   Work out the value of
  (i) x,   (ii) y.

(b)   Show how regular
hexagons tessellate.

(c)   Explain why
regular pentagons
will not tessellate.

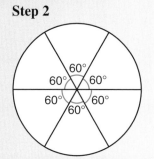

**Not drawn
accurately**

Edexcel

3   Part of a regular polygon
is shown.

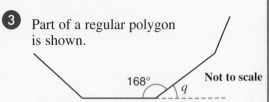

168°   **Not to scale**

q

(a)   What is the size of angle q?

(b)   How many sides has the polygon?

4   Copy each of the following diagrams
onto squared paper and draw six more
shapes to form a tessellation.

(a)

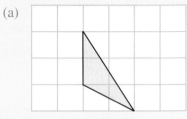

(b)

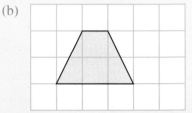

5 *ABCDE* is a regular pentagon.

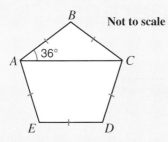

B   **Not to scale**

A 36°   C

E   D

Given that ∠*BAC* = 36°,
explain why *AC* is parallel to *ED*.

6 The diagram shows three regular
polygons.

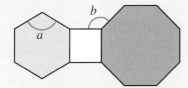

b

a

Work out the size of each lettered angle.

7 Work out the size of angle *x*.

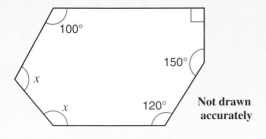

100°

150°

x

x   120°   **Not drawn
accurately**

8 The diagram shows a regular 9-sided
polygon.

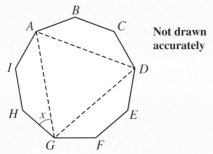

B
A   C   **Not drawn
accurately**
I   D

H   x
E
G   F

(a) What type of triangle is *ADG*?
Give a reason for your answer.
(b) What is the size of the angle
marked *x*?

9 A regular octagon, drawn below, has
eight sides.
One side of the octagon has been extended
to form angle *p*.

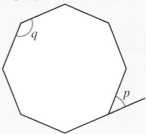

q

p

(a) Work out the size of angle *p*.
(b) Work out the size of angle *q*.

10 *ABCDEF* is a regular polygon.

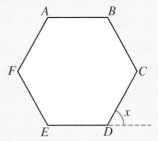

A   B

F   C

x
E   D

(a) What name is given to this polygon?
(b) What is the size of the exterior angle
marked *x*?
(c) What is the sum of the interior angles?

11 The diagram shows a regular decagon
which has been divided into three parts.

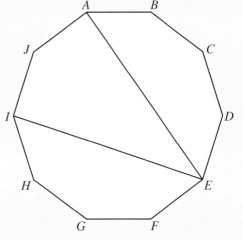

A   B

J   C

I   D

H   E

G   F

(a) What name is given to the
quadrilateral *AEIJ*?
(b) What name is given to the shape
ABCDE?
(c) Work out the size of angle *AED*?
(d) What is the size of angle *AEI*?

Circle Properties

Circles

A **circle** is the shape drawn by keeping a pencil the same distance from a fixed point on a piece of paper.
Compasses can be used to draw circles accurately.

It is important that you understand the meaning of the following words:

Circumference – special name used for the perimeter of a circle.

Radius – distance from the centre of the circle to any point on the circumference.

Diameter – distance right across the circle, passing through the centre point. Notice that the diameter is twice as long as the radius.

Chord – a line joining two points on the circumference.
The longest chord of a circle is the diameter.

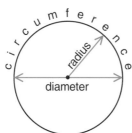

Tangent – a line which touches the circumference of a circle at one point only.

Arc – part of the circumference of a circle.

Segment – a chord divides a circle into two segments.

Sector – two radii divide a circle into two sectors.

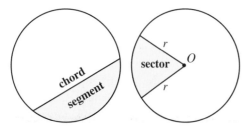

Activity

Measure the marked angles in these diagrams.
What do you notice?

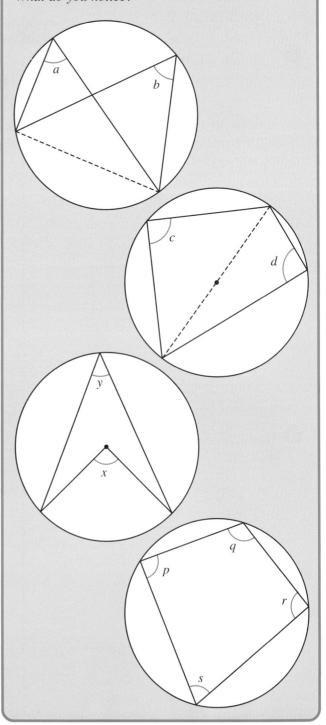

Circle properties

The angle in a semi-circle is a right angle

Angles which are:
    at the circumference,
    standing on a diameter,
are equal to 90°.

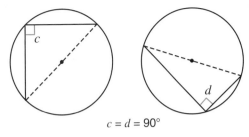

$c = d = 90°$

The angle at the centre is twice the angle at the circumference

If two angles are standing on the same chord, the angle at the centre of the circle is twice the angle at the circumference.

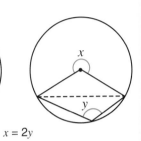
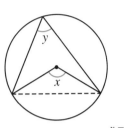

$x = 2y$

Angles in the same segment are equal

Angles which are:
    at the circumference,
    standing on the same chord,
    in the same segment,
are equal.

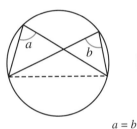
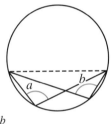

$a = b$

Opposite angles of a cyclic quadrilateral are supplementary

A quadrilateral whose vertices lie on the circumference of a circle is called a **cyclic quadrilateral**.

The opposite angles of a cyclic quadrilateral are supplementary (add up to 180°).

$p + r = 180°$
and
$q + s = 180°$

EXAMPLE

The diagram has not been drawn accurately.
O is the centre of the circle. Find the marked angles.

$a = 56°$ (angles in the same segment)

$b = 2 \times 56$ ($\angle$ at centre = twice $\angle$ at circum.)
$b = 112°$

$c = 180 - 56$ (opp. $\angle$s of a cyclic quad.)
$c = 124°$

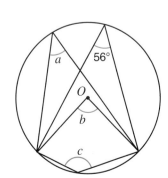

The diagrams in this exercise have not been drawn accurately.
Do not use a protractor or a calculator for this exercise.

1 The following diagrams show triangles drawn in semi-circles.
Work out the size of the marked angles.

(a)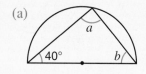

(b)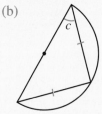

(c)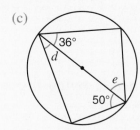

(d)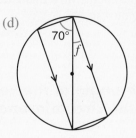

2 *O* is the centre of the circle.
Work out the size of the marked angles.

(a)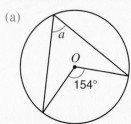

(b)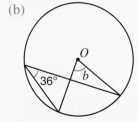

(c)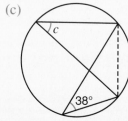

(d)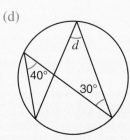

(e)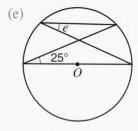

(f)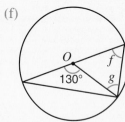

(g)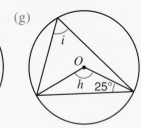

(h)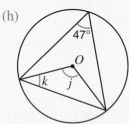

3 *O* is the centre of the circle.
Work out the size of the marked angles.

(a)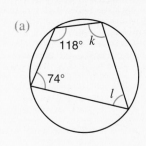

(b)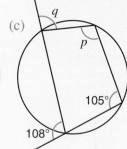

(c)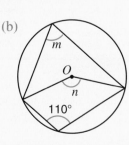

(d)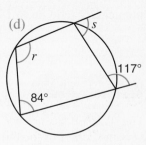

(e)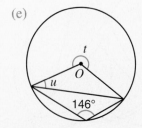

(f)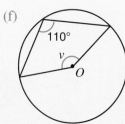

(g)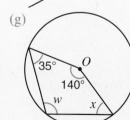

(h)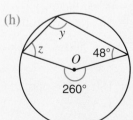

4 In the diagram BD is a diameter.
Angle ACD = 43°.
Calculate angle x.

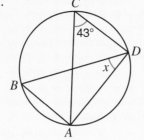

5 ABCD is a cyclic quadrilateral, with
BA produced (extended) to E.
Angle EAD = 70° and angle CDB = 34°.
Calculate angles BCD and CAD.

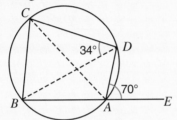

6 PQ is a diameter.
Angle RPQ = 29°.
Calculate
angle PSR.

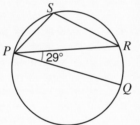

7 In the diagram, O is the centre of the circle.
Angle PSQ = 28° and angle QSR = 47°.
Calculate angle PQR
and angle QRS.

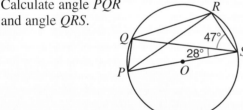

8 P, Q, R, S and T are points on a circle.
∠QRS = 105°, ∠PTS = 140°,
∠PQR = 135° and PT = TS.
Calculate ∠PSR and ∠TPQ.

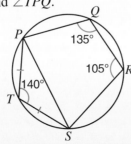

9 In the figure, O is the centre of the circle.
Angle ORP = 20°.
Calculate (a) angle POR, (b) angle PQR.

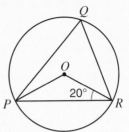

10 In the figure, O is the centre of the circle.
AC = CB.
Calculate the angles
(a) DOE, (b) ABD, (c) DBE.

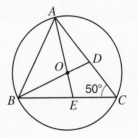

11 The centre of the circle is O.
Calculate the value of x.

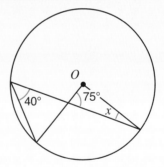

12 In the circle, centre O, QR is a diameter.
The line QS is a common chord of the
two circles and points T, S and R are
collinear. Find angle QPT.

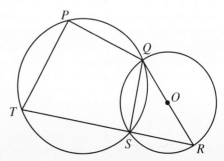

Tangents

The diagram shows a tangent drawn from a point P to touch the circle, centre O, at T.

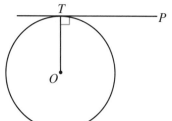

A tangent to a circle is a straight line which touches the circumference at one point only.

A tangent is perpendicular to the radius at the point of contact.

This diagram shows two tangents drawn from a point P to touch the circle, centre O, at points A and B.

Tangents drawn to a circle from the same point are equal, $PA = PB$.
OP bisects angle APB.

What is the name given to the shape OAPB?

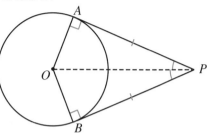

EXAMPLE

The diagram has not been drawn accurately.
O is the centre of the circle. Find the marked angles.

$a = 29°$ (SX and TX are tangents from X,
so $\angle TXO = \angle SXO$.)

$b = 90°$ (Tangent perpendicular to radius at T.)

$c = 180 - 90 - 29$
$c = 61°$

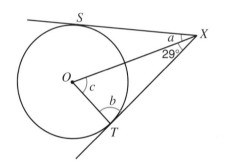

Exercise 25.2

The diagrams in this exercise have not been drawn accurately.
Do not use a protractor or a calculator for this exercise.

1 O is the centre of the circle. Work out the size of the marked angles.

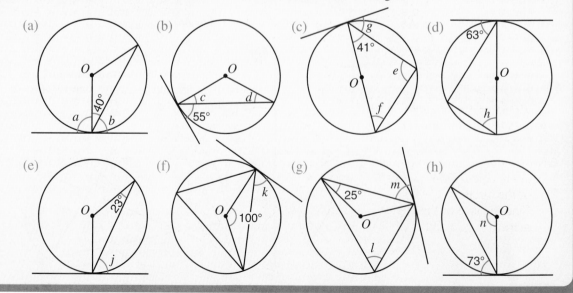

2 O is the centre of the circle. Work out the size of the marked angles.

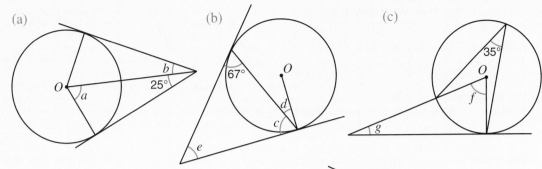

(a)

(b)

(c)

3 AB and AD are tangents to the circle centre O.
COD is a diameter and angle $CBO = 48°$.

Calculate   (a)   angle BOC,
                    (b)   angle BDO,
                    (c)   angle BAD.

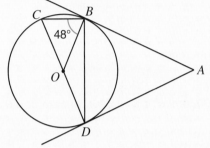

4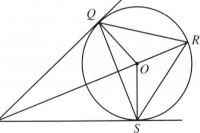

In the diagram, O is the centre of the circle.
TP is a tangent.
Angle $TPA = 42°$ and angle $ABP = 42°$.

Calculate   (a)   angle PAB,
                    (b)   angle PTA.

5 In the diagram, PQ and PS are tangents to the circle centre O.
POR is a straight line.
Angle $SRQ = 50°$.

Calculate   (a) $\angle SOQ$,
                    (b) $\angle SPO$,
                    (c) $\angle RSO$.

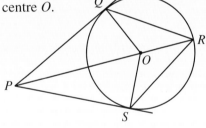

6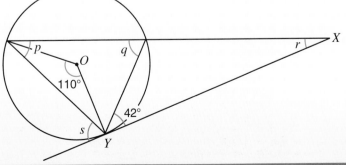

PQ and PS are tangents to the circle centre O.
POR is a straight line.
Angle $SPO = 18°$.

Calculate   (a) $\angle POS$,
                    (b) $\angle OSR$,
                    (c) $\angle SQR$.

7 The line XY is a tangent to the
circle and O is the centre
of the circle.
Find the size of the angles
marked p, q, r and s.

- A **circle** is the shape drawn by keeping a pencil the same distance from a fixed point on a piece of paper.

- The meaning of the following words:
  Circumference – special name used for the perimeter of a circle.
  Radius – distance from the centre of the circle to any point on the circumference. The plural of radius is **radii**.
  Diameter – distance right across the circle, passing through the centre point.
  The diameter is twice as long as the radius.
  Chord – a line joining two points on the circumference.
  The longest chord is the diameter.
  Tangent – a line which touches the circumference of a circle at one point only.
  Arc – part of the circumference of a circle.
  Segment – a chord divides a circle into two segments
  Sector – two radii divide a circle into two sectors.

- The vertices of a **cyclic quadrilateral** lie on the circumference of a circle.

- **Circle properties**

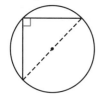

The angle in a semi-circle is a right angle.

Angles in the same segment are equal.

$x = 2y$
The angle at the centre is twice the angle at the circumference.

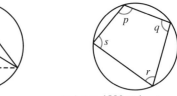

$p + r = 180°$ and $q + s = 180°$
Opposite angles of a cyclic quadrilateral are supplementary.

- A tangent is perpendicular to the radius at the point of contact.

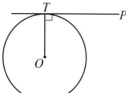

- Tangents drawn to a circle from the same point are equal in length.

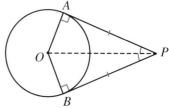

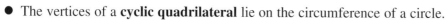

The diagrams in this exercise have not been drawn accurately.

1. O is the centre of the circle. Work out the size of the marked angles.

(a)

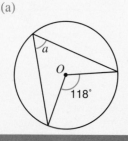

(b)

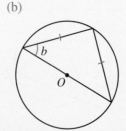

(c)

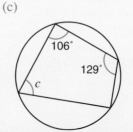

(d)

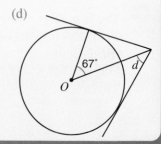

2 P, Q, R and S are four points on the circumference of a circle.
PR is a diameter of the circle and PQ is parallel to SR.
Angle QPR = 37°.
Calculate the size of the angles marked x, y and z.

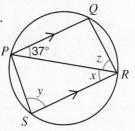

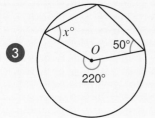

3 In the diagram, O is the centre of the circle.
Find x.

4 O is the centre of the circle.
Tangents are drawn from T to touch the circle at A and B.
Angle OBA = 35°.

Explain why angle ATB = 70°.

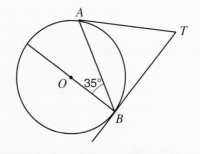

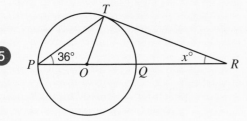

5 In the diagram, O is the centre of the circle and TR is the tangent to the circle at T. Calculate x.

6 RP is the diameter of the circle O.
Work out the size of angles PQS, QRP, QSP and QOP.

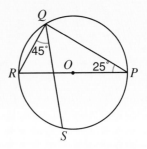

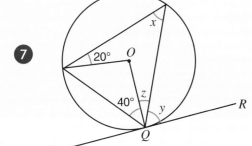

7 In the diagram, O is the centre of the circle and PQR is a tangent to the circle.
Find the values of the angles marked x, y and z.

8 O is the centre of the circle.
ABC is a tangent to the circle at B.
Work out the size of angles x, y and z.

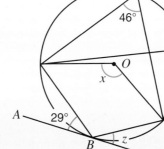

Circles and Other Shapes

Activity

Draw a circle with radius 2 cm.
Use thread or the edge of a strip of paper to measure the circumference of your circle.
Draw circles with radii 3 cm, 4 cm and so on.
Measure the circumference of each circle and write your results in a table.
What do you notice?

Radius (cm)	2	3	4	5	6	7	8
Diameter (cm)							
Circumference (cm)							

The Greek letter π

The circumference of any circle is just a bit bigger than three times the diameter of the circle.
The Greek letter π is used to represent this number.
We use an approximate value for π, such as 3, $3\frac{1}{7}$, 3.14, or the π key on a calculator, depending on the accuracy we require.

Circumference of a circle

The diagram shows a circle with radius r and diameter d.

The **circumference** of a circle can be found using the formulae:

$$C = \pi \times d$$

or $\quad C = 2 \times \pi \times r$

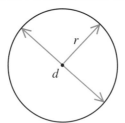

Remember: $\quad d = 2 \times r$

○○○○○○○○○○○○○○○○○○○
Chapter 25 looked at angle properties of circles.
In this chapter we look at various calculations involving lengths and areas associated with circles.

These formulae can be rearranged to find the radius, or diameter, when given the circumference.

For $\ C = 2\pi r$

$$r = \frac{C}{2\pi}$$

For $\ C = \pi d$

$$d = \frac{C}{\pi}$$

○○○○○○○○○○○○○○○○○○○○○○
Short but accurate
We sometimes use letters in place of words.
C is short for circumference.
r is short for radius.
d is short for diameter.

EXAMPLES

1 Find the circumference of a circle with diameter 80 cm.
Take π to be 3.14.
Give your answer to the nearest centimetre.

$C = \pi \times d$
$\quad = 3.14 \times 80 \text{ cm}$
$\quad = 251.2 \text{ cm}$
Circumference is 251 cm to the nearest centimetre.

2 A circle has circumference 37.2 cm. Find the radius of the circle, giving your answer to the nearest millimetre.
Take $\pi = 3.14$.

$C = 2 \times \pi \times r$
$37.2 = 2 \times 3.14 \times r$
$37.2 = 6.28 \times r$
$\quad r = \frac{37.2}{6.28}$
$\quad r = 5.923...$
$\quad r = 5.9 \text{ cm}$, to the nearest millimetre.

Do not use a calculator for questions 1 and 2.

1 Estimate the circumference of these circles.
Use the approximate rule: Circumference = 3 × diameter.

(a)

4 cm

(b)

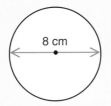

8 cm

(c)

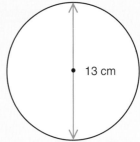

13 cm

2 Use the approximate rule to estimate the circumference of these circles.

Remember: diameter = 2 × radius.

(a)

2.5 cm

(b)

5 cm

(c)

6.4 cm

In questions 3 to 15, take π to be 3.14 or use the π key on your calculator.

3 Calculate the circumference of these circles.
Use the formula $C = \pi \times d$.

(a)

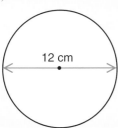

12 cm

(b)

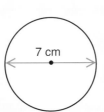

7 cm

(c)

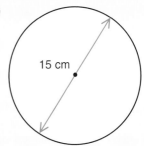

15 cm

4 Calculate the circumference of these circles.
Use the formula $C = 2 \times \pi \times r$.

(a)

4.5 cm

(b)

5.6 cm

(c)

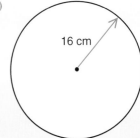

16 cm

5 A circle has a diameter of 9 cm.
Calculate the circumference of the circle.
Give your answer correct to the nearest
whole number.

6 A circular biscuit tin has a diameter of 24 cm.
What is the circumference of the tin?

7 A dinner plate has a radius of 13 cm.
Calculate the circumference of the plate.
Give your answer to an appropriate degree
of accuracy.

8 A circle has a radius of 6.5 cm.
Calculate the circumference of the circle.
Give your answer correct to one decimal
place.

9 Stan marks the centre
circle of a football pitch.
The circle has a radius
of 9.15 m.
What is the
circumference of
the circle?

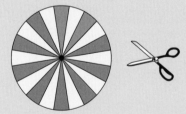

10 The radius of a tractor wheel is 0.8 m.
Calculate the circumference of the wheel.

11 Two cyclists go once round a circular track.
Eddy cycles on the inside of the track
which has a radius of 20 m.
Reg cycles on the outside of the track
which has a radius of 25 m.
How much further does Reg cycle?

12 A circular mug has a circumference of
24 cm. Find the radius of the mug, giving
your answer to the nearest millimetre.

13 The circumference of a copper pipe
is 94 mm.
Find, to the nearest millimetre, the
diameter of the pipe.

14 The circumference of a
bicycle wheel is 190 cm.
Find the diameter of
the wheel, giving your
answer to the nearest
centimetre.

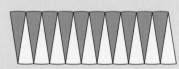

15 The circumference of the London Eye is
approximately 420 metres.
What is the radius?.
Give your answer correct to the nearest
metre.

Area of a circle

Activity

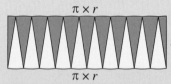

Cut out the 20 sectors.
Arrange them like this.

Draw a circle.
Divide it into 20 equal **sectors**.
Colour the sectors using two colours.

$\pi \times r$

Take the end sector and cut it in half.
Place one piece at each end of the pattern

The circumference of a circle is given by $2 \times \pi \times r$.
Half of the circumference is $\pi \times r$.
So the length of the rectangle is $\pi \times r$.
The width of the rectangle is the same as the radius of the
circle, r.

Using area of a rectangle = length $\times$ breadth

area of a circle = $\pi \times r \times r$

area of a circle = $\pi \times r^2$

Area of a circle

The area of a circle can be found using the formula:

$$A = \pi \times r^2$$

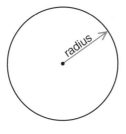

This formula can be rearranged to find the radius when given the area of the circle.

For $A = \pi r^2$

$$r^2 = \frac{A}{\pi}$$

$$r = \sqrt{\frac{A}{\pi}}$$

For more accurate calculations use the π key on your calculator.

EXAMPLES

1 Estimate the area of a circle with radius of 6 cm.
Take π to be 3.

$A = \pi \times r \times r$
$= 3 \times 6 \times 6$
$= 108 \text{ cm}^2$
Area is approximately 108 cm².

2 Calculate the area of a circle with diameter 9 cm.
Give your answer correct to the nearest whole number.

$A = \pi \times r \times r$
$= \pi \times 4.5 \times 4.5$
$= 63.617... \text{ cm}^2$
Area is 64 cm² to the nearest whole number.

Remember
$$r = \frac{d}{2}$$

3 The top of a tin of cat food has an area of 78.5 cm².
What is the radius of the tin?
Take $\pi = 3.14$.

$A = \pi \times r^2$
Substitute values for A and π.
$78.5 = 3.14 \times r^2$
Solve this equation to find r.
Divide both sides of the equation by 3.14.
$\frac{78.5}{3.14} = r^2$
$r^2 = 25$
Take the square root of both sides.
$r = 5$
The radius of the tin is 5 cm.

Exercise 26.2

Do not use a calculator for questions 1 and 2.

1 Estimate the areas of these circles.
Use the approximate rule:
Area = 3 × (radius)².

(a)
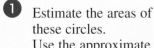
5 cm

(b)
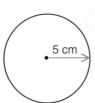
7 cm

(c)
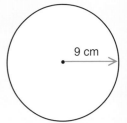
9 cm

2 Estimate the areas of these circles.
Take π to be 3.

Remember:
$$\text{Radius} = \frac{\text{diameter}}{2}$$

(a)

6 cm

(b)
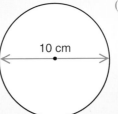
10 cm

(c)
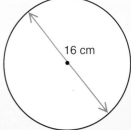
16 cm

In questions 3 to 12, take π to be 3.14 or use the π key on your calculator.

3 Calculate the areas of these circles. Give your answers to the nearest whole number.

(a)

4 cm

(b)

6.5 cm

(c)

12 cm

4 Calculate the areas of these circles. Give your answers correct to one decimal place.

(a)

6.4 cm

(b)

7.6 cm

(c)

26 cm

5 Find the areas of circles with:
(a)   radius 0.4 m,
(b)   diameter 365 mm.

6 The letter O is cut from card.

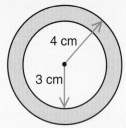

4 cm

3 cm

The inside radius of the letter is 3 cm.
The outside radius of the letter is 4 cm.
Calculate the area of the letter.

7 The diameter of a bicycle wheel is 66 cm.
A plastic spoke cover is made for the wheel.
What is the area of the spoke cover?

66 cm

8 A dinner plate has a diameter of 25 cm.
Find the area of the plate.
Give your answer correct to the nearest whole number.

9 A circular rug has a radius of 0.5 m.
Calculate the area of the rug.
Give your answer correct to two decimal places.

10 A circle has an area of 50 cm².
Calculate the radius of the circle.

11 A circular flower bed has an area of 40 m².
Calculate the diameter of the flower bed.
Give your answer to a suitable degree of accuracy.

12 The face of a circular coin has an area of 5.3 cm².
Calculate the radius of the coin.
Give your answer to the nearest millimetre.

Mixed questions involving circumferences and areas of circles

Some questions will involve finding the area and some the circumference of a circle.

Remember: Choose the correct formula for area or circumference.
   You need to think about whether to use the radius or the diameter.

EXAMPLES

1 Find the perimeter of this shape.
Take $\pi = 3.14$.

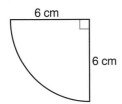

6 cm

6 cm

Find the circumference of a circle with radius 6 cm.

$$C = 2 \times \pi \times r$$
$$= 2 \times 3.14 \times 6 \text{ cm}$$
$$= 37.68 \text{ cm}$$

Perimeter $= \frac{1}{4} \times$ circumference + two radii
$$= \frac{1}{4} \times 37.68 + (2 \times 6) \text{ cm}$$
$$= 9.42 + 12$$
$$= 21.42 \text{ cm}$$

Perimeter $= 21.4$ cm, correct to 3 sig. figs.

2 A circle has an area of $81\pi \text{ cm}^2$.
Calculate the circumference of the circle, giving your answer in terms of π.

First, find the radius of the circle.
The area of a circle is given by:
$A = \pi r^2$
Substitute $A = 81\pi$.
$81\pi = \pi \times r^2$
Divide both sides by π.
$r^2 = 81$
$r = 9$
The radius of the circle is 9 cm.
The circumference of a circle is given by:
$C = 2\pi r$
Substitute $r = 9$.
$C = 2 \times \pi \times 9$.
$C = 18\pi$

The circumference of the circle is 18π cm.

Exercise 26.3

In this exercise take π to be 3.14 or use the π key on your calculator.

1 The top of a tin of cat food is a circle of diameter 8.4 cm.
(a) Calculate the circumference of the tin.
Give your answer correct to the nearest whole number.
(b) Calculate the area of the top of the tin.
Give your answer correct to one decimal place.

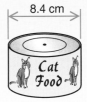

8.4 cm

Cat
Food

2 Find (a) the perimeters, and (b) the areas of these shapes.
Give your answers correct to one decimal place.

(i)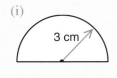

3 cm

(ii)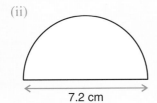

7.2 cm

(iii)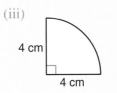

4 cm

4 cm

(iv)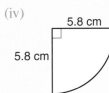

5.8 cm

5.8 cm

3 A circle is drawn inside a square, as shown.
The square has sides of length 10 cm.
Calculate the area of the shaded region.

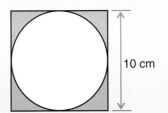

10 cm

4 Thirty students join hands to form a circle.
The diameter of the circle is 8.5 m.
(a) Find the circumference of the circle.
Give your answer to the nearest metre.
(b) What area is enclosed by the circle?
Give your answer to an appropriate degree of accuracy.

5 Which has the greater area:
a circle with radius 4 cm, or
a semi-circle with diameter 11 cm?
You must show all your working.

6 The radius of a circular plate is 15 cm.
(a) What is its area?
(b) What is its circumference?
Give your answers in terms of π.

7 A bicycle wheel has a diameter of 66 cm.
(a) What is the circumference of the wheel?
(b) Adrian cycles a distance of 1000 cm. How many complete rotations does the wheel make?

8 The front wheel on Nick's tricycle has a diameter of 18 cm.

(a) Calculate the circumference of the front wheel.
(b) How far does Nick have to cycle for the front wheel to make 20 complete turns?

9 A circular flower bed has diameter 12 m.
(a) How much edging is needed to go right round the bed?
(b) The gardener needs one bag of fertiliser for each 7 m². How many bags of fertiliser are needed for this bed?

10 The wheel of a wheelbarrow rotates 60 times when it is pushed a distance of 50 m.

Calculate the radius of the wheel.

11 Calculate the area of a semi-circle with a diameter of 6.8 cm.

12 Calculate the perimeter of a semi-circle with a radius of 7.5 cm.

13 A circle has a circumference of 64 cm. Calculate the area of the circle.

14 A circle has an area of 128 cm². Calculate the circumference of the circle.

15 A circle has a circumference of 14π cm. Calculate the area of the circle in terms of π.

16 A circle has an area of 144π cm². Calculate the circumference of the circle in terms of π.

17 The diagram shows a small circle drawn inside a larger circle.

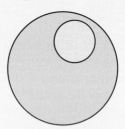

The shaded area is 55π cm².
The small circle has a radius of 3 cm.
Calculate the radius of the larger circle.

18 The diagram shows a small circle drawn inside a larger circle.

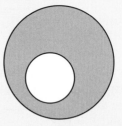

The small circle has an area of 16π cm².
The larger circle has a circumference of 18π cm.
Calculate the shaded area.
Give your answer in terms of π.

Areas of shapes

Here is a reminder of the formulae used to find the areas of other shapes.

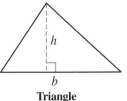
Triangle
$A = \frac{1}{2} \times b \times h$

Rectangle
$A = lb$

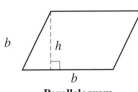
Parallelogram
$A = bh$

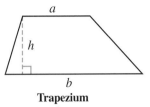
Trapezium
$A = \frac{1}{2}(a+b)h$

Compound shapes

Shapes formed by joining different shapes together are called **compound shapes**.
To find the area of a compound shape we must first divide the shape up into rectangles, triangles, circles, etc and find the area of each part.
Shapes can be divided in different ways, but they should all give the same answer.

EXAMPLES

1

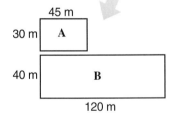

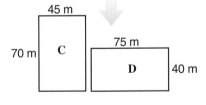

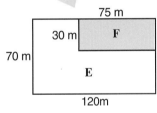

Area of shape is given by:
Area A + Area B
$= (45 \times 30) + (120 \times 40)$
$= 1350 + 4800$
$= 6150 \, \text{m}^2$

Area of shape is given by:
Area C + Area D
$= (45 \times 70) + (75 \times 40)$
$= 3150 + 3000$
$= 6150 \, \text{m}^2$

Area of shape is given by:
Area (E + F) − Area F
$= (120 \times 70) - (75 \times 30)$
$= 8400 - 2250$
$= 6150 \, \text{m}^2$

All the methods give the same answer so use the method you find easiest.

2 Find the area of this metal plate.

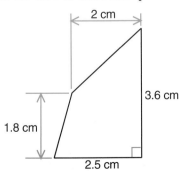

The plate can be split into a rectangle, A, and two triangles, B and C.

Area A $= 2 \times 1.8 = 3.6 \, \text{cm}^2$

Area B $= \dfrac{2 \times 1.8}{2} = 1.8 \, \text{cm}^2$

Area C $= \dfrac{0.5 \times 1.8}{2} = 0.45 \, \text{cm}^2$

Total area $= 3.6 + 1.8 + 0.45 = 5.85 \, \text{cm}^2$

Note: There are other methods. Try one!

1 Find the areas of these shapes which are made up of rectangles.

(a)

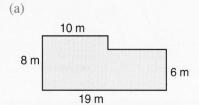

10 m

8 m

6 m

19 m

(b)

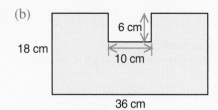

6 cm

18 cm

10 cm

36 cm

(c)

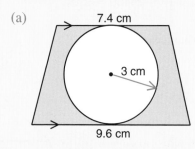

18 km

6 km

12 km

24 km

12 km

12 km

2 Find the areas of these shapes.

(a)

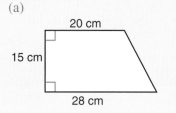

20 cm

15 cm

28 cm

(b)

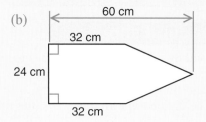

60 cm

32 cm

24 cm

32 cm

(c)

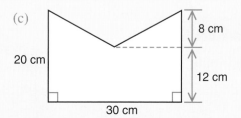

8 cm

20 cm

12 cm

30 cm

3 Find the areas of these shapes.

(a)

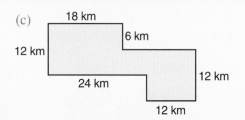

6 cm

12 cm

(b)

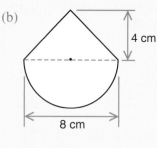

4 cm

8 cm

(c)

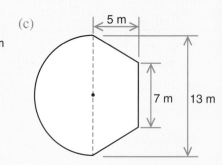

5 m

7 m   13 m

4 Calculate the shaded areas in each of these shapes.

(a)

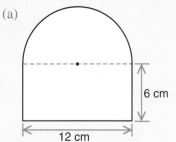

7.4 cm

3 cm

9.6 cm

(b)

12.8 cm

(c)

2.4 cm

8.4 cm

10 cm

5 A rectangle measures 8 cm by 32 cm.
Four circles are drawn inside the rectangle, as shown.
What area of the rectangle is not shaded?

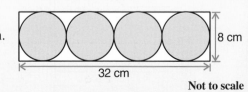

8 cm

32 cm

Not to scale

6 Find the area of the shaded square.

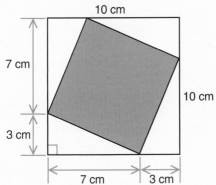
10 cm
7 cm
10 cm
3 cm
7 cm   3 cm

7 A window is made in the shape of a semicircle of radius 0.2 m on top of a rectangle of height 0.8 m.

(a) What is the area of glass in the window?

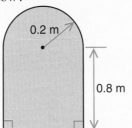
0.2 m
0.8 m

(b) A plastic strip is made to go right round the edge of the window. How long is the strip?

8 Find the area and perimeter of the shaded shape.

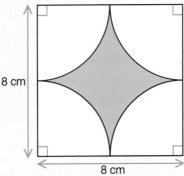
8 cm
8 cm

9 A right-angled triangle has sides 6 cm, 8 cm and 10 cm.
Semicircles are drawn on each side.

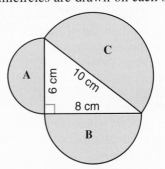
C
A
6 cm
10 cm
8 cm
B

Find the areas of A, B and C.
What do you notice about the areas of the three semicircles?

What you need to know

- A **circle** is the shape drawn by keeping a pencil the same distance from a fixed point on a piece of paper.

- Diameter $= 2 \times$ radius

- The **circumference** of a circle is given by:
  $C = \pi \times d$ or $C = 2 \times \pi \times r$

- The **area** of a circle is given by:
  $A = \pi \times r^2$

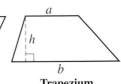
circumference
radius
diameter

- Shapes formed by joining different shapes together are called **compound shapes**.
  To find the area of a compound shape we must first divide the shape up into rectangles, triangles, circles, etc and find the area of each part.
  Here is a reminder of the formulae used to find the areas of other shapes.

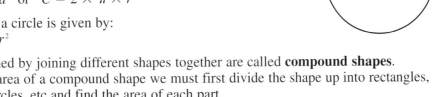

Triangle	Rectangle	Parallelogram	Trapezium
$A = \frac{1}{2} \times b \times h$	$A = lb$	$A = bh$	$A = \frac{1}{2}(a+b)h$

Take π to be 3.14 or use the π key on your calculator.

1 The diagram shows two pulleys.
The larger pulley has radius 5 cm.
The smaller pulley has diameter 8 cm.

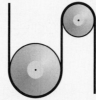

(a) What is the area of the larger pulley?
(b) What is the circumference of the smaller pulley?

2 A new wire mesh fence is to be put round a **circular** training ring.
The radius of the ring is 45 m.

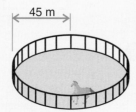

45 m

(a) Calculate, to the nearest metre, the length of fence needed.
(b) Calculate, to the nearest 10 square metres, the area of the ring.   Edexcel

3 Susie has a new bike.
The radius of its wheels is 30 cm.
(a) Work out the circumference of one of the wheels.

Susie rides her bike to school which is 1 km from her home.
(b) How many times will one of the wheels of Susie's bike turn on the way to school?   Edexcel

4 The diagram shows the plan of a kitchen floor.

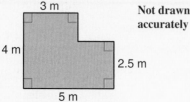

3 m

Not drawn accurately

4 m

2.5 m

5 m

Work out the area of the floor.

5

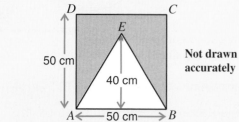

D   C

E

50 cm

40 cm

Not drawn accurately

A ← 50 cm → B

ABCD is a square of side 50 cm.
E is a point inside the square.
E is 40 cm from the line *AB*.
Work out the area of the shaded region.   Edexcel

6 The diagram shows a car park.
Calculate the area of the car park.

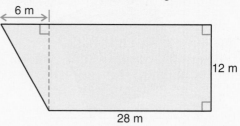

6 m

12 m

28 m

7

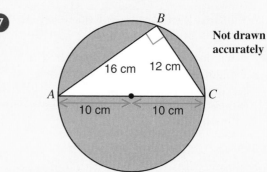

B

Not drawn accurately

16 cm   12 cm

A   C
10 cm   10 cm

The diagram shows a right-angled triangle *ABC* and a circle.
A, *B* and *C* are points on the circumference of the circle.
AC is a diameter of the circle.
The radius of the circle is 10 cm.
AB = 16 cm and *BC* = 12 cm.

Work out the area of the shaded part of the circle.
Give your answer correct to the nearest cm².   Edexcel

8 Four semicircles are drawn on the line *AB*, as shown.

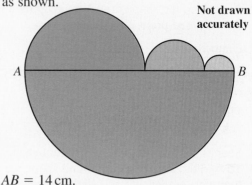

Not drawn accurately

A   B

AB = 14 cm.
(a) Work out the perimeter of the shape.
Give your answer in terms of π.
Explain how your worked out your answer.
(b) The radii of the semicircles are in the ratio 7 : 4 : 2 : 1.
Calculate the area of the shape.
Give your answer in terms of π.

Loci and Constructions

Following rules

Three students are given rules to follow.

> **John**
> Walk so that you are always 2 metres from the lamp post.

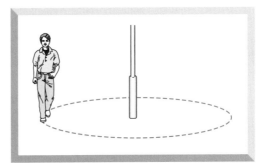

His path is a circle, radius 2 metres.

> **Hanif**
> Walk along a straight road.
> You must keep 30 cm from the edge of the road and stay on the pavement.

His path is a straight line.

> **Sarah**
> Start from the corner of the lawn.
> Walk across the lawn so that you are always the same distance from two sides.

Her path is a straight line.
The line cuts the angle in two.

Locus

The path of a point which moves according to a rule is called a **locus**.
If we talk about more than one locus we call them **loci**.

| EXAMPLES | Draw sketches to show the loci of John, Hanif and Sarah. |

John

Hanif

Sarah

① Adam goes down this slide.
Make a sketch of the slide as viewed from the
side and show the locus of Adam's head as he
goes down the slide.

② The diagram shows part of a rectangular lawn.
Starting from the wall, Sally walks across the
lawn so that she is always the same distance
from both hedges.
Draw a sketch to show the locus of Sally's path.

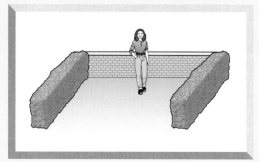

③ *PQRS* is a square of side 8 cm.
A point *X* is inside the square.

X is less than 8 cm from *P*.
X is nearer to *PQ* than to *SR*.

Make a sketch showing where *X* could be.

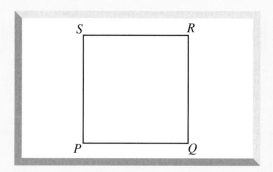

④ A ball is rolled down a step, as shown.
Copy the diagram, and sketch the locus of *P*,
the centre of the ball, as it rolls from *X* to *Y*.

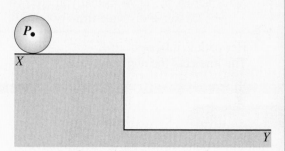

⑤ A wire is stretched between two posts.
A ring slides along the wire and a dog is attached to the ring by a rope.
Make a sketch to show where the dog can go.

⑥ A point *P* is 1 cm from this shape.
Copy the diagram, and draw an accurate
locus of **all** the positions of *P*.

Sometimes it is necessary to construct loci accurately.
You are expected to use only a ruler and compasses.
Here are the methods for two constructions.

To draw the perpendicular bisector of a line

This means to draw a line at right angles to a given line dividing it into two equal parts.

1 Draw line *AB*.

2 Open your compasses to just over half the distance *AB*. Mark two arcs which cross at *C* and *D*.

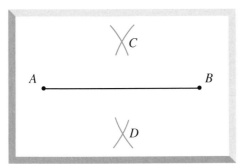

3 Draw a line which passes through the points *C* and *D*.

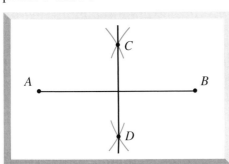

This line is the locus of a point which is the same distance from *A* and *B*.
Points on the line *CD* are **equidistant** (the same distance) from points *A* and *B*.
The line *CD* is at right angles to *AB*.
CD is sometimes called the **perpendicular bisector** of *AB*.

To draw the bisector of an angle

This means to draw a line which divides an angle into two equal parts.

1 Draw the angle *A*.
Use your compasses, centre *A*, to mark points *B* and *C* which are the same distance from *A*.

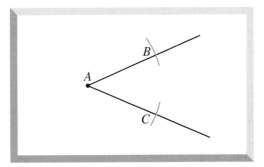

2 Use points *B* and *C* to draw equal arcs which cross at *D*.

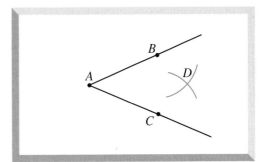

3 Draw a line which passes through the points *A* and *D*.

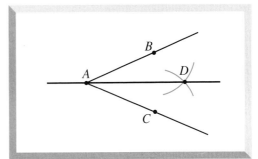

This line is the locus of a point which is the same distance from *AB* and *AC*.
Points on the line *AD* are **equidistant** from the lines through *AB* and *AC*.
The line *AD* cuts angle *BAC* in half.
AD is sometimes called the **bisector** of angle *BAC*.

1 Mark two points, *A* and *B*, 10 cm apart.
Construct the perpendicular bisector of
AB.

2 Use a protractor to draw an angle of 60°.
Construct the bisector of the angle.
Check that both angles are 30°.

3 Draw a triangle in the middle of a new
page.
Construct the perpendicular bisectors of
all three sides.
They should meet at a point, *Y*.

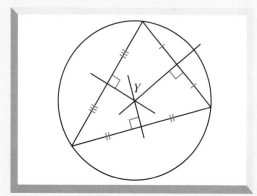

Put the point of your compasses on *Y* and
draw the circle which goes through all
three vertices of the triangle.
This construction is sometimes called the
circumscribed circle of a triangle.

4 Draw another triangle on a new page.
Bisect each angle of the triangle.
The bisectors should meet at a point, *X*.

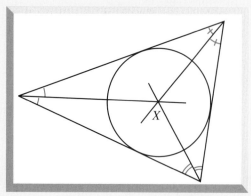

Put the point of your compasses on
point *X* and draw the circle which just
touches each side of the triangle.
This construction is sometimes called the
inscribed circle of a triangle.

5 Using a circle of
radius 4 cm,
copy the
diagram.
Draw the
perpendicular
bisectors of the
chords *WX* and *YZ*.
What do you notice about
the perpendicular bisectors?

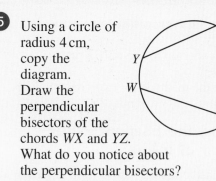

> The perpendicular bisector of a
> chord always passes through the
> centre of a circle.

6 Two trees are 6 metres apart. Alan walks
so that he is always the same distance
from each tree. Draw a scale diagram to
show his path.

7 *ABC* is an equilateral triangle with sides
4 cm.

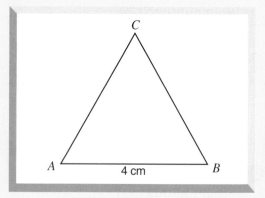

A point *X* is in the triangle.
It is nearer to *AB* than to *BC*.
It is less than 3 cm from *A*.
It is less than 2 cm from *BC*.

Shade the region in which *X* could lie.

8 Draw a rectangle *ABCD* with
AB = 6 cm and *AD* = 4 cm.

(a) Mark, with a thin line, the locus of
a point which is 1 cm from *AB*.

(b) Mark, with a dotted line, the locus
of a point which is the same
distance from *A* and *B*.

(c) Mark, with a dashed line, the locus
of a point which is 3 cm from *A*.

9 Draw a right-angled triangle with sides of 6 cm, 8 cm and 10 cm.

A point X is in the triangle.
It is 4 cm from B.
It is the same distance from A and B.

Mark accurately, the position of X.

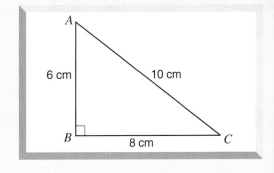

10 Copy the diagram and draw the locus of a point which is the same distance from PQ and RS.

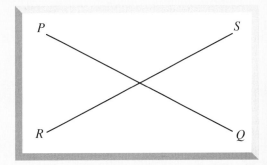

11 Triangle ABC is isosceles with AB = BC = 7 cm and AC = 6 cm.
(a) Construct triangle ABC.
(b) Point X is equidistant from A, B and C. Mark accurately the position of X.

12 (a) The diagram shows the sketch of a field. Make a scale drawing of the field using 1 cm to represent 100 m.
(b) A tree is 400 m from corner D and 350 m from corner C. Mark the position of the tree on your drawing.
(c) John walks across the field from corner D, keeping the same distance from AD and CD. Show his path on your diagram.
(d) Does John walk within 100 m of the tree in crossing the field?

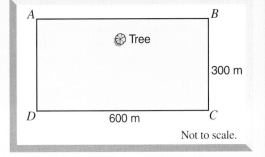

13 Part of a coast line is shown.

A boat is:
(i) equidistant from X and Z, and
(ii) equidistant from XY and YZ.

Copy the diagram and mark the position of the boat.

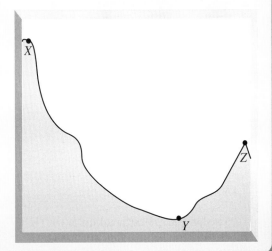

To draw the perpendicular from a point to a line

This means to draw a line at right angles to a given line, from a point that **is not on the line**.

1 Open your compasses so that from point *A* you can mark two arcs on the line *PQ*.

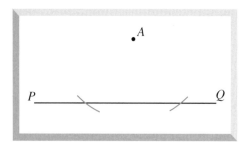

2 Use points *B* and *C* to draw equal arcs which cross at *D*.

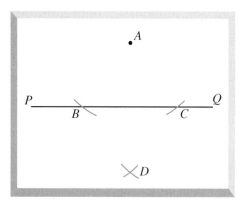

3 Draw a line from *A* to *D*.

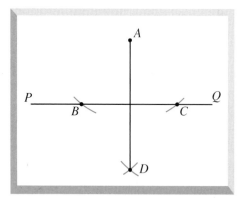

The line *AD* is perpendicular (at right angles) to the line *PQ*.

To draw the perpendicular from a point on a line

This means to draw a line at right angles to a given line, from a point that **is on the line**.

Keep your compasses at the same setting whilst doing this construction.

1 From *A*, draw an arc which cuts the line *PQ*.

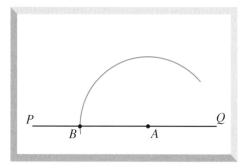

2 From *B*, draw an arc to cut the first arc at *C*. Then from *C*, draw an arc to cut the first arc at *D*.

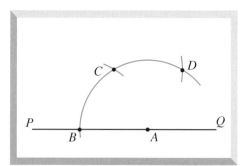

3 From *C* and *D*, draw arcs to meet at *E*. Draw the line *AE*.

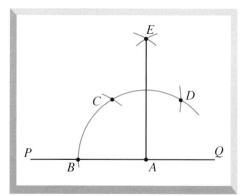

The line *AE* is perpendicular (at right angles) to the line *PQ*.

① Draw a line *PQ*, 8 cm long.
Mark a point *A*, about 5 cm above the line.
Draw the line which passes through *A* and is perpendicular to line *PQ*.

② Draw a line *PQ*, 8 cm long.
Mark a point *A*, somewhere on the line.
(a) Using your compasses, mark points
B and *C*, which are 3 cm from *A* on the
line *PQ*.
(b) Set your compasses to 5 cm.
Draw arcs from *B* and *C* which intersect
at *D*.
(c) Draw the line *AD*.

*This is another method of constructing a
perpendicular from a given point on a line.*

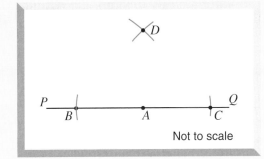

Not to scale

③ Using ruler and compasses only, make an
accurate drawing of the triangle shown in
this sketch.

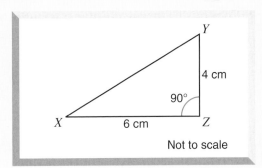

Not to scale

④ (a) Make an accurate drawing of this triangle.
(b) The **altitude** of the triangle is a line
perpendicular to a side which passes
through the opposite corner of the triangle.
Draw the altitude of the triangle *ABC*
which passes through point *B*.

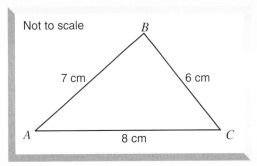

⑤ (a) Copy the diagram.
(b) Mark all points inside the rectangle that
are less than 2 cm from the line *AB*.

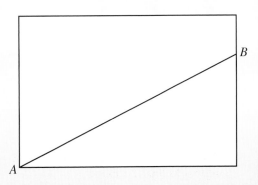

6 Draw a line *PQ*, 5 cm long.
Using compasses, draw an arc centre *P* to cut *PQ* at *X*.
With your compasses at the same setting draw another arc, centre *X*, to cut the first arc at *Y*.
Draw a line through *PY*.
Measure angle *XPY*. What do you find?

Show how you can use this construction to draw angles of 30° and 120°.

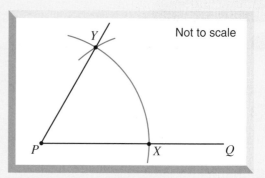

Not to scale

What you need to know

- The path of a point which moves according to a rule is called a **locus**.

- The word **loci** is used when we talk about more than one locus.

Using a ruler and compasses you should be able to:

- Construct the **perpendicular bisector of a line**.

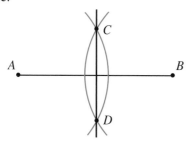

Points on the line *CD* are **equidistant** from the points *A* and *B*.

- Construct the **bisector of an angle**.

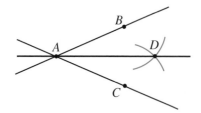

Points on the line *AD* are **equidistant** from the lines *AB* and *AC*.

- Construct the **perpendicular from a point to a line**.

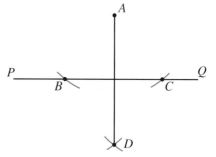

- Construct the **perpendicular from a point on a line**.

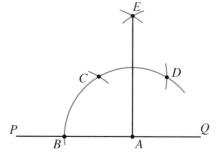

IDEAS FOR INVESTIGATION

A coin is rolled along a line.
Sketch the locus of a point which starts off at the bottom.

What is the locus of the point if the coin rolls around another coin, or if the coins are not round, or … ?
Investigate.

1 The diagram shows the position of points X and Y.   X ●

The point Z is   (a)   less than 3 cm from Y,
                    (b)   nearer to X than Y.
Copy the diagram and shade the region which
contains all the points which satisfy both of
these conditions.

● Y

2 A point T is 3 cm from the line AB.
Copy the line and draw the locus of all the positions of T.

A ———————————————————— B

3 A rectangle measures 4 cm by 3 cm.

A point P is outside the rectangle and 2 cm from the
edge of the rectangle.
Copy the rectangle and draw the locus of all the positions of P.

4 (a)   Use ruler and compasses only to construct a parallelogram ABCD, with AB = 5 cm,
            AD = 7 cm and angle BAD = 60°.
    (b)   The bisector of angle ADC meets BC at E.
            Construct the bisector of angle ADC and measure BE.

5 PQR is an equilateral triangle with sides of length 6 cm.
    (a)   Use ruler and compasses only to construct triangle PQR.
    (b)   O is the centre of the circle which passes through P, Q and R.
            Find, by construction, the radius of this circle.

6 Triangle ABC is shown. Copy the triangle.
    (a)   Draw accurately the locus of the points which are 3 cm from B.
    (b)   Draw accurately the locus of the points which are the same distance from BA as they
            are from BC.

T is a point inside triangle ABC.
T is 3 cm from B.
T is the same distance from BA as
it is from BC.
    (c)   On your diagram, mark the point T
            clearly with a cross.
            Label it with the letter T.

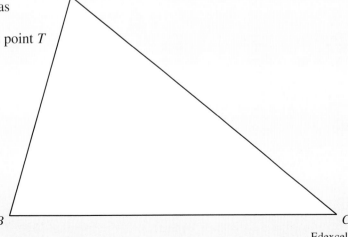

Edexcel

7 A treasure chest is buried on an island.
P and *Q* are two trees on this island.

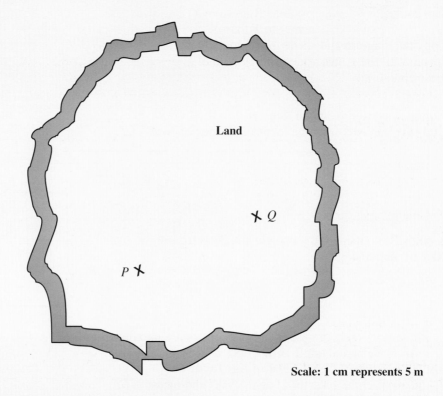

Scale: 1 cm represents 5 m

The treasure chest is buried the same distance from *P* as it is from *Q*.

(a) Copy the diagram and draw accurately the locus of points which are the same distance from *P* as they are from *Q*.

On the diagram, 1 centimetre represents 5 metres.
The treasure chest is buried 20 metres from *P*.

(b) Draw accurately the locus which represents all the points which are 20 metres from *P*.

(c) Find the point where the treasure chest is buried.
On your diagram, mark the point clearly with a *T*.

Edexcel

8 (a) Use ruler and compasses only to construct an equilateral triangle of side 4 cm.

(b) A point *P* is 1 cm from the edge of the triangle.
Draw an accurate locus of all the possible positions of *P*.

9 *PQRS* shows a sketch of a park.

(a) Use ruler and compasses only to construct a plan of the park using a scale of 1 cm to represent 100 m.

A fountain is:
(i) equidistant from *P* and *Q*,
(ii) equidistant from *PS* and *SR*.

(b) Draw the locus for (i) and (ii) on your plan, and hence find the position of the fountain. Label it with the letter *F*.

(c) Find the distance, in metres, of the fountain from *R*.

CHAPTER 28

Transformations

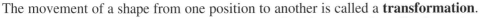

The movement of a shape from one position to another is called a **transformation**.
The change in position of the shape can be described in terms of a **reflection**, a **rotation** or a **translation**.
Later in the chapter you will meet another transformation, called an **enlargement**.

Reflection

Look at this diagram.
It shows a **reflection** of a shape in the line *AB*.
The line *AB* is sometimes called a **mirror line**.
Place a mirror on the line *AB* and look at
the reflection.
You should see that the image of the
shape is the same distance from the
mirror as the original.

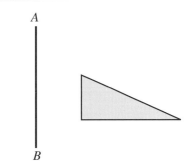

In this diagram the shape *WXYZ* has been
reflected in the line *AB* to $W_1X_1Y_1Z_1$.

If you join the points *W* and W_1:
  the distance from *W* to the mirror line is the same
  as the distance from the mirror line to W_1,
  the line WW_1 is at right angles to the mirror line.

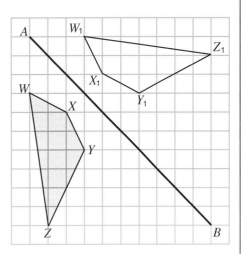

Notation
When the shape *WXYZ* is reflected onto $W_1X_1Y_1Z_1$, we
can say that shape $W_1X_1Y_1Z_1$ is the **image** of *WXYZ*.
We can also say that *WXYZ* is **mapped** onto $W_1X_1Y_1Z_1$.

EXAMPLE

Copy the shape *P* onto squared paper.
Draw the reflection of shape *P* in the *y* axis.

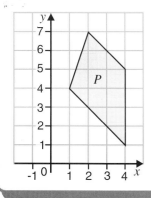

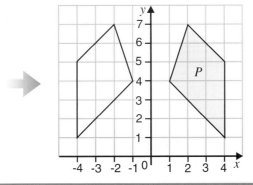

Notice that:
$(1, 4) \rightarrow (-1, 4)$
$(2, 7) \rightarrow (-2, 7)$
$(4, 5) \rightarrow (-4, 5)$
$(4, 1) \rightarrow (-4, 1)$
Can you see a pattern?

1 Copy each of the following shapes and draw the reflection of the shape in the line *AB*.

(a)

(b)

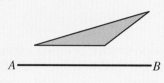

(c)

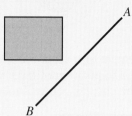

2 Copy each of the following shapes onto squared paper and draw the image of the shape after reflection in the line *AB*.

(a)

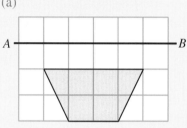

(b)

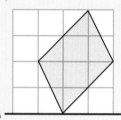

(c)

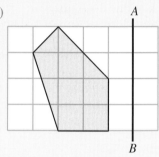

(d)

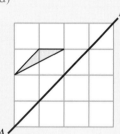

(e)

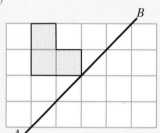

(f)

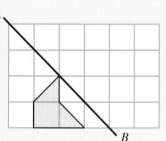

3 Copy each of the following diagrams onto squared paper and draw the reflection of each shape in the line given.

(a)

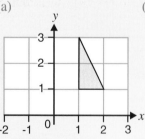

Reflect in the *y* axis.

(b)

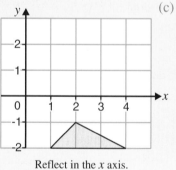

Reflect in the *x* axis.

(c)

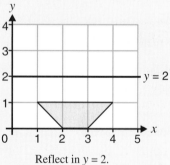

Reflect in *y* = 2.

(d)

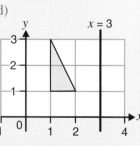

Reflect in *x* = 3.

(e)

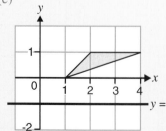

Reflect in *y* = −1.

(f)

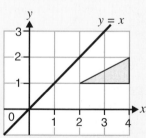

Reflect in *y* = *x*.

4 Copy the diagram onto squared paper.
Draw the image of the shape after:
  (a) a reflection in the x axis,
  (b) a reflection in the y axis,
  (c) a reflection in the line $x = 3$,
  (d) a reflection in the line $x = -1$,
  (e) a reflection in the line $y = x$.

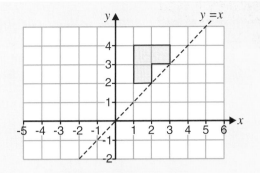

5 In the diagram, P is the point $(2, 1)$.
Find the coordinates of the image of P under a reflection in:
  (a) the x axis,
  (b) the y axis,
  (c) the line $x = 1$,
  (d) the line $y = -1$,
  (e) the line $y = x$.

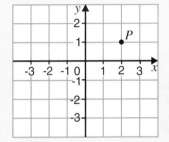

6 The diagram shows a quadrilateral $ABCD$.
Give the coordinates of B after:
  (a) a reflection in the x axis,
  (b) a reflection in the y axis,
  (c) a reflection in the line $x = 4$,
  (d) a reflection in the line $x = -1$,
  (e) a reflection in the line $y = x$.

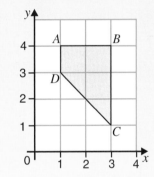

Rotation

Look at this diagram.
It shows the **rotation** of a shape P through
$90°$ anticlockwise about O (the origin).

P is mapped onto P_1.

All points on the shape P are turned through
the same angle about the same point.
This point is called the **centre of rotation**.

When a shape is rotated it stays the same
shape and size but its **orientation** on the page
changes.

For a rotation we need:
  a centre of rotation,
  an amount of turn,
  a direction of turn.

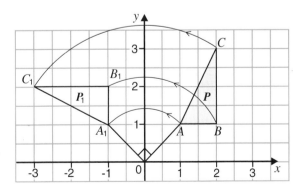

$$A \rightarrow A_1$$
$AO = A_1O$ and $\angle AOA_1 = 90°$.
What happens to points B and C?

Copy triangle *ABC* onto squared paper.
Draw the image of triangle *ABC* after it has been rotated through 90° clockwise about the point *P* (1, 1).
Label the image $A_1 B_1 C_1$.

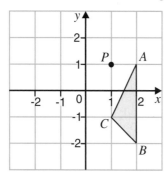

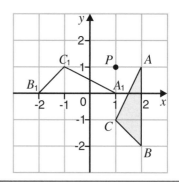

Exercise 28.2

1 Copy each of these shapes onto squared paper.
Draw the new position of each shape after the rotation given.

(a)

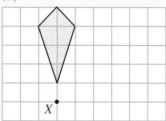

$\frac{1}{4}$ turn clockwise about centre *X*.

(b)

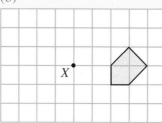

$\frac{1}{2}$ turn clockwise about centre *X*.

(c)

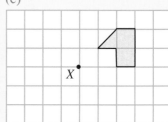

$\frac{1}{4}$ turn anticlockwise about centre *X*.

(d)

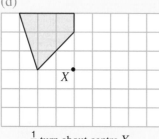

$\frac{1}{2}$ turn about centre *X*.

(e)

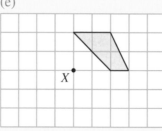

$\frac{3}{4}$ turn clockwise about centre *X*.

(f)

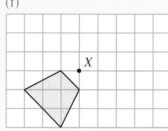

$\frac{3}{4}$ turn anticlockwise about centre *X*.

2 Copy each of the following shapes onto squared paper.
Draw the new position of the shape after it has been rotated through 90° clockwise about the origin (0, 0).

(a)

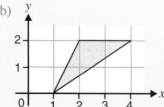

(b)

(c)

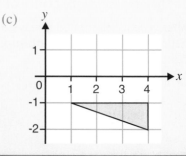

3 Copy each of the following shapes onto squared paper and then draw the new position of the shape after it has been rotated through 180°, about the point *X*.

(a)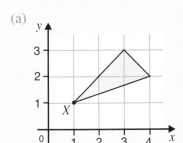

(b)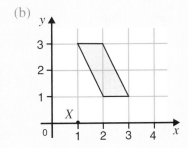

(c)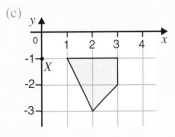

4 The diagram shows a quadrilateral *ABCD*.

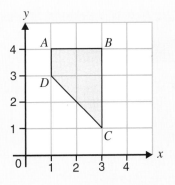

Give the coordinates of *B* after:
(a) a rotation through 90°, clockwise about (0, 0),
(b) a rotation through 90°, anticlockwise about (0, 0),
(c) a rotation through 180°, about (0, 0),
(d) a rotation through 90°, clockwise about (3, 1),
(e) a rotation through 90°, anticlockwise about (3, 1),
(f) a rotation through 180°, about (3, 1).

Translation

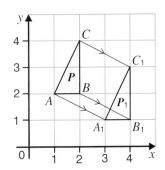

Look at this diagram.

It shows a **translation** of a shape *P* with vector $\begin{pmatrix} 2 \\ -1 \end{pmatrix}$.

P is mapped onto P_1.

All points on the shape *P* are moved the same distance in the same direction without turning.

A translation can be given:

● in terms of a **distance** and a **direction**,
  e.g. 2 units to the right and 1 unit down.

● with a vector, e.g. $\begin{pmatrix} 2 \\ -1 \end{pmatrix}$.

$A\,(1, 2) \rightarrow A_1(3, 1)$
$B\,(2, 2) \rightarrow B_1(4, 1)$
$C\,(2, 4) \rightarrow C_1(4, 3)$
Can you see a pattern?

When a **vector** is used to describe a translation:
the top number describes the **horizontal** part of the movement:
  $+$ = to the right, $-$ = to the left

the bottom number describes the **vertical** part of the movement:
  $+$ = upwards, $-$ = downwards

When a shape is translated it stays the same shape and size and has the same orientation.

EXAMPLE

Copy triangle P onto squared paper.

Draw the image of triangle P after it has been translated with vector $\begin{pmatrix} -3 \\ 2 \end{pmatrix}$.

Label the image P_1.

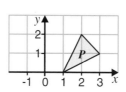

Exercise 28.3

1 Copy the shape onto squared paper.

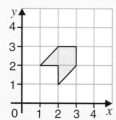

Draw the new position of the shape after each of the following translations:
(a) 2 units to the right and 3 units up,
(b) 1 unit to the right and 2 units down,
(c) 3 units to the left and 2 units up,
(d) 1 unit to the left and 3 units down.

2 Copy the shape onto squared paper.

Draw the new position of the shape after each of the following translations.

(a) $\begin{pmatrix} 3 \\ 2 \end{pmatrix}$ (b) $\begin{pmatrix} 2 \\ -3 \end{pmatrix}$ (c) $\begin{pmatrix} -2 \\ 3 \end{pmatrix}$ (d) $\begin{pmatrix} -2 \\ -3 \end{pmatrix}$

3 The diagram shows a quadrilateral $ABCD$.

Give the coordinates of B after the shape has been translated with vector:

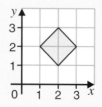

(a) $\begin{pmatrix} 2 \\ 1 \end{pmatrix}$ (b) $\begin{pmatrix} -2 \\ 2 \end{pmatrix}$ (c) $\begin{pmatrix} 1 \\ -3 \end{pmatrix}$ (d) $\begin{pmatrix} -2 \\ -3 \end{pmatrix}$

4 The translation $\begin{pmatrix} 2 \\ -1 \end{pmatrix}$ maps $S(5, 3)$ onto T.

What are the coordinates of T?

5 Write down the translation which maps:
(a) $X(1, 1)$ onto $P(3, 2)$,
(b) $X(1, 1)$ onto $Q(2, -1)$,
(c) $X(1, 1)$ onto $R(-2, 2)$,
(d) $X(1, 1)$ onto $S(-2, -1)$.

6 The diagram shows quadrilateral S.
Copy S onto squared paper.

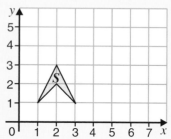

(a) The translation $\begin{pmatrix} 3 \\ 2 \end{pmatrix}$ maps S onto T.
    Draw and label T.
(b) Write down the translation which maps T onto S.

7 The translation $\begin{pmatrix} 2 \\ -1 \end{pmatrix}$ maps $P(3, 2)$ onto Q.

The translation $\begin{pmatrix} -3 \\ 2 \end{pmatrix}$ maps Q onto R.

(a) What are the coordinates of R?
(b) Write down the translation which maps R onto P.

Enlargement

This diagram shows another transformation, called an **enlargement**.
It shows an enlargement of a shape P with scale factor 2 and centre O.

P is mapped onto P_1.

When a shape is enlarged:
    angles remain unchanged,
    all **lengths** are multiplied by a **scale factor**.

Scale factor $= \dfrac{\text{new length}}{\text{original length}}$

For an enlargement we need:
    a centre of enlargement,
    a scale factor.

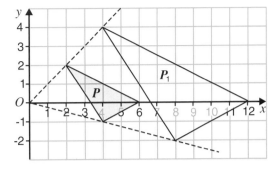

Using a centre of enlargement

A slide projector makes an enlargement of a picture.
The light bulb is the **centre of enlargement.**

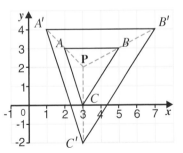

To enlarge a shape using a centre of enlargement:
Draw a line from the centre of enlargement, P, to one corner, A.
Extend this line to A' so that the length of $PA' =$ the scale factor $\times$ the length of PA.
Do the same for other corners of the shape.
Join up the corners to make the enlarged shape. Label the diagram.

EXAMPLES

1   Draw an enlargement of triangle ABC, centre $P(0, 1)$ and scale factor 3.

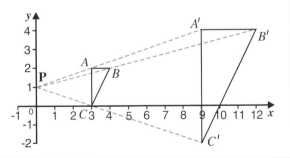

2   Use centre $P(3, 2)$ and a scale factor of 2 to enlarge triangle ABC.

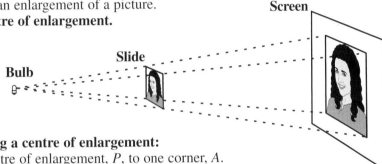

To find the centre and scale factor of an enlargement:
Join pairs of corresponding points.
Extend the lines until they meet. This point is the centre of enlargement.
Measure a pair of corresponding lengths.

Scale factor $= \dfrac{\text{new length}}{\text{original length}}$

Find the centre of enlargement and the scale factor when triangle XYZ is mapped onto triangle $X'Y'Z'$.

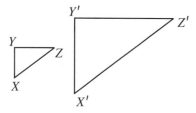

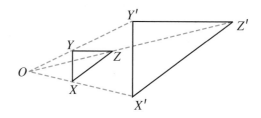

$$\text{Scale factor} = \frac{X'Y'}{XY} = \frac{2.0}{0.8} = 2.5$$

The centre of enlargement is the point O.

Exercise 28.4

1 Copy each diagram onto squared paper and enlarge it using the centre and scale factor given. You will need longer axes than those shown below.

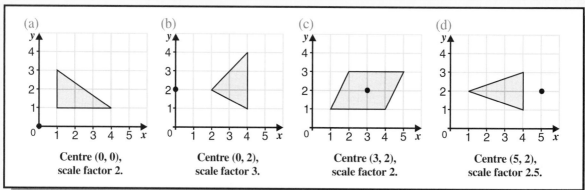

(a) Centre (0, 0), scale factor 2.

(b) Centre (0, 2), scale factor 3.

(c) Centre (3, 2), scale factor 2.

(d) Centre (5, 2), scale factor 2.5.

2 The diagram shows a quadrilateral $ABCD$.
Give the coordinates of B after an enlargement:
  (a) scale factor 2, centre (0, 0),
  (b) scale factor 3, centre (0, 0),
  (c) scale factor 2, centre (0, 2),
  (d) scale factor 3, centre C (3, 1),
  (e) scale factor 2, centre D (1, 3),
  (f) scale factor 2, centre A (1, 4).

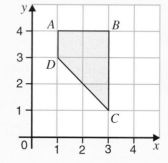

3 For each of the following diagrams find the scale factor and the coordinates of the centre of enlargement.

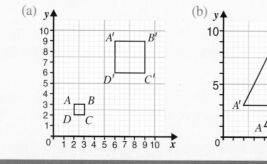

(a)

(b)

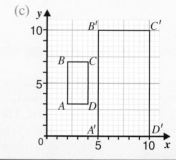

(c)

310

Using a scale factor which is a fraction

When the scale factor is a value between 0 and 1, such as 0.5 or $\frac{1}{3}$, the new shape is smaller than the original shape. Even though the shape gets smaller it is still called an enlargement.

EXAMPLE Draw an enlargement of this shape with centre (0, 1) and scale factor $\frac{1}{3}$.

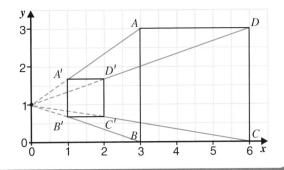

Exercise 28.5

1 Copy the following shapes onto squared paper and draw the enlargement given.

(a) Scale factor $\frac{1}{2}$, centre (1, 2).

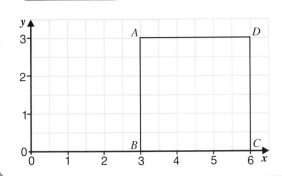

(b) Scale factor $\frac{1}{3}$, centre (0, 0).

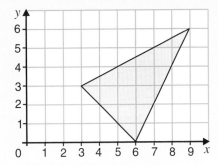

2 For each of the following diagrams give the centre of enlargement and the scale factor.

(a)
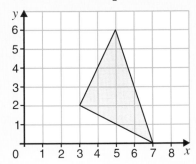

(b)
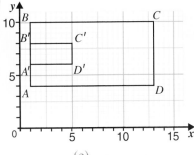

(c)
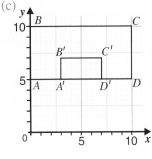

(d)
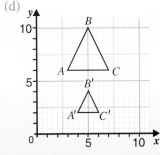

(e)
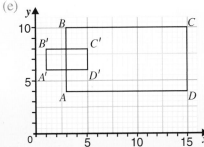

Describing transformations

Look at the shapes in this diagram.

We can describe the single transformation which maps A onto B as a **reflection** in the line $x = 3$.

We can describe the single transformation which maps A onto C as a **rotation** of $180°$ about $(2, 1)$.

We can describe the single transformation which maps A onto D as a **translation** with vector $\begin{pmatrix} 2 \\ -3 \end{pmatrix}$.

We can describe the single transformation which maps D onto E as an **enlargement**, scale factor 2, centre $(2, 0)$.

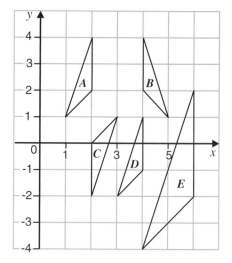

The flow chart below can be used to decide what type of transformation has taken place. The details required to fully describe each type of transformation are also given.

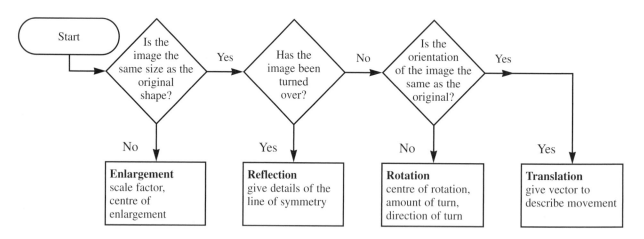

Try following the flow chart for the diagram above.

To find a line of reflection

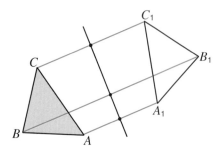

1 Join each point to its image point.
2 Put a mark halfway along each line.
3 Use a ruler to join the marks.

To find the centre and angle of rotation

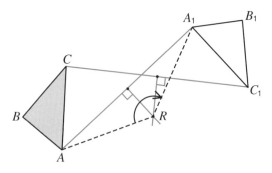

1 Join each point to its image point.
2 Put a mark halfway along each line.
3 Use a set-square to draw a line at right angles to each line. The point where the lines cross is the centre of rotation, R.
4 Join one point and its image to the centre of rotation.
5 The angle of rotation is given by the size of the angle ARA_1.

Exercise 28.6

1 Describe fully the single transformation which takes L_1 onto L_2, L_3, L_4, L_5 and L_6.

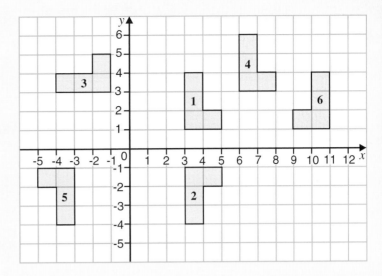

2 Describe fully the single transformation which maps
(a) T onto U,
(b) T onto V,
(c) T onto W.

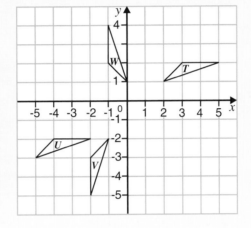

3 Describe fully the single transformation which maps
(a) A onto B,
(b) A onto C,
(c) A onto D.

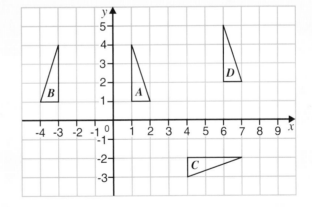

4 Describe the single transformation which maps $ABCD$ onto $PQRS$.

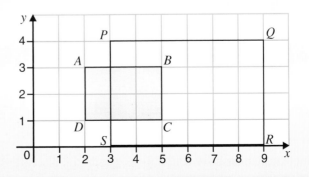

5 Describe fully the single transformation which maps *ABC* onto *XYZ*.

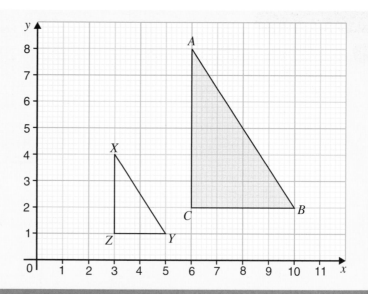

Combinations of transformations

Look at this diagram.

P has been mapped onto P_1 by a reflection in the *x* axis.

Then P_1 has been mapped onto P_2 by a reflection in the *y* axis.

Describe the single transformation which maps P onto P_2.

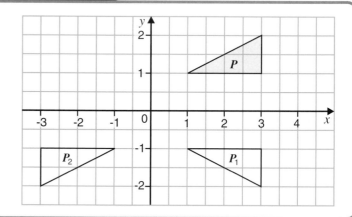

> **EXAMPLE**   Copy triangle *Q* onto squared paper.

(a) *Q* is mapped onto Q_1 by a rotation through 90°, clockwise about (0, 0). Draw and label Q_1.
(b) Q_1 is mapped onto Q_2 by a reflection in the line *y* = 0. Draw and label Q_2.
(c) Describe the single transformation which maps *Q* onto Q_2.

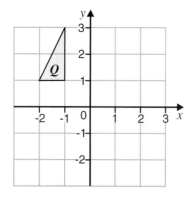

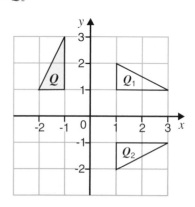

(c)   The single transformation which maps *Q* onto Q_2 is a reflection in the line *y* = *x*.

314

1 The diagram shows a quadrilateral
labelled *A*.
Copy the diagram onto squared paper.

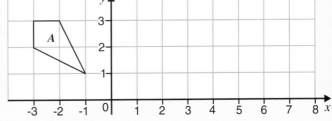

(a) *A* is mapped onto A_1 by a
reflection in the line $x = 0$.
Draw and label A_1.

(b) A_1 is mapped onto A_2 by a
reflection in the line $x = 4$.
Draw and label A_2.

(c) Describe fully the single transformation which maps *A* onto A_2.

2 The diagram shows a triangle labelled *P*.
Copy the diagram onto squared paper.

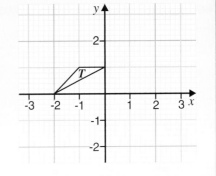

(a) *P* is mapped onto P_1 by a reflection in the
line $y = x$.
Draw and label P_1.

(b) P_1 is mapped onto P_2 by a reflection in the
line $x = 5$.
Draw and label P_2.

(c) Describe fully the single transformation
which maps *P* onto P_2.

3 The diagram shows a triangle labelled *T*.
Copy the diagram onto squared paper.

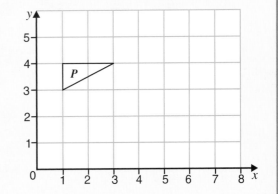

(a) Rotate *T* through 90° clockwise about (0, 0) to T_1.
Draw and label T_1.

(b) Reflect T_1 in the line $y = 0$ to T_2.
Draw and label T_2.

(c) Reflect T_2 in the line $x = 0$ to T_3.
Draw and label T_3.

(d) Describe fully the single transformation which
maps *T* onto T_3.

4 The diagram shows a quadrilateral labelled *Q*.
Copy the diagram onto squared paper.

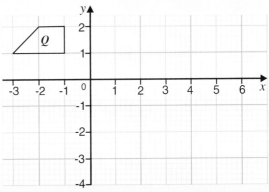

(a) *Q* is mapped onto Q_1 by a rotation
through 90°, anticlockwise about
(0, 0).
Draw and label Q_1.

(b) Q_1 is mapped onto Q_2 by a rotation
through 90°, anticlockwise about
(2, 0).
Draw and label Q_2.

(c) Describe fully the single
transformation which maps *Q* onto Q_2.

Transformations . . . Transformations . . . Transformations . . .

5 The diagram shows a shape labelled S.
Copy the diagram onto squared paper.

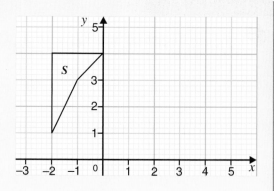

(a) The translation $\begin{pmatrix} 4 \\ 2 \end{pmatrix}$ maps S onto S_1.
Draw and label S_1.

(b) The translation $\begin{pmatrix} -8 \\ 1 \end{pmatrix}$ maps S_1 onto S_2.
Draw and label S_2.

(c) Describe fully the single transformation which maps S onto S_2.

6 The diagram shows a triangle labelled R.
Copy the diagram onto squared paper.

(a) R is mapped onto R_1 by a rotation through $90°$, anticlockwise about $(0, 0)$.
Draw and label R_1.

(b) R_1 is mapped onto R_2 by a reflection in the line $y = -x$.
Draw and label R_2.

(c) R_2 is mapped onto R_3 by a reflection in the line $x = 3$.
Draw and label R_3.

(d) Describe fully the single transformation which maps R onto R_3.

What you need to know

- The movement of a shape from one position to another is called a **transformation**.
- **Single transformations** can be described in terms of a reflection, a rotation, a translation or an enlargement.
- **Reflection**: The image of the shape is the same distance from the mirror line as the original.
- **Rotation**: All points are turned through the same angle about the same point, called a centre of rotation.
- **Translation**: All points are moved the same distance in the same direction without turning.
- **Enlargement**: All lengths are multiplied by a scale factor.

  $$\text{Scale factor} = \frac{\text{new length}}{\text{original length}} \qquad \text{New length} = \text{scale factor} \times \text{original length}$$

  The size of the original shape is:
  increased by using a scale factor greater than 1,
  reduced by using a scale factor which is a fraction, i.e. between 0 and 1.

- How to fully describe a transformation.

Transformation	Image same shape and size?	Details needed to describe the transformation
Reflection	Yes	Mirror line, sometimes given as an equation.
Rotation	Yes	Centre of rotation, amount of turn, direction of turn.
Translation	Yes	Vector: Top number = horizontal movement, bottom number = vertical movement.
Enlargement	No	Centre of enlargement, scale factor.

1 Copy the diagram.

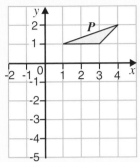

Shape P is reflected in the line $y = -1$.
Draw the new position of P on your diagram.

2 Copy the diagram.

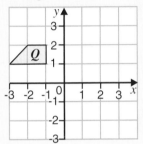

Shape Q is rotated 90° anticlockwise about
centre (0, 0).
Draw the new position of Q on your diagram.

3 Copy the diagram.

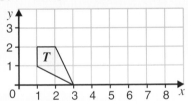

Shape T is translated 3 units to the right and
2 units up.
Draw the new position of T on your diagram.

4 Copy the shaded shape onto squared paper.

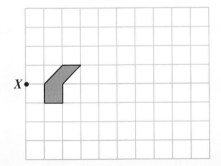

Draw an enlargement of the shaded shape,
scale factor 3, centre X.

5 The diagram shows the position of
shape **A**.

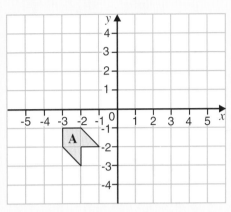

Copy the diagram.
(a) Reflect shape **A** in the y axis.
  Label the image **B**.
(b) Rotate shape **A** through 180°
  about (0, 0).
  Label the image **C**.
(c) (i) The translation, with vector
    $\begin{pmatrix} -2 \\ 4 \end{pmatrix}$ maps shape **A** onto **D**.
    Draw and label **D**.
  (ii) Describe the translation
    which maps shape **D** onto **A**.

6 The diagram shows triangles P, Q, R, S
and T.

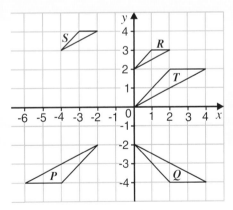

Describe fully the single
transformation which maps
(a) P onto Q,
(b) T onto Q,
(c) R onto S,
(d) S onto R,
(e) R onto T,
(f) T onto R.

Transformations · · · Transformations · · ·

7

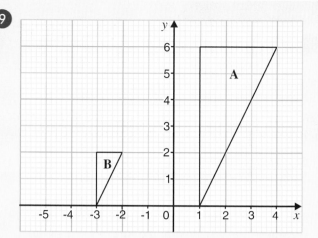

(a) Describe fully the single transformation that maps shape **P** onto shape **Q**.

(b) Rotate shape **P** 90° anticlockwise about the point *A* (1, 1).   Edexcel

8 Copy the diagram onto squared paper.

Draw the enlargement of the shape with scale factor $\frac{1}{2}$, centre *C*.

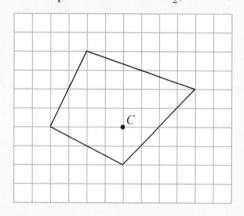

9

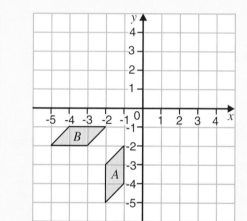

Describe fully the single transformation which maps triangle **A** to triangle **B**.   Edexcel

10

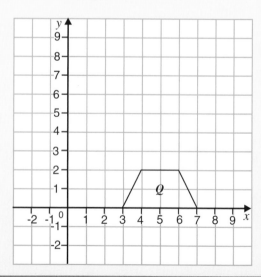

(a) Describe fully the single transformation which maps *A* onto *B*.

(b) Copy shape *A* onto squared paper.

   (i) Draw the enlargement of shape *A*, scale factor 3, centre (−3, −4). Label the image *C*.

   (ii) Describe fully the single transformation which maps *C* onto *A*.

11 The diagram shows a trapezium labelled *Q*. Copy the diagram onto squared paper.

(a) *Q* is mapped onto Q_1 by a reflection in the *x* axis.

   Draw and label Q_1.

(b) Q_1 is mapped onto Q_2 by a translation with vector $\begin{pmatrix} 2 \\ 4 \end{pmatrix}$.

   Draw and label Q_2.

(c) Q_2 is mapped onto Q_3 by a reflection in the line *y* = *x*.

   Draw and label Q_3.

(d) Describe fully the single transformation which maps *Q* onto Q_3.

CHAPTER 29

Volumes and Surface Areas

3-dimensional shapes (or solids)

These are all examples of 3-dimensional shapes.

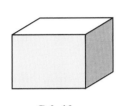

Cuboid   **Cylinder**   **Sphere**   **Pyramid with square base**   **Cone**

What other 3-dimensional shapes do you know?

Making and drawing 3-dimensional shapes

Nets

3-dimensional shapes can be made using **nets**.

This is the net of a cube.

The net can be folded to make a cube.

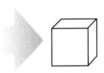

There are 12 different nets which can be used to make a cube. See how many of them you can draw.

2-dimensional drawings of 3-dimensional shapes

Isometric drawings are used to draw 3-dimensional shapes.
Here are two isometric drawings of a cube of side 2 cm.

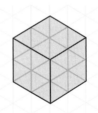
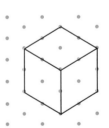

Naming parts of a solid shape

Each flat surface is called a **face**.
Two faces meet at an **edge**.
Edges of a shape meet at a corner, or point, called a **vertex**.
The plural of vertex is **vertices**.

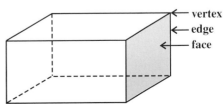

← vertex
← edge
← face

1 A cube has edges of length 3 cm.
Use squared paper to draw an accurate net of the cube.

2 The diagram shows part of a net of a cube.

(a) In how many different ways can
you complete the net?
Draw each of your nets.

(b) Explain why the diagram above
is **not** the net of a cube.

3 Use squared paper to draw an accurate net of this cuboid.

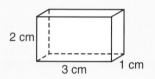

2 cm

3 cm   1 cm

4 Draw an accurate net for each of these 3-dimensional shapes.

(a)

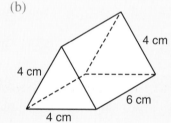

1 cm

1 cm

2 cm

5 cm

2 cm

(b)

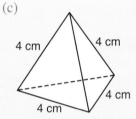

4 cm

4 cm

6 cm

4 cm

(c)

4 cm   4 cm

4 cm

4 cm

5 The diagram shows a pyramid.
A model of the pyramid is to be made using straws.
The straws are each 10 cm long and are joined using pipe cleaners.

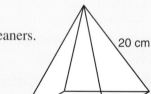

20 cm

10 cm

10 cm

(a) How many edges does the pyramid have?
(b) How many vertices does the pyramid have?
(c) How many straws are needed to make the pyramid?
(d) What is the total length of the edges of the pyramid?

6 Draw these 3-dimensional shapes on isometric paper.
(a) (i)   A cube of side 3 cm.
    (ii) A 3 cm by 2 cm by 1 cm cuboid.
    (iii) A 3 cm by 4 cm by 5 cm cuboid.
(b) Draw a net for each of the 3-dimensional shapes.

7 There are 8 different 3-dimensional shapes which can be made
using 4 linking cubes.
One of them is shown.

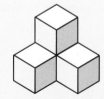

(a) Make all the 3-dimensional shapes using linking cubes.
(b) Draw the 3-dimensional shapes on isometric paper.

Plans and Elevations

When an architect designs a building he has to draw diagrams to show what the building will look like from different directions.
These diagrams are called **plans and elevations**.

The view of a building looking from above is called the **plan**.
The views of a building from the front or sides are called **elevations**.

To show all the information about a 3-dimensional shape we often need to draw several diagrams.

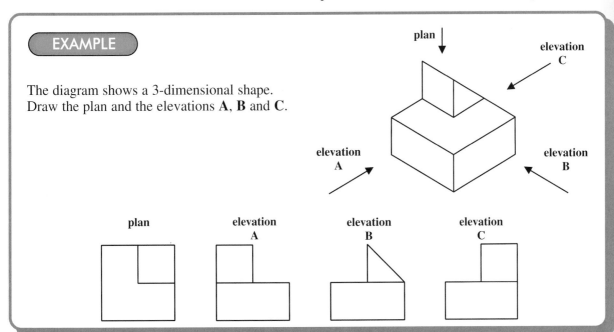

EXAMPLE

The diagram shows a 3-dimensional shape.
Draw the plan and the elevations **A**, **B** and **C**.

Exercise 29.2

1   Draw a sketch to show the plan view of each of these 3-dimensional shapes.

(a)   **a staircase**   (b)   **a pyramid**   (c)   **a cup**

2   Each of these 3-dimensional shapes has been made using 5 linking cubes of side 1 cm.
On squared paper, draw diagrams to show the plan and the elevations **A**, **B** and **C** of each shape.

(a)   (b)   (c)

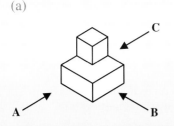 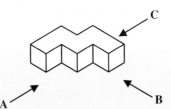 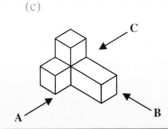

3   The diagram shows a plastic cylinder of height 3 cm and radius 2 cm with a hole of radius 1 cm drilled through the centre.
Draw the plan and a side elevation of the cylinder.

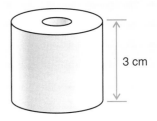

3 cm

4 The diagram shows an open box containing 3 balls of radius 2 cm.

    (a) Draw a plan of the box.
    (b) Draw an elevation of the box from the direction marked **A**.

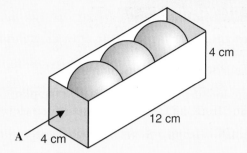

4 cm

12 cm

A   4 cm

5 The plans and elevations of 3-dimensional shapes made from linking cubes of side 1 cm are shown. Draw each of the 3-dimensional shapes on isometric paper.

(a)   **Plan**   **Left - side elevation**   **Front elevation**   **Right - side elevation**

(b)   **Plan**   **Left - side elevation**   **Front elevation**   **Right - side elevation**

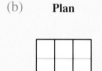

(c)   **Plan**   **Left - side elevation**   **Front elevation**   **Right - side elevation**

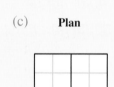 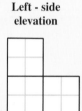 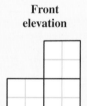 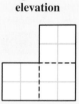

Volume

Volume is the amount of space occupied by a three-dimensional shape.

1 cm
1 cm
1 cm

Volume = 1 cm³

This **cube** is 1 cm long, 1 cm wide and 1 cm high.
It has a volume of **1 cubic centimetre**. The volume of this cube can be written as 1 cm³.

Small volumes can be measured using cubic millimetres (mm³).
Large volumes can be measured using cubic metres (m³).

Volume of a cuboid

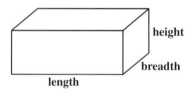

height
breadth
length

The formula for the volume of a cuboid is:
    Volume = length × breadth × height

This formula can be written using letters as:
    $V = lbh$

Volume of a cube
A cube is a special cuboid in which the length, breadth and height all have the same measurement.
Volume = length × length × length
    $V = l^3$

Surface area of a cuboid

Opposite faces of a cuboid are the same shape and size.

To find the surface area of a cuboid find the areas of the six rectangular faces and add the answers.

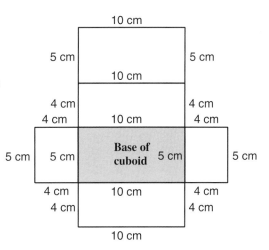

The surface area of a cuboid can also be found by finding the area of its net.

EXAMPLE

Find the volume and surface area of a cuboid measuring 30 cm by 15 cm by 12 cm.

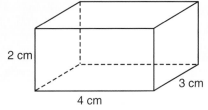

Volume = lbh
= 30 cm × 15 cm × 12 cm
= 5400 cm³

Surface area = $(2 \times 30 \times 15) + (2 \times 15 \times 12) + (2 \times 30 \times 12)$
= 900 + 360 + 720
= 1980 cm²

Exercise 29.3

Do not use a calculator for questions 1 to 5.

1 This is a cuboid.
(a) Draw a net of the cuboid on one-centimetre squared paper.
(b) Calculate the area of the net.
(c) What is the surface area of the cuboid?

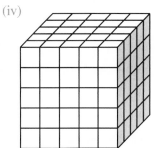

2 Large cubes are made from small cubes of edge 1 cm.
(a) How many small cubes are in each of the large cubes?
(b) What is the surface area of each large cube?

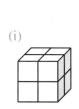
(i)

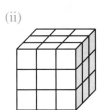
(ii)

(iii)

(iv)

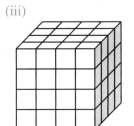

3 Calculate the volumes and surface areas of these cubes and cuboids.

(a)

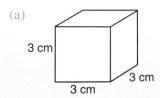

(b)

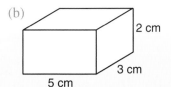

(c)

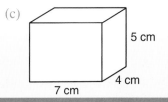

29

Volumes and Surface Areas

323

4 This **cuboid** is made using 24 one-centimetre cubes.

A cuboid made from 24 one-centimetre cubes has a volume of 24 cm³.
(a)   What other different cuboids can you make with 24 cubes?
There are 5 others. Which cuboid has the smallest surface area?
(b)   How many different cuboids can you make with 36 cubes?
What are the dimensions of the cuboid with the largest surface area?

5 Shapes are made using one-centimetre cubes. Find the volume and surface area of each shape.

(a)   (b)   (c)   (d)   (e)   (f)

    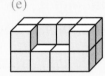

6 Calculate the volumes and surface areas of these cuboids.
Where necessary give your answer to an appropriate degree of accuracy.
(a)   3 cm by 5 cm by 10 cm.
(b)   2.4 cm by 3.6 cm by 6 cm.
(c)   18 cm by 24 cm by 45 cm.
(d)   3.2 cm by 4.8 cm by 6.3 cm.
(e)   5.8 cm by 10.6 cm by 14.9 cm.

9 A cuboid has a volume of 2250 cm³.
The length of the cuboid is 25 cm.
The height of the cuboid is 12 cm.
Calculate the surface area of the cuboid.

7 A cuboid has a volume of 76.8 cm³.
The length of the cuboid is 3.2 cm.
The breadth of the cuboid is 2.4 cm.
What is the height of the cuboid?

10 The surface area of
this cuboid is 197 cm².

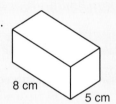

8 cm   5 cm

Calculate the volume of the cuboid.

8 A cuboid has a square base of side 3.6 cm.
The volume of the cuboid is 58.32 cm³.
Calculate the height of the cuboid.

Prisms

These shapes are all **prisms**.

 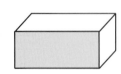 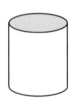 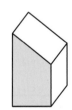 

What do these 3-dimensional shapes have in common?
Draw a different 3-dimensional shape which is a prism.

Explain why these shapes are not prisms.

 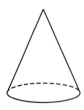 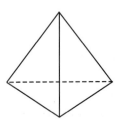

Volume of a prism

The formula for the volume of a prism is:
Volume = area of cross-section × length.

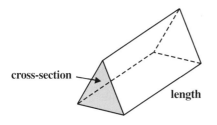

cross-section

length

Volume of a cylinder

A **cylinder** is a prism.
The **volume of a cylinder** can be written as:
Volume = area of cross-section × height
$$V = \pi r^2 h$$

Notice that length has been replaced by height.

EXAMPLES   Find the volumes of these prisms.

(a)

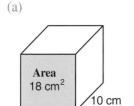

Area 18 cm²

10 cm

Volume = area of cross-
        section × length
      = 18 × 10
      = 180 cm³

(b)

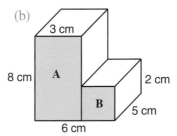

3 cm

8 cm   **A**

2 cm

B

6 cm   5 cm

Area A = 8 × 3 = 24 cm²
Area B = 3 × 2 = 6 cm²
Total area = 30 cm²
Volume = 30 × 5 = 150 cm³

(c)

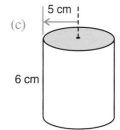

5 cm

6 cm

$V = \pi r^2 h$
  $= \pi \times 5^2 \times 6$
  $= 471.238...$
  $= 471$ cm³, correct to 3 s.f.

Exercise 29.4

You should be able to do questions 1 to 3 without using a calculator.
Having completed them you can use your calculator to check your answers.

1 Find the volumes of these prisms.

(a)

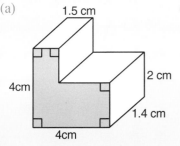

Area = 20 cm²

2 cm

(b)

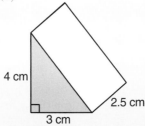

Area 28 cm²

5 cm

(c)

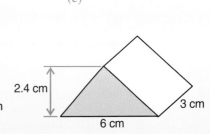

Area 9.6 cm²   10 cm

2 Calculate the shaded areas and the volumes of these prisms.

(a)

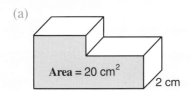

1.5 cm

2 cm

4cm

1.4 cm

4cm

(b)

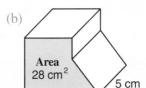

4 cm

3 cm   2.5 cm

(c)

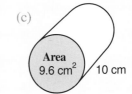

2.4 cm

6 cm   3 cm

3 Calculate the shaded areas and the volumes of these prisms.

(a)

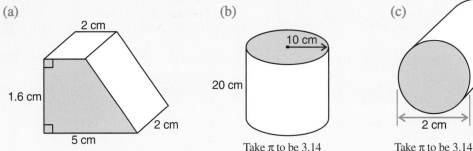

2 cm

1.6 cm

5 cm

2 cm

(b)

10 cm

20 cm

Take π to be 3.14

(c)

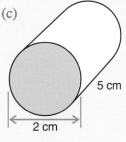

5 cm

2 cm

Take π to be 3.14

4 Find the volumes of these prisms.
Where necessary take π to be 3.14 or use the π key on your calculator.

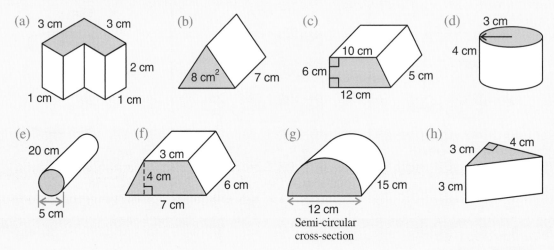

(a) 3 cm   3 cm

2 cm

1 cm   1 cm

(b)

8 cm²   7 cm

(c)

10 cm

6 cm   5 cm

12 cm

(d) 3 cm

4 cm

(e)

20 cm

5 cm

(f)

3 cm

4 cm   6 cm

7 cm

(g)

15 cm

12 cm
Semi-circular
cross-section

(h)

4 cm

3 cm

3 cm

5 Which tin holds more cat food?

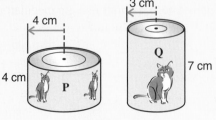

3 cm

4 cm

4 cm   P

Q   7 cm

6 The radius of a cylinder is 5 cm. It has a volume of 900 cm³.
Calculate the height of the cylinder, giving your answer correct to 1 decimal place.

7 A cylinder is 8 cm high. It has a volume of 183 cm³.
Calculate the radius of the cylinder correct to 1 decimal place.

8 A cylinder has a diameter of 10.6 cm. The volume of the cylinder is 1060 cm³.
Calculate the height of the cylinder.
Give your answer to an appropriate degree of accuracy.

9 A cylinder with a radius of 3 cm and a height of 8 cm is full of water.
The water is poured into another cylinder with a diameter of 8 cm.
Calculate the height of the water.

Surface area of a cylinder

The top and bottom of a cylinder are circles.
The curved surface of a cylinder is a rectangle.

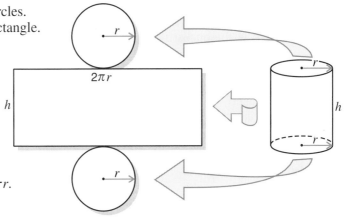

The rectangle has the same height, h,
as the cylinder.
The length of the rectangle must be
just long enough to "wrap around"
the circle.
The lid of the cylinder has radius r and
circumference $2\pi r$.
So the length of the rectangle is also $2\pi r$.

Area of lid $= \pi r^2$ Area of rectangle = length × breadth
Area of base $= \pi r^2$ $= 2\pi r \times h$
Area of lid and base $= 2\pi r^2$ $= 2\pi rh$

If a cylinder has radius, r, and height, h, then
the formula for the surface area is:

$$\text{Surface area} = 2\pi r^2 + 2\pi rh$$

Area of the top   Area of the
and bottom   rectangle

The formula for the
surface area is sometimes
given as:
Surface area $= 2\pi r(r + h)$

EXAMPLE

Find the surface area of a cylinder with radius 4 cm
and height 6 cm. Take π to be 3.14.

$$\begin{aligned}
\text{Area} &= 2\pi rh + 2\pi r^2 \\
&= 2 \times \pi \times 4 \times 6 + 2 \times \pi \times 4^2 \\
&= 150.796 \ldots + 100.530 \ldots \\
&= 251.327 \ldots \\
&= 251.3 \text{ cm}^2, \text{ correct to 1 d.p.}
\end{aligned}$$

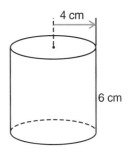

4 cm

6 cm

Exercise 29.5

Take π to be 3.14 or use the π key on your calculator.

1 Find the surface areas of these cylinders.

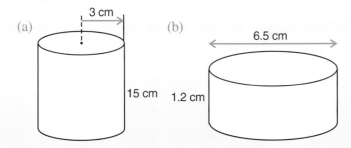

(a) 3 cm

15 cm   1.2 cm

(b) 6.5 cm

2 Show that the curved
surface area of this can
is approximately 75 cm².

3 cm

4 cm   BEANZ

Volumes and Surface Areas

3 A bucket is in the shape of a cylinder.

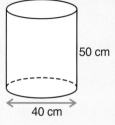

50 cm

40 cm

(a) Calculate the area of the bottom of the bucket.
(b) Calculate the curved surface area of the bucket.
(c) What is the volume of the bucket?

4 A cylinder is 15 cm high.
The curved surface area of the cylinder is 377 cm².
Calculate the volume of the cylinder.

5 A cylinder has a radius of 3.6 cm.
The volume of the cylinder is 346 cm³.
Calculate the total surface area of the cylinder.
Give your answer to an appropriate degree of accuracy.

6 A concrete pipe is 150 cm long.
It has an internal radius of 15 cm and an external radius of 20 cm.
Calculate, giving your answers to 3 significant figures,
(a) the area of the curved surface inside of the pipe,
(b) the curved surface area of the outside of the pipe.

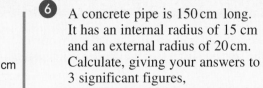

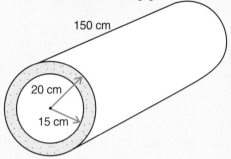

150 cm

20 cm

15 cm

What you need to know

- **Faces**, **vertices** (corners) and **edges**.
  For example, a cube has 6 faces, 8 vertices and 12 edges.

  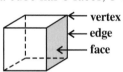

  vertex
  edge
  face

- A **net** can be used to make a solid shape.

- **Isometric paper** is used to make 2-dimensional drawings of 3-dimensional shapes.

  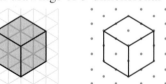

- Volume is the amount of space occupied by a 3-dimensional shape.

- Plans and Elevations.
  The view of a 3-dimensional shape looking from above is called a **plan**.
  The view of a 3-dimensional shape from the front or sides is called an **elevation**.

- The formula for the volume of a **cuboid** is:
  Volume = length × breadth × height
  $$V = l \times b \times h$$

  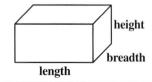

  height
  breadth
  length

- To find the **surface area** of a cuboid find the area of the six rectangular faces and add the answers together.

- Volume of a **cube** is:
  Volume = (length)³
  $$V = l^3$$

- If you make a cut at right angles to the length of a **prism** you will always get the same cross-section.

  cross-section
  length

- Volume of a prism
  = area of cross-section × length

- A **cylinder** is a prism.
  Volume of a cylinder is: $V = \pi \times r^2 \times h$

  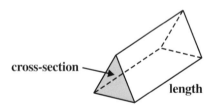

  r

  h

  Surface area of a cylinder is:
  Surface area = $2\pi r^2 + 2\pi rh$

328

3-dimensional coordinates

One coordinate identifies a point on a line.
Two coordinates identify a point on a plane.
Three coordinates identify a point in space.

The diagram shows a cuboid drawn in 3-dimensions.

Using the axes x, y and z shown:

Point A is given as (0, 2, 0).

Point B is given as (2, 2, 0).

Point C is given as (2, 2, 3).

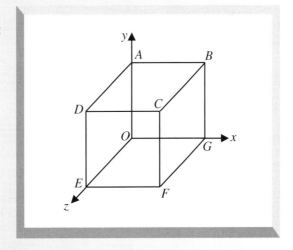

Give the 3-dimensional coordinates of points, D, E, F, and G.

3-dimensional noughts and crosses

The diagram shows a 3-dimensional game which can be used by two people to play "noughts" and "crosses".

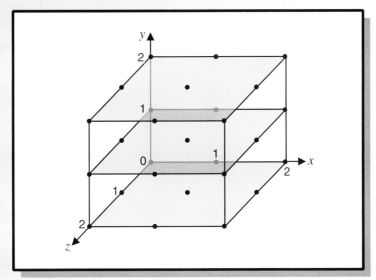

To play the game each player takes it in turn to give the 3-dimensional coordinates of a point. The first player to get three points in a line wins.

Winning lines can be horizontal, vertical or diagonal.
eg. (1, 0, 1), (1, 1, 1) and (1, 2, 1) would be a winning line.

Use a copy of the diagram to play "3-dimensional noughts and crosses".

Do not use a calculator for questions 1 to 7.

1 Two views of a model are shown.

The model is made
using one centimetre cubes.
(a)   What is the volume of the model?
(b)   What is the surface area of the model?

2 The diagram shows
a cuboid.

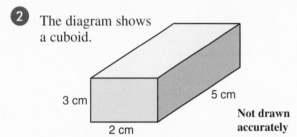

3 cm   5 cm

**Not drawn
accurately**

2 cm

(a)   Work out the volume of the cuboid.
(b)   On isometric paper, make an accurate
      full-size drawing of the cuboid.   Edexcel

3 (a)   Which of these diagrams is the net of a
           cube?

A   B

C   D

(b)   How many cubes of edge 2 cm can be
      packed into a cuboid with dimensions
      7 cm by 12 cm by 6 cm?

4 The diagram shows a pyramid with a square
base of side 3 cm.
The length of each sloping edge is 4 cm.
Draw an accurate net of the pyramid.

**Not drawn
accurately**

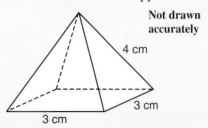

4 cm

3 cm

3 cm

5 This 3-dimensional shape has been
made using linking cubes of side 1 cm.

On squared paper, draw diagrams to
show the plan and the elevation
from **X**.

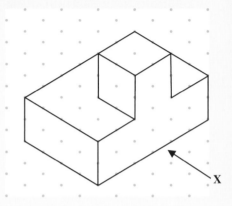

X

6 A block of wood measures 15 cm by
8 cm by 3 cm.
A letter F is cut out of the block of
wood, as shown.

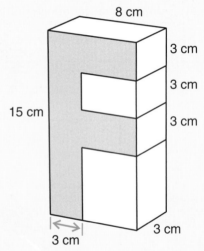

8 cm

3 cm

3 cm

15 cm

3 cm

3 cm

3 cm

(a)   Calculate the shaded area.
(b)   Calculate the volume of the
      letter F.

7 Matt has two pieces of wood.

A cuboid which measures 6 cm by
5 cm by 4 cm.
A cube of edge 5 cm.

(a)   Which piece of wood has the
      larger volume?
(b)   Which piece of wood has the
      larger surface area?
Show working for each of your
answers.

8 A sketch of a prism is shown.
The cross-section of the prism is a trapezium.

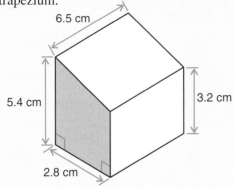

Calculate the volume of the prism.
Give your answer to a suitable degree of accuracy.

9 The surface area of a cube is 1350 cm².
What is the volume of the cube?

10 The diagram shows two packets of salt.
Alika says, "Packet B holds more salt."
Is she right?
Explain your answer.

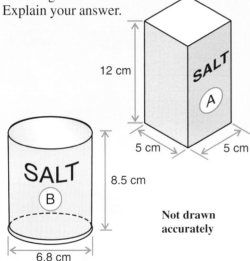

11 Tennis balls are sold in two types of container; a cylinder and a cuboid.
Both containers are just big enough to hold four balls, as shown.

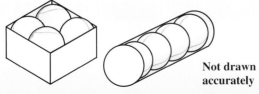

Not drawn accurately

A tennis ball has a diameter of 6.4 cm.
Calculate the volume of each container.

12 Lentil soup is sold in cylindrical tins.
Each tin has a base radius of 3.8 cm and a height of 12.6 cm.

Not to scale

Calculate the surface area of a tin.
Give your answer to a suitable degree of accuracy.

13 A cylinder can has a radius of 6 cm.

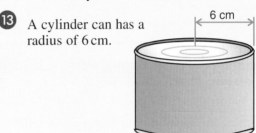

(a) Calculate the area of the circular end of the can.

The capacity of the can is 2000 cm³.
(b) Calculate the height of the can.
Give your answer correct to 1 decimal place.   Edexcel

14 Orange juice is poured from a box into a jug, as shown.

The box is a cuboid measuring 19 cm by 8.8 cm by 6 cm.
The jug is a cylinder with a diameter of 9.4 cm.
What is the depth of orange in the jug when a full box of juice has been poured in?

Enlargements and Similar Figures

Enlargement

When a shape is enlarged:
> all **lengths** are multiplied by a **scale factor**,
> **angles** remain unchanged.

For example:
> Shape **B** is an enlargement of Shape **A**.
> The scale factor is 2.

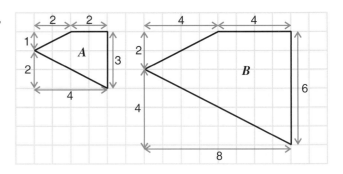

> Scale factor $= \dfrac{\text{new length}}{\text{original length}}$
>
> This can be rearranged to give
> new length = original length $\times$ scale factor.

Similar figures

When one figure is an enlargement of another, the two figures are **similar**.

Sometimes one of the figures is rotated or reflected.
For example:
> Figures **C** and **E** are enlargements of figure **A**.
> Figures **A**, **C** and **E** are similar.

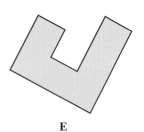

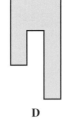

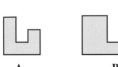

A	B	C	D	E

When two figures are **similar**:
> their **shapes** are the same,
> their **angles** are the same,
> corresponding **lengths** are in the same ratio,
> this ratio is the **scale factor** of the enlargement.

Activity

Figures X and Y are similar.
Y is an enlargement of X.
The ratio (or scale factor) is given by

$$\frac{\text{new length}}{\text{original length}}$$

Check that this ratio is the same for all four pairs
of corresponding sides.
Check that the angles are the same in the two figures.

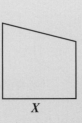

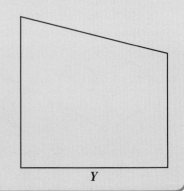

1 A photo has width 6 cm and height 10 cm.
An enlargement is made, which has width 8 cm.
Calculate the height of the enlargement.

Scale factor = $\frac{8}{6}$

$h = 10 \times \frac{8}{6}$

$h = 13.3$ cm, correct to 1 d.p.

2 These two figures are similar.
Calculate the lengths of x and y.
Write down the size of the angle marked a.

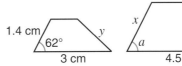

The scale factor $= \frac{4.5}{3} = 1.5$

Lengths in the large figure are given by:
length in small figure $\times$ scale factor
$x = 1.4 \times 1.5$
$x = 2.1$ cm

Lengths in the small figure are given by:
length in large figure $\div$ scale factor
$y = 2.7 \div 1.5$
$y = 1.8$ cm

The angles in similar figures are the same, so $a = 62°$.

Exercise **30.1**

1 Copy each diagram onto squared paper and draw an enlargement with the given scale factor.

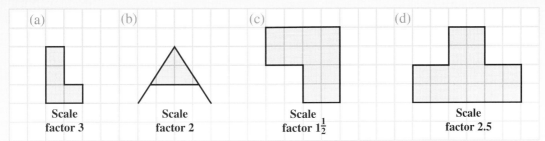

(a)	(b)	(c)	(d)
Scale factor 3	Scale factor 2	Scale factor $1\frac{1}{2}$	Scale factor 2.5

2 The shapes in this question have been drawn accurately.
(a) Explain why these two shapes are not similar to each other.

(b) Which two of these shapes are similar to each other?

P   Q   R

3 Which of the following must be similar to each other?
(a) Two circles. (b) Two kites. (c) Two parallelograms. (d) Two squares. (e) Two rectangles.

4 These two kites are similar.
  (a) What is the scale factor of their lengths?
  (b) Find the length of the side marked x.
  (c) What is the size of angle a?

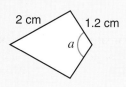

5 In each part, the two figures are similar. Lengths are in centimetres.
Calculate the lengths and angles marked with letters.

(a)

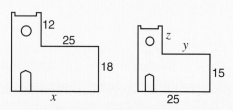

(b)

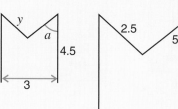

(c)

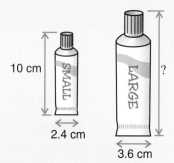

6 These two tubes are similar.

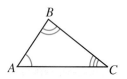 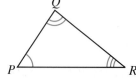

The width of the small size is 2.4 cm
and the height of the small size is 10 cm.
The width of the large size is 3.6 cm.
Calculate the height of the large size.

7 A shape has width 0.8 cm and length 2.4 cm.
It is enlarged to give a new shape with width
1 cm. Calculate the length of the new shape.

8 A castle has height 30 m. The height of the
castle wall is 6 m. A scale model of the castle
has height 25 cm. Calculate the height of the
castle wall in the scale model.

9 The dimensions of three sizes of paper are given.

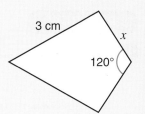

Length (cm)	24	30	y
Width (cm)	x	20	32

All the sizes are similar.
Calculate the values of x and y.

Similar triangles

For any pair of similar triangles:
  corresponding lengths are opposite equal angles,
  the scale factor is the ratio of corresponding sides.

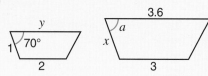

$$\frac{AB}{PQ} = \frac{BC}{QR} = \frac{CA}{RP} = \text{scale factor}$$

EXAMPLES

1 These two triangles are similar, with the equal angles marked.

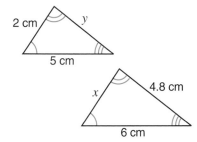

Calculate the lengths x and y.

Scale factor $= \frac{6}{5} = 1.2$

$x = 2 \times 1.2$
$x = 2.4 \, \text{cm}$

$y = 4.8 \div 1.2$
$y = 4 \, \text{cm}$

2 Triangles ABC and PQR are similar. Calculate the lengths of AC and PQ.

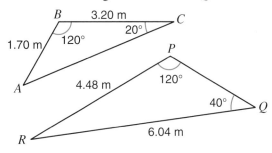

BC and PR are corresponding sides.

Scale factor $= \frac{4.48}{3.20} = 1.4$

$AC = 6.04 \div 1.4$
$AC = 4.31 \, \text{m}$, correct to 2 d.p.

$PQ = 1.70 \times 1.4$
$PQ = 2.38 \, \text{m}$

Exercise 30.2

Question 1 should be done without a calculator.

1 In each part, the triangles are similar, with equal angles marked. Lengths are in centimetres. Calculate lengths x and y.

(a)
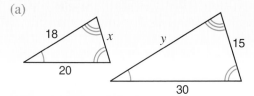

(b)
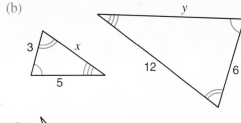

(c)
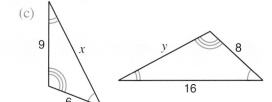

(d)
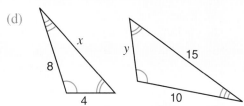

2 Triangles ABC and ADE are similar. Lengths are in centimetres.
$\angle AED = \angle ACB$.

Calculate the lengths of AB and AE.

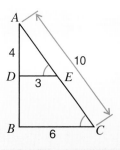

3 In each part the triangles are similar. Calculate the unknown lengths in both triangles.

(a)

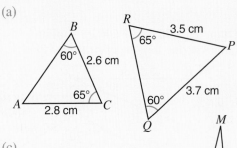
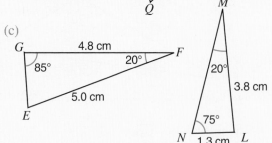

(b)

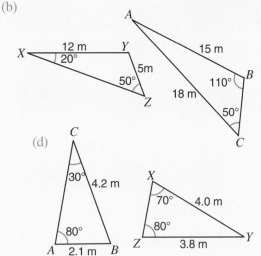

(c)

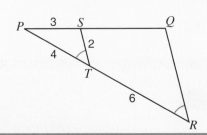

(d)

4 Triangles *PST* and *PQR* are similar.
Lengths are in centimetres.
∠*PTS* = ∠*PRQ*.

(a) Write down the length of *PR*.
(b) Calculate *QR*, *PQ* and *QS*.

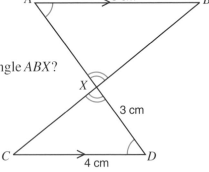

Showing that two triangles are similar

To show that two triangles are similar you have to show that:
either they have equal angles **or** corresponding lengths are all in the same ratio.
If you can show that one of these conditions is true then the other one is also true.

EXAMPLE

1 *AB* and *CD* are parallel lines. *AD* and *BC* meet at *X*.
(a) Prove that triangles *ABX* and *DCX* are similar.
(b) Which side in triangle *DCX* corresponds to *AX* in triangle *ABX*?
(c) Calculate the length of *AX*.

(a) ∠*BAX* = ∠*CDX* (alternate angles)
∠*AXB* = ∠*DXC* (vertically opposite angles)
Triangles *ABX* and *DCX* contain two pairs of equal
angles and so they are similar.
*If two pairs of angles are equal then the third pair
must be equal. Why?*
(b) ∠*ABX* = ∠*DCX*.
Sides *AX* and *DX* are opposite these equal angles.
So *DX* corresponds to *AX*.
(c) $\frac{AX}{3} = \frac{5}{4}$ (or scale factor = $\frac{5}{4}$)

$AX = \frac{5}{4} \times 3$

$AX = 3.75\,\text{cm}$

○○○○○○○○○○○○○○○
You **must** give reasons for any
statements you make.
Alternate angles, corresponding
angles and vertically opposite
angles were covered in Chapter 20.

EXAMPLE

2 Show that these two triangles are similar.

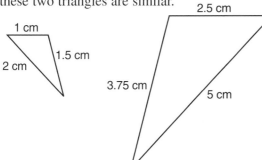

$\frac{5}{2} = 2.5$

$\frac{3.75}{1.5} = 2.5$

$\frac{2.5}{1} = 2.5$

All three pairs of corresponding sides are in the same ratio, so the triangles are similar.

Exercise 30.3

1 *BC* is parallel to *PQ*. Show that triangles *ABC* and *APQ* are similar and calculate the required lengths.

(a)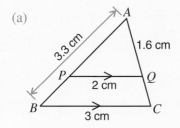

Calculate *AC* and *AP*.

(b)

Calculate *AC* and *BP*.

(c)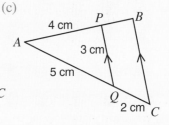

Calculate *BC* and *BP*.

(d)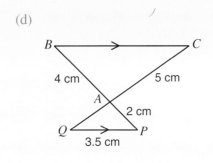

Calculate *AQ* and *BC*.

(e)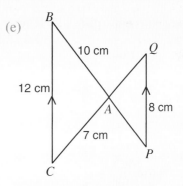

Calculate *AQ* and *BP*.

2 Show that these pairs of triangles are similar and find angle *x*.

(a)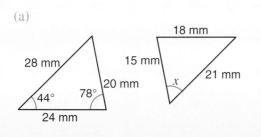

(b)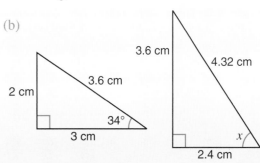

3 All marked lengths are in centimetres.

(a) In each part show that triangles ABC and APQ are similar and find angle x.

(i)

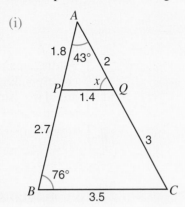

(ii)

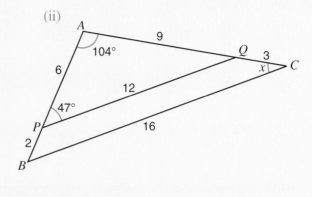

(b) In each part find the perimetres of triangles ABC and APQ.
What do you notice about the ratio of the perimeters of the triangles and the ratio of the lengths of corresponding sides?

4 (a) Explain why triangles ABC and PQR are similar.
(b) Calculate the length of AB.
(c) The perimeter of triangle ABC is 7.5 cm.
Find the perimeter of triangle PQR.

Not drawn accurately

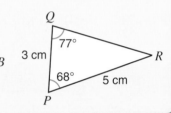

What you need to know

- When a shape is **enlarged**:   all **lengths** are multiplied by a **scale factor**,
  angles remain unchanged.

- When two figures are **similar**:
  their **shapes** are the same,
  their **angles** are the same,
  corresponding **lengths** are in the same ratio,
  this ratio is the **scale factor** of the enlargement.

- Scale factor $= \dfrac{\text{new length}}{\text{original length}}$

- All circles are similar to each other.

- All squares are similar to each other.

- For **similar triangles**:
  corresponding lengths are opposite equal angles,
  the scale factor is the ratio of the corresponding sides.

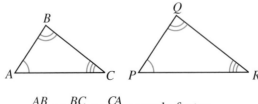

$$\frac{AB}{PQ} = \frac{BC}{QR} = \frac{CA}{RP} = \text{scale factor}$$

①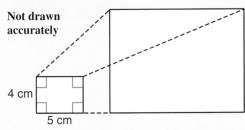

Not drawn accurately

4 cm

5 cm

The diagram represents two photographs.
(a) Work out the area of the small photograph.

The photograph is to be enlarged by scale factor 3.
(b) Write down the measurements of the enlarged photograph.
(c) How many times bigger is the area of the enlarged photograph than the area of the small photograph? Edexcel

② Explain why triangles *ABX* and *PQX* are similar.

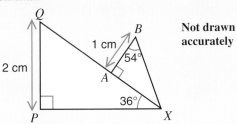

Not drawn accurately

Q

B

1 cm

54°

2 cm

A

36°

P

X

③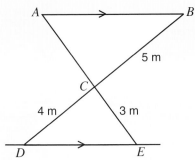

A

B

5 m

C

4 m

3 m

D

E

In the diagram *CD* = 4 metres, *CE* = 3 metres and *BC* = 5 metres.
AB is parallel to *DE*.
ACE and *BCD* are straight lines.

(a) Explain why triangle *ABC* is similar to triangle *EDC*.
(b) Calculate the length of *AC*. Edexcel

④ There triangles are similar.
The ratio of *AC* : *PR* is 2 : 3.
(a) Calculate the length of *AB*.
(b) Calculate the length of *QR*.

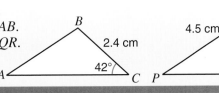

B

2.4 cm

42°

A   *C*   *P*

Q

4.5 cm

42°

R

Not drawn accurately

⑤ These shapes are similar.
Not drawn accurately

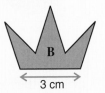

A

B

2 cm

3 cm

The height of shape **A** is 1.6 cm.
(a) What is the height of shape **B**?

The perimeter of shape **B** is 13.5 cm.
(b) Find the perimeter of shape **A**.

⑥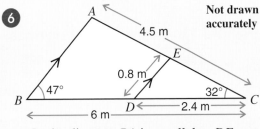

A

4.5 m

Not drawn accurately

E

0.8 m

47°

32°

B

D   2.4 m   *C*

6 m

In the diagram *BA* is parallel to *DE*.
AEC and *BDC* are straight lines.
AC = 4.5 m, *DE* = 0.8 m, *CD* = 2.4 m, *BC* = 6 m.
Angle *ABC* = 47°, angle *BCA* = 32°.
(a) (i)   Calculate the size of angle *DEC*.
     (ii) Explain your answer.
(b) Calculate the length of *EC*.
(c) Calculate the length of *AB*. Edexcel

⑦ *BC* is parallel to *DE*.
AB is twice as long as *BD*.
AD = 36 cm and *AC* = 27 cm.

(a) Work out the length of *AB*.
(b) Work out the length of *AE*.

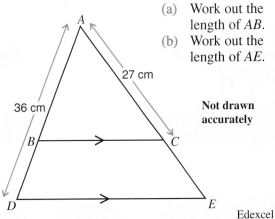

A

27 cm

36 cm

Not drawn accurately

B   *C*

D   *E*

Edexcel

CHAPTER 31

Pythagoras' Theorem

The longest side in a right-angled triangle is called the **hypotenuse**.

In any right-angled triangle it can be proved that:
"The square on the hypotenuse is equal to the sum of the squares on the other two sides."

This is known as the **Theorem of Pythagoras**, or **Pythagoras' Theorem**.

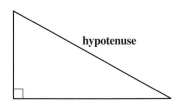

Checking the Theorem of Pythagoras

Look at this triangle.

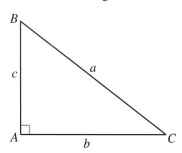

Notice that: the side opposite angle A is labelled a,
the side opposite angle B is labelled b,
the side opposite angle C is labelled c.

ABC is a right-angled triangle because $\angle BAC = 90°$.
$a = 5\,cm$, so $a^2 = 25\,cm^2$.
$b = 4\,cm$, so $b^2 = 16\,cm^2$.
$c = 3\,cm$, so $c^2 = 9\,cm^2$.

$a^2 = b^2 + c^2$

Activity

Use a ruler and a pair of compasses to draw the following triangles accurately.

(a)

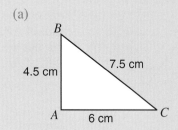

(b)

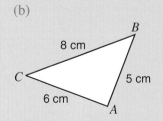

(c)

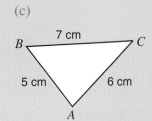

(d)

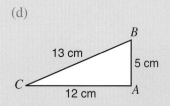

(e)

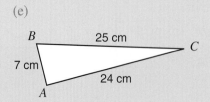

(f)

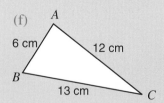

For each triangle: Measure angle BAC.
Is angle $BAC = 90°$?
Does $a^2 = b^2 + c^2$?
Explain your answers.

When we know the lengths of two sides of a right-angled triangle, we can use the Theorem of Pythagoras to find the length of the third side.

Finding the hypotenuse

EXAMPLE

The roof of a house is 12 m above the ground. What length of ladder is needed to reach the roof, if the foot of the ladder has to be placed 5 m away from the wall of the house?

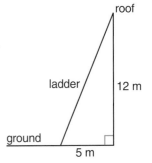

Using Pythagoras' Theorem.
$$l^2 = 5^2 + 12^2$$
$$l^2 = 25 + 144$$
$$l^2 = 169$$

Take the square root of both sides.
$$l = \sqrt{169}$$
$$l = 13\,\text{m}$$

The ladder needs to be 13 m long.

Exercise 31.1

1 These triangles are right-angled.
Calculate the length of the hypotenuse.

(a)

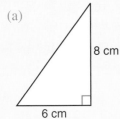

6 cm, 8 cm

(b)

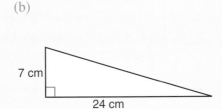

7 cm, 24 cm

(c)

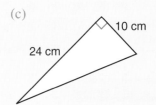

24 cm, 10 cm

2 These triangles are right-angled.
Calculate the length of side a to one decimal place.

(a)

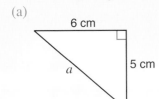

6 cm, 5 cm, a

(b)

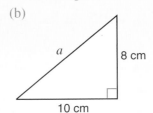

a, 8 cm, 10 cm

(c)

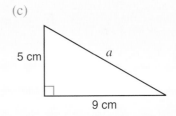

5 cm, a, 9 cm

3 AB and CD are line segments, drawn on a centimetre-squared grid.
Calculate the exact length of (a) AB, (b) CD.

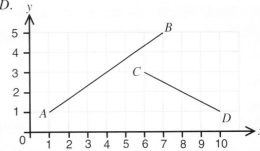

4 Calculate the distance between the following points.
(a) $A(2, 0)$ and $B(6, 3)$.
(b) $C(6, 3)$ and $D(0, 10)$.
(c) $E(2, 2)$ and $F(-3, -10)$.
(d) $G(-2, -2)$ and $H(-6, 5)$.
(e) $I(3, -1)$ and $J(-3, -5)$.

5 The coordinates of the vertices of a parallelogram are $P(1, 1)$, $Q(3, 5)$, $R(x, y)$ and $S(7, 3)$.
(a) Find the coordinates of R.
(b) X is the midpoint of PQ. Find the coordinates of X.
(c) Y is the midpoint of PS. Find the coordinates of Y.
(d) Calculate the distance XY.

Finding one of the shorter sides

To find one of the shorter sides we can rearrange the Theorem of Pythagoras.

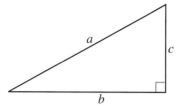

To find b we use: $\quad$ To find c we use:
$$b^2 = a^2 - c^2 \qquad c^2 = a^2 - b^2$$

To find the length of a shorter side of a right-angled triangle: Subtract the square of the known short side from the square on the hypotenuse. Take the square root of the result.

EXAMPLE

A wire used to keep a radio aerial steady is 9 metres long. The wire is fixed to the ground 4.6 metres from the base of the aerial. Find the height of the aerial, giving your answer correct to one decimal place.

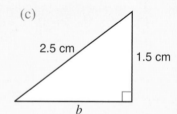

Using Pythagoras' Theorem.
$$9^2 = h^2 + 4.6^2$$
Rearranging this we get:
$$h^2 = 9^2 - 4.6^2$$
$$h^2 = 81 - 21.16$$
$$h^2 = 59.84$$
Take the square root of both sides.
$$h = \sqrt{59.84}$$
$$h = 7.735\ldots$$
$$h = 7.7 \text{ m, correct to 1 d.p.}$$

The height of the aerial is 7.7 m, correct to 1 d.p.

Exercise 31.2

1 Work out the length of side b.

(a)

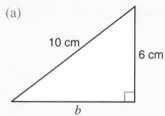

(b)

6.5 cm

b

2.5 cm

(c)

2.5 cm $\quad$ 1.5 cm

b

2 Work out the length of side c, correct to one decimal place.

(a)

8 cm $\quad$ 4 cm

c

(b)

5 cm $\quad$ 12 cm

c

(c)

10 cm $\quad$ 3 cm

c

3 Two boats A and B are 360 m apart. Boat A is 120 m due east of a buoy. Boat B is due north of the buoy. How far is boat B from the buoy?

4 The diagram shows a right-angled triangle, *ABC*, and a square, *ACDE*.

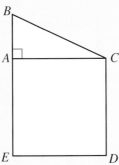

AB = 2.5 cm and *BC* = 6.5 cm.
Calculate the area of the square *ACDE*.

5 The diagram shows a right-angled triangle, *ABC*, and a square, *XYBA*.

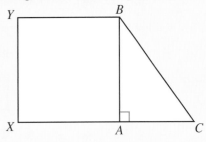

BC = 6 cm.
The square *XYBA* has an area of 23.04 cm².
Calculate the length of *AC*.

Problems involving the use of Pythagoras' Theorem

Questions leading to the use of Pythagoras' Theorem often involve:

Understanding the problem.
  What information is given?
  What are you required to find?

Drawing diagrams.
  In some questions a diagram is not given.
  Drawing a diagram may help you to understand the problem.

Selecting a suitable right-angled triangle.
  In more complex problems you will have to select a right-angled triangle which can be used to answer the question. It is a good idea to draw this triangle on its own, especially if it has been taken from a three-dimensional drawing.

EXAMPLE

The diagram shows the side view of a swimming pool.
It slopes steadily from a depth of 1 m to 3.6 m.
The pool is 20 m long.
Find the length of the sloping bottom of the pool,
giving the answer correct to three significant figures.

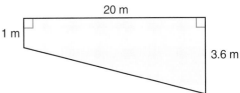

$\triangle CDE$ is a suitable right-angled triangle.
$CD = 3.6 - 1 = 2.6$ m

Using Pythagoras' Theorem in $\triangle CDE$.

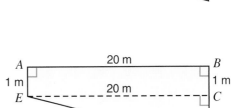

$DE^2 = CD^2 + CE^2$
$DE^2 = 2.6^2 + 20^2$
$DE^2 = 6.76 + 400$
$DE^2 = 406.76$
$DE = \sqrt{406.76}$ m
$DE = 20.1682...$ m

The length of the sloping bottom of the pool is 20.2 m, correct to 3 sig. figs.

1 In each of the following, work out the length of the side marked x.

(a)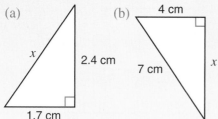

(b)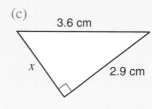
4 cm
7 cm
2.4 cm
1.7 cm
x

(c)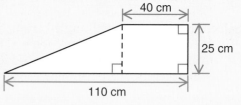
3.6 cm
x
2.9 cm

(d)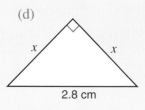
x x
2.8 cm

2 A rectangle is 8 cm wide and 15 cm long.
Work out the length of its diagonals.

3 The length of a rectangle is 24 cm. The diagonals of the rectangle are 26 cm.
Work out the width of the rectangle.

4 A square has sides of length 6 cm. Work out the length of its diagonals.

5 The diagonals of a square are 15 cm. Work out the length of its sides.

6 The height of an isosceles triangle is 12 cm. The base of the triangle is 18 cm.
Work out the length of the equal sides.

7 An equilateral triangle has sides of length 8 cm.
Work out the height of the triangle.

8 The diagram shows the side view of a car ramp.
The ramp is 110 cm long and 25 cm high.
The top part of the ramp is 40 cm long.
Calculate the length of the sloping part of the ramp.

40 cm
25 cm
110 cm

9 The top of a lampshade has a diameter of 10 cm.
The bottom of the lampshade has a diameter of 20 cm.
The height of the lampshade is 12 cm.
Calculate the length, l, of the sloping sides.

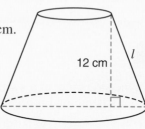
12 cm
l

10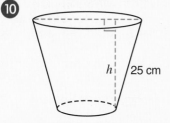
h 25 cm

The top of a bucket has a diameter of 30 cm.
The bottom of the bucket has a diameter of 16 cm.
The sloping sides are 25 cm long.
How deep is the bucket?

11 *ABCD* is a kite.
$AB = 8.5$ cm, $BC = 5.4$ cm and $BD = 7.6$ cm.
(a) Calculate the length of *AC*.
(b) Calculate the area of the kite.

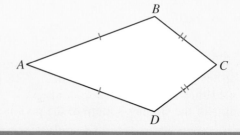
B
A
C
D

What you need to know

- The longest side in a right-angled triangle is called the **hypotenuse**.

- The **Theorem of Pythagoras** states:
  "In any right-angled triangle the square on the hypotenuse is equal to the sum of the squares on the other two sides."

  $a^2 = b^2 + c^2$
  Rearranging gives:
  $b^2 = a^2 - c^2$
  $c^2 = a^2 - b^2$

  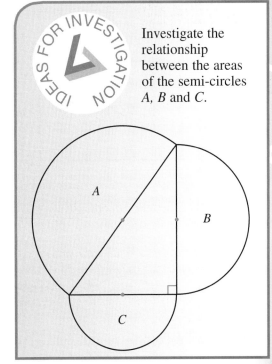

- When we know the lengths of two sides of a right-angled triangle, we can use the Theorem of Pythagoras to find the length of the third side.

IDEAS FOR INVESTIGATION

Investigate the relationship between the areas of the semi-circles *A*, *B* and *C*.

Pythagoras' Theorem

Review Exercise

Do not use a calculator for questions 1 to 3.

1 A walker on Dartmoor is 8 km south of Princetown and 6 km east of Princetown. How far is the walker from Princetown?

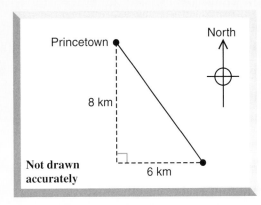

2 The diagram shows a triangle *KLM*, with *LX* perpendicular to *KM*.
$KL = 5$ cm, $KM = 5$ cm and $XM = 2$ cm.
Find the **exact** length of *LM*.

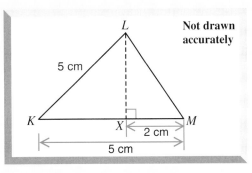

3 A sketch of a right-angled triangle is shown. The triangle has an area of 54 cm². Calculate the perimeter of the triangle.

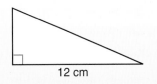

12 cm

4 PQR is a right-angled triangle.

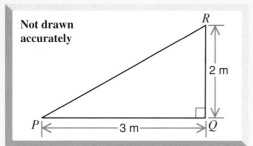

Not drawn accurately

P 3 m Q 2 m R

PQ is of length 3 m and QR is of length 2 m.
Calculate the length of PR.   Edexcel

5

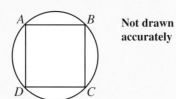

Not drawn accurately

A, B, C and D are four points on the circumference of a circle.
$ABCD$ is a square with sides 20 cm long.

Work out the diameter of the circle.
Give your answer correct to 3 significant figures.   Edexcel

6 John is standing 200 m due west of a power station and 300 m due north of a pylon.
Calculate the distance of the power station from the pylon.

7 The diagram shows a trapezium $ABCD$.

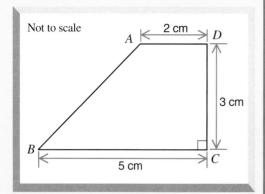

Not to scale

Calculate the **exact** length of the line AB.

8 The diagram shows a sketch of triangle PQR.

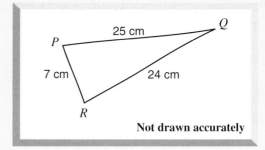

Not drawn accurately

Show that PQR is a right-angled triangle.

9 The sketch shows the positions of M and N.
M has coordinates $(-2, 1)$.
N has coordinates $(4, 5)$.

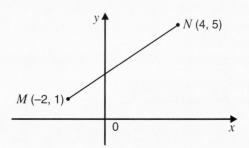

Calculate the length of MN.

10 A helicopter flies from its base on a bearing of 045° for 20 km before landing.
How far east of its base is the helicopter when it lands?

11 The diagram consists of two right-angled triangles.

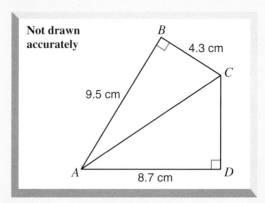

Not drawn accurately

$AB = 9.5$ cm, $BC = 4.3$ cm and $AD = 8.7$ cm.
Calculate the length of CD.
Give your answer to an appropriate degree of accuracy.

CHAPTER 32

Trigonometry

We use **trigonometry** to find the lengths of sides and the sizes of angles in right-angled triangles.

We already know that the longest side of a right-angled triangle is called the **hypotenuse**.

In order to understand the relationships between sides and angles the other sides of the triangle also need to be named.

The **opposite** side is the side directly opposite the angle being used and the **adjacent** side is the side next to the angle.

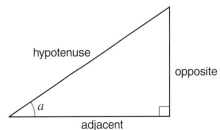

Look at this diagram.
It shows how the height of a kite changes as more and more string is let out.

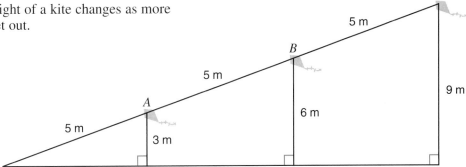

When the kite is at A, the string is 5 m long and the kite is 3 m high.

At A, the ratio $\frac{\text{height of kite}}{\text{length of string}}$, is therefore $\frac{3}{5} = 0.6$.

Calculate the value of the same ratio at B and C.

What do you notice?

When the kite is flying at angle a, the ratio $\frac{\text{height of kite}}{\text{length of string}}$ will always be the same whatever the length of the kite string and is called the **sine** of angle a.

Finding the length of the opposite side

The sine ratio

For any right-angled triangle:

$$\sin a = \frac{\text{opposite}}{\text{hypotenuse}}$$

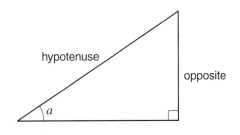

The sine ratio links three pieces of information:
the size of an **angle**,
the length of the side **opposite** the angle,
the length of the **hypotenuse**.
If we are given the values for two of these we can find the value of the third.

EXAMPLE

Find the height of a kite when it is flying at an angle of $40°$ and the kite string is $12\,\text{m}$ long. Give the answer correct to 3 significant figures.

$$\sin a = \frac{\text{opp}}{\text{hyp}}$$

Substitute known values.

$$\sin 40° = \frac{h}{12}$$

Multiply both sides by 12.

$$h = 12 \times \sin 40°$$

Using your calculator, press:

[1] [2] [×] [sin] [4] [0] [=]

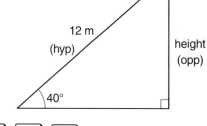

Mathematical shorthand	
Word	**Abbreviation**
sine	sin
opposite	opp
hypotenuse	hyp

$h = 7.713\ldots$
$h = 7.71\,\text{m}$, correct to 3 s.f.

The height of the kite is $7.71\,\text{m}$, correct to 3 s.f.

Exercise 32.1

1 Find the height, h, of these kites.
Give your answers correct to 3 significant figures.

(a)

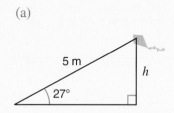

(b)

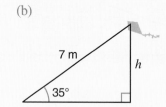

(c)

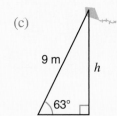

2 Calculate the lengths marked x.
Give your answers correct to 3 significant figures.

(a)

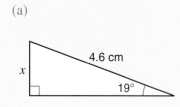

(b)

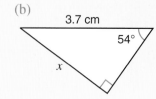

(c)

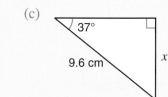

3 In $\triangle ABC$, angle $ACB = 90°$.
  (a) If $\angle BAC = 47.5°$ and $AB = 4.6\,\text{m}$ find BC.
  (b) If $\angle ABC = 67.4°$ and $AB = 12.4\,\text{m}$ find AC.
  (c) If $\angle BAC = 15.8°$ and $AB = 17.4\,\text{cm}$ find BC.
  (d) If $\angle BAC = 35°$ and $AB = 8.5\,\text{cm}$ find the size of $\angle ABC$ and then find AC.
Give your answers correct to 3 significant figures.

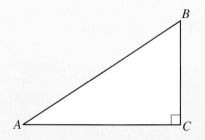

Finding an angle

If you are given the sine of an angle and asked to find the angle, use the inverse sine function, $\sin^{-1}$, on your calculator.

Using your calculator, press: `sin` `3` `0`
The display should read 0.5.
Clear the display and press: `sin⁻¹` `0` `.` `5` `=`
What do you notice?

EXAMPLE

Find the size of angle a when the kite string is 12 m long and the kite is flying 7 m above the ground.
Give the answer correct to one decimal place.

$$\sin a = \frac{\text{opp}}{\text{hyp}}$$

Substitute known values.

$$\sin a° = \frac{7}{12}$$

$$a = \sin^{-1} \frac{7}{12}$$

Using your calculator, press: `sin⁻¹` `(` `7` `÷` `1` `2` `)` `=`

$a = 35.685...$

$a = 35.7°$, correct to 1 d.p.

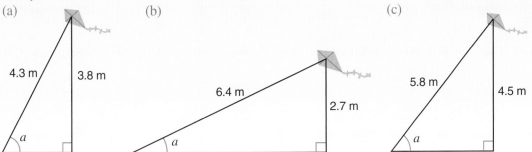

Exercise 32.2

1 Find the size of angle a for each of these kites.
Give your answers correct to one decimal place.

(a)   (b)   (c)

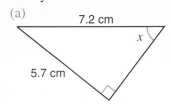

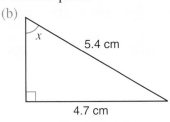

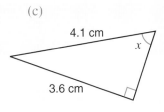

2 Find the size of angle x in each of these triangles.
Give your answers correct to one decimal place.

(a)   (b)   (c)

7.2 cm

x

5.7 cm

x

5.4 cm

4.7 cm

4.1 cm

x

3.6 cm

3 In $\triangle PQR$ angle $PQR = 90°$.
(a) If $QR = 4$ m and $PR = 10$ m find the size of $\angle QPR$.
(b) If $PQ = 4.7$ cm and $PR = 5.2$ cm find the size of $\angle PRQ$.
(c) If $QR = 7.2$ m and $PR = 19.4$ m find the size of $\angle QPR$.
(d) If $PQ = 3.7$ cm and $PR = 9.1$ cm find the size of $\angle QRP$ and then find the size of $\angle QPR$.
Give your answers correct to one decimal place.

R

P

Q

Finding the hypotenuse

Find the length of the string, l, when a kite is 6 m high and the string makes an angle of 50° with the ground.

Give the answer correct to 3 significant figures.

$$\sin a = \frac{\text{opp}}{\text{hyp}}$$

Substitute known values.

$$\sin 50° = \frac{6}{l}$$

Multiply both sides by l.

$$l \times \sin 50° = 6$$

Divide both sides by $\sin 50°$.

$$l = \frac{6}{\sin 50°}$$

Using your calculator, press: 　6　÷　sin　5　0　=

$l = 7.832...$

$l = 7.83$ m, correct to 3 s.f.

The length of the string is 7.83 m, correct to 3 s.f.

Exercise 32.3

1 Find the lengths, l, of these kite strings.
Give your answers correct to 3 significant figures.

(a)

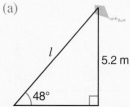

5.2 m, 48°

(b)

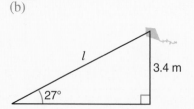

3.4 m, 27°

(c)

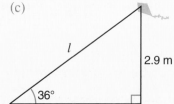

2.9 m, 36°

2 Calculate the length of side x in each of these triangles.
Give your answers correct to two decimal places.

(a)

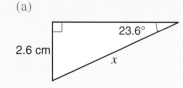

23.6°, 2.6 cm, x

(b)

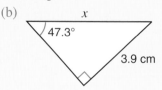

x, 47.3°, 3.9 cm

(c)

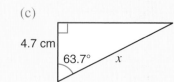

4.7 cm, 63.7°, x

3 In $\triangle ABC$ angle $ACB = 90°$.
(a) If $\angle BAC = 36.2°$ and $BC = 4.5$ m find AB.
(b) If $\angle ABC = 64.7°$ and $AC = 15.8$ cm find AB.
(c) If $\angle BAC = 12.7°$ and $BC = 14.7$ cm find AB.
(d) If $\angle BAC = 72.8°$ and $AC = 7.6$ m find the size of $\angle ABC$ and then find AB.
Give your answers correct to 3 significant figures.

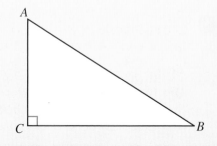

The cosine and tangent ratios

We have found that **sine** is the ratio $\dfrac{\text{opposite}}{\text{hypotenuse}}$.

In a similar way we can find two other ratios, the **cosine** of angle a and the **tangent** of angle a.

The cosine ratio

For any right-angled triangle:

$$\cos a = \frac{\text{adjacent}}{\text{hypotenuse}}$$

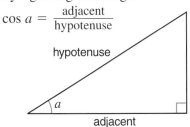

The cosine ratio links three pieces of information:
    the size of an **angle**,
    the length of the side **adjacent** to the angle,
    the length of the **hypotenuse**.
If we are given the values of two of these we can find the value of the third.

The tangent ratio

For any right-angled triangle:

$$\tan a = \frac{\text{opposite}}{\text{adjacent}}$$

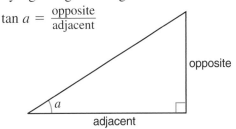

The tangent ratio links three pieces of information:
    the size of an **angle**,
    the length of the side **opposite** to the angle,
    the length of the side **adjacent** to the angle.
If we are given the values of two of these we can find the value of the third.

EXAMPLE

1   Write down the sin, cos and tan ratios for angle a in the triangle.

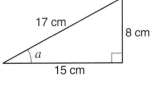

$$\sin a = \frac{\text{opp}}{\text{hyp}} = \frac{8}{17}$$

$$\cos a = \frac{\text{adj}}{\text{hyp}} = \frac{15}{17}$$

$$\tan a = \frac{\text{opp}}{\text{adj}} = \frac{8}{15}$$

Mathematical shorthand

Word	Abbreviation
adjacent	adj
opposite	opp
hypotenuse	hyp
sine	sin
cosine	cos
tangent	tan

How to select and use the correct ratio

There are only 3 different types of question for each of the ratios.
Selecting the correct ratio is most important.
To do this:

1. Go to the angle you know (or want to find).
2. Name sides (opp, adj, hyp).
   If you are trying to find the length of a side, name that side first together with one other side of known length.
   If you are trying to find the size of an angle, name two sides of known length.
3. Select the correct ratio and write it down.

$$\sin a = \frac{\text{opp}}{\text{hyp}} \quad \cos a = \frac{\text{adj}}{\text{hyp}} \quad \tan a = \frac{\text{opp}}{\text{adj}}$$

   One way to remember the ratios is to use the initial letters, SOHCAHTOA.
   You may know another method.

4. Substitute known values from the question.
5. Rearrange to isolate the angle, or side, you are trying to find.
6. Use your calculator to find the size of the angle, or side, writing down more figures than you need for the final answer.
7. Correct to the required degree of accuracy.
8. Give the answer, stating the degree of approximation and giving the correct units. When giving the answer to a problem you should use a short sentence.

2 Find the length, h, giving the answer to 3 significant figures

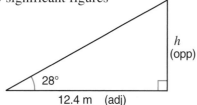

$$\tan a = \frac{\text{opp}}{\text{adj}}$$

Substitute known values.

$$\tan 28° = \frac{h}{12.4}$$

Multiply both sides by 12.4.

$$h = 12.4 \times \tan 28°$$

Using your calculator, press:

[1] [2] [.] [4] [×] [tan] [2] [8] [=]

$$h = 6.593\ldots$$
$$h = 6.59\,\text{m, correct to 3 s.f.}$$

3 Find the size of angle a, correct to one decimal place.

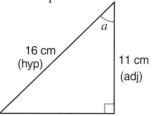

$$\cos a = \frac{\text{adj}}{\text{hyp}}$$

Substitute known values.

$$\cos a° = \frac{11}{16}$$

$$a = \cos^{-1} \frac{11}{16}$$

Using your calculator, press:

[cos⁻¹] [(] [1] [1] [÷] [1] [6] [)] [=]

$$a = 46.56\ldots$$
$$a = 46.6°\text{, correct to 1 d.p.}$$

Exercise **32.4**

1 Write down the sin, cos and tan ratios for angle p in each of the following triangles.

(a)

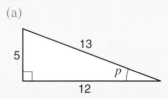

(b)

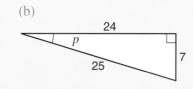

(c)

2 By choosing the correct ratio, calculate angle p in each of the following triangles. Give your answers correct to one decimal place.

(a)

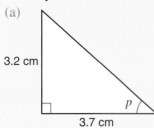

(b)

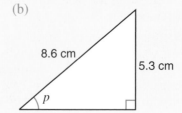

(c)

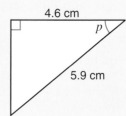

(d)

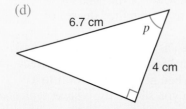

(e)

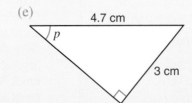

(f)

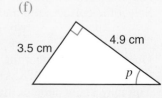

3 By choosing the correct ratio, calculate side *a* in each of the following triangles.

(a)
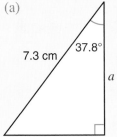
7.3 cm, 37.8°, *a*

(b)
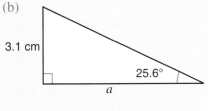
3.1 cm, 25.6°, *a*

(c)
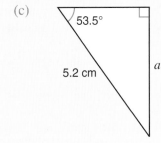
53.5°, 5.2 cm, *a*

(d)
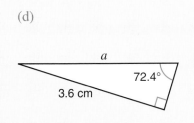
a, 72.4°, 3.6 cm

(e)
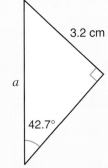
3.2 cm, *a*, 42.7°

(f)
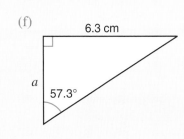
6.3 cm, *a*, 57.3°

4 An equilateral triangle has sides of length 5 cm. Calculate the height of the triangle.

5 An isosceles triangle has sides of length 10 cm, 10 cm and 6 cm. Calculate the angles of the triangle.

6 Calculate
(a) the length of *AC*,
(b) the length of *CE*.

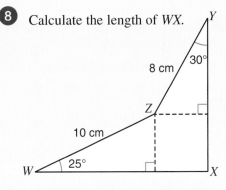
C, 5 cm, 20°, *D*, *E*, 50°, *B*, 5 cm, *A*

7
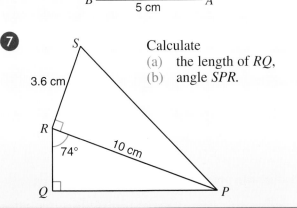
S, 3.6 cm, *R*, 74°, 10 cm, *Q*, *P*

Calculate
(a) the length of *RQ*,
(b) angle *SPR*.

8 Calculate the length of *WX*.

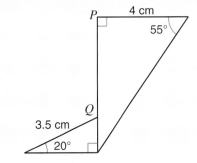
Y, 30°, 8 cm, *Z*, 10 cm, *W*, 25°, *X*

9 Calculate the length of *PQ*.

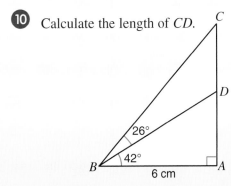
P, 4 cm, 55°, *Q*, 3.5 cm, 20°

10 Calculate the length of *CD*.

C, *D*, 26°, *B*, 42°, 6 cm, *A*

Trigonometry . . . Trigonometry . . . Trigonometry . . .

Angles of elevation and depression

When we look **up** from the horizontal the angle we turn through is called an **angle of elevation**.

When we look **down** from the horizontal the angle we turn through is called an **angle of depression**.

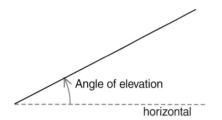

Angle of elevation
horizontal

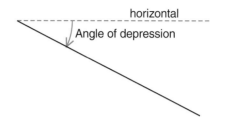

horizontal
Angle of depression

EXAMPLES

1 From a point on the ground, 30 m from the base of a pylon, the angle of elevation to the top of the pylon is 50°.

Find the height of the pylon.

$\tan a = \dfrac{\text{opp}}{\text{adj}}$

$\tan 50° = \dfrac{h}{30}$

$h = 30 \times \tan 50°$

$h = 35.75\ldots$

$h = 35.8$ m, correct to 3 s.f.

The height of the pylon is 35.8 m, correct to 3 s.f.

h
(opp)

50°

30 m (adj)

2 Staten Island Ferry is 270 m away from the base of the Statue of Liberty.
The ferry can be seen from a viewing point in the lantern, 85 m above the ground.

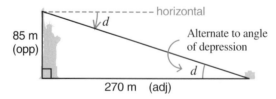

horizontal
d

85 m
(opp)

Alternate to angle of depression

d

270 m (adj)

What is the angle of depression to the ferry from the viewing point?

$\tan a = \dfrac{\text{opp}}{\text{adj}}$

$\tan d° = \dfrac{85}{270}$

$d = \tan^{-1} \dfrac{85}{270}$

$d = 17.47\ldots$

$d = 17.5°$, correct to 1 d.p.

The angle of depression to the ferry from the viewing point is 17.5°, correct to 1 d.p.

Exercise 32.5

1 From a point on the ground 20 m from the base of a tree, the angle of elevation of the top of the tree is 47°.
Calculate the height of the tree.

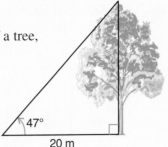

47°
20 m

2 From a point on the ground 10 m from a block of flats, the angle of elevation of the top of the block is 76°.
Calculate the height of the block of flats.

3 A fishing boat is 200 m from the bottom of a vertical cliff.
From the top of the cliff the angle of depression to the fishing boat is 34°.
(a) Calculate the height of the cliff.
(b) A buoy is 100 m from the bottom of the cliff. Calculate the angle of depression to the buoy from the top of the cliff.

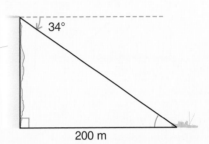

34°

200 m

4 A yacht is 20 m from the bottom of a lighthouse.
From the top of the lighthouse the angle of depression to the yacht is 48°.
Calculate the height of the lighthouse.

5 A cat is on the ground 25 m from the foot of a house. A bird is perched on the gutter of the house 15 m from the ground.
Calculate the angle of elevation from the cat to the bird.

6 A tree, 6 m high, casts a shadow of 4.8 m on horizontal ground.
Calculate the angle of elevation of the sun.

7 From a point, A, on the ground, the angle of elevation to a hot air balloon is 9°.
The balloon is 150 m above the ground.
Calculate the distance from A to the balloon.

8 From the top of a cliff, 36 m high, the angles of depression of two boats at sea are 17° and 25°. The boats are in a straight line from the foot of the cliff. Calculate the distance between the two boats.

Three-figure bearings

Remember:
Bearings are used to describe the direction in which you must travel to get from one place to another. They are measured from the North line in a clockwise direction. A bearing can be any angle from 0° to 360° and is written as a three-figure number.

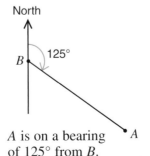

North

B   125°

A is on a bearing of 125° from B.

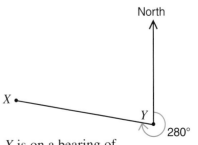

North

X

Y

280°

X is on a bearing of 280° from Y.

Trigonometry . . . Trigonometry . . . Trigonometry . . .

A plane flies 300 km on a bearing of 132° from an airport.
How far South and East is it from the airport?
Give the answers correct to 3 significant figures.

x is the distance South.
y is the distance East.
Using supplementary angles:
$\angle PAB = 180° - 132° = 48°$.

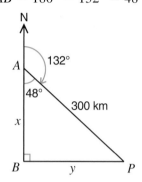

To find x

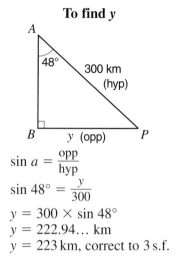

$$\cos a = \frac{\text{adj}}{\text{hyp}}$$
$$\cos 48° = \frac{x}{300}$$
$$x = 300 \times \cos 48°$$
$$x = 200.73\ldots \text{ km}$$
$$x = 201 \text{ km, correct to 3 s.f.}$$

To find y

$$\sin a = \frac{\text{opp}}{\text{hyp}}$$
$$\sin 48° = \frac{y}{300}$$
$$y = 300 \times \sin 48°$$
$$y = 222.94\ldots \text{ km}$$
$$y = 223 \text{ km, correct to 3 s.f.}$$

The plane is 201 km South and
223 km East of the airport,
correct to 3 s.f.

*How can you use Pythagoras'
Theorem to check the answer?*

Sketch diagrams
Drawing a sketch diagram may help you to
understand the question.
More information can be added to the diagram as you
answer the question.

Exercise 32.6

1 A plane flies 250 km on a bearing of 052.6°.
 (a) How far north is it from its original position?
 (b) How far east is it from its original position?

2 A helicopter leaves its base and flies 23 km on a bearing of 285°.
 How far west is it from its base?

3 A ship at A is 3.8 km due north of a lighthouse.
 A ship at B is 2.7 km due east of the same lighthouse.
 What is the bearing of the ship at B from the ship at A?

4 A helicopter has flown from its base on a bearing of 153°. Its distance east of base is 19 km.
 How far has the helicopter flown?

5 A fishing boat leaves port and sails on a straight course. After 2 hours its distance south of
 port is 24 km and its distance east of port is 7 km. On what bearing did it sail?

6 A yacht sails 15 km on a bearing of 053°, then 7 km on a bearing of 112°.
 How far north is the yacht from its starting position?

7 A plane flies 307 km on a bearing of 234°, then 23 km on a bearing of 286°.
 How far south is the plane from its starting position?

8 Jayne sails 1.5 km on a bearing of 050°. She then changes course and sails 2 km on a bearing
 of 140°. On what bearing must she sail to return to her starting position?

What you need to know

- **Trigonometry** is used to find the lengths of sides and the sizes of angles in right-angled triangles.

- You must learn the **sine**, **cosine** and **tangent** ratios.

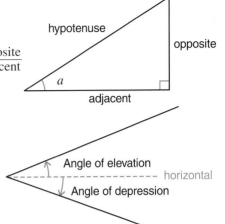

$$\sin a = \frac{\text{opposite}}{\text{hypotenuse}} \quad \cos a = \frac{\text{adjacent}}{\text{hypotenuse}} \quad \tan a = \frac{\text{opposite}}{\text{adjacent}}$$

- Each ratio links the size of an angle with the lengths of two sides. If we are given the values for two of these we can find the value of the third.

- When we look **up** from the horizontal the angle we turn through is called the **angle of elevation**.

- When we look **down** from the horizontal the angle we turn through is called the **angle of depression**.

- **Three-figure bearings.**
  Bearings are used to describe the direction in which you must travel to get from one place to another. They are measured from the North line in a clockwise direction. A bearing can be any angle from 0° to 360° and is written as a three-figure number.

Review Exercise

1. When Jayne is 10 m from a haystack, the angle of elevation to the top of the haystack is 18°. Calculate h, the height of the haystack.

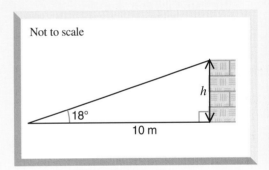

Not to scale

2. Madge places a marker 20 m from a tree.

   From the marker the angle of elevation to the top of the tree is 27°.

   Calculate the height of the tree.

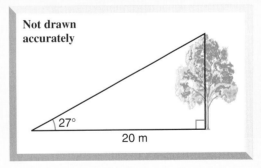

Not drawn accurately

Edexcel

3. **Calculate** the length of the line AB.

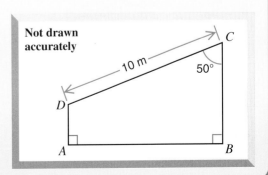

Not drawn accurately

Edexcel

4 An aircraft takes off from an airport at *A*. After flying 4000 m the aircraft is 360 m above the ground.
Calculate the angle of elevation of the aircraft from *A*.

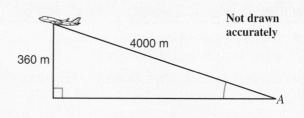

Not drawn accurately

4000 m

360 m

A

5 *AB* and *BC* are two sides of a rectangle.
AB = 120 cm and *BC* = 148 cm.
D is a point on *BC*.
Angle *BAD* = 15°.

Work out the length of *CD*.
Give your answer correct to the nearest centimetre.

Edexcel

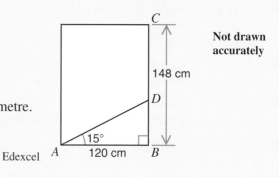

C

Not drawn accurately

148 cm

D

15°

A   120 cm   *B*

6 Paul flies his helicopter from Ashwell.
He flies due west for 4.8 km.
He then flies due south for 7.4 km to Birton.

Calculate the three-figure bearing of Birton from Ashwell.

Edexcel

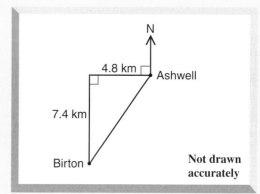

N

4.8 km   Ashwell

7.4 km

Birton

Not drawn accurately

7 In a building, the 1st floor is 5.2 m above the ground floor.
An escalator links the ground floor to the 1st floor.
The escalator slopes at an angle of 37.5° to the horizontal.
Calculate the length of the escalator.

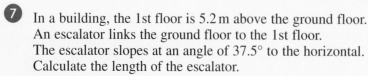

1st Floor

5.2 m

Ground Floor   37.5°

8 The diagram shows a quadrilateral *ABCD* which has been divided into two right-angled triangles.
BC = 3.6 cm, *BD* = 7.2 cm and angle *BAD* = 59°.

(a) Calculate angle *BDC*.
(b) Calculate the length of *AB*.

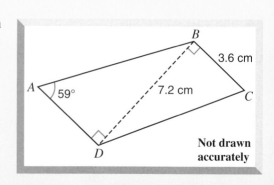

B

3.6 cm

A   59°   7.2 cm   *C*

D

Not drawn accurately

9 In triangle ABC the ratio of $AC : BC$ is $4 : 3$.
Show that $\cos BAC = 0.8$.

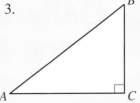

10 $\cos PQR = \frac{12}{13}$

(a) Find (i) $\tan PQR$,
(ii) $\sin PQR$.

(b) $PQ = 6\,\text{cm}$.
What are the lengths of QR and PR?

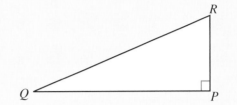

11

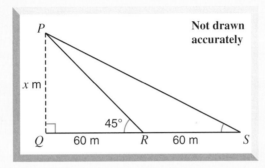

Not drawn accurately

A boat is anchored at point P. Point P is x metres from the beach, QS.
Raja walks along the edge of the beach for $60\,\text{m}$ from point Q to a point R.
Angle QRP is $45°$.
(a) Write down the value of x.

Raja walks for another $60\,\text{m}$ along the beach to the point S. QS is a straight line.
(b) **Calculate** the size of angle QSP.
Give your answer to the nearest degree.

Edexcel

12 A plane flies $120\,\text{km}$ from A to B on a bearing of $048°$.
The plane then changes course and flies $60\,\text{km}$ due south from B to C.
A sketch of its journey is shown.

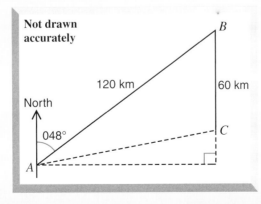

Find the distance of C east and north of A and hence calculate the bearing on which the plane must fly to return to A.

Understanding and Using Measures

Units of measurement

Different units can be used to measure the same quantity. For example:

The same **length** can be measured using centimetres, kilometres, inches, miles, …

The same **mass** can be measured using grams, kilograms, pounds, ounces, …

The same **capacity** can be measured using litres, millilitres, gallons, pints, …

There are two sorts of units in common use − **metric** units and **imperial** units.

Activity

Which of the units mentioned in these statements are metric and which are imperial?

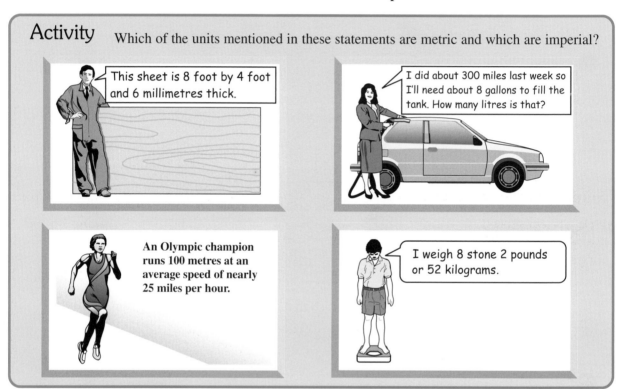

Metric units

The common metric units used to measure length, mass (weight) and capacity (volume) are shown below.

Length	Mass	Capacity and volume
1 kilometre (km) = 1000 metres (m)	1 tonne (t) = 1000 kilograms (kg)	1 litre = 1000 millilitres (ml)
1 m = 100 centimetres (cm)	1 kg = 1000 grams (g)	1 cm³ = 1 ml
1 m = 1000 millimetres (mm)		1 m³ = 1000 litres
1 cm = 10 mm		

Kilo means thousand, 1000.   So, a **kilo**gram is one thousand grams.

For example: 3 kilograms = 3000 grams.

Centi means hundredth, $\frac{1}{100}$.   So, a **centi**metre is one hundredth of a metre.

For example: 2 centimetres = $\frac{2}{100}$ metre.

Milli means thousandth, $\frac{1}{1000}$.   So, a **milli**litre is one thousandth of a litre.

For example: 5 millilitres = $\frac{5}{1000}$ litre.

Changing from one metric unit to another

Changing from one metric unit to another involves multiplying, or dividing, by a power of 10 (10, 100 or 1000). Multiplying and dividing by powers of 10 was covered in Chapter 2.

EXAMPLES

1

| 1 centimetre (cm) = 10 millimetres (mm) |

(a) Change 6.3 cm into millimetres.

To change centimetres into millimetres, multiply by 10.
6.3 × 10 = 63
6.3 cm = 63 mm

(b) Change 364 mm into centimetres.

To change millimetres into centimetres, divide by 10.
364 ÷ 10 = 36.4
364 mm = 36.4 mm

2

| 1 kilogram (kg) = 1000 grams (g) |

(a) Change 19.4 kg into grams.

To change kilograms into grams, multiply by 1000.
19.4 × 1000 = 19 400
19.4 kg = 19 400 g

(b) Change 245 g into kilograms.

To change grams into kilograms, divide by 1000.
245 ÷ 1000 = 0.245
245 g = 0.245 kg

Exercise 33.1   Do not use a calculator.

1 Change each of the following lengths into millimetres.
(a) 8.6 cm   (b) 0.8 cm   (c) 0.08 cm

2 Change each of the following lengths into centimetres.
(a) 90 mm   (b) 210 mm   (c) 2 mm

3 Change each of the following lengths into metres.
(a) 200 cm   (b) 4550 cm   (c) 66 cm

4 Change each of the following lengths into centimetres.
(a) 6 m   (b) 0.9 m   (c) 0.07 m

5 Change each of the following lengths into kilometres.
(a) 4000 m   (b) 35 000 m   (c) 455 m

6 Change each of the following lengths into metres.
(a) 6 km   (b) 650 km   (c) 0.35 km

7 Change each of the following masses into grams.
(a) 2 kg   (b) 7.5 kg   (c) 0.6 kg

8 Change each of the following masses into kilograms.
(a) 3000 g   (b) 32 000 g   (c) 220 g

9 Copy and complete each of the following.
(a) 320 000 ml = ... l
(b) 0.32 t   = ... kg = ... g
(c) 3200 g   = ... kg = ... t
(d) 320 mm   = ... cm = ... m
(e) 32 000 cm = ... m = ... km
(f) 3.2 km   = ... m = ... cm

10 Find the number of kilograms in:
(a) 6 t   (b) 800 g   (c) 0.65 t

11 Find the number of metres in:
(a) 8000 mm   (b) 8.6 cm   (c) 0.04 km

12 Find the number of millilitres in:
(a) 2 l   (b) 0.85 l   (c) 0.03 l

13 Which two lengths are the same?
2000 m   20 km   200 m   2 km   0.02 km

14 Which two weights are the same?
8 g   8 kg   8000 g   0.8 kg   80 kg

15 Which length is the longest?

0.5 km   50 m   5000 mm   500 cm

16 Which weight is the heaviest?

0.3 t   3000 g   3 kg   30 kg

17 (a) How many metres are there in 3123 mm?

(b) How many centimetres are there in 4.5 m?

(c) How many litres are there in 400 ml?

18 A can of coke contains 330 ml.
How many litres of coke are there in 6 cans?

19 One lap of a running track is 400 m.
How many laps are run in an 8 km race?

20 Twenty children at a party share equally 1 kg of fruit pastilles.
How many grams of pastilles does each child receive?

21 To make a dozen biscuits uses 240 g of flour.
James has 1.2 kg of flour.
How many biscuits can he make?

22 Ben takes two 5 ml doses of medicine four times a day.
Ben stops taking the medicine after 5 days.
Originally, there was $\frac{1}{4}$ of a litre of medicine.
How much medicine is left?

Changing units - lengths, areas and volumes

$$1 \text{ m} = 100 \text{ cm}$$
$$1 \text{ m}^2 = 100 \times 100 \text{ cm}^2 = 10\ 000 \text{ cm}^2$$
$$1 \text{ m}^3 = 100 \times 100 \times 100 \text{ cm}^3 = 1\ 000\ 000 \text{ cm}^3$$

How many mm equal 1 cm?

How many mm² equal 1 cm²?

How many mm³ equal 1 cm³?

Estimating with sensible units using suitable degrees of accuracy

It is a useful skill to be able to estimate length, mass and capacity.
These facts might help you.

Length
Most adults are between 1.5 m and 1.8 m tall.
The door to your classroom is about 2 m high.
Find some more facts which will help you to estimate length and distance.

Mass
A biro weighs about 5 g.
A standard bag of sugar weighs 1 kg.
Find some more facts which will help you to estimate weight or mass.

Capacity
A teaspoon holds about 5 ml.
A can of pop holds about 330 ml.
Find some more facts which will help you to estimate volume and capacity.

EXAMPLES

1 The Great Wall of China, the longest man-made structure in the world, is about 2350 km long.
Degree of accuracy: nearest 50 km.

2 Earthquake shock waves travel through rock at a speed of approximately 25 000 km/hour.
Degree of accuracy: nearest 1000 km/hour.

3 The smallest mammal is the Kitti's hog-nosed bat.
It weighs about 1.5 g.
Degree of accuracy: nearest 0.1 g.

4 The current Olympic record for the men's 100 m is 9.92 seconds.
Degree of accuracy: nearest 0.01 seconds.

Exercise **33.2**

1 Which of the following is the best estimate for the mass of a banana?

1 kg   5 g   250 g
30 g   3 kg   750 g

2 Which of the following is the best estimate for the diameter of a football?

2 m   50 mm   30 cm
1.5 m   0.6 m   800 mm

3 Which of the following would be the best estimate for the capacity of a mug?

15 ml   1200 ml   2 *l*
0.5 *l*   200 ml   800 ml

4 Give a sensible estimate using an appropriate unit for the following measures:
(a) the length of a matchstick,
(b) the length of a football pitch,
(c) the weight of a 30 cm ruler,
(d) the weight of a double decker bus.
In each case state the degree of accuracy you have chosen for your estimate.

5 The diagram, which is drawn to scale, shows a man standing next to a tree. Using an appropriate metric unit estimate the height of the tree. State the degree of accuracy that you have used in making your estimate.

6 How much milk is in this jug?

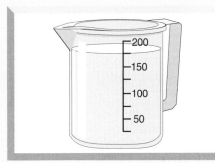

Give your answer in an appropriate unit and state the degree of accuracy you have used.

7 "My teacher's height is about 1.7 mm."
This statement is incorrect.

It can be corrected by changing the unit:
"My teacher's height is about 1.7 m",
or it can be corrected by changing the quantity.
"My teacher's height is about 1700 mm".

Each of these statements is also incorrect.
"Tyrannosaurus, a large meat-eating dinosaur, is estimated to have been about 12 cm long".
"The tallest mammal is the giraffe which grows up to about 5.9 mm tall".
"My car used 5 ml of petrol on a journey of 35 miles".
"The area of the school hall is about 500 mm²".

Correct each statement:
(a) by changing the unit,
(b) by changing the quantity.
For each statement give the degree of accuracy that is used.

Imperial units

The following imperial units of measurement are in everyday use.

Length	**Mass**	**Capacity and volume**
1 foot = 12 inches	1 pound = 16 ounces	1 gallon = 8 pints
1 yard = 3 feet	14 pounds = 1 stone	
1 mile = 1760 yards	2240 pounds = 1 ton	

Metric and imperial conversions

In order to convert to and from metric and imperial units you need to know these facts.

Length	**Mass**	**Capacity and volume**
5 miles is about 8 km	1 kg is about 2.2 pounds	1 litre is about 1.75 pints
1 inch is about 2.5 cm		1 litre is about 0.2 gallons
1 foot is about 30.5 cm		
1 m is about 39 inches		

1 Convert 40 cm to inches.

1 inch is about 2.5 cm.
40 cm is about 40 ÷ 2.5 inches.
40 cm is about 16 inches.

2 How many pints are there in a
4 litre carton of milk?

1 litre is about 1.75 pints.
4 litres is about 4 × 1.75 pints.
4 litres is about 7 pints.

3 Change 5 kg to pounds.

1 kg is about 2.2 pounds.
5 kg is about 5 × 2.2 pounds.
5 kg is about 11 pounds.

4 Tim is 6 feet 2 inches tall.
Estimate Tim's height in centimetres.

6 feet 2 inches = 6 × 12 + 2 = 74 inches.
74 inches is about 74 × 2.5 cm.
6 feet 2 inches is about 185 cm.

5 The capacity of a car's petrol tank is
12 gallons.
How much does the petrol tank hold in litres?

1 litre is about 0.2 gallons.
12 gallons is about 12 ÷ 0.2 litres.
12 gallons is about 60 litres.

6 How far is 32 km in miles?

There are 32 ÷ 8 = 4 lots of 8 km in 32 km.
So there must be 4 lots of 5 miles in 32 km.
4 × 5 = 20.
There are 20 miles in 32 km.

Exercise 33.3

1 Change the following lengths into
centimetres.
(a) 2 inches   (b) 2 feet

2 Change the following lengths into inches.
(a) 2 m   (b) 20 cm

3 Change the following lengths into kilometres.
(a) 5 miles   (b) 45 miles

4 Change the following lengths into miles.
(a) 8 km   (b) 40 km

5 Change the following weights into pounds.
(a) 25 kg   (b) 1 t

6 Change the following masses into kilograms.
Give your answers to the nearest kilogram.
(a) 100 pounds   (b) 6 stones 11 pounds

7 Estimate the number of litres in each of the
following.
(a) 5 pints   (b) 2 gallons 3 pints

8 Convert each quantity to the units given.
(a) 15 kg to pounds.
(b) 20 litres to pints.
(c) 5 metres to inches.
(d) 6 inches to millimetres.
(e) 50 cm to inches.

9 A box contains 200 balls.
Each ball weighs 50 g.
Estimate the total weight of the balls in
pounds.

10 James is 5 feet 8 inches tall.
Estimate James' height in centimetres.

11 James weighs 10 stones 6 pounds.
Estimate James' weight in kilograms.

12 Estimate:
(a) the number of metres in 2000 feet,
(b) the number of kilometres in
3 miles,
(c) the number of feet in
150 centimetres,
(d) the number of pounds in
1250 grams.

13 A sheet of card measures 12 inches by
20 inches.
What is the area of the card in
square centimetres?

14 Lauren says 10 kg of potatoes weighs
the same as 20 lb of sugar.
Is she correct?
Show all your working.

15 Alfie cycles 6 miles.
Jacob cycles 10 kilometres.
Alfie claims that he has cycled further than Jacob. Is he correct?
Show all your working.

16 Convert the following speeds to kilometres per hour.
(a) 30 miles per hour.
(b) 50 miles per hour.
(c) 30 metres per second.

17 Convert the following speeds to miles per hour.
(a) 60 km per hour.
(b) 40 metres per second.

18 Convert a speed of 60 miles per hour to metres per second.
Give your answer to a suitable degree of accuracy.

19 (a) A car does 40 miles to the gallon.
How many kilometres does it do per litre?
(b) A car does 9.6 kilometres to the litre.
How many miles does it do per gallon?

20 30 g of grass seed is needed to sow 1 m² of lawn.
What weight of grass seed is needed to sow a rectangular lawn measuring 40 foot by 30 foot?

21 Concrete is sold by the cubic metre.
A path, 31 feet long, 5 feet wide and 1 foot 6 inches deep, is to be made of concrete.
How many cubic metres of concrete are needed?

Discrete and continuous measures

Discrete measures

Discrete measures can only take particular values.

For example: The number of people on a bus is 42.
Two ice skating judges give scores of 5.1 and 5.2.

The number of people on a bus must be a whole number.
The ice skating scores show that a discrete measure does not need to be a whole number.
They are discrete because scores are not given between numbers like 5.1 and 5.2.

Continuous measures

James was 14 on the day of his 14th birthday.
He will still be called 14 years old right up to the day before his 15th birthday.
So, although James is 14, his actual age is any age within a range of 1 year.

Jenny is **not** exactly 14 years and 3 months old.
However, Jenny's age is given to a greater degree of accuracy than James' age because the range of possible ages in her case is smaller.
What is the range of possible ages in Jenny's measurement of her age?

Measures which can lie within a range of possible values are called **continuous measures**.
The value of a continuous measure depends on the accuracy of whatever is making the measurement.

1 Jane is 160 cm tall to the nearest 10 cm. What are the limits between which her true height lies?

When rounding to the nearest 10:
The smallest value that rounds to 160 is 155.
155 cm is the smallest height that Jane can be.
The largest value that rounds to 160 is $164.\dot{9}$.
$164.\dot{9}$ cm is the largest height that Jane can be.
For ease the value $164.\dot{9}$ is normally called 165 (even though 165 rounds to 170).

So Jane's actual height is any height from 155 cm to 165 cm.
This can be written as the inequality:
155 cm ≤ Jane's height < 165 cm

2 Jane is 162 cm tall to the nearest 1 cm. What are the limits between which her true height lies?

When rounding to the nearest 1:
The smallest value that rounds to 162 is 161.5.
161.5 cm is the smallest height that Jane can be.
The largest value that rounds to 162 is $162.4\dot{9}$.
$162.4\dot{9}$ cm is the largest height that Jane can be.
For ease the value $162.4\dot{9}$ is normally called 162.5 (even though 162.5 rounds to 163).

So Jane's actual height is any height from 161.5 cm to 162.5 cm.
This can be written as the inequality:
161.5 cm ≤ Jane's height < 162.5 cm

Exercise 33.4

1 State whether each of the following are discrete or continuous measures.
 (a) The volume of wine in a wine glass.
 (b) The votes cast for the Independent Party candidate in a local election.
 (c) The number of pages in a newspaper.
 (d) The time it takes to walk to school.
 (e) The number of beds in a hospital.
 (f) The weight of your best friend.

2 For each of the following measures state whether the value given is an exact value or give the limits within which it could lie.
 (a) A book has 224 pages.
 (b) A bus was 5 minutes late.
 (c) Tom has two brothers.
 (d) I weigh 63 kg.
 (e) Judy is 153 cm tall.

3 What are the slowest and fastest possible times:
 (a) of Derek who runs exactly 100 metres in 13 seconds measured to the nearest second,
 (b) of Jan who swims exactly 100 metres in 82.6 seconds measured to the nearest tenth of a second?

4 Tina is 1.53 m tall.
 (a) To what degree of accuracy is Tina's height given?
 (b) What are the limits between which her true height lies?

5 (a) What is the minimum weight of a 62 kg parcel measured to the nearest kilogram?
 (b) What is the minimum length of a 2.3 m shelf measured to the nearest 0.1 m?
 (c) What is the minimum time for a race timed at 12.63 seconds measured to the nearest one hundredth of a second?

6 What degree of accuracy has been used to make these estimates of the length of a corridor:
 (a) About 120 m.
  The smallest possible length is 115 m.
 (b) About 100 m.
  The smallest possible length is 75 m.
 (c) About 200 m.
  The smallest possible length is 150 m.

Dimensions and formulae

Formulae can be used to calculate perimeters, areas and volumes of various shapes.
By analysing the **dimensions** involved it is possible to decide whether a given formula represents a perimeter, an area or a volume.

Length (L) has **dimension 1**.
Length (L) $\times$ Length (L) = **Area** (L^2) has **dimension 2**.
Length (L) $\times$ Length (L) $\times$ Length (L) = **Volume** (L^3) has **dimension 3**.

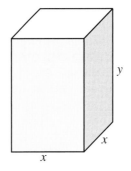

The size of this square based cuboid depends on:
    x, the length of the side of the square base,
    y, the height of the cuboid.

The total **length** of the edges of the cuboid is given by the formula:
    $E = 8x + 4y$
This formula involves:
Numbers: 8 and 4
Lengths (L): x and y
The formula has **dimension 1**.

The total **surface area** of the cuboid is given by the formula:
    $S = 2x^2 + 4xy$
This formula involves:
Numbers: 2 and 4
Areas (L^2): $x \times x$ and $x \times y$
The formula has **dimension 2**.

The **volume** of the cuboid is given by the formula:
    $V = x^2y$
This formula involves:
Volume (L^3): $x \times x \times y$
This formula has **dimension 3**.

EXAMPLE

In each of these expressions the letters a, b and c represent lengths.
Use dimensions to check whether the expressions could represent a perimeter, an area or a volume.
(a) $2a + 3b + 4c$ (b) $3a^2 + 2b(a + c)$
(c) $2a^2b + abc$ (d) $3a + 2ab + c^3$

(a) $2a + 3b + 4c$
     Write this using dimensions.
     $L + L + L \equiv 3L \equiv L$
     $2a + 3b + 4c$ has dimension 1 and could represent a perimeter.

(b) $3a^2 + 2b(a + c)$
     Write this using dimensions.
     $L^2 + L(L + L)$
     $\equiv$ $L^2 + L(2L)$
     $\equiv$ $L^2 + 2L^2$
     $\equiv$ $3L^2$
     $\equiv$ L^2
     $3a^2 + 2b(a + c)$ has dimension 2 and could represent an area.

Note
When checking formulae and expressions, numbers can be ignored because they have no dimension.
$\equiv$ means 'is equivalent to'.

(c) $2a^2b + abc$
     Write this using dimensions.
     $L^2 \times L + L \times L \times L$
     $\equiv$ $L^3 + L^3$
     $\equiv$ $2L^3$
     $\equiv$ L^3
     $2a^2b + abc$ has dimension 3 and could represent a volume.

(d) $3a + 2ab + c^3$
     Write this using dimensions.
     $L + L \times L + L^3$
     $\equiv$ $L + L^2 + L^3$
     The dimensions are **inconsistent**.
     $3a + 2ab + c^3$ does not represent a perimeter, an area or a volume.

Understanding and Using Measures

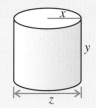

1 p, q, r and x, y, z represent lengths.
For each formula state whether it represents
a length, an area or a volume.

(a) pq (b) $2\pi x$ (c) $p + q + r$ (d) πz

(e) pqr (f) $2(pq + qr + pr)$ (g) $\pi x^2 y$ (h) $2\pi x(x + y)$

2 In each of the expressions below, x, y and z represent lengths.
By using dimensions decide whether each expression could represent a perimeter, an area, a
volume or none of these.
Explain your answer in each case.

(a) $x + y + z$ (b) $xy + xz$ (c) xyz (d) $x^2(y^2 + z^2)$

(e) $x(y + z)$ (f) $\dfrac{x^2}{y}$ (g) $\dfrac{xz}{y}$ (h) $x + y^2 + z^3$

(i) $xy(y + z)$ (j) $x^3 + x^2(y + z)$ (k) $xy(y^2 + z)$ (l) $x(y + z) + z^2$

3 The diagram shows a discus.
x and y are the lengths shown on the diagram.
These expressions could represent certain quantities
relating to the discus.

$\pi(x^2 + y^2)$ $\pi x^2 y^2$ πxy $2\pi(x + y)$

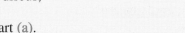

(a) Which of them could be an expression for:
   (i) the longest possible distance around the discus,
   (ii) the surface area of the discus.

(b) Use dimensions to explain your answers to part (a).

4 x, y and z represent lengths.

(a) $A = xyz + z(x - y) + 2y$
This is not a formula for perimeter, area
or volume.
Use dimensions to explain why.

(b) $P = 3z(x + y)$
This could be a formula for area.
Use dimensions to explain why.

(c) $V = x^2 y + z^2(2x - y) + 2y^3$
This could be a formula for volume.
Use dimensions to explain why.

5 p, q, r and s represent the lengths of the
edges of this triangular prism.

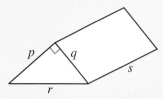

Match the formulas to the measurements.

Formulas

$\frac{1}{2} pqs$ $2\left(p + q + r + \frac{3s}{2}\right)$ $s(p + q + r) + pq$

Measurements

Edge length   Surface area   Volume

6 These arrows are similar.

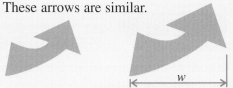

w represents the width of any arrow.
k and c are numbers.
H represents the height of the arrow and
A its area.
Which of the following statements could
be correct and which **must** be wrong.

(a) $H = kw$ (b) $H = ckw$

(c) $H = kw + c$ (d) $A = cw$

(e) $A = kw^2$ (f) $A = kw^3$

Give a reason for each of your answers
and where you think the formula **must**
be wrong suggest what it might be for.

7 In these formulae a, b and c represent
lengths and A represents an area.

(a) $a = b + c$ (b) $a^2 = bc$

(c) $A = a^2 + bc$ (d) $c = A + ab$

(e) $Ab = a^3$ (f) $A = \dfrac{a^2}{c} + b^2$

Which of the formulae have consistent
dimensions?

What you need to know

- The common units – both **metric** and **imperial** – used to measure **length**, **mass** and **capacity**.
- How to convert from one unit to another. This includes knowing the connection between one metric unit and another and the approximate equivalents between metric and imperial units.

Metric Units	Imperial Units	Conversions
Length	**Length**	**Length**
1 kilometre (km) = 1000 metres (m)	1 foot = 12 inches	5 miles is about 8 km
1 m = 100 centimetres (cm)	1 yard = 3 feet	1 inch is about 2.5 cm
1 m = 1000 millimetres (mm)	1 mile = 1760 yards	1 foot is about 30.5 cm
1 cm = 10 mm		1 m is about 39 inches
Mass	**Mass**	**Mass**
1 tonne (t) = 1000 kilograms (kg)	1 pound = 16 ounces	1 kg is about 2.2 pounds
1 kg = 1000 grams (g)	14 pounds = 1 stone	
	2240 pounds = 1 ton	**Capacity and volume**
Capacity and volume		1 litre is about 1.75 pints
1 litre = 1000 millilitres (ml)	**Capacity and volume**	1 litre is about 0.2 gallons
1 cm³ = 1 ml	1 gallon = 8 pints	
1 m³ = 1000 litres		

- How to change between units of area. For example $1 \text{ m}^2 = 10\,000 \text{ cm}^2$.
- How to change between units of volume. For example $1 \text{ m}^3 = 1\,000\,000 \text{ cm}^3$.
- How to estimate measurements using sensible units and a suitable degree of accuracy.
- A **discrete measure** can only take a particular value and a **continuous measure** lies within a range of possible values which depends upon the degree of accuracy of the measurement.
- By analysing the **dimensions** of a formula it is possible to decide whether a given formula represents a **length** (dimension 1), an **area** (dimension 2) or a **volume** (dimension 3).

 IDEAS FOR INVESTIGATION

Shoe size is a discrete measure. Foot size is a continuous measure.
Investigate the connection between foot size and shoe size.

Review Exercise

1 How many magazines, each 0.6 cm thick, will fit on a bookcase shelf which is exactly 1.2 m wide?

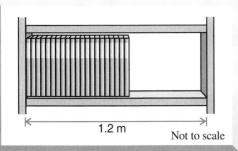

1.2 m

Not to scale

2 One glass of lemonade contains 300 ml. How many glasses of lemonade can be poured from a jug which contains 2.4 litres?

3 (a) How many metres are there in 2.65 kilometres?
(b) The distance from Calais to Paris is 280 km. What is this distance in miles?

4 Tim is 5 feet 10 inches tall and weighs 72 kg. Sam is 165 cm tall and weighs 11 stone 7 pounds. Who is taller? Who is heavier?

5 (a) Which is longer: 10 000 metres
or 6 miles?

(b) Which is shorter: $\frac{3}{8}$ of an inch
or 10 mm?

(c) Which is more: 2 gallons of milk
or 10 litres of milk?

(d) Which is less: 200 lb of coal
or 100 kg of coal?

Show working for each of your answers.

6 Percy buys 7 lb of potatoes at 35 pence
per kilogram.
Calculate the cost of the potatoes to an
appropriate degree of accuracy.

7 Convert an area of 25 m² to:

(a) cm², (b) square feet.

8 What is 48 kilometres per hour in

(a) miles per hour,

(b) metres per second?

9 James runs at an average speed of
12 miles/hour. Tim runs at an average
speed of 320 m/minute.
Who runs faster?

10 According to the instructions Vinyl
Matt paint covers about 13 m²/litre.

(a) Estimate the area covered with
2 gallons of paint?

(b) Estimate how many litres of paint
is needed to cover a wall which
measures 18 feet by 10 feet.

11 The total surface area of the Earth's
oceans is 362 million square kilometres.
To what degree of accuracy is this
measurement given?

12 Which of these measurements is
discrete and which is continuous?

(a) Two pints of milk.

(b) Two 1 pint bottles of milk.

Explain your answer.

13 Karen has a pencil that has a length of
10 centimetres, correct to the nearest
centimetre. Write down

(a) the minimum length the pencil
could be,

(b) the maximum length the pencil
could be. *Edexcel*

14 A blue whale weighs 140 tonnes to the
nearest 10 tonnes.
What is the smallest possible weight of
a blue whale?

15 When measured to the nearest 100 ml the
volume of a container was found to be 600 ml.
When measured to the nearest 10 ml the
volume of the same container was found to be
650 ml.
Give an example of a volume that agrees with
both of these measurements.

16 One of these formulae gives the total surface
area of the hexagonal prism.

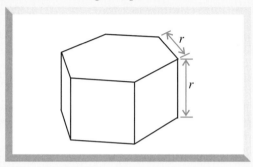

$11.2r^3$ $11.2r^2$ $11.2r$

(a) Which is the correct formula?

(b) Explain your answer.

17 The expressions shown in the table can be used
to calculate lengths, areas and volumes of
various shapes.

π, 2, 4 and $\frac{1}{2}$ are numbers which have no
dimensions.
The letters r, l, b and h represent lengths.
Copy the table and put a tick in the box
underneath those expressions that can be used
to calculate a volume.

$2\pi r$	$4\pi r^2$	$\pi r^2 h$	πr^2	lbh	$\frac{1}{2} bh$

Edexcel

18

A	**B**	**C**	**D**
$p^3 + 3q^2$	$p^2 + 2q$	$2p + 3q$	$3p^2 + 3pq$

The boxes **A**, **B**, **C** and **D** show 4 expressions.
The letters p and q represent lengths.
2 and 3 are numbers which have no dimensions.

(a) Write **one** of the letters **A**, **B**, **C** or **D** for
the expression which represents

(i) an area, (ii) a length.

The box **X** shows an expression.
The letters p and q represent
lengths.
n is a number.

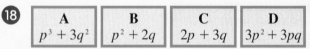

X
$p^n(p + q)$

The expression represents a volume.

(b) Find the value of n. *Edexcel*

1 Find the size of the angles *a*, *b* and *c*.

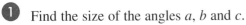

2

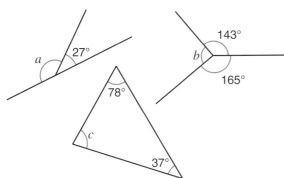

This pattern is from the tiled floor of the Taj Mahal in India.
The pattern is made from these 2 shapes.

    A   **B**

(a) (i) Write down the order of rotational symmetry of shape **A**.

     (ii) Write down the number of lines of symmetry of shape **B**.

(b) Show how shape **B** will tessellate. You should draw at least 5 shapes. Edexcel

3

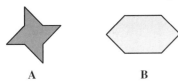

This signpost is on the road from Paris to Dijon. Work out the approximate distance, in miles, from the signpost to Paris. Edexcel

4 This 3-dimensional shape has been made using linking cubes of side 1 cm. On squared paper, draw diagrams to show the plan and the elevation from **X**.

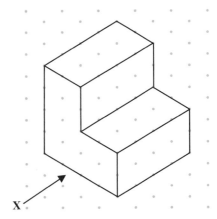

5 The diagram shows a parallelogram and a rectangle.
Both shapes have the same area.
Calculate the length of the rectangle.

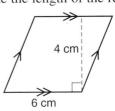

6 By drawing at least six shapes show how this shape can be used to make a tessellation.

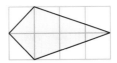

7 A triangle has sides of length 7 cm, 5 cm and 4 cm.

(a) Make an accurate drawing of the triangle.

(b) Work out the area of the triangle.

371

8 The diagram shows triangles **P**, **Q** and **R**.

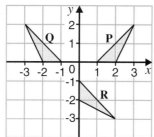

(a) Describe the single transformation which takes **P** onto **Q**.

(b) Describe the single transformation which takes **P** onto **R**.

Copy triangle **P** onto squared paper.

(c) Draw an enlargement of triangle **P** with scale factor 2, centre (0, 0).

9 (a) Which of these shapes are similar to each other?

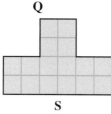

P   **Q**

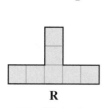

R   **S**

(b) This shape is enlarged with scale factor 2.

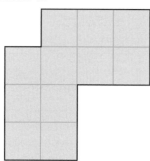

(i) What is the perimeter of the enlarged shape?

(ii) What is the area of the enlarged shape?

10 (a) Adrian is 6 feet 3 inches tall. Calculate Adrian's height in centimetres.

(b) Adrian weighs 78 kg, correct to the nearest kilogram. What are the limits between which his true weight must lie?

11 (a) The diagram shows a pair of parallel lines. The lines marked with the arrows are parallel. Work out the size of the angles marked $e°$, $f°$ and $g°$.

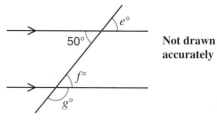

Not drawn accurately

(b) Work out the size of the angle marked $h°$.

Not drawn accurately

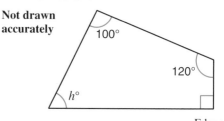

Edexcel

12 A table top is a circle of radius 50 cm.

(a) Calculate the circumference of the table top.

(b) Calculate the area of the table top.

13 The diagram represents the positions of Wigan and Manchester.

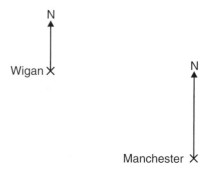

(a) Measure and write down the bearing of Manchester from Wigan.

(b) Find the bearing of Wigan from Manchester.

Edexcel

14 Y is 50 m from X on a bearing of 080°. Z is 70 m from Y on a bearing of 110°.

(a) Make a scale drawing to show the positions of X, Y and Z. Use a scale of 1 cm to 10 m.

(b) Find by measurement the distance and bearing of X from Z.

15 Copy the diagram.

Enlarge the trapezium *PQRS* using a scale factor of $\frac{1}{2}$.

Use the point *O* as the centre of enlargement.

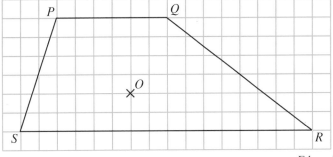

Edexcel

16 The diagram shows a tin of treacle.
The tin is a cylinder.
The radius of the base is 4 cm.
The height is 7.5 cm.

(a) Calculate the volume of treacle in the tin when it is full.

(b) Kath uses 75 cm³ of treacle to make a tart.
Calculate the depth of the treacle left in the tin.

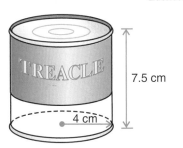

17

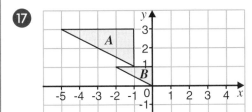

(a) Describe fully the single transformation which maps *A* onto *B*.

(b) *B* is mapped onto *C* by a translation with vector $\begin{pmatrix} 3 \\ -2 \end{pmatrix}$.

Draw a diagram to show the positions of *B* and *C*.

18 The diagram shows part of a garden path.
Each shape in the path is a regular polygon.
Work out the size of each lettered angle.

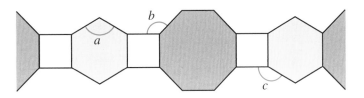

19 Two straight roads are shown on the diagram.
A new gas pipe is to be laid from Bere equidistant from the two roads.
The diagram is drawn to a scale of 1 cm to 1 km.

(a) Copy the diagram and construct the path of the gas pipe.

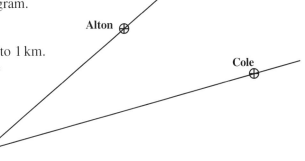

(b) The gas board needs a construction site depot.
The depot must be equidistant from Bere and Cole.
The depot must be less than 2 km from Alton.
Draw loci on the diagram to represent this information.

(c) The depot must be nearer the road through Cole than the road through Alton.
Mark on your diagram, with a cross, a possible position for the site depot which satisfies all these conditions.

20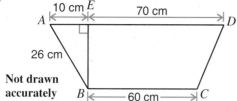

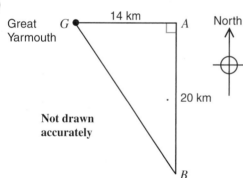

In triangle *ABE*, *AB* = 26 cm,
AE = 10 cm and angle *AEB* = 90°.
(a) Calculate the length of *BE*.
(b) Calculate the area of the trapezium
ABCD.

ABCD is the cross section of a trough
used in a village competition.
The trough is a prism of length 200 cm.
(c) Calculate the volume of the trough.

Edexcel

21

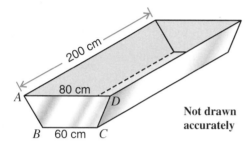

The diagram represents Nelson's voyage
from Great Yarmouth to position *B*.
Nelson's boat sails due East from Great
Yarmouth for 14 km to a position *A*.
The boat then changes course and sails
for 20 km to a position *B*.
On a map, the distance between *G* and *A*
is 56 cm.

(a) Work out the scale of the map.
Give your answer in the form 1 : *n*,
where *n* is an integer.
(b) Calculate the distance, in km, of *B*
from Great Yarmouth.
(c) Calculate the bearing of
Great Yarmouth from *B*. Edexcel

22 *O* is the centre of the circle.
XP and *XQ*
are tangents
to the circle at
P and *Q*.

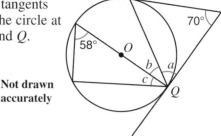

Find the size of the angles marked *a*, *b* and *c*.
Give a reason for each of your answers.

23 The diagram shows a right-angled triangle.
Sin $y = \frac{4}{5}$

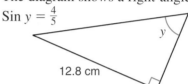

Calculate the area of the triangle.
Give your answer to a suitable degree of
accuracy.

24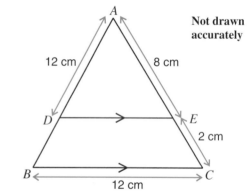

DE is parallel to *BC*.
ADB and *AEC* are straight lines.
AD = 12 cm.   *BC* = 12 cm.
AE = 8 cm.   *EC* = 2 cm.
Calculate the length of
(a) *DE*,   (b) *DB*. Edexcel

25 A hemisphere of radius
r cm fits exactly on top
of a cylinder of height
h cm to form the solid
shown opposite.
Tony worked out a
formula for the volume,
V cm³, of the solid.

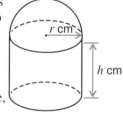

His formula was $V = \frac{2}{3} \pi r^2 + \pi r h$.
Explain why Tony's formula cannot be
correct. Edexcel

CHAPTER 34

Collection and Organisation of Data

To answer questions such as:

Which is the most popular colour of car?

Is it going to rain tomorrow?

Which team won the World Cup in 1998?

we need to collect data.

Primary and secondary data

When data is collected by an individual or organisation to use for a particular purpose it is called **primary data**.

Primary data is obtained from experiments, investigations, surveys and by using questionnaires.

Data which is already available or has been collected by someone else for a different purpose is called **secondary data**.

Sources of secondary data include the Annual Abstract of Statistics, Social Trends and the Internet.

Data

Data is made up of a collection of **variables**.
Each variable can be described, numbered or measured.

Data which can only be **described** in words is **qualitative**. Such data is often organised into categories, such as make of car, colour of hair, etc.

Data which is given **numerical** values, such as shoe size or height, is **quantitative**.
Quantitative data is either **discrete** or **continuous**.

> **Discrete** data can only take certain values, usually whole numbers, but may include fractions (e.g. shoe sizes).

> **Continuous** data can take any value within a range and is measurable (e.g. height, weight, temperature, etc.).

EXAMPLES

The taste of an orange is a qualitative variable.

The number of pips in an orange is a discrete quantitative variable.

The surface area of an orange is a continuous quantitative variable.

Exercise 34.1

State whether the following data is qualitative or quantitative.
If the data is quantitative state whether it is discrete or continuous.

1 The colours of cars in a car park.

2 The weights of eggs in a carton.

3 The numbers of desks in classrooms.

4 The names of students in a class.

5 The sizes of spanners in a toolbox.

6 The depths that fish swim in the sea.

7 The numbers of goals scored by football teams on a Saturday.

8 The brands of toothpaste on sale in supermarkets.

9 The sizes of ladies dresses in a store.

10 The heights of trees in a wood.

Collection of data

Data can be collected in a variety of ways; by observation, by interviewing people and by using questionnaires. The method of collection will often depend on the type of data to be collected.

Data collection sheets

Data collection sheets are used to record data.

To answer the question, "Which is the most popular colour of car?", we could draw up a simple data collection sheet and record the colours of passing cars by observation.

EXAMPLE

A **data collection sheet** for colour of car is shown, with some cars recorded.

Colour of car	Tally	Frequency
Black	‖	2
Blue	卌 卌 ‖‖	13
Green	‖‖‖	4
Red	卌 卌 ‖	
Silver	卌 ‖	
White	卌 卌 ‖‖‖	
	Total	

The colour of each car is recorded in the **tally** column by a single stroke.

To make counting easier, groups of 5 are recorded as 卌.

How many red cars are recorded?
How many cars are recorded altogether?

The total number of times each colour appears is called its **frequency**.
A table for data with the totals included is called a **frequency distribution**.

For large amounts of discrete data, or for continuous data, we organise the data into **groups** or **classes**. When data is collected in groups it is called a **grouped frequency distribution** and the groups you put the data into are called **class intervals**.

EXAMPLE

The weights of 20 boys are recorded in the grouped frequency table shown below.

Weight w kg	Tally	Frequency
$50 \leqslant w < 55$	‖	1
$55 \leqslant w < 60$	‖‖	3
$60 \leqslant w < 65$	卌 ‖‖‖	9
$65 \leqslant w < 70$	卌 ‖	6
$70 \leqslant w < 75$	‖	1
	Total	20

Weights are grouped into class intervals of equal width.

$55 \leqslant w < 60$ means 55 kg, or more, but less than 60 kg.

John weighs 54.9 kg. *In which class interval is he recorded?*
David weighs 55.0 kg. *In which class interval is he recorded?*

What is the width of each class interval?

376

1 The colours of 40 cars in a car park are shown.

red	red	blue	green	white	grey
blue	red	red	grey	white	green
red	white	white	blue	red	white
blue	blue	green	black	white	blue
red	silver	silver	blue	red	red
silver	white	white	red	blue	green
red	blue	silver	white		

(a) Make a frequency table for the data.
(b) Which colour of car is most popular?

2 The days of the week on which some students were born are recorded.

Monday	Monday	Sunday	Wednesday	Thursday
Friday	Saturday	Tuesday	Monday	Friday
Thursday	Sunday	Monday	Friday	Tuesday
Thursday	Wednesday	Tuesday	Monday	Wednesday
Friday	Monday	Saturday	Friday	Thursday
Tuesday	Thursday	Monday	Sunday	Tuesday
Saturday	Wednesday	Friday	Thursday	Tuesday
Monday	Wednesday	Friday	Sunday	Thursday
Tuesday	Wednesday	Sunday		

(a) Make a frequency table for the data.
(b) How many students are included?
(c) On which day of the week did most births occur?

3 The ages of 40 people are shown below.

27	34	54	57	3	12
15	19	29	30	33	47
35	20	39	28	9	11
26	42	50	26	10	7
33	49	21	18	1	25
24	34	19	20	27	37
43	56	37	34		

(a) Copy and complete the grouped frequency table for the data given.

Age	Tally	Frequency
0 - 9		
10 - 19		
20 - 29		

(b) What is the width of each class interval?
(c) How many people are in the class interval 30–39?
(d) How many people are less than 20 years old?
(e) How many people are 40 or older?

Collection and Organisation of Data

4 The heights, in centimetres, of 36 girls are recorded as follows.

148	161	175	156	155	160	178	159	170
163	147	150	173	169	170	174	166	163
162	158	155	165	168	154	156	163	167
172	170	165	160	164	172	157	173	161

(a) Copy and complete the grouped frequency table for the data.

Height h cm	Tally	Frequency
$145 \leqslant h < 150$		
$150 \leqslant h < 155$		

(b) What is the width of each class interval?
(c) How many girls are in the class interval $155 \leqslant h < 160$?
(d) How many girls are less than 160 cm?
(e) How many girls are 155 cm or taller?

5 Draw up a data collection sheet to record the month in which people were born. Collect data from 50 people.
(a) Make a frequency table for the data.
(b) In which month did most births occur?

Databases

If we need to collect data for more than one type of information, for example; the make, colour, registration letter and mileage of cars; we will need to collect data in a different way.

We could create a **data collection card** for each car.

Car	1
Make	Vauxhall
Colour	Grey
Registration letter	T
Mileage	18 604

Alternatively, we could use a data collection sheet and record all the information about each car on a separate line.

This is an example of a simple **database**.

Car	Make	Colour	Registration letter	Mileage
1	Vauxhall	Grey	T	18 604
2	Ford	Blue	R	33 216
3	Ford	White	S	27 435
4	Nissan	Red	P	32 006

When all the data has been collected, separate frequency or grouped frequency tables can be drawn up.

Exercise 34.3

1 The database gives information about the babies born at a maternity hospital one day.

Baby's name	Time of birth	Weight (kg)	Length (cm)
Alistair	0348	3.2	44
Francis	0819	3.5	48
Louisa	1401	3.7	47

(a) Which baby is the longest?
(b) Which baby is the heaviest?
(c) Which baby was born first?

2 A database of cars is shown.

Car	Make	Colour	Registration letter	Mileage
1	Vauxhall	Grey	T	18 604
2	Ford	Blue	R	33 216
3	Ford	White	S	27 435
4	Nissan	Red	P	32 006
5	Vauxhall	Blue	R	31 598
6	Ford	Green	P	37 685
7	Vauxhall	Red	T	21 640
8	Nissan	White	R	28 763
9	Ford	White	S	30 498
10	Vauxhall	White	T	9 865
11	Nissan	Red	X	7 520
12	Vauxhall	Grey	T	16 482

(a) (i) Draw up separate frequency tables for make, colour and registration letter.
    (ii) Draw up a grouped frequency table for mileage.
       Use class intervals of 5000 miles, starting at $0 \leqslant m < 5000$, $5000 \leqslant m < 10\,000, \ldots$
(b) (i) Which make of car is the most popular?
    (ii) How many Ford cars are white?
    (iii) How many cars have a mileage of 30 000 or more?
    (iv) How many cars have a T registration letter?

3 Use data collection cards to collect information about students in your class.
Include gender, height, shoe size and pulse rate.
(a) What is the smallest shoe size for students in your class?
(b) What is the gender of the student with the highest pulse rate?
(c) What is the difference between the highest pulse rate and the lowest pulse rate?
(d) What is the height of the tallest student?
(e) What differences are there in the data collected for male and female students?

4 (a) Design a data collection card to collect information on the leisure time activities of students.
(b) Draw up frequency or grouped frequency tables for the data.
(c) Which leisure time activity is the most popular?
(d) What differences are there in the leisure time activities of male and female students?

Collection and Organisation of Data

Questionnaires are frequently used to collect data. In business they are used to get information about products or services and in politics they are frequently used to test opinion on a range of issues and personalities.

When constructing questions for a questionnaire you should:

(1) use simple language, so that everyone can understand the question;

(2) ask short questions which can be answered precisely, with a "yes" or "no" answer, a number, or a response from a choice of answers;

(3) provide tick boxes, so that questions can be answered easily;

(4) avoid open-ended questions, like: "What do you think of education?" which might produce long rambling answers which would be difficult to collate or process;

(5) avoid leading questions, like: "Don't you agree that there is too much bad language on television?" and ask instead:
"Do you think that there is too much bad language on television?"

Yes ☐   No ☐

(6) ask questions in a logical order.

Multiple-response questions

In many instances a choice of responses should be provided.

Instead of asking "How old are you?" which does not indicate the degree of accuracy required and many people might consider personal, we could ask instead:

Which is your age group?

under 18 ☐
18 to 40 ☐
41 to 65 ☐
over 65 ☐

Notice there are no gaps and only **one** response applies to each person.

Sometimes we invite **multiple responses** by asking questions, such as:

Which soaps do you watch?

Coronation Street ☐
EastEnders ☐
Emmerdale ☐
Brookside ☐
Hollyoaks ☐

Tick as many as you wish.

Exercise 34.4

1 Susan wants to find out what people think about the Health Service.
Part of the questionnaire she has written is shown.

> Q4. What is your date of birth?
>
> Q5. Don't you agree that waiting lists for operations are too long?
>
> Q6. How many times did you visit your doctor last year?
>
> ☐ less than 5   ☐ 5 - 10   ☐ 10 or more

(a) Why should Q4 not be asked?
(b) Give a reason why Q5 is unsuitable.
(c) (i)   Explain why Q6 is unsuitable in its present form.
     (ii) Rewrite the question so that it could be included in the questionnaire.

2 In preparing the questions for a questionnaire on radio listening habits the following questions were rejected.
(a) When do you listen to the radio?
(b) What do you like about radio programmes?
(c) Don't you agree that the radio gives the best news reports.
Explain why each question is unsuitable and rewrite the question so that it could be included in the questionnaire.

3 In preparing questions for a survey on the use of a library the following questions were considered. Explain why each question in its present form is unsuitable and rewrite the question.
  (a) How old are you?
  (b) How many times have you used the library?
  (c) Which books do you read?
  (d) How could the library be improved?

4 A mobile phone company wants to carry out a survey. It wants to find out the distribution of the age and sex of customers and the frequency with which they use the phone.
  The company intends to use a questionnaire.
  Write three questions and responses that will enable the company to carry out the survey.

5 A school is to conduct a homework survey. Suggest five questions which could be included.

6 A survey of reading habits is to be conducted. Suggest five questions which could be included.

7 A survey of eating habits is to be conducted. Suggest five questions which could be included.

Hypothesis

A **hypothesis** is a statement that may or may not be true.
To test a hypothesis we can construct a questionnaire, carry out a survey and analyse the results.

EXAMPLE

A questionnaire to test the hypothesis, "People think it is better to give than to receive" could include questions like these.

1. **Gender:** male ☐   female ☐

2. **Age:** 11 - 16 ☐   17 - 21 ☐   22 - 59 ☐   60 & over ☐

3. **Do you think it is better to give than to receive?**
   Yes ☐   No ☐

4. **To which of the following have you given in the last year?**
   School ☐   Charities ☐   Church ☐
   Hospital ☐   Special appeals ☐   Homeless ☐

   Other (please list) _____

Suggest another question which could be included.

Sampling

When information is required about a small group of people it is possible to survey everyone.
When information is required about a large group of people it is not always possible to survey everyone and only a **sample** may be asked. The sample chosen should be large enough to make the results meaningful and representative of the whole group or the results may be **biased**.
For example, to test the hypothesis, "Girls are more intelligent than boys", you would need to ask equal numbers of boys and girls from various age groups.
The results of a survey may also be biased if there is any form of deliberate selection or if the sample is incomplete.

Two-way tables

We have already seen that the results of a survey can be recorded on data collection sheets and then collated using frequency or grouped frequency tables. We can also illustrate data using **two-way tables**.

A two-way table is used to illustrate the data for two different features (variables) in a survey.

EXAMPLE   The following two-way table shows the results of a survey.

(a)   How many boys wear glasses?
(b)   How many children wear glasses?
(c)   How many children were surveyed?

	Wear Glasses	
	Yes	No
Boys	4	14
Girls	3	9

(a)   4   (b)   7   (c)   30

Do the results of the survey prove or disprove the hypothesis, "More boys wear glasses than girls"? Explain your answer.

Exercise 34.5

1   George is investigating the cost of return journeys by train.
He plans to ask ten passengers who are waiting at a station at midday the cost of their return journeys.
Give two reasons why he might get biased results.

2   Judy is investigating shopping habits.
She plans to interview 50 women at her local supermarket on a Tuesday morning.
Give three reasons why she might get biased results.

3   State one advantage and one disadvantage of a postal survey.

4   Design a questionnaire to test the hypothesis:
"Children watch more television than adults".
Consider:
(a)   does gender affect people's opinions?
(b)   do people's opinions change with age?

5   Design a questionnaire to test the hypothesis:
"People think that everyone should take part in sport".
Describe the sample you could use to test this hypothesis.

6   Design a questionnaire to test the hypothesis:
"People think that animals should not be used to test drugs".
Describe the sample you could use to test this hypothesis.

7   Design a questionnaire to test the hypothesis:
"Children have too much homework".
Describe the sample you could use to test this hypothesis.

8   The two-way table shows information about the ages of people in a retirement home.

	Age				
	60 - 64	65 - 69	70 - 74	75 - 79	80 and over
Men	0	2	5	8	1
Women	2	5	6	5	6

(a)   How many men are aged 75 - 79?
(b)   How many men are included?
(c)   How many people are aged 75 or more?
(d)   How many people are included?
(e)   What percentage of these people are aged 75 or more?

9 A group of 25 students were each asked how many brothers and sisters they had. The table shows the results.

Number of sisters

		0	1	2	3
Number of brothers	0	5	1	2	0
	1	4	3	2	1
	2	2	3	1	0
	3	0	1	0	0

(a) How many students have no brothers or sisters?
(b) How many students have one sister?
(c) How many students have one brother and one sister?
(d) How many students have more brothers than sisters?

10 The two-way table shows information about a class of pupils.

	Can swim	Cannot swim
Boys	14	6
Girls	8	2

(a) How many boys can swim?
(b) How many boys are in the class?
(c) What percentage of the boys can swim?
(d) What percentage of the girls can swim?
(e) Do the results prove or disprove the hypothesis:
"More boys can swim than girls"?
Explain your answer.

11 The two-way table shows the results of a survey to test the hypothesis: "More girls are left-handed than boys".
Do the results prove or disprove the hypothesis?
Explain your answer.

	Left-handed	
	Yes	No
Boys	3	18
Girls	2	12

12 The two-way table shows the results of a survey.

Grade in Mathematics		E	D	C	B	A
	A			1	2	2
	B		1	2	5	2
	C		1	8	3	
	D		3	3	2	
	E	2	1	2		

Grade in English

(a) How many students achieved the same grade in both subjects?
(b) How many students got a grade A, B or C in Mathematics?
(c) Do the results prove or disprove the hypothesis:
"Students get better grades in English than Mathematics"? Explain your answer.

13 Suggest a hypothesis of your own.
(a) Design a suitable questionnaire to test your hypothesis.
(b) Choose a suitable sample and collect data.
(c) Does the data prove your hypothesis?

14. The two-way table shows the number of boys and girls in families taking part in a survey.

Number of girls	4					
	3	1		2		
	2	1	2	3		
	1	5	9		1	1
	0		3		2	
		0	1	2	3	4

Number of boys

(a) (i) How many families have two children?
   (ii) Does the data support the hypothesis: "More families have less than 2 children than more than 2 children"? Explain your answer.
(b) (i) How many girls are included in the survey?
   (ii) Does the data support the hypothesis: "More boys are born than girls"? Explain your answer.

15. The two-way table shows the age and gender of people taking part in a survey.

	Age				
	Under 18	18 to 25	26 to 40	41 to 64	65 and over
Female	0	2	7	9	7
Male	0	4	17	19	10

Give a reason why the data collected may not be representative of the whole population.

What you need to know

- **Primary data** is data collected by an individual or organisation to use for a particular purpose. Primary data is obtained from experiments, investigations, surveys and by using questionnaires.

- **Secondary data** is data which is already available or has been collected by someone else for a different purpose. Sources of secondary data include the Annual Abstract of Statistics, Social Trends and the Internet.

- **Qualitative** data – Data which can only be described in words.

- **Quantitative** data – Data that has a numerical value. Quantitative data is either **discrete** or **continuous**. **Discrete** data can only take certain values. **Continuous** data has no exact value and is measurable.

- **Data Collection Sheets** – Used to record data during a survey.

- **Tally** – A way of recording each item of data on a data collection sheet. A group of five is recorded as ⊥⊥⊥⊥.

- **Frequency Table** – A way of collating the information recorded on a data collection sheet.

- **Grouped Frequency Table** – Used for continuous data or for discrete data when a lot of data has to be recorded.

- **Database** – A collection of data.

- **Class Interval** – The width of the groups used in a grouped frequency distribution.

- **Questionnaire** – A set of questions used to collect data for a survey. Questionnaires should:
  (1) use simple language,
  (2) ask short questions which can be answered precisely,
  (3) provide tick boxes,
  (4) avoid open-ended questions,
  (5) avoid leading questions,
  (6) ask questions in a logical order.

- **Hypothesis** – A hypothesis is a statement which may or may not be true.

- When information is required about a large group of people it is not always possible to survey everyone and only a **sample** may be asked. The sample chosen should be large enough to make the results meaningful and representative of the whole group (population) or the results may be **biased**.

- **Two-way Tables** – A way of illustrating two features of a survey.

Review Exercise

1 Karl's and Eleanor's school is near a busy main road.
They decide to carry out a survey of the different types of vehicles that travel on the main road.
Design a suitable data sheet so that they can collect their data easily. *Edexcel*

2 The times, in seconds, taken by 20 students to complete a task are shown.

| 4.3 | 12.9 | 10.0 | 5.7 | 18.2 | 14.0 | 11.6 | 14.9 | 8.5 | 16.0 |
| 15.0 | 13.4 | 3.7 | 6.0 | 10.5 | 11.6 | 15.4 | 3.7 | 8.0 | 9.3 |

(a) Copy and complete the frequency table shown, using intervals of 5 seconds.

Time (t seconds)	Tally	Frequency
$0 \leqslant t < 5$		
$5 \leqslant t < 10$		

(b) Which is the modal class?

3 In a factory there are 79 male and 74 female managers.
Managers can be either junior or senior. There are 28 male senior managers.
There is a total of 93 junior managers.

(a) Construct a two-way table to show the
number of male and female managers
in junior and senior management.

	Male	Female
Junior management		
Senior management		

(b) Comment on the proportion of women
in junior and senior management. *Edexcel*

4 Fred is conducting a survey into television viewing habits.
One of the questions in his survey is:
"How much television do you watch?"

His friend Sheila tells him that it is not a very good question.
Write down two ways in which Fred could improve his question. *Edexcel*

5 The table shows the age and gender of people taking part in a survey to test the hypothesis
"Children have too much homework".

	Age				
	Under 11	11 to 16	17 to 25	26 to 50	Over 50
Male	0	4	6	5	5
Female	0	0	0	0	0

Give three reasons why the sample is biased.

6 John wants to find out what students think about the library service at his college.
Part of the questionnaire he has written is shown.

Q1.   What is your name? ....

Q2.   How many times a week do you go to the library?
　　　☐ Often　　　☐ Sometimes　　　☐ Never

(a) Why should Q1 not be asked?
(b) What is wrong with the choices offered in Q2?

7 Alfie is writing a questionnaire to survey opinion on whether nightclubs should be allowed to stay open all night.

(a) Which one of the following points is important when he is writing his questionnaire?
  P Write questions for people who go to nightclubs only.
  Q Write questions that do not require long answers.
  R Write as many questions as he can think of.

(b) Which one of the following points is important when he is deciding which people to ask?
  X Ask older people only.
  Y Ask people outside a nightclub.
  Z Ask some men and some women.

(c) Alfie wants to know the age distribution of respondents.
   He considers the following questions.
  A What is your age?
  B Are you older than: ☐25 ☐45 ☐65?
  (i) Give a reason why Question **A** is unsuitable.
  (ii) Give a reason why Question **B** is unsuitable.

8 Terry is carrying out a survey on the shopping habits of people at a superstore.
He says, "People who travel further to the store will come less often and spend more money per visit."
Write three questions which would help him test his statement.

9 The two-way table shows the results of a survey to test the hypothesis
"A higher proportion of detached houses have garages than semi-detached houses"?

	Garage	No garage
Semi-detached houses	27	9
Detached houses	16	4

Do the results prove or disprove the hypothesis?
Explain your answer.

10 A travel agent says "More women prefer holidays abroad than men".
The table shows the results of a survey to test this statement.

	Men	Women
Prefer holidays abroad	18	21
Prefer holidays in the UK	6	7

Do these results support the statement made by the travel agent?
Explain your answer.

11 Sylvia asks a number of women how many boys and girls they each have.
Her findings are shown in the table.
(a) How many women were included in Syvlia's survey?
(b) How many children did these women have altogether?

Number of boys

	0	1	2	3	4
4		1			
3	2	1			
2	3	1			
1	1	3	2	1	
0	5	2	1		1

Number of girls

Most people find numerical data easier to understand if it is presented in a pictorial or diagrammatical form. For this reason television reports, newspapers and advertisements frequently use graphs and diagrams to present data.

Bar charts

Bar charts are a simple but effective way of displaying data.
Bars can be drawn either horizontally or vertically.

EXAMPLE

The table shows how a group of boys travelled to school one day.

Method of travel	Bus	Cycle	Car	Walk
Number of boys	2	7	1	5

The bar chart below shows this information.

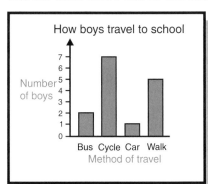

Notice that:
Bars are the same width.

There are gaps between the bars because data that can be counted is discrete.

The height of each bar gives the **frequency**.

The tallest bar represents the most frequent variable (category).

The most frequently occurring variable is called the **mode** or **modal category**. Cycle is the modal category for these boys.

Bar-line graphs

Instead of drawing bars to show frequency we could draw vertical lines.
Such graphs are called **bar-line graphs** or **vertical line graphs**.
The lines can be drawn horizontally or vertically.

EXAMPLE

The graph shows the number of goals scored by a football team in 10 matches.

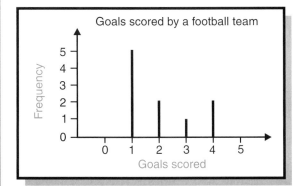

The frequency represents the number of matches played.

In how many matches was only one goal scored?

What is the difference between the largest number of goals scored in a match and the smallest number of goals scored?

The difference between the largest and smallest variable is called the **range**.
The range for the number of goals scored is $4 - 1 = 3$.

1 The bar chart shows the time Jim spent watching television each day last week.

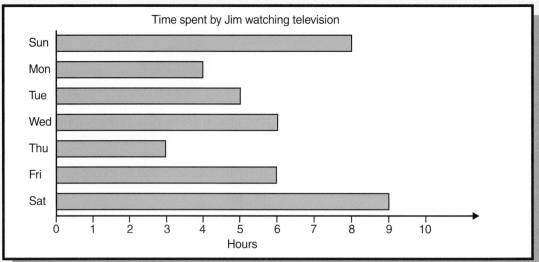

Time spent by Jim watching television

(a) On which day did Jim watch the most television?
(b) How many hours did Jim spend watching television on Tuesday?
(c) How many hours did Jim spend watching television last week?
(d) On which day did Jim spend a third of the day watching television?
(e) What fraction of the day did Jim spend watching television on Wednesday?
(f) What is the range of the number of hours per day Jim spent watching television?

2 The table shows the amount of pocket money given each week to a number of Year 11 girls.

Amount (£)	1	2	3	4	5	6	7	8	9	10
Number of girls	0	0	1	5	10	4	0	3	0	7

(a) Draw a bar-line graph of the data.
(b) What is the modal amount of pocket money?
(c) What is the range of the amount of pocket money given each week?
(d) What percentage of the girls got less than £5?

3 The bar-line graph illustrates the number of goals scored per match by a hockey team.

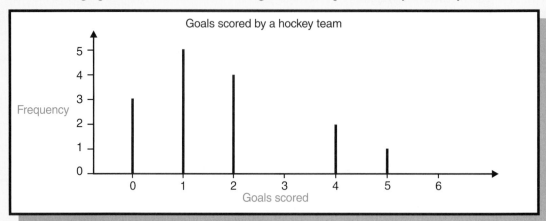

Goals scored by a hockey team

(a) How many matches have the team played?
(b) Which number of goals scored is the mode?
(c) What is the range of the number of goals scored?
(d) In what percentage of games were no goals scored?

4 The bar chart shows the day of birth for a group of children.

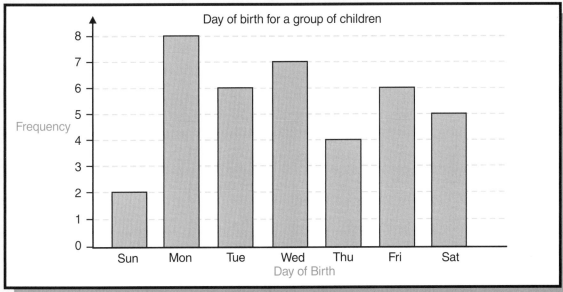

(a) How many children are in the group? (b) Which day of birth is the mode?

The table shows the day of birth for the girls.

Day of birth	Sun	Mon	Tue	Wed	Thu	Fri	Sat
Number of girls	1	5	2	3	3	1	4

(c) Draw up a table to show the day of birth for the boys.

5 Record the day of birth for all the students in your class.
Draw a bar chart of the data. Compare your data with the data given in question 4.

Comparing data

Bar charts can also be used to compare data.

EXAMPLE The table shows how a class of children travelled to school one day.

Method of travel	Bus	Cycle	Car	Walk
Boys	2	7	1	5
Girls	3	1	5	6

To make it easier to compare information for boys and girls we can draw both bars on the same diagram, as shown.

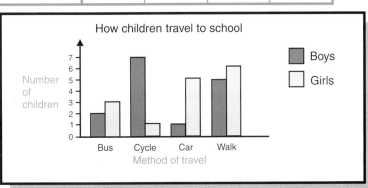

Eight children cycle to school. *How many children travel to school by car?*

Walking is the most popular method of travelling to school. *Which method of travel is the least popular?*

What percentage of girls walk to school?

Compare and comment on the method of travel of these boys and girls.

1. A group of children were asked how many hours they had spent watching television on a particular Sunday. The bar chart shows the results.

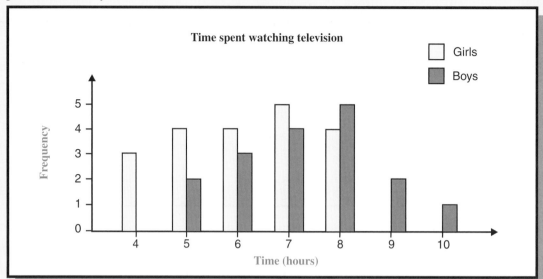

(a) What was the modal time for the girls?
(b) What was the range in time for the boys?
(c) How many boys watched television for more than 8 hours?
(d) (i) How many girls were included in the survey?
    (ii) What percentage of the girls watched television for 6 hours?
(e) Compare and comment on the time spent watching television for these boys and girls.

2. The bar chart shows the results of a survey of the shoe sizes of pupils in a Year 9 class.

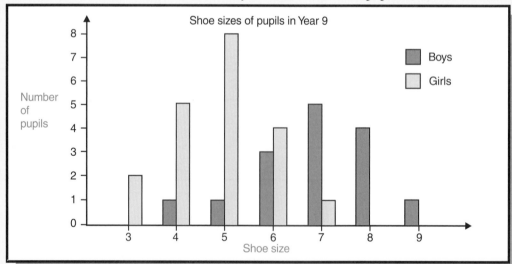

(a) Which size of shoe is the mode for the girls?
(b) Which size of shoe is the mode for the boys?
(c) How many pupils have shoe size 6?
(d) What percentage of boys have shoe size 8 or 9?
(e) What percentage of girls have shoe size 3 or 4?
(f) What is the range of shoe size for girls?
(g) What is the range of shoe size for boys?
(h) Compare and comment on the shoe sizes of boys and girls.

Pie charts

Bar charts are useful for comparing the various types of data (categories) with each other.
To compare each category with **all** the data collected we use a **pie chart**.

A pie chart is a circle which is divided up into sectors.
The whole circle represents the total frequency and each sector represents the frequency of one part (category) of the data.

Drawing pie charts

The table shows the ways in which some children like to eat eggs.

Method of cooking	Poached	Boiled	Scrambled	Fried
Number of children	5	8	6	11

To show this information in a pie chart we must find the angles of the sectors which represent each category. First calculate the angle which represents each child.
30 children are represented by 360°.
1 child is represented by $360° \div 30 = 12°$.
Sector angle = Number of children in category $\times 12°$

Method of cooking	Poached	Boiled	Scrambled	Fried	**Total**
Number of children	5	8	6	11	**30**
Sector angle	60°	96°	72°	132°	**360°**

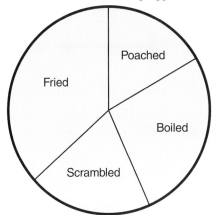

Method of Cooking Eggs

Using a table allows you to keep your work tidy and to make checks.

The whole circle represents the total frequency of 30.

Each sector represents the frequency of one category (method of cooking).

Exercise **35.3**

1 The table shows information about the trees in a wood.

Type of tree	Ash	Beech	Maple
Number of trees	20	25	15

Draw a pie chart for this data.

2 The colour of eyes of 90 people were recorded.
The table shows the results.

Colour of eyes	Brown	Blue	Green	Other
Number of people	40	25	15	10

Draw a pie chart for this data.

3 The table shows the sales of ice-cream cornets at a kiosk one day.

Ice-cream cornet	Vanilla	Strawberry	99
Frequency	94	37	49

Draw a pie chart for this data.

4 The table shows the results of a survey to find the most popular takeaway food.

Type of takeaway	Fish & chips	Chicken & chips	Chinese meal	Pizza
Number of people	165	204	78	93

Draw a pie chart for this data.

5 The results of a survey to find the most popular terrestrial television channel are shown.

Television channel	BBC1	BBC2	ITV	Ch4	Ch5
Percentage of people	33	14	32	13	8

Show the information in a pie chart.

6 The breakfast cereal preferred by some adults is shown.

Breakfast cereal	Cornflakes	Muesli	Porridge	Branflakes
Number of adults	25	20	12	15

Show the information in a pie chart.

Interpreting pie charts

Pie charts are useful for showing and comparing proportions of data. However, they do not show frequencies. Such information can be found by interpreting the pie chart.

To interpret a pie chart we need to know:
- the sector angles (which can be measured from an accurately drawn pie chart), **and**
- the total frequency represented by the pie chart, **or**
  the frequency represented by one of the sectors.

EXAMPLE

The pie chart shows the makes of 120 cars.
(a) Which make of car is the mode?
(b) How many of the cars are Ford?

(a) The sector representing Vauxhall is the largest.
Therefore, Vauxhall is the mode.

(b) The angle of the sector representing Ford is 72°.
The number of Ford cars = $\frac{72}{360} \times 120 = 24$.

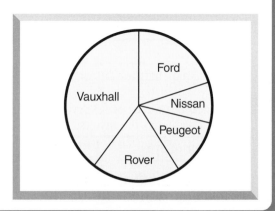

Exercise **35.4**

1 The pie chart shows the type of holiday chosen by 36 people.

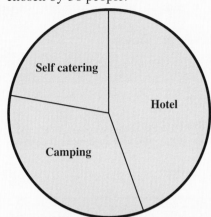

(a) How many people chose a camping holiday?

(b) How many people chose a self-catering holiday?

(c) What type of holiday is the mode?

2 The pie chart shows the resorts chosen by 60 skiers to Italy.

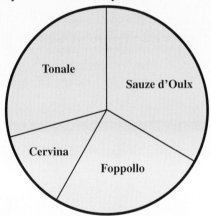

(a) How many skiers chose Sauze d'Oulx?

(b) How many skiers chose Foppollo?

(c) Which resort is the mode?

3 The pie chart shows the holiday destinations of 180 people.

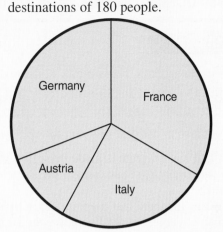

(a) Which holiday destination is the mode?

(b) How many people went to Italy?

(c) How many people went to Germany?

(d) How many people went to Austria?

4 The pie chart shows the membership of an international committee.

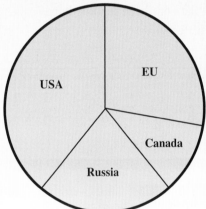

The USA has 7 committee members.

(a) How many committee members has the EU?

(b) How many committee members has Canada?

(c) How many committee members are there altogether?

5 The pie chart shows the different types of tree in a forest.

There are 54 oak trees and these are represented by a sector of 27°.

(a) The pine trees are represented by an angle of 144°.
How many pine trees are there?

(b) There are 348 silver birch trees.
Calculate the angle of the sector representing silver birch trees.

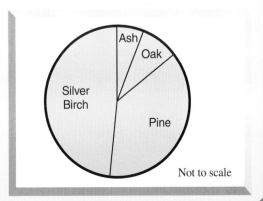

Not to scale

Stem and leaf diagrams

Data can also be represented using a **stem and leaf diagram**.

EXAMPLE

The times, in seconds, taken by 20 students to complete a puzzle are shown.

15	9	23	32	17	12	27	19	26	15
20	11	24	31	10	17	15	28	33	18

Construct a stem and leaf diagram to represent this information.

A stem and leaf diagram is made by splitting each number into two parts.
As the data uses 'tens' and 'units', the stem will represent the 'tens' and the leaf will represent the 'units'.
To draw the stem and leaf diagram begin by drawing a vertical line.
The digits to the left of the line make the **stem**.
The digits to the right of the line are the **leaves**.

The first number is 15.
Next to the stem of 1 record 5.

9 is recorded as 0 9

```
0 │ 9
1 │ 5  7  2  9  5  1  0  7  5  8
2 │ 3  7  6  0  4  8
3 │ 2  1  3
```

Once the data has been recorded, it is usual to redraw the diagram so that the leaves are in numerical order.

```
                    1 │ 5   means 15 seconds
0 │ 9
1 │ 0  1  2  5  5  5  7  7  8  9
2 │ 0  3  4  6  7  8
3 │ 1  2  3
```

Stem and leaf diagrams are often drawn without column headings in which case a key is necessary.
e.g. 1│5 means 15 seconds

Exercise 35.5

1 The amount of petrol, in litres, bought by 20 motorists is shown.

16	23	27	10	35	42	26	25	24	17
23	41	33	35	25	19	16	31	12	29

Construct a stem and leaf diagram to represent this information.

2 The times, in seconds, taken to answer 24 telephone calls are shown.

3.2	5.6	2.4	3.5	4.3	3.6	2.8	5.8	3.3	2.6	3.2	2.8
5.6	3.5	4.2	1.5	2.7	2.5	3.7	3.1	2.9	4.2	2.4	3.0

Copy and complete the stem and leaf diagram to represent this information.

```
              3 │ 2   means 3.2 seconds
1 │
2 │
3 │ 2
4 │
5 │
```

For this data
the stem represents 'units',
the leaf represents 'tenths'.

3 The number of press-ups completed by 18 students in one minute is shown.

21 36 41 25 18 32 40 36 22
9 16 24 33 36 27 32 20 28

Draw a stem and leaf diagram to represent this information.

4 The heights, in centimetres, of the heels on 20 different pairs of shoes are shown.

2.7 3.4 2.0 6.0 4.5 3.6 3.1 2.4 4.2 1.8
3.5 2.5 2.6 2.1 4.0 3.5 4.2 2.6 3.9 5.4

Construct a stem and leaf diagram to represent this information.

5 David did a survey to find the cost, in pence, of a loaf of bread.
The stem and leaf diagram shows the results of his survey.

```
                    2 | 7   means 27 pence
2 | 7 9
3 | 1 1 2 9 9 9
4 | 2 5 9
5 | 0
```

(a) How many loaves of bread are included in the survey?
(b) What is the range of the prices?
(c) Which price is the mode?

Back to back stem and leaf diagrams

Back to back stem and leaf diagrams can be used to compare two sets of data.

EXAMPLE

The results for examinations in Mathematics and English for a group of students are shown. The marks are given as percentages.

Mathematics: 91 27 55 69 83 25 45 53 67 71
30 52 45 59 86 73 65 47 54 38

English: 45 40 48 65 75 55 36 85 76 69
64 58 47 64 67 72 83 74 62 51

(a) Construct a back to back stem and leaf diagram for this data.
(b) Compare and comment on the results in Mathematics and English.

(a)
```
    Mathematics              English        3 | 6  means 36%
            7 5 | 2 |
            8 0 | 3 | 6
        7 5 5 | 4 | 0 5 7 8
    9 5 4 3 2 | 5 | 1 5 8
        9 7 5 | 6 | 2 4 4 5 7 9
        3 1 | 7 | 2 4 5 6
        6 3 | 8 | 3 5
          1 | 9 |
```

For Mathematics:
5 | 2 means 25%

(b) The range of marks in Mathematics is larger than in English.
The modal group in English is 60 to 69, in Mathematics it is 50 to 59.

1 The stem and leaf diagram shows the distribution of marks for a test marked out of 50.

Boys						Girls		1	7 means 17 marks

Boys					Stem	Girls					
					0	9					
			6	2	1	0	1	2	7		
	7	6	4	3	2	1	3	5	5	6 7 8
9	5	3	2	0	3	2	5	9		
			5	1	4	1				
				0	5					

(a) What is the lowest mark for the girls?
(b) What is the highest mark for the boys?
(c) How many pupils scored more than 25 marks?
(d) Compare and comment on the marks for boys and girls.

2 The time taken to complete a computer game is recorded to the nearest tenth of a minute. The times for a group of 20 adults and 20 children are shown.

Adults					Children				
7.9	8.2	7.3	9.2	6.4	6.4	5.4	4.9	6.6	7.1
6.5	6.1	8.2	7.8	7.0	5.1	6.5	6.3	7.4	6.5
9.4	8.0	7.3	5.4	7.7	8.2	7.7	5.9	6.8	7.6
10.1	5.9	6.7	7.3	6.0	5.3	6.2	8.0	4.7	7.9

(a) Construct a back to back stem and leaf diagram for this data.
(b) Compare and comment on the times for adults and children.

What you need to know

- **Bar chart**. Used for data which can be counted.
  Often used to compare quantities of data in a distribution.
  Bars can be drawn horizontally or vertically.
  Bars are the same width and there are gaps between bars.
  The length of each bar represents frequency.
  The longest bar represents the **mode**.
  The difference between the largest and smallest variable is called the **range**.

- **Bar-line graph**. Instead of drawing bars, horizontal or vertical lines are drawn to show frequency.

- **Pie chart**. Used for data which can be counted.
  Often used to compare proportions of data, usually with the total.
  The whole circle represents all the data.
  The size of each sector represents the frequency of data in that sector.
  The largest sector represents the **mode**.

- **Stem and leaf diagrams**. Used to represent data in its original form.
  Data is split into two parts. The part with the higher place value is the stem,
  e.g. 15 stem 1 leaf 5.
  The data is shown in numerical order on the diagram.

  e.g. 2|3 5 9 represents 23, 25, 29. A key is given to show the value of the data.

  e.g. 3|4 means 34 cm or 3|4 means 3.4 cm etc.

  Back to back stem and leaf diagrams can be used to compare two sets of data.

① Some families on holiday at a seaside resort were questioned about their holiday accommodation.

Type of accommodation	Hotel	Bed & Breakfast	Self-catering	Caravan	Camping	Other
Number of families	9	17	11	8	2	3

(a) Draw a bar chart to show this information.
(b) What type of accommodation is the mode?
(c) How many families were questioned?
(d) What percentage of these families had Bed & Breakfast?

② 30 people used a Sports Centre one evening. Here is a frequency table of the activities in which they took part.

Draw a pie chart to show this information.

Activity	Frequency
Gym	12
Swimming	3
Squash	6
Aerobics	9

Edexcel

③ 720 students were asked how they travelled to school. The pie chart shows the results of this survey.

Work out how many of the students travelled to school by bus.

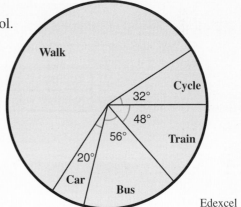

Edexcel

④ The pie chart shows the five types of fruit trees sold by a garden centre.
21 apple trees were sold.

(a) How many plum trees were sold?
(b) How many fruit trees were sold altogether?

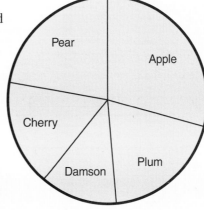

⑤ The weights in grams of 20 cherry tomatoes are shown.

    5.4   4.6   6.7   3.9   4.2   5.0   6.3   5.4   4.8   3.5
    4.6   5.6   5.8   6.0   2.8   4.4   4.7   5.6   5.1   4.8

Draw a stem and leaf diagram to represent this information.

6 A butcher keeps a record of the fresh and frozen poultry he sells each day.
Of the poultry sold one Saturday he finds:

$\frac{7}{12}$ were chickens, $\frac{1}{3}$ were turkeys and the rest were ducks.

(a) Draw a pie chart to represent this information.

(b) He sold 21 chickens.
How much poultry did he sell altogether?

(c) The bar chart shows the frozen poultry he sold.

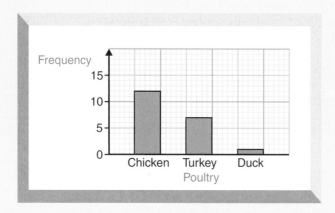

Copy and complete the table to show the fresh poultry he sold.

Poultry	Chicken	Turkey	Duck
Number sold			

7 The frequency diagram shows the distribution of marks for a class of 30 pupils in a mental arithmetic test.

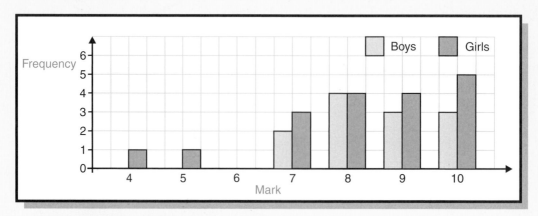

(a) What is the ratio of boys to girls in the class?
Give your answer in its simplest form.

(b) The test is marked out of 10.
What percentage of the class scored full marks?
Give your answer to a suitable degree of accuracy.

(c) By comparing the mode and range for the girls with the mode and range for the boys comment on the marks scored.

CHAPTER 36

Averages and Range

Activity

Some friends went on a school trip. They each brought different amounts of spending money, as follows:

Penny £15	Keith £35	Nishpal £40	Jayne £10	Stephen £50	Ben £60
Charlotte £35	Suzie £50	Dan £55	Vicki £35	Jack £55	

Ben brought the most and Jayne the least.
What was the difference in the amounts of spending money Ben and Jayne brought?
Which was the most common amount of money?
Who brought the middle amount of money? How much was this?
If the friends shared out their money equally, how much would each person get?

Range

The difference between the highest and lowest amounts is called the **range**.
Range = highest amount − lowest amount

Types of average

The most common amount is called the **mode**.
When the amounts are arranged in order of size, the middle one is called the **median**.
When the money is shared out equally, the amount each person gets is called the **mean**.

EXAMPLE

The price, in pence, of a can of cola in different shops is shown.
33, 34, 31, 32, 30, 31, 31, 35.
Find (a) the mode, (b) the median, (c) the mean price.

(a) The **mode** is the most common amount.
The most common price is 31.
The mode is 31 pence.
We sometimes say the modal price is 31p.

(b) The **median** is found by arranging the data in order of size and taking the middle amount.
Arrange the data in order of size.
30, 31, 31, 31, 32, 33, 34, 35.

The middle amount is $\frac{31 + 32}{2} = 31.5$

The median is 31.5 pence.

> Where there are an even number of values the median is the average of the middle two.

(c) The **mean** is found by finding the total of all the data and dividing the total by the number of data values.
Add the data.
33 + 34 + 31 + 32 + 30 + 31 + 31 + 35 = 257

The mean = $\frac{257}{8} = 32.125$

The mean is 32.125 pence.

1   Tony recorded the number of birthday cards sold each day.

     3   4   8   1   4   1 3 4 4 8

   (a)   Work out the range of the number of cards sold each day.

   (b)   Write down the mode.

   (c)   Find the median number of cards sold each day.

2   Claire recorded the number of e-mail messages she received each day.

     2   1   7   4   1   1 1 2 4 7   15

   (a)   Write down the mode.

   (b)   Find the median number of messages received each day.

   (c)   Calculate the mean number of messages received each day.

3   Gail noted the number of stamps on parcels delivered to her office.

     3   2   4   5   7   3   4   3   5   3

   (a)   Write down the mode.

   (b)   Find the range of the number of stamps on a parcel.

   (c)   Find the median number of stamps on a parcel.

   (d)   Calculate the mean number of stamps on a parcel.

4   Sanjay played a computer game 8 times and recorded his scores.

     140   135   125   125   130   135   140   135

   (a)   Which score is the mode?

   (b)   Calculate the median of his scores.

   (c)   Find the mean score. Give your answer to the nearest whole number.

5   Frank counted the number of books on different shelves in a library.
He recorded the following numbers.

     38   40   26   49   37   43

   (a)   Find the median number of books on a shelf.

   (b)   What is the range of the number of books on a shelf?

   (c)   Calculate the mean number of books on a shelf.
Give your answer correct to one decimal place.

6   The weights of 8 men in a rowing team are:

86 kg   95 kg   89 kg   93 kg   84 kg   78 kg   91 kg   79 kg

Calculate the mean of their weights correct to one decimal place.

7   The mean of six numbers is 5. Five of the numbers are 2, 3, 7, 8 and 6.
What is the other number?

8   The mean length of 8 rods is 75 cm. An extra rod is added.
The total length of the 9 rods is 729 cm. What is the length of the extra rod?

Frequency distributions

A **frequency distribution table** is used to present data.

Johti measured the lengths of some twigs. He recorded the following results.

     2   3   2   6   3   6   2

     3   5   4   3   2   2   3

     5   6   2   6   5   6   2

His results are shown in this frequency distribution table.

Length (cm)	2	3	4	5	6
Number of twigs (frequency)	7	5	1	3	5

EXAMPLE

Find the mode, median, mean and range of the lengths of the twigs that Johti measured.

To find the mode:
The mode is the amount with the greatest frequency.
There were 7 twigs of length 2 cm.
This is more than any other length of twigs.
The mode of the lengths is 2 cm.

To find the median:
The median is the middle amount.
We could list the 21 twigs in order of length and split them up like this:

10 shortest twigs	middle twig	10 longest twigs

This shows that the median length is the length of the 11th twig.
From the table we can see that:
    the first 7 twigs are each 2 cm long,
    and the next 5 twigs are each 3 cm long.
So the 11th twig is 3 cm long.
The median length is 3 cm.

To find the mean:

$$\text{Mean} = \frac{\text{Total of all lengths}}{\text{Number of lengths}}$$

The best way to do this is to use a table.

Length (cm) x	Number of twigs (frequency) f	Frequency $\times$ Number of twigs $f \times x$
2	7	14
3	5	15
4	1	4
5	3	15
6	5	30
Totals	$\Sigma f = 21$	$\Sigma fx = 78$

$$\text{Mean} = \frac{\text{Total of all lengths}}{\text{Number of lengths}} = \frac{\Sigma fx}{\Sigma f}$$

Mean $= \frac{78}{21} = 3.714 \ldots$
Mean length $= 3.7$ cm, correct to 1 decimal place.

To find the range:
Range = longest length − shortest length
    $= 6 - 2$
    $= 4$ cm

Mathematical shorthand

Σ is the Greek letter 'sigma'.

Σf means the sum of frequencies.

Σfx means the sum of the values of fx

$$\text{Mean} = \frac{\Sigma fx}{\Sigma f}$$

Calculating averages from diagrams

EXAMPLE

Calculate the range, mode, median and mean of the ages for the data shown in the bar chart.

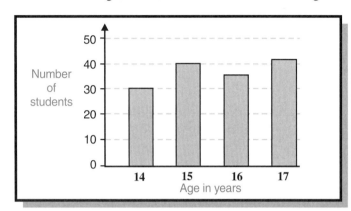

The range is the difference between the highest and lowest ages.
Range = 17 - 14
= 3 years

The most common age is shown by the tallest bar.
So the modal age is 17 years.

Use a table to find the median and the mean.

Age x	Frequency f	Frequency × Age $f \times x$
14	30	420
15	40	600
16	36	576
17	41	697
Totals	$\Sigma f = 147$	$\Sigma fx = 2293$

The middle student is given by:
$$\frac{147 + 1}{2} = 74$$
The 74th student in the list has the median age.
The first 70 students are aged 14 or 15 years.
The 74th student has age 16 years.
Median age is 16 years.

$$\text{Mean} = \frac{\text{Total of all ages}}{\text{Number of students}} = \frac{\Sigma fx}{\Sigma f}$$

$$\text{Mean} = \frac{2293}{147} = 15.598\ldots$$

Mean age is 15.6 years, correct to 1 d.p.

Exercise 36.2

Try to do questions 1 and 4 without using a calculator.

1 Hilary observed customers using the express checkout at a supermarket.

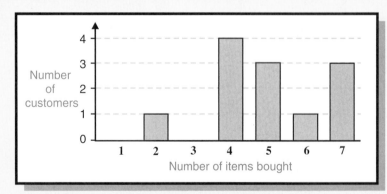

(a) Find the range of the number of items bought.
(b) What is the mode of the number of items bought?
(c) Work out the median number of items bought.
(d) Calculate the mean number of items bought.

2 Mark asked some students, "How many keys do you have on your key ring?"
The data collection sheet shows the responses he recorded.

Number of keys	Tally
2	I I
3	I I I
4	ⱵⱵⱵ I I I
5	ⱵⱵⱵ
6	I I

(a) Use Mark's data to make a frequency distribution table.
(b) How many students did Mark ask?
(c) Write down the mode of the number of keys on a key ring.
(d) Find the median number of keys.
(e) Calculate the mean number of keys on a key ring.

3 Pat recorded the weekly earnings of a group of students. Her results were as follows:

£15   £30   £20   £35   £15   £15   £20   £25   £35   £15
£25   £20   £25   £25   £25   £20   £25   £15   £35

(a) Show the data in a frequency distribution table.
(b) Find the range of the weekly earnings.
(c) What is the modal weekly earnings?
(d) How many people were in the group?
(e) What is the median weekly earnings?
(f) Calculate the total weekly earnings of the group.
(g) Calculate the mean weekly earnings. Give your answer to the nearest penny.

4 A group of students took part in a quiz on the Highway Code. The bar chart shows their scores.

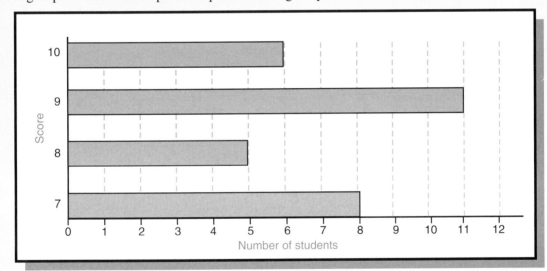

(a) Which score is the mode?
(b) What is the median score?
(c) How many students took part in the quiz?
(d) Calculate the mean score.

5 Find the mode, median and mean for the following sets of data.

(a)

Number of letters delivered	1	2	3	4	5	6
Number of days	6	9	6	6	2	1

(b)

Number of siblings	0	1	2	3	4	5
Frequency	1	4	10	4	1	1

(c)

Number of days absent in a year	0	1	2	3	4	5	6	7	8	9	10	11
Number of students	56	0	0	4	14	10	24	11	21	15	8	2

Grouped frequency distributions

When there is a lot of data, or the data is continuous, **grouped frequency distributions** are used.

Calculating the mean

For a grouped frequency distribution the true value of the mean cannot be found as the actual values of the data are not known.

To **estimate the mean**, we assume that all the values in each class are equal to the midpoint of the class.

$$\text{Estimated mean} = \frac{\Sigma\ (\text{frequency} \times \text{midpoint})}{\text{Total frequency}} = \frac{\Sigma fx}{\Sigma f}$$

Modal class

For a grouped frequency distribution with equal class width intervals, the **modal class** is the class (or group) with the highest frequency.

EXAMPLE

The table shows the masses of a group of children.
(a) Calculate an estimate of the mean mass.
(b) Find the modal class.

Mass (m kg)	Frequency
$40 \leqslant m < 50$	3
$50 \leqslant m < 60$	10
$60 \leqslant m < 70$	6
$70 \leqslant m < 80$	12

(a)

Mass (m kg)	Midpoint x	Frequency f	Frequency × Midpoint $f \times x$
$40 \leqslant m < 50$	45	3	135
$50 \leqslant m < 60$	55	10	550
$60 \leqslant m < 70$	65	6	390
$70 \leqslant m < 80$	75	12	900
	Totals	$\Sigma f = 31$	$\Sigma fx = 1975$

Midpoint of
40 - 50 kg class is
given by:
$\frac{40 + 50}{2} = \frac{90}{2} = 45$

Estimate of mean $= \dfrac{\Sigma fx}{\Sigma f} = \dfrac{1975}{31} = 63.709\ldots$

Estimate of mean mass $= 63.7$ kg, correct to 3 sig. figs.

(b) The modal class is 70 - 80 kg.

Exercise 36.3

1 Give the modal class and calculate an estimate of the mean for each of the following.

(a)

Salary (s) (£000's)	$10 \leqslant s < 15$	$15 \leqslant s < 20$	$20 \leqslant s < 25$	$25 \leqslant s < 30$	$30 \leqslant s < 35$
Number of employees	79	32	14	0	2

(b)

Time spent watching TV per week (hours)	0 -	10 -	20 -	30 -	40 - 50
Number of students	2	8	5	14	7

2 The table shows the distribution of the weights of some turkeys.
Calculate an estimate of the mean weight of these turkeys.
Give your answer correct to one decimal place.

Weight (w kg)	Frequency
$2 \leqslant w < 4$	7
$4 \leqslant w < 6$	9
$6 \leqslant w < 8$	5
$8 \leqslant w < 10$	3

3 The table shows the distribution of the prices of houses for sale in a particular neighbourhood.

Price (p £000's)	$60 \leqslant p < 80$	$80 \leqslant p < 100$	$100 \leqslant p < 120$	$120 \leqslant p < 140$
Number of houses	3	7	4	1

Calculate an estimate of the mean price of these houses.
Give your answer to an appropriate degree of accuracy.

4 The table shows the distribution of the heights of trees in a wood.
Calculate an estimate of the mean height.

Height in metres (to nearest 0.1 m)	Number of trees
3.0 - 3.4	12
3.5 - 3.9	10
4.0 - 4.4	23
4.5 - 4.9	18
5.0 - 5.4	13

5 The table shows the distribution of marks in a test.
Calculate an estimate of the mean mark.
Notice that the class intervals are not all equal.

Mark	Number of students
0 - 19	12
20 - 29	23
30 - 34	25
35 - 39	14
40 - 50	3

Comparing distributions

By answering the following questions, compare the marks obtained by boys and girls in a test.

Mark (out of 10)	7	8	9	10
Number of boys	2	5	3	0
Number of girls	4	0	2	1

(a) What was the highest mark?

A girl got the highest mark of 10.

(b) Which set of marks was more spread out?

Range = highest mark − lowest mark
Boys: Range = 9 − 7 = 2
Girls: Range = 10 − 7 = 3
The girls' marks were more spread out.

(c) Were the marks for the boys or the girls better overall?

Calculate the mean for each set of marks.

Boys:
Mean $= \dfrac{2 \times 7 + 5 \times 8 + 3 \times 9 + 0 \times 10}{10}$

$= \dfrac{81}{10} = 8.1$

Girls:
Mean $= \dfrac{4 \times 7 + 0 \times 8 + 2 \times 9 + 1 \times 10}{7}$

$= \dfrac{56}{7} = 8$

The boys did better overall.

Note:
To compare the overall standard, the median could be used instead of the mean.

1. The weights of a sample of Cherry tomatoes have a range of 30 g and a mean of 45 g.
   The weights of a sample of Moneymaker tomatoes have a range of 90 g and a mean of 105 g.
   Compare and comment on the weights of Cherry and Moneymaker tomatoes.

2. The times, in minutes, taken by 8 boys to swim 50 metres are shown.
   1.8   2.0   1.7   2.2   2.1   1.9   1.8   2.1
   (a) (i)   What is the range of these times?
        (ii) Calculate the mean time.

   The times, in minutes, taken by 8 girls to swim 50 metres are shown.
   2.1   1.9   1.8   2.3   1.6   2.0   2.6   1.9
   (b) Comment on the times taken by these boys and girls to swim 50 m.

3. Use the mean and the range to compare the number of goals scored per match by these teams.

   Jays

Number of goals scored per hockey match	Number of matches
0	3
1	5
2	2
3	2
4	1
5	2

   Wasps

Number of goals scored per hockey match	Number of matches
0	0
1	2
2	3
3	1
4	2
5	0

4. Use the mean and the range to compare the number of visits to the cinema by these women and men.

Number of visits to the cinema last month	0	1	2	3	4	5	6	More than 6
Number of women	8	9	7	3	2	1	1	0
Number of men	0	12	7	1	0	0	0	0

5. Deepak thought that the girls in his class wore smaller shoes than the boys on average, but that the boys' shoe sizes were less varied than the girls'.
   He did a survey to test his ideas. The table shows his results. Was he correct?

Shoe size	$4\frac{1}{2}$	5	$5\frac{1}{2}$	6	$6\frac{1}{2}$	7	$7\frac{1}{2}$	8	$8\frac{1}{2}$	9	$9\frac{1}{2}$
Number of boys	1	0	5	4	4	2	1	0	1	0	0
Number of girls	0	2	0	2	3	0	2	0	3	1	1

6. (a) Find the modal class for the ages of customers in each of these two restaurants.
   (b) Which restaurant attracts more younger people?
   (c) Explain why it is only possible to find an approximate value for the range.

Age range	0 - 9	10 - 19	20 - 29	30 - 39	40 - 49	50 - 59	60 - 69	70 - 79	80 - 89
MacQuick	8	9	10	7	1	1	3	1	0
Pizza Pit	2	4	12	15	5	3	3	2	1

7 The graphs show the monthly sales of bicycles before and after a marketing campaign.
Calculate the medians and the ranges. Use your results to compare 'Before' with 'After'.

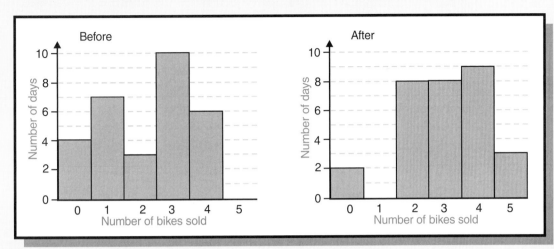

Which is the best average to use?

Many questions in mathematics have definite answers. This one does not.
Sometimes the mean is best, sometimes the median and sometimes the mode. It all depends on the situation and what you want to use the average for.

EXAMPLES

1 A youth club leader gets a discount on cans of drinks if she buys all one size.
She took a vote on which size people wanted.
The results were as follows:

Size of can (ml)	100	200	330	500
Number of votes	9	12	19	1

Mode = 330 ml
Median = 200 ml
Mean = 245.6 ml, correct to one decimal place.

Which size should she buy?

The mean is no use at all because she can't buy cans of size 245.6 ml.
Even if the answer is rounded to the nearest whole number (246 ml), it's still no use.
The median is possible because there is an actual 200 ml can.
However, only 12 out of 41 people want this size.
In this case the **mode** is the best average to use, as it is the most popular size.

2 A lecturer sets a unit test. He wants to choose a minimum mark for a distinction so that 50% of his students get this result. Should he use the modal mark, the median mark or the mean mark?

The median mark is the middle mark, so half the students will get the median mark or higher.
The lecturer must use the median mark.
Explain why the modal mark and the mean mark are not suitable.
The median mark cannot be decided until after the test.
Explain why.

In questions 1 to 3 find all the averages possible. State which is the most sensible and why.

1 On a bus: 23 people are wearing trainers,
10 people are wearing boots,
8 people are wearing lace-up shoes.

2 20 people complete a simple jigsaw. Their times, in seconds, are recorded.
5, 6, 8, 8, 9, 10, 11, 11, 12, 12, 12, 15, 15, 15, 15, 18, 19, 20, 22, 200.

3 Here are the marks obtained by a group of 11 students in a mock exam. The exam was marked out of 100.
5, 6, 81, 81, 82, 83, 84, 85, 86, 87, 88.

4 The times for two swimmers to complete each of ten 25 m lengths are shown below.

Swimmer A	30.1	30.1	30.1	30.6	30.7	31.1	31.1	31.5	31.7	31.8
Swimmer B	29.6	29.7	29.7	29.9	30.0	30.0	30.1	30.1	30.1	44.6

Which is the better swimmer? Explain why.

5 The table shows the number of runs scored by two batsmen in several innings.

Batsman A	0	0	10	12	20	22	50	51	81	104	
Batsman B	0	24	25	27	28	30	33	34	44	45	46	96

Which is the better batsman? Explain why.

What you need to know

- There are three types of **average**: the **mode**, the **median** and the **mean**.
  The **mode** is the most common amount.
  The **median** is the middle amount (or the mean of the two middle amounts) when the amounts are arranged in order of size.
  $$\textbf{Mean} = \frac{\text{Total of all amounts}}{\text{Number of amounts}}$$

- The **range** is a measure of **spread**.
  Range = highest amount − lowest amount

- To find the mean of a **frequency distribution** use:
  $$\text{Mean} = \frac{\text{Total of all amounts}}{\text{Number of amounts}} = \frac{\Sigma fx}{\Sigma f}$$

- To find the mean of a **grouped frequency distribution**, first find the value of the midpoint of each class. Then use:
  $$\text{Estimated mean} = \frac{\text{Total of all amounts}}{\text{Number of amounts}} = \frac{\Sigma fx}{\Sigma f}$$

- Choosing the best average to use:
  When the most **popular** value is wanted use the **mode**.
  When **half** of the values have to be above the average use the **median**.
  When a **typical** value is wanted use either the **mode** or the **median**.
  When all the **actual** values have to be taken into account use the **mean**.
  When the average should not be distorted by a few very small or very large values do **not** use the mean.

1 The lateness of 12 buses is recorded.
The results, in minutes, are shown.

5   6   7   8   8   10   10   10   11   12   13   14

(a) (i) What is the range of lateness for these buses?
    (ii) Calculate the mean lateness for these buses.
The lateness of 12 trains is also recorded.
The range in lateness for these trains in 14 minutes and the mean lateness is 5 minutes.
(b) Compare and comment on the lateness for these buses and trains.

2 (a) Find the range and mode of these prices.
    (b) Calculate the median and mean price of a bottle of milk.

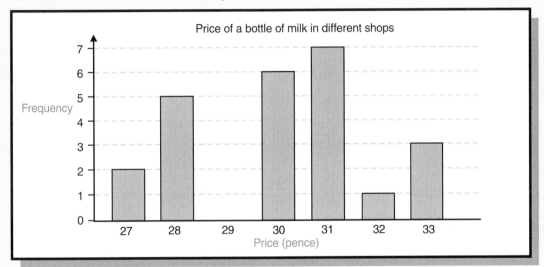

3 The temperatures at midnight in January 1995 in Shiverton were measured and recorded.
The results were used to construct the frequency table.

Temperature in °C	0	1	2	3	4	5	6	7	8
Number of nights	4	5	5	3	3	7	3	0	1

(a) Work out the range of the temperatures.
(b) Work out the mean temperature.
    Give your answer correct to 1 decimal place.   Edexcel

4 The number of words in each sentence of a newspaper story were counted.
The frequency table shows the results.

Number of words	Frequency
6 to 10	5
11 to 15	12
16 to 20	7
21 to 25	5
26 to 30	3

(a) Which is the modal class interval?
(b) In which class interval is the median?
(c) Calculate an estimate of the mean number of words in a sentence.

5 A class took a test. The mean mark of the 20 boys in the class was 17.4.
The mean mark of the 10 girls in the class was 13.8.
(a) Calculate the mean mark for the whole class.

5 pupils in another class took the test.
Their marks, written in order, were 1, 2, 3, 4 and x.
The mean of these 5 marks is equal to twice the median of these 5 marks.
(b) Calculate the value of x.

Edexcel

6 Phillip and Elizabeth collected information about the heights and weights of their friends.
They calculated the mean, median and mode of their results.

	Mean	Median	Mode
Phillip's friends	Height 180 cm	Height 175 cm	Height 177 cm
	Weight 50 kg	Weight 45 kg	Weight 40 kg
Elizabeth's friends	Height 175 cm	Height 175 cm	Height 172 cm
	Weight 45 kg	Weight 50 kg	Weight 50 kg

Philip says that most of his friends do not weigh as much as most of Elizabeth's friends.
(a) Explain why this may not be true.

Elizabeth says that all Phillip's friends are taller than her friends.
(b) Explain why this may not be true.

Edexcel

7 The graph shows the results of a survey of the number of faults in cars before and after servicing.

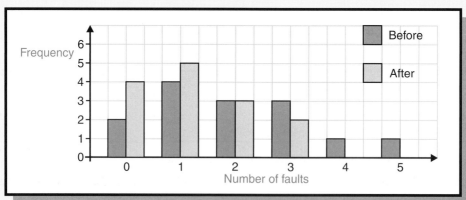

(a) A mechanic says, "The survey shows all cars have fewer faults after servicing."
Is this true? Explain your answer.

(b) A customer says, "The survey shows the average number of faults in cars before and after servicing is the same." Which average is being used?

(c) A report on the survey says, "The average number of faults per car before servicing is 2."
Which average is being used?
Use the same average to find the average number of faults per car after servicing.

8 The table gives information about the
weights of a sample of 20 packets
of prepacked cheese.
Use the table to calculate an estimate
of the mean weight of a packet of
prepacked cheese.

Weight (g grams)	Frequency
$150 \leqslant g < 200$	3
$200 \leqslant g < 250$	5
$250 \leqslant g < 300$	4
$300 \leqslant g < 350$	6
$350 \leqslant g < 400$	2

Presentation of Data 2

Time series

The money spent on shopping **each day**, the gas used **each quarter** and the rainfall **each month** are all examples of **time series**.
A time series is a set of readings taken at time intervals.

A time series is often used to monitor progress and to show the **trend** (increases and decreases) so that future performance can be predicted.
The type of graph used in this situation is called a **line graph**.

EXAMPLE

The table shows the temperature of a patient taken every half-hour.

Time	0930	1000	1030	1100	1130	1200
Temperature °C	36.9	37.1	37.6	37.2	36.5	37.0

Draw a line graph to illustrate the data.

To draw a line graph of this information, the given values are plotted and then joined to show the trend.

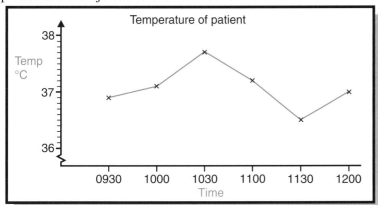

Only the plotted points show **known values**.

Lines are drawn to show the **trend**.

What is the highest temperature recorded?

*Explain why the graph can only be used to give an **estimate** of the patient's temperature at 1115.*

Exercise 37.1

 The midday temperature at a seaside resort was recorded each day for one week.
The line graph shows the results.

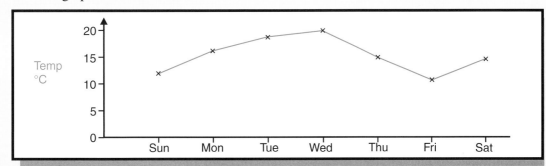

(a) What was the midday temperature on Thursday?
(b) Explain why you cannot use this line graph to estimate the temperature at midnight on Monday.

2 The number of cars sold by a car dealer is recorded each month.
The line graph shows the results for the first six months of 2000.

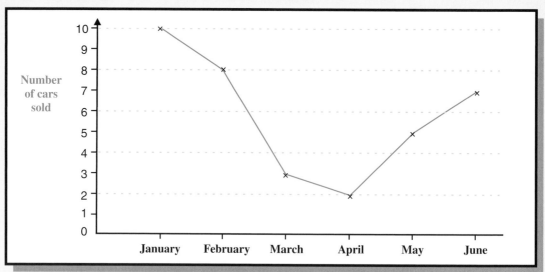

(a) How many cars were sold in February?
(b) In which months were more than 5 cars sold?
(c) Explain why you cannot estimate how many cars were sold halfway through April.

3 Each year, on his birthday, a teenager records his height.
The table shows the results.

Age (yrs)	13	14	15	16	17	18	19
Height (cm)	145	151	157	165	174	179	180

(a) Draw a line graph to represent this information.
(b) Use your graph to estimate:
   (i) the height of the teenager when he was $14\frac{1}{2}$ years of age,
   (ii) the age of the teenager when he reached 160 cm in height.

4 Joan is a member of Weight Watchers.
She records her weight at the beginning of each week.
The line graph shows a record of her weight for six weeks.

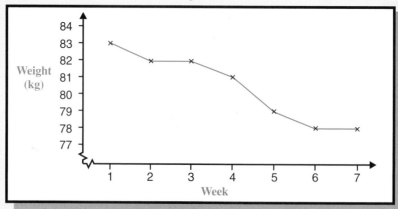

(a) What was Joan's weight at the beginning of Week 2?
(b) What was Joan's weight at the end of Week 2?
(c) How much weight did Joan lose in 6 weeks?
(d) In which week did Joan's weight first fall below 80 kg?

Seasonal variation

The graph below shows the amount of gas used by a householder each quarter over a period of 3 years.

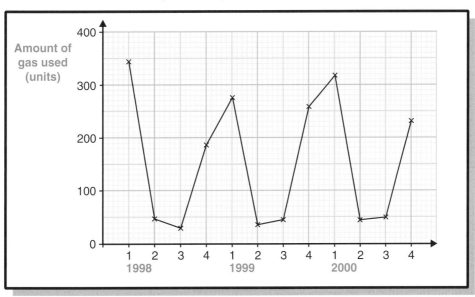

The graph shows high points for winter months and low points for summer months. These ups and downs occur because more (or less) gas is used at certain times of the year. As these ups and downs vary with the seasons of the year they are called **seasonal variations**.

To get a better idea of the average number of units of gas used each quarter we need to smooth out these seasonal variations.

Moving averages

To smooth out seasonal variations we need to find the average for every four quarters moving forward one quarter at a time. These are called **moving averages**.

The first moving average is found by calculating the mean for the four quarters of 1998.

$$\frac{345+49+30+188}{4} = \frac{612}{4} = 153$$

The second moving average is found by calculating the mean of the last three quarters in 1998 and the first quarter in 1999.

$$\frac{49+30+188+277}{4} = \frac{544}{4} = 136$$

This process is repeated moving forward one quarter at a time. Because these averages are calculated for four consecutive quarters at a time they are called **4-point moving averages**.

The table opposite shows a useful way of setting out the calculations.

Copy and complete the table.

The number of points chosen for the moving average depends on the pattern in the data. In the example given a 4-point moving average was chosen because the pattern was repeated every 4 quarters.

Gas used			Moving average calculations			
Year	Quarter	Units				
1998	1	345	345			
	2	49	49	49		
	3	30	30	30	30	
	4	188	188	188	188	
1999	1	277		277	277	
	2	37			37	
	3	46				
	4	260				
2000	1	319				
	2	45				
	3	50				
	4	232				
4-point moving sum			612	544	532	
4-point moving average			153	136		

1 These values have been taken at equal time intervals.
Calculate the 3-point moving averages.
17   58   30   14   61   33   23   55   42

2 These values have been taken at equal time intervals.
Calculate the 5-point moving averages.
27   26   15   34   42   26   24   17   44   54

3 The number of new cars sold each quarter by a garage for the last three years is shown.

Year	1998				1999				2000			
Quarter	1	2	3	4	1	2	3	4	1	2	3	4
Number of cars sold	20	15	25	12	18	13	21	8	14	9	17	5

Calculate the 4-quarterly moving averages.

4 Calculate the value of the third average in a 5-point moving average for these values.
5   7   10   4   1   7   11   13   6   7

5 These values have been taken at equal time intervals.
160   640   310   145   670   355   175   640   385
Calculate an appropriate moving average.

Moving average graphs

Moving averages are calculated in order to investigate the general **trend** in a time series.

To investigate the trend the moving averages are plotted on the same diagram as the original graph.

Each moving average is plotted at the midpoint of the period to which it refers, so in the case of the gas used, the first moving average is plotted midway between the 2nd and 3rd quarters of 1998, the second is plotted midway between the 3rd and 4th quarters of 1998 and so on.

When all the points have been plotted a line of best fit is drawn for the moving averages to show the general **trend**.

The graph below shows the moving average values and trend line for the amount of gas used over a three-year period.

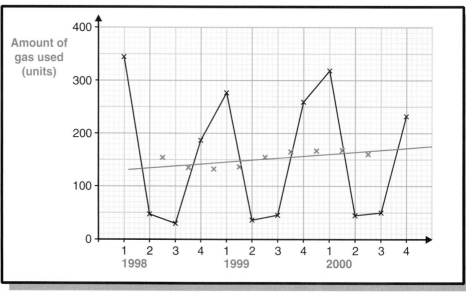

The trend shows a slight increase in the amount of gas used.

1 The table shows the amount of water used every 6 months by a householder over a period of 5 years.

Year	1996		1997		1998		1999		2000	
Month	Feb	Sept	Feb	Sept	Feb	Sept	Feb	Sept	Feb	Sept
Water used (cubic metres)	46	57	33	55	46	57	72	83	42	57

(a) Plot these values on graph paper.
(b) Calculate a 2-point moving average.
(c) Plot the moving averages on your graph.
(d) Comment on the trend in the amount of water used.

2 The table shows the quarterly electricity bills for a householder

Quarterly electricity bills

		Feb	May	Aug	Nov
	1998	£54.75	£62.16	£47.71	£57.80
Year	1999	£50.51	£64.43	£36.33	£57.39
	2000	£71.39	£65.69	£38.24	£51.65

(a) Use the data to draw a graph.
(b) Calculate a 4-point moving average.
(c) Plot the moving averages on your graph.
(d) Comment on the trend in the cost of electricity.

3 The table shows the termly absences from school for a class over a four-year period.

Termly absences

		Autumn	Spring	Summer
	Year 8	19	54	32
	Year 9	22	132	35
Year	Year 10	28	57	47
	Year 11	25	51	62

(a) Use the data to draw a graph.
(b) Calculate the values of a suitable moving average.
(c) Plot the moving averages on your graph.
(d) Comment on the trend in the number of absences for this class.

4 The table gives the daily sales (in £100's) for a new shop during the first three weeks of trading.

Daily sales

	Mon	Tue	Wed	Thu	Fri	Sat
Week 1	57	39	27	34	56	74
Week 2	38	34	28	32	61	83
Week 3	43	37	31	43	67	92

(a) Plot these values on graph paper.
(b) Calculate a 6-point moving average.
(c) Plot the moving averages on the same graph.
(d) Draw a trend line.
(e) Comment on the trend in sales.
(f) Estimate the daily sales for Monday in week 4.

5 The number of new homes completed each quarter by a builder for the last three years is shown.

Year	1998				1999				2000			
Quarter	1	2	3	4	1	2	3	4	1	2	3	4
Number of new homes	21	35	36	18	19	23	28	14	15	19	22	9

(a) Plot these values on graph paper.
(b) Calculate the values of a suitable moving average.
(c) Plot the moving averages on the same graph.
(d) Draw a trend line by eye.
(e) Comment on the trend.
(f) Estimate the number of new homes completed by the builder in the first quarter of 2001.

Frequency diagrams

We use **bar charts** when data can be counted and there are only a few different items of data.
If there is a lot of data, or the data is continuous, we draw a **histogram** or **frequency polygon**.

Histograms

Histograms are used to present information contained in **grouped frequency distributions**. In this section we will only be drawing histograms for grouped frequency distributions that have equal class width intervals.

> Histograms with equal class width intervals look like bar charts with no gaps.

Frequency polygons

Frequency polygons are often used instead of histograms when we need to compare two, or more, groups of data.
To draw a frequency polygon:
- plot the frequencies at the midpoint of each class interval,
- join successive points with straight lines.

To compare data, frequency polygons for different groups of data can be drawn on the same diagram.

EXAMPLE

1 The frequency distribution of the heights of some boys is shown.

Height (cm)	130 -	140 -	150 -	160 -	170 -	180 -
Frequency	1	7	12	9	3	0

> **Note:**
> 130 - means 130 or more but less than 140.

Draw a histogram and a frequency polygon to illustrate the data.

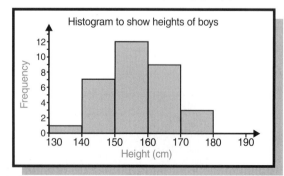

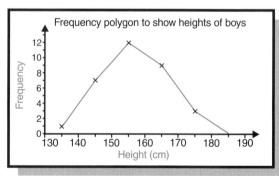

Individual bars are not labelled because the horizontal axis represents a **continuous** variable.

EXAMPLE

2 A supermarket opens at 0800. The frequency diagram shows the distribution of the times employees arrive for work.
 (a) How many employees arrive before 0730?
 (b) How many employees arrive between 0730 and 0800?
 (c) How many employees arrive after 0800?
 (d) What is the modal class?

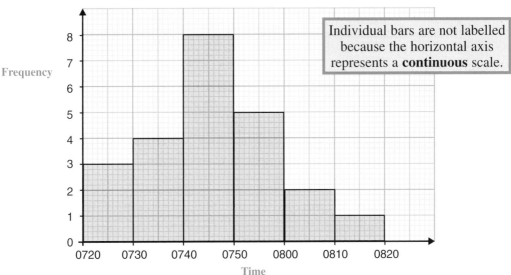

> Individual bars are not labelled because the horizontal axis represents a **continuous** scale.

 (a) 3 employees arrive before 0730.
 (b) Between 0730 and 0740, 4 employees arrive.
  Between 0740 and 0750, 8 employees arrive.
  Between 0750 and 0800, 5 employees arrive.
  Employees arriving between 0730 and 0800 = 4 + 8 + 5 = 17.
 (c) 3 employees arrive after 0800.
 (d) The modal class is the time interval with the highest frequency.
  The class interval 0740 to 0750 has the highest frequency.
  The modal class is therefore, "0740 and less than 0750".

Exercise 37.4

1 The frequency diagram shows information about the weights of 100 people.
 (a) How many people weigh between 60 kg and 70 kg?
 (b) How many people weigh less than 60 kg?
 (c) How many people weigh 70 kg or more?

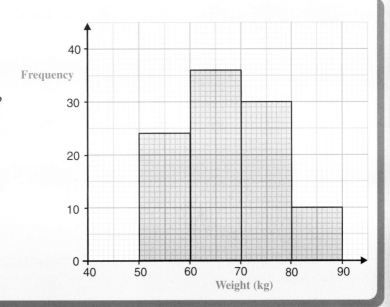

2 The frequency polygon shows the distribution of the distances travelled to work by the employees at a supermarket.

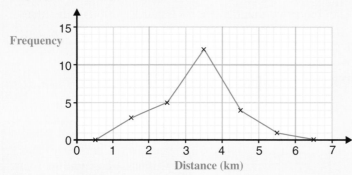

When drawing frequency polygons, frequencies are plotted at the midpoints of the class intervals.

(a)   How many employees travel between 2 km and 3 km to work?
(b)   How many employees travel more than 4 km to work?

3 The distances, in metres, recorded in a long jump competition are shown.

5.46	5.80	5.97	5.43	6.72	5.93	6.26	6.64
5.13	6.05	6.36	6.88	6.11	5.50	6.38	5.71
6.55	6.10	5.84	5.49	6.20	5.67	6.34	6.00

(a)   Copy and complete the following frequency distribution table.

Distance (m metres)	$5.00 \leqslant m < 5.50$	$5.50 \leqslant m < 6.00$	$6.00 \leqslant m < 6.50$	$6.50 \leqslant m < 7.00$
Frequency				

(b)   Draw a histogram to illustrate the data.
(c)   Which is the modal class?

4 The table shows the grouped frequency distribution of the marks of 200 students.

Mark (%)	1 - 10	11 - 20	21 - 30	31 - 40	41 - 50	51 - 60	61 - 70	71 - 80	81 - 90	91 - 100
Number of Students	0	2	16	24	44	50	35	20	8	1

Draw a frequency diagram to show these results.

5 A frequency distribution of the heights of some girls is shown.

Height (h cm)	$130 \leqslant h < 140$	$140 \leqslant h < 150$	$150 \leqslant h < 160$	$160 \leqslant h < 170$	$170 \leqslant h < 180$
Frequency	3	5	12	4	1

Draw a histogram to illustrate the data.

6 The frequency polygon shows the distribution of the ages of pupils who attend a village school.

(a)   How many pupils are under 4 years of age?
(b)   How many pupils are between 5 and 6 years of age?
(c)   How many pupils are over 7 years of age?
(d)   How many pupils attend the school?

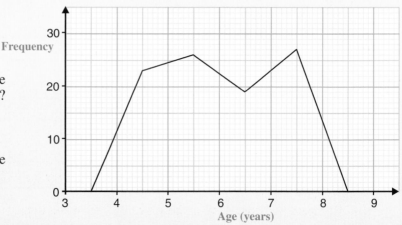

7 The frequency polygon shows the distribution of the marks scored in a science test.

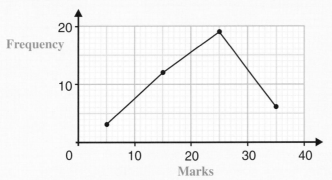

Copy and complete the frequency distribution table for these results.

Mark	Frequency
0 and less than 10	
10 and less than 20	
20 and less than 30	
30 and less than 40	

8 Here are the marks of pupils for a test in French.

44	23	36	60	50	45	35	56	41	37
31	57	43	29	67	45	34	54	29	25
46	52	27	36	39	45	41	54	49	37

(a) Copy and complete the frequency distribution table for these results.

Mark	Tally	Frequency
20 and less than 30		
30 and less than 40		
40 and less than 50		
50 and less than 60		
60 and less than 70		

(b) Which is the modal class?
(c) Draw a frequency polygon to illustrate the data.

9 The table shows the distances travelled to school by 100 children.

Distance (km)	0 -	2 -	4 -	6 -	8 -	10 -	12 -	14 -
Frequency	26	32	22	10	6	3	1	0

Draw a frequency polygon to illustrate this information.

10 The frequency distribution of the weights of some students is shown.

Weight (kg)	40 -	50 -	60 -	70 -	80 -	90 - 100
Number of males	0	6	11	5	2	1
Number of females	3	14	8	0	0	0

(a) On the same diagram draw a frequency polygon for the males and a frequency polygon for the females.
(b) Compare and comment on the weights of male and female students.

11 The table shows the results of students in tests in English and Mathematics.

Marks	English	Mathematics
0 and less than 10	0	1
10 and less than 20	4	4
20 and less than 30	9	9
30 and less than 40	12	7
40 and less than 50	0	4

(a) Draw a frequency polygon for the English marks.
(b) On the same diagram draw a frequency polygon for the Mathematics marks.
(c) Compare and comment on the marks of the students in these two tests.

12 The table shows the results for competitors in the 1999 and 2000 Schools' Javelin Championship.
Only the best distance thrown by each competitor is shown.

Distance thrown (m metres)	Number of competitors 1999	Number of competitors 2000
$10 \leqslant m < 20$	0	1
$20 \leqslant m < 30$	3	4
$30 \leqslant m < 40$	14	19
$40 \leqslant m < 50$	21	13
$50 \leqslant m < 60$	7	11
$60 \leqslant m < 70$	0	2

(a) On the same diagram draw a frequency polygon for the 1999 results and then a frequency polygon for the 2000 results.
(b) Compare and comment on the results.

Misleading graphs

Television programmes, newspapers and advertisements frequently use graphs and diagrams to present information.
Many of the graphs and diagrams they use are well presented and give a fair interpretation of the facts, others are deliberately drawn to mislead.

Look at the graph below.
Why is it misleading?

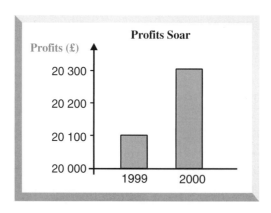

You should notice that the vertical scale does not begin at zero.
The actual increase in profits is only £200 but the graph makes it appear much more.

1 The following graph is misleading. Explain why.

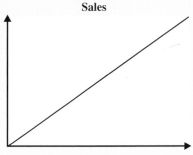

Sales

2 This graph is drawn to compare the money raised for charity by two schools.

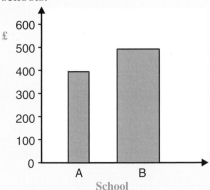

School A has raised £400.
School B has raised £500.
Why is the graph misleading?

3 This graph shows how the price of a litre of petrol has increased.

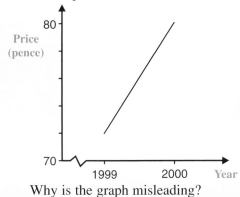

Why is the graph misleading?

4

> **PASS WITH US**
> Our learners only need an average of 8 lessons before they can take the driving test.

Give a reason why this advertisement may be misleading.

5 This diagram is used to compare the average price of a house in two different years.

Big growth in house prices

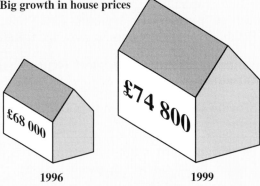

Why is the diagram misleading?

6 The graph shows the number of "Home" supporters and the number of "Away" supporters at a football match.
Why is the graph misleading?

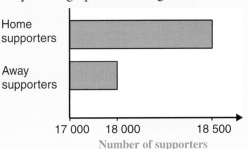

7 Why is this diagram misleading?

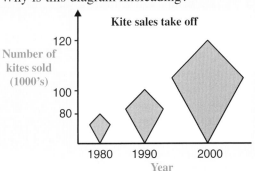

8 The graph shows the votes cast for a political party in five elections.

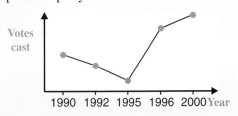

Why is the graph misleading?

What you need to know

- A **time series** is a set of readings taken at time intervals.

- A **line graph** is used to show a time series.
  Only the plotted points represent actual values.
  Points are plotted by lines to show the **trend**.

- Variations in a time series which recur with the seasons of the year are called **seasonal variations**.

- **Moving averages** are used to smooth out variations in a time series so that the trend can be seen.

- **Histogram**. Used to illustrate **grouped frequency distributions.**
  The horizontal axis is a continuous scale.

- **Frequency polygon**. Used to illustrate grouped frequency distributions.
  Often used to compare two or more distributions on the same diagram.
  Frequencies are plotted at the midpoints of the class intervals and joined with straight lines.
  The horizontal axis is a continuous scale.

- **Misleading graphs**
  Graphs may be misleading if:

  > the scales are not labelled,
  > the scales are not uniform,
  > the frequency does not begin at zero.

Review Exercise

1 Jim bought his house in 1985.
The table shows the value of Jim's house on January 1st at 5 yearly intervals.

Year	1985	1990	1995	2000
Value of house (£)	60 000	95 000	68 000	84 000

(a) Draw a line graph to show this information.
(b) Estimate the value of Jim's house on July 1st 1988.
(c) Jim uses the graph to estimate the value of his house on January 1st 2005.
Give a reason why his estimate may not be very accurate.

2 A factory operates 5 days a week.
The table shows the number of workers' absent each day over the last 3 weeks.

Week	1					2					3				
Day	M	Tu	W	Th	F	M	Tu	W	Th	F	M	Tu	W	Th	F
Number of absences	6	5	2	3	11	4	3	1	4	13	5	3	2	4	12

(a) Plot these values on graph paper.
(b) Calculate a 5-point moving average.
(c) Plot the moving averages on the same graph.
(d) Draw a trend line by eye.
(e) Comment on the trend.

3 The following is a record of the heights, in centimetres, of 40 guinea pigs.

21	22	11	16	22	13	11	25	9	17
21	24	27	25	12	14	8	12	6	17
23	7	12	26	14	8	12	26	17	19
23	29	21	19	26	26	18	21	13	9

(a) Copy and complete the frequency table, using intervals of 5 cm.

Height (h cm)	Tally	Frequency
$5 \leqslant h < 10$		
$10 \leqslant h < 15$		

(b) Draw a frequency diagram for this information.
(c) How many guinea pigs were under 15 cm in height?
(d) Write down the modal class interval of the heights.

Edexcel

4 Aimee does a survey of the distances people travel to work.
The frequency diagram shows the results.

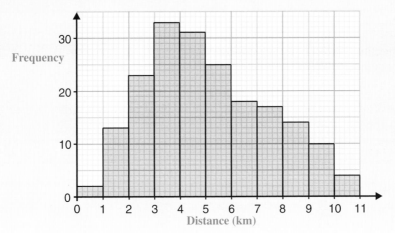

(a) Which is the modal class?
(b) How many people travel between 4 km and 5 km?
(c) How many people were included in the survey?

5 The frequency polygon illustrates the time taken by students to complete a puzzle.
Copy and complete the table for the data.

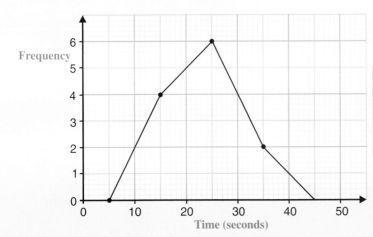

Time (seconds)	Frequency
10 and less than 20	
20 and less than 30	
30 and less than 40	

6

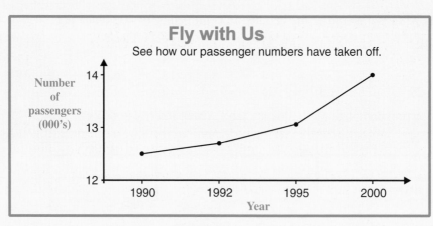

Write down two ways in which the graph is misleading

7 The grouped frequency table shows the results of a survey about the distance travelled to work by people each day.

Distance (km)	0 -	4 -	8 -	12 -	16 -	20 - 24
Number of people	10	24	30	8	7	1

(a) Draw a histogram to illustrate this information.
(b) How many people travelled less than 8 kilometres?

8 Mrs Mathers marks the French essays of a large number of boys and girls.
The table shows the distribution of marks given.

Marks	1 to 5	6 to 10	11 to 15	16 to 20	21 to 25
Frequency	2	18	46	35	6

The frequency polygon shows the distribution of marks for the boys.

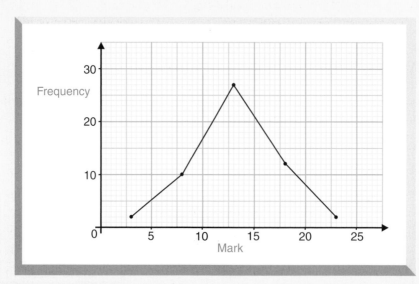

Copy the graph.
(a) On the same axes draw a frequency polygon for the girls.
(b) Use the frequency polygons to compare the distribution of marks given to boys and girls.

When we investigate statistical information we often find there are connections between sets of data, for example height and weight. In general taller people weigh more than shorter people.

To see if there is a connection between two sets of data we can plot a **scatter graph**.
The scatter graph below shows information about the heights and weights of ten boys.

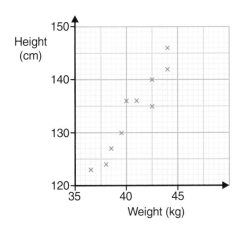

Each cross plotted on the graph represents the weight and height of one boy.

The diagram shows that taller boys generally weigh more than shorter boys.

1. The scatter graph shows the shoe sizes and heights of a group of girls.

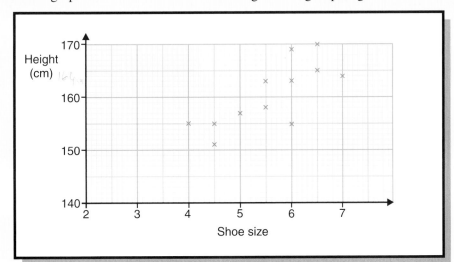

  (a) How many girls wear size $6\frac{1}{2}$ shoes?
  (b) How tall is the girl with the largest shoe size?
  (c) Does the shortest girl wear the smallest shoes?
  (d) What do you notice about the shoe sizes of taller girls compared to shorter girls?

2 The scatter graph shows the marks obtained by a group of students in a test in English and a test in French.

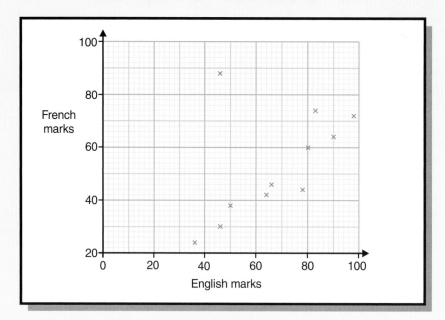

(a) Janice got the top mark in English. What mark did she get in French?
(b) The results of one student look out of place.
   (i) What marks did the student get in English and in French?
   (ii) Give a possible reason why this student has different results from the rest of the group.

3 The scatter graph shows the pulse rates of a group of women after doing aerobics for one minute and their weight.

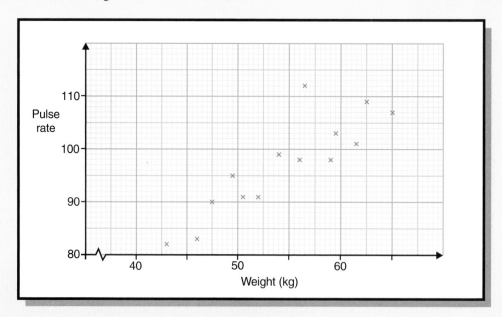

(a) How many of these women weigh less than 50 kg?
(b) What is the weight of the woman with the lowest pulse rate?
(c) What do you notice about the pulse rates of heavier women compared to lighter women?

Correlation

The relationship between two sets of data is called **correlation**.

In general the scatter graph of the heights and weights shows that as height increases, weight increases. This type of relationship shows there is a **positive correlation** between height and weight.

But if as the value of one variable increases the value of the other variable decreases, then there is a **negative correlation** between the variables.

When no relationship exists between two variables there is **zero correlation**.

The following graphs show types of correlation.

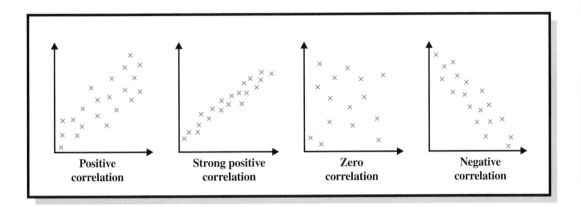

As points get closer to a straight line the stronger the correlation.
Perfect correlation is when all the points lie on a straight line.

Exercise 38.2

 (a) Which of these graphs shows the strongest positive correlation?
(b) Which of these graphs shows perfect negative correlation?
(c) Which of these graphs shows the weakest correlation?

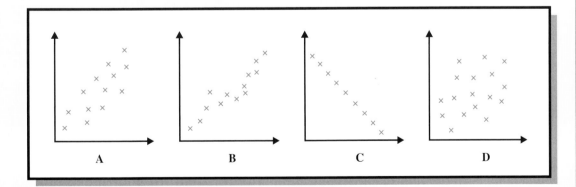

2 Describe the type of correlation you would expect between:
(a) the age of a car and its secondhand selling price,
(b) the heights of children and their ages,
(c) the shoe sizes of children and the distance they travel to school,
(d) the number of cars on the road and the number of road accidents,
(e) the engine size of a car and the number of kilometres it can travel on one litre of fuel.

③ The table shows the distance travelled and time taken by motorists on different journeys.

Distance travelled (km)	30	45	48	80	90	100	125
Time taken (hours)	0.6	0.9	1.2	1.2	1.3	2.0	1.5

(a) Draw a scatter graph for the data.
(b) What do you notice about distance travelled and time taken?
(c) Give one reason why the distance travelled and the time taken are not perfectly correlated.

④ Tyres were collected from a number of different cars. The table shows the distance travelled and depth of tread for each tyre.

Distance travelled (1000 km)	4	5	9	10	12	15	18	25	30
Depth of tread (mm)	9.2	8.4	7.6	8	6.5	7.4	7	6.2	5

(a) Draw a scatter graph for the data.
(b) What do you notice about the distance travelled and the depth of tread?
(c) Give one reason why the distance travelled and the depth of tread are not perfectly correlated.

Line of best fit

We have seen that **scatter graphs** can be used to illustrate two sets of data and from the distribution of points plotted an indication of the relationship which exists between the data can be seen.

The scatter graph of heights and weights has been redrawn below and a **line of best fit** has been drawn, by eye, to show the relationship between height and weight.

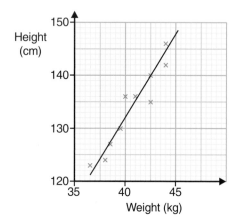

Lines of best fit
● The slope of the line shows the trend of the points.
● A line is only drawn if the correlation (positive or negative) is strong.
● The line does not have to go through the origin of the graph.

Where there is a relationship between the two sets of data the line of best fit can be used to estimate other values.

A boy is 132 cm tall.
Using the line of best fit an estimate of his weight is 40 kg.

In a similar way we can use the line to estimate the height of a boy when we know his weight.
A boy weighs 43 kg. Estimate his height.

1 The table shows the ages and weights of ten babies.

Age (weeks)	2	4	9	7	13	5	6	1	10	12
Weight (kg)	3.5	3.3	4.2	4.7	5	3.8	4	3	5	5.5

(a) Use this information to draw a scatter graph.
(b) What type of correlation is shown on the scatter graph?
(c) Draw a line of best fit.
(d) Mrs Wilson's baby is 11 weeks old.
Use the graph to estimate the weight of her baby.

2 The table shows the temperature of water as it cools in a freezer.

Time (minutes)	5	10	15	20	25	30
Temperature (°C)	36	29	25	20	15	8

(a) Use this information to draw a scatter graph.
(b) What type of correlation is shown?
(c) Draw a line of best fit.
(d) Use the graph to estimate the time when the temperature of the water reaches 0°C.

3 The table shows the weights and fitness factors for a number of women.
The higher the fitness factor the fitter a person is.

Weight (kg)	45	48	50	54	56	60	64	72	99	112
Fitness Factor	41	48	40	40	35	40	34	30	17	15

(a) Use this information to draw a scatter graph.
(b) What type of correlation is shown on the scatter graph?
(c) Draw a line of best fit.
(d) Use the graph to estimate:
  (i) the fitness factor for a woman whose weight is 80 kg,
  (ii) the weight of a woman whose fitness factor is 22.

4 The following table gives the marks obtained by some candidates taking examinations in French and German.

Mark in French	53	35	39	53	50	59	36	43
Mark in German	64	32	44	70	56	68	40	48

(a) (i) Use this information to draw a scatter graph.
  (ii) Draw the line of best fit by eye.
(b) Use the graph to estimate:
  (i) the mark in German for a candidate who got 70 in French,
  (ii) the mark in French for a candidate who got 58 in German.
(c) Which of the two estimates in (b) is likely to be more reliable?
Give a reason for your answer.

What you need to know

- A **scatter graph** can be used to show the relationship between two sets of data.

- The relationship between two sets of data is referred to as **correlation**.

- You should be able to recognise **positive** and **negative** correlation.

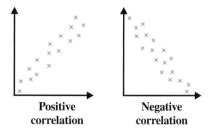

Positive correlation   Negative correlation

- When there is a relationship between two sets of data a **line of best fit** can be drawn on the scatter graph.
  The correlation is stronger as points get closer to a straight line.
  Perfect correlation is when all the points lie on a straight line.

 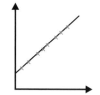 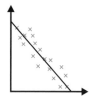

- The line of best fit can be used to **estimate** the value from one set of the data when the corresponding value of the other set is known.

Shoe size and height
Record the heights and shoe sizes of 20 male students.

Plot a scatter graph of "shoe size" against "height".

What type of correlation exists between the shoe sizes and heights of these students?

Take the shoe size of another student.
Can you use the graph to estimate the height of the student?

Investigate further.
You might like to consider age and gender.

Review Exercise

1. The data from a survey of cars was used to plot several scatter graphs.

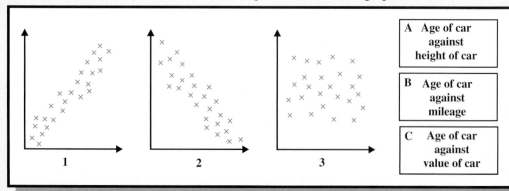

A	Age of car against height of car
B	Age of car against mileage
C	Age of car against value of car

Match each scatter graph to the correct description.

2 The scatter graph shows the number of books read by some children and the reading ages of these children.

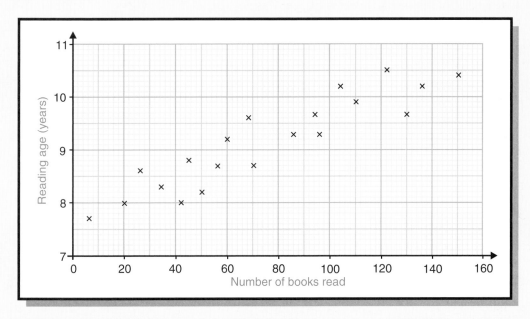

(a) How many children have read more than 100 books?
(b) One of these children has read 50 books.
What is the reading age of this child?
(c) Describe the relationship shown by the scatter graph.

3 A park has an outdoor swimming pool.
The scatter graph shows the maximum temperature and the number of people who used the pool on ten Saturdays in the summer.

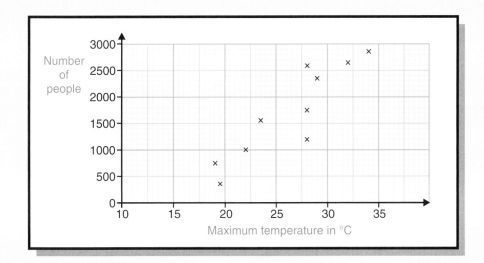

(a) Describe the correlation between the maximum temperature and the number of people who used the pool.
(b) Copy the scatter graph and draw a line of best fit.

The weather forecast for another Saturday gives a maximum temperature of 27°C.
(c) Use your line of best fit to estimate the number of people who will use the pool.

Edexcel

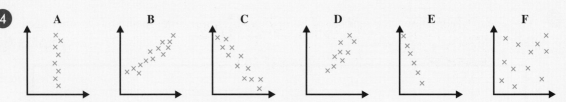

4

Sketches of six scatter diagrams **A** to **F** are shown.
(a)   Which scatter diagrams show
  (i)   positive correlation,   (ii)   negative correlation,   (iii)   no correlation?

The table gives information on underground railway ('tube') systems in 7 cities.

City	Kilometres of route (x)	Passenger journeys per year (millions) (y)
London	395	780
New York	390	1060
Paris	200	1190
Tokyo	155	1930
San Francisco	115	70
Washington DC	125	140
Kyoto	10	45

(b)   Plot a scatter diagram to show this information.

Los Angeles hopes to open an underground railway. There will be 28 km of route.
(c)   Can you use your scatter diagram to estimate the number of passenger journeys per year?
  Explain your answer.
Edexcel

5   The table shows the number of units of electricity used in heating a house on ten different days and the average temperature for each day.

Average temperature (°C)	6	2	0	6	3	5	10	8	9	12
Units of electricity used	28	38	41	34	31	31	22	25	23	22

(a)   Draw a scatter graph to show the information in the table.
(b)   Describe the **correlation** between the number of units of electricity used and the average temperature.
(c)   Draw a line of best fit on your scatter graph.
(d)   Use your line of best fit to estimate
  (i)   the average temperature if 35 units of electricity are used,
  (ii)   the units of electricity used if the average temperature is 7°C.
Edexcel

6   The table gives information about the age and value of a number of cars of the same type.

Age (years)	1	$4\frac{1}{2}$	6	3	5	2	4
Value (£)	8200	4900	3800	6200	4500	7600	5200

(a)   Use the information to draw a scatter graph.
(b)   What type of correlation is there between the age and value of these cars?
(c)   Draw a line of best fit.
(d)   Jo has a car of this type which is 7 years old and is in average condition.
  Use the graph to estimate its value.

CHAPTER 39

Cumulative Frequency

Cumulative frequency tables

This **frequency table** shows the masses of some stones recorded during an experiment.

Mass (kg)	20 -	30 -	40 -	50 -	60 - 70
Frequency	3	5	10	8	4

The first class is 20 - 30 kg.
The **upper class boundary** of this class is 30 kg.
What are the upper class boundaries of the other classes?

The information given in a frequency table can be used to make a **cumulative frequency table**.

Mass (kg), less than	20	30	40	50	60	70
Cumulative frequency	0	3	8	18	26	30

Note
If the question does not give the upper class boundaries, then the upper class boundary of each class is equal to the lower class boundary of the next class.

Mass of stone (less than)	Number of stones
20 kg	0
30 kg	0 + 3 = 3
40 kg	0 + 3 + 5 = 8
50 kg	0 + 3 + 5 + 8 + 10 = 18

Cumulative frequency graph

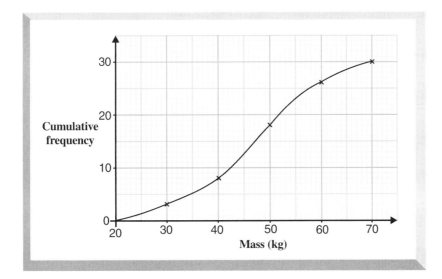

To draw a **cumulative frequency graph**:
1. Draw and label:
   the **variable** on the horizontal axis,
   cumulative frequency on the vertical axis.

2. Plot the cumulative frequency against the upper class boundary of each class.

3. Join the points with a smooth curve.

Median

The median of 13 numbers is the 7th number.
The median of 14 numbers is between the 7th and
8 th numbers.
We could call this the "$7\frac{1}{2}$ th" number.

For n numbers, the rule for finding the median is:

$$\text{Median} = \tfrac{1}{2}(n + 1)\text{th number}$$

> The median of a frequency distribution is the value of the middle number.
> On a cumulative frequency graph this value is read from the horizontal axis.

Interquartile range

The **range** of a set of data was covered in Chapter 35 and again in Chapter 36.
It measures how spread out the data is.
Range = highest value − lowest value.
The range is influenced by extreme high or low values of data and can be misleading.

A better way to measure spread is to find the range of the
middle 50% of the data.
This is called the **interquartile range**.
Interquartile range IQR = Upper Quartile − Lower Quartile

For n numbers the rules for finding the quartiles are:

Lower Quartile $= \tfrac{1}{4}(n + 1)$th number

Upper Quartile $= \tfrac{3}{4}(n + 1)$th number

> On a cumulative frequency graph the values of the Upper Quartile and the Lower Quartile are read from the horizontal axis.

EXAMPLE

Using the cumulative frequency graph from the previous
page, estimate:
(a)   the median mass of the stones,
(b)   the interquartile range of the masses of the stones.

> **When n is large**
> When the total frequency, n, is 'large' you need not bother with '+1' in the rules for the median, lower quartile and upper quartile.
>
> Instead use:
>
> median $= \tfrac{1}{2}\, n$ th number
>
> lower quartile $= \tfrac{1}{4}\, n$ th number
>
> upper quartile $= \tfrac{3}{4}\, n$ th number
>
> 'Large' means greater than 50.
>
> *Explain why.*

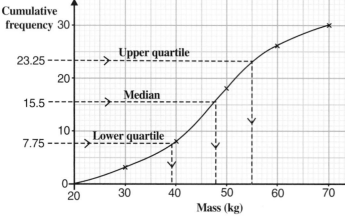

(a)   There are 30 stones.
$\tfrac{1}{2}(30 + 1) = 15.5$, so the median is the
mass of the 15.5th stone.
Read along from 15.5 on the vertical axis
and down to the horizontal axis.
This is shown on the graph.
Median = 48 kg.

*Why are the values for the median and
interquartile range only estimates?*

(b) $\tfrac{1}{4}(30 + 1) = 7.75$, so the lower quartile
is the mass of the 7.75th stone.
$\tfrac{3}{4}(30 + 1) = 23.25$, so the upper quartile
is the mass of the 23.25th stone.
Read these values from the graph.

IQR = Upper Quartile − Lower Quartile
$= 55 − 39$
$= 16$ kg
The interquartile range is 16 kg.

Exercise 39.1

1 Silvia made a record of the times students took to walk to school in the morning.

Time (minutes)	0 -	5 -	10 -	15 -	20 -	25 - 30
Number of students	4	12	18	15	8	3

(a) Copy and complete this cumulative frequency table.

Time (minutes), less than	0	5	10	15	20	25	30
Cumulative frequency							

(b) Draw a cumulative frequency graph for the data.
(c) Use your graph to find:
   (i) the median time,
   (ii) the upper quartile time,
   (iii) the lower quartile time.
(d) Calculate the interquartile range of the times.

2 A secretary weighed a sample of letters to be posted.

Weight (g)	20 -	30 -	40 -	50 -	60 -	70 -	80 - 90
Number of letters	2	4	12	7	8	16	3

(a) How many letters were in the sample?
(b) Draw a cumulative frequency graph for the data.
(c) Use your graph to find:
   (i) the median weight of a letter,
   (ii) the interquartile range of the weights.

3 The times spent by students on mobile phones one day is shown.

Time (t minutes)	$0 \leqslant t < 5$	$5 \leqslant t < 10$	$10 \leqslant t < 15$	$15 \leqslant t < 20$	$20 \leqslant t < 25$
Number of students	34	22	12	8	4

(a) Draw a cumulative frequency graph for the data.
(b) Use your graph to find (i) the median time,
   (ii) the interquartile range of the times.

Another look at cumulative frequency graphs

Some variables are discrete and can only take certain values.
In many cases these are whole numbers. For these variables there are gaps between the classes.

For example, this frequency distribution table shows the number of spelling mistakes found in some essays.

Number of mistakes	0 - 5	6 - 10	11 - 15	16 - 20
Number of essays	9	17	8	3

The first class ends at 5. The highest number of spelling mistakes in the class 0 - 5 is 5.
The second class starts at 6.
We take the upper class boundary for the class 0 - 5 to be halfway between 5 and 6, at 5.5.
What are the upper class boundaries for the other classes?

In the following example there are gaps between the classes, because the lengths are measured to the nearest centimetre.

In an experiment Sophie measured and recorded the longest roots of plants.

Length (to nearest cm)	0 - 2	3 - 5	6 - 8	9 - 11	12 - 14
Number of plants	0	14	35	23	10

(a)   Make a cumulative frequency table for the data Sophie collected.
(b)   Draw a cumulative frequency graph for the data.
(c)   Use your graph to find:
    (i)   the median length,
    (ii)   the interquartile range of lengths.
(d)   How many plants had roots at least 11.2 cm long?

The class 3 - 5 includes measurements from 2.5 cm to 5.5 cm. The upper class boundary is 5.5.

(a)

Length (cm) less than	2.5	5.5	8.5	11.5	14.5
Cumulative frequency	0	14	47	70	80

(b)

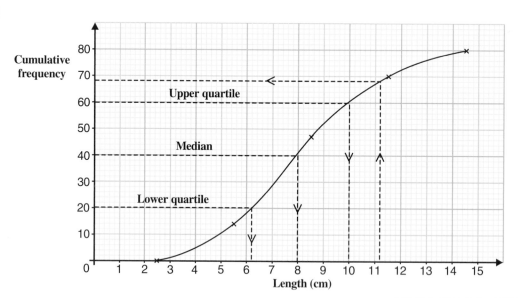

(c)   (i)   There are 80 plants.
$\frac{1}{2}$ of 80 = 40, so the median is the length of the roots of the 40th plant.
Median = 8.0 cm

(ii)   For the lower quartile use $\frac{1}{4}$ of 80 = 20.
Lower quartile = 6.2 cm
For the upper quartile use $\frac{3}{4}$ of 80 = 60.
Upper quartile = 10.0 cm
IQR = Upper Quartile − Lower Quartile
= 10.0 − 6.2
= 3.8 cm

Remember
Cumulative frequency is plotted against the upper class boundary for each class.

(d)   From 11.2 on the horizontal axis read upwards to the graph and across to the vertical axis.
There are 68 plants of length less than 11.2 cm.
So the number of plants with roots at least 11.2 cm long is 80 − 68 = 12 plants.

Exercise **39.2**

1 The times taken by competitors to complete the crossword in an annual competition were recorded to the nearest minute.

Time (minutes)	10 - 14	15 - 19	20 - 24	25 - 29	30 - 34
Frequency	7	21	37	12	3

(a) Copy and complete the cumulative frequency table.

Time (minutes)	< 9.5	< 14.5	< 19.5	< 24.5	< 29.5	< 34.5
Cumulative frequency						

(b) Draw a cumulative frequency graph for the data.
(c) Use your graph to find:
    (i) the interquartile range of times,
    (ii) the number of competitors who took less than last year's winning time of 16 minutes to complete the crossword.

2 Draw a cumulative frequency graph for the results shown in this table.

Number of marks	0 - 20	21 - 25	26 - 30	31 - 40
Number of students	10	17	23	14

(a) Find the median mark.
(b) Find the interquartile range of marks.
(c) The minimum mark for a Grade A is 33.
    What percentage of students gained Grade A?
(d) 10% of students failed.
    What was the minimum mark for a pass?

3 A survey was made of the heights of plants produced by a batch of seed.

Height (h cm)	$80 \leqslant t < 85$	$85 \leqslant t < 90$	$90 \leqslant t < 95$	$95 \leqslant t < 100$	$100 \leqslant t < 105$
Frequency	20	35	15	11	14

(a) How many plants were measured in the survey?
(b) Draw a cumulative frequency graph for the data.
    Label the horizontal axis from 70 cm to 110 cm.
(c) Use your graph to estimate:
    (i) the median height,
    (ii) the interquartile range of heights,
    (iii) the number of plants taller than 97.5 cm.
(d) The shortest 10 plants are used for testing.
    Estimate the height of the tallest of these 10 plants.

4 The times spent listening to the radio last week by some students is shown.

Time (t hours)	$0 \leqslant t < 5$	$5 \leqslant t < 10$	$10 \leqslant t < 15$	$15 \leqslant t < 20$	$20 \leqslant t < 30$	$30 \leqslant t < 40$
Number of students	7	15	18	24	12	4

(a) Draw a cumulative frequency graph for the data.
(b) Use your graph to find the interquartile range of times.
(c) What percentage of the students spent more than 25 hours per week listening to the radio?

5 The heights of a number of men are shown in the table.
Draw a cumulative frequency graph for the data.
Use your graph to find:

(a) the median and interquartile range of heights,
(b) the number of men less than 155 cm,
(c) the number of men at least 163 cm,
(d) the maximum height of the shortest 20 men,
(e) the minimum height of the tallest 10% of men.

Height (h cm)	Frequency
$140 \leqslant h < 150$	1
$150 \leqslant h < 160$	6
$160 \leqslant h < 170$	8
$170 \leqslant h < 180$	21
$180 \leqslant h < 190$	14

Comparing distributions

EXAMPLE

A firm tested a sample of electric motors produced by an assembly line. They kept a running total of the numbers of motors which had failed at any time. This cumulative frequency graph was plotted using the data collected.

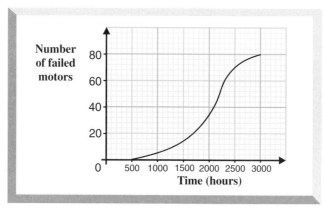

(a) Find the median lifetime of a motor.

(b) Find the interquartile range of lifetimes.

(c) A sample of motors, produced by another assembly line, was tested and found to have:
   Median lifetime = 1900 hours
   Upper quartile = 2000 hours
   Lower quartile = 1700 hours
Compare the two samples of motors.

(a) Median lifetime = 2100 hours

(b) IQR = Upper Quartile − Lower Quartile
   = 2300 − 1700
   = 600 hours

(c) For the second sample:
   Median = 1900 hours
   IQR = 2000 − 1700 = 300 hours
   The first sample has a greater median time.
   On average, they lasted 200 hours longer than motors in the second sample.

   The spread of the second sample (given by the IQR) is much smaller.
   It is 300 hours, compared with 600 hours for the first sample.

1 The heights of a group of boys and a group of girls were recorded separately.
   The results are shown by the cumulative frequency graphs.

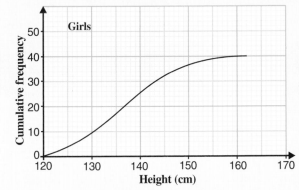 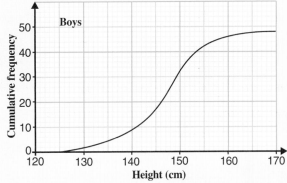

(a) How many girls were measured?
(b) Find the interquartile range of heights of the girls.
(c) Find the interquartile range of heights of the boys.
(d) Use your answers to parts (b) and (c) to comment on the heights of the girls compared with the boys.
(e) How many boys are taller than the tallest girl?

2 The milk yields of a herd of cows is shown in the table below.

Milk yield (x litres)	$5 \leqslant x < 10$	$10 \leqslant x < 15$	$15 \leqslant x < 20$	$20 \leqslant x < 25$	$25 \leqslant x < 30$
Number of cows	15	28	37	26	25

(a) Use the data to draw a cumulative frequency graph.
(b) Use your graph to estimate:
    (i) the median milk yield,   (ii) the interquartile range of milk yields.
(c) A neighbouring farmer calculated the following results for his herd of cows.
    Median yield = 22 litres, Lower quartile = 9 litres, Upper quartile = 28 litres.
    Compare and comment on the data for the two herds.

3 A sample of potatoes of Variety X and a sample of potatoes of Variety Y are weighed.
   The cumulative frequency graphs show information about the weight distribution of each sample.

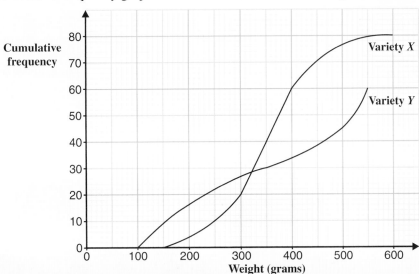

By finding the median and interquartile range of each sample, compare and comment on the weights of these varieties of potato.

Box plots (or **box and whisker diagrams**) provide a useful way of representing the range, the median and the quartiles of a set of data.

They are also useful for comparing two (or more) distributions.

The graph shows the cumulative frequency distribution of the masses of 80 fish.

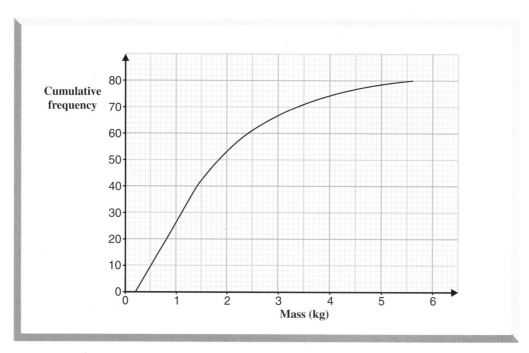

From the graph we can read off the following information:

- the minimum mass is $0.2\,kg$,
- the maximum mass is $5.6\,kg$,
- the median mass is $1.4\,kg$,
- the lower quartile is $0.8\,kg$,
- the upper quartile is $2.4\,kg$.

This information can now be represented as a box plot.

Begin by drawing a horizontal line and marking a scale from 0 to $6\,kg$.
Above your line, draw a box from the lower quartile to the upper quartile and mark in the median with a line across the box.
Draw lines (sometimes called whiskers) from the lower end of the box to $0.2\,kg$ and from the upper end of the box to $5.6\,kg$ to represent the range.

A box plot for the masses of these fish is shown below.

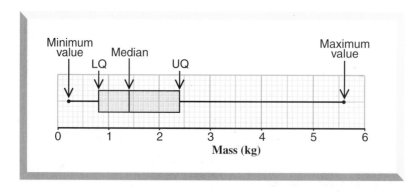

The box plot shows how the masses of these fish are spread out and how the middle 50% are clustered.

EXAMPLE

The number of points scored by the 11 players in a basketball team during a competition are shown.

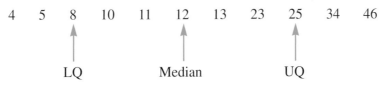

13   12   5   34   8   10   11   46   25   23   4

Draw a box plot to illustrate the data.

Begin by putting the data in order and then locate the median, lower quartile and upper quartile.

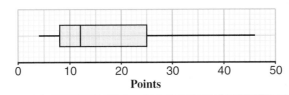

4   5   8   10   11   12   13   23   25   34   46

LQ   Median   UQ

Then use these values to draw the box plot.

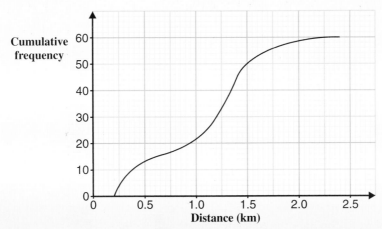

0   10   20   30   40   50

Points

Exercise **39.4**

1 The midday temperatures, in °C, for 11 cities around the world are:

9   12   20   24   25   28   28   30   31   32   35

Draw a box plot to represent these temperatures.

2 A group of 15 people were asked to estimate the weight of a large tortoise. Their estimates, in kilograms, are shown.

2.8   3.0   3.2   3.3   3.5   3.6   3.8   3.8
4.0   4.0   4.2   4.2   4.4   4.5   4.7

Draw a box plot to represent these estimates.

3 The cumulative frequency graph shows information about the distances travelled by children to get to school.

Cumulative frequency

60
50
40
30
20
10
0

0   0.5   1.0   1.5   2.0   2.5

Distance (km)

Draw a box plot to illustrate the data.

4 A sample of 23 people were asked to record the amount they spent on food last week.
The amounts, in £'s, are shown.

37	46	55	63	19	63	16	22	42	47	23	18
51	38	27	33	42	64	56	48	57	37	22	

(a) Find the median and quartiles of this distribution.
(b) Draw a box plot to represent the data.

5 The box plot illustrates the reaction times of a group of people.

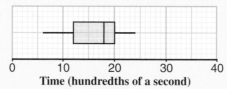

Time (hundredths of a second)

(a) What was the minimum reaction time?
(b) What is the value of the interquartile range?

6 A group of students took examinations in Mathematics and English.
The box plots illustrate the results.

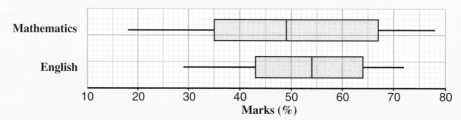

Marks (%)

(a) What was the highest mark scored in English?
(b) What was the lowest mark scored in Mathematics?
(c) Which subject has the higher median mark?
(d) What is the value of the interquartile range for English?
(e) Comment on the results of these examinations.

7 The cumulative frequency graphs show the times taken by students to run 100 m.

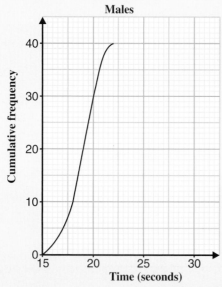

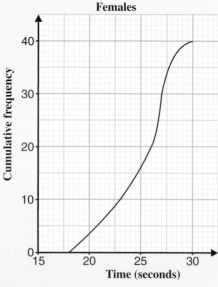

(a) Draw box plots to compare the times for males and females.
(b) Comment on the times for males and females.

What you need to know

- The information given in a frequency table can be used to make a **cumulative frequency table**.

- To draw a **cumulative frequency graph**:

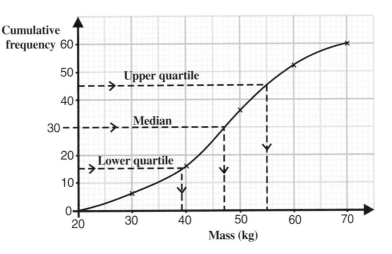

1. Draw and label: the variable on the horizontal axis,
     cumulative frequency on the vertical axis.
2. Plot the cumulative frequency against the upper class boundary of each class.
3. Join the points with a smooth curve.

- If the question does not give the upper class boundaries, then the upper class boundary of each class is equal to the lower class boundary of the next class.

- When the classes have gaps between them then the upper class boundary is halfway between the end of one class and the beginning of the next.

- The **median** is the value of the middle number.

  The **lower quartile** is the value located at $\frac{1}{4}$ of the total frequency.

  The **upper quartile** is the value located at $\frac{3}{4}$ of the total frequency.

  The **interquartile range** measures the spread of the middle 50% of the data.

  Interquartile range = Upper Quartile − Lower Quartile

- A **box plot** is used to represent the range, the median and the quartiles of a distribution.

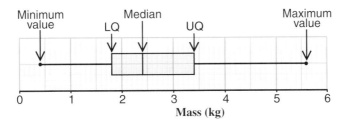

- The box plot shows how the data is spread out and how the middle 50% of data is clustered.

- Box plots can be used to compare two (or more) distributions.

1 The cumulative frequency graph shows the finishing times of people taking part in a 10 km race for charity.

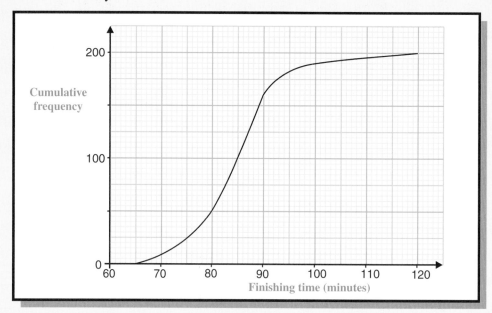

(a) How many people took part in the race?

(b) What percentage of people took more than 90 minutes to finish the race?

(c) Use the graph to estimate:
   (i) the median finishing time,
   (ii) the interquartile range.

(d) Give a reason why the interquartile range is a better measure of spread than the range for this data.

2 At a supermarket, members of staff recorded the lengths of time that 80 customers had to wait in the queues at the check-outs.
The waiting times are grouped in the frequency table below.

Waiting time (t seconds)	Frequency
$0 < t \leqslant 50$	4
$50 < t \leqslant 100$	7
$100 < t \leqslant 150$	10
$150 < t \leqslant 200$	16
$200 < t \leqslant 250$	30
$250 < t \leqslant 300$	13

(a) Copy and complete the cumulative frequency table.

(b) Draw a cumulative frequency graph for this data.

(c) Use your graph to work out an estimate for
   (i) the median waiting time,
   (ii) the number of these customers who had to wait for more than 3 minutes.

Waiting time (t seconds)	Cumulative frequency
$0 < t \leqslant 50$	
$0 < t \leqslant 100$	
$0 < t \leqslant 150$	
$0 < t \leqslant 200$	
$0 < t \leqslant 250$	
$0 < t \leqslant 300$	

Edexcel

3 A group of people took a fitness test.
They exercised hard.
Then they were timed to see how long their pulses took to return to normal.
The time taken for a pulse to return to normal is called the RECOVERY TIME.
The recovery times for the group are shown in the table below.

Recovery time (seconds)	Frequency	Cumulative frequency
0 up to but not including 20	0	0
20 up to but not including 40	7	7
40 up to but not including 60	9	16
60 up to but not including 80	18	34
80 up to but not including 90	13	47
90 up to but not including 100	12	59
100 up to but not including 120	9	68
120 up to but not including 140	6	74

(a) Use the figures in the table to draw a cumulative frequency curve.
(b) Use your cumulative frequency curve to estimate the value of
   (i) the median,
   (ii) the interquartile range.

A second group of people took the fitness test.
The recovery times of people in this group had a median of 61 seconds and an interquartile
range of 22 seconds.
(c) Compare the fitness results of the two groups.   Edexcel

4 A survey was made of the heights of plants produced
by a batch of seed.
(a) How many plants were measured in the survey?
(b) Draw a cumulative frequency graph for the data.
(c) Use your graph to estimate:
   (i) the median height,
   (ii) the interquartile range of heights,
   (iii) the number of plants taller than 97.5 cm.
(d) The shortest 10 plants are used for testing.
   Estimate the height of the tallest of these 10 plants.

Height (h cm)	Frequency
$80 \leqslant h < 85$	20
$85 \leqslant h < 90$	35
$90 \leqslant h < 95$	15
$95 \leqslant h < 100$	11
$100 \leqslant h < 105$	14

5 The box plot shows information about the price of a pint of milk in a number of shops.

(a) What is the range in price?
(b) What is the median price?
(c) What is the value of the interquartile range?

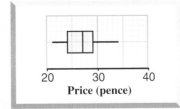

6 The times taken by students to access a website gave the following information.

Maximum time   5.1 minutes   Lower quartile   2.8 minutes
Minimum time   1.5 minutes   Upper quartile   4.2 minutes
Median time   3.8 minutes

Draw a box plot to represent this information.

What is probability?

Probability, or **chance**, involves describing how likely something is to happen.
For example:
How likely is it to rain tomorrow?

We often make forecasts, or judgements, about how likely things are to happen.
When trying to forecast tomorrow's weather the following **outcomes** are possible:
sun, cloud, wind, rain, snow, …
We are interested in the particular **event**, rain tomorrow.

> The chance of an event happening can be described using these words:
> **Impossible   Unlikely   Evens   Likely   Certain**

Use one of the words in the box to describe the chance of rain tomorrow.

Probability words
In any situation, the possible things that can happen are called **outcomes**. An outcome of particular interest is called an **event**.

Probability and the probability scale

Estimates of probabilities can be shown on a **probability scale**. The scale goes from 0 to 1.
A **probability of 0** means that an event is **impossible**.
A **probability of 1** means that an event is **certain**.
Probabilities are written either as a fraction, a decimal or a percentage.

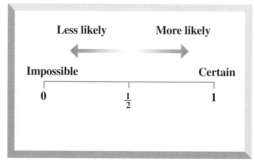

Describe the likelihood that an event will occur if it has a probability of $\frac{1}{2}$.

Exercise 40.1

1. Describe each of the following events as:
   Impossible   Unlikely   Evens   Likely   Certain
   (a) You roll a normal dice and get an odd number.
   (b) You roll a normal dice and get a 7.
   (c) A 6 is scored at least 80 times when a normal dice is rolled 600 times.
   (d) It will rain on three days running in August.
   (e) Somewhere in the world it is raining today.
   (f) A coin is tossed five times and lands heads up on each occasion.
   (g) A coin is tossed five times and lands heads up at least once.

446

2 The probabilities of four events have been marked on a probability scale.
Copy the probability scale.

Event V   A coin lands 'heads' up.
Event W   A person is over 3 metres tall.
Event X   Rolling an ordinary dice and getting a score less than 7.
Event Y   There is a 35% chance that it will rain tomorrow.

Label the arrows on your diagram to show which event they represent.

Calculating probabilities using equally likely outcomes

Probabilities can be **calculated** in situations where each outcome is **equally likely** to occur.

In such situations, the probability of an event, X, occurring is given by:

$$P(X) = \frac{\text{Number of possible outcomes in the event}}{\text{Total number of possible outcomes}}$$

In this book $P(X)$ stands for the probability of X.

Probability words
In many probability situations things are taken or picked at **random**.
For example:
A boy is picked at random from a group.
This means that any boy in the group is equally likely to be picked.

EXAMPLES

1 A fair dice is rolled.
What is the probability of getting
(a) a 6,
(b) an odd number,
(c) a 2 or a 3?

Total number of possible outcomes is 6 (1, 2, 3, 4, 5 and 6).
The dice is fair so each of these outcomes is equally likely.

(a) The number of outcomes in the event getting a 6 is 1.

$$P(6) = \tfrac{1}{6}$$

(b) The total number of outcomes in the event is 3 (1, 3, 5).

$$P(\text{an odd number}) = \tfrac{3}{6} = \tfrac{1}{2}$$

(c) The total number of outcomes in the event is 2 (2, 3).

$$P(2 \text{ or } 3) = \tfrac{2}{6} = \tfrac{1}{3}$$

2 This table shows how 100 counters are coloured red or blue and numbered 1 or 2.

	Red	Blue
1	23	19
2	32	26

The 100 counters are put in a bag and a counter is taken from the bag at random.
(a) Calculate the probability that the counter is red.
(b) Calculate the probability that the counter is blue and numbered 1.

Total number of possible outcomes = 100
(a) Red counters = 23 + 32 = 55

$$P(\text{red}) = \tfrac{55}{100} = \tfrac{11}{20}$$

This could be written as 0.55 or 55%.

(b) There are 19 counters that are blue and numbered 1.

$$P(\text{blue and 1}) = \tfrac{19}{100}$$

This could be written as 0.19 or 19%.

1 A bag contains a red counter, a blue counter and a green counter.
A counter is taken from the bag at random.
What is the probability of taking:
(a) a red counter,
(b) a red or a green counter,
(c) a counter that is not blue?

2 A bag contains 3 red sweets and 7 black sweets.
A sweet is taken from the bag at random.
What is the probability of taking:
(a) a red sweet,
(b) a black sweet?

3 This fair spinner is used in a game.

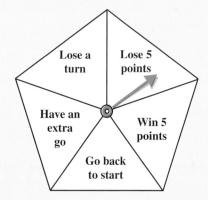

In the game a player spins the arrow.
What is the probability that the player:
(a) loses a turn,
(b) wins 5 points or loses 5 points?

4 The eleven letters of the word MISSISSIPPI are written on separate tiles.
The tiles are placed in a bag and mixed up. One tile is selected at random.
What is the probability that the tile selected shows:
(a) the letter M,
(b) the letter I,
(c) the letter P?

5 The letters of the word TRIGONOMETRY are written on separate cards. The cards are shuffled and dealt, face down, onto a table. A card is selected at random. What is the probability that the card shows:
(a) the letter Y,
(b) the letter R?
Write your answers in their simplest form.

6 A card is taken at random from a full pack of 52 playing cards with no jokers.
What is the probability that the card:
(a) is red,
(b) is a heart,
(c) is the ace of hearts?

7 A bag contains 4 red counters, 3 white counters and 3 blue counters.
A counter is taken from the bag at random.
What is the probability that the counter is:
(a) red,
(b) white or blue,
(c) red, white or blue,
(d) green?

8 In a hat there are twelve numbered discs.

Nina takes a disc from the hat at random.
What is the probability that Nina takes a disc:
(a) with at least one 4 on it,
(b) that has not got a 4 on it,
(c) that has a 3 or a 4 on it?

9 This table shows how fifty counters are numbered either 1 or 2 and coloured red or blue.

	Red	Blue
1	12	8
2	8	22

One of the counters is chosen at random.
What is the probability that the counter is:
(a) a 1,
(b) blue,
(c) blue and a 1?

A blue counter is chosen at random.
(d) What is the probability that it is a 1?

A counter numbered 1 is chosen at random.
(e) What is the probability that it is blue?

10 The table shows the way that 120 pupils from Year 7 travel to Linfield School.

A pupil from Year 7 is chosen at random.
What is the probability that the pupil:
(a) walks to school,
(b) is a girl who travels by car,
(c) is a boy who does not travel by bus?

A girl from Year 7 is chosen at random.
What is the probability that:
(d) she walks to school,
(e) she does not travel by car?

	Boys	Girls
Walk	23	17
Bus	15	20
Car	12	8
Bike	20	5

A Year 7 pupil who travels by bike is chosen at random.
(f) What is the probability that the pupil is a boy?

11 Tim plays a friend at Noughts and Crosses.
He says: 'I can either win, draw or lose, so the probability that I will win must be $\frac{1}{3}$'.
Explain why Tim is wrong.

Estimating probabilities using relative frequency

In question 11 in Exercise 40.2, probabilities **cannot** be calculated using equally likely outcomes.
In such situations probabilities can be estimated using the idea of **relative frequency**.

It is not always necessary to perform an experiment or make observations.
Sometimes the information required can be found in past records.

> The relative frequency of an event is given by:
>
> Relative frequency = $\dfrac{\text{Number of times the event happens in an experiment (or in a survey)}}{\text{Total number of trials in the experiment (or observations in the survey)}}$

EXAMPLE

1 Jamie does the following experiment with a bag containing 2 red and 8 blue counters.

> Take a counter from the bag at random.
> Record the colour then put the counter back in the bag.
> Repeat this for 100 trials.

Jamie calculates the relative frequency of getting a red
counter every 10 trials and shows his results on a graph.
Draw a graph showing the results that Jamie might get.
This is the sort of graph that Jamie might get.

P(Red) = $\frac{2}{10}$ = 0.2
This is shown on the
graph by the dotted line.

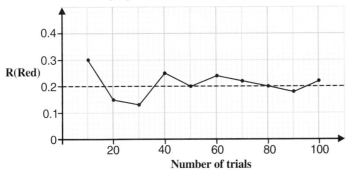

Jamie's graph illustrates:
as the number of trials
increases, relative
frequency gives a better
estimate of calculated
probability.

Try Jamie's experiment yourself and see what sort of results you get.

2 In an experiment a drawing pin is dropped for 100 trials.
The drawing pin lands "point up" 37 times.
What is the relative frequency of the drawing pin landing "point up"?

Relative frequency $= \frac{37}{100}$

$\qquad\qquad\qquad = 0.37$

Relative frequency gives a better estimate of probability the larger the number of trials.

3 A counter was taken from a bag of counters and replaced.
The relative frequency of getting a blue counter was found to be 0.4.
There are 20 counters in the bag.
Estimate the number of blue counters.

Relative frequency of taking a blue counter is 0.4.
Total number of counters in the bag = 20
Number of blue counters = 20 × 0.4 = 8
There are 8 blue counters in the bag.

Exercise 40.3

1 50 cars are observed passing the school gate.
14 red cars are observed.
What is the relative frequency of a red car passing the school gate?

2 Rainfall records show that in April it rained in Newcastle on 24 days in 1998.
Estimate the probability of rain in Newcastle on a day in April.

3 Gemma keeps a record of her chess games with Helen.
Out of the first 10 games, Gemma wins 6. Out of the first 30 games Gemma wins 21.
Estimate the probability that Gemma will win her next game of chess with Helen.

4 There are 50 cars in the school car park.
5 of the cars are black.
(a)   What is the relative frequency of a black car in the car park?

The relative frequency of a red car in the school car park is 0.2.
(b)   How many red cars are in the car park?

5 The results of games of chess played by four children at a chess club are shown in this table.

Player	Games won	Games drawn	Games lost
Tom	4	2	6
Sam	8	1	7
Kim	3	0	1
Pam	9	2	9

(a)   Calculate the relative frequency of a win for each player.
(b)   Which of these relative frequencies is most likely to give the best estimate of the probability that the child will win their next game?
Explain your answer.
(c)   If Tom plays Pam, who do you think is more likely to win?
Explain your answer.

6 A counter was taken from a bag of counters and replaced.
The relative frequency of getting a red counter was found to be 0.3.
There are 30 counters in the bag.
Estimate the number of red counters.

7 500 tickets are sold for a prize draw.
(a) Samantha buys one ticket.
What is the probability that she wins first prize?
(b) The probability that Greg wins first prize is $\frac{1}{20}$.
How many tickets did he buy?

8 A bypass is to be built to avoid a town.
There are three possible routes that the road can take.
A survey was carried out in the town.

Route	A	B	C
Relative frequency	0.4	0.5	0.1

30 people opted for Route C.
(a) How many people were surveyed altogether?
(b) How many people opted for Route A?
(c) How many people opted for Route B?

9 Rachel selects 40 holiday brochures at random.
The relative frequency of the brochure being for a holiday in Italy is 0.2.
How many brochures did Rachel select for holidays in Italy?

10 A counter is taken from a bag at random. Its colour is recorded and the counter is then put back in the bag.
This is repeated 300 times.
The number of red counters taken from the bag after every 100 trials is shown in the table.

Number of trials	Number of red counters
100	52
200	102
300	141

(a) Calculate the relative frequency after each 100 trials.
(b) Estimate the probability of taking a red counter from the bag.

11 The diagram shows a spinner which is spun a number of times.
The graph shows the relative frequency of the spinner landing on the number 1 plotted against the number of times the spinner is spun.

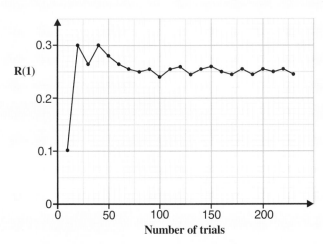

(a) The spinner is a fair spinner.
How can you tell from the graph?

(b) How might the relative frequency of the spinner landing on the number 3 change with the number of trials?
Show your answer on a graph with relative frequency plotted after every 20 trials.

Events which **cannot happen at the same time** are called **mutually exclusive events**.
For example, the event 'Heads' cannot occur at the same time as the event 'Tails'.

> When A and B are events which cannot happen at the same time:
> P(A or B) = P(A) + P(B)

The probability of an event not happening

> The events A and not A cannot happen at the same time.
> Because the events A and not A are certain to happen:
> P(not A) = 1 − P(A)

EXAMPLES

1 A bag contains 3 red (R) counters, 2 blue (B) counters and 5 green (G) counters.
A counter is taken from the bag at random.
What is the probability that the counter is:
(a) red,
(b) green,
(c) red or green?
Find the total number of counters in the bag.
$5 + 2 + 3 = 10$
Total number of possible outcomes = 10.
(a) Number of possible outcomes = 3.
$$P(R) = \tfrac{3}{10}$$
(b) Number of possible outcomes = 5.
$$P(G) = \tfrac{5}{10} = \tfrac{1}{2}$$
(c) Events R and G cannot happen at the same time.
$$P(R \text{ or } G) = P(R) + P(G)$$
$$= \tfrac{3}{10} + \tfrac{5}{10} = \tfrac{8}{10} = \tfrac{4}{5}$$

2

A bag contains 10 counters.
3 of the counters are red (R).
A counter is taken from the bag at random.
What is the probability that the counter is:
(a) red,
(b) not red?
Total number of possible outcomes = 10.
(a) Number of possible outcomes = 3.
$$P(R) = \tfrac{3}{10}$$
(b) $P(\text{not } R) = 1 - P(R)$
$$= 1 - \tfrac{3}{10} = \tfrac{7}{10}$$

Exercise 40.4

1 A fish is taken at random from a tank.
The probability that the fish is black is $\tfrac{2}{5}$.
What is the probability that the fish is not black?

2 Tina has a bag of beads.
She takes a bead from the bag at random.
The probability that the bead is white is 0.6.
What is the probability that the bead is not white?

3 The probability of a switch working is 0.96.
What is the probability of a switch not working?

4 Six out of every 100 men are taller than 1.85 m.
A man is picked at random.
What is the probability that he is not taller than 1.85 m?

5 A bag contains red, white and blue balls.
A ball is taken from the bag at random.
The probability of taking a red ball is 0.4.
The probability of taking a white ball is 0.35.
What is the probability of taking a white ball or a blue ball?

6 Tom and Sam buy some tickets in a raffle.
The probability that Tom wins 1st prize is 0.03.
The probability that Sam wins 1st prize is 0.01.
(a) What is the probability that Tom or Sam win 1st prize?
(b) What is the probability that Tom does not win 1st prize?

7 A spinner can land on red, white or blue.
The probability of the spinner landing on red is 0.2.
The probability of the spinner landing on red or on blue is 0.7.
The spinner is spun once.
What is the probability that the spinner lands:
(a) on blue,
(b) on white?

8 A bag contains red, green, blue, yellow and white counters.
The table shows the probabilities of obtaining each colour when a counter is taken from the bag at random.

Red	Green	Blue	Yellow	White
30%	25%	20%	20%	10%

(a) (i) How can you tell that there is a mistake in the table?
    (ii) The probability of getting a white counter is wrong. What should it be?

A counter is taken from the bag at random.
(b) (i) What is the probability that it is either green or blue?
    (ii) What is the probability that it is either red, green or blue?
    (iii) What is the probability that it is not yellow?

9 Some red, white and blue cubes are numbered 1 or 2.
The table shows the probabilities of obtaining each colour and number when a cube is taken at random.

	Red	White	Blue
1	0.1	0.3	0
2	0.3	0.1	0.2

A cube is taken at random.
(a) What is the probability of taking a red cube?
(b) What is the probability of taking a cube numbered 2?
(c) State whether or not the following pairs of events are mutually exclusive.
    Give a reason for each answer.
    (i) Taking a cube numbered 1 and taking a blue cube.
    (ii) Taking a cube numbered 2 and taking a blue cube.
(d) (i) What is the probability of taking either a blue cube or a cube numbered 1 (or both)?
    (ii) What is the probability of taking either a blue cube or a cube numbered 2 (or both)?

EXAMPLES

1 A fair coin is thrown twice.
Identify all of the possible outcomes and write down their probabilities.

Method 1
List the outcomes systematically.
1st throw   **2nd throw**
Head (H)   Head (H)
Head (H)   Tail (T)
Tail (T)   Head (H)
Tail (T)   Tail (T)

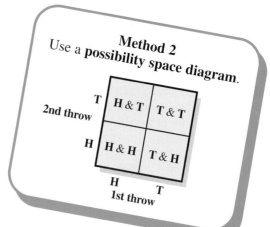

Use a **possibility space diagram**. **Method 2**

When a fair coin is tossed twice, there are four possible outcomes.
Because the coin is fair all the possible outcomes are **equally likely**.
Because all the outcomes are equally likely their probabilities can be worked out.

Method 3
Use a **tree diagram**.

1st throw	2nd throw	Outcome
H	H	H and H
	T	H and T
T	H	T and H
	T	T and T

The lines are called the **branches** of the tree diagram.

P(H and H) = P(H and T) = P(T and H) = P(T and T) = $\frac{1}{4}$.

2 A fair dice is rolled twice.
Use a possibility space diagram to show all the possible outcomes.
What is the probability of getting a 'double six'?
What is the probability of getting any 'double'?
What is the probability that exactly one 'six' is obtained?

2nd roll

6	1 and 6	2 and 6	3 and 6	4 and 6	5 and 6	6 and 6
5	1 and 5	2 and 5	3 and 5	4 and 5	5 and 5	6 and 5
4	1 and 4	2 and 4	3 and 4	4 and 4	5 and 4	6 and 4
3	1 and 3	2 and 3	3 and 3	4 and 3	5 and 3	6 and 3
2	1 and 2	2 and 2	3 and 2	4 and 2	5 and 2	6 and 2
1	1 and 1	2 and 1	3 and 1	4 and 1	5 and 1	6 and 1
	1	**2**	**3**	**4**	**5**	**6**

1st roll

The dice is fair so there are 36 equally likely outcomes.

P(double 6)
There is one outcome in the event (6 and 6).
P(double 6) = $\frac{1}{36}$

P(any double)
The 6 outcomes in the event are shaded blue.
P(any double) = $\frac{6}{36} = \frac{1}{6}$

P(exactly one six)
The 10 outcomes in the event are shaded grey.
P(exactly one six) = $\frac{10}{36} = \frac{5}{18}$

454

Exercise 40.5

1 A red car (R), a blue car (B) and a green car (G) are parked on a narrow drive, one behind the other.
  (a) List all the possible orders in which the three cars could be parked.
  The cars are parked on the drive at random.
  (b) What is the probability that the blue car is the first on the drive?

2 Two fair dice are rolled and the numbers obtained are added.
  (a) Draw a possibility space diagram to show all of the possible outcomes.
  (b) Use your diagram to work out:
      (i)   the probability of obtaining a total of 10,
      (ii) the probability of obtaining a total greater than 10,
      (iii) the probability of obtaining a total less than 10.
  (c) Explain why the probabilities you worked out in (b) should add up to 1.

3 A fair coin is tossed and a fair dice is rolled.
  Copy and complete the table to show all the possible outcomes.

Dice

		1	2	3	4	5	6
Coin	H		H2				
	T						

What is the probability of obtaining:
  (a) a head and a 5,   (b) a tail and an even number,
  (c) a tail and a 6,   (d) a tail and an odd number,
  (e) a head and a number more than 4,   (f) an odd number?

4 Sanjay has to travel to school in two stages.
  Stage 1: he can go by bus or train or he can get a lift.
  Stage 2: he can go by bus or he can walk.

  (a) List all the different ways that Sanjay can travel to school.

  Sanjay decides the way that he travels on each stage at random.
  (b) What is the probability that he goes by bus in both stages?

5 The diagram shows an unbiased spinner.
  It is divided into four equal sections numbered as shown.
  The spinner is spun twice and the numbers the arrow lands on each time are added to obtain a score.
  (a) Copy and complete this table to show all the possible scores.

2nd spin

		1	2	3	4
	1	2	3		
1st	2	3			
spin	3				
	4				

  (b) Calculate the probability of getting a score of:
      (i) 2,   (ii) 3,   (iii) 6.

6 Bag A contains 2 red balls and 1 white ball.
Bag B contains 2 white balls and 1 red ball.
A ball is drawn at random from each bag.

Bag A

	R	R	W
W	RW		
W			
R			

(a) Copy and complete the table to show all possible pairs of colours.

(b) Explain why the probability of each outcome is $\frac{1}{9}$.

Bag B

(c) Calculate the probability that the two balls are the same colour.

7 The diagram shows two sets of cards A and B.

One card is taken at random from set A. One card is taken at random from set B.
(a) List all the possible outcomes.

The two numbers are added together.
(b) (i) What is the probability of getting a total of 5?
(ii) What is the probability of getting a total that is not 5?

All the cards are put together and one of them is taken at random.
(c) What is the probability that it is labelled A or 2 (or both)?

8 Students at a college must choose to study two subjects from the list:
Maths   English   Science   Art
(a) Write down all the possible pairs of subjects that the students can choose.

David chooses both subjects at random.
(b) What is the probability that one of the subjects he chooses is Maths?

James chooses Maths and one other subject at random.
(c) What is the probability that he chooses Maths and Science?

9 A spinner has an equal probability of landing on either red, green, blue, yellow or white.
The spinner is spun twice.
(a) List all the possible outcomes.
(b) (i) What is the probability that, on both spins, the spinner lands on white?
(ii) What is the probability that, on both spins, the spinner lands on white at least once?
(iii) What is the probability that, on both spins, the spinner lands on the same colour?

10 The diagram shows two unbiased spinners.
Each spinner is divided into equal sections and numbered as shown.
Each spinner is spun and the numbers that each arrow lands on are added together.
(a) Draw a possibility space diagram to show all the possible outcomes.
(b) Calculate the probability of getting a total of 2.
(c) Calculate the probability of getting a total of 6.

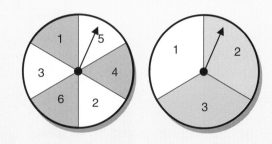

Independent events

When two coins are tossed, the outcome of the first toss has no effect on the outcome of the second toss.
One person being left-handed does not influence another person being left-handed.
These are examples of events which can happen together but which do not affect each other.
Events like this are called **independent** events.

> When A and B are **independent** events then the probability of A and B occurring is given by:
> $$P(A \text{ and } B) = P(A) \times P(B)$$
>
> This rule can be extended to any number of independent events. For example:
> $$P(A \text{ and } B \text{ and } C) = P(A) \times P(B) \times P(C)$$

Using tree diagrams to work out probabilities

A **tree diagram** can be used to find all the possible outcomes when two or more events are combined.
It can also be used to help calculate probabilities when outcomes are not equally likely.

EXAMPLE

1   **Box A** contains 1 red ball (R) and
1 blue ball (B).
Box B contains 3 red balls (R) and
2 blue balls (B).
A ball is taken at random from
Box A.
A ball is then taken at random
from Box B.

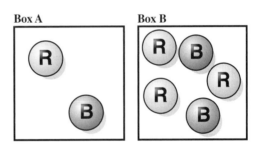

(a)   Draw a tree diagram to show
all the possible outcomes.

(b)   Calculate the probability that
two red balls are taken.

(a)

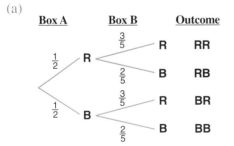

Remember:
When drawing a tree diagram
probabilities must be put on the branches.
Using equally likely outcomes:
In Box A
$P(R) = \frac{1}{2}$ $P(B) = \frac{1}{2}$
In Box B
$P(R) = \frac{3}{5}$ $P(B) = \frac{2}{5}$

(b)   The numbers of red and blue balls are unequal in Box B.
This means that the outcomes RR, RB, BR and BB are not equally likely.

Multiply the probabilities along the branches of the tree diagram.

$$P(RR) = \frac{1}{2} \times \frac{3}{5} = \frac{1 \times 3}{2 \times 5} = \frac{3}{10}$$

The probability that two red balls are taken is $\frac{3}{10}$.

2 The probability that Amanda is late for school is 0.4.
Use a tree diagram to find the probability that on two days running:
(a)   she is late twice,   (b)   she is late exactly once.

Day 1	Day 2	Probability

```
                          0.4    late      0.4 × 0.4 = 0.16
                   late
            0.4
                          0.6    not late  0.4 × 0.6 = 0.24

                          0.4    late      0.6 × 0.4 = 0.24
            0.6
                   not late
                          0.6    not late  0.6 × 0.6 = 0.36
```

(a)   The probability that Amanda is late twice.

The outcome included in this event is:
   (late **and** late)
P(late twice) = 0.16

(b)   The probability that Amanda is late exactly once.

The outcomes included in this event are:
   (late **and** not late) **or** (not late **and** late)
These outcomes are mutually exclusive.
P(late exactly once) = 0.24 + 0.24 = 0.48

Exercise **40.6**

1 A bag contains 3 red counters and 2 blue counters.
A counter is taken at random from the bag and then replaced.
Another counter is taken at random from the bag.

(a)   Copy and complete the tree diagram to show all the possible outcomes. Write the probability of each of the events on the branches of the tree diagram.

(b)   (i)   Calculate the probability that both counters taken are blue.
   (ii)   Calculate the probability that at least one counter taken is blue.

```
1st          2nd
counter      counter

        3/5    red
    
              blue
```

2 A manufacturer makes an electrical circuit which contains two switches.
The probability that a switch is faulty is 0.1.

(a)   Copy and complete the tree diagram.
Write the probability of each of the events on the branches of the tree diagram.

(b)   (i)   Calculate the probability that both switches are faulty.
   (ii)   Calculate the probability that exactly one switch is faulty.

The circuit works if both switches are not faulty.
(c)   The manufacturer makes 1000 circuits.
Estimate the number that work.

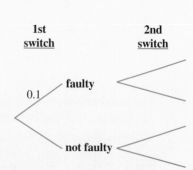

```
1st          2nd
switch       switch

        0.1    faulty

              not faulty
```

3 Five people in a group of 50 people are left handed.
There are 20 females in the group.
A person is picked at random from the group.

(a) (i) What is the probability that the person is left handed?
(ii) What is the probability that the person is right handed?
(iii) What is the probability that the person is female?
(iv) What is the probability that the person is male?
(b) Copy and complete the tree diagram.
Write the probability of each of the events on the branches of the tree diagram.
(c) (i) Calculate the probability that the person picked is a left handed female.
(ii) Calculate the probability that the person picked is a left handed female or is a right handed male.

left handed

right handed

4 Bag A contains 3 blue counters, 5 red counters and 2 white counters.
Bag B contains 2 blue counters and 3 red counters.
A ball is taken at random from Bag A.
A ball is taken at random from Bag B.

(a) Copy and complete the tree diagram to show the possible pairs of colours.
Write the probability of each of the events on the branches.
(b) Calculate the probability that a blue counter is taken from Bag A and a red counter is taken from Bag B.
(c) Calculate the probability that both counters are the same colour.

Bag A   **Bag B**

blue

red

blue

red

white

5 The probability that a car fails an MOT test on lights is $\frac{1}{10}$.

The probability that a car fails an MOT test on brakes is $\frac{1}{5}$.

A car is stopped at random and given an MOT test.
The tree diagram shows the possible outcomes.

(a) Copy and complete the tree diagram.

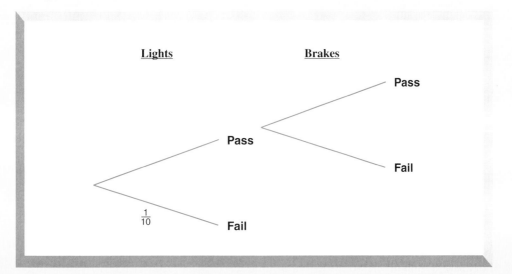

Lights   Brakes

Pass

Pass

Fail

$\frac{1}{10}$

Fail

(b) Calculate the probability that the car will fail the MOT test on lights or brakes.

6 A fair spinner can land on either black or white.
The probability that it lands on white when it is spun is 0.3.
(a) What is the probability that it lands on black when it is spun?
The spinner is spun twice.
(b) Find the probability of getting two blacks.
(c) Find the probability of getting the same colour on both spinners.

7 In box A there are 3 red and 5 blue counters.
In box B there are 2 red and 3 blue counters.
A counter is taken at random from each box.
Calculate the probability that:
(a) both counters are red,
(b) at least one of the counters is red.

8 Colin takes examinations in Maths and in English.
The probability that he passes Maths is 0.7.
The probability that he passes English is 0.8.
The results in each subject are independent of each other.
Calculate the probability that:
(a) he passes Maths and fails English,
(b) he fails both subjects.

9 Dice A and Dice B are two normal dice.
Dice A is a fair dice.
Dice B is biased so that the probability of getting an even number is $\frac{2}{3}$.
Both of the dice are tossed.
Find the probability that:
(a) an odd number is scored on dice A and an even number on dice B,
(b) an odd number is scored on one dice and an even number on the other.

10 A box contains cubes which are coloured red (R), white (W) or blue (B) and numbered 1, 2 or 3.
The table shows the probabilities of obtaining each colour and each number when a cube is taken from the box at random.

A single cube is taken from the box at random.
(a) What is the probability that the cube is:
   (i) red and numbered 2,
   (ii) white or numbered 1 (or both),
   (iii) white or numbered 3 (or both)?

Colour of cube

		R	W	B
Number on cube	1	0.2	0	0.1
	2	0.1	0.3	0
	3	0	0.1	0.2

A cube is taken from the box at random and then replaced.
Another cube is then taken from the box at random.
(b) Calculate the probability that:
   (i) both cubes are blue and numbered 1,
   (ii) both cubes are blue.

11 A bag contains red, white and blue cubes.
The cubes are numbered 1, 2, 3 and 4.
The probabilities of taking cubes from the box at random are shown in the table.

A single cube is taken from the box at random.
(a) What is the probability that:
   (i) the cube is white,
   (ii) the cube is red and numbered 4,
   (iii) the cube is white or numbered 3 (or both)?

Colour of cube

		Red	White	Blue
Number on cube	1	0.1	0	0
	2	0.1	0.1	0.1
	3	0	0.2	0.2
	4	0.1	0	0.1

A cube is taken from the box at random and then replaced.
Another cube is then taken from the box at random.
(b) Calculate the probability that both cubes are the same colour.

- You need to know the meaning of these terms:
    impossible, unlikely, evens, likely, certain
    outcome, event   fair, unbiased, biased, taken at random
    equally likely outcomes   trial

- **Probability** describes how likely or unlikely it is that an event will occur.
  Probabilities can be shown on a probability scale.
  Probability **must** be written as a fraction, a decimal or a percentage.

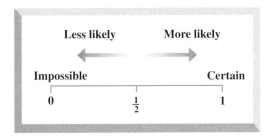

- How to work out probabilities using **equally likely outcomes**.
  The probability of an event is given by:

$$\text{Probability} = \frac{\text{Number of outcomes in the event}}{\text{Total number of possible outcomes}}$$

- How to estimate probabilities using **relative frequency**.
  The relative frequency of an event is given by:

$$\text{Relative frequency} = \frac{\text{Number of times the event happens in an experiment (or in a survey)}}{\text{Total number of trials in the experiment (or observations in the survey)}}$$

- How to use probabilities to **estimate** the number of times an event occurs in an **experiment** or **observation**.
    Estimate = total number of trials (or observations) $\times$ probability of event

- **Mutually exclusive events** cannot occur at the same time.
  When A and B are mutually exclusive events:

$$P(A \text{ or } B) = P(A) + P(B)$$

- A general rule for working out the probability of an event, A, **not happening** is:

$$P(\text{not } A) = 1 - P(A)$$

- How to find all the possible outcomes when two events are combined.
    By **listing** the outcomes systematically.
    By using a **possibility space diagram**.
    By using a **tree diagram**.

- The outcomes of **independent events** do not influence each other.
  When A and B are independent events:

$$P(A \text{ and } B) = P(A) \times P(B)$$

1 A game is played with two fair spinners.

In each turn of the game both spinners are spun and the numbers are added to get a score.

(a) Copy and complete the following table to show each possible score.

	1	2	3	4
1				
2				
3				

(b) What is the probability of:
  (i) scoring 6,
  (ii) not scoring 6?

(c) To start the game a player needs to score either 2 or 5.
What is the probability that the game starts on the first throw?

2 Patrick has 20 marbles in a bag.
8 of the marbles are red.
7 of the marbles are blue.
The rest of the marbles are yellow.

(a) He takes one marble out of the bag at random.
  (i) What is the probability that it is blue?
  (ii) What is the probability that it is red or blue?
  (iii) What is the probability that it is not blue?
  Give your answers as fractions in their simplest form.

(b) He takes two marbles out of the bag at random.
List all the possible colour combinations.   Edexcel

3 A machine makes compact discs.
The probability that a perfect compact disc will be made by this machine is 0.85.
Work out the probability that a compact disc made by this machine will not be perfect.   Edexcel

4 Georgina is watching a football match.
She says, "The probability that the team I support will win is $\frac{1}{3}$ because there are only three possible results: win, lose or draw."
Explain why her statement may be wrong.

5 Jane has four red beads and six blue beads.
She picks beads one at a time at random.
(a) What is the probability that the first bead she picks is red?
The first bead she picks is blue.
(b) What is the probability that the second bead she picks is red?

6 Helen has a set of blue cards and a set of red cards, as shown.

(a) A card is chosen at random from each set.
List all the possible combinations.
(b) What is the probability that both cards are 2's?

7 The results from 20 spins of a numbered spinner are:

2 1 4 3 2 1 3 4 5 2
1 5 3 4 2 3 3 3 2 4

(a) Find the relative frequency of 2.

The results from another 20 spins are:

1 2 2 3 2 1 2 4 5 2
2 3 4 2 1 5 3 3 5 3

(b) Use the results from all 40 spins to estimate the number of times a 2 will occur in 500 spins.

8 A fair dice is thrown 600 times.
Estimate the number of times a prime number is thrown.

9 The probability that a person stopped at random will be wearing glasses is $\frac{2}{5}$.
Two people are stopped at random.
Work out the probability that they will both be wearing glasses.

10 The Orange Party, the Yellow Party and the Purple Party stand in a school election.
The table shows the voting intentions of a sample of students before the election.

Voting intentions

	Orange Party	Yellow Party	Purple Party
Boys	4	5	6
Girls	5	7	3

(a) A student in the sample is chosen at random.
What is the probability that the person chosen intends to vote for the Orange Party?

(b) A girl in the sample is chosen at random.
What is the probability that she intends to vote for the Purple Party?

(c) There are 960 students in the school.
Use the results of the sample to estimate the number of students in the school who intend to vote for the Yellow Party.

11 Helen and Joan are going to take a swimming test.
The probability that Helen will pass the swimming test is 0.95.
The probability that Joan will pass the swimming test is 0.8.
The two events are independent.

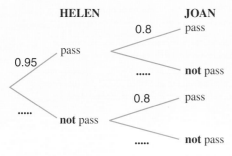

HELEN   JOAN

0.8 — pass

pass

0.95

..... — **not** pass

0.8 — pass

.....

not pass

..... — **not** pass

(a) Copy and complete the probability tree diagram.

(b) Work out the probability that both Helen and Joan will pass the swimming test.

(c) Work out the probability that one of them will pass the swimming test and the other one will **not** pass the swimming test. *Edexcel*

12 Chris is going to roll a biased dice.
The probability that he will get a six is 0.09.

(a) Work out the probability that he will **not** get a six.

Chris is going to roll the dice 30 times.

(b) Work out an estimate for the number of sixes he will get.

Tina is going to roll the same biased dice twice.

(c) Work out the probability that she will get
  (i) **two** sixes,
  (ii) **exactly one** six. *Edexcel*

13

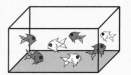

Tank A   **Tank B**

There are two fish tanks in a pet shop.
In tank **A** there are four white fish and one black fish.
In tank **B** there are three white fish and four black fish.
One fish is to be taken out of tank **A** at random.
One fish is to be taken out of tank **B** at random.

Using a tree diagram, or otherwise, calculate the probability that

(a) the two fish will both be white,

(b) the two fish will be of different colours. *Edexcel*

14 Sita puts 5 balls in Box A and 4 balls in box B.
The balls in each box are numbered as shown.

Box A   **Box B**

A ball is taken from each box at random.

(a) What is the probability that both balls have odd numbers?

(b) What is the probability that the sum of the numbers on the balls is less than 5?

Section Review - Handling Data

1 (a) The graph shows the results of a survey of the times people had to wait at airports for their flights.

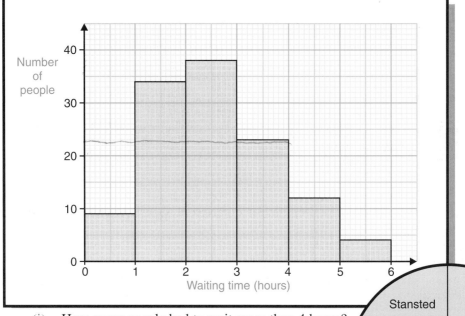

Number of people

Waiting time (hours)

    (i)   How many people had to wait more than 4 hours?
    (ii) How many people had to wait between 2 and 3 hours?
 (b) The pie chart shows the departure airports of these people.
    (i)   Which airport is the mode?
    (ii) 60 people departed from Heathrow. How many people departed from Gatwick?
 (c) How many people were included in the survey?

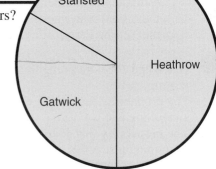

Stansted

Heathrow

Gatwick

2

Game	Number of students
Badminton	8
Basketball	15
Squash	6
Volleyball	16

A group of students was given a choice of four games to play.
The table shows the numbers choosing each game.
Draw a pie chart to show this information.

3 Jo measures the lengths, in centimetres, of a sample of runner beans.
The stem and leaf diagram shows the results.
 (a) How many runner beans are included in the sample?
 (b) What is the range of their lengths?
 (c) Which length is the mode?

```
                        1 | 3  means  13 cm

1 |  3   5   7   9

2 |  0   3   4   6   6   6   7   8

3 |  0   1   1
```

4 A shop employs 8 men and 2 women.
The mean weekly wage of the 10 employees is £396.
The mean weekly wage of the 8 men is £400.
Calculate the mean weekly wage of the 2 women.

Edexcel

5 A group of students were each asked how many books they had read last month.
The frequency diagram shows the results.

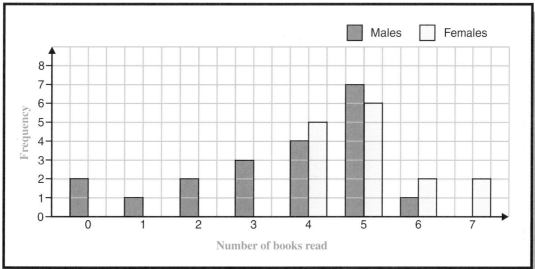

(a) How many students were included?
(b) What is the range in the number of books read by females?
(c) Calculate the mean number of books read by females.
(d) Compare and comment on the number of books read by males and the number of books read by females.

6 The diagram shows two sets of cards A and B.

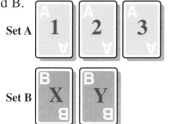

Set A   1   2   3

Set B   X   Y

One card is taken from set A and one card is taken from set B.
List all the possible outcomes.

7 A box contains 20 plastic ducks.
3 of the ducks are green, 10 are blue and the rest are yellow.
A duck is taken from the box at random.
(a) What is the probability that it is green?
(b) What is the probability that it is yellow?

8 A class survey found the probability of having brown eyes is 0.6.
(a) What is the probability of not having brown eyes?
(b) There are 30 children in the class. Estimate the number with brown eyes.

9 The table shows information about a group of children.

	Can swim	Cannot swim
Boys	16	4
Girls	19	6

(a) One of these children is chosen at random.
What is the probability that the child can swim?
(b) A girl in the group is chosen at random.
What is the probability that she cannot swim?
(c) Tony says, "These results show a higher proportion of girls can swim."
Is he correct?
Give reasons for your answer.

10 A spinner is labelled as shown.
The results of the first 30 spins are given below.

1 2 3 3 5 1 3 2 2 4
5 3 2 1 2 5 2 4 1 5
1 5 2 2 4 2 5 4 2 3

(a) What is the relative frequency of getting the number 1?
(b) Is the spinner fair?
Give a reason for your answer.

Section Review . . . . Section Review . . . . Section Review . . .

11 Laurie is designing a survey to find out about people who use a superstore near her home. One of the things Laurie wants to find out is how far people have travelled to get to the superstore.

(a) Decide which question below is best to ask. Give **two** reasons for your decision.

> **[A]** How far have you travelled to get here today?
>
> **[B]** Where do you live?
>
> **[C]** Do you live far from here?
>
> **[D]** Please show me on this map where you have travelled from.

Laurie decides to do her survey one Friday evening outside the superstore.

(b) Give **one** reason why this would give a biased sample.   Edexcel

12 The table gives you the marks scored by pupils in a French and in a German test.

French	15	35	34	23	35	27	36	34	23	24	30	40	25	35	20
German	20	37	35	25	33	30	39	36	27	20	33	35	27	32	28

(a) Draw a scatter graph of the marks scored in the French and German tests.
(b) Describe the relationship between the marks scored in the two tests.
(c) Draw a line of best fit on the diagram.

Abigail scored 32 in the French test.
(d) Use the scatter graph to estimate the mark she scored in the German test.   Edexcel

13 Four scatter diagrams are shown.

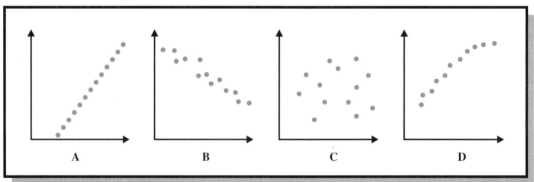

(a) Which diagram shows negative correlation?
(b) Which diagram shows no correlation?
(c) Which diagram could show the relationship between the engine size of cars and their top speeds?

14 Samples of two different varieties of onion were weighed. The box plots show the results.

(a) Find the medians and interquartile ranges for each variety.

(b) Comment on the differences between the two varieties.

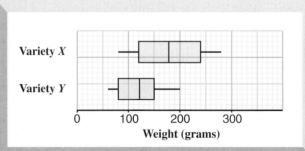

15 Nick travels to work by train on two days.
The probability that the train is late on any day is 0.3.
(a) Draw a tree diagram to show all the possible outcomes for the two days.
(b) What is the probability that the train is late on at least one of the two days?

16 Bronwen owns a pet shop.
The table gives information about the weights of hamsters in Bronwen's shop.

Weight of hamsters (w grams)	$28 \leqslant w < 30$	$30 \leqslant w < 32$	$32 \leqslant w < 34$	$34 \leqslant w < 36$
Numbers of hamsters	9	5	4	2

Calculate an estimate for the mean weight of the hamsters in Bronwen's shop.   Edexcel

17 The speeds, in miles per hour (mph), of 200 cars travelling on the A320 road were measured.
The results are shown in the table.

Speed (mph) not exceeding	20	25	30	35	40	45	50	55	60
Cumulative frequency	1	5	14	28	66	113	164	196	200

(a) Draw a cumulative frequency graph to show these figures.
(b) Use your graph to find an estimate for
    (i) the median speed (in mph),
    (ii) the interquartile range (in mph),
    (ii) the percentage of cars travelling less than 48 miles per hour.   Edexcel

18 The number of mobile phones sold each quarter by a retailer for the last three years is shown.

Year	1998				1999				2000			
Quarter	1	2	3	4	1	2	3	4	1	2	3	4
Number of phones sold	18	28	22	36	20	32	28	42	24	42	40	76

(a) Plot these values on graph paper.
(b) Calculate the 4-quarterly moving averages.
(c) Plot the moving averages on the same graph.
(d) Draw a trend line by eye.
(e) Comment on the trend.
(f) Estimate the number of mobile phones sold by the retailer in the first quarter of 2001.

19 A bag contains some red, some white and some blue counters.
A counter is picked at random.
The probability that it will be red is 0.2.
The probability that it will be white is 0.3.

(a) What is the probability that a counter picked at random will be either red or white?
(b) What is the probability that a counter picked at random will be either red or blue?

A counter will be picked at random. Its colour will be recorded. The counter will be put back in the bag. A second counter will be picked at random. Its colour will be recorded.
(c) (i) Calculate the probability that the first counter will be red and the second counter will be white.
    (ii) Calculate the probability that both counters will be white.   Edexcel

Exam Practice - Non-calculator Paper

Do not use a calculator for this exercise.

1 The diagram shows a target.

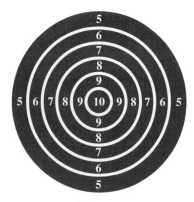

Score	Frequency
5	2
6	1
7	3
8	1
9	2
10	1

Billy fires at the target ten times.
The frequency table gives information about his scores.
Work out his total score. *Edexcel*

2 Steven pays 96 pence for 3 oranges and 2 grapefruit.
A grapefruit costs 27 pence.
How much is an orange?

3 (a) Work out $32.4 - 14.9$.
(b) Work out $23.6 \div 8$.

4 (a) Simplify $b \times b \times b$.
(b) Multiply out $2(a - 3)$.
(c) Drinks cost 35 pence each.
How much will d drinks cost?

5 23 pupils did a sponsored spelling test. Their **total** score was 345 spellings correct.
(a) Work out the mean number of spellings correct per pupil.
(b) Show how you can **check** that your answer is about right by using approximations for the numbers. *Edexcel*

6 (a) $p = -8$ and $q = -3$.
Work out the value of $p - 2q$.

(b) Work out $\dfrac{-14 + 2}{-0.2}$.

(c) Work out $\dfrac{5}{7} - \dfrac{1}{3}$. *Edexcel*

7 A sequence begins 15, 7, 3, …
The rule for continuing the sequence is shown.

> Subtract 1 from the last number and then divide by 2.

Write down the next three numbers in the sequence.

8 (a) Calculate the volume of this cuboid.

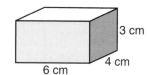

3 cm
6 cm
4 cm

(b) Calculate the surface area of the cuboid.

9 (a) Work out 0.1×0.4.
(b) Write down the value of 7^2.
(c) What is the value of $\sqrt{81}$?
(d) What is the reciprocal of $\frac{3}{2}$?

10 (a) What is the value of $2x^2$ when $x = -3$?
(b) Simplify $3t - t - 3$.
(c) Solve $2(x - 3) = 8$.

11 A triangle has sides of length 6 cm, 5 cm and 4 cm.
(a) Make an accurate drawing of the triangle.
(b) By taking measurements from your diagram, calculate the area of the triangle.

12 A vase contains 5 red tulips and 4 yellow tulips.
A tulip is taken from the vase at random.
What is the probability that it is red?

13 In the diagram, PQR is an isosceles triangle. The lines PQ and RS are parallel.

Not to scale

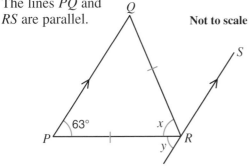

(a) Work out the size of angle x.
(b) (i) What is the size of angle y?
    (ii) Give a reason for your answer.

14 (a) Write these fractions in order of size.
    $$\frac{2}{5} \quad \frac{5}{8} \quad \frac{1}{3} \quad \frac{3}{10}$$
(b) Write $\frac{2}{5}$ as a percentage.
(c) Calculate $\frac{5}{8}$ of 32.

15 Joyce wants to calculate $\dfrac{59.6}{20.2 - 4.9}$.

By writing each of the numbers in Joyce's calculation to the nearest whole number estimate the answer.

16

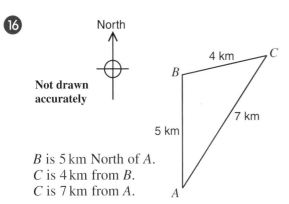

Not drawn accurately

B is 5 km North of A.
C is 4 km from B.
C is 7 km from A.

(a) Make an accurate scale drawing of triangle ABC.
    Use a scale of 1 cm to 1 km.
(b) From your accurate scale drawing, measure the bearing of C from A.
(c) Find the bearing of A from C.   Edexcel

17 (a) A tin contains 60 toffees.
    Jacob eats 15% of the toffees.
    What fraction of the toffees are left?
    Give your answer in its simplest form.
(b) A box contains milk and plain chocolates in the ratio 2 : 1.
    The box contains 24 chocolates.
    How many are plain?

18 Work out   (a) $\frac{5}{6} - \frac{2}{3}$ (b) $\frac{4}{5} + \frac{3}{4}$

19 Factorise   (a) $2m - 4n$,   (b) $t^2 - 2t$.

20 Solve the equations.
(a) $4x + 2 = 26$ (b) $19 + 4y = 9 - y$
    Edexcel

21 (a) A sequence begins 5, 8, 11, 14, …
    (i) What is the next term in the sequence?
    (ii) Write an expression in terms of n for the nth term in the sequence.
(b) Another sequence begins
    2, 5, 8, 11, …
    Write an expression, in terms of n, for the nth term of this sequence.

22 (a) Use the equation $y = x + 3$ to complete the table of values.

x	-3	-2	-1	0	1	2	3
y	0			3		5	

(b) Use the equation $y = x^2$ to complete the table of values.

x	-3	-2	-1	0	1	2	3
y						4	

(c) Draw the graphs of
    $y = x + 3$ and $y = x^2$.   Edexcel

23 An examination in history is marked out of 60 marks.
Reg gets 54 marks.
What percentage of the marks does he get?

24 A travel company carried out a survey of the ages of its customers.
The results of the survey are shown in the table.

Age group (years)	Percentage of customers in this age group
11 - 20	8
21 - 30	28
31 - 40	19
41 - 50	21
51 - 60	13
61 - 70	11

(a) Draw a frequency polygon to show this information.
(b) In which age group is the median age?
    Edexcel

A and **B** are two fair spinners.
Jane spins the two spinners together once.
(a)   Copy and complete the table below to show
all the possible results **and** the total scores.

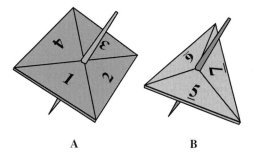

Spinner **A**	Spinner **B**	Total score

A   B

(b)   Use your table to find the probability that Jane will get a total score of 7.

Tom spins the two spinners together 60 times.
(c)   Work out the number of times your would expect Tom to get a total score of 7.   Edexcel

26

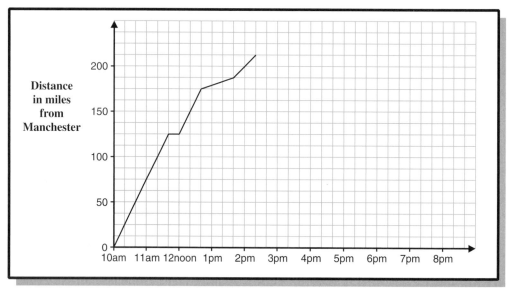

The graph represents part of Mrs. Hinton's journey from Manchester to London.
Mrs. Hinton stopped for a rest at a service station.
(a)   (i)   Write down the time at which she stopped.   (ii)   For how long did she stop?

For part of her journey Mrs. Hinton had to slow down because of a traffic queue.
(b)   For how many miles did she travel at a slower speed?

Mrs. Hinton spent an hour at a meeting in London.
She then returned home to Manchester, travelling at a steady speed of 50 miles per hour.
(c)   Copy and complete the graph of her journey.   Edexcel

27   The diagram shows a sketch
of triangle *ABC*.

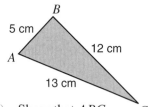

(a)   Show that *ABC*
is a right-angled triangle.
(b)   Calculate the area of
triangle *ABC*.

28
(a)   Work out an estimate for $\dfrac{3.08 \times 693.89}{0.47}$

The length of a rod is 98 cm correct to the nearest
centimetre.
(b)   (i)   Write down the maximum length that the rod
could be.
(ii)   Write down the minimum length that the rod
could be.   Edexcel

29   A box contains 24 pens and some pencils.
The ratio of pens to pencils in the box is 4 : 5.
30% of the pencils need sharpening.
How many pencils need sharpening?

30 (a) Draw the graph of $y = 6 - x^2$ for values of x from -3 to 3.
(b) Use your graph to solve the equation $6 - x^2 = 0$.

31 The diagram shows the positions of shapes T, M and N.

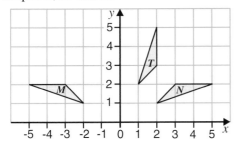

(a) Describe fully the single transformation which maps T onto M.
(b) Describe fully the single transformation which maps T onto N.
(c) M is mapped onto P by an enlargement, scale factor 2, centre $(-5, 1)$. Draw a diagram to show the positions of M and P.

32 (a) List the values of n, where n is a whole number, such that $3 < 2n + 1 \leqslant 7$.
(b) Solve the simultaneous equations $x + 2y = -1$ and $4x - 2y = -9$.
(c) Solve the equation $x^2 - 5x = 0$.

33 Solve the simultaneous equations:
$$3x + 2y = 11$$
$$x - y = 7$$
Edexcel

34 (a) Simplify
(i) $5p^3 \times 3p^2$, (ii) $8p^6 \div 4p^3$.
(b) Factorise fully $3x^2 - 6xy$.

35 Factorise completely:
(a) $6a^2b^3 - 15a^3b$ (b) $x^2 - 7x + 6$
Edexcel

36 In triangle LMN, $\cos L = \frac{3}{5}$.
Calculate the length of NL.

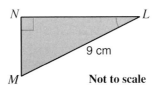

9 cm

Not to scale

37 (a) Work out $4 \times 10^3 \times 5 \times 10^5$.
Give your answer in standard form.
(b) Work out $\dfrac{4 \times 10^3}{5 \times 10^5}$.
Give your answer in standard form.

38 In a sale prices are reduced by 10%.
The sale price of a tennis racket is £36.
What was the original price of the tennis racket?

39 Here are some expressions.
$$\frac{ab}{h} \qquad 2\pi b^2 \qquad (a + b)ch \qquad 2\pi a^3$$
$$\pi ab \qquad 2(a^2 + b^2) \qquad \pi a^2 b$$

The letters a, b, c and h represent lengths. π and 2 are numbers that have no dimensions.
Which three expressions could represent areas?
Edexcel

40

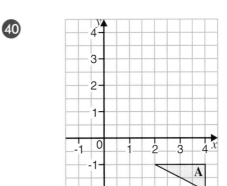

Copy the diagram.
(a) Reflect triangle A in the x axis. Label the reflection B.
(b) Reflect triangle B in the line $y = x$. Label the reflection C.
(c) Describe fully the single transformation which maps triangle A onto triangle C.
(d) Write down the equation of the line which is parallel to $y = x$ and passes through the point $(0, 8)$.

This line crosses the x axis at the point P.
(e) Calculate the coordinates of P.

41 (a) Using the measurements shown in the diagram, calculate the length of the line AB.

A

7.5 m

C ←2.5 m→ *D*

Not drawn accurately

x°

O ← 3.2 m → *B*

Angle $AOB = x°$.
(b) Write down the value of $\tan x°$.
Edexcel

Exam Practice - Calculator Paper

You may use a calculator for this exercise.

1 Laura buys 18 cartons of juice.
She pays with a £10 note.
She gets £2.98 change.
How much is each carton of juice?

2 Rosie gets on a bus at 1745 and gets off
the bus at 1806.
How long was she on the bus?

3 Les writes down six numbers.
    4   6   7   9   10   24
  (a) Which of these numbers are
       factors of 12?
  (b) Which of these numbers is a
       multiple of 12?
  (c) Which of these numbers is a prime
       number?

4 (a) Simplify $t + 2t + 3t$.
  (b) Solve $4x + 3 = 5$.

5 A caretaker is paid at a basic rate of
£7.76 per hour for 36 hours a week.
Overtime is paid at one and a half times
the basic rate.
One week the caretaker works 42 hours.
How much is the caretaker paid that
week?

6 The diagram shows a rectangle.

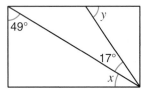

Work out the size of angles x and y.

7 A candle weighs x grams.
  (a) Write an expression, in terms of x,
       for the weight of 20 candles.
  (b) A box of 20 candles weighs
       3800 grams.
       The box weighs 200 grams.
       What is the weight of a candle?

8 (a) On graph paper draw and label the
       lines $y = 2x$ and $y = 6 - x$ for
       values of x from -1 to 4.
  (b) Solve the equation $2x = 6 - x$.

9 (a) Work out 20% of £25.
  (b) Work out $\frac{3}{8}$ of 6 metres.   Edexcel

10

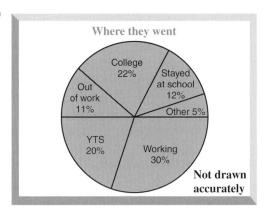

300 young people were asked what they did
after completing Year 11 at school.
The pie chart shows the results of the survey.
  (a) How many of the young people were
       working?

Gwen made an accurate drawing of the pie
chart.
She first drew the sector representing the
young people out of work.
  (b) Calculate the size of the angle of this
       sector.
       Give your answer correct to the nearest
       degree.
  (c) Change to a decimal the percentage
       going to college.
  (d) What fraction of the young people stayed
       at school?
       Give your answer in its simplest form.
                            Edexcel

11 A shop sells two brands of flour.
Brand A: weight 500 g, cost 39 pence.
Brand B: weight 800 g, cost 59 pence.
Which brand of flour gives more grams
per penny?
You **must** show all your working.

12 A garden is a rectangle measuring
26 m by 11.5 m.
Grass covers 67% of the area of the garden.
Calculate the area of grass.
Give your answer to a suitable degree of
accuracy.

13 Work out $\dfrac{0.36 \times 0.89}{47 - 3.9}$

Give your answer correct to
2 significant figures.

14 $AB = BC$.
Angle $ACB = 63°$.
ACE and BCD are straight lines.

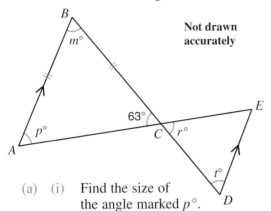

Not drawn accurately

(a) (i) Find the size of
the angle marked $p°$.
(ii) Give a reason for your answer.
(b) Work out the size of
(i) the angle marked $m°$,
(ii) the angle marked $r°$.

AB is parallel to DE.
(c) (i) Find the size of the angle
marked $t°$.
(ii) Explain how your worked out
your answer.   Edexcel

15

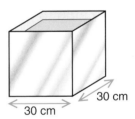

Water is stored in a tank in the shape of a
cuboid with a square base.
The sides of the base are 30 cm long.
The depth of the water is 20 cm.
(a) Work out the volume of the water.

More water is put in the tank.
The depth of the water rises to 21.6 cm.
(b) Calculate the percentage increase in
the volume of the water in the tank.
Edexcel

16 (a) Write 72 as a product of its prime
factors.
(b) What is the least common multiple of
48 and 72?

17 A fair six-sided dice and a fair coin are
thrown together.
(a) List all the possible outcomes.
(b) What is the probability of getting a tail
and an even number?
(c) What is the probability of getting a tail
or an even number or both?

18 Sticks are used to make patterns of
triangles.

Pattern 1   Pattern 2   Pattern 3

Write an expression, in terms of n, for the
number of sticks used to make Pattern n.

19 Aisha is carrying out a survey into radio
listening habits.
One of the questions she writes is:
"How often do you listen to the radio?"

A friend tells her that this question is
unsuitable.
Write down two ways in which this
question could be improved.

20 Carpet tiles measure
45 cm by 45 cm.

How many tiles are needed to cover a floor
which measures 4.05 m by 5.4 m?

21 (a) Work out $\sqrt{8}$.
Give your answer correct to
2 decimal places.
(b) Work out 8^5.
(c) Find the value of $\dfrac{1}{x} + y^3$
when $x = 5$ and $y = 0.5$.

22 (a) Solve $3x - 9 = 7 - 2x$.
(b) Factorise $3a - 6b$.
(c) Simplify $5x - 2(x + 3)$.

23 (a) A kilogram of strawberries costs £1.70.
Estimate, to the nearest £, the cost of
5 lbs of strawberries.
(b) A bowl of strawberries and cream
weighs 210 grams.
The ratio, by weight, of strawberries
to cream is 5 : 1.
What is the weight of the cream?

24 The stem and leaf diagram shows the results of measuring some leaves.

					4 | 3 means 4.3 cm
4	7	9			
5	0	3	6	8	
6	1	4	5	5	7
7	2				

(a) How many leaves were measured?
(b) What is the range in the lengths of these leaves?
(c) Calculate the mean length of these leaves.

25 Calculate the area of a semi-circle, radius 15 cm.

15 cm

26 Craig puts £200 into his bank account. He is paid simple interest at 4% per year. How much interest does he get if he withdraws his money after 9 months?

27 Ben asked 50 people how much they paid for a new computer.
The results are shown in this frequency table.

Price (£P)	Number of computers
$0 < P \leq 500$	7
$500 < P \leq 1000$	20
$1000 < P \leq 1500$	11
$1500 < P \leq 2000$	9
$2000 < P \leq 2500$	3

(a) Calculate an estimate for the mean price paid for a new computer.

By the end of each year, the value of a computer falls by 15% of its value at the start of that year.
A new computer has a value of £1200.
(b) Calculate its value by the end of the third year.

Edexcel

28 (a) Solve (i) $\dfrac{x - 7}{3} = -2$
   (ii) $8 - 3x = 2(x + 5)$.
(b) Use trial and improvement to solve the equation $x^3 + 2x = 400$.
Show all your trials.
Give your answer correct to one decimal place.

29 Helen tries to win a coconut at the fair. She throws a ball at a coconut.

If she knocks a coconut off its stand, she wins the coconut. Helen has two throws.

The probability that she will win a coconut with her first throw is 0.2.
The probability that she will win a coconut with her second throw is 0.3.

Work out the probability that, with her two throws, Helen will win
(a) 2 coconuts,
(b) exactly 1 coconut.

Edexcel

30 O is the centre of the circle.
Work out the size of angles a, b and c.

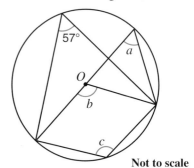

57°

Not to scale

31

Not drawn accurately

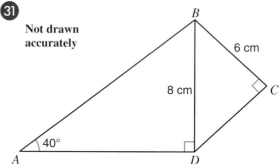

B

6 cm

8 cm

C

40°

A

D

$ABCD$ is a quadrilateral.
Angle $BDA = 90°$, angle $BCD = 90°$, angle $BAD = 40°$.
$BC = 6$ cm, $BD = 8$ cm.

(a) Calculate the length of DC.
Give your answer correct to 3 significant figures.
(b) Calculate the size of angle DBC.
Give your answer correct to 3 significant figures.
(c) Calculate the length of AB.
Give your answer correct to 3 significant figures.

Edexcel

(a) Solve the simultaneous equations. $3y = 2x - 5$
$$y = x - 4$$

(b) Use the formula $y = \dfrac{(x - c)}{\sqrt{(m^2 + 6)}}$ to calculate the value of y when $x = 20$, $c = 4.7$ and $m = \frac{1}{2}$.

(c) Solve the inequality $2x - 5 < 8$.

Edexcel

33 The last 10 gas bills for a householder are shown in the table.

Date of bill	Jul. 1998	Oct. 1998	Jan. 1999	Apr. 1999	Jul. 1999	Oct. 1999	Jan. 2000	Apr. 2000	Jul. 2000	Oct. 2000
Amount (£)	18	20	133	100	23	27	123	127	27	33

(a) Draw a time series graph to illustrate the data.
(b) Calculate the four-quarterly moving averages.
(c) Plot the values of the moving average on the same graph.
(d) Use your graph to estimate the next gas bill.

34 In a survey, 100 retired people were asked how many hours of sleep they had during one week.
The table shows the results.

(a) Draw a cumulative frequency graph to illustrate the data.

Sleep (t hours)	Frequency
$35 \leqslant t < 40$	3
$40 \leqslant t < 45$	7
$45 \leqslant t < 50$	12
$50 \leqslant t < 55$	28
$55 \leqslant t < 60$	40
$60 \leqslant t < 65$	8
$65 \leqslant t < 70$	2

(b) Use the graph to estimate:
  (i) the median,
  (ii) the interquartile range.
(c) A similar survey of people aged 18 to 21 found that they had a median of 55 hours sleep and an interquartile range of 5 hours.
  Use this information to comment on the sleeping habits of these two groups of people.

35 You are given the formula $s = \frac{1}{3}at^2$.
(a) Calculate the value of s when $t = 2\frac{1}{4}$ and $a = 0.8$.
(b) Rearrange the formula to give t in terms of s and a.

36
$$F = \frac{ab}{a - b}$$

Imran uses this formula to calculate the value of F.
Imran estimates the value of F without using a calculator.
$a = 49.6$ and $b = 30.6$.

(a) (i) Write down approximate values for a and b that Imran could use to estimate the value of F.
  (ii) Work out the estimate for the value of F that these approximations give.
  (iii) Use your calculator to work out the accurate value for F.
  Use $a = 49.8$ and $b = 30.6$.
  Write down all the figures on your calculator display.

Imran works out the value of F with two new values for a and b.
(b) Calculate the value of F when $a = 9.6 \times 10^{12}$ and $b = 4.7 \times 10^{11}$.
  Give your answer in standard form, correct to two significant figures. Edexcel

37 In 1999, a charity sold $2\frac{1}{4}$ million lottery tickets at 25p each.
80% of the money was kept by the charity.
(a) Calculate the amount of money kept by the charity.

In 2000, the price of a lottery ticket fell by 20%.
Sales of lottery tickets increased by 20%.
80% of the money was kept by the charity.
(b) Calculate the percentage change in the amount of money kept by the charity. Edexcel

Answers

CHAPTER 1

Exercise 1.1 — Page 1

1. (a) 396   (b) 5010
   (c) 70 200   (d) 9 002 051
   (e) 762 504 019   (f) 20 202 020

2. (a) eighty-four
   (b) twenty-three thousand five hundred and ninety
   (c) ninety-three million one hundred and forty-five thousand six hundred and seventy
   (d) seven hundred and sixty-four thousand eight hundred and nine
   (e) six thousand and forty-nine
   (f) nine million eighty thousand and four

3. (a) 1004   (b) 1035   (c) 1086

4. (a) 30   (b) 3 000 000   (c) 600
   (d) 2000   (e) 4000   (f) 6

5. (a) 203   (b) 28

6. (a) 39, 74, 168, 421
   (b) 3801, 3842, 3874, 4765, 5814

7. (a) 429, 425, 399, 103, 84
   (b) 9951, 9653, 9646, 9434

8. (a) 76541 (digits in descending order)
   (b) 14567 (digits in ascending order)

9. (a) 9654   (b) 4569

10.
3458	4358	5348	8345
3485	4385	5384	8354
3548	4538	5438	8435
3584	4583	5483	8453
3845	4835	5834	8534
3854	4853	5843	8543

6 numbers beginning with 8

Exercise 1.2 — Page 2

1. (a) 28   (b) 33

2. (a) 29   (b) 31   (c) 43
   (d) 43   (e) 53   (f) 46

3. (a) 91   (b) 4   (c) 55
   (d) 63   (e) 38   (f) 17

4. (a) 788   (b) 83   (c) 174
   (d) 952   (e) 2002   (f) 12 203
   (g) 201   (h) 1541   (i) 3451
   (j) 1 000 000

5. (a) 27   (b) 56   (c) 35
   (d) 54   (e) 74   (f) 70
   (g) 120   (h) 112

6. 112 miles   7. £539   8. £276

9. (a) 141   (b) 132   (c) 133
   (d) 406

10. (a) 1378   (b) 2269   11. 81 030

Exercise 1.3 — Page 3

1. (a) 33   (b) 27

2. (a) 28   (b) 46   (c) 25
   (d) 35

3. (a) 5   (b) 92   (c) 43
   (d) 68   (e) 76   (f) 17
   (g) 59   (h) 21

4. (a) 16   (b) 17   (c) 50
   (d) 49   (e) 90   (f) 105
   (g) 150   (h) 301   (i) 575
   (j) 4

5. (a) 354   (b) 428   (c) 1284
   (d) 158   (e) 2224   (f) 469
   (g) 6268   (h) 3277

6. 89   7. 384

8. Car C
   Car A 8479, Car B 11 643, Car C 13 859

9. (a) £74   (b) £60

Exercise 1.4 — Page 5

1. 40   2. 72   3. 144   4. £5.52

5. (a) 84   (b) 85   (c) 252
   (d) 549   (e) 2112   (f) 15 895
   (g) 24 072   (h) 42 084

6. (a) 1320   (b) 12 300
   (c) 47 000   (d) 38 400

7. (a) 2310   (b) 514   (c) 100

8. (a) 240   (b) £3.90

9. (a) 210   (b) 140   (c) 350
   (d) 280

10. (a) 300   (b) 420   (c) 1200
    (d) 7200

11. 960   12. 10 000

13. (a) 7590   (b) 7140   (c) 21 480
    (d) 12 300   (e) 13 020   (f) 21 510
    (g) 32 960   (h) 9940   (i) 18 960
    (j) 13 000

14. (a) E.g. To multiply by 200, multiply by 2 and then by 100.

(b) E.g. To multiply by 2000, multiply by 2 then by 1000.

Exercise **1.5** Page 7

1. (a) 16 (b) 20 (c) 8

2. (a) 17 (b) 157 (c) 136
(d) 75 remainder 5 (e) 393 remainder 2
(f) 206 (g) 1098 (h) 20 140

3. (a) 456 (b) 465 (c) 64
(d) 654

4. (a) 100 (b) 702 000 (c) 10

5. (a) 8 (b) 15 (c) 12
(d) 5 (e) 7

6. (a) 253 (b) 79 (c) 537
(d) 126 (e) 45 (f) 613

7. (a) E.g. To divide by 200, divide by 100 then by 2.
(b) (i) 26 (ii) 293 (iii) 412

Exercise **1.6** Page 8

1. 1344
2. 2432
3. 4862
4. 11 130
5. 38 772
6. 76 812
7. 345 015
8. 6 620 544
9. 463
10. 158
11. 123
12. 256
13. 504
14. 654
15. 406
16. 208
17. £1392

18. (a) £1764 (b) £3427 (c) £9866
19. 1416 **20.** (a) 16 rem 10 (b) 25 rem 7
(c) 17 rem 35

21. 17, 7p change **22.** (a) 41 (b) 16

Exercise **1.7** Page 9

1. (a) 37 (b) 3 (c) 9 (d) 58
(e) 6 (f) 30 (g) 5 (h) 19
(i) 14 (j) 20 (k) 24 (l) 4
(m) 0 (n) 56 (o) 56 (p) 6
(q) 28 (r) 0

2. (a) $5 \times 6 + 7 = 37$
(b) $5 + 6 \times 7 = 47$
(c) $15 + 8 \times 9 = 87$
(d) $15 \times 8 + 9 = 129$
(e) $15 \times 8 - 9 = 111$
(f) $15 \div 5 + 3 = 6$
(g) $5 - 24 \div 6 = 1$
(h) $19 \div 19 + 7 \times 0 = 1$
(i) $4 \times 4 + 7 \times 2 = 30$

3. Many answers, for example:
$6 - 3 \times 2 + 1 = 1$ $6 - 3 - 2 + 1 = 2$
$6 \div 3 + 2 - 1 = 3$ $6 \div 3 + 2 \times 1 = 4$
$6 - 3 + 2 \times 1 = 5$ $6 + 3 - 2 - 1 = 6$
$6 + 3 - 2 \times 1 = 7$ $6 \times 3 \div 2 - 1 = 8$
$6 \times 3 \div 2 \times 1 = 9$ $6 + 3 + 2 - 1 = 10$

4. 25 **5.** 148 cm **6.** (a) 63 (b) 75

Review Exercise **1** Page 10

1. (a) eight hundred and seventy thousand three hundred and two
(b) 3 027 409

2. (a) 987 542 (b) 245 789

3. (a) 97, 404 (b) 114, 306
(c) 92, 209

4. (a) 2059 (b) 587

5. (a) 73 500 (b) 6420
(c) 3020 (d) 462

6. 298 miles

7. (a) 6462 (b) 241

8. (a) 50 (b) 50 (c) 10 (d) 2

9. £2175

10. 14 664 **14.** (a) 163
(b) £3 200 000
11. 120
12. (a) 166 (b) 4 **15.** £17
13. £16 297 **16.** 136

CHAPTER 2

Exercise **2.1** Page 13

1. (a) $7 + 0.6 + 0.02$
(b) $30 + 7 + 0.9 + 0.02 + 0.008$
(c) $7 + 0.5 + 0.04 + 0.001$
(d) $20 + 0.5 + 0.003$

2. (a) 0.4 (b) 0.009
(c) 80 (d) 0.05

3. (a) 1.68 (b) 1.39 (c) 1.04

4. (a) 0.07 (b) 0.6

5. (a) A 10.5, B 11 (b) C 5.2, D 5.6
(c) E 0.54, F 0.59 (d) G 0.751, H 0.757

6. (a) 3.001, 3.01, 3.1, 3.15, 3.2
(b) 3.567, 3.576, 3.657, 3.675
(c) 0.1, 0.15, 0.45, 0.5, 0.55

7. (a) 9.87, 9.78, 8.97, 8.79
(b) 1.5, 0.15, 0.015, 0.00015
(c) 2.701, 2.7, 2.67, 2.599

8. 47.5074 **9.** 93.07

1. (a) (i) 8.86 (ii) 12.449 (iii) 17.49
   (b) (i) $8.86 - 3.72 = 5.14$
     (ii) $12.449 - 5.384 = 7.065$
     (iii) $17.49 - 5.69 = 11.8$

2. (a) (i) 6.23 (ii) 24.32 (iii) 24.68
   (b) (i) $6.23 + 3.24 = 9.47$
     (ii) $24.32 + 13.28 = 37.6$
     (iii) $24.68 + 20.36 = 45.04$

3. (a) 10.9 (b) 1.65 (c) 0.9
   (d) 11 (e) 1.2 (f) 0.6
   (g) 0.24 (h) 8.9

4. (a) 6.84 (b) 86.33 (c) 5.22
   (d) 5.003 (e) 3 (f) 1.24
   (g) 15.781 (h) 8.28 (i) 16.033
   (j) 6.273

5. (a) (i) £3.30 (ii) £1.70
   (b) (i) £11.24 (ii) £3.76
   (c) (i) £0.83 (ii) £9.17
   (d) (i) £16.24 (ii) £33.76

6. 4.35 kg   **7.** 4.88 m   **8.** 1.55 m

9. (a) Team A 148.93 s
      Team B 149.08 s
      Team C 149.53 s
   (b) A, B, C

10. 0.719 s

11. (a) 95.21 s (b) 47.72 s

1. (a) 250.6 (b) 2506 (c) 25 060
   (d) 9.3 (e) 93 (f) 930
   (g) 0.623 (h) 6.23 (i) 62.3
   (j) 94.51 (k) 945.1 (l) 9451

2. (a) 3.77 (b) 0.377 (c) 0.0377
   (d) 0.027 (e) 0.0027 (f) 0.00027
   (g) 18.902 (h) 1.8902 (i) 0.18902
   (j) 0.9 (k) 0.09 (l) 0.009

3. (a) (i) 0.64 (ii) 6.4 (iii) 64
   (b) (i) 0.64 (ii) 0.064 (iii) 0.0064

4. (a) £13.50 (b) £135 (c) £1350

5. (a) £2.50 (b) £25 (c) £250

6. (a) 5.04 km (b) 50.4 km (c) 504 km

7. (a) £7.95 (b) £0.12 (c) 66.9p

8. 12.3×1000 and $12.3 \div 0.001$
   $12.3 \div 100$ and 12.3×0.01
   12.3×0.1 and $12.3 \div 10$
   $12.3 \div 0.01$ and 12.3×100
   12.3×10 and $12.3 \div 0.1$
   12.3×0.001 and $12.3 \div 1000$

1. (a) 8.5 (b) 0.36 (c) 1.3
   (d) 0.48 (e) 0.06 (f) 1.44

2. (a) 8.75 (b) 54.53
   (c) 1.03 (d) 29.808
   (e) 0.0007 (f) 0.01
   (g) 0.0001 (h) 97.82
   (i) 57.78 (j) 0.000 177 6

3. (a) (i) 3 (ii) 1.5 (iii) 0.24 (iv) 15
   (b) Each answer is less than the original
      number.

4. (a) 21p (b) £1.84 (c) 78p

5. (a) £13.93 (b) £10.08 (c) £54.21
   (d) £26.24

6. (a) (i) 35.1 fr (b) (i) $12.30
     (ii) 5.85 fr   (ii) $1.23
     (iii) 528.45 fr   (iii) $59.86

7. (a) £4.34 (b) £5.12 (c) £2.60
   (d) £2.34

1. (a) 4 (b) 15 (c) 15
   (d) 4 (e) 50

2. (a) 1.75 (b) 1.6 (c) 2.4
   (d) 1.75 (e) 1.125

3. (a) 12.3 (b) 2.92 (c) 6.05
   (d) 1430 (e) 0.05 (f) 12.5
   (g) 6.54 (h) 37.5

4. (a) 37 (b) 5.6 (c) 43.75
   (d) 46.9 (e) 10.62 (f) 34.2

5. (a) (i) 10 (ii) 6 (iii) 0.3
   (b) Each answer is greater than the original
      number.

6. 67   **7.** 45

8. (a) 47p (b) £1.35 (c) 11p
   (d) 9p (e) 66.8p

1. (a) $\frac{1}{4}$ (b) $\frac{1}{2}$ (c) $\frac{3}{4}$ (d) $\frac{1}{10}$

2. (a) $\frac{7}{10}$ (b) $\frac{2}{5}$ (c) $\frac{1}{100}$ (d) $\frac{1}{5}$
   (e) $\frac{1}{20}$ (f) $\frac{3}{20}$ (g) $\frac{13}{25}$ (h) $\frac{7}{100}$
   (i) $\frac{1}{8}$ (j) $\frac{13}{20}$ (k) $\frac{3}{5}$ (l) $\frac{19}{20}$

3. (a) $1\frac{7}{10}$ (b) $2\frac{3}{10}$ (c) $1\frac{2}{5}$ (d) $3\frac{1}{4}$
   (e) $4\frac{4}{5}$ (f) $12\frac{1}{10}$ (g) $16\frac{3}{4}$ (h) $5\frac{1}{20}$

4. (a) $\frac{2}{3}$ (b) $\frac{1}{9}$ (c) $\frac{5}{9}$

1. (a) (i) 20.745   (b) (i) 0.87
        (ii) 14.407   (ii) 4.33
        (iii) 179.22   (iii) 1.53

2. 40 s   **3.** 2.37 m

4. (a) (i) 76.2   (b) (i) 0.762
        (ii) 762   (ii) 0.0762
        (iii) 7620   (iii) 0.007 62

5. (a) (i) 1746   (b) (i) 4.365
        (ii) 2619   (ii) 2.91
        (iii) 3492   (iii) 2.1825

6. (a) £247.50 (b) £7.99

7. (a) 46.62   (b) 10.152   (c) 105.9

8. (a) 7.2   (b) 1235   (c) 13 700

9. 18   **10.** £9.03   **11.** 20.8

12. 18.8125   **13.** 3.378 (3 d.p.)

CHAPTER 3

1. (a) 4870   (b) 4900   (c) 5000

2. (a) 7430   (b) 7400   (c) 7000

3.

Number	Nearest 10	Nearest 100	Nearest 1000
7613	7610	7600	8000
977	980	1000	1000
61 115	61 120	61 100	61 000
9714	9710	9700	10 000
623	620	600	1000
9949	9950	9900	10 000
5762	5760	5800	6000
7501	7500	7500	8000
7500	7500	7500	8000
7499	7500	7500	7000

4. (a) 19 000 (nearest thousand)
   (b) 260 (nearest ten)
   (c) 140 (nearest ten)
   (d) £50 (nearest pound)
   (e) 130 (nearest ten)
   (f) 24 100 (nearest hundred)
   (g) 309 000 km² (nearest thousand km²)
   (h) 190 km (nearest ten kilometres)
   (i) £51 (nearest pound)
   (j) 700 (nearest hundred)

5. (a) 745, 746, 747, 748, 749
   (b) 750, 751, 752, 753, 754
   (c) Any number from 8450 to 8499
   (d) Any number from 8500 to 8549

6. 42 500   **7.** 135, 144   **8.** 2749

1. 4   **4.** 5   **7.** 29   **10.** 7

2. 5   **5.** 9   **8.** 19   **11.** 5

3. 10   **6.** 24   **9.** 5

1. (a) 3.962   (b) 3.96   (c) 4.0

2. (a) 567.65   (b) 567.7   (c) 568

3. Missing entries:
   0.96, 0.97, 15.281, 0.06, 4.99, 5.00

4. 4.86

5. (a) (i) 46.1   (ii) 59.7
       (iii) 569.4   (iv) 17.1   (v) 0.7
   (b) (i) 46.14   (ii) 59.70
       (iii) 569.43 (iv) 17.06 (v) 0.66
   (c) (i) 46.145 (ii) 59.697
       (iii) 569.434 (iv) 17.059 (v) 0.662

6. (a) £12.16, nearest penny
   (b) £3.57, nearest penny
   (c) £2.37, nearest penny
   (d) 35.7 cm, nearest millimetre
   (e) £1.33, nearest penny
   (f) £12.70, nearest penny

1. (a) 20 (b) 500 (c) 0.3 (d) 0.02 (e) 20

2.

Number	sig. fig.	Answer
456 000	2	460 000
454 000	2	450 000
7 981 234	3	7 980 000
7 981 234	2	8 000 000
1290	2	1300
19 602	1	20 000

3.

Number	sig. fig.	Answer
0.000567	2	0.00057
0.093748	2	0.094
0.093748	3	0.0937
0.093748	4	0.09375
0.010245	2	0.010
0.02994	2	0.030

4. 485.7

5. (a) (i) 83 000 (ii) 83 (iii) 1000
(iv) 0.0073 (v) 0.0019
(b) (i) 82 700 (ii) 82.7 (iii) 1000
(iv) 0.00728 (v) 0.00190
(c) (i) 82 660 (ii) 82.66 (iii) 1001
(iv) 0.007281 (v) 0.001899

6. 472 m² (3 s.f.)

7. (a) 51 cm² (2 s.f.) (b) 157 cm² (3 s.f.)
(c) 6100 m² (2 s.f.) (d) 1.23 m (nearest cm)
(e) 154 000 m² (3 s.f.)

Exercise **3.5** Page 30

1. (a) $30 \times 40 = 1200$, 1312
(b) $10 \times 70 = 700$, 792
(c) $60 \times 30 = 1800$, 1972
(d) $70 \times 50 = 3500$, 3240
(e) $30 \times 80 = 2400$, 2652
(f) $20 \times 200 = 4000$, 3723
(g) $300 \times 60 = 18\,000$, 16 296
(h) $300 \times 20 = 6000$, 7176

2. (a) $600 \div 20 = 30$, 33
(b) $600 \div 20 = 30$, 29
(c) $300 \div 20 = 15$, 16
(d) $800 \div 40 = 20$, 24

3. (a) $4 \times 2 = 8$, 7.56
(b) $9 \times 3 = 27$, 27.59
(c) $50 \times 4 = 200$, 202.02
(d) $100 \times 3 = 300$, 299.86

4. (a) $10 \div 5 = 2$, 2.2
(b) $20 \div 4 = 5$, 4.8
(c) $30 \div 3 = 10$, 9.5
(d) $200 \div 5 = 40$, 39.9

5. (a) 30 is bigger than 29 and 50 is bigger
than 48.
So, 30×50 is bigger than 29×48
(b) $200 \div 10 = 20$, 14, estimate is bigger

6. (a) £5000 + £800 = £5800 (b) £6112

7. (a) $500 + 1300 = 1800$
(b) $3000 - 1800 = 1200$

8. (a) 6.4, 6.41875 (b) 20, 18.709677…
(c) 20, 20.45631…

9. (a) Meadow View 66 m², Park View 61 m²
(b) Meadow View 65.72 m²,
Park View 60.07 m²

Review Exercise **3** Page 31

1. (a) 8480 (b) 8500 (c) 8000

2. (a) 315 (b) 310 (c) 314.6 (d) 300

3. (a) 3 967 000 (b) 4 000 000

4. (a) $\dfrac{200 - 50}{3}$ (b) 50

5. $2000 \div 50 = 40$

6. (a) $400 \times 4 = 1600$
(b) $10 \times £500 = £5000$

7. $500 \times £2 = £1000$

8. (a) 700 francs (b) £600 **9.** £6000

10. 7 **11.** 39 **12.** (a) 25.6 (b) 30

13. (a) 9.2 (b) 9.18 **14.** (a) 1 (b) 1.5

15. (a) 600×300 (b) 180 000 (c) 5016

16. 49.7

17. (a) 2, 1.99972… (b) 10, 9.85276…
(c) 6, 5.6283…

18. (a) 17.8 is less than 18 **and** (b) $\dfrac{40 \times 60}{300}$
0.97 is less than 1,
so answer is less than 18.

19. $\dfrac{6 \times 200}{0.5} = 2400$

20. (a) 203.056 cm³ (b) 203 cm³, measurements
only accurate to 1 d.p.

21. (a) 18.3312 m² (b) 18.4 m², measurements
accurate to 2 d.p. so area
must be rounded up.

CHAPTER 4

Exercise **4.1** Page 34

1. (a) Warmer (b) Colder
(c) Warmer (d) Colder

2. (a) Less (b) More
(c) Less (d) More

3. (a) Colombo (b) Moscow
(c) $-22°C$, $-17°C$, $-7°C$, $0°C$, $3°C$, $15°C$,
$21°C$.

4. (a) $-28°C$, $-13°C$, $-3°C$, $19°C$, $23°C$.
(b) $-11°C$, $-9°C$, $-7°C$, $0°C$, $10°C$, $12°C$.
(c) $-29°C$, $-15°C$, $2°C$, $18°C$, $27°C$.
(d) $-20°C$, $-15°C$, $-5°C$, $0°C$, $10°C$, $20°C$.

5. (a) -78, -39, -16, -9, 11, 31, 51.
(b) -5, -3, -2, -1, 0, 1, 2, 4, 5.
(c) -103, -63, -19, -3, 5, 52, 99, 104.
(d) -50, -30, -20, 0, 10, 30, 40.
(e) -30, -15, -10, 0, 8, 17, 27.

Exercise **4.2** Page 35

1. (a) -3 (b) -4 (c) -7 (d) -32 (e) 0
(f) -27 (g) -61 (h) -1

2. (b) (i) -1 (ii) -4 (iii) -4

3. (a) 9 (b) 1 (c) 12 (d) -10 (e) 30 (f) 15

4. (a) $-£75$ (£75 overdrawn)
(b) £40 (£40 in credit)

5. (a) $-80\,\text{m}$ (b) $-200\,\text{m}$ (c) $60\,\text{m}$
    (d) $60\,\text{m}$ (e) $120\,\text{m}$ (f) $70\,\text{m}$
    (g) $300\,\text{m}$ (h) $50\,\text{m}$ (i) $130\,\text{m}$
    (j) $240\,\text{m}$ (k) $250\,\text{m}$

Exercise 4.3   Page 36

1. (a) 2   (b) 1   (c) -9
   (d) 8   (e) 4   (f) -5
   (g) -7 (h) 7   (i) 1
   (j) -15 (k) -3 (l) -6

2. (a) 13   (b) 6   (c) 7
   (d) 7   (e) 5   (f) -12
   (g) -1 (h) 13   (i) -11
   (j) 11   (k) 9   (l) 0

3. (a) 5   (b) 3   (c) 3
   (d) -7 (e) -6 (f) -1

4. (a) 6   (b) -8 (c) -28
   (d) 0   (e) -35 (f) 19

5. (a) 7   (b) -1 (c) 36
   (d) -6 (e) 38   (f) 15
   (g) -15 (h) 25   (i) 15
   (j) -6

6. (a) $3°\text{C}$ (b) $10°\text{C}$ (c) $5°\text{C}$
   (d) $6°\text{C}$ (e) $37°\text{C}$

7. $-15°\text{C}$

Exercise 4.4   Page 38

1. (a) 35   (b) -35 (c) 35
   (d) 10   (e) -10 (f) 10
   (g) 1   (h) -24 (i) -24
   (j) -45 (k) 64   (l) -42
   (m) 42   (n) -80 (o) -80
   (p) 32

2. (a) -20 (b) 60   (c) -30
   (d) 60   (e) -60 (f) -100

3. (a) -4 (b) 4   (c) 5
   (d) -5 (e) -5 (f) 5
   (g) 6   (h) -6 (i) 4
   (j) -8 (k) 6   (l) -5

4. (a) -1.8 (b) 3   (c) -1.6
   (d) 3.2   (e) -20 (f) 12
   (g) -10 (h) 5

5. (a) -0.5 (b) -0.8 (c) 0.7
   (d) -15 (e) -4 (f) 4

Review Exercise 4   Page 38

1. $-20, -5, 0, 15, 25.$

2. (a) -18 (b) 4   (c) 4

3. (a) Poole   (b) Selby

4. (a) -2 (b) -2

---

5. (a) 13 degrees   (b) $-8°\text{C}$

6. 5 degrees   7. 4191 m

8. (a) $8°\text{C}$ (b) $18°\text{C}$ (c) $26°\text{C}$

9. $7°\text{C}$ 10. $-£33.55$ (£33.55 overdrawn)

11. (a) 24   (b) -24 (c) -24
    (d) 24   (e) 40   (f) -40
    (g) -40 (h) 40

12. (a) -5 (b) 2   (c) -6 (d) 4

13. (a) (i) -1 (ii) 6   (iii) 5
    (b) (i) 6   (ii) 2

14. (a) $21°\text{C}$ (b) $24.8°\text{F}$

15. (a) -20
    (b) Naomi
      Tim: $10 \times 2 + 10 \times (-1) = 10$
      Naomi: $8 \times 2 + 5 \times (-1) = 11$

CHAPTER 5

Exercise 5.1   Page 41

1. (a) 3, 6, 9, 12, 15.
   (b) 7, 14, 21, 28, 35.
   (c) 20, 40, 60, 80, 100.
   (d) 12, 24, 36, 48, 60.
   (e) 19, 38, 57, 76, 95.

2. (a) 20   (b) 70   (c) Third
   (d) Eleventh   (e) 5   (f) 5

3. (a) Second   (b) Second   (c) Fifth
   (d) Third

4. (a) (i) Answers are even numbers.
      (ii) Answers are even numbers.
      (iii) Answers are even numbers.
      (iv) Answers are odd numbers.

   (b) (i)

$\times$	2	3	6	7	9
2	E	E	E	E	E
3	E	O	E	O	O
6	E	E	E	E	E
7	E	O	E	O	O
9	E	O	E	O	O

      (ii)

$\times$	O	E
O	O	E
E	E	E

5. (a) $1 \times 18, 2 \times 9, 3 \times 6$
   (b) 1, 2, 3, 6, 9, 18

6. (a) $1 \times 20, 2 \times 10, 4 \times 5$
   (b) 1, 2, 4, 5, 10, 20

7. (a) 1, 2, 4, 8, 16
(b) 1, 2, 4, 7, 14, 28
(c) 1, 2, 3, 4, 6, 9, 12, 18, 36
(d) 1, 3, 5, 9, 15, 45
(e) 1, 2, 3, 4, 6, 8, 12, 16, 24, 48
(f) 1, 2, 5, 10, 25, 50
(g) 1, 2, 3, 4, 5, 6, 10, 12, 15, 20, 30, 60
(h) 1, 2, 4, 5, 8, 10, 16, 20, 40, 80

8. (a) (i) 1, 2   (ii) 1, 3   (iii) 1, 5
    (iv) 1, 7   (v) 1, 11   (vi) 1, 13
(b) 17, 19, 23, 29, 31, …

9. (a) (i) 1, 2, 4   (ii) 1, 3, 9
    (iii) 1, 5, 25   (iv) 1, 7, 49
(b) 121, 169, 289, 361, …

10. (a) (i) 1, 2, 3, 6   (ii) 1, 2, 5, 10
    (iii) 1, 2, 7, 14   (iv) 1, 2, 13, 26
    (v) 1, 5, 11, 55   (vi) 1, 2, 19, 38
(b) 15, 21, 22, 33, 35, …

11. (a) 4 (6, 12, 18, 36)
(b) 8 (5, 10, 15, 20, 30, 40, 60, 120)
(c) 6 (2, 4, 10, 20, 50, 100)
(d) 8 (4, 8, 12, 16, 24, 32, 48, 96)

12. (a) 14, 35   (b) 4, 5, 20   (c) 3, 5

13. (i) 2, 3, 5, 7, 11, 13, 17, 19, 23, 29, 31, 37, 41, 43, 47.
Prime number

Exercise 5.2   Page 44

1. (a) 4^4 (b) 3^8 (c) 8^7
(d) 0.3^3 (e) 1.6^5 (f) 12^7

2. (a)

Expression	Index form	Value
$10 \times 10 \times 10 \times 10 \times 10 \times 10$	10^6	1 000 000
$10 \times 10 \times 10 \times 10 \times 10$	10^5	100 000
$10 \times 10 \times 10 \times 10$	10^4	10 000
$10 \times 10 \times 10$	10^3	1000
10×10	10^2	100
10	10^1	10
1	10^0	1

(b) (i)

Expression	Index form	Value
$5 \times 5 \times 5 \times 5 \times 5 \times 5$	5^6	15 625
$5 \times 5 \times 5 \times 5 \times 5$	5^5	3125
$5 \times 5 \times 5 \times 5$	5^4	625
$5 \times 5 \times 5$	5^3	125
5×5	5^2	25
5	5^1	5
1	5^0	1

(ii)

Expression	Index form	Value
$4 \times 4 \times 4 \times 4 \times 4 \times 4$	4^6	4096
$4 \times 4 \times 4 \times 4 \times 4$	4^5	1024
$4 \times 4 \times 4 \times 4$	4^4	256
$4 \times 4 \times 4$	4^3	64
4×4	4^2	16
4	4^1	4
1	4^0	1

(c) 1

3. (a) 8   (b) 36   (c) 81
(d) 144   (e) 625   (f) 10 000 000

4. (a) $2^2 \times 3^2$ (b) $2 \times 3^3 \times 5$
(c) $2 \times 3 \times 5^2$ (d) $2^4 \times 3 \times 5^2$
(e) $3^4 \times 5^2 \times 7$

Exercise 5.3   Page 45

1. (a) 2, 3   (b) 2, 5   (c) 2, 7
(d) 3, 5   (e) 2, 3, 11

2. (a) $2^2 \times 3$ (b) $2^2 \times 5$ (c) $2^2 \times 7$
(d) $3^2 \times 5$ (e) $2 \times 3 \times 11$

3. (a) 1, 2, 2×3, 2×3^2, 2×3^3, 2^2, $2^2 \times 3$,
$2^2 \times 3^2$, $2^2 \times 3^3$, 2^3, $2^3 \times 3$, $2^3 \times 3^2$,
$2^3 \times 3^3$, 2^4, $2^4 \times 3$, $2^4 \times 3^2$, $2^4 \times 3^3$, 2^5,
$2^5 \times 3$, $2^5 \times 3^2$, $2^5 \times 3^3$, 3, 3^2, 3^3
(b) 1, 5, 5×7, 5×7^2, 5×7^3, 5×7^4, 5^2,
$5^2 \times 7$, $5^2 \times 7^2$, $5^2 \times 7^3$, $5^2 \times 7^4$, 5^3,
$5^3 \times 7$, $5^3 \times 7^2$, $5^3 \times 7^3$, $5^3 \times 7^4$, 7, 7^2,
7^3, 7^4

4. 1000   1 000 000   2700
56 250 000   3 294 225   926 859 375

5. 2700, 3528, 4500

6. 56, 88, 104

7. 126, 132, 150

Exercise 5.4   Page 46

1. (a) 24   (b) 160   (c) 20
(d) 90   (e) 90   (f) 24
(g) 40   (h) 630

2. (a) 6   (b) 8   (c) 2
(d) 4   (e) 11   (f) 4
(g) 3   (h) 15

4. (a) 3   (b) 2×3^4
(c) 54   (d) 324

5. (a) $2^3 \times 3^3$ (b) $2^5 \times 3^2$
(c) 72   (d) 864

6. 9.18 am

1. (a) 1, 4, 9, 16, 25, 36, 49, 64, 81, 100, 121, 144, 169, 196, 225, 256, 289, 324, 361, 400
(c) $21^2 = 400 + 41 = 441$

2. (a) 1, 8, 27, 64, 125, 216, 343, 512, 729, 1000

3. (a) (i) 9 (ii) -8 (iii) 16 (iv) -125
(b) The result of squaring a negative number is a positive number.
The result of cubing a negative number is a negative number.

4. 64

5. (a) 44.89 (b) 39.304 (c) 0.49
(d) 0.000064 (e) 0.16 (f) -0.125

6. (a) 1 (b) 0.027 (c) 0.4 (d) 0.25

7. (a) 1.69 (b) 4.913 (c) 1 (d) 4.8

8. (a) (i) 169 (ii) 289 (iii) 6.25
(iv) 0.64 (v) 94.09
(b) (i) 216 (ii) 3375 (iii) 13.824
(iv) 0.343 (v) 175.616
(c) (i) 2187 (ii) 16 807 (iii) 531 441
(iv) 0.0625 (v) 792.35168

9. (a) 79.62624 (b) -1.728 (c) 0.49
(d) 90 (e) 60 (f) 864
(g) 1944 (h) 128 (i) 8192
(j) 0.860 518 4

10. (a) 30 (b) 66
(c) 2592 (d) 1440
(e) 1080 (f) 6.770 83…
(g) 126 216 (h) 0.281 25
(i) 20 000

11. (a) (i) 0.5 (ii) 0.2 (iii) 0.1
(iv) 2 (v) 10 (vi) 5
(b) (i) 0.25 (ii) 0.05 (iii) 0.04
(iv) 4 (v) 2.5 (vi) 6.25

13. (a) 0.5 (b) 0.25 (c) 1.25 (d) 4

14. (a) 3 (b) 0 (c) 1 (d) 2
(e) 6 (f) 3 (g) 4 (h) 3

1. (a) 5 (b) 10 (c) 8 (d) 7

2. (a) 2 (b) 4 (c) 5 (d) 3

3. (a) 4.5 (b) 3.6 (c) 10.4 (d) 5.8

4. 7.42 m **5.** 16.51 mm

1. (a) 2^7 (b) 4^9 (c) 6^3
(d) 8^7 (e) $9^0 = 1$ (f) 2^{-2}
(g) 5^{-2} (h) 3^{-1} (i) 8^{-5}

2. (a) 2^3 (b) 4^2 (c) 6
(d) 8 (e) 3^6 (f) 2^{-4}
(g) 5^{12} (h) 11^{-5} (i) 7^{-1}

3. (a) 8^2 (b) 7^{-5} (c) 2.5^{-1}
(d) $4^0 = 1$ (e) 10^{-1} (f) 6^{-4}
(g) 0.1^{-12} (h) 5^{-15} (i) 4^5

4. (a) $4^2 \times 8^7$ (b) 4×5^{-2}
(c) $2^{-2} \times 5^5$ (d) $3^{-3} \times 8^4$

5. (a) 2^3 (b) 3 (c) 5^3

1. (a) $\sqrt{2}$ surd (b) $\sqrt{9} = 3$
(c) $\sqrt{7}$ surd (d) $\sqrt{1} = 1$
(e) $\sqrt{18}$ surd (f) $\sqrt{25} = 5$

2. (a) $2\sqrt{2}$ (b) $2\sqrt{3}$ (c) $2\sqrt{7}$
(d) $3\sqrt{3}$ (e) $5\sqrt{3}$ (f) $3\sqrt{5}$
(g) $2\sqrt{5}$ (h) $6\sqrt{2}$

3. (a) $2\sqrt{2}$ (b) $\sqrt{5}$ (c) $7\sqrt{3}$ (d) $2\sqrt{2}$

4. (a) $\frac{3}{2}$ (b) $\frac{5}{4}$ (c) $\frac{\sqrt{6}}{2}$
(d) $\sqrt{2}$ (e) $\frac{2}{\sqrt{5}}$

5. (a) 3 (b) 6 (c) 6 (d) 4
(e) 6 (f) 6 (g) $5\sqrt{2}$ (h) $3\sqrt{2}$

1. (a) 1, 2, 3, 4, 6, 12
(b) 1, 2, 3, 5, 6, 10, 15, 30
(c) 1, 2, 3, 4, 6, 8, 12, 16, 24, 32, 48, 96

2. Only two factors, 1 and 19.

3. (a) 16 (b) 4 (c) 7, 13, 19

4. 36 **5.** (a) 9 (b) 8 (c) 11

6. (a) 8: 1, 2, 4, 8
9: 1, 3, 9
11: 1, 11
17: 1, 17
121: 1, 11, 121
(b) (i) 11, 17 (ii) prime numbers
(c) (i) 9, 121 (ii) square numbers

7. (a) 2 (b) 1, 2, 3, 4, 6, 9, 12, 18, 36 (c) 108
(d) One factor is the square root of the number.

8. (a) (i) $2 \times 3^2 \times 7$ (b) 630
(ii) $2 \times 3^2 \times 5$ (c) 18
(iii) $2 \times 3 \times 5 \times 7$

9. (a) 2^5 (b) $2^3 \times 3^2$ (c) 4 (d) 288

10. 90 seconds   12. (a) 49   (b) 9

11. (a) $n = 3, p = 37$ 13. 3

14. (a) 125   (b) 6   (c) 72

15. (a) $2\sqrt{5}$ (b) $\frac{6}{5}$ (c) 6

16. $\sqrt{400}$. $\sqrt{400} = 20$, $2^5 = 32$

17. (a) 0.04   (b) 0.729

18. (a) 2.65   (b) 7   (c) 343

19. 7.1   21. (a) 32 768   (b) 0.167

20. 5.8   22. 2.84

23. (a) 10^2 (b) 10^6 (c) 10^0
    (d) 10^{-1} (e) 10^{-3}

24. (a) 1   (b) 625   (c) 272
    (d) 90   (e) 500   (f) 50
    (g) 50   (h) 40

25. (a) $x = 4$ (b) $x = 4$ (c) $x = 0$

26. (a) 31 104   (b) 0.02943
    (c) 0.00006561   (d) 8145
    (e) -16384 (f) 786 432

27. (a) 3^8 (b) 5^{11}
    (c) 9^6 (d) 4^5
    (e) 7^5 (f) 6^4
    (g) 2^{-3} (h) 5^{-7}
    (i) 4^{-3} (j) $2^{-7} \times 7^2$
    (k) 3^9

28. (a) 3.7   (b) 5^{-1}

CHAPTER 6

Exercise 6.1   Page 58

1. Missing entries:
    (a) 7.5×10^4
    (b) 800 000 000, 8×10^8
    (c) 35 000 000 000 000,
      $3.5 \times 10\ 000\ 000\ 000\ 000$
    (d) $6.23 \times 10\ 000\ 000\ 000\ 000$, 6.23×10^{13}
    (e) 5 400 000 000, $5.4 \times 1\ 000\ 000\ 000$
    (f) 69 300 000, 6.93×10^7
    (g) $4.531 \times 100\ 000\ 000\ 000$, 4.53×10^{11}
    (h) 697 000, $6.97 \times 100\ 000$
    (i) $4.5312 \times 100\ 000$, 4.5312×10^5
    (j) 109 700, 1.097×10^5

2. (a) 6 E 13, 6×10^{13}, 60 000 000 000 000
    (b) 9.6 E 12, 9.6×10^{12}, 9 600 000 000 000
    (c) 1.05 E 13, 1.05×10^{13},
      10 500 000 000 000
    (d) 1.3 E 14, 1.3×10^{14},
      130 000 000 000 000

    (e) 2.4 E 14, 2.4×10^{14},
      240 000 000 000 000
    (f) 2.5 E 12, 2.5×10^{12}, 2 500 000 000 000
    (g) 1.408 E 16, 1.408×10^{16},
      14 080 000 000 000 000
    (h) 2.288 E 14, 2.288×10^{14},
      228 800 000 000 000
    (i) 8.073 E 11, 8.073×10^{11},
      807 300 000 000
    (j) 1.1 E 15, 1.1×10^{15},
      1 100 000 000 000 000

3. (a) 3×10^{11} (b) 8×10^7
    (c) 7×10^8 (d) 2×10^9
    (e) 4.2×10^7 (f) 2.1×10^{10}
    (g) 3.7×10^9 (h) 6.3×10^2
    (i) 3.219×10^9 (j) 6.5412×10^8
    (k) 8.97213×10^5 (l) 4.267×10^{10}

4. (a) 600 000   (b) 2000
    (c) 50 000 000   (d) 900 000 000
    (e) 3 700 000 000   (f) 28
    (g) 99 000 000 000   (h) 71 000
    (i) 397   (j) 817.2
    (k) 7 431 200   (l) 1 234 000 000

5. (a) (i) 4.5×10^3 (ii) 7.8×10^7
      (iii) 5.3×10^5 (iv) 3.25×10^4
    (b) (i) 4500   (ii) 78 000 000
      (iii) 530 000   (iv) 32 500

Exercise 6.2   Page 60

1. (a) -1 (b) -5 (c) -9
    (d) -3 (e) -11 (f) -13

2. Missing entries:
    (b) 7.5×10^{-3}
    (c) 8.75×10^{-6}
    (d) $3.5 \times 0.000\ 000\ 001$, 3.5×10^{-9}
    (e) $6.23 \times 0.000\ 000\ 000\ 001$, 6.23×10^{-12}
    (f) $5 \times 0.000\ 000\ 1$, 5×10^{-7}
    (g) $4.725 \times 0.000\ 000\ 01$, 4.725×10^{-8}
    (h) 5×0.01, 5×10^{-2}
    (i) $7.85 \times 0.000\ 001$, 7.85×10^{-6}

3. (a) 0.35
    (b) 0.0005
    (c) 0.000 072
    (d) 0.0061
    (e) 0.000 000 000 117
    (f) 0.000 000 813 5
    (g) 0.064 62
    (h) 0.000 000 004 001

4. (a) 7×10^{-3} (b) 4×10^{-2}
    (c) 5×10^{-9} (d) 8×10^{-4}
    (e) 2.3×10^{-9} (f) 4.5×10^{-8}
    (g) 2.34×10^{-2} (h) 2.34×10^{-9}
    (i) 6.7×10^{-3} (j) 3×10^{-1}
    (k) 7.395×10^{-8} (l) 3.4×10^{-13}

5. (a) 0.000 005 5   (b) 0.000 000 065
    (c) 32 000 000   (d) 290
    (e) 0.000 000 000 031 67   (f) 11 150
    (g) 0.000 014 12   (h) 40

6. (a) $6\,E-12$, 6×10^{-12}, 0.000 000 000 006
    (b) $1.35\,E-10$, 1.35×10^{-10},
       0.000 000 000 135
    (c) $3\,E-11$, 3×10^{-11}, 0.000 000 000 03
    (d) $1.15\,E-10$, 1.15×10^{-10},
       0.000 000 000 115
    (e) $4.24\,E-09$, 4.24×10^{-9},
       0.000 000 004 24
    (f) $9.728\,E-11$, 9.728×10^{-11},
       0.000 000 000 097 28
    (g) $2.891\,E-13$, 2.891×10^{-13},
       0.000 000 000 000 289 1
    (h) $3\,E-10$, 3×10^{-10}, 0.000 000 000 3
    (i) $1.055\,E\,11$, 1.055×10^{11},
       105 500 000 000
    (j) $9.25\,E\,11$, 9.25×10^{11}, 925 000 000 000

Exercise 6.3   Page 62

1. (a) 262 500
    (b) 105 000 000 000 000
    (c) 72 250 000 000 000
    (d) 0.000 000 125
    (e) 30 000 000 000
    (f) 263 160 000 000 000 000 000

2. (a) 9.38×10^{19} (b) 1.6×10^{1}
    (c) 2.25×10^{26} (d) 1.25×10^{-37}
    (e) 2.4×10^{20} (f) 5×10^{-2}

3. (a) 2.088×10^{9} (b) $1.525\,965 \times 10^{16}\,\text{km}$

4. (a) Pluto, Jupiter, Saturn
    (b) $1.397 \times 10^{5}\,\text{km}$, 139 700 km

5. (a) $9.273 \times 10^{6}\,\text{km}^2$ (b) $4.93 \times 10^{5}\,\text{km}^2$

6. 2.52×10^{12}

7. 2.2×10^{-5} **9.** 2.85×10^{-3}

8. 2.3×10^{-7} **10.** 9×10^{-28} grams

11. (a) 4.55×10^{9} years
    (b) About 6.6×10^{3} times

Exercise 6.4   Page 63

1. (a) 5.2×10^{3} (b) 8.4×10^{6}
    (c) 4×10^{4} (d) 5×10^{4}

2. (a) 2.8×10^{3} (b) 9×10^{5}
    (c) 3×10^{7} (d) 9.5×10^{8}

3. (a) 8×10^{7} (b) 6×10^{7}
    (c) 2.4×10^{8} (d) 2.7×10^{15}

4. (a) 3×10^{3} (b) 3×10^{3}
    (c) 5×10^{1} (d) 2×10^{11}
    (e) 4×10^{5} (f) 3×10^{-3}

5. (a) 1.5×10^{0} (b) 2.7×10^{13}
    (c) 4.5×10^{4} (d) 1.25×10^{-13}
    (e) 6×10^{8}

6. (a) 1.5×10^{11} (b) 2.4×10^{3}
    (c) 4.2×10^{-8} (d) 6.4×10^{7}
    (e) 5×10^{1} (f) 3×10^{9}
    (g) 6.25×10^{-6} (h) 2.5×10^{4}

Review Exercise 6   Page 64

1. (a) 7.8×10^{6} (b) 5×10^{-6}
    (c) (i) 170 000   (ii) 0.0032

2. (a) 3.5×10^{3} (b) 1.4×10^{8}
    (c) 210 000   (d) 0.0006

3. (a) 8×10^{4} (b) 0.0000125

4. (a) 1.6×10^{8} (b) 28 000

5. (a) 2.5×10^{5} (b) 2.69×10^{-3}

6. (a) 1.47×10^{8} (b) 2.1×10^{3}
    (c) $£7 \times 10^{4}$

CHAPTER 7

Exercise 7.1   Page 66

1. (a) $\frac{4}{9}$ (b) $\frac{2}{8} = \frac{1}{4}$ (c) $\frac{8}{16} = \frac{1}{2}$ (d) $\frac{3}{12} = \frac{1}{4}$

2. E.g. $\frac{15}{24}, \frac{30}{48}, \frac{45}{72}, \ldots, \frac{10}{16}, \frac{20}{32}, \ldots$
    simplest form $\frac{5}{8}$

3. (a) **P**   (b) **P**   (c) **R**
    (d) **R**   (e) **Q**   (f) **S**

4. (a) $\frac{1}{3}$ (b) $\frac{1}{3}$ (c) $\frac{1}{3}$ (d) $\frac{1}{3}$ (e) $\frac{1}{2}$

5. (a) E.g. $\frac{2}{6}, \frac{3}{9}, \frac{4}{12}$

    (b) E.g. $\frac{4}{18}, \frac{6}{27}, \frac{8}{36}$

    (c) E.g. $\frac{10}{16}, \frac{15}{24}, \frac{20}{32}$

    (d) E.g. $\frac{8}{10}, \frac{12}{15}, \frac{16}{20}$

    (e) E.g. $\frac{6}{20}, \frac{9}{30}, \frac{12}{40}$

    (f) E.g. $\frac{14}{24}, \frac{21}{36}, \frac{28}{48}$

6. (a) 2   (b) 3   (c) 6   (d) 3   (e) 8   (f) 7

7. (a) $\frac{3}{4}$ (b) $\frac{4}{5}$ (c) $\frac{2}{3}$ (d) $\frac{2}{9}$

    (e) $\frac{2}{3}$ (f) $\frac{2}{5}$ (g) $\frac{6}{25}$ (h) $\frac{4}{5}$

8. (a) $\frac{1}{5}$ (b) $\frac{1}{4}$ (c) $\frac{2}{3}$ (d) $\frac{2}{5}$ (e) $\frac{4}{7}$

9. (a) $\frac{7}{10}$ (b) $\frac{1}{5}$

10. (a) 24   (b) $\frac{1}{6}$

Exercise 7.2 — Page 68

1. (a) $1\frac{3}{10}$ (b) $1\frac{1}{2}$ (c) $2\frac{1}{8}$
   (d) $3\frac{3}{4}$ (e) $4\frac{3}{5}$ (f) $4\frac{6}{7}$

2. (a) $\frac{27}{10}$ (b) $\frac{8}{5}$ (c) $\frac{35}{6}$
   (d) $\frac{63}{20}$ (e) $\frac{41}{9}$ (f) $\frac{53}{7}$

3. (a) 3   (b) 4   (c) 3   (d) 8
   (e) 8   (f) 9   (g) 12   (h) 20

4. (a) $2\frac{2}{5}$ (b) $7\frac{1}{2}$ (c) $7\frac{1}{2}$ (d) $9\frac{3}{5}$

5. £60   6. 28   7. £48   8. £92   9. £132.50

10. (a) 9   (b) 10   (c) $\frac{5}{24}$

11. (a) (i) 10   (ii) 25   (iii) 12
   (b) $\frac{13}{60}$

12. £743.75

Exercise 7.3 — Page 70

1. (a) $\frac{3}{8}$ (b) $\frac{7}{12}$ (c) $\frac{7}{10}$ (d) $\frac{8}{15}$ (e) $\frac{9}{14}$

2. (a) $\frac{1}{8}$ (b) $\frac{1}{12}$ (c) $\frac{3}{10}$ (d) $\frac{2}{15}$ (e) $\frac{5}{14}$

3. (a) $1\frac{1}{4}$ (b) $1\frac{1}{2}$ (c) $1\frac{11}{20}$ (d) $1\frac{8}{21}$ (e) $1\frac{5}{24}$

4. (a) $\frac{1}{8}$ (b) $\frac{8}{15}$ (c) $\frac{5}{8}$
   (d) $\frac{17}{45}$ (e) $\frac{5}{24}$ (f) $\frac{19}{48}$

5. (a) $4\frac{1}{4}$ (b) $3\frac{5}{6}$ (c) $4\frac{3}{8}$
   (d) $5\frac{17}{20}$ (e) $6\frac{13}{30}$ (f) $5\frac{9}{20}$

6. (a) $1\frac{1}{10}$ (b) $\frac{5}{12}$ (c) $\frac{5}{8}$
   (d) $3\frac{3}{10}$ (e) $1\frac{27}{40}$ (f) $\frac{47}{48}$

7. $\frac{4}{15}$

8. (a) $\frac{7}{20}$ (b) $\frac{17}{20}$ 10. (a) $\frac{27}{80}$ (b) Andy

9. $\frac{7}{60}$ 11. $\frac{3}{10}$

Exercise 7.4 — Page 72

1. (a) $\frac{1}{6}$ (b) $\frac{1}{20}$ (c) $\frac{1}{10}$ (d) $\frac{5}{21}$
   (e) $\frac{1}{6}$ (f) $\frac{1}{4}$ (g) $\frac{4}{5}$ (h) $\frac{7}{16}$

2. (a) $\frac{3}{8}$ (b) $\frac{3}{10}$ (c) $\frac{1}{3}$ (d) $\frac{1}{3}$
   (e) $\frac{3}{16}$ (f) $\frac{2}{35}$ (g) $\frac{1}{2}$ (h) $\frac{1}{4}$
   (i) $\frac{1}{6}$ (j) $\frac{1}{6}$

3. (a) $1\frac{1}{8}$ (b) 2   (c) $3\frac{3}{4}$ (d) $3\frac{17}{20}$
   (e) $4\frac{7}{8}$ (f) $1\frac{13}{15}$ (g) 14   (h) $13\frac{1}{2}$
   (i) $2\frac{7}{10}$ (j) $8\frac{3}{4}$

4. (a) $2\frac{3}{5}$ (b) $3\frac{1}{2}$ (c) $5\frac{2}{5}$ (d) $2\frac{1}{2}$
   (e) $1\frac{1}{3}$ (f) $3\frac{4}{7}$ (g) $\frac{2}{3}$ (h) $1\frac{1}{3}$

5. (a) $\frac{4}{15}$ (b) 15

Exercise 7.5 — Page 74

1. (a) $\frac{1}{10}$ (b) $\frac{3}{8}$ (c) $\frac{1}{10}$ (d) $\frac{1}{3}$
   (e) $\frac{4}{7}$ (f) $\frac{4}{9}$

2. (a) 2   (b) $\frac{2}{5}$ (c) $2\frac{5}{8}$ (d) $3\frac{1}{3}$
   (e) 22   (f) $7\frac{1}{3}$

3. (a) $\frac{5}{6}$ (b) $\frac{9}{16}$ (c) $\frac{4}{5}$ (d) $1\frac{1}{3}$
   (e) $\frac{2}{3}$ (f) $1\frac{1}{2}$ (g) $\frac{2}{3}$ (h) $1\frac{1}{6}$
   (i) $1\frac{1}{2}$ (j) $1\frac{4}{5}$

4. (a) $\frac{2}{3}$ (b) $1\frac{3}{8}$ (c) $1\frac{1}{7}$ (d) $4\frac{2}{3}$
   (e) $13\frac{1}{2}$ (f) $\frac{4}{5}$ (g) $1\frac{1}{2}$ (h) $1\frac{1}{4}$
   (i) $2\frac{2}{7}$ (j) $3\frac{6}{25}$

5. (a) $21, \frac{17}{20}$ cm   (b) $23, \frac{1}{2}$ cm

6. (a) $\frac{32}{45}$ (b) $2\frac{2}{5}$

7. $\frac{16}{21}$

Exercise 7.6 — Page 74

1. £3.20   3. £3.20   5. 96 cm
2. 70 km   4. £5   6. 189

Exercise 7.7 — Page 77

1. (a) $\frac{3}{25}$ (b) $\frac{3}{5}$ (c) $\frac{8}{25}$ (d) $\frac{7}{40}$
   (e) $\frac{9}{20}$ (f) $\frac{13}{20}$ (g) $\frac{11}{50}$ (h) $\frac{101}{500}$
   (i) $\frac{7}{25}$ (j) $\frac{111}{200}$ (k) $\frac{5}{8}$ (l) $\frac{21}{25}$

2. (a) (i) 0.25   (ii) 0.5   (iii) 0.75
   (b) (i) 0.1   (ii) 0.3   (iii) 0.7
   (c) (i) 0.4   (ii) 0.6   (iii) 0.8

3. (a) (i) 0.15   (ii) 0.35   (iii) 0.95
   (b) (i) 0.16   (ii) 0.36   (iii) 0.92
   (c) (i) 0.07   (ii) 0.23   (iii) 0.53

4. (a) 0.125   (b) 0.625
   (c) 0.225   (d) 0.725

5. (a) $0.\dot{7}$ (b) $0.\dot{1}$ (c) $0.\dot{3}\dot{6}$
    (d) $0.8\dot{2}$ (e) $0.1\dot{3}\dot{5}$ (f) $0.\dot{2}1\dot{6}$
    (g) $0.1\dot{6}$ (h) $0.\dot{2}8571\dot{4}$

6. (a) $0.\dot{8}$ (b) $0.\dot{4}$ (c) $0.\dot{5}\dot{1}$
    (d) $0.7\dot{2}$ (e) $0.\dot{1}42857\dot{}$ (f) $0.\dot{8}5714\dot{2}$
    (g) $0.0\dot{3}$ (h) $0.4\dot{6}$ (i) $0.8\dot{3}$
    (j) $0.7\dot{7}\dot{2}$

7. (a) 0.33   (b) 0.67   (c) 0.43
    (d) 0.45   (e) 0.78   (f) 0.38

Review Exercise 7   Page 78

1. (a) 24 (b) 10 (c) 4   **2.** 15   **3.** £25.80

4. (a) $\frac{11}{12}$ (b) $\frac{11}{40}$ **5.** $\frac{4}{15}$ **6.** $\frac{7}{10}$

7. (a) $\frac{2}{5}$ (b) $\frac{6}{25}$ (c) $\frac{9}{20}$ (d) $\frac{1}{8}$ **8.** $\frac{1}{4}$

9. (a) $6\frac{1}{12}$ (b) $4\frac{10}{63}$ (c) $2\frac{1}{10}$ (d) $2\frac{19}{30}$
   (e) $4\frac{1}{2}$ (f) 10   (g) $1\frac{5}{7}$ (h) $2\frac{1}{2}$

10. (a) $2\frac{1}{12}$ m (b) $\frac{1}{4}$ m²   **11.** $\frac{1}{10}$ **12** £80

13. (a) 0.8 (b) 0.45 (c) 0.42 (d) 0.402

14. E.g. $\frac{3}{8}$, $\frac{5}{16}$

15. (a) 64 (b) $\frac{7}{16}$ **17.** 384 km

16. (a) 0.17 (b) $\frac{3}{8}$ **18.** (a) £5.40 (b) $\frac{3}{20}$

CHAPTER 8

Exercise 8.1   Page 80

1. Entries are: 10%, 20%, 25%, 30%, 40%, 50%, 60%, 70%, 75%, 80%, 90%

2. (a) 34% (b) 48% (c) 15% (d) 80%
   (e) 27% (f) 65% (g) $66\frac{2}{3}$% (h) $22\frac{2}{9}$%

3. (a) $\frac{1}{10}$ (b) $\frac{1}{4}$ (c) $\frac{9}{50}$ (d) $\frac{13}{25}$
   (e) $\frac{23}{100}$ (f) $\frac{1}{8}$ (g) $\frac{57}{200}$ (h) $\frac{29}{40}$

4. (a) 20% (b) 45% (c) 32% (d) 12.5%
   (e) 7% (f) 112% (g) 1.5% (h) 33.3%

5. (a) 0.8   (b) 0.15   (c) 0.47
   (d) 0.72   (e) 0.875   (f) 1.5

6. 0.42, $\frac{17}{40}$, 43%, $\frac{9}{20}$

7. 28%, 0.2805, $\frac{57}{200}$, $\frac{23}{80}$ **8.** 80%

9. (a) 90% (b) 85% (c) 88% (d) 80%

10. B   **11.** Team A

Exercise 8.2   Page 81

1. (a) 60% (b) 16% (c) 70%
   (d) 21% (e) 21%

2. (a) 32% (b) 12.5% (c) 50%
   (d) 90% (e) 30%

3. 32%   **6.** (a) 40% (b) 60%

4. 20%   **7.** 12.5%

5. 30%   **8.** 37.5%   **9.** 6%

10. (a) $33\frac{1}{3}$% (b) $66\frac{2}{3}$% (c) $11\frac{1}{9}$%
   (d) $42\frac{1}{2}$% (e) $56\frac{1}{2}$%

11. 9.5%   **12.** 25%

Exercise 8.3   Page 83

1. (a) £16 (b) £15 (c) £66
   (d) £52.50 (e) £25 (f) £30
   (g) £27 (h) 4 m (i) 24 kg
   (j) 280 (k) £11.25 (l) 12

2. (a) 60 (b) 105 (c) 45%

3. £20   **4.** 270

5. (a) £42 (b) £70.50

6. £1.95   **7.** £4.50

8. (a) 660 (b) 198   **9.** 24 g

10. (a) £480 (b) £420 (c) £2800
   (d) £1080 (e) £3450 (f) £1260
   (g) £80 (h) £13 (i) £16.50
   (j) £57.50

11. (a) £420 (b) £600 (c) £2000
   (d) £150 (e) £10 200 (f) £4550
   (g) £510 (h) £5.50 (i) £33.60
   (j) £40.95

12. 24p per minute   **15.** 759 g

13. £215   **16.** £11 625

14. £18.45   **17.** 8400 cm²

Exercise 8.4   Page 84

1. £19.38

2. (a) £14 541.75 (b) 83.9p per litre
   (c) 32p per pint

3. (a) £244.64 (b) £4706 (c) £2372.50

4. $83\frac{1}{3}$%   **5.** (a) £10 530 (b) 17.3%

6. £91 814   **7.** (a) £34.13 (b) £41.39

8. (a) 36.3% (b) 23.7% (c) 37.8%

9. 1.35×10^9 km³   **11.** 30%

10. 1.49×10^9 square miles   **12.** 2.53%

Exercise 8.5
Page 86

1. 20%   **2.** 20%   **3.** 25%

4. Becky
Sam's increase = 32%
Becky's increase = 40%

5. (a) $12\frac{1}{2}\%$ (b) 12%
Rent went up by a greater percentage.

6. 16.7%   **8.** Car A 13.8%, Car B 18.2%

7. 12%   **9.** 1995 - 1996 (9.2%)

10. 19.5%

11. 3.51%   **14.** 8% increase

12. 18.6%   **15.** 19%

13. (a) 6.27 cm² (b) 6.1%   **16.** 3.5%

Exercise 8.6
Page 87

1. 600 ml   **7.** 67.5 mg

2. £600   **8.** £1420

3. £220   **9.** £1600

4. (a) 50   **10.** School A 425,
(b) 90   School B 450

5. 1.89 m   **11.** £400

6. £312 500   **12.** £150

Review Exercise 8
Page 89

1. (a) 18 (b) 20%   **4.** 180

2. £8.82   **5.** 62.5%

3. 90%   **6.** 65

7. (a) £17.50   (b) 11%

8. 80 kg   **11.** 35%

9. 25%   **12.** 43 200

10. (a) 45% (b) 60   **13.** £80

14. (a) (i) £360   (ii) £230.40
(b) £375

15. £212.31

CHAPTER 9

Exercise 9.1
Page 91

1. (a) 1030 (b) 2230 (c) 0145
(d) 1345 (e) 0750 (f) 2350

2. (a) 2.15 pm (b) 5.25 am (c) 11.20 pm
(d) 10.05 am (e) 9.40 am (f) 5.05 pm

3. (a) 1835, 1920, 2000, 2050
(b) 40 minutes   (c) 45 minutes

4. (a) 1.15 pm   (b) 2 hours 50 minutes

5. (a) 1325   (b) 4 hours 15 minutes

6. (a) 1.30 pm   (b) 1330

7. (a) 1441   (b) 2.41 pm

Exercise 9.2
Page 92

1. (a) 49 minutes   (b) 1 hour 35 minutes
(c) 1.42 pm   (d) 0815

2. (a) 1215   (b) 1 hour 48 minutes
(c) 5.42 pm

3. (a) 0900   (b) 44 minutes
(c) 2 hours 20 minutes

4. (a) (i) 1520   (ii) 1610
(b) 1650

Exercise 9.3
Page 94

1. 36 hours

2. £313.60   **5.** £10.20   **8.** £1100

3. £272   **6.** £15 600   **9.** £800 000

4. £203.40   **7.** £23 220   **10.** £1440

Exercise 9.4
Page 95

1. £121.50   **4.** £94.91   **7.** £3630.07

2. £11.36   **5.** £18.91   **8.** £11 578

3. £4069.30   **6.** £245.61   **9.** £7122

Exercise 9.5
Page 96

1. £15.99   **3.** £1.60

2. 50p   **4.** 90p   **5.** £4.80

6. (a) £47   (b) 10 days

7. (a) £39   (b) 120 miles

8. £26   **9.** £638   **10.** £165   **11.** £40.50

Exercise 9.6
Page 97

1. (a) 0.5p   (b) 5.25p

2. Small: 5.2 g per penny.
Large: 5.1 g per penny.
Small tin is better buy.

3. Small pot

4. 700 g   **7.** Medium

5. Large pot   **8.** 1.5 litre bottle

6. 1 kg   **9.** Medium

10. (a) Daisy's £448, Alfie's £438
(b) Alfie's

Exercise 9.7 — Page 98

1. (a) £300   (b) £25
2. £74.84   4. £6.30   6. £46.76
3. 810   5. £112   7. £334.90
8. (a) £57   (b) £81   (c) £84 000
    (d) £95   (e) £226   (f) £108
9. £12 400

Exercise 9.8 — Page 100

1. £6
2. (a) £3.50   (b) £73.50
3. (a) £59.50   (b) £399.50
4. (a) £15.75   (b) £105.75
5. (a) £8.97   (b) £188.50
6. £291.40
7. £170.37   10. £428.87   13. £1.60
8. £216.20   11. £69.32   14. £293.75
9. £44.13   12. £183.75   15. £2928.10

Exercise 9.9 — Page 102

1. £10   5. £48
2. (a) £30   (b) £15   6. £225
3. £2   7. £242
4. £225   8. £330.75
9. (a) earns 78p more interest
10. (a) £11 576.25   (b) £11 910.16
    (c) £12 250.43   (d) £12 597.12
11. (a) £2420   (b) £1938.66

Exercise 9.10 — Page 102

1. (a) 1420.50 francs   (b) 426 marks
    (c) 74 700 drachmas   (d) 422 400 lira
    (e) 35 850 pesetas   (f) 241.50 dollars
2. (a) £9.50   (b) £5.23   (c) £25
    (d) £21.74   (e) £39.77   (f) £18.07
3. (a) 71 marks   (b) £14.79
4. (a) 337 920 lira   (b) £28.40
5. (a) £251.05   (b) 7170 pesetas
6. (a) £211.19   (b) 426.15 francs
7. (a) 805 dollars   (b) £74.64
8. £132.16
9. France: £5596.62,   Germany: £5809.86
    Cheaper in France
10. (a) 17.09 Euros   (b) 585.10 francs

Review Exercise 9 — Page 104

1. (a) (i) 4.03 pm   (ii) 25 minutes
    (b) 1540
2. 56p
3. £68.40   6. 231 miles
4. £252.74   7. £6.20
5. (a) £720   (b) £60   8. £40.20
9. 400 g: 0.54 g per penny
    125 g: 0.51 g per penny
    400 g jar is better value
10. £586.32   12. 4 hours
11. £77   13. 1974.60 francs
14. (a) 76.75 marks   (b) £13.68
15. (a) £3   (b) 5%
16. £5.76
17. £2450.09
18. (a) £61.80   (b) 1.225043

CHAPTER 10

Exercise 10.1 — Page 106

1. (a) 8 SMILERS and 2 GLUMS
    (b) (i) 8 SMILERS and 4 GLUMS
       (ii) 3 SMILERS and 9 GLUMS
    (c) (i) 16 SMILERS and 4 GLUMS
       (ii) 8 SMILERS and 12 GLUMS
2. (a) (i) 75   (ii) 200
    (b) (i) 12   (ii) 32
    (c) (i) 56   (ii) 140
3. (a) (i) 16   (ii) 80
    (b) (i) 9   (ii) 45
    (c) (i) 84   (ii) 112
4. (a) (i) 14 SMILERS and 6 GLUMS
       (ii) 35 SMILERS and 15 GLUMS
    (b) (i) 9 SMILERS and 6 GLUMS
       (ii) 30 SMILERS and 20 GLUMS

Exercise 10.2 — Page 108

1. (a) E.g. 12 : 2, 18 : 3, 24 : 4,
    (b) E.g. 14 : 4, 21 : 6, 28 : 8,
    (c) E.g. 6 : 10, 9 : 15, 12 : 20.
2. (a) 1 : 2   (b) 1 : 3   (c) 3 : 4
    (d) 2 : 5   (e) 3 : 4   (f) 2 : 5
    (g) 3 : 7   (h) 9 : 4   (i) 4 : 9
    (j) 7 : 3
3. (a) 12   (b) 28   (c) 100   (d) 20
4. 198 cm   5. 400 g   6. 64

7. 18 years   **9.** 40 : 9

8. 2 : 3   **10.** 1 : 250   **11.** 1 : 1500

12. (a) 4 : 1   (b) 2 : 25   (c) 11 : 2
    (d) 5 : 2   (e) 4 : 1   (f) 40 : 17
    (g) 9 : 20   (h) 3 : 4   (i) 5 : 1
    (j) 4 : 1   (k) 1 : 15   (l) 2 : 1

13. (a) 100 ml   (b) 4 : 1

14. 2 : 3   **15.** 3 : 7   **16.** 3 : 2

Exercise 10.3   Page 109

1. (a) 6, 3   (b) 15, 5   (c) 7, 28
    (d) 90, 10   (e) 60, 40

2. 18   **4.** $\frac{1}{4}$

3. Sunny £36, Chandni £12   **5.** 80%

6.

	4 : 1	3 : 2
(a)	32, 8	24, 16
(b)	16, 4	12, 8
(c)	64 kg, 16 kg	48 kg, 32 kg
(d)	160 g, 40 g	120 g, 80 g
(e)	£960, £240	£720, £480

7. (a) £14, £21   (b) £32, £24   (c) £3.50, £2

8. 45

9. $\frac{5}{8}$ **12.** £192

10. 60%   **13.** 2 033 000

11. 48%   **14.** 170 000 km²

15. (a) Jenny 50, Tim 30   (b) 10

16. (a) 5 : 2   (b) 6   (c) 55
    (d) 32 is not a multiple of 5 + 2 = 7

17. 8 cm, 12 cm, 18 cm   **19.** 40°, 60°, 80°

18. 200 kg   **20.** 45%

21. (a) $12\frac{1}{2}$%, $37\frac{1}{2}$%, 50%   (b) $\frac{1}{3}$ (c) $\frac{3}{5}$

Exercise 10.4   Page 111

1. (a) 16p   (b) £1.28

2. (a) £6   (b) £60   **3.** £2.85

4. (a) 120 cm   (b) 2 kg   **5.** £201.60

6. (a) 250 g   (b) 150 g

7. £36   **8.** £2.85   **9.** £14.76

10. (a) 50 g   (b) 720 g

11. £44.64   **12.** £32.29

13. (a) £1.54   (b) 12 minutes

14. (a) 180 g   (b) 637.5 ml   (c) 210 g

15. (a) 12 minutes   (b) 16 miles

16. (a) 12 m²   (b) 12 litres

17. (a) £130   (b) 32   **18.** $17\frac{1}{2}$ minutes

19. (a) 168.75 g   (b) 36   (c) 540 ml

20. £8.35

Review Exercise 10   Page 113

1. 3 : 4   **3.** 200 g flour, 25 g sugar

2. 9   **4.** 12

5. (a) 2 : 1   (b) 75 g   (c) 75 g

6. Tracey £4000, Wayne £3200

7. (a) £15   (b) 40%   **8.** 1 : 200 000

9. (a) 24   (b) 5 : 3

10. Red 1.5 litres, yellow 0.9 litres

11. 306 075   **12.** £5.19

13. (a) 6 oz flour, 4 oz sugar, 4 oz margarine,
    5.3 oz dried fruit, 2 eggs   (b) 27

14. 112.5 litres   **15.** £504

CHAPTER 11

Exercise 11.1   Page 115

1. 8 miles per hour

2. (a) 20 km/h   (b) 10 m/s   (c) 50 km/h
    (d) 20 cm/s   (e) 300 m/min

3. 8 km

4. (a) 150 km   (b) 90 km   (c) 400 m
    (d) 1500 m   (e) 40 km

5. 15 minutes

6. (a) 3 hours   (b) 2 minutes
    (c) 10 seconds   (d) 100 minutes
    (e) 4 hours

7. 8 km/h   **10.** 25 m per minute

8. 3 km   **11.** 6 km

9. $2\frac{1}{4}$ hours   **12.** 27 minutes

13. (a) $2\frac{1}{2}$ hours   (b) 50 minutes

14. (a) 57.5 km/hour   (b) 1 hour

15. (a) 8 m/s   (b) 100 km   (c) 12 cm
    (d) 1 hour   (e) 1 s

16. (a) 300 km   (b) 5 hours   (c) 60 km/h

17. 5 m/s   **18.** 10 km/hour

19. 10.14 m/s, 9.37 m/s, 9.20 m/s, 8.22 m/s,
    7.77 m/s, 7.05 m/s

20. 10.30 am   **21.** 11.09 am

22. (a) 13.8 km/h (b) 1.10 pm

23. 4.81 m/s **24.** 3×10^8 m/s

25. 2 hours 17 minutes

Exercise 11.2 Page 117

1. (a) 1005 (b) 24 miles (c) 3

2. (a) 1042 (b) 28 km
(c) (i) 1115 (ii) 8 km

3. (a) 50 km/h (b) 20 m/s
(c) 9 miles/hour

4. (a) 10 km/h (b) 6.7 km/h (c) 8 km/h

5. (a) (b) (i)

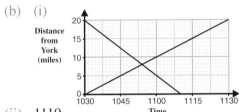

(b) (ii) 1110

6. (a) 1118 (b) 1230 (c) Twice
(d) 42 minutes
(e) Between 1200 and 1230
(f) 4 km/h

7. (a) 9 miles/hour
(b) (i)

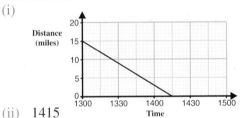

(ii) 1415

8. (a)

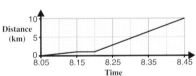

(b) 15 km/h

9. (a)

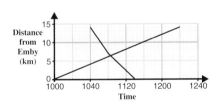

(b) (i) 1220 (ii) 1102 (iii) 14 km/hour

Exercise 11.3 Page 121

1. 8 g/cm³ **5.** 9360 g

2. 9 g/cm³ **6.** 2000 cm³

3. 28.6 g/cm³ **7.** 0.8 g/cm³

4. 7200 g **8.** 100 g

9. 118.3 people/km²

10. (a) 30 530 km² (b) 104.2 people/km²
(c) 5.74×10^7

Review Exercise 11 Page 122

1. 240 miles

2. (a) 9 km/h (b) 36 minutes

3. 94 km/h

4. (a) 142.9 seconds (b) 252 m

5. 20 km/h

6. 63.3 miles per hour

7. 5 hours 42 minutes

8. (a) 50 mph (b) 55 mph

9. (a) 24 000 m/hour (b) 24 km/hour

10.

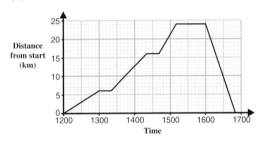

11. (a) (i) 1300 (ii) 20 km/h
(b)

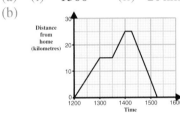

12. (a) 125 km (b) 1 hour
(c) To Leeds, steeper gradient.

13. 11 500 g

14. Steel 2.5 g/cm³, Concrete 1600 cm³,
Foam 200 g

15. 0.067 people per square mile.

Section Review Page 124

1. (a) (i) 3 (ii) 2
(b) −9, −3, 0.6, 2, 10 (c) 0.06

2. £3978 **3.** (a) 120 (b) 250

4. (a) 11 degrees Celsius (b) −2°C

5. (a) (i) 6000 (ii) 26 600
(b) (i) 2 (ii) 2, 5 (iii) 9
(iv) 8 (v) 25 698

6. 62p **7.** 11.20 am

8. (a) 3040 (b) 2736

9. (a) 60 × 30 (b) 1800 (c) 88

10. (a) £1.92 (b) £1.80

11. (a) Any decimal between 0.25 and 0.3̇. (b) $\frac{1}{2}$

12. (a) 72p (b) £78 **13.** (a) 13 (b) 24.9

14. (a) 14 (b) 48

15. (a) 3^5 is smaller. $3^5 = 243$, $5^3 = 125$

16. (a) (i) $\frac{1}{20}$ (ii) $1\frac{7}{8}$ (b) 0.25 $\left(\frac{1}{4}\right)$

(c) $6^2 \div 0.6 = 60$

17. 15

18. (a) $2^2 \times 3^2$ (b) $a = 4$, $b = 1$
(c) 12 (d) 144

19. (a) 1.5×10^3 (b) 6×10^5

20. (a) 0945 (b) 38 miles
(c) 2 (d) 23 miles per hour

21. (a) £8.60
(b) 250 g pot.
145 g pot: 3.71 g/p, 250 g pot: 3.79 g/p

22. (a) £9.40 (b) 75 (c) 37.5%

23. £1660 **24.** £107.50 **25.** 9.8

26. (a) flour 345 g, butter 225 g, sugar 150 g, eggs 3.
(b) 177°C (c) 130

27. £16.80 **28.** (a) £284.24 (b) 5 hours

29. 2197 marks

30. (a) 1 953 125 (b) 0.143

31. 3.21

32. (a) $x = 4$, $y = 2$ (b) $3^3 \times 5^2$
(c) $2^4 \times 3^5 \times 5^3$

33. 31.6% **34.** (a) 6.5 (b) 1.27 seconds

35. £3434.70 **36.** (a) 100 km/h (b) 50 mph

37. (a) 1.8×10^9 (b) £720
(c) 2.2×10^6

38. (a) 9.1×10^{-25} (b) 4.55×10^{-18} g

39. 5 104 000

CHAPTER 12

Exercise 12.1

1. $n + 4$ **6.** $8m$

2. $n - 3$ **7.** $p - 1$ **11.** $5b$ pence

3. $3n$ **8.** $p + 5$ **12.** $\frac{c}{3}$ pence

4. $m + 6$ **9.** $25p$ **13.** $\frac{a}{5}$ pence

5. $m - 12$ **10.** $6k$ **14.** $\frac{36}{g}$

15. (a) $2t$ (b) $10t$

Exercise 12.2
Page 130

1. (a) $2y$ (b) $3c$ (c) $5x$
(d) $7p$ (e) $2t$ (f) $3d$
(g) $3n$ (h) $5y$ (i) $10g$
(j) $8m$ (k) $13z$ (l) $2r$
(m) $5t$ (n) $4y$ (o) $3j$
(p) $4c$ (q) $7x$ (r) w
(s) 0 (t) $-5y$ (u) $-5x$
(v) $-14a$ (w) $6b$ (x) $2m$

2. (a) $4x$ (b) $6a$ (c) $9y$ (d) $6u$

3. (a) Can be simplified, $2v$.
(b) Cannot be simplified, different terms.
(c) Can be simplified to $3v + 4$.
(d) Cannot be simplified, different terms.

4. (a) $8x + y$ (b) $w + 2v$ (c) $2a - 2b$
(d) $5x + 3y$ (e) $3 + 7u$ (f) $p + 4q$
(g) $3d - 7c$ (h) $2y + 1$ (i) $a + b$
(j) $4m + n$ (k) $9c - d$ (l) $x + y$
(m) $6p$ (n) $5 - 5k$ (o) $a + 3$

5. (a) $8a + 3b$ (b) $3p + 3q$ (c) $3m + 2n$
(d) $x - 2y$ (e) $2x + 3y$ (f) $d + 3$
(g) $3b - 2a$ (h) 7 (i) $a + 2b$
(j) $-2f$ (k) $v - 4w$ (l) $-2 - 5t$
(m) $4q - 4p$ (n) $1 - 7k$ (o) $c - d + 11$

6. (a) $4x + 2$ (b) $4a + 6b$ (c) $3x$
(d) $6y + 9$

7. (a) $2xy$ (b) $2pq$ (c) $3ab$
(d) $2x^2$ (e) $9y^2$ (f) $4a^2$
(g) $2d^2 - 3g^2$ (h) $5t^2 - t$
(i) $6m - m^2$ (j) $2p^2 - p$

Exercise 12.3
Page 131

1. (a) $3a$ (b) $7b$ (c) $8c$
(d) $9d$ (e) $4e$ (f) $8f$
(g) $6p$ (h) $15q$ (i) r^2
(j) g^2 (k) $2g^2$ (l) $6g^2$
(m) $4t^2$ (n) $12t^2$ (o) $15u^2$
(p) $9d^2$

2. (a) $-3y$ (b) $-5y$ (c) $2y$ (d) $-6y$
(e) $-t^2$ (f) $-2t^2$ (g) $-10t^2$ (h) $10t^2$

3. (a) $5a$ (b) $4b$ (c) 12 (d) 20
(e) $2y$ (f) 8 (g) 2 (h) 18
(i) $3p$ (j) 3 (k) 9 (l) 6
(m) 4 (n) 5 (o) 4 (p) 9

4. (a) $-2y$ (b) $-3y$ (c) -5 (d) m
(e) -3 (f) -2 (g) -3 (h) 1

5. (a) ab (b) xy (c) y^2 (d) $2pq$
(e) $2a^2$ (f) $3xy$ (g) $6ab$ (h) $12gh$
(i) $6d^2$ (j) $3g^2$ (k) $5ab$ (l) $6gh$
(m) abc (n) m^3 (o) $2d^3$ (p) $3g^3$
(q) $6x^3$ (r) $10m^2n$ (s) $3abc$ (t) $18pqr$

6. (a) a^2 (b) $4x^2$ (c) $6g^2$ (d) $10y^2$

1. (a) y^3 (b) t^5 (c) a^6
    (d) g^{10} (e) a^4 (f) m^6
    (g) $2y^3$ (h) $6d^5$ (i) $8x^5$
    (j) $25y^6$ (k) $6t^5$ (l) $24r^6$
    (m) m^3n^2 (n) a^4b^2 (o) $6r^3s^4$
    (p) $10x^5y^3$

2. (a) t^6 (b) y^6 (c) g^9
    (d) x^8 (e) $9a^2$ (f) $8h^3$
    (g) $2m^6$ (h) $4m^6$ (i) $3d^6$
    (j) $9d^6$ (k) $27a^6$ (l) $8k^9$
    (m) x^2y^2 (n) m^3n^6 (o) $8s^3t^3$
    (p) $9p^4q^2$

3. (a) y^2 (b) a   (c) 1
    (d) t^4 (e) g^{-1} (f) h^{-2}
    (g) $6b^2$ (h) $5m$ (i) $4x^6$
    (j) $4t$ (k) $5y^4$ (l) $3h^{-1}$
    (m) y (n) m^2n^{-1} (o) $\frac{2}{3}p^2q^{-1}$
    (p) $3rs^2$

4. (a) t (b) g^{-1} (c) m^2 (d) y
    (e) y^2 (f) m^{-1} (g) $2t^2$ (h) 3

1. (a) $2x + 10$ (b) $3a + 18$ (c) $8y + 12$

2. (a) $3x + 6$ (b) $2y + 10$ (c) $4x + 2$
    (d) $3p + 3q$

3. (a) $a^2 + a$ (b) $2d + d^2$ (c) $2x^2 + x$

4. (a) $2x + 8$ (b) $4b + 4$
    (c) $8x + 4$ (d) $3t - 6$
    (e) $20 - 4a$ (f) $6 - 12p$
    (g) $6b + 12c$ (h) $6m - 15n$

5. (a) $x^2 + 3x$ (b) $2y + y^2$
    (c) $t^2 - 5t$ (d) $2g^2 + 3g$
    (e) $2m - 3m^2$ (f) $3a^2 + 4a$
    (g) $2p^2 + 6p$ (h) $6d - 9d^2$
    (i) $2x^2 + 2xy$ (j) $5xy - 10y^2$

6. (a) $2x + 5$ (b) $3a + 11$
    (c) $6w - 17$ (d) $10 + 2p$
    (e) $3q$ (f) $7 - 3t$
    (g) $5z + 8$ (h) $8t + 15$
    (i) $2c - 6$ (j) $5a - 9$
    (k) $3y - 10$ (l) $2x + 6$
    (m) $8a + 23$ (n) $10x - 12$
    (o) $2p - 11$ (p) $5a + 2b$
    (q) $3x + y$ (r) $2p - 5q$
    (s) $5x - x^2$ (t) $a^2 - 2a$
    (u) $2y$

7. (a) $5x + 8$ (b) $5a + 13$
    (c) $9y + 23$ (d) $9a + 5$
    (e) $26t + 30$ (f) $5z + 13$
    (g) $12q + 16$ (h) $11x - 3$
    (i) $20e - 16$ (j) $12d + 6$
    (k) $3m^2 - 3m$ (l) $5a^2 - 4a$

8. (a) $-3x + 6$ (b) $-3x + 6$
    (c) $-2y + 10$ (d) $-6 + 2x$
    (e) $-15 + 3y$ (f) $-4 - 4a$
    (g) $3 - 2a$ (h) $2d + 6$
    (i) $2b - 6$ (j) $-6p - 9$
    (k) $m - 6$ (l) $5d + 1$
    (m) $-a^2 + 2a$ (n) $d - d^2$
    (o) $2x^2$ (p) $-6g^2 - 9g$
    (q) $7t^2 - 6t$ (r) $8m - 2m^2$

1. (a) $2(x + y)$ (b) $3(a - 2b)$
    (c) $2(3m + 4n)$ (d) $x(x - 2)$
    (e) $a(b + 1)$ (f) $x(2 - y)$
    (g) $2a(b - 2)$ (h) $2x(2x + 3)$
    (i) $dg(1 - g)$

2. (a) $2(a + b)$ (b) $5(x - y)$
    (c) $3(d + 2e)$ (d) $2(2m - n)$
    (e) $3(2a + 3b)$ (f) $2(3a - 4b)$
    (g) $4(2t + 3)$ (h) $5(a - 2)$
    (i) $2(2d - 1)$ (j) $3(1 - 3g)$
    (k) $5(1 - 4m)$ (l) $4(k + 1)$

3. (a) $x(y - z)$ (b) $g(f + h)$
    (c) $b(a - 2)$ (d) $q(3 + p)$
    (e) $a(1 + b)$ (f) $g(h - 1)$
    (g) $a(a + 3)$ (h) $t(5 - t)$
    (i) $d(1 - d)$ (j) $m(m + 1)$
    (k) $r(5r - 3)$ (l) $x(3x + 2)$

4. (a) $3(y + 2)$ (b) $t(t - 1)$
    (c) $2d(d + 2)$ (d) $3m(1 - 2n)$
    (e) $2g(f + 2g)$ (f) $4q(p - 2)$
    (g) $3y(2 - 5y)$ (h) $2x(3x + 2y)$
    (i) $2n(3n - 1)$ (j) $2b(2a + 3)$
    (k) $\frac{1}{2}a(1 - a)$ (l) $x(w + 2 - x)$

1. $6t$ pence   **2.** $x + 3$ years old

3. (a) $5n$ pence   (b) $n - 15$ pence
    (c) $5n - 45$ pence

4. (a) $2x$ cm   (b) $x + 3$ cm
    (c) $4x + 3$ cm

5. $18n + 5g$ pence

6. (a) (i) $2n + 3$ (ii) $6n^2$
    (b) $5 - 2x$ (c) $3(x - 2)$

7. (a) $3ab$ (b) $a^2 + 2a$
    (c) $2x - 6$

8. (a) mp pence   (b) $5 - 4x$

9. (a) (i) $3w$ (ii) $w + 2$ (iii) w^2
    (b) $7d + 3$

10. (a) $t(t - 3)$ (b) $3a(2 + b)$

11. (a) $4a$ (b) $2a + 2b$ (c) $7a + 17$

12. (a) $3n - 5$ (b) $a - 7$ (c) $x(2x + y)$

13. (a) $6a^3$ (b) $24a^2b$ (c) $2a^2b$

14. (a) $13 - 2x$ (b) $2y(3x - 1)$ (c) $5m^2$

15. (a) a^9 (b) b^3 (c) c^2 **16.** $3a^2$

17. (a) $3(2x - 5)$ (b) $y(y + 7)$

18. (a) $2x^2 - x$ (b) $1 - 3x$

19. (a) $6y^5$ (b) $2t^3$ (c) $8a^3$

20. (a) (i) $3y(2x - y)$ (ii) $2m(2m + 3)$
     (b) (i) $10y^5$ (ii) $3x^4$

21. (a) x^8 (b) y^4 (c) $4w^2$

CHAPTER 13

Exercise 13.1   Page 137

1. (a) 3   (b) 4   (c) 9   (d) 16
   (e) 5   (f) 3   (g) 18   (h) 21

2. (a) 6   (b) 6   (c) 14   (d) 3
   (e) 2   (f) 8   (g) 8   (h) 15
   (i) 4

3. (a) $a = 3$ (b) $y = 8$ (c) $c = 5$
   (d) $d = 16$

4. (a) $x = 8$ (b) $x = 7$ (c) $x = 5$
   (d) $x = 28$ (e) $x = 3$ (f) $x = 5$
   (g) $x = 4$ (h) $x = 9$ (i) $x = 1$

5. (a) $y = 2$ (b) $d = 5$ (c) $a = 9$
   (d) $a = 9$

Exercise 13.2   Page 139

1. 3   **4.** 3   **7.** 5

2. 5   **5.** 8   **8.** (a) 2   (b) $2x + 6$

3. 6   **6.** 4   **9.** $3x - 6$

10. (a) 21   (b) -9 (c) $3x + 6$

11. (a) (i) $M = 15$ (ii) $M = 37.5$ (iii) $M = 11.25$

   (b) $K = 16$ (c) $K = 51.2$ (d) $M = \dfrac{5K}{8}$

12. (a) 140 minutes   (b) 2 kg
   (c) $C = 40k + 20$

13. (a) £13   (b) $C = 2k + 3$

14. (a) £44   (b) £80   (c) $C = 12x + 8$

Exercise 13.3   Page 141

1. (a) $x = 6$ (b) $e = 15$ (c) $d = 11$
   (d) $q = 7$ (e) $n = 16$ (f) $y = 17$
   (g) $a = 4$ (h) $p = 3$ (i) $p = 8$
   (j) $x = 15$ (k) $a = 2$ (l) $y = 8$
   (m) $p = 4$ (n) $t = 3$ (o) $h = 7$
   (p) $b = 2$ (q) $d = 10$ (r) $x = 6$

2. (a) $c = 7$ (b) $x = 4$ (c) $y = 4$
   (d) $x = 2$ (e) $b = 6$ (f) $x = 4$
   (g) $k = 2$ (h) $b = 3$ (i) $r = 24$
   (j) $z = 10$ (k) $t = 20$ (l) $a = 2$

3. (a) $x = -2$ (b) $y = -3$ (c) $t = -2$
   (d) $a = -2$ (e) $d = -3$ (f) $g = -3$
   (g) $t = \frac{1}{2}$ (h) $x = 7\frac{1}{2}$ (i) $d = 1\frac{2}{5}$
   (j) $a = 1\frac{1}{2}$ (k) $g = \frac{1}{5}$ (l) $b = 4\frac{1}{2}$

4. (a) $p = -10$ (b) $a = 2\frac{1}{2}$ (c) $t = 7$
   (d) $n = 4$ (e) $c = -0.3$ (f) $h = 0.7$
   (g) $x = 3$ (h) $y = -0.8$ (i) $y = 12$
   (j) $m = -3$ (k) $t = -18$ (l) $v = 9$
   (m) $t = -0.9$ (n) $p = -1.5$ (o) $x = -18$

Exercise 13.4   Page 142

1. (a) $x = 3$ (b) $a = 2$ (c) $t = 2$
   (d) $y = 0$ (e) $e = 5$ (f) $x = 2$

2. (a) $p = 5$ (b) $c = 6$ (c) $x = 3$
   (d) $y = 9$ (e) $g = 11$ (f) $q = 8$

3. (a) $a = 4$ (b) $b = 6$ (c) $c = 1$
   (d) $d = 9$ (e) $e = 5$ (f) $f = 4$

4. (a) $w = 2$ (b) $s = 3$ (c) $x = 2$
   (d) $g = 3$ (e) $q = 4$ (f) $t = 3$
   (g) $w = 4$ (h) $x = 3$ (i) $y = 5$

5. (a) $p = -1$ (b) $d = -2$ (c) $g = -2$
   (d) $x = 8\frac{1}{2}$ (e) $y = \frac{2}{5}$ (f) $t = \frac{1}{2}$
   (g) $t = 1\frac{3}{4}$ (h) $a = 2\frac{1}{2}$ (i) $m = 2\frac{3}{5}$

Exercise 13.5   Page 143

1. (a) $x = 5$ (b) $q = 2$ (c) $t = 3$
   (d) $e = 3$ (e) $g = 4$ (f) $y = 1$
   (g) $x = 2$ (h) $k = 1$ (i) $a = 4$
   (j) $p = 6$ (k) $m = 2$ (l) $d = 5$
   (m) $y = 5$ (n) $u = 3$ (o) $q = 0$

2. (a) $d = 8$ (b) $q = 3$ (c) $c = 2$
   (d) $t = 3$ (e) $w = 2$ (f) $e = 3$
   (g) $g = 5$ (h) $z = 4$ (i) $m = 6$
   (j) $a = 5$ (k) $x = 4$ (l) $y = 3$

3. (a) $m = -4$ (b) $t = -2$ (c) $p = -2$
   (d) $x = 3\frac{1}{2}$ (e) $a = \frac{1}{2}$ (f) $b = \frac{4}{5}$
   (g) $y = \frac{4}{5}$ (h) $d = \frac{3}{4}$ (i) $f = -3\frac{1}{2}$

4. (a) $t = -5$ (b) $y = 2$ (c) $s = \frac{1}{2}$
   (d) $p = -\frac{1}{3}$ (e) $a = 1.8$ (f) $c = 0.11$
   (g) $p = 5$ (h) $x = -6$ (i) $x = 32$

5. (a) $n = 2$ (b) $z = 6$ (c) $w = 3$
   (d) $m = 4$ (e) $h = 2$ (f) $x = -3$
   (g) $w = 3$ (h) $y = 1\frac{1}{2}$ (i) $v = -8$
   (j) $c = -1\frac{1}{2}$ (k) $x = -18$ (l) $x = -7$

1. (a) 3 (b) 8 (c) 12 (d) 15

2. (a) $x = 6$ (b) $y = 8$ (c) $a = 24$
   (d) $d = -10$ (e) $a = 6$ (f) $x = 4\frac{1}{2}$
   (g) $m = -2$ (h) $t = \frac{4}{9}$

3. (a) $h = 11$ (b) $x = 8$ (c) $a = -3$
   (d) $d = -3$ (e) $x = \frac{3}{4}$ (f) $a = \frac{1}{10}$
   (g) $d = 5\frac{1}{2}$ (h) $h = 1\frac{1}{2}$ (i) $x = -3$
   (j) $x = \frac{7}{9}$ (k) $a = 5$ (l) $x = 1\frac{1}{4}$

4. (a) $x = 1\frac{1}{3}$ (b) $x = 12$ (c) $x = -1\frac{3}{5}$
   (d) $x = -4$ (e) $x = 1$ (f) $x = 19$
   (g) $x = -1$ (h) $x = -1$ (i) $x = 3\frac{1}{2}$

1. (a) $4y + 7$ cm (b) $y = 8$
2. (a) $12x$ (b) $x = 15$
3. (a) $x - 4$ cm (b) $4x - 8$ cm
   (c) $x = 7$
4. (a) 410 (b) $b = 3n + 50$ (c) 140
5. (a) £51 (b) $T = 15d + 6$ (c) 6 days
6. (a) £295 (b) $C = 45n + 70$ (c) 9 days
7. (a) 8 (b) 3
   (c) $A = 3x - 7$ (d) $x = 14$
8. (a) $x + 10$ pence (b) $3x + 20$ pence
   (c) 15 pence
9. (a) $9x + 4$ cm (b) $x = 6$ (c) 24 cm
10. (a) $7x - 4$ cm (b) $x = 9$
    (c) 13 cm, 17 cm, 29 cm
11. (a) $18x = 540°$ (b) $150°$
12. (a) $6x + 3$ cm² (b) $x = 4.5$
13. (a) $6t - 3$ cm (b) $3t + 6$ cm
    (c) $t = 3$
14. (a) $6x + 16$ cm (b) $x = 2$ (c) 28 cm
15. (a) 105 cm²

1. (a) 4 (b) 3 (c) 6 (d) 4
2. (a) $a = 10$ (b) $a = 5$
3. (a) $y = 2$ (b) $t = -3$
   (c) $g = \frac{1}{2}$ (d) $x = \frac{3}{5}$

4. (a) $y = 3$ (b) $y = -1$
5. (a) $m = 7$ (b) $t = 5$
6. (a) $a = 2$ (b) $b = 4$ (c) $c = -5$
7. (a) $a = -5$ (b) $x = 0.8$
   (c) $x = -0.5$
8. $x = -1$
9. (a) $x = 6$ (b) $x = 12$
10. (a) $T = hx + 20$ (b) £6
11. (a) £17 (b) $C = 0.15n + 5$
    (c) 480
12. (a) $3x - 5$ (b) -8 (c) 7
13. (a) $5x + 24$ (b) $x = 5$
14. (a) (i) $x + 7$ pence (ii) $3x + 7$ pence
    (b) $x = 30$, cake costs 37p
15. (a) $n - 7$ pence (b) 18 pence
16. (a) (i) $P = 10x + 4$ (ii) $A = 6x^2 + 4x$
    (b) $A = 112$
17. (a) $9x + 5 = 4x + 20$ (b) 3 kg
18. (a) (i) $6x - 15$ cm (ii) $4x - 8$ cm
    (b) (i) $6x - 15 = 4x - 8$
        $x = 3.5$ (ii) 2 cm

CHAPTER 14

1. (a) $5y$ pence (b) $y + 8$ pence
2. $12e$
3. (a) $a + 1$ years old (b) $a - 4$ years old
   (c) $a + n$ years old
4. $b - 3$
5. $h + 12$ cm
6. (a) $2d$ (b) $2d + 5$
7. (a) $P = y + 5$ (b) $P = y - 2$
   (c) $P = 2y$
8. Ben: $A = d - 2$ Charlotte: $A = 2d$
   Erica: $A = \frac{d}{2}$
9. (a) $P = 4g$ (b) $P = 4y + 4$
   (c) $P = 3x - 1$ (d) $P = 2a + 2b$
10. $C = 25d$
11. (a) 17 (b) 145 (c) 101
    (d)

n	$n + 1$	$n + 2$
$n + 10$		

    (e) $S_n = 4n + 13$

12. (a) 115   (b) 175   (c) 45

(d)

n	$n+1$	$n+2$
	$n+11$	
	$n+21$	

(e) $S_n = 5n + 35$

Exercise 14.2   Page 153

1. (a) 5   (b) 10   (c) 1
2. (a) 20   (b) 28   (c) -12
3. (a) 1   (b) 2   (c) -6
4. (a) 2   (b) -2 (c) 8
5. (a) 13   (b) -7
6. (a) -2 (b) 10
7. (a) 2   (b) 1   (c) $\frac{1}{2}$
8. (a) 1   (b) 1.5   (c) 2.5
9. (a) 6   (b) 5.8
10. (a) 0   (b) 1
11. (a) 3.5   (b) 4
12. $F = 75$ **13.** $V = 26$ **14.** $P = -9$
15. (a) $C = 104$ (b) $C = 32$
16. (a) $S = 40$ (b) $S = -2$ (c) $S = 6$
17. (a) $T = 35$ (b) $T = -2$
(c) $T = -18$ (d) $T = 6$
18. (a) $K = -1$ (b) $K = 13$
19. (a) $L = 10$ (b) $L = -11$
20. 33
21. (a) 96 m   (b) 720 m   (c) 36 m
22. (a) $-10°C$ (b) $-20°C$ (c) $-30°C$
(d) $-40°C$
23. (a) $50°F$ (b) $14°F$ (c) $-22°F$
(d) $-40°F$
24. 138 minutes
25. 240 volts   **27.** £40.14
26. $F = 4100$ **28.** 0.3

Exercise 14.3   Page 154

1. (a) $S = 9$ (b) $S = 9$
2. (a) $S = 18$ (b) $S = 18$
3. (a) $S = 36$ (b) $S = 36$
4. (a) $S = 32$ (b) $S = 32$
5. (a) $S = 16$ (b) $S = 16$
6. (a) 39   (b) 66
(c) 39   (d) 66

7. (a) 27   (b) -27
(c) 125   (d) -125
8. (a) 128   (b) -128
9. (a) -2 (b) 2
10. (a) $\frac{3}{4}$ (b) $1\frac{1}{2}$
11. (a) 4   (b) 1.5   (c) -3
12. (a) $L = 10$ (b) $L = 0.5$
13. (a) 26.0   (b) 3.2
14. (a) 12   (b) 1.4
15. $F = 144$ **16.** $h = 307.5$
17. (a) $T = 1.80$ (b) $T = 2.5$
18. (a) $v = 6.3$ (b) $v = 7.4$

Exercise 14.4   Page 156

1. (a) $m = a - 5$ (b) $m = a - x$
(c) $m = a + 2$ (d) $m = a + b$
(e) $m = 2 - a$ (f) $m = x - a$

2. (a) $x = \frac{y}{4}$ (b) $x = \frac{y}{a}$
(c) $x = -\frac{y}{a}$ (d) $x = 2y$
(e) $x = ay$ (f) $x = -ay$
(g) $x = \frac{2}{y}$ (h) $x = -\frac{n}{y}$

3. (a) $p = \frac{1}{2}y - 3$ (b) $p = \frac{t - q}{5}$
(c) $p = \frac{m + 2}{3}$ (d) $p = \frac{q + r}{4}$
(e) $p = \frac{3 - a}{2}$ (f) $p = \frac{g - d}{3}$
(g) $p = 2m - 6$ (h) $p = 3y - 3x$
(i) $p = 5t + 10$ (j) $p = 2h - 2g$
(k) $p = \frac{3}{s - q}$ (l) $p = \frac{a}{x - y}$

4. $K = \frac{P}{0.45}$ **6.** $n = \frac{C - 35}{24}$

5. $c = \frac{F - 32}{1.8}$ **7.** $a = \frac{2A}{h} - b$

8. (a) $c = \pm\sqrt{y}$ (b) $c = y^2$
(c) $c = \pm\sqrt{\frac{y}{d}}$ (d) $c = 9y^2$
(e) $c = \pm\sqrt{y - x}$ (f) $c = (y - x)^2$
(g) $c = \pm\sqrt{dy - dx}$ (h) $c = (ax + ay)^2$

9. (a) $V = IR$ (b) $m = \dfrac{E}{c^2}$

   (c) $x = \pm\sqrt{\dfrac{y - b}{a}}$ (d) $v = \pm\sqrt{\dfrac{2e}{m}}$

10. (a) $a = b - c^2$ (b) $a = \pm\sqrt{b}$

   (c) $a = 2b + \frac{1}{4}c$ (d) $a = \frac{1}{3}b$

   (e) $a = \dfrac{4b}{15}$ (f) $a = \dfrac{3b}{2}$

   (g) $a = \dfrac{p - d}{m}$ (h) $a = \pm\sqrt{\dfrac{F}{m}}$

11. (a) $x = \dfrac{3a}{2}$ (b) $x = \dfrac{3b - 2a}{5}$

   (c) $x = \dfrac{8}{a - 2}$ (d) $x = \dfrac{ab}{3 - a}$

   (e) $x = \dfrac{3a}{6 - a}$ (f) $x = \dfrac{ab}{a + b}$

Exercise 14.5   Page 157

1. (a) $d = \dfrac{P}{4}$ (b) $d = 0.7\,\text{cm}$

2. (a) $l = \dfrac{A}{b}$ (b) $l = 6\,\text{cm}$

3. (a) (i) $D = ST$ (ii) $D = 24\,\text{km}$

   (b) (i) $T = \dfrac{D}{S}$ (ii) $T = 1.25$ hours

4. (a) $p = \dfrac{2A}{3q}$ (b) $p = 3.2\,\text{cm}$

5. (a) $b = \frac{1}{2}P - l$ (b) $b = 4.2\,\text{cm}$

6. (a) $x = \dfrac{y - c}{m}$ (b) $x = 3$

7. (a) $b = \dfrac{2A}{h}$ (b) $b = 23$

8. (a) $d = \pm\sqrt{\dfrac{C}{I}}$ (b) $d = \pm 1.17$

9. (a) $q = \pm\sqrt{p^2 - r^2}$ (b) $q = \pm 6.8$

10. (a) $r = \sqrt[3]{\dfrac{3V}{4\pi}}$ (b) $r = 33.7$

11. (a) $x = \pm\sqrt{ab}$ (b) $x = \pm 4.0 \times 10^4$

12. (a) $n = \dfrac{1 - m}{1 + m}$ (b) $n = 8.4 \times 10^{-1}$

Review Exercise 14   Page 158

1. 4   **2.** $V = 7$

3. (a) 1   (b) 5   (c) -5 (d) -6

4. $P = 7.5$ **5.** $S = -14$ **6.** 108

7. (a) 6   (b) -6 **8.** $C = 100 - 29n$

9. (a) $2a + 4b + 2c$ (b) 22

10. (a) $C = 15$ (b) $-15°\text{C}$

11. $A = 75$ **12.** 15 hours   **13.** $1\frac{1}{6}$

14. (a) £169

   (b) (i) $r = \dfrac{C - 25}{3}$ (ii) $35\,\text{cm}$

15. (a) $C = 2900$ (b) $R = 8$

   (c) 6   (b) $R = \dfrac{C - 2000}{180}$

16. $s = -8$

17. (a) $a = -2.5$ (b) $d = \dfrac{3a}{b + c}$

18. (a) $p = 7.2$ (b) $s = \dfrac{q - p}{r}$

19. (a) $p = 6.5$ (b) $q = 15$

20. (a) 7.6×10^3 (b) $M = \dfrac{Rv^2}{G}$

21. $v = \pm\sqrt{\dfrac{t - u}{s}}$

CHAPTER   15

Exercise 15.1   Page 160

1. (a) 17, 21, 25   (b) 14, 16, 18
   (c) 16, 13, 10   (d) 28, 33, 38
   (e) 48, 96, 192   (f) $1\frac{1}{2}$, $1\frac{3}{4}$, 2
   (g) 2, 1, $\frac{1}{2}$ (h) 0.9, 1.0, 1.1
   (i) 2, 0, -2 (j) 5, 2.5, 1.25
   (k) 21, 28, 36   (l) 29, 47, 76

2. (a) 8, 14   (b) 10, 22
   (c) 8, 32   (d) 16, -2
   (e) 16, 36   (f) 8, 21
   (g) 2, 20, 26   (h) 2.0, 1.6, 1.2

3. (a) Add 7; 37, 44
   (b) Add 2; 13, 15
   (c) Add 4; 21, 25
   (d) Subtract 5; 11, 6
   (e) Divide by 2; 2, 1
   (f) Multiply by 3; 81, 243
   (g) Add 0.2; 1, 1.2
   (h) Add $\frac{3}{4}$; $3\frac{3}{4}$, $4\frac{1}{2}$
   (i) Add 2 more than last time; 34, 46
   (j) Subtract 3; -5, -8

Exercise 15.2   Page 162

1. (a) 1, 5, 9, 13, 17   (b) 1, 2, 4, 8, 16
   (c) 40, 35, 30, 25, 20   (d) 4, 5, 7, 11, 19
   (e) 47, 23, 11, 5, 2   (f) 2, 6, 4, 5, 4.5

2. (a) 2, 4, 8   (b) 6, 12, 24
   (c) $-2, -4, -8$

3. (a) 4, 10, 22   (b) 8, 18, 38
   (c) $-4, -6, -10$

4. (a) (i) 21 (ii) 3 (b) 37

5. (a) (i) 36 (ii) 123 (b) 10

6. $-6, -27$

Exercise **15.3**   Page 164

1. (a) 3 (b) 3 (c) 6 (d) 8 (e) -2

2. (a) $3n$ (b) $8n$ (c) $12n$ (d) $2n$

3. (a) 3 (c) $3n + 1$ (d) 25

4. (a) 2 (c) $2n + 7$ (d) 47

5. (a) -4 (c) $24 - 4n$

6. (a) $3n - 2$ (b) $22 - 3n$ (c) $4n + 1$
(d) $4n$ (e) $2n - 1$ (f) $4n + 3$
(g) $8 - 2n$ (h) $3n + 2$ (i) $5n - 2$
(j) $45 - 5n$ (k) $n - 1$ (l) $2n - 3$

7. (a) 49, 97 (b) 1537

Exercise **15.4**   Page 167

1. (a) 10 (b) 27 is an odd number (c) $2p$

2. (a) 17 (b) 4 (c) $4n + 1$

3. (a) (i) 15 (ii) 30 (iii) 300 (b) $3n$

4. (a) (i) 18 (ii) 82
(b) Pattern 7 (c) $4n + 2$

5. (a) (i) 51 (ii) 100
(b) (i) $x + 1$ (ii) $2x$

6. (a) $22\,\text{cm}^2$ (b) $42\,\text{cm}^2$ (c) $4n + 2\,\text{cm}^2$

7. (a) 27 (b) $T = 5n + 2$
(c) 52 (d) 15

8. (a) 11 (b) Pattern 18
(c) $m = 2p + 1$

9. (a) 25 (b) $4^2 = 16, 5^2 = 25$
(c) n^2 (d) 225

10. (a) (i) 37, add 2 more than last time.
(ii) 35, add 2 more than last time.
(iii) 39, add 2 more than last time.
(iv) 72, add 4 more than last time.
(v) 42, add 2 more than last time.
(b) (i) $n^2 + 1$ (ii) $n^2 - 1$ (iii) $n^2 + 3$
(iv) $2n^2$ (v) $n^2 + n$

11. (a) $T = n^2 + n = n(n + 1)$ (b) 110

12. (a) 15 (b) $\dfrac{4 \times 5}{2} = 10, \dfrac{5 \times 6}{2} = 15$
(c) $\dfrac{n(n + 1)}{2}$ (d) 55

13. (a) 32 (b) $2^4 = 16, \quad 2^5 = 32$
(c) 2^n (d) 1024 (c) 8th

14. (a) 10, 100, 1000, 10 000, 100 000
(b) 10^n (c) 10^6

15. (a) 3^n (b) 59 049

Review Exercise **15**   Page 170

1. (a) 26, 37 (b) $\dfrac{1}{3}, \dfrac{1}{9}$

2. (a) 16
(b) No. Not (multiple of 3) + 1.
(c) 103

3. (a) 9 (b) 12 (c) 10

4. (a) 7 (b) $-5, -13$

5. (a) 14, 7, 12
(b) Repeats 6, 3, 8, 4, 2, 1

6. (a) 21
(b) Add one more than last time.

7. $x - 4$

8. (a) 13 (b) 3 (c) $3n + 1$

9. (a) $2n + 1$ (b) 201

10. (a) (i) 2, -1
(ii) Subtract 3 from last term.
(b) $20 - 3n$
(c) -130

11. (a) n^2 (b) $n^2 - 1$

12. (a) 50 (b) $2n^2$ (c) Pattern 8

CHAPTER 16

Exercise **16.1**   Page 172

1. (1) $y = 4$ (4) $y = -1$
(2) $x = -3$ (5) $y = x$
(3) $x = 1$

2.

3. (a)

x	1	2	3
(i) y	3	4	5
(ii) y	2	4	6

4.

x	-2	-1	0	1	2	3
(a) y	-3	-2	-1	0	1	2
(b) y		-2	1	4	7	10

5. (b) Same slope, parallel
y-intercept is different

6. (b) Same slope, parallel
y-intercept is different

7. (b) Same *y*-intercept, 3
Different slope

9. (b) $x = 0.5$

10. (a) Missing entries: 6, 4, 3
(b) (i) $y = 2.5$ (ii) $y = 4.5$

11. (b) (i) $y = -2$ (ii) $x = 0.5$

Exercise 16.2
Page 174

1. (a) gradient 3, *y*-intercept -1

2. $y = 3x$, $y = 3x + 2$

3. gradients: 4, 3, 2, -2, $\frac{1}{2}$, 2, 0, $-\frac{1}{2}$

y-intercepts: 3, 5, -3, 4, 3, 0, 3, 4

4. (1) C (2) D (3) B (4) A

5. (a) $y = 5x - 4$ (b) $y = -\frac{1}{2}x + 6$

6. (a) $y = x - 2$ (b) $y = 2x - 2$
(c) $y = -2x - 2$

7. (c) 1 (d) $(0, -4)$ (e) $y = x - 4$

8. (c) $y = -2x - 1$

9. (a) Line slopes up from left to right.
(b) Line slopes down from left to right.
(c) Line is horizontal.

10. $y = 3x$

11. $y = 3x + 8$

12. (a) £25 (b) £15 per hour
(c) $y = 15x + 25$ (d) £145

13. $y = 13 - 3x$

14. (a) $f = 0.8d + 2.4$ (b) £6.40

15. (a) $l = 0.06w + 8$ (b) 26 mm

Exercise 16.3
Page 177

1. $y = \frac{3x}{2} + 3$

2. (a) $y = -\frac{1}{2}x + 2$ (b) $y = -\frac{4}{5}x + 4$
(c) $y = -\frac{2}{3}x + \frac{4}{3}$ (d) $y = \frac{2}{7}x - 2$

3. (a) $\frac{1}{2}$ (b) 1 (c) 2
(d) $-\frac{1}{3}$ (e) $\frac{3}{4}$ (f) $-\frac{2}{5}$

4. (a) $a = 0$ (b) $a = \frac{1}{2}$ (c) $a = -2$
(d) $a = 2\frac{1}{2}$ (e) $a = 2$ (f) $a = \frac{2}{5}$

5. (a) $y = x + $ (any number)
(b) $y = 2x + $ (any number)
(c) $y = \frac{1}{2}x + $ (any number)

6. $y = -\frac{3}{2}x + $ (any number)

7. (a) $\frac{4}{5}$ (b) 2 (c) $y = $ (any number)$x + 2$

8. (a) $(0, 5)$ (b) $(3, 0)$

9. (a) $(0, 4), (5, 0)$
(b) $(0, -2), (0.5, 0)$
(c) $(0, 5), (7.5, 0)$

10. (a) $A(0, 2), B(-4, 0)$ (b) $\frac{1}{2}$
(c) (ii) $y = \frac{1}{2}x + $ (any number)

11. (a) $P(0, 3), Q(6, 0)$ (b) $-\frac{1}{2}$
(c) (ii) $y = -\frac{1}{2}x + $ (any number)

Exercise 16.4
Page 179

1. (a)

x	1	2	3
$y = x + 2$	3	4	5
$y = 5 - x$	4	3	2

(c) $x = 1.5$

2. (b) $x = 2.5$

3. (b) $x = 0.5$

4. $x = 1.2$

5. (b) $y = 9$ (c) $x = 3$

6. (c) The number of hours for which the two firms charge the same amount.

7. (d) B (e) A (f) 6 days

Exercise 16.5
Page 181

1. B

2. (a)

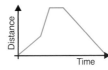

3. 1. C 2. B 3. E 4. A

4.

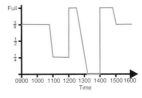

5.

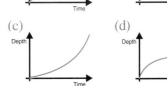

6. (a) 1. D 2. A 3. C 4. B

1. (a) $y = 4$ (b) $x = -1$
    (c) No. $3 \times 10 - 2 \neq 27$

2. (a)

x	-2	-1	0	1	2
y	0	1	2	3	4

    (b)

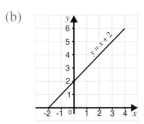

    (c) $a = 5, b = -3$

3. (a)

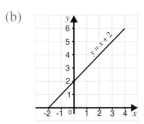

    (b) $(1, 3)$

4. (a)

x	-2	-1	0	1	2	3
y	-5	-3	-1	1	3	5

    (c) (i) $y = -3.8$ (ii) $x = 2.4$

5. (b) $(2, 3)$

6. (b) Same gradient, 2.

7. (a) $(0, -3)$
    (b) (i) $m = 2$ (ii) $c = -1$

8. $y = -2x + 4$

9. (b) £40   (c) $y = 0.2x + 40$
    (d) £1040

10. (a) $c = 2, m = 3$ (b) $(0, -4)$

11.

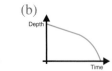

12. (a) Brian   (b) Afzal
    (c) 600 m   (d) Afzal

13. (a)   (b)

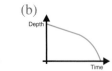

14. **A**: Graph **R**, **B**: Graph **S**

15. (a) $A(0, 3), B(-1.5, 0)$
    (b) $y = 2x - 2$

CHAPTER 17

1. $x = 4, \; y = 2$ **4.** $x = 2, \; y = 3$

2. $x = 3, \; y = 5$ **5.** $x = 3, \; y = 1$

3. $x = 2, \; y = 3$ **6.** $x = 4, \; y = 3$

1. (a) Both lines have gradient -1.
    (b) Both lines have gradient 4.
    (c) Both lines are the same.
    (d) Both lines have gradient 0.4.

2. (a) $y = -2x + 6, \; y = -2x + 3$
    (b) $y = 2x + 3.5, \; y = 2x + 2$
    (c) $y = 2.5x - 4, \; y = 2.5x + 1.75$
    (d) $y = -3x + 1.25, \; y = -3x + 0.5$

3. (b) and (d) have no solution.
    (a) $x = 0.4, \; y = 4$
    (c) $x = -0.125, \; y = 1.875$

1. $x = 1, \; y = 2$ **11.** $x = 4, \; y = 1$

2. $x = 3, \; y = 4$ **12.** $x = 4, \; y = 2$

3. $x = 2, \; y = 1$ **13.** $x = 2, \; y = 3$

4. $x = 1, \; y = 7$ **14.** $x = 4, \; y = -2$

5. $x = 3, \; y = 1$ **15.** $x = 2, \; y = -1.5$

6. $x = 2, \; y = 3$ **16.** $x = -1, \; y = 3$

7. $x = 5, \; y = 2$ **17.** $x = -5, \; y = 6$

8. $x = 4, \; y = 2$ **18.** $x = 2.5, \; y = -1$

9. $x = 5, \; y = 4$ **19.** $x = -6, \; y = 2.5$

10. $x = 3, \; y = 2$ **20.** $x = 3, \; y = -1.5$

1. $x = 2, \; y = 1$ **13.** $x = 5, \; y = 2$

2. $x = 2, \; y = 3$ **14.** $x = 1, \; y = -2$

3. $x = 3, \; y = 1$ **15.** $x = -1, \; y = 2$

4. $x = 4, \; y = 2$ **16.** $x = 2, \; y = 1$

5. $x = 2, \; y = -1$ **17.** $x = -1, \; y = 1$

6. $x = 4, \; y = -3$ **18.** $x = -2, \; y = 3$

7. $x = 4, \; y = 0.5$ **19.** $x = -1, \; y = 7$

8. $x = -3, \; y = 0.5$ **20.** $x = 4, \; y = -1$

9. $x = 4, \; y = 1$ **21.** $x = 2.5, \; y = 3$

10. $x = 2.2, \; y = 5.6$ **22.** $x = 2, \; y = -1$

11. $x = 1.5, \; y = 2$ **23.** $x = 1, \; y = -2$

12. $x = 1, \; y = 2$ **24.** $x = -2, \; y = 0.5$

Exercise 17.5 — Page 192

1. $x = 2$, $y = 6$
2. $x = 9$, $y = 18$
3. $x = 8$, $y = 2$
4. $x = 3$, $y = 6$
5. $x = 2$, $y = 13$
6. $x = 0$, $y = 2$
7. $x = 2$, $y = 4$
8. $x = 7$, $y = 6$
9. $x = 4$, $y = 8$
10. $x = 10.5$, $y = 0.5$
11. $x = -68$, $y = -122$
12. $x = 8$, $y = 6$

Exercise 17.6 — Page 193

1. (a) $6x + 3y = 93$, $2x + 5y = 91$
   (b) Pencil 8p, pen 15p
2. (a) $5x + 30y = 900$, $10x + 15y = 1260$
   (b) Apples £1.08 per kg, oranges 12p each
3. $x = 95$, $y = 82$
4. 32 children, 3 adults
6. Coffee 50p, Tea 40p
5. $x = 100$, $y = 70$
7. $x = 160$, $y = 120$

Review Exercise 17 — Page 194

1. (b) $x = 1.8$, $y = 0.8$
2. (a) $x = 3$, $y = 7$ (b) $x = 4.5$, $y = 1.25$
3. $x = 2$, $y = 4$
4. (a) $x = 3$, $y = 2$ (b) $x = 4$, $y = -2$
   (c) $x = 1$, $y = 2$ (d) $x = -2$, $y = 1$
5. $x = 7$ $y = 3$
6. $x = 7$, $y = 0.5$
7. $x = 3$, $y = -2$
8. (a) Same gradient, 2
      $y = 2x - 2$, $y = 2x + \frac{3}{2}$
   (b) Same gradient, $\frac{1}{4}$
      $y = \frac{1}{4}x + \frac{1}{4}$, $y = \frac{1}{4}x + \frac{3}{8}$
   (c) $a = 3$, b = any number, except 2
   (d) $\frac{q}{p} = -3$, $\frac{r}{p} \neq 2$
9. (a) $3x + 2y = 26$, $4x + y = 28$
   (b) Blouse £6
10. (a) $4x + y = 58$, $6x + 2y = 92$
    (b) $x = 12$, $y = 10$

CHAPTER 18

Exercise 18.1 — Page 196

1. (a) True (b) True (c) True (d) False
   (e) True (f) False (g) False (h) True
2. (a) E.g. 5, 4, 3, ... (b) E.g. $-2, -1, 0$ ...
   (c) E.g. 5, 4, 3, ... (d) E.g. 7, 6, 5, ...
   (e) E.g. 11, 12, 13, ... (f) -1
   (g) 5 (h) One of: $-6, -5, -4, -3, -2$
3. (a) 2, 3, 4 (b) $-1, 0, 1, 2, 3$
   (c) $-4, -3, -2, -1$ (d) $-1, 0, 1, 2$

4. (a) $x \geq 2$ (b) $-6 \leq x < -2$
   (c) $-2 < x < 1$ (d) $x < 5$ and $x \geq 8$
5. (a)
   (b)
   (c)

Exercise 18.2 — Page 197

1. (a) $n > 2$ (b) $a < 4$
   (c) $d \leq 3$ (d) $t < -3$
   (e) $g > -2$ (f) $y \geq 0$

2. (a) $a < 4$ (b) $b \geq 1$
   (c) $b \leq 1$ (d) $c > 5$
   (e) $d < -3$ (f) $a \geq 6$
   (g) $b < 15$ (h) $c \leq 3$
   (i) $d > 4$ (j) $f < -2$
   (k) $g \leq \frac{1}{2}$ (l) $h < 2$
   (m) $j \geq 2\frac{1}{2}$ (n) $k > -4$
   (o) $m > -6\frac{1}{2}$ (p) $n \leq 2$
   (q) $p > 8$ (r) $q > 1$
   (s) $r \geq -1\frac{1}{2}$ (t) $t > 13$
   (u) $u \leq 9$ (v) $v < -1\frac{1}{2}$
   (w) $w > 8$ (x) $x < 1\frac{2}{5}$

Exercise 18.3 — Page 198

1. $a < -2$
2. $b \geq 3$
3. $c \leq -4$
4. $d > -1$
5. $e \geq 2$
6. $f < 1$
7. $g > -4$
8. $h \geq 2$
9. $j \leq 1$
10. $k > -\frac{1}{3}$
11. $m < -3$
12. $n > -4$
13. $p \geq \frac{5}{9}$
14. $q > -2\frac{1}{5}$
15. $n < 9$

Exercise 18.4 — Page 199

1. (a) $1 < x \leq 5$ (b) $-1 \leq x < 9$
   (c) $-7 < x \leq 4$
2. (a) $1 < x \leq 3$ (b) $-2 \leq x < 4$
   (c) $3 < x < 4\frac{1}{2}$ (d) $-\frac{1}{3} \leq x \leq 4$
   (e) $2 < x \leq 5$ (f) $-3 \leq x < 6$
   (g) $-2 < x < 2$ (h) $3 \leq x < 6$
   (i) $-4\frac{1}{2} \leq x \leq -1$
3. (a) 6, 7, 8 (b) $-2, -1, 0, 1, 2, 3, 4$
   (c) 0, 1, 2 (d) 4, 5, 6, 7
   (e) 5 (f) 2, 3
   (g) $-2, -1, 0$ (h) $-1, 0, 1, 2, 3$
   (i) $-4, -3, -2, -1, 0, 1, 2, 3, 4, 5, 6$
   (j) 8, 9, 10, 11, 12, 13, 14, 15, 16
   (k) $-4, -3, -2, -1, 0, 1, 2, 3$
   (l) -6

Exercise **18.6**   Page 201

3. A : ③,

    B : ①,

    C : ④,

    D : ②,

4.

5. $y \geqslant 1, \quad y \leqslant x$

6. $x \geqslant 1, \quad y < 5 \quad$ and $\quad y > x + 2$

7. $y < 4, \quad x \leqslant 3, \quad y \leqslant 2x \quad$ and $\quad y > x$

8. $x \leqslant 2, \quad x + y > 3, \quad y \leqslant x + 3$

9. (a) 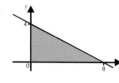   (b) (2, 2), (3, 2)

Review Exercise **18**   Page 203

1. (a) $x \geqslant -5$ (b) $x < 3$
    (c) $x \leqslant 6$ (d) $x > -2$

2. (a)

    (b)

    (c)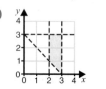

3. 3, 4, 5   4. $-1, 0, 1, 2$

5. (a) $x < 4$ (b) $-1 < x \leqslant 2$
    (c) $-1 \leqslant x < 1$ (d) $-3 < x < -1$

6. (a) $x < -2$ (b) $x \geqslant 5$ (c) $x \leqslant 3$

7. (a) $-1, 0, 1, 2, 3, 4$ (b) $-3, -2, -1, 0, 1$
    (c) $-2, -1$

8. (a) $-1, 0, 1$
    (b) (i) $n > -\frac{8}{3}$ (ii) -2

9. $-2, -1, 0, 1$ 10. $a < \frac{3}{5}$

11. (a) $x < -6$ (b) $x < 4\frac{1}{2}$

12. (a) $n \leqslant 5$ (b) 5

13. (a) $x < 3$ (b) 3, 4, 5

14. (a)   (b)   (c)

15.   16. (a) $x \leqslant 2, \quad y \leqslant 4$
    and $\quad x + y \leqslant 4$

    (b)

17.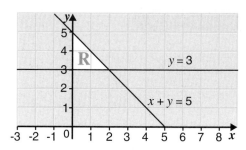

18. (a)

    (b)

    (c)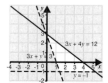

CHAPTER 19

Exercise **19.1**   Page 206

1. $x^2 + 7x + 12$ 13. $2x^2 + x - 3$

2. $x^2 + 6x + 5$ 14. $3x^2 + 14x - 5$

3. $x^2 - 3x - 10$ 15. $12x^2 + 14x - 10$

4. $2x^2 - 3x - 2$ 16. $x^2 - 9$

5. $3x^2 - 20x + 12$ 17. $x^2 - 25$

6. $6x^2 + 7x + 2$ 18. $x^2 - 49$

7. $x^2 + 6x - 16$ 19. $x^2 - 100$

8. $x^2 + 3x - 10$ 20. $x^2 + 6x + 9$

9. $x^2 + 2x - 3$ 21. $x^2 + 10x + 25$

10. $x^2 - 5x + 6$ 22. $x^2 - 6x + 9$

11. $x^2 - 5x + 4$ 23. $x^2 - 14x + 49$

12. $x^2 - 5x - 14$ 24. $4x^2 - 12x + 9$

Exercise **19.2**   Page 208

1. (a) $x(x + 5)$ (b) $x(x - 7)$
    (c) $y(y - 6)$ (d) $2y(y - 6)$
    (e) $t(5 - t)$ (f) $y(8 + y)$
    (g) $x(x - 20)$ (h) $3x(x - 20)$

2. (a) $(x - 3)(x + 3)$ (b) $(x - 9)(x + 9)$
(c) $(y - 5)(y + 5)$ (d) $(y - 1)(y + 1)$
(e) $(x - 8)(x + 8)$ (f) $(10 - x)(10 + x)$
(g) $(6 - x)(6 + x)$ (h) $(x - a)(x + a)$

3. (a) $(x + 5)(x + 1)$ (b) $(x + 7)(x + 2)$
(c) $(x + 2)(x + 4)$ (d) $(x + 3)(x + 6)$
(e) $(x - 5)(x - 1)$ (f) $(x - 5)(x - 2)$
(g) $(x - 4)(x - 3)$ (h) $(x + 4)(x - 1)$
(i) $(x + 7)(x - 2)$ (j) $(x - 5)(x + 1)$

4. (a) $(x + 1)(x + 2)$ (b) $(x + 1)(x + 7)$
(c) $(x + 3)(x + 5)$ (d) $(x + 2)(x + 6)$
(e) $(x + 1)(x + 11)$ (f) $(x + 4)(x + 5)$
(g) $(x + 4)(x + 6)$ (h) $(x + 4)(x + 9)$

5. (a) $(x - 3)^2$ (b) $(x - 4)(x - 2)$
(c) $(x - 10)(x - 1)$ (d) $(x - 15)(x - 1)$
(e) $(x - 5)(x - 3)$ (f) $(x - 8)(x - 2)$
(g) $(x - 10)(x - 2)$ (h) $(x - 8)(x - 3)$

6. (a) $(x - 3)(x + 2)$ (b) $(x - 6)(x + 1)$
(c) $(x - 4)(x + 6)$ (d) $(x - 3)(x + 8)$
(e) $(x - 5)(x + 3)$ (f) $(x - 3)(x + 6)$
(g) $(x - 8)(x + 5)$ (h) $(x - 6)(x + 2)$

7. (a) $(x - 2)^2$ (b) $(x + 5)(x + 6)$
(c) $(x - 2)(x + 4)$ (d) $(x - 7)(x + 3)$
(e) $(x - 4)(x + 5)$ (f) $(x + 3)(x + 4)$
(g) $(x + 4)^2$ (h) $(x - 1)^2$
(i) $(x - 7)(x + 7)$ (j) $t(t + 12)$
(k) $(x - 2)(x - 7)$ (l) $(x - 6)(x - 1)$
(m) $(x + 2)(x + 9)$ (n) $(x + 3)(x + 8)$
(o) $(x + 1)(x + 18)$ (p) $(x - y)(x + y)$
(q) $(x + 3)(x - 2)$ (r) $y(y + 4)$
(s) $(y - 5)^2$ (t) $(x - 6)^2$

Exercise 19.3　　　　Page 209

1. $3(x + 4y)$ **11.** $3(m - 2)(m + 2)$
2. $(t - 4)(t + 4)$ **12.** $(v - 3)(v + 2)$
3. $(x + 1)(x + 3)$ **13.** $a(x - y)(x + y)$
4. $y(y - 1)$ **14.** $-2(4 + x)$
5. $2(d^2 - 3)$ **15.** $(2 - k)^2$
6. $(p - q)(p + q)$ **16.** $2(3 - x)(3 + x)$
7. $a(a - 2)$ **17.** $2(5 - x)(5 + x)$
8. $(x - 1)^2$ **18.** $3(2x - 3y)(2x + 3y)$
9. $2y(y - 4)$ **19.** $3a(2a - 1)$
10. $(a - 3)^2$ **20.** $(x - 7)(x - 8)$

Exercise 19.4　　　　Page 210

1. (a) $2d + 3$ (b) $3x + 2$
(c) $4a + 5b$ (d) $3m - 2n$
(e) $4x - 2y$ (f) $a + b$
(g) $x - 1$ (h) $x^2 - 2$
(i) $\dfrac{x}{3x - 2}$ (j) $\dfrac{x}{2x^2 - 1}$

(k) $\dfrac{1}{2x - 1}$ (l) $\dfrac{1}{3x}$

(m) $\dfrac{3}{2}$ (n) $\dfrac{m}{3}$

(o) $\dfrac{x - 3}{x + 2}$ (p) $-\dfrac{5}{3}$

2. (a) **E** (b) **C** (c) **B** (d) **A** (e) **D**

3. (a) $\dfrac{x}{x + 1}$ (b) $\dfrac{x + 2}{x + 3}$ (c) $\dfrac{x}{x + 3}$

(d) $\dfrac{x - 5}{x + 3}$ (e) $\dfrac{x - 2}{x - 3}$ (f) $\dfrac{x - 5}{x + 4}$

(g) $x - 1$ (h) $\dfrac{1}{x + 2}$ (i) $\dfrac{x + 1}{2}$

Exercise 19.5　　　　Page 211

1. (a) $x = 2$ or 3 (b) $x = -4$ or -6
(c) $x = 3$ or -1 (d) $x = 5$ or -2
(e) $x = 0$ or 4 (f) $x = 0$ or -2

2. (a) $x = 1$ or 2 (b) $y = -3$ or -4
(c) $m = 4$ or -2 (d) $a = 3$ or -4
(e) $n = 9$ or -4 (f) $z = 6$ or 3
(g) $k = -3$ or -5 (h) $c = -7$ or -8
(i) $b = 4$ or -5 (j) $v = 12$ or -5
(k) $w = 4$ or -12 (l) $p = 9$ or -8

3. (a) $x = 0$ or 5 (b) $y = 0$ or -1
(c) $p = 0$ or -3 (d) $a = 0$ or 4
(e) $t = 0$ or 6 (f) $g = 0$ or 4

4. (a) $x = 2$ or -2 (b) $y = 12$ or -12
(c) $a = 3$ or -3 (d) $d = 4$ or -4
(e) $x = 10$ or -10 (f) $x = 6$ or -6
(g) $x = 7$ or -7 (h) $x = 1.5$ or -1.5

5. (a) $y = 5$ or -1 (b) $x = 0$ or 1
(c) $x = 4$ (d) $x = 5$ or -3
(e) $n = 12$ or -2 (f) $m = 7$ or 1
(g) $a = 8$ or -3 (h) $x = 1$ or 3

6. (a) $x(x - 4) = 21$
(b) $x = 7$ (x cannot equal -3)

7. $x = 9$ or -7 **8.** 7 and 8

Exercise 19.6　　　　Page 213

1. (a)

x	-3	-2	-1	0	1	2	3
y	9	4	1	0	1	4	9

(c) $y = 2.25$

2. (a)

x	-3	-2	-1	0	1	2	3
y	7	2	-1	-2	-1	2	7

(c) $y = 0.25$ (d) $(-1.4, 0), (1.4, 0)$

3. (a)

x	-3	-2	-1	0	1	2	3
y	5	0	-3	-4	-3	0	5

(c) $y = -1.75$ (d) $x = -2$ and $x = 2$

4. Graphs have same shape, different positions.

503

5. (b) $y = 7.25$ (c) $x = -1.7$ and $x = 1.7$

6. (a) Entries are: 8, 2, 0, 2, 8
   (c) $x = \pm 1.6$

7. (a) Entries are: 6, 2, 0, 0, 2, 6
   (c) $x = -1$ or 0 (d) $\left(-\frac{1}{2}, -\frac{1}{4}\right)$

8. (a) Entries are: 5, 1, −1, −1, 1, 5
   (c) $x = -0.6$ or 1.6

9. (a) Entries are: −3, 7, 13, 15, 13, 7, −3
   (c) $x = \pm 2.7$

10. (b) $x = -3$ or 1

11. (a) Entries are: −6, 1, 6, 9, 10, 9, 6, 1, −6
   (c) $x = \pm 3.2$ (d) (0, 10)

12. (a) $x = \pm 2.8$ (b) $x = \pm 2.2$
   (c) $x = 0$ (d) $x = \pm 2.4$

14. (a) Entries are: −24, 0, 8, 6, 0, −4, 0, 18
   (c) $x = -3$ or 0 or 2

15. (a) Entries are: −6, 8, 10, 6, 2, 4, 18
   (c) $x = -2.7$

Exercise 19.7 — Page 215

1. $x = 3.8$ **3.** $x = 3.2$
2. (a) $w = 4.2$ (b) $x = 2.3$ **4.** $x = 9.4$
5. (a) $x = 6.2$ (b) $x = 6.22$
6. (a) $2x^2(x + 2)$ (b) $x = 5.3$
7. $x = 1.82$

Review Exercise 19 — Page 216

1. $x^2 - 3x - 10$
2. (a) (i) $t(t - 4)$ (ii) $t = 0$ or 4
   (b) (i) $(y + 1)(y + 2)$ (ii) $y = -1$ or −2
3. (a) $2x^2 + 9x + 4$ (b) $2x(2x - 3)$
4. $x = 2$ or −1 **5.** $x = 2$ or −4
6. (a) $x = +3$ or −3 (b) $x = 9$ or −1
7. (a) $(x - 3)(x + 4) = 78$
   (b) (i) $x^2 + x - 12 = 78$, $x^2 + x - 90 = 0$
   (ii) $x = 9$ or −10
   (iii) Length 13 cm, width 6 cm
8. (a)

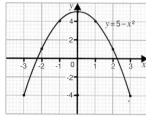

9. (a) B
   (b) A

   (b) (i) 5 (ii) $x = 2.24$ or −2.24

10. (a)

x	0.5	1	1.5	2	2.5	3
V	0.5	2	4.5	8	12.5	18

   (c) $x = 2.2$

11. $x = 2.59$

504

Section Review — Page 217

1. (b) $M(-1, 1)$
2. (a) $2a + 1$ (b) $2y^2 - y$
3. (a) $3x$ pence (b) $x + 7$ pence
4. (a) $x = 2$ (b) $x = 4$
   (c) $x = 12$
5. (a) −2 (b) $2(x - 3)$
   (c) 3
6. 6.5
7. (a) −5 (b) 15
8. (a) 17 (b) $x - 4$
9. (a) $2a - b + 3ab$ (b) $2x + 3$
10. (a) −8 (b) $\frac{1}{8}$
11. (a) $x = 3$ (b) $n = 7$
12. (a) 14 (b) $3n - 1$
13. (a) (i) $x = 3.2$ (ii) $t = 1.5$
   (b) $2(3 + 2a)$
14. (a) $2x$ pence (b) $3x - 15$ pence
   (c) 22 pence
15. (a) $x = 4$ (b) 27 cm
16. (a) −3 (b) $9 - 2n$
17. (a) (c)

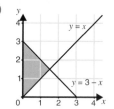

   (b) Where graphs cross.
18. (a) $x = 5$ (b) $x = 0.5$, $y = -2.5$
19. (a) (i) $x = 5$ (ii) $y = 4$
   (iii) $p = 3.2$ (iv) $x = -4.5$
   (b) $x \leqslant 2.5$
20. (a) $3(2p - 1)$ (b) $p(p + 2)$
21. (a) $6n - 5$ (b) $n^2 + 2$
22. (b) (i) $y = 5.8$ (ii) $x = \pm 1.9$
23. (a) $x > 3$ (b) −3, −2
24. (a) −28°C (b) 39 000 feet
25. (a) $V = \pm 0.7$ (b) $P = RV^2$
26. (a) $x < -0.5$
   (b) $x^2 - 10x + 25$
   (c) (i) $3m(m - 2)$
   (ii) $(t - 4)(t + 3)$
27. (b) (i) −4.25 (ii) $x = -1.6$ and 2.6
28. (a) $y = 20x + 18$ (b) £118

29.

30. (a) $2x$
(b) $15a^5$
(c) $25t^6$

31. (a) $x = 3$
(b) $x = 3, \quad y = -2$
(c) $-2, -1$

32. (a) $r = \sqrt[3]{\dfrac{3V}{4\pi}}$ (b) $r = 6$

33. $x = 2.6$

34. (a) $x^2 - 5x + 6$ (b) $x = 1$ or -8

35. (a) $8x + 14$ metres
(b) $(2x + 4)(2x + 3) - 12$
$= 4x^2 + 14x + 12 - 12$
$= 4x^2 + 14x$
(c) $22.56\,\mathrm{m^2}$

36. (a) $y = 0$ or -5 (b) $m = 3$ or 4

37. $x(15 - x) = 54$
$15x - x^2 = 54$
$x^2 - 15x + 54 = 0$

38. (a) $\dfrac{a}{5}$ (b) $2(x - 3)(x + 3)$

39. $(x + 2)(x + 1) = 6$
$x^2 + 3x + 2 = 6$
$x^2 + 3x - 4 = 0$

CHAPTER 20

Exercise 20.1   Page 221

1. (a) $180°$ (b) $90°$ (c) $270°$
(d) $90°$ (e) $120°$ (f) $6°$
(g) $42°$ (h) $720°$ (i) $540°$
(j) $810°$

2. (a) $45°$ (b) $315°$ **3.** (a) $45°$ (b) $360°$

4. Acute: **A, G**   Obtuse: **B, C, F, H**
Reflex: **D, I**   Right: **E**

Exercise 20.2   Page 222

1. (a) $39°$ (b) $118°$ (c) $42°$

2. (a) $217°$ (b) $234°$

Exercise 20.3   Page 224

1. (a) $a = 30°$ (b) $b = 150°$
(c) $c = 42°$ (d) $d = 20°$
(e) $e = 126°$ (f) $f = 203°$
(g) $g = 133°, \quad h = 47°$ (h) $i = 112°$
(i) $j = 127°, \quad k = 53°, \quad l = 37°$
(j) $m = 96°$
(k) $n = 47°, \quad p = 43°$

2. (a) $45°$ (b) $30°$ (c) $60°$ (d) $36°$
(e) $40°$ (f) $80°$ (g) $20°$ (h) $30°$

Exercise 20.4   Page 227

1. (a) $a = 65°$ (b) $b = 115°$
(c) $c = 105°$ (d) $d = 100°$

2. (a) $a = 130°, \quad b = 130°$
(b) $c = 60°, \quad d = 120°$
(c) $e = 40°, \quad f = 40°$
(d) $g = 65°, \quad h = 65°$

3. (a) $a = 63°$ (b) $b = 68°, \quad c = 112°$
(c) $d = 87°$ (d) $e = 124°$
(e) $f = 65°$ (f) $g = 54°$
(g) $h = 113°$ (h) $i = 124°$

4. (a) $a = 125°, \quad b = 125°$
(b) $c = 62°, \quad d = 118°, \quad e = 62°$
(c) $f = 74°, \quad g = 106°$
(d) $h = 52°, \quad i = 128°$

5. (a) $m = 84°, \quad n = 116°$
(b) $p = 56°, \quad q = 116°$
(c) $r = 61°$
(d) $s = 270°$

Exercise 20.5   Page 228

1. (a) $\angle BAC$ (b) $\angle RQS$ (c) $\angle XZY$

2. $a = \angle QPS, \quad b = \angle PQS, \quad c = \angle RQS,$
$d = \angle QRS, \quad e = \angle QSR, \quad f = \angle PSQ$

3. (a) $93°$ (b) $108°$ (c) $52°$ (d) $110°$
(e) $65°$ (f) $295°$ (g) $283°$ (h) $326°$

4. (a) (i) $43°$ (ii) supplementary angles
(b) (i) $125°$ (ii) vertically opposite angles
(c) (i) $63°$ (ii) corresponding angles

5. (a) $132°$ (b) $126°$ (c) $141°$
(d) $85°$ (e) $65°$
(f) $\angle QSP = 105°, \quad \angle STU = 105°$

6. (a) $\angle AOB = 153°, \quad \angle COD = 37°$
(b) $\angle QTU = 48°, \quad \angle QTS = 132°$
(c) reflex $\angle TUV = 280°$

Exercise 20.6   Page 230

1. (a) $45°$ (b) $135°$ (c) $90°$
(d) $90°$ (e) $180°$

2. (a) South   (b) North

3. (a) North-west   (b) North-east

4. Entries are: south-east, south-east, south, north-west

Exercise 20.7   Page 232

1. (a) $065°$ (b) $140°$ (c) $249°$
(d) $228°$ (e) $300°$ (f) $090°$

2. (b) (i) $230°$ (ii) $305°$ (iii) $015°$
(iv) $080°$ (v) $125°$ (vi) $355°$

3.

4. (a) 315°
(b) 135°
(c) 285°
(d) 105°
(e) 230°
(f) 050°

1. 16.8 km   **2.** 3.2 cm   **3.** (a) 7 m (b) 30 cm

4. 12.5 m   **5.** 70 cm

6. (a) 1 : 20   (b) 5.8 m   (c) 22.5 cm

7. (a) (i) 128°   (ii) 308°
   (b) (i) 4.7 cm (ii) 47 km

8. (a) 240 m   (b) 063°   **9.** 19.8 km

10. (a) 8 km   (b) 114°   (c) 294°

11. (a) 6300 km   (b) 248°

12. (a) 50 km   (b) 347°   (c) 167°

1. (a) $a = 57°$, supplementary angles
   (b) $x = 30°$

2. (a) $y = 50$

3. (a) Corresponding angles
   (b) $r = 80°$
   (c) (i) $x = 80°$ (ii) alternate angles

4. (a) $x = 30°$

5. (a) (i) 153° (ii) 63°   (b) $\angle BOQ$

6. (a) 230°   (b) 140°
   (c) (i) 3.7 cm (ii) 740 m

7. (b) 245°   (c) (i) 64 km   (ii) 197°

CHAPTER   **21**

1. (a) Yes   (b) Yes   (c) No
   (d) No   (e) Yes   (f) No

2. (a) Yes, obtuse-angled   (b) No
   (c) Yes, acute-angled
   (d) Yes, right-angled
   (e) Yes, obtuse-angled   (f) No

3. (a) $a = 70°$ (b) $b = 37°$ (c) $c = 114°$
   (d) $d = 43°$ (e) $e = 63°$ (f) $f = 13°$

1. (a) $a = 120°$ (b) $b = 110°$ (c) $c = 50°$
   (d) $d = 80°$ (e) $e = 88°$ (f) $f = 55°$

2. (a) $a = 32°, b = 148°$ (b) $c = 63°$
   (c) $d = 52°, e = 64°$

1. (a) Isosceles (b) Equilateral (c) ΔBCE

2. (b) (i) Acute-angled, scalene
     (ii) Right-angled, scalene
     (iii) Acute-angled, isosceles
     (iv) Obtuse-angled, isosceles

3. $AC = BC \; \angle BAC = \angle ABC$ **4.** (6, 2), (6, 8)

5. (a) $a = 60°$ (b) $a = 85°$
   (c) $a = 75°$ (d) $a = 50°$

6. $a = 40°, \; b = 120°, \; c = 62°, \; d = 128°,$
   $e = 18°, \; f = 144°, \; g = 85°, \; h = 116°,$
   $i = 26.5°, \; j = 153.5°$

7. (a) Isosceles   (b) 74°   (c) 46°

8. (a) $\angle BCD = 120°$
   (b) $\angle PRQ = 80°, \; \angle QRS = 160°$
   (c) $\angle MNX = 50°$

5. (b) 9.3 cm   (c) 39°

1. (a) 13 cm   (b) 13.3 cm (c) 19.9 cm

2. $\Delta PQR = 33$ cm, $\Delta QRS = 32$ cm,
   $\Delta RST = 35$ cm. ΔRST has greatest perimeter

3. (a) $a = 7$ cm (b) $d = 3.8$ cm (c) $f = 3$ cm

4. (a) 9 cm²   (b) 6 cm²   (c) 3.6 cm²
   (d) 7.2 cm²   (e) 4.16 cm² (f) 11.52 cm²

5. (a) 3.8 cm²   (b) 8 cm²   (c) 3.24 cm²

6. (a) $a = 8$ cm (b) $b = 4$ cm (c) $c = 16$ cm

7. 67.5 cm²   **8.** 30 cm   **9.** 4 cm

1. (b) (i) Isosceles   (ii) 8 cm²
   (c) Point S on line $y = 5$.

2. (a) $x = 70°$ (b) $y = 110°$

3. (a) $\angle DCA = 53°$ (b) $\angle BAC = 50°$

4. (b) (i) $\angle BAC = 50°$ (ii) acute angle

5. (a) 28 cm²   (b) 7 cm²   (c) 21 cm²

6. 9.6 cm²   **7.** (b) 16 cm²

8. (a) 45 cm   (b) 75 cm²   (c) 10 cm

CHAPTER   **22**

3. (a) 5 (b) 3 (c) 0   **4.** 1, 1, 1, 2, 0

5. (a) 2 (b) 3 (c) 4 (d) 2 (e) 6 (f) 8

6. (a) MY   (b) NZ   (c) NXZ   (d) JP

7. (a) 1   (b) (i)   (ii)

8. (a) 1   (b) (i)   (ii) 3

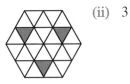

9. (a) (i) 0 (ii) 2   (b) (i) 1 (ii) 1
(c) (i) 2 (ii) 2   (d) (i) 0 (ii) 4
(e) (i) 1 (ii) 1

Exercise 22.2   **Page 251**

1. 9

2. (a) 4   (b) 4   (c) 2   (d) Infinite

3. (a) 2   (b) 2   (c) 4

4. (a) 4   (b) 1, 4

5. (a) 4   (b) 4

Exercise 22.3   **Page 252**

1. A, O F, L C, G H, J D, P   **2.** **D**, **E**

3. (a) ΔCED (b) $CBFE$

4. (a) ΔAXZ and ΔZYC, ΔBXZ and ΔZYB

Exercise 22.4   **Page 253**

1. **A**, **D** (SSS)   **2.** **A**, **D** (ASA)

3. (a) Yes, ASA   (b) No
(c) Yes, SAS   (d) Yes, SSS
(e) No   (f) Yes, RHS
(g) Yes, SAS   (h) No
(i) Yes, ASA

4. (a) No   (b) No
(c) Yes, RHS   (d) No
(e) Yes, ASA   (f) Yes, ASA
(g) Yes, SSS   (h) Yes, SAS
(i) Yes, ASA

5. No lengths given, one triangle is larger than the other.

6. $DE = PQ$ (given) $DF = PR$ (given)
$\angle EDF = \angle QPR$ (70°)   Congruent, SAS

7. (a) $\angle BDC = 25°$
(b) BD is common
$AB = CD$ (7 cm)
$\angle ABD = \angle BDC$ (alt. $\angle$s)
Congruent, SAS
(c) $\angle ADB$

Review Exercise 22   **Page 255**

1.

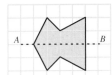

2. (a) Y   (b) Z

3. (a) **Y**   (b) **Z**
(c) **X**

4. (a)

(b)

5. (a) 4   (b) 2

6. (a) E.g.

(b) E.g.

7. (a) ΔCDE
(b) ΔCEF
(c) $CDEF$

8. **A** and **D**, SSS

9. **A** and **C**, SAS

CHAPTER   **23**

Exercise 23.1   **Page 259**

1. (b) (i) Isosceles trapezium
(ii) Parallelogram
(iii) Rhombus (iv) Kite (v) Square

2. M (1, 4)   **4.** C (5, 4)   **6.** A (1, 3)

3. S (3, 1)   **5.** Y (6, 4)   **7.** L (2, 3)

8. (3, 1), (3, 5)

9. (a) $a = 62°$ (b) $b = 54°$, $c = 36°$
(c) $d = 62°$ (d) $e = 116°$, $f = 86°$
(e) $g = 124°$ (f) $h = 75°$
(g) $i = 38°$, $j = 42°$
(h) $k = 55°$, $l = 45°$

10. (a) 25°   (b) 50°   (c) 130°

11. $\angle WXY = 72°$, $\angle XYZ = 108°$

12.

A	B	C	D	E	F	G	H	I
1	0	1	4	2	2	0	0	1
1	1	1	4	2	2	1	2	1

13. (a) 4   (b) 2   (c) 1

14. (a) 2   (b) 2   (c) 1

15. (b) Two lines of symmetry.   (c) 2

Exercise 23.2   **Page 262**

1. (a) **B** and **C**   (b) **B** and **D**

2. **A** 8 cm² **B** 12 cm² **C** 12 cm² **D** 9 cm²
E 8 cm² **F** 12 cm²

3. (a) 8 cm, 3.75 cm²   (b) 8 cm, 2.79 cm²
(c) 11.2 cm, 7.84 cm²   (d) 5.6 cm, 1.96 cm²

4. (a) 12.25 cm² (b) 3.92 cm² (c) 4.68 cm²
(d) 12.24 cm² (e) 4.35 cm² (f) 5.75 cm²

5. $14\,\text{m}^2$ **7.** $4\,\text{cm}$ **9.** $8\,\text{cm}$

6. $84\,\text{cm}^2$ **8.** $20\,\text{cm}^2$ **10.** $4\,\text{cm}$

11. $h = 5.4\,\text{cm}, l = 9\,\text{cm}$

12. (a) $a = 4\,\text{cm}$ (b) $b = 5\,\text{cm}$ (c) $c = 10\,\text{cm}$
    (d) $d = 4\,\text{cm}$ (e) $e = 3\,\text{cm}$ (f) $f = 11\,\text{cm}$
    (g) $g = 8\,\text{cm}$ (h) $h = 10\,\text{cm}$ (i) $i = 8\,\text{cm}$
    (j) $j = 2\,\text{cm}$

Review Exercise 23   Page 265

1. (a) 2   (b) **A**   (c) 2   **2.** $S(-2, 0)$

3. $a = 30°$, $b = 60°$, $c = 42°$, $d = 78°$

4. $a = 35°$. Sum of angles is $360°$.

5. (a) 1   (b) (i) $a = 110°$, $b = 100°$
            (ii) $c = 95°$

6. (a) $a = 115°$, $b = 44°$

7. $1\,\text{cm}$ by $28\,\text{cm}$, $2\,\text{cm}$ by $14\,\text{cm}$, $4\,\text{cm}$ by $7\,\text{cm}$

8. $64\,\text{cm}^2$ **10.** $29.4\,\text{cm}$

9. $25\,\text{cm}^2$ **11.** $20\,\text{cm}$ **12.** $7.2\,\text{cm}$

CHAPTER 24

Exercise 24.1   Page 267

1. (a) $a = 63°$ (b) $b = 55°$, $c = 62°$
    (c) $d = 95°$, $e = 76°$

2. (a) $a = 60°$ (b) $b = 103°$
    (c) $c = 100°$ (d) $d = 128°$

3. (a) $a = 120°$ (b) $b = 62°$
    (c) $c = 76°$ (d) $d = 120°$, $e = 50°$

4. (a) $540°$ (b) $900°$
    (c) $1080°$ (d) $1260°$

5. (a) $d = 60°$ (b) $e = 120°$
    (c) $f = 130°$

Exercise 24.2   Page 269

1. (a) (i) $120°$ (ii) $90°$
      (iii) $60°$ (iv) $45°$
    (b) (i) $60°$ (ii) $90°$
      (iii) $120°$ (iv) $135°$

2. 20   **3.** (a) 40 (b) 15 (c) 9 (d) 6

4. 8   **5.** (a) 5 (b) 20 (c) 40 (d) 4

6. (a) $72°$ (b) $108°$ (c) $540°$

7. (a) $a = 90°$, $b = 60°$, $c = 210°$
    (b) $d = 90°$, $e = 120°$, $f = 150°$
    (c) $g = 90°$, $h = 135°$, $i = 135°$
    (d) $j = 105°$ (e) $k = 162°$
    (f) $l = 192°$ (g) $m = 132°$
    (h) $n = 96°$

8. (a) $a = 60°$ (b) $b = 135°$, $c = 45°$
    (c) $d = 36°$, $e = 72°$

9. (a) $a = 720°$ (b) $1080°$

10. $y = 180 - \dfrac{360}{x}$

11. (a) $150°$ (b) $210°$ (c) $240°$
    (d) $210°$ (e) $330°$

12. (a) 5, 5   (b) 6, 6

Exercise 24.3   Page 270

4. At any vertex, sum of angles cannot equal $360°$.

Review Exercise 24   Page 272

1. (a) 6
    (b) (i) $\angle AOB = 60°$
       (ii) Equilateral triangle

2. (a) (i) $x = 72°$ (ii) $y = 54°$
    (b) E.g.

    (c) At any vertex, sum of angles cannot
       equal $360°$.

3. (a) $q = 12°$ (b) 30 sides

5. $\angle AED = 108°$ (int. $\angle$ of a pentagon)
    $\angle CAE = 108° - 36° = 72°$
    $\angle CAE + \angle AED = 180°$ (allied angles)
    So AC is parallel to ED.

6. $a = 120°$, $b = 135°$

7 $x = 130°$

8. (a) Equilateral. Three sides equal.
    (b) $x = 40°$

9. (a) $p = 45°$ (b) $q = 135°$

10. (a) Hexagon   (b) $x = 60°$
    (c) $720°$

11. (a) Kite   (b) Pentagon
    (c) $\angle AED = 54°$ (d) $\angle AEI = 36°$

CHAPTER 25

Exercise 25.1   Page 276

1. (a) $a = 90°$, $b = 50°$ (b) $c = 45°$
    (c) $d = 40°$, $e = 54°$ (d) $f = 20°$

2. (a) $a = 77°$ (b) $b = 72°$
    (c) $c = 38°$ (d) $d = 40°$
    (e) $e = 25°$ (f) $f = 65°$, $g = 65°$
    (g) $h = 130°$, $i = 65°$
    (h) $j = 94°$, $k = 43°$

3. (a) $k = 106°$, $l = 62°$
   (b) $m = 70°$, $n = 140°$
   (c) $p = 108°$, $q = 105°$
   (d) $r = 117°$, $s = 84°$
   (e) $t = 292°$, $u = 56°$
   (f) $v = 140°$
   (g) $w = 110°$, $x = 75°$
   (h) $y = 130°$, $z = 82°$

4. $47°$ **5.** $\angle BCD = 70°$, $\angle CAD = 76°$

6. $119°$ **7.** $\angle PQR = 105°$, $\angle QRS = 118°$

8. $\angle PSR = 45°$, $\angle TPQ = 95°$

9. (a) $140°$ (b) $70°$

10. (a) $100°$ (b) $40°$ (c) $25°$

11. $25°$ **12.** $90°$

Exercise 25.2 — Page 278

1. (a) $a = 90°$, $b = 50°$
   (b) $c = 35°$, $d = 35°$
   (c) $e = 90°$, $f = 49°$, $g = 49°$
   (d) $h = 63°$
   (e) $j = 67°$
   (f) $k = 50°$
   (g) $l = 65°$, $m = 65°$
   (h) $n = 146°$

2. (a) $a = 65°$, $b = 25°$
   (b) $c = 67°$, $d = 23°$, $e = 46°$
   (c) $f = 70°$, $g = 20°$

3. (a) $84°$ (b) $42°$ (c) $84°$

4. (a) $48°$ (b) $6°$

5. (a) $100°$ (b) $40°$ (c) $25°$

6. (a) $72°$ (b) $36°$ (c) $54°$

7. $p = 42°$, $q = 55°$, $r = 13°$, $s = 55°$

Review Exercise 25 — Page 280

1. (a) $a = 59°$ (b) $b = 45°$
   (c) $c = 51°$ (d) $d = 23°$

2. $x = 37°$, $y = 90°$, $z = 53°$

3. $x = 60°$

4. $\angle TBO = 90°$ (tangent perpendicular to radius)
   $\angle TBA = 55°$ (complementary $\angle$'s)
   ΔABT is isosceles
   $\angle ABT = 180 - (55 + 55) = 70°$

5. $x = 18°$

6. $\angle PQS = 45°$, $\angle QRP = 65°$
   $\angle QSP = 65°$, $\angle QOP = 130°$

7. $x = 50°$, $y = 60°$, $z = 30°$

8. $x = 92°$, $y = 46°$, $z = 17°$

Exercise 26.1 — Page 283

1. (a) $12\,cm$ (b) $24\,cm$ (c) $39\,cm$

2. (a) $15\,cm$ (b) $30\,cm$ (c) $38.4\,cm$

3. (a) $37.7\,cm$ (b) $22.0\,cm$ (c) $47.1\,cm$

4. (a) $28.3\,cm$ (b) $35.2\,cm$ (c) $100.5\,cm$

5. $28\,cm$ **9.** $57.5\,m$

6. $75.4\,cm$ **10.** $5.03\,m$ **13.** $30\,mm$

7. $81.7\,cm$ **11.** $31.4\,m$ **14.** $60\,cm$

8. $40.8\,cm$ **12.** $3.8\,cm$ **15.** $67\,m$

Exercise 26.2 — Page 285

1. (a) $75\,cm^2$ (b) $147\,cm^2$ (c) $243\,cm^2$

2. (a) $27\,cm^2$ (b) $75\,cm^2$ (c) $192\,cm^2$

3. (a) $50\,cm^2$ (b) $133\,cm^2$ (c) $452\,cm^2$

4. (a) $32.2\,cm^2$ (b) $45.4\,cm^2$ (c) $531\,cm^2$

5. (a) $0.503\,m^2$ (b) $105\,000\,mm^2$

6. $22.0\,cm^2$

7. $3421\,cm^2$ **9.** $0.79\,m^2$ **11.** $7.14\,m$

8. $491\,cm^2$ **10.** $4.0\,cm$ **12.** $1.3\,cm$

Exercise 26.3 — Page 287

1. (a) $26\,cm$ (b) $55.4\,cm^2$

2. (a) (i) $15.4\,cm$ (ii) $18.5\,cm$
       (iii) $14.3\,cm$ (iv) $20.7\,cm$
   (b) (i) $14.1\,cm^2$ (ii) $20.4\,cm^2$
       (iii) $12.6\,cm^2$ (iv) $26.4\,cm^2$

3. $21.5\,cm^2$ **4.** (a) $27\,m$ (b) $56.7\,m^2$

5. Circle: $50.3\,cm^2$ Semi-circle: $47.5\,cm^2$
   The circle is bigger.

6. (a) $225\,\pi\,cm^2$ (b) $30\,\pi\,cm$

7. (a) $207\,cm$ (b) 4

8. (a) $56.5\,cm$ (b) $11.3\,m$

9. (a) $37.7\,m$ (b) 17

10. $13.3\,cm$ **13.** $326\,cm^2$ **16.** $24\,\pi\,cm$

11. $18.2\,cm^2$ **14.** $40.1\,cm$ **17.** $8\,cm$

12. $38.6\,cm$ **15.** $49\,\pi\,cm^2$ **18.** $65\,\pi\,cm^2$

Exercise 26.4 — Page 290

1. (a) $134\,m^2$ (b) $588\,cm^2$ (c) $396\,km^2$

2. (a) $360\,cm^2$ (b) $1104\,cm^2$ (c) $480\,cm^2$

3. (a) 129 cm²   (b) 41.1 cm²   (c) 116 m²

4. (a) 22.7 cm²   (b) 17.6 cm²   (c) 23.9 cm²

5. 54.9 cm²

6. 58 cm²

7. (a) 0.383 m²   (b) 2.63 m

8. 13.7 cm², 25.1 cm

9. A   14.1 cm²   B   25.1 cm²
    C   39.3 cm²   A + B = C

Review Exercise 26   Page 292

1. (a) 78.5 cm²   (b) 25.1 cm

2. (a) 283 m   (b) 6360 m²

3. (a) 188.5 m   (b) 530

4. 17 m²   **6.** 372 m²

5. 1500 cm²   **7.** 218 cm²

8. (a) 14π cm
     Perimeter is equivalent to the
     circumference of a circle with
     diameter 14 cm.
    (b) 35π cm²

CHAPTER 27

Exercise 27.2   Page 296

5. Perpendicular bisectors pass through the
    centre of the circle.

7.   **8.**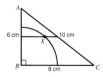

9.   **12.**
                             (d) Yes

Review Exercise 27   Page 301

1.   **2.**

X•   A ——— B

              •Y

---

3.   **8.**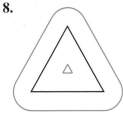

4. (b) $BE = 2$ cm

5. (b) 3.5 cm

6.   **9.**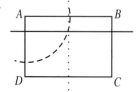

7. 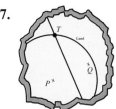   (c) 380 m

CHAPTER 28

Exercise 28.1   Page 304

5. (a) $(2, -1)$ (b) $(-2, 1)$ (c) $(0, 1)$
    (d) $(2, -3)$ (e) $(1, 2)$

6. (a) $(3, -4)$ (b) $(-3, 4)$ (c) $(5, 4)$
    (d) $(-5, 4)$ (e) $(4, 3)$

Exercise 28.2   Page 306

4. (a) $(4, -3)$ (b) $(-4, 3)$ (c) $(-3, -4)$
    (d) $(6, 1)$ (e) $(0, 1)$ (f) $(3, -2)$

Exercise 28.3   Page 308

3. (a) $(5, 5)$ (b) $(1, 6)$ (c) $(4, 1)$
    (d) $(1, 1)$

4. $T (7, 2)$

5. (a) $\begin{pmatrix} 2 \\ 1 \end{pmatrix}$ (b) $\begin{pmatrix} 1 \\ -2 \end{pmatrix}$

    (c) $\begin{pmatrix} -3 \\ 1 \end{pmatrix}$ (d) $\begin{pmatrix} -3 \\ -2 \end{pmatrix}$

6. (b) $\begin{pmatrix} -3 \\ -2 \end{pmatrix}$

7. (a) $(2, 3)$ (b) $\begin{pmatrix} 1 \\ -1 \end{pmatrix}$

Exercise 28.4   Page 310

2. (a) $(6, 8)$ (b) $(9, 12)$ (c) $(6, 6)$
    (d) $(3, 10)$ (e) $(5, 5)$ (f) $(5, 4)$

3. (a) scale factor 3, centre $(0, 0)$
    (b) scale factor 3, centre $(5, 0)$
    (c) scale factor 2.5, centre $(0, 5)$

Exercise 28.5 — Page 311

2. (a) scale factor $\frac{1}{3}$, centre (5, 7)

   (b) scale factor $\frac{1}{3}$, centre (1, 7)

   (c) scale factor $\frac{2}{5}$, centre (5, 5)

   (d) scale factor $\frac{1}{2}$, centre (5, −2)

   (e) scale factor $\frac{1}{3}$, centre (0, 7)

Exercise 28.6 — Page 313

1. L_2: reflection in x axis
   L_3: rotation, 90° anticlockwise, about (0, 0)
   L_4: translation, 3 units right and 2 units up
   L_5: rotation, 180°, about (0, 0)
   L_6: reflection in $x = 7$

2. (a) translation $\begin{pmatrix} -7 \\ -4 \end{pmatrix}$

   (b) reflection in $y = -x$

   (c) rotation, 90° anticlockwise, about (1, 0)

3. (a) reflection in $x = -1$

   (b) rotation, 90° clockwise, about (1, −2)

   (c) translation $\begin{pmatrix} 5 \\ 1 \end{pmatrix}$

4. enlargement, scale factor 2, centre (1, 2)

5. enlargement, scale factor $\frac{1}{2}$, centre (0, 0)

Exercise 28.7 — Page 315

1. (c) translation $\begin{pmatrix} 8 \\ 0 \end{pmatrix}$

2. (c) rotation, 90° anticlockwise, about (5, 5)

3. (d) rotation, 90° anticlockwise, about (0, 0)

4. (c) rotation, 180°, about (1, −1)

5. (c) translation $\begin{pmatrix} -4 \\ 3 \end{pmatrix}$

6. (d) translation $\begin{pmatrix} 6 \\ 0 \end{pmatrix}$

Review Exercise 28 — Page 317

1.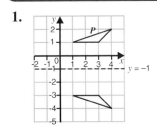

2.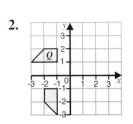

3.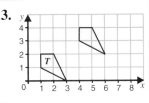

5.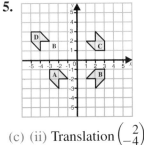

   (c) (ii) Translation $\begin{pmatrix} 2 \\ -4 \end{pmatrix}$

6. (a) reflection in $x = -1$

   (b) reflection in $y = -1$

   (c) translation $\begin{pmatrix} -4 \\ 1 \end{pmatrix}$ (d) translation $\begin{pmatrix} 4 \\ -1 \end{pmatrix}$

   (e) enlargement, scale factor 2, centre (0, 4)

   (f) enlargement, scale factor $\frac{1}{2}$, centre (0, 4)

7. (a) Rotation,   (b)
      180° about (0, 0)

8. Enlargement, scale factor $\frac{1}{3}$,
   centre (−5, 0)

10. (a) reflection in $y = x$

    (b) (i) enlargement, scale factor $\frac{1}{3}$,
           centre (−3, −4)

11.   (d) rotation,
                                90° anticlockwise,
                                about (1, 3)

CHAPTER 29

Exercise 29.1 — Page 320

2. (a) 4   (b) 2 faces overlap

5. (a) 8   (b) 5   (c) 12   (d) 120 cm

Exercise 29.2 — Page 321

1. (a)   (b)   (c)

2. (a)

   (b)

511

(c)

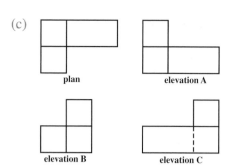

plan elevation A

elevation B elevation C

3.

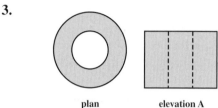

plan elevation A

4. (a)

(b)

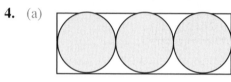

5. (a) (b)

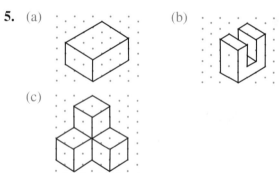

(c)

Exercise 29.3   Page 323

1. (b) 52 cm²   (c) 52 cm²

2. (a) (i) 8   (ii) 27
       (iii) 64   (iv) 125
    (b) (i) 24 cm²   (ii) 54 cm²
       (iii) 96 cm²   (iv) 150 cm²

3. (a) 27 cm³,   54 cm²
    (b) 30 cm³,   62 cm²
    (c) 140 cm³,   166 cm²

4. (a) 1 cm × 4 cm × 6 cm,
       1 cm × 2 cm × 12 cm,
       1 cm × 3 cm × 8 cm,
       2 cm × 2 cm × 6 cm,
       2 cm × 3 cm × 4 cm
       Smallest SA: 2 × 3 × 4, 52 cm²
    (b) 9
       Largest SA: 1 × 1 × 36, 146 cm²

5. (a) 4 cm³,   18 cm²   (b) 5 cm³,   20 cm²
    (c) 8 cm³,   28 cm²   (d) 7 cm³,   24 cm²
    (e) 14 cm³,   42 cm²   (f) 10 cm³,   32 cm²

6. (a) 150 cm³,   190 cm²
    (b) 51.8 cm³,   89.3 cm²
    (c) 19 440 cm³,   4644 cm²
    (d) 96.8 cm³,   132 cm²
    (e) 916 cm³,   612 cm²

7. 10 cm   **8.** 4.5 cm   **9.** 1155 cm²   **10.** 180 cm³

Exercise 29.4   Page 325

1. (a) 40 cm³   (b) 140 cm³   (c) 96 cm³

2. (a) 11 cm²,   15.4 cm³
    (b) 6 cm²,   15 cm³
    (c) 7.2 cm²,   21.6 cm³

3. (a) 5.6 cm²,   11.2 cm³
    (b) 314 cm²,   6280 cm³
    (c) 3.14 cm²,   15.7 cm³

4. (a) 10 cm³   (b) 56 cm³   (c) 330 cm³
    (d) 113 cm³   (e) 393 cm³   (f) 120 cm³
    (g) 848 cm³   (h) 18 cm³

5. P   **7.** 2.7 cm

6. 11.5 cm   **8.** 12.0 cm   **9.** 4.5 cm

Exercise 29.5   Page 327

1. (a) 339 cm²   (b) 90.9 cm²

3. (a) 1260 cm²   (b) 6280 cm²   (c) 62 800 cm³

4. 754 cm³   **5.** 274 cm²

6. (a) 14 100 cm²   (b) 18 800 cm²

Review Exercise 29   Page 330

1. (a) 12 cm³
    (b) 40 cm²

2. (a) 30 cm³
    (b)

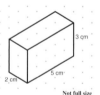

Not full size

3. (a) C
    (b) 54

4.

Not full size

5.

6. (a) 75 cm²
    (b) 225 cm³

7. (a) Cube.
       Cuboid: 120 cm³,
       cube: 125 cm³.
    (b) Cube.
       Cuboid: 148 cm²,
       cube: 150 cm².

8. 78.3 cm³

9. 3375 cm³

10. Yes. A holds 300 cm³, B holds 308.7 cm³

11. Cuboid: 1048.6 cm³, Cylinder: 823.5 cm³

12. 392 cm²   **13.** (a) 113.1 cm² (b) 17.7 cm

14. 14.5 cm

CHAPTER 30

Exercise 30.1 — Page 333

2. (a) Corresponding lengths not in same ratio.
   (b) **P** and **R**

3. (a) Two circles   (d) Two squares

4. (a) Scale factor = $\frac{3}{2}$ = 1.5
   (b) $x = 1.8$ cm   (c) $a = 120°$

5. (a) $x = 1.5$ cm, $y = 2.4$ cm, $a = 70°$
   (b) $x = 5$ cm, $y = 1.5$ cm, $a = 53°$
   (c) $x = 30$ cm, $y = 20.8$ cm, $z = 10$ cm

6. 15 cm   **7.** 3 cm   **8.** 5 cm   **9.** $x = 16$, $y = 48$

Exercise 30.2 — Page 335

1. (a) $x = 10$ cm, $y = 27$ cm
   (b) $x = 6$ cm, $y = 10$ cm
   (c) $x = 12$ cm, $y = 12$ cm
   (d) $x = 12$ cm, $y = 5$ cm

2. $AB = 8$ cm, $AE = 5$ cm

3. (a) $AB = 2.96$ cm, $QR = 3.25$ cm
   (b) $XZ = 14.4$ m, $BC = 6.25$ m
   (c) $EG = 1.6$ cm, $MN = 4.0$ cm
   (d) $AC = 4.0$ m, $XZ = 2.0$ m

4. (a) $PR = 10$ cm
   (b) $QR = 5$ cm, $PQ = 7.5$ cm,
       $QS = 4.5$ cm

Exercise 30.3 — Page 337

1. (a) $AC = 2.4$ cm, $AP = 2.2$ cm
   (b) $AC = 4.5$ cm, $BP = 1$ cm
   (c) $BC = 4.2$ cm, $BP = 1.6$ cm
   (d) $AP = 2.5$ cm, $BC = 7$ cm
   (e) $AQ = 4\frac{2}{3}$ cm, $BQ = 16\frac{2}{3}$ cm

2. (a) $x = 58°$ (b) $x = 56°$

3. (a) (i) 61°   (ii) 29°
   (b) (i) 13 cm, 5.2 cm   (ii) 36 cm, 27 cm
       same

4. (b) $AB = 1.8$ cm   (c) 12.5 cm

Review Exercise 30 — Page 339

1. (a) 20 cm²   (b) 12 cm by 15 cm   (c) 9

2. $\angle PQX = 54°$, $\angle AXB = 36°$
   Both triangles have same angles. $PQ = 2AB$
   Triangles are similar.

3. (a) $\angle BAC = \angle CED$ (alt. $\angle$s)
       $\angle ABC = \angle CDE$ (alt. $\angle$s)
       $\angle ABC = \angle DCE$ (vert. opp. $\angle$s)
       Δs ABC and EDC are similar,
       equal angles.
   (b) $AC = 3.75$ m

4. (a) $AB = 3$ cm   (b) $QR = 3.6$ cm

5. (a) 2.4 cm   (b) 9 cm

6. (a) (i) 101°
       (ii) $\angle DEC = \angle ABC$ (corres. $\angle$s)
           $\angle DEC = 180° - 47° - 32° = 101°$
   (b) $EC = 1.8$ m   (c) $AB = 2$ m

7. (a) $AB = 24$ cm   (b) $AE = 40.5$ cm

CHAPTER 31

Exercise 31.1 — Page 341

1. (a) 10 cm   (b) 25 cm   (c) 26 cm

2. (a) 7.8 cm   (b) 12.8 cm   (c) 10.3 cm

3. (a) $\sqrt{52}$ cm   (b) $\sqrt{20}$ cm

4. (a) 5 (b) 9.22 (c) 13 (d) 8.06 (e) 7.21

5. (a) $R(9, 7)$ (b) $X(2, 3)$ (c) $Y(4, 2)$ (d) 2.24

Exercise 31.2 — Page 342

1. (a) 8 cm   (b) 6 cm   (c) 2 cm

2. (a) 6.9 cm   (b) 10.9 cm   (c) 9.5 cm

3. 339 m   **4.** 36 cm²   **5.** 3.6 cm

Exercise 31.3 — Page 344

1. (a) 2.9 cm (b) 5.7 cm (c) 2.1 cm (d) 2.0 cm

2. 17 cm   **5.** 10.6 cm   **8.** 74.3 cm

3. 10 cm   **6.** 15 cm   **9.** 13 cm

4. 8.5 cm   **7.** 6.9 cm   **10.** 24 cm

11. (a) 11.4 cm   (b) 43.5 cm²

Review Exercise 31 — Page 345

1. 10 km   **4.** 3.6 cm

2. $\sqrt{20}$ cm   **5.** 28.3 cm

3. 36 cm   **6.** 361 m   **7.** $\sqrt{18}$ cm

8. $25² = 24² + 7²$ ΔPQR is right-angled at R.

9. 7.2   **10.** 14.1 km   **11.** 5.7 cm

CHAPTER 32

Exercise 32.1 — Page 348

1. (a) $h = 2.27$ m   (b) $h = 4.02$ m
   (c) $h = 8.02$ m

2. (a) $x = 1.50$ cm   (b) $x = 2.99$ cm
    (c) $x = 5.78$ cm

3. (a) $BC = 3.39$ m   (b) $AC = 11.4$ m
    (c) $BC = 4.74$ cm
    (d) $\angle ABC = 55°$, $AC = 6.96$ cm

Exercise 32.2   Page 349

1. (a) $a = 62.1°$ (b) $a = 25.0°$ (c) $a = 50.9°$
2. (a) $x = 52.3°$ (b) $x = 60.5°$ (c) $x = 61.4°$
3. (a) $\angle QPR = 23.6°$ (b) $\angle PRQ = 64.7°$
    (c) $\angle QPR = 21.8°$
    (d) $\angle QRP = 24.0°$, $\angle QPR = 66.0°$

Exercise 32.3   Page 350

1. (a) $l = 7.00$ m   (b) $l = 7.49$ m
    (c) $l = 4.93$ m
2. (a) $x = 6.49$ cm   (b) $x = 5.31$ cm
    (c) $x = 10.61$ cm
3. (a) $AB = 7.62$ m   (b) $AB = 17.5$ cm
    (c) $AB = 66.9$ cm
    (d) $\angle ABC = 17.2°$, $AB = 25.7$ m

Exercise 32.4   Page 352

1.

	$\sin p$	$\cos p$	$\tan p$
(a)	$\frac{5}{13}$	$\frac{12}{13}$	$\frac{5}{12}$
(b)	$\frac{7}{25}$	$\frac{24}{25}$	$\frac{7}{24}$
(c)	$\frac{4}{5}$	$\frac{3}{5}$	$\frac{4}{3}$

2. (a) $p = 40.9°$ (b) $p = 38.0°$
    (c) $p = 38.8°$ (d) $p = 53.3°$
    (e) $p = 39.7°$ (f) $p = 35.5°$
3. (a) $a = 5.77$ cm   (b) $a = 6.47$ cm
    (c) $a = 4.18$ cm   (d) $a = 3.78$ cm
    (e) $a = 4.72$ cm   (f) $a = 4.04$ cm
4. 4.33 cm   **5.** 72.5°, 72.5°, 34.9°
6. (a) 5.96 cm   (b) 1.71 cm
7. (a) 2.76 cm   (b) 19.8°
8. 13.06 cm   **9.** 4.52 cm   **10.** 9.45 cm

Exercise 32.5   Page 355

1. 21.4 m **2.** 40.1 m **3.** (a) 135 m (b) 53.5°
4. 22.2 m   **5.** 31.0°   **6.** 51.3°
7. 959 m   **8.** 40.5 m

Exercise 32.6   Page 356

1. (a) 152 km   (b) 199 km   **2.** 22.2 km
3. 145°   **4.** 41.9 km   **5.** 164°
6. 6.40 km   **7.** 174 km   **8.** 283°

Review Exercise 32   Page 357

1. 3.25 m   **4.** 5.2°
2. 10.2 m   **5.** 116 cm
3. 7.66 m   **6.** 213°   **7.** 8.5 m
8. (a) $\angle BDC = 26.6°$ (b) $AB = 8.4$ cm
9. $AB : AC : BC$ is $5 : 4 : 3$ (Pythagoras)
    $\text{Cos } BAC = \frac{AC}{AB} = \frac{4}{5} = 0.8$
10. (a) (i) $\frac{5}{12}$ (ii) $\frac{5}{13}$
    (b) $QR = 6.5$ cm, $PR = 2.5$ cm
11. (a) $x = 60$ (b) $\angle QSP = 27°$
12. East 89.2 km, North 20.3 km.
    257°

CHAPTER 33

Exercise 33.1   Page 361

1. (a) 86 mm   (b) 8 mm   (c) 0.8 mm
2. (a) 9 cm   (b) 21 cm   (c) 0.2 cm
3. (a) 2 m   (b) 45.5 m   (c) 0.66 m
4. (a) 600 cm   (b) 90 cm   (c) 7 cm
5. (a) 4 km   (b) 35 km   (c) 0.455 km
6. (a) 6000 m   (b) 650 000 m (c) 350 m
7. (a) 2000 g   (b) 7500 g   (c) 600 g
8. (a) 3 kg   (b) 32 kg   (c) 0.22 kg
9. (a) 320 000 ml = 320*l*
    (b) 0.32t = 320 kg = 320 000 g
    (c) 3200 g = 3.2 kg = 0.0032t
    (d) 320 mm = 32 cm = 0.32 m
    (e) 32 000 cm = 320 m = 0.32 km
    (f) 3.2 km = 3200 m = 320 000 cm
10. (a) 6000 kg (b) 0.8 kg   (c) 650 kg
11. (a) 8 m   (b) 0.086 m   (c) 40 m
12. (a) 2000 ml (b) 850 ml   (c) 30 ml
13. 2000 m and 2 km   **15.** 0.5 km
14. 8 kg and 8000 g   **16.** 0.3 t
17. (a) 3.123 m   (b) 450 cm   (c) 0.4 *l*
18. 1.98 *l* **19.** 20 **20.** 50 g **21.** 60 **22.** 50 ml

Exercise 33.2   Page 363

1. 250 g   **2.** 30 cm   **3.** 200 ml
5. 6.4 m, nearest 0.1 m
6. 175 ml, nearest 5 ml

7. (a) 12 m, nearest metre
5.9 m, nearest 100 cm
5 l, nearest litre
500 m², nearest 50 m²
(b) 1200 cm, nearest 100 cm
5900 mm, nearest 100 mm
5000 ml, nearest 1000 ml
500 000 000 mm², nearest 50 000 000 mm²

Exercise 33.3 — Page 364

1. (a) 5 cm (b) 61 cm
2. (a) 78 inches (b) 8 inches
3. (a) 8 km (b) 72 km
4. (a) 5 miles (b) 25 miles
5. (a) 55 pounds (b) 2200 pounds
6. (a) 45 kg (b) 43 kg
7. (a) 3 litres (b) 11 litres
8. (a) 33 pounds (b) 35 pints
(c) 195 inches (d) 150 mm
(e) 20 inches
9. 22 pounds **10.** 170 cm **11.** 66.4 kg
12. (a) 610 m (b) 4.8 km
(c) 5 feet (d) 2.75 pounds
13. 1500 cm² **14.** No. 10 kg is about 22 pounds.
15. No. 6 miles is about 9.6 km.
16. (a) 48 km/hour (b) 80 km/hour
(c) 108 km/hour
17. (a) 37.5 miles per hour
(b) 90 miles per hour
18. 27 metres per second
19. (a) 12.8 km/litre (b) 30 miles per gallon
20. 3.35 kg, nearest 10 g **21.** 6.8 m³, 1 d.p.

Exercise 33.4 — Page 366

1. (a) continuous (b) discrete
(c) discrete (d) continuous
(e) discrete (f) continuous
2. (a) exact (b) 4.5 mins $\leqslant t <$ 5.5 mins
(c) exact (d) 62.5 kg $\leqslant w <$ 63.5 kg
(e) 152.5 cm $\leqslant$ J $<$ 153.5 cm
3. (a) 12.5 s $\leqslant t <$ 13.5 s
(b) 82.55 s $\leqslant t <$ 82.65 s
4. (a) nearest 0.01 m (centimetre)
(b) 1.525 m $\leqslant h <$ 1.535 m
5. (a) 61.5 kg (b) 2.25 m (c) 12.625 s
6. (a) nearest 10 m (b) nearest 50 m
(c) nearest 100 m

Exercise 33.5 — Page 368

1. (a) area (b) length
(c) length (d) length
(e) volume (f) area
(g) volume (h) area
2. (a) perimeter (b) area
(c) volume (d) none
(e) area (f) perimeter
(g) perimeter (h) none
(i) volume (j) volume
(k) none (l) area
3. (a) (i) $2\pi(x + y)$
(ii) $\pi(x^2 + y^2)$, πxy
5. $\frac{1}{2}pqs$, volume
$2\left(p + q + r + \frac{3s}{2}\right)$, edge length
$s(p + q + r) + pq$, surface area
6. (a) correct (b) correct (c) correct
(d) wrong (e) correct (f) wrong
7. (a), (b), (c), (e)

Review Exercise 33 — Page 369

1. 200 **2.** 8 full glasses
3. (a) 2650 m (b) 175 miles
4. Taller: Tim by about 10 cm,
heavier: Sam by about 1 kg
5. (a) 10 000 m (6 miles = 9600 m)
(b) 10 mm $\left(\frac{3}{8}\text{ inch} = 9.5\text{ mm}\right)$
(c) 10 litres (2 gallons = 9.14 l)
(d) 200 lb (100 kg = 220 lb)
6. £1.11
7. (a) 250 000 cm² (b) 270 square feet
8. (a) 30 mph (b) 13.3 m/s
9. Both same speed
10. (a) 120 m² (b) 1.3 litres
11. nearest 1 million square kilometres
12. (a) continuous (b) discrete
13. (a) 9.5 cm (b) 10.4$\dot{9}$ cm
14. 135 tonnes
15. Any volume from 645 ml up to, but not
including, 650 ml.
16. (a) 11.2r^2
(b) Surface area has dimension 2.
17. Volume: $\pi r^2 h$, lbh
18. (a) (i) **D** (ii) **C**
(b) $n = 2$

　　　　Page 371

1. $a = 153°$,
　　$b = 52°$,
　　$c = 65°$

2. (a) (i) 4　(ii) 2
　　(b)
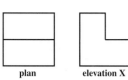

3. 85 miles

4.
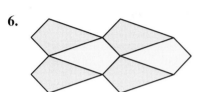
plan　　elevation X

5. 8 cm

6.
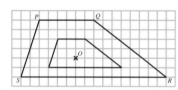

7. (b) 9.8 cm²

8. (a) Reflection in the y axis
　　(b) Rotation, 90° clockwise, about (0, 0)

9. (a) **P** and **S**　(b) (i) 32 cm　(ii) 44 cm²

10. (a) 190.5 cm　(b) $77.5 \text{ kg} \leqslant w < 78.5 \text{ kg}$

11. (a) $x = 50°$, $f = 50°$, $g = 130°$
　　(b) $h = 50°$

12. (a) 314 cm　(b) 7854 cm²

13. (a) 121°　(b) 301°

14. (b) 116 m, 276°

15.
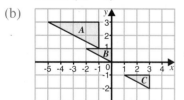

16. (a) 377 cm³　(b) 6.0 cm

17. (a) Enlargement, scale factor $\frac{1}{2}$,
　　centre (1, −1)
　　(b)
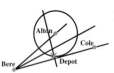

18. $a = 120°$, $b = 135°$, $c = 150°$

19.
　　Alton　Cole
　　Bere　Depot

20. (a) 24 cm
　　(b) 1680 cm²
　　(c) 336 000 cm³

21. (a) 1 : 25 000　(b) 24.4 km　(c) 325°

22. $a = 55°$, ΔPQX is isosceles
　　$b = 35°$, $\angle OQX = 90°$
　　$c = 32°$, angle in a semicircle = 90°

23. 61.4 cm²

24. (a) $DE = 9.6$ cm
　　(b) $DB = 3$ cm

25. Formula given has dimension 2.
　　Volume should have dimension 3.

CHAPTER 34

Exercise 34.1　　**Page 375**

1. qualitative

2. quantitative, continuous

3. quantitative, discrete

4. qualitative

5. quantitative, discrete

6. quantitative, continuous

7. quantitative, discrete

8. qualitative

9. quantitative, discrete

10. quantitative, continuous

Exercise 34.2　　**Page 377**

1. (a)

Colour of car	Colour of car
Black	1
Blue	9
Green	4
Grey	2
Red	11
Silver	4
White	9
Total	40

　　(b) red

2. (a)

Day	Frequency
Monday	8
Tuesday	7
Wednesday	6
Thursday	7
Friday	7
Saturday	3
Sunday	5
Total	43

　　(b) 43　(c) Monday

3. (a)

Age	Tally	Frequency
0 - 9	||||	4
10 - 19	⪫⪫⪫ ||	7
20 - 29	⪫⪫⪫ ⪫⪫⪫ |	11
30 - 39	⪫⪫⪫ ⪫⪫⪫	10
40 - 49	||||	4
50 - 59	||||	4

(b) 10 years   (c) 10   (d) 11   (e) 8

4. (a)

Height h cm	Frequency
$145 \leqslant h < 150$	2
$150 \leqslant h < 155$	2
$155 \leqslant h < 160$	7
$160 \leqslant h < 165$	9
$165 \leqslant h < 170$	6
$170 \leqslant h < 175$	8
$175 \leqslant h < 180$	2
Total	36

(b) 5 cm   (c) 7   (d) 11   (e) 32

Exercise 34.3   Page 379

1. (a) Francis   (b) Louisa   (c) Alistair

2. (a) (i)

Make	Frequency
Ford	4
Nissan	3
Vauxhall	5
Total	12

Colour	Frequency
Blue	2
Green	1
Grey	2
Red	3
White	4
Total	12

Registration letter	Frequency
P	2
R	3
S	2
T	4
X	1
Total	12

(ii)

Mileage (m)	Frequency
$0 \leqslant m < 5000$	0
$5000 \leqslant m < 10\,000$	2
$10\,000 \leqslant m < 15\,000$	0
$15\,000 \leqslant m < 20\,000$	2
$20\,000 \leqslant m < 25\,000$	1
$25\,000 \leqslant m < 30\,000$	2
$30\,000 \leqslant m < 35\,000$	4
$35\,000 \leqslant m < 40\,000$	1
Total	12

(b) (i) Vauxhall   (ii) 2   (iii) 5   (iv) 4

Exercise 34.4   Page 380

1. (a) Too personal   (b) Leading
    (c) (i) Groups overlap
        (ii) ☐ less than 5   ☐ 5 to 9
            ☐ 10 or more
2. (a) Too open   (b) Too open   (c) Leading
3. (a) Too personal   (b) Too open
    (c) Too open   (d) Too open

Exercise 34.5   Page 382

1. Small sample.   One data collection time.
2. Women only.   One location.
    One data collection time.
3. Advantage: confidential, wider circulation, etc
    Disadvantage: slow, non-response, etc
8. (a) 8   (b) 16   (c) 20   (d) 40   (e) 50%
9. (a) 5   (b) 8   (c) 3   (d) 10
10. (a) 14   (b) 20   (c) 70%   (d) 80%
    (e) Disprove. 80% is greater than 70%.
11. Disprove,   Boys $\frac{3}{21} = \frac{1}{7}$,   Girls $\frac{2}{14} = \frac{1}{7}$,
                same proportion
12. (a) 20   (b) 27
    (c) Prove, Maths ABC = 27,
        English ABC = 32, English > Maths
14. (a) (i) 10   (ii) No. Less 8, More 12
    (b) (i) 37   (ii) No. Girls 37, Boys 37, same
15. Fewer females than males, no-one under 18.

Review Exercise 34   Page 385

1. For example:

Type of vehicle	Tally	Frequency
Car		
Lorry		
Bus		

2. (a)

Time (t seconds)	Frequency
$0 \leq t < 5$	3
$5 \leq t < 10$	5
$10 \leq t < 15$	8
$15 \leq t < 20$	4

(b) $10 \leq t < 15$

3. (a)

	Male	Female
Junior management	51	42
Senior management	28	32

(b) A higher proportion of female managers are in senior management, than for male managers.

4. How many hours of television do you watch each week?
Less than 20 ☐ 20 to 30 ☐ More than 30 ☐
How many days a week do you watch TV?
Every day ☐ 4 to 6 ☐ 1 to 3 ☐ 0 ☐

5. Only males asked. No-one under 11.
Mainly adults surveyed.

6. (a) Replies should be anonymous.
(b) Not specific.

7. (a) **Q** (b) **Z** (c) (i) Too open
(ii) Not enough boxes

8. How far do you travel to the superstore?
Less than 5 km ☐ 5 km to 10 km ☐
More than 10 km ☐
How often do you come to the superstore each week? 1 ☐ 2 ☐ 3 ☐ More than 3 ☐
How much, on average, do you spend per visit?
Less than £20 ☐ £20 to £30 ☐
£50 or more ☐

9. Prove. Semi-detached 75%, Detached 80%.

10. Do not support.
Women 75% Men 75% Same proportion

11. (a) 24 (b) 49

CHAPTER 35

1. (a) Saturday (b) 5 hours (c) 41 hours
(d) Sunday (e) $\frac{1}{4}$ (f) 6 hours

2. (b) £5 (c) £7 (d) 20%

3. (a) 15 (b) 1 (c) 5 (d) 20%

4. (a) 38 (b) Monday
(c)

Day of birth	S	M	T	W	T	F	S
Number of boys	1	3	4	4	1	5	1

1. (a) 7 hours (b) 5 hours (c) 3
(d) (i) 20 (ii) 20%
(e) E.g. boys have higher mode and larger range.

2. (a) 5 (b) 7 (c) 7 (d) $33\frac{1}{3}$%
(e) 35% (f) 4 (g) 5
(h) Boys have higher mode and larger range.

1.

Tree	Ash	Beech	Maple
Angle	120°	150°	90°

2.

Colour	Brown	Blue	Green	Other
Angle	160°	100°	60°	40°

3.

Ice cream	Vanilla	Strawberry	99
Angle	188°	74°	98°

4.

Takeaway	Fish & Chips	Chicken & Chips	Chinese Meal	Pizza
Angle	110°	136°	52°	62°

5.

TVChannel	BBC1	BBC2	ITV	CH4	CH5
Angle	119°	50°	115°	47°	29°

6.

Cereal	Cornflakes	Muesli	Porridge	Bran Flakes
Angle	125°	100°	60°	75°

1. (a) 12 (b) 8 (c) Hotel
2. (a) 20 (b) 15 (c) Sauze d'Oulx
3. (a) France (b) 45 (c) 55 (d) 20
4. (a) 5 (b) 2 (c) 18
5. (a) 288 (b) 174°

1.

					1	0 means 10 litres
1	0	2	6	6	7	9
2	3	3	4	5	5	6 7 9
3	1	3	5	5		
4	1	2				

2.

					3	2 means 3.2 seconds
1	5					
2	4	4	5	6	7	8 8 9
3	0	1	2	2	3	5 5 6 7
4	2	2	3			
5	6	6	8			

3.

	1	6 means 16 press-ups					

0	9
1	6 8
2	0 1 2 4 5 7 8
3	2 2 3 6 6 6
4	0 1

4.

	2 | 7 means 2.7 cm

1	8
2	0 1 4 5 6 6 7
3	1 4 5 5 6 9
4	0 2 2 5
5	4
6	0

5. (a) 12
(b) 23 pence
(c) 39 pence

Exercise 35.6 Page 396

1. (a) 9
(b) 50
(c) 17
(d) Highest mark scored by a boy.
Lowest mark scored by a girl.
Boys have a greater range of marks.

2. (a)

Adults		Children	4 | 7 means 4.7 mins
	4	7 9	
9 4	5	1 3 4 9	
7 5 4 1 0	6	2 3 4 5 5 6 8	
9 8 7 3 3 3 0	7	1 4 6 7 9	
2 2 0	8	0 2	
4 2	9		
1	10		

(b) Adults have larger range.
Fastest time recorded by child,
slowest time recorded by adult.

Review Exercise 35 Page 397

1. (b) Bed & Breakfast
(c) 50
(d) 34%

2.

Activity	Gym	Swimming	Squash	Aerobics
Angle	144°	36°	72°	108°

3. 112

4. (a) 14   (b) 72

5.

	5 | 4 means 5.4 grams

2	8
3	5 9
4	2 4 6 6 7 8 8
5	0 1 4 4 6 6 8
6	0 3 7

6. (a)

Poultry	Chicken	Turkey	Duck
Angle	210°	120°	30°

(b) 36

(c)

Poultry	Chicken	Turkey	Duck
Number sold	9	5	2

7. (a) 2 : 3   (b) 27%
(c) Boys: mode 8, range 3.
Girls: mode 10, range 6.
Boys have a lower modal mark but a
smaller range of marks than the girls.

CHAPTER 36

Exercise 36.1 Page 400

1. (a) 7   (b) 4   (c) 4
2. (a) 1   (b) 2   (c) 3
3. (a) 3   (b) 5   (c) 3.5   (d) 3.9
4. (a) 135   (b) 135   (c) 133
5. (a) 39   (b) 23   (c) 38.8
6. 86.9 kg   **7.** 4   **8.** 129 cm

Exercise 36.2 Page 402

1. (a) 5   (b) 4   (c) 5   (d) 5

2. (a)

Number of keys	2	3	4	5	6
Frequency	2	3	8	5	2

(b) 20   (c) 4   (d) 4   (e) 4.1

3. (a)

Wage (£)	15	20	25	30	35
Frequency	5	4	6	1	3

(b) £20   (c) £25   (d) 19
(e) £25   (f) £440   (g) £23.16

4. (a) 9   (b) 9   (c) 30   (d) 8.5
5. (a) 2, 2.5, 2.7   (b) 2, 2, 2.1
(c) 0, 5, 4.5

Exercise 36.3 Page 404

1. (a) £10 000 ≤ s < £15 000, £15 200
(b) 30 - 40 hours, 29.4 hours

2. 5.3 kg

3. £94 000

4. 4.3 m

5. 27.7

1. Moneymaker larger range and higher mean than Cherry.

2. (a) (i) 0.5 minutes (ii) 1.95 minutes
(b) Girls a little slower on average and more varied.

3. Jays: mean 1.9, range 5
Wasps: mean 2.4, range 3
Wasps scored more on average and had less spread.

4. Women: mean 1.6, range 6
Men: mean 1.5, range 2
Women made more visits to the cinema, though the number of visits is more spread.

5. Average: Boys 6.2, Girls 7.2
Range: Boys 4, Girls $4\frac{1}{2}$
No. Girls' average greater than boys'.
Correct about variation.

6. (a) MacQuick 20 - 29, Pizza Pit 30 - 39
(b) MacQuick - mean 26 years
(Pizza Pit 36.5 years)
(c) Exact ages not known.

7. Before: median 3, range 4
After: median 3, range 5
Would have been better to calculate the means. Before 2.2, After 3.0

1. Mode trainers. Cannot calculate others.

2. Mode 15s, median 12s, mean 22.75s
Median most sensible, not affected by 200 as is mean, mode not much use.

3. Mode 81, median 83, mean 69.8
Median most sensible, not affected by 5 & 6 as is mean, mode not much use.

4. Swimmer A.
Mean is lower (A 30.88s, B 31.38s)
Range less (A 1.7s, B 15s)
Median is higher (A 30.9s, B 30.0s)

5. Batsman B
Higher median (B 31.5, A 21)
Higher mean (B 36, A 35)

1. (a) (i) 9 minutes (ii) 9.5 minutes
(b) Trains are more variable, but less late on average.

2. (a) Range 6p, mode 31p
(b) Median 30p, mean 30.1p

3. (a) 8°C (b) 3.1°C

4. (a) 11 to 15 (b) 11 to 15
(c) 16.3

5. (a) 16.2 (b) $x = 20$

6. (a) Mean weight of Phillip's friends is greater than Elizabeth's friends.
(b) Both groups of friends have the same median height.

7. (a) No. Only 2 of the 4 cars that had one fault before servicing now have no faults.
(b) Mode.
(c) Mean.
After servicing mean = 1.2 (1 d.p.).

8. 272.5 g

1. (a) 15°C
(b) Temperature variations during each day are not known.
Line only indicates trend in midday temperatures.

2. (a) 8 (b) Jan, Feb, June
(c) No information given about when cars are sold during the month.

3. (b) (i) 154 cm (ii) 15 years 4 months

4. (a) 82 kg (b) 82 kg (c) 5 kg (d) Week 4

1. 35, 34, 35, 36, 39, 37, 40

2. 28.8, 28.6, 28.2, 28.6, 30.6, 33

3. 18, 17.5, 17, 16, 15, 14, 13, 12, 11.25 **4.** 6.6

5. 3-point moving averages are:
370, 365, 375, 390, 400, 390, 400

1. (a) (c)

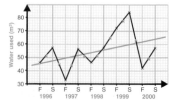

(b) 51.5, 45, 44, 50.5, 51.5, 64.5, 77.5, 62.5, 49.5
(d) There is an upward trend in the amount of water used.

2. (a) (c)

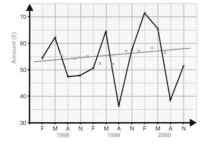

(b) £55.61, £54.55, £55.11, £52.27, £52.16, £57.39, £57.70, £58.18, £56.74

(d) There is an upward trend in the quarterly bills.

3. (a) (c)

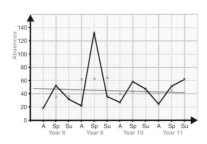

(b) 3-point moving averages are:
35, 36, 62, 63, 65, 40, 44, 43, 41, 46

(d) Trend shows steady level of absence, greatly affected by Spring figure for Year 9.

4. (a) (c) (d)

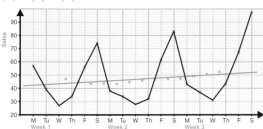

(b) 47.8, 44.7, 43.8, 44, 43.6, 44.5, 46, 46.8, 47.3, 47.8, 49.7, 50.7, 52.2

(e) The trend shows a general increase in sales.

(f) £4800

5. (a) (c) (d)

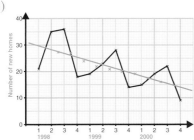

(b) 4-point moving averages are:
27.5, 27, 24, 22, 21, 20, 19, 17.5, 16.25

(e) The trend shows a general decrease in the number of new homes being built.

(f) 11

1. (a) 36   (b) 24
(c) 40

2. (a) 5   (b) 5

3. (a) Entries are: 4, 7, 9, 4
(c) 6.00 and less than 6.50

6. (a) 0   (b) 26
(c) 27   (d) 95

7.

Mark	0 - 9	10 - 19	20 - 29	30 - 39
Frequency	3	12	19	6

8. (a)

Mark	Frequency
20 and less than 30	5
30 and less than 40	8
40 and less than 50	9
50 and less than 60	6
60 and less than 70	2

(b) 40 and less than 50

10. (b) Females have smaller range in weight than males.
Males have higher modal class.

11. (c) English results have smaller range.
English modal class is higher.

12. (b) 2000 results have a larger range.
1999 results have higher modal class.

1. Axes not labelled.

2. Bars not equal width.

3. Vertical axis does not begin at zero.

4. Pass rate not given.
Advert implies you "pass" after 8 lessons.

5. 10% increase in price, disproportionate increase in diagram size.

6. Horizontal axis does not begin at zero and is not a uniform scale.

7. Vertical scale not uniform.
Size of diagrams disproportionate to increase in sales.

8. Horizontal scale not uniform.
Vertical scale not calibrated.

1. (b) £87 000
   (c) Prices of houses rise and fall, future prices unpredictable.

2. (a) (c) (d)

   (b) 5.4, 5, 4.6, 4.4, 4.6, 5, 5.2, 5.2, 5.4, 5.4, 5.2
   (e) Trend shows no change in the number of absences.

3. (a)

Height (h cm)	Frequency
$5 \leqslant h < 10$	6
$10 \leqslant h < 15$	10
$15 \leqslant h < 20$	7
$20 \leqslant h < 25$	9
$25 \leqslant h < 30$	8

   (c) 16   (d) $10 \leqslant h < 15$

4. (a) 3 but less than 4   (b) 31   (c) 190

5.

Time (seconds)	Frequency
10 and less than 20	4
20 and less than 30	6
30 and less than 40	2

6. Vertical scale does not begin at zero. Horizontal scale is not uniform.

7. (b) 34

8. (a) Girls:

Marks	Frequency
1 - 5	0
6 - 10	8
11 - 15	19
16 - 20	23
21 - 25	4

   (b) Girls have a smaller range of marks. Boys have a lower modal class.

CHAPTER **38**

Exercise **38.1** — Page 425

1. (a) 2   (b) 164 cm   (c) No
   (d) Taller girls usually have larger shoe sizes than shorter girls.

2. (a) 72
   (b) (i) English 46, French 88
       (ii) French could be her first language.

3. (a) 4   (b) 43 kg   (c) Tend to be higher

Exercise **38.2** — Page 427

1. (a) **B**   (b) **C**   (c) **D**

2. (a) Negative   (b) Positive   (c) Zero
   (d) Positive   (e) Negative

3. (b) Positive correlation
   (c) Different conditions, types of road, etc.

4. (b) Negative correlation
   (c) Different road surfaces, driving styles, etc.

Exercise **38.3** — Page 429

1. (b) Positive correlation   (d) 4.8 to 4.9 kg

2. (b) Negative correlation   (d) 38 minutes

3. (b) Negative correlation
   (d) (i) 27 to 28   (ii) 91 to 92 kg

4. (b) (i) 88 - 89   (ii) 49 - 50
   (c) (ii), as estimated value is within the range of known values.

Review Exercise **38** — Page 430

1. 1 B, 2 C, 3 A

2. (a) 6   (b) 8.2 years
   (c) Children who read more tend to have a higher reading age.

3. (a) Positive correlation.
       When the temperature is higher, more people tend to use the pool.
   (c) 1800 to 1900 people.

4. (a) (i) **B, D**   (ii) **A, C, E**   (iii) **F**
   (c) No. Points scattered, no linear correlation.

5. (b) Negative correlation.
       As the average temperature increases, fewer units of electricity tend to be used.
   (d) (i) 2.5°C   (ii) 28 units

6. (b) Perfect negative correlation.
   (d) £2600 - £3000

CHAPTER 39

Exercise **39.1** — Page 435

1. (a) Entries are: 0, 4, 16, 34, 49, 57, 60
   (c) (i) 14 mins   (ii) 18 to 19 mins
       (iii) 9 to 10 mins
   (d) 9 mins

2. (a) 52   (c) (i) 61 g   (ii) 28 g

3. (b) (i) 6 to 7 mins   (ii) 8 mins

Exercise **39.2** — Page 437

1. (a) Entries are: 0, 7, 28, 65, 77, 80
   (c) (i) 6 minutes   (ii) 12

2. (a) 26 to 27   (b) 7 to 8 marks
     (c) 15 to 16%   (d) 17

3. (a) 95
     (c) (i) 89 cm (ii) 10 to 11 cm (iii) 19
     (d) 83 cm

4. (b) 9 to 10 hours   (c) 12%

5. (a) 175 cm, 14.5 cm   (b) 3   (c) 41
     (d) 172.5 cm   (e) 185.5 cm

Exercise **39.3**   Page 439

1. (a) 40   (b) 13 cm   (c) 8.5 cm
     (d) Girls heights are more varied, etc.   (e) 1

2. (b) (i) 18 litres   (ii) 10 litres
     (c) Neighbour's cows have higher average
        yield, but the yield is more varied, etc.

3. Variety X, median 350 g, IQR 100 g.
    Variety Y, median 350 g, IQR 220 g.
    Same median, but weight of Variety Y is more
    varied, etc.

Exercise **39.4**   Page 441

1.
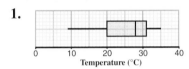

2.
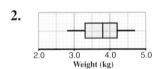

3.
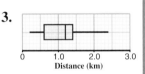

4. (a) median = £42, lower quartile = £23,
       upper quartile = £55

5. (a) 0.06 s   (b) 0.08 s

6. (a) 72% (b) 18% (c) English (d) 21%
     (e) English mark has a higher median,
        Maths marks more spread.

7. (b) Males have lower median time and not
       spread out. Females have higher median
       time and greater variation.

Review Exercise **39**   Page 444

1. (a) 200   (b) 20%
     (c) (i) 85 mins   (ii) 9 mins
     (d) Range is affected by a few very slow
        times.

2. (a) Entries are: 4, 11, 21, 37, 67, 80
     (c) (i) 205 seconds (ii) 51 customers

3. (b) (i) 82 seconds   (ii) 33 to 34 seconds
     (c) The second group is fitter, with lower
        median and less variation in recovery
        times.

4. (a) 95
     (c) (i) 89 cm (ii) 10 to 11 cm
     (d) 83 cm

5. (a) 13p   (b) 27p   (c) 5p

6.
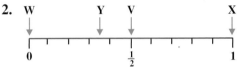

CHAPTER   **40**

Exercise **40.1**   Page 446

1. (a) Evens   (b) Impossible
     (c) Likely   (d) Unlikely
     (e) Certain   (f) Unlikely
     (g) Likely

2.
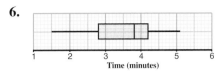

Exercise **40.2**   Page 448

1. (a) $\frac{1}{3}$ (b) $\frac{2}{3}$ (c) $\frac{2}{3}$

2. (a) $\frac{3}{10}$ (b) $\frac{7}{10}$

3. (a) $\frac{1}{5}$ (b) $\frac{2}{5}$

4. (a) $\frac{1}{11}$ (b) $\frac{4}{11}$ (c) $\frac{2}{11}$

5. (a) $\frac{1}{12}$ (b) $\frac{1}{6}$

6. (a) $\frac{1}{2}$ (b) $\frac{1}{4}$ (c) $\frac{1}{52}$

7. (a) $\frac{2}{5}$ (b) $\frac{3}{5}$ (c) 1 (d) 0

8. (a) $\frac{2}{3}$ (b) $\frac{1}{3}$ (c) $\frac{3}{4}$

9. (a) $\frac{2}{5}$ (b) $\frac{3}{5}$ (c) $\frac{4}{25}$ (d) $\frac{4}{15}$
     (e) $\frac{2}{5}$

10. (a) $\frac{1}{3}$ (b) $\frac{1}{15}$ (c) $\frac{11}{24}$ (d) $\frac{17}{50}$
     (e) $\frac{21}{25}$ (f) $\frac{4}{5}$

11. The events are not equally likely.

Exercise **40.3**   Page 450

1. $\frac{7}{25}$ **2.** $\frac{4}{5}$ **3.** $\frac{21}{30} = \frac{7}{10}$

4. (a) $\frac{1}{10}$ (b) 10

5. (a) Tom $\frac{1}{3}$, Sam $\frac{1}{2}$, Kim $\frac{3}{4}$, Pam $\frac{9}{20}$

(b) Pam - because she has played the most games.

(c) Pam - because $\frac{9}{20}$ is greater than $\frac{1}{3}$.

6. 9   **7.** (a) $\frac{1}{500}$ (b) 25

8. (a) 300   (b) 120   (c) 150

9. 8

10. (a) $\frac{52}{100} = 0.52$ $\frac{102}{200} = 0.51$ $\frac{141}{300} = 0.47$

(b) 0.47

11. (a) Relative frequency close to theoretical probability (0.25).
(b) Varies around 0.5

Exercise **40.4**   Page 452

1. $\frac{3}{5}$ **2.** 0.4   **3.** 0.04   **4.** $\frac{47}{50}$ **5.** 0.6

6. (a) 0.04   (b) 0.97   **7.** (a) 0.5   (b) 0.3

8. (a) (i) The probabilities add to 105%
(ii) 5%
(b) (i) 45%   (ii) 75%   (iii) 80%

9. (a) 0.4   (b) 0.6
(c) (i) Yes (ii) No
(d) (i) 0.6 (ii) 0.6

Exercise **40.5**   Page 455

1. (a) RBG, RGB, GBR, GRB, BGR, BRG

(b) $\frac{1}{3}$

2. (a)

	1	2	3	4	5	6
1	2	3	4	5	6	7
2	3	4	5	6	7	8
3	4	5	6	7	8	9
4	5	6	7	8	9	10
5	6	7	8	9	10	11
6	7	8	9	10	11	12

(b) (i) $\frac{1}{12}$ (ii) $\frac{1}{12}$ (iii) $\frac{5}{6}$

(c) They cover all possible scores.

3.   Dice

Coin		1	2	3	4	5	6
	H	H1	H2	H3	H4	H5	H6
	T	T1	T2	T3	T4	T5	T6

(a) $\frac{1}{12}$ (b) $\frac{1}{4}$ (c) $\frac{1}{12}$
(d) $\frac{1}{4}$ (e) $\frac{1}{6}$ (f) $\frac{1}{2}$

4. (a)

Stage 1	Stage 2
Bus	Bus
Bus	Walk
Train	Bus
Train	Walk
Lift	Bus
Lift	Walk

(b) $\frac{1}{6}$

5. (a)   **2nd spin**

		1	2	3	4
	1	2	3	4	5
1st	2	3	4	5	6
spin	3	4	5	6	7
	4	5	6	7	8

(b) (i) $\frac{1}{16}$ (ii) $\frac{1}{8}$ (iii) $\frac{3}{16}$

6. (a)   Bag A

		R	R	W
Bag B	W	RW	RW	WW
	W	RW	RW	WW
	R	RR	RR	WR

(c) $\frac{4}{9}$

7. (a)

A	1	1	2	2	3	3
B	2	3	2	3	2	3

(b) (i) $\frac{2}{6} = \frac{1}{3}$ (ii) $\frac{4}{6} = \frac{2}{3}$ (c) $\frac{4}{5}$

8. (a) Maths, English
Maths, Science
Maths, Art
English, Science
English, Art
Science, Art

(b) $\frac{3}{6} = \frac{1}{2}$ (c) $\frac{1}{3}$

9. (a)

	W	RW	GW	BW	YW	WW
2nd spin	Y	RY	GY	BY	YY	WY
	B	RB	GB	BB	YB	WB
	G	RG	GG	BG	YG	WG
	R	RR	GR	BR	YR	WR
		R	G	B	Y	W

                     1st spin

(b) (i) $\frac{1}{25}$ (ii) $\frac{9}{25}$ (iii) $\frac{5}{25} = \frac{1}{5}$

10. (a)

	1	2	3	4	5	6
1	2	3	4	5	6	7
2	3	4	5	6	7	8
3	4	5	6	7	8	9

(b) $\frac{1}{18}$ (c) $\frac{1}{6}$

Exercise 40.6   Page 458

1. (a)

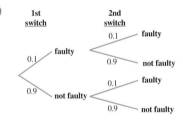

(b) (i) $\frac{4}{25}$ (ii) $\frac{16}{25}$

2. (a)

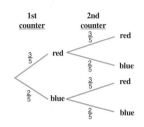

(b) (i) 0.01   (ii) 0.18
(c) 810

3. (a) (i) $\frac{5}{50} = \frac{1}{10}$ (ii) $\frac{45}{50} = \frac{9}{10}$

(iii) $\frac{20}{50} = \frac{2}{5}$ (iv) $\frac{30}{50} = \frac{3}{5}$

(b)

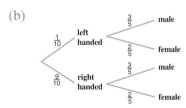

(c) (i) $\frac{2}{50} = \frac{1}{25}$ (ii) $\frac{29}{50}$

4. (a)

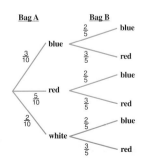

(b) $\frac{9}{50}$ (c) $\frac{21}{50}$

---

5. (a)

Lights   Brakes
$\frac{9}{10}$ Pass $\frac{4}{5}$ Pass $\frac{1}{5}$ Fail
$\frac{1}{10}$ Fail

(b) $\frac{7}{25}$

6. (a) 0.7   (b) 0.49   (c) 0.58

7. (a) $\frac{3}{20}$ (b) $\frac{5}{8}$

8. (a) 0.14   (b) 0.06

9. (a) $\frac{1}{3}$ (b) $\frac{1}{2}$

10. (a) (i) 0.1   (ii) 0.7   (iii) 0.6
(b) (i) 0.01   (ii) 0.09

11. (a) (i) 0.3   (ii) 0.1   (iii) 0.5
(b) 0.34

Review Exercise 40   Page 462

1. (a)

	1	2	3	4
1	2	3	4	5
2	3	4	5	6
3	4	5	6	7

(b) (i) $\frac{2}{12} = \frac{1}{6}$ (ii) $\frac{10}{12} = \frac{5}{6}$

(c) $\frac{4}{12} = \frac{1}{3}$

2. (a) (i) $\frac{7}{20}$ (ii) $\frac{3}{4}$ (iii) $\frac{13}{20}$

(b) Red, Blue   Blue, Yellow
Red, Yellow   Blue, Blue
Red, Red   Yellow, Yellow

3. 0.15

4. The events are not equally likely.

5. (a) $\frac{2}{5}$ (b) $\frac{4}{9}$

6. (a) AA   A2
1A   12
2A   22

(b) $\frac{2}{9}$

7. (a) $\frac{5}{20} = \frac{1}{4}$ (b) 150   **8.** 300   **9.** $\frac{4}{25}$

10. (a) $\frac{9}{30} = \frac{3}{10}$ (b) $\frac{3}{15} = \frac{1}{5}$ (c) 384

11. (a)

HELEN   JOAN
0.95 pass   0.8 pass   0.2 not pass
0.05 not pass   0.8 pass   0.2 not pass

(b) 0.76   (c) 0.23

12. (a) 0.91   (b) 3
     (c) (i) 0.0081   (ii) 0.1638

13. (a) $\frac{12}{35}$ (b) $\frac{19}{35}$

14. (a) $\frac{3}{10}$ (b) $\frac{3}{10}$

Section Review   Page 464

1. (a) (i) 16   (ii) 38
    (b) (i) Heathrow   (ii) 40
    (c) 120

2.

Game	Angle
Badminton	64°
Basketball	120°
Squash	48°
Volleyball	128°

3. (a) 15   (b) 18 cm   (c) 26 cm

4. £380

5. (a) 35   (b) 3   (c) 5.1
    (d) Males have greater range,
     7 compared with 3.
     Females have greater average,
     5.1 compared with 3.6.

6. Set A   1   1   2   2   3   3
    Set B   X   Y   X   Y   X   Y

7. (a) $\frac{3}{20}$ (b) $\frac{7}{20}$

8. (a) 0.4   (b) 18

9. (a) $\frac{7}{9}$ (b) $\frac{6}{25}$
    (c) Can swim: girls 0.76, boys 0.8.
     Not true. 0.8 > 0.76

10. (a) $\frac{1}{6}$ (b) Probably not, as 2 occurs twice as
                    many times as any other number.

11. (a) **D**. Exact location known.
     Distances can be calculated later.
    (b) Mainly after work shoppers.

12. (b) Positive correlation   (d) 32

13. (a) **B**   (b) **C**   (c) **D**

14. (a) X median: 180 g, IQR: 120 g
     Y median: 120 g, IQR: 70 g
    (b) Variety X has higher median weight and
     more variation in weight.

15. (a)

Day 1   Day 2   (b) 0.51

0.7 On time
0.7 On time
0.3 Late
0.3 Late
0.7 On time
0.3 Late

16. (a) 30.9 g

17. (b) (i) 44 mph   (ii) 11 mph   (iii) $72\frac{1}{2}$%

18. (b) 26, 26.5, 27.5, 29, 30.5, 31.5, 34, 37, 45.5
    (e) Upward trend in sale of phones.
    (f) 30

19. (a) 0.5   (b) 0.7
    (c) (i) 0.06   (ii) 0.09

Non-calculator Paper   Page 468

1. 73   **2.** 14 pence

3. (a) 17.5   (b) 2.95

4. (a) b^3 (b) $2a - 6$ (c) $35d$ pence

5. (a) 15   (b) $300 \div 20 = 15$

6. (a) -2 (b) 60   (c) $\frac{8}{21}$

7. $1, 0, -\frac{1}{2}$ **8.** (a) 72 cm³   (b) 108 cm²

9. (a) 0.04   (b) 49   (c) 9   (d) $\frac{2}{3}$

10. (a) 18   (b) $2t - 3$ (c) $x = 7$

11. 9.9 cm²   **12.** $\frac{5}{9}$

13. (a) $x = 54°$
    (b) (i) $y = 63°$ (ii) alternate angles

14. (a) $\frac{3}{10}, \frac{1}{3}, \frac{2}{5}, \frac{5}{8}$ (b) 40%   (c) 20

15. 4   **16.** (b) 035°   (c) 215°

17. (a) $\frac{17}{20}$ (b) 8   **18.** (a) $\frac{1}{6}$ (b) $1\frac{11}{20}$

19. (a) $2(m - 2n)$ (b) $t(t - 2)$

20. (a) $x = 6$ (b) $y = -2$

21. (a) (i) 17   (ii) $3n + 2$ (b) $3n - 1$

22. (a) Entries for y: 0, 1, 2, 3, 4, 5, 6
    (b) Entries for y: 9, 4, 1, 0, 1, 4, 9

23. 90%   **24.** (b) 31 - 40

25. (a)

A	B	Total	A	B	Total
1	5	6	3	5	8
1	6	7	3	6	9
1	7	8	3	7	10
2	5	7	4	5	9
2	6	8	4	6	10
2	7	9	4	7	11

    (b) $\frac{2}{12} = \frac{1}{6}$ (c) 10

26. (a) (i) 11.40 am   (ii) 20 minutes
    (b) $12\frac{1}{2}$ miles
    (c)

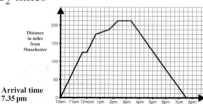

27. (a) $13^2 = 12^2 + 5^2$
So $\triangle ABC$ is right-angled at B
(b) $30\,\text{cm}^2$

28. (a) $\dfrac{3 \times 700}{0.5} = 4200$
(b) (i) $98.4\dot{9}\,\text{cm}$ (ii) $97.5\,\text{cm}$

29. 9   **30.** (b) $x = \pm 2.4$

31. (a) Rotation, 90° anticlockwise, centre $(0, 0)$.
(b) Reflection in $y = x$.
(c)

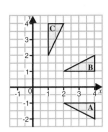

32. (a) 2, 3   (b) $x = -2$, $y = 0.5$
(c) $x = 0$ or 5

33. $x = 5$, $y = -2$

34. (a) (i) $15p^5$ (ii) $2p^3$ (b) $3x(x - 2y)$

35. (a) $3a^2b(2b^2 - 5a)$ (b) $(x - 1)(x - 6)$

36. $5.4\,\text{cm}$ **37.** (a) 2×10^9 (b) 8×10^{-3}

38. £40   **39.** $2\pi b^2$, πab, $2(a^2 + b^2)$

40. (a) (b)

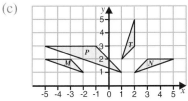

(c) Rotation, 90° anticlockwise, about $(0, 0)$.
(d) $y = x + 8$ (e) $P(-8, 0)$

41. (a) $AB = 9.6\,\text{m}$ (b) $\tan x° = 3$

Calculator Paper   Page 472

1. 39p

2. 21 minutes

3. (a) 4, 6   (b) 24   (c) 7

4. (a) $6t$ (b) $x = \dfrac{1}{2}$

5. £349.20

6. $x = 41°$, $y = 58°$

7. (a) $20x$ grams   (b) 180 grams

8. (b) $x = 2$

9. (a) £5   (b) $2.25\,\text{m}$

10. (a) 90   (b) 40°   (c) 0.22   (d) $\dfrac{3}{25}$

11. Brand A 12.8 g/p, Brand B 13.6 g/p.
Brand B gives more grams per penny.

12. $200\,\text{m}^2$ **13.** 0.0074

14. (a) (i) $p = 63°$
(ii) $\triangle ABC$ is isosceles,
$\angle BAC = \angle BCA$.
(b) (i) $m = 54°$ (ii) $r = 63°$
(c) (i) $t = 54°$
(ii) $\angle ABC = \angle CDE$ (alt. $\angle$s)

15. (a) $18\,000\,\text{cm}^3$ (b) 8%

16. (a) $2 \times 2 \times 2 \times 3 \times 3 = 2^3 \times 3^2$ (b) 144

17. (a) 1H, 2H, 3H, 4H, 5H, 6H,
1T, 2T, 3T, 4T, 5T, 6T.
(b) $\dfrac{1}{4}$ (c) $\dfrac{3}{4}$

18. $2n + 1$

19. How many hours a week do you listen to the radio?

Less than 10 ☐   10 to 20 ☐   More than 20 ☐

On how many days each week do you listen to the radio?

Every day ☐   4 to 6 ☐   1 to 3 ☐   0 ☐

20. 108

21. (a) 2.83   (b) 32 768   (c) 0.325

22. (a) $x = 3.2$ (b) $3(a - 2b)$ (c) $3x - 6$

23. (a) £4   (b) 35 g

24. (a) 12   (b) $2.5\,\text{cm}$ (c) $5.89\,\text{cm}$

25. $353\,\text{cm}^2$

26. £6

27. (a) £1060   (b) £736.95

28. (a) (i) $x = 1$ (ii) $x = -\dfrac{2}{5}$ (b) $x = 7.3$

29. (a) 0.06   (b) 0.38

30. $a = 57°$, $b = 114°$, $c = 123°$

31. (a) $DC = 5.29\,\text{cm}$ (b) $\angle DBC = 41.4°$
(c) $AB = 12.4\,\text{cm}$

32. (a) $x = 7$, $y = 3$ (b) $y = 6.12$
(c) $x = < 6.5$

33. (b) 67.75, 69, 70.75, 68.25, 75, 76, 77.5
(d) £133

34. (b) (i) 55 hours   (ii) 7 hours
(c) Same median, but retired people have a larger spread (IQR)

35. (a) 1.35   (b) $t = \pm\sqrt{\dfrac{3s}{a}}$

36. (a) (i) $a = 50$, $b = 30$ (ii) $F = 75$
(iii) $F = 79.36875$
(b) 4.9×10^{11}

37. (a) £450 000   (b) 4%

Index